To Mo, *my mother-in-law, who always gave me such
a lot to think about!*

Child, Family, and Community

Family-Centered Early Care and Education

Fifth Edition

Janet Gonzalez-Mena

Napa Valley College, Emerita

Merrill
is an imprint of

Upper Saddle River, New Jersey
Columbus, Ohio

Library of Congress Cataloging-in-Publication Data
Gonzalez-Mena, Janet.
    Child, family, and community : family-centered early care and education / Janet Gonzalez-Mena.—5th ed.
       p. cm.
    Rev. ed. of: The young child in the family and the community. 4th ed. c2006.
    ISBN 978-0-13-513230-2
    1. Socialization.   2. Child rearing.   3. Family.   I. Gonzalez-Mena, Janet. Young child in the
family and the community.   II. Title.
    HQ783.G59 2009
    649'.1—dc22

                                                                                    2008002831

Vice President and Executive Publisher: Jeffery W. Johnston
Acquisitions Editor: Julie Peters
Editorial Assistant: Tiffany Bitzel
Senior Managing Editor: Pamela D. Bennett
Senior Project Manager: Linda Hillis Bayma
Production Coordination: Elm Street Publishing Services
Design Coordinator: Diane C. Lorenzo
Photo Coordinator: Valerie Schultz
Cover Designer: Jeff Vanik
Cover image: SuperStock
Operations Specialist: Laura Messserly
Director of Marketing: Quinn Perkson
Marketing Manager: Erica DeLuca
Marketing Coordinator: Brian Mounts

This book was set in Nouarese BK by Integra Software Services. It was printed and bound by R.R. Donnelley & Sons Company. The cover was printed by R.R. Donnelley & Sons Company.

Photo Credits for Chapter Openers: Todd Yarrington/Merrill, p. 2; Scott Cunningham/Merrill, pp. 24, 104; Tim Gonzalez-Mena, p. 50; Anne Vega/Merrill, pp. 76, 270; Frank Gonzalez-Mena, pp. 132, 154, 226; Laura Zahner, pp. 176, 344; PH College, p. 202; Jim Darter, p. 246; George Dodson/PH College, p. 298; Pearson Learning Photo Studio, p. 318.

Pearson® is a registered trademark of Pearson plc
Merrill® is a registered trademark of Pearson Education, Inc.

Pearson Education Ltd., London   Pearson Education North Asia, Ltd., Hong Kong
Pearson Education Singapore, Pte. Ltd.   Pearson Educación de Mexico, S.A. de C.V.
Pearson Education Canada, Inc.   Pearson Education Malaysia, Pte. Ltd.
Pearson Education–Japan   Pearson Education Upper Saddle River, New Jersey
Pearson Education Australia PTY., Limited

Merrill
is an imprint of

                                                    10 9 8 7 6
                                                    ISBN 13: 978-0-13-513230-2
                                                    ISBN 10:   0-13-513230-4

Preface

This fifth edition of *Child, Family, and Community: Family-Centered Care and Education* includes a number of significant changes, including an altered title and a shift in focus. It's still a book written to the reader directly from the author and is still about the socialization and education of young children in child rearing, caring, and educational contexts from birth to 8 years of age. The shift in focus puts working with families in early care and education settings in the spotlight as the central theme and includes practical advice in every chapter about how to do that.

FOUNDATIONAL IDEAS SUPPORTING THIS BOOK

Parents have always been an important feature of this book, but this edition suggests the reader expand from child-centered care and education programs to family-centered ones, taking into account that the child always comes to school in a context, a fact that can't be ignored. Urie Bronfenbrenner's ecological model of human development is introduced and discussed in Chapter 1, to emphasize the numerous influences on children, including families, teachers, schools, communities, and so forth.

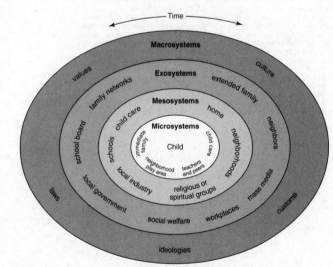

This book goes beyond mere parent involvement to something bigger and more inclusive. Partnering with parents isn't about simply educating the adults in children's lives or requiring them to become involved in the program. The partnership is a *collaboration* with shared power and working relationships. Communication skills, which are emphasized throughout the book, are the key to those partnerships.

As before, the book examines developmental theory and adds diverse perspectives from a base of solid academics, constructivist theory, and my own experience. The point of the book was always for the reader to think of the child in context, but dividing it into three parts seemed to separate the different contexts. In this edition the three parts have been eliminated because the child, family, and community are integrated throughout the book—and always from the view of working with parents and other family members.

ENCOURAGES REFLECTION ABOUT PERSONAL EXPERIENCES

Readers will find the text full of real-life examples and personal insights. They are also asked to bring their own ideas, experiences, and insights to their reading, in accordance with Jean Piaget's ideas about learners attaching new knowledge to existing knowledge. In other words, readers are encouraged to reach into their own experiences to make sense of new information in terms of what they already know. They are helped to see how that same approach works equally well when relating to families and conveying information to them. Respect for one's own background, experiences, knowledge, ideas, and insights is important whether a student, a teacher, or a parent.

Because whatever we read always filters through our own subjective experiences, this text acknowledges that fact and capitalizes on it. Thus, students can feel at home and find their own voices. They are asked to do the same for families when working with them. I too, as the author, let my voice come through as I tell personal stories and share insights. All readers are asked regularly to look at the issues, information, and examples in light of their own ideas, feelings, and experiences. Examples are designed to appeal to both traditional and nontraditional students, reflecting the changing demographics of the United States today.

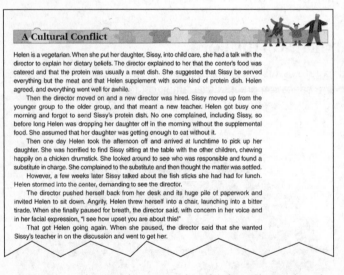

A Cultural Conflict

Helen is a vegetarian. When she put her daughter, Sissy, into child care, she had a talk with the director to explain her dietary beliefs. The director explained to her that the center's food was catered and that the protein was usually a meat dish. She suggested that Sissy be served everything but the meat and that Helen supplement with some kind of protein dish. Helen agreed, and everything went well for awhile.

Then the director moved on and a new director was hired. Sissy moved up from the younger group to the older group, and that meant a new teacher. Helen got busy one morning and forgot to send Sissy's protein dish. No one complained, including Sissy, so before long Helen was dropping her daughter off in the morning without the supplemental food. She assumed that her daughter was getting enough to eat without it.

Then one day Helen took the afternoon off and arrived at lunchtime to pick up her daughter. She was horrified to find Sissy sitting at the table with the other children, chewing happily on a chicken drumstick. She looked around to see who was responsible and found a substitute in charge. She complained to the substitute and then thought the matter was settled.

However, a few weeks later Sissy talked about the fish sticks she had had for lunch. Helen stormed into the center, demanding to see the director.

The director pushed herself back from her desk and its huge pile of paperwork and invited Helen to sit down. Angrily, Helen threw herself into a chair, launching into a bitter tirade. When she finally paused for breath, the director said, with concern in her voice and in her facial expression, "I see how upset you are about this!"

That got Helen going again. When she paused, the director said that she wanted Sissy's teacher in on the discussion and went to get her.

The book is written for all those who work with young children or will work with them, including early childhood students who plan to be preschool, kindergarten, and primary teachers, infant care teachers, caregivers, child care workers, school-age child care program administrators or staff, family child care providers, or parents. Because of the variety of jobs and job titles, I tried to use *early educator* instead of always using the term *teacher*. Instead of *school*, I also often use *early care and education program* to include the variety of settings for young children and their families. If I only wrote about schools and teachers, some readers would conclude that programs specifically designed as child care for working or student families might not be included. That's not the case. I'm trying hard to make the point that care and education are linked—you can't have quality education without care being a part of it, just as you can't have quality care without education being included.

WHAT IS NEW IN THIS EDITION

- *A broader array of theories underlying parent relations practices.* In this edition I've expanded my discussions of Bronfenbrenner's ecological theory of human development and Maslow's hierarchy of human needs to help explain children's motivations and behavior to readers. These first appear in Chapter 1. Discussions of Erikson's psychological stages of development have always been covered in this book because all young children pass through them. Explanations of these theories help students understand how children are affected by their environment (their "ecology") and what causes them to act in ways that they do.

- *Expanded ages covered: Infancy through school-age.* Because some states' teacher training programs extend through third or fourth grade, and also because the School-Age Child Care Certificate is growing nationally, I included coverage of older, primary-grade children in this edition. Chapter 5 is a new chapter, titled Working with Families of School-Age Children. We discuss not only how to make kindergarten and primary-grade and after-school programs more family-centered, but also how children of these ages learn morals and values; the use of adult affirmations, praise, and attention; and how to work with parents to teach children prosocial behaviors.

Strategy Box 3.1

When Conflicts Arise: Strategies for Working with Families

- In the face of differing ideas about care practices, seek to establish common ground with individual families without simply imposing regulations, rules, and restrictions.
- The first step in looking for common ground is to suspend judgment. Make your goal to talk about the differences and see the family's point of view.
- Develop appreciation for contrasting patterns of care and understand that they need not be mutually exclusive.
- Aim for consensus in the face of conflicts and differences in perception.
- If you are feeling highly emotional about a particular issue, do some self-reflection to understand why this is a particular "hot button" for you. Gaining insights into your personal issues may help you better understand the family's perspective.

- *More strategies on partnering with parents.* This edition includes more practical strategies on ways to communicate with, understand, and partner with parents. Strategy Boxes highlight this addition.

- *Related Web Sites.* To support the notion of basing our actions on research and evidence in the field of early childhood education, I included some related Web Sites and descriptions in this edition. Reviewing these Web Sites will expand your understanding of our field and thereby increase your professionalism. A number of these

---

WEB SITES

Child Development Institute
http://www.childdevelopmentinfo.com/parenting/helping_children_cope_with_separation.shtml
This Web site has an article on helping children cope with separation and loss of all sorts, but focusing particularly on death.

Early Head Start National Resource Center
http://www.ehsnrc.org/
The Early Head Start National Resource Center Web site contains a database of all the Early Head Start Program sites as well as valuable tips and strategies for trainers and many full-text documents on a range of infant- and toddler-related topics.

Pikler Institute
http://www.pikler.org
and
International Pikler Association
http://www.aipl.org
Both Web sites give information on the Pikler approach used at the Pikler Institute, a residential nursery in Budapest, Hungary.

Program for Infant/Toddler Caregivers (PITC)
http://www.pitc.org
The Program for Infant/Toddler Caregivers supports and promotes quality care for infants and toddlers through resources, information, and training. The site includes information on brain research and

are included at the end of each chapter and can be used for homework and assignments in addition to browsing for information.

- *Combined former Chapter 4 with former Chapter 10.* Chapter 4, Self-Esteem, has been combined with former Chapter 10, Strokes and Affirmations, to keep relevant and somewhat overlapping content together.
- *Updated and expanded ancillary package.* This edition provides the following in instructor support: online Instructor's Manual, online Test Bank, online Power-Point slides, TestGen, WebCT Test Bank, and Blackboard Test Bank. These can be downloaded from the Instructor Resource Center at www.pearsonhighered.com.

CHANGES IN THE FIFTH EDITION

Chapter 1, The Child in Context of Family and Community, is a new chapter in this edition and now includes the theories of Bronfenbrenner and Maslow. Family systems theory is also included and is new to this edition. Other subjects in this chapter are meeting the needs of what has been called *the whole child* and issues of school readiness. The chapter starts with an exploration of the notion of *context*, which comes from Bronfenbrenner's ecological theory. The child is examined in the context of developmental theory, which comes in the context of family, which lies in the context of community. All of these contexts can be thought of as environments or settings that hold people, that influence each other, and that are influenced by culture. Recognizing the importance of context is a step to exploring why making family-centered early care and education important and what the benefits are for children, families, and early educators. A quick history of the family-centered approach to care and education shows that the idea has been around for a long time, yet still hasn't become widespread. The changes in this book are related to the fact that the time is ripe for the early care and education field as a whole to make a shift in focus, just as this edition has done.

Chapter 2, Supporting Families Around Issues of Attachment, explores how Erikson's stage of trust versus mistrust affects infants and their families. Implications for working with parents around attachment issues have been added throughout the chapter. A section on infant mortality and the effect of attachment has been removed because it didn't seem to fit the new focus on family-centered care and education. The rest of the chapter has been updated, but much of the same information is still there, only with a new focus. Building relationships and meeting needs continue to be important themes of this chapter, which looks at parenting as well as infants in early care and education programs. Issues of attachment in group care are examined, and the Pikler approach in Budapest, Hungary, is explored. Inclusion and the related feelings of belonging are discussed, including the implications of Vygotsky's work to inclusion programs. The attachment of a baby who was exposed to drugs while still in the womb is a sidelight of this chapter.

Chapter 3, Supporting Families with Autonomy-Seeking Youngsters, has implications for working with families who have toddlers in early care and education programs. This chapter explores the toddler behaviors that indicate the push toward becoming a separate independent individual—behaviors such as rebellion and neg-ativity, exploration, self-help skills, and a sense of possession. A new section dis-cusses how some families don't see the push for autonomy in the same way that teachers who have learned about Erikson's stages of psychosocial development regard autonomy. This is because of differences between the culture of the teacher and the culture of some families. Loss and separation and helping toddlers develop the skills needed to cope are also features of this chapter. Partnering with parents is a main feature. A story about a teen parent is a sidelight of the chapter.

Chapter 4, Sharing Views of Initiative with Families, has strategies for working with families whose children are enrolled in child care or preschool programs. This chapter explores the development of a conscience and focuses mainly on Erikson's third stage of psychosocial development—initiative versus guilt. The text acknowl-edges that all families don't share the same views of encouraging initiative that the teachers trained in Erikson's psychosocial stages of development have. Also featured are the role of imagination and fantasy, a look at shy children and aggressive children, and how to empower *all* children, including those with special needs. Discussion of play and how to make it more accessible for children with special needs are part of this chapter as well as Vygotsky's ideas about how peer relationships contribute to learning (language development, cognitive development) through play. Sidelights of the chapter include a look at a child with attention deficit/hyperactivity disorder (ADHD); differing perspectives on child rearing; and addressing the roots of violence by teaching problem-solving skills.

Chapter 5, Working with Families of School-Age Children, is a new chapter to this edition. This chapter focuses on children in kindergarten through third grade and includes Erikson's stage of industry, but also looks at the child in transition from the stage of initiative, which is where most kindergartners and some first graders are. Some of its features include how family-centered kindergartens can help ease the transition into "real school" as well as how parent–teacher partnerships work in schools. Ways of working with parents around teaching children prosocial behaviors are a major part of this chapter and are looked at in the context of how children learn morals and values. The power of adult attention and the use of affirmations are also included, as well as a close look at praise. Resilience in children is another feature of this chapter.

Chapter 6, Understanding Families' Goals, Values, and Culture, still looks at cul-tural differences in goals and values, plus the relationship of those goals and values to child rearing. It explores contrasting cultural patterns, which show up as two pat-terns as in the old edition, but this edition has the added focus of working with par-ents around issues that arise between parents and professionals. Conflict resolution is discussed after showing a number of conflicts mostly related to the two patterns. Also new to this chapter is an added piece about the early educator's need for self-reflection and discovering personal "hot buttons" that cause defensive reactions and move the person toward an argumentative stance and away from dialoguing. A side-light of this chapter is a comparison of the values of independence and interdepen-dence and how they show up in child-rearing practices.

Chapter 7, Working with Families on Guidance Issues, has a new focus. Instead of being just a chapter on discipline, the chapter now takes a look at differing perspectives on discipline and gives some ideas about how to relate to parents around differences in perspectives. The chapter still looks at seven ways to *prevent* the need for guiding children's behavior and then examines seven ways to respond to unacceptable behavior. Sidelights of this chapter are the story of one mother who stopped using punishment and started using consequences to guide the behavior of her son; the story of a mother who has abused her child; and the story of what one town did to work toward preventing physical abuse of its children.

Chapter 8, Working with Families on Addressing Feelings and Problem Solving, follows the guidance chapter, focusing specifically on working with families around issues that come up as children are expressing feelings. Problem solving now follows in the same chapter, instead of having its own chapter as it did in the fourth edition. The link is that feelings are a way to give energy to problem solving. The problem-solving scenes were removed from home and family settings and placed in school settings with teachers working with children around problem solving and helping parents see the benefits of a problem-solving approach. The chapter also explores how to look at feelings and problem solving from more than one perspective. Sidelights of this chapter show how Marcie, a stepmother, learns to cope with her anger in healthy ways and how Julie, another mother, learns to let go of responsibility for her child's feelings.

Chapter 9, Working with Families to Support Self-Esteem, combines Chapter 4 from the fourth edition, Self-Esteem, with Chapter 10 from that edition, Strokes and Affirmations. The chapter includes some ways to promote self-esteem, what happens when the media stereotype in negative ways, and why always being positive is not a way to raise children's self-esteem. It also includes discussion of *scaffolding* in learning situations as a way to help children develop self-esteem. Also discussed are *affirmations*, recognition by another person, as another way to support self-esteem development, which relates to *self-fulfilling prophecies*, an important concept for both teachers and parents to understand. The chapter also explores how cultural differences can affect the way parents perceive self-esteem.

Chapter 10, Working with Families Around Gender Issues, now has suggestions for working with parents around some of the hot issues brought up in this chapter such as research on how parents, preschool teachers, and primary teachers influence the development of differentiated gender roles. Also, issues of equity are brought up in the chapter, and suggestions are given for understanding parents' perspectives on those issues. Guidelines for teaching young children about gender equity end the chapter, and suggestions are given for creating discussion with parents around those guidelines. The chapter also explores the choice of toys, language issues, and differential socialization. A sidelight of this chapter is a discussion about cultural differences in sex roles, and questions about where traditional roles end and oppression begins.

Chapter 11, Stress and Success in Family Life, has an expanded section on the factors that make a family successful, and family systems theory is also woven into the chapter. Information from family systems theory was already there in the fourth edition, but wasn't named before. The chapter still looks at what it takes to be a healthy family and examines the lives of six families, who, in spite of many stresses, are struggling to be successful. The chapter touches on the issues of substance abuse, divorce, child custody, and poverty. It examines the influence of family structure and makeup and defines the family broadly so there is room for all kinds of families in the definition: nuclear families as well as single-parent families, stepfamilies, blended families, extended families, families with teen parents, and families with children who have special needs. A sidelight of this chapter looks at what families do in early childhood that helps ensure later school success.

Chapter 12, Early Care and Education Programs as Community Resources, used to be Chapter 6 on child care in the fourth edition. Now it is broadened to look at early care and education programs in general—beyond just child care. The chapter starts out looking at the whole range of programs and explaining them, including the movement toward what's called Universal Pre-K. Later the chapter focuses more specifically on child care because of the particular issues that come up when families have their children in out-of-home care all day, five days a week, year round. That's different from Head Start or other half-day preschool programs. It is also different from kindergarten and the primary grades. This chapter views early care and education programs as important community resources for families. The gap between home and school is discussed, and there is an exploration of the relations between parents and early childhood professionals, with the ideal being parent–professional partnerships, keeping in mind this is especially important when the family has a child who has special needs. Sidelights of this chapter are the stories of Debbie, Walt, and Sean, who are looking for child care for their children.

Chapter 13, Other Community Resources, explores what other contributions besides early care and education programs the community makes to support the six families introduced in Chapter 11. There is added material on working with families to connect them with each other to form a community and also to connect them with community resources. There's the addition of an exercise about support systems that readers can do themselves and teachers can use for parent meetings. Family system theory is discussed again in this chapter with an example of different issues around boundaries. More mention is made of such resources as public libraries. The chapter is still about the way the community serves and supports families through social networks and institutions and shows how the six families in Chapter 11 connect to the resources in their community. The subject of child abuse is also explored. A sidelight of the chapter is a description of various ways that families find and connect to community resources.

Chapter 14, Societal Influences on Children and Families, used to be Socializing Agents in the fourth edition. New to the chapter is a section on institutionalized racism that was suggested by a reviewer. Head Start testing and the issues around the testing involved with No Child Left Behind (NCLB) are mentioned, but because the picture is changing while this edition is being prepared, they aren't expanded on. The chapter looks at societal influences such as peer groups, schools, and the media. It also examines factors in socialization—such as inequity and diversity, classism, and racism. It also explores some stories of what can happen when parents and teachers are adversaries instead of partners. Sidelights of the chapter include a look into what "ready to learn" really means and recommendations regarding television and young children.

Chapter 15, Social Policy Issues, has been updated and new topics added. The push for getting children ready to learn is joined by NCLB and Universal Pre-K issues. There is still the material on what a community can do to ensure that all children get an equal chance to feel good about themselves and fulfill themselves in our society. This chapter examines a range of social policy issues that affect families, children, and the programs that serve them. A feature of the chapter is a discussion of the movement toward inclusion of children with special needs in programs with their typically developing peers. Child advocacy is an important part of the chapter. There's now a whole section on conflict, violence, and what they do to children, families, and communities. The book now ends with a plea to move from dominator models of getting along and replacing them with equity models. Peace isn't something that is won, but rather something that is made. We can each become a peacemaker and we can teach children. Sidelights of the chapter include culturally responsive care and statistics responding to the question: Does every child get an equal start?

ACKNOWLEDGMENTS

Over the years of writing and revising this text, my list of people to acknowledge got too long for me to name everybody without leaving someone out. I do want to acknowledge Julie Peters and the staff at Pearson/Merrill for their help and support. Thank you, Julie, for being patient with me while I was going through a difficult time during the preparation of this revision.

I also want to thank the following reviewers for their insights and comments: John M. Chavez, California State University, East Bay; Patricia Dilko, Cañada College; Sydney Fisher Larson, College of the Redwoods; Donna Rafanello, Long Beach City College; and Bob Sasse, Palomar College.

Last but not least, I thank my family and especially my husband, Frank Gonzalez-Mena, who has given me firsthand experience of what it is like to live in a multicultural family.

Brief Contents

Chapter 1   The Child in Context of Family and Community   2

Chapter 2   Supporting Families Around Issues of Attachment   24

Chapter 3   Supporting Families with Autonomy-Seeking Youngsters   50

Chapter 4   Sharing Views of Initiative with Families   76

Chapter 5   Working with Families of School-Age Children   104

Chapter 6   Understanding Families' Goals, Values, and Culture   132

Chapter 7   Working with Families on Guidance Issues   154

Chapter 8   Working with Families on Addressing Feelings and Problem Solving   176

Chapter 9   Working with Families to Support Self-Esteem   202

Chapter 10   Working with Families Around Gender Issues   226

Chapter 11   Stress and Success in Family Life   246

Chapter 12   Early Care and Education Programs as Community Resources   270

Chapter 13   Other Community Resources   298

Chapter 14   Societal Influences on Children and Families   318

Chapter 15   Social Policy Issues   344

NAEYC: Where We Stand   367

References   370

Index   388

Contents

CHAPTER 1 **The Child in Context of Family and Community**   **2**

Looking at Context Through Ecological Theory   5
  Bronfenbrenner's Ecological Model   6
Implications for Early Education: Family-Centered
  Approaches   8
  Family-Centered Defined   9
  The Benefits of Family-Centered Programs for Children   9
  The Benefits of Family-Centered Programs for Teachers   10
  The Benefits of Family-Centered Programs for Families   10
  Mutual Benefits   11
History of Family-Centered Care and Education   11
  Challenges to Creating Partnerships with Families   15
Other Lenses Through Which to Look at Family-Centered
  Approaches   16
  The Family Systems Theory Lens   16
  The Whole Child Lens   18
Abraham Maslow's Hierarchy of Needs   19
Looking Back and Looking Forward   21
For Discussion   22
Web Sites   22
Further Reading   23

CHAPTER 2 **Supporting Families Around Issues of Attachment**   **24**

Attachment and Trust   27
How Attachment Occurs   30
Attachment Behaviors   32
  Signs of Attachment in Parents   32
  Signs of Attachment in Infants   32
Obstacles to Attachment   33
  Temperament and Attachment   34
  Developmental Differences   35
Learning to Cope with Feelings of Loss   36

Varying Attachment Patterns   39
    Bowlby and Ainsworth's Research   39
    Questions About Classic Attachment Research   40
Judging Attachment in a Cross-Cultural Situation   42
Child Care and Attachment   42
    Effects of Child Care on Attachment   43
    How Caregiver and Parent Roles Differ   44
    Attachment in Full-Inclusion Programs   46
Looking Back and Looking Forward   47
For Discussion   47
Web Sites   47
Further Reading   48

CHAPTER 3   **Supporting Families with Autonomy-Seeking Youngsters   50**

Toddlers and Autonomy   52
Signs of Developing Autonomy   53
    Negativity   53
    Exploration   53
    Self-Help Skills   55
    A Sense of Possession   59
Dealing with Issues of Power and Control   61
    Set Up a Developmentally Appropriate Environment   61
    Appreciate Play   62
    Encourage Self-Help Skills   64
    Give Choices   65
    Provide Control   65
    Set Limits   67
Coping with Loss and Separation   68
    Taking Separation in Small Steps   69
    Entering Child Care   69
Partnering with Parents of Toddlers   72
Looking Back and Looking Forward   73
For Discussion   73
Web Sites   74
Further Reading   74

CHAPTER 4   **Sharing Views of Initiative with Families   76**

What Initiative Looks Like in a 4-Year-Old   78
Analyzing Initiative in a 4-Year-Old   80
Developmental Conflicts   82
    Autonomy Versus Shame and Doubt   82
    Initiative Versus Guilt   82

Imagination and Fantasy   84
The Value of Play of All Sorts   84
How the Environment Contributes to a Sense
    of Initiative   86
    Dimensions of Play Environments   88
How Adults Contribute to Children's Initiative   89
Special Considerations for Children with Disabilities   90
The Shy Child   91
A Look at Aggression   93
    Causes of Aggression   93
Teaching Young Children Problem-Solving Skills   96
Empowering the Preschool-Age Child   98
Looking Back and Looking Forward   101
For Discussion   101
Web Sites   102
Further Reading   103

CHAPTER 5   **Working with Families of School-Age
Children   104**

A Family-Centered Approach to Kindergarten   107
Erikson's Stages of Development   108
Differences Families Notice Between School and
    Preschool   111
    Constructivist Approach   111
    Role of Recess   111
How Do You Find Out What Families Want for Their
    Children?   113
Teaching Prosocial Skills   115
Looking at the Decision-Making Process as a Way of Exploring
    Morals   116
The Power of Adult Attention   118
What Are Affirmations?   120
    Children's Response to Positive Adult Attention   121
Teaching Morals by Promoting Prosocial Development   127
Looking Back and Looking Forward   129
For Discussion   129
Web Sites   130
Further Reading   131

CHAPTER 6   **Understanding Families' Goals, Values,
and Culture   132**

Cultural Differences in Goals and Values   135
Contrasting Cultural Patterns   137

When Families and Early Educators Have Conflicting Goals
    and Values   138
What to Do When Conflicts Arise   141
    Build Relationships   146
    Know Yourself   146
    Work to Bring Differences Out in the Open   146
    Discuss Differences   147
    Become an Effective Cross-Cultural Communicator   147
    Problem Solve   147
    Commit Yourself to Education   148
Helping Children Understand and Value Cultural
    Pluralism   148
Looking Back and Looking Forward   149
For Discussion   150
Web Sites   150
Further Reading   151

CHAPTER 7   **Working with Families on Guidance
                     Issues   154**

Defining the Word Discipline   157
Problems with Using Punishment to Teach   159
Guidelines for Disciplining Young Children   160
    Discipline as Preventing Unacceptable Behavior   162
    Guidance as Responding to Unacceptable Behavior   165
Looking Back and Looking Forward   172
For Discussion   173
Web Sites   173
Further Reading   174

CHAPTER 8   **Working with Families on Addressing Feelings
                     and Problem Solving   176**

Feelings   178
What Are Feelings?   181
    All Feelings Are Positive   181
Learning Feelings   182
    Social Referencing   182
    Cultural Scripts   184
    The Importance of Accepting Feelings   185
    Teaching Children Healthy Expressions of Feelings   187
Teaching Children to Cope with Feelings   189
    Developing Self-Calming Skills   189
    Coping by Playing Pretend   190

Coping with Simultaneous Feelings   191
Coping with Fear   191
Coping with Anger   193
Problem Solving   194
Using the RERUN *Problem-Solving*
Process with a Child   195
Problem Solving as a Cultural Issue   195
Problem Solving and Parenting Styles   196
The Authoritarian Approach   196
The Permissive Approach   197
The Authoritative Approach   198
A Deeper Look at the Three Parenting Styles   198
Looking Back and Looking Forward   199
For Discussion   199
Web Sites   200
Further Reading   200

CHAPTER 9   **Working with Families to Support Self-Esteem   202**

Portrait of a Person with High Self-Esteem   204
Definition of Self-Esteem   205
Dimensions of Self-Esteem   206
Significance   206
Competence   207
Power   207
Virtue   208
The Role of Beliefs and Expectations in
Self-Esteem   208
Where Does Self-Esteem Come From?   209
Promoting Self-Esteem   210
Give More Honest Feedback and Encouragement Than
Praise   211
Give Children Opportunities to
Experience Success   211
Children Learn from Failure   214
Celebrating Differences: An Antibias Approach   215
Bias Can Hurt   216
Cultural Differences and Self-Esteem   217
Changing Negative Messages to Positive Ones   221
Looking Back and Looking Forward   222
For Discussion   223
Web Sites   223
Further Reading   224

CHAPTER 10   **Working with Families Around Gender Issues   226**

Why Think About Teaching Gender Roles?   228
The Women of Today   229
Gender Equity and Child Rearing   230
  Toys and Gender Roles   230
  The Power of Language   232
Using Modeling to Teach   233
Differential Socialization   234
  Differential Treatment from Parents   236
  Differential Treatment in Preschool   236
  Differential Treatment in Elementary School   237
The Role of Biology in Creating Differences Between Boys and Girls   239
Guidelines for Parents and Early Childhood Educators   242
Looking Back and Looking Forward   244
For Discussion   244
Web Sites   244
Further Reading   245

CHAPTER 11   **Stress and Success in Family Life   246**

Successful Families   250
Traits of Successful Families   251
  Sara's Family   254
  Roberto's Family   255
  Junior's Family   256
  Michael's Family   256
  Courtney's Family   257
  The Jackson Family   258
  Comparing the Six Families   259
Stress as a Positive Force   261
What We Can Learn from Studies of Resilient Children   262
Helping All Children Become Resilient Children   264
Looking Back and Looking Forward   266
For Discussion   267
Web Sites   267
Further Reading   267

CHAPTER 12   **Early Care and Education Programs as Community Resources   270**

Early Care and Education Programs as Child-Rearing Environments   276

Affordability and Availability   278
     Status and Salaries   279
The State of Child Care in America Today   280
Looking at Quality   281
Adult-Child Interactions in Child Care and Early Education
     Settings   282
Including Everybody: Children with
     Special Needs   285
Partnering with Parents   286
Questions Concerning Continuity Between Child Care and
     Home   287
Parent–Professional Partnerships   290
     Roadblocks to Mutual Appreciation, Respect,
       and Support   290
Looking Back and Looking Forward   293
For Discussion   294
Web Sites   295
Further Reading   295

CHAPTER 13   **Other Community Resources**   **298**
Social Networks   300
     Developing a Broad Base of Support   301
     Forms Social Networks May Take   302
     Community Institutions That Serve Families   303
Families Using Community Resources   304
     Sara's Family   304
     Roberto's Family   305
     Junior's Family   306
     Michael's Family   307
     Courtney's Family   308
     The Jackson Family   309
Connections to the Community   310
     A Summary of Community Resources   311
     Availability of Community Resources   313
Looking Back and Looking Forward   315
For Discussion   315
Web Sites   315
Further Reading   316

CHAPTER 14   **Societal Influences on Children and**
        Families   **318**
Socialization and the Family   320
     The Issue of Bias   321

Schools as Socializing Agents   326
  Getting into Kindergarten   327
  Classroom Behavior   330
  Responding to Diversity   331
  Inequity and Schools   332
The Peer Group as an Agent of Socialization   333
  Functions of the Peer Group   334
The Media as an Influence on Socialization   335
  Commercial Advertising   337
  Violence   338
Looking Back and Looking Forward   340
For Discussion   341
Web Sites   341
Further Reading   342

CHAPTER 15   Social Policy Issues   344

Who Is Responsible for America's Children?   346
  Does Every Child Get an Equal Start?   346
Ready to Learn: A Goal for All of America's Children   348
  Head Start   350
  Child Care   351
Moving Toward Full-Inclusion Programs   354
Economic Development   354
Adequate Health Services and Nutrition for All   355
Taking a Preventive Approach   356
Advocacy   357
Violence and Its Effect on Children and Families   359
Looking Back and Looking Forward   362
For Discussion   363
Web Sites   363
Further Reading   364

NAEYC: Where We Stand   367

References   370

Index   388

Note: Every effort has been made to provide accurate and current Internet information in this book. However, the Internet and information posted on it are constantly changing, so it is inevitable that some of the Internet addresses listed in this textbook will change.

Child, Family, and Community

Family-Centered
Early Care and Education

CHAPTER 1

The Child in Context of Family and Community

In this chapter you'll discover . . .

- Why this book is called *Child, Family, and Community*
- What ecological theory is
- Why making early care and education programs family-centered is important
- The benefits of family-centered programs for children, families, and teachers
- The history of the family-centered approach to care and education
- Some of the challenges of partnering with families
- What family systems are
- How to meet the needs of the "whole child"

Why is the title of this book, the *Child, Family, and Community*? Here's why. Many people go into the profession of early care and education because they love children. They find they relate well to children, and they enjoy being with them. When these individuals start taking classes, they find that their early childhood studies focus on the development and education of children. The course for which this book is designed also focuses on the child, but with a difference. This book takes the position that children must be looked at in context—meaning that each child must be viewed in the context of his or her family, and each family must be viewed in the context of the community to which it belongs. Taking this larger view of each child will help readers remember to always keep the context in mind, no matter what aspect of child development or early education they study.

What are the various contexts that families come in? Culture is certainly one context, as are race, ethnicity, socioeconomic level, family structure, and all the other variables that make this particular family what it is. Immigrant status, if any, is also a context. In one sense we are all immigrants. If you believe evolutionary theory, we all started in Africa. But let's jump forward a few eons and look at the people who were on this continent first, the individuals who can be considered indigenous. Their descendents are still here. The rest of the population is made up of immigrants, whether willing or unwilling, whether the family came this year, within the last century, or a few hundred years ago. When the family immigrated, and under what circumstances, has had an influence on the immigrants' lives and those of their descendents. This list of influences on families represents just the tip of the iceberg. It's a sample of all the ways in which families differ from each other by the contexts they are in.

Another huge influence on children is the community. The child and family are always placed in a community context. What community a family is in makes a big difference. My husband's family moved

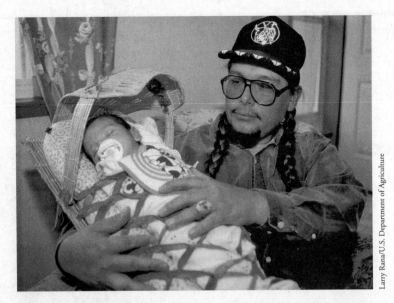

Larry Rana/U.S. Department of Agriculture

What are the contexts that families come in? Certainly their culture is one as are race, ethnicity, socioeconomic level, family structure, and all the other variables that make this particular family what it is.

from Puebla, Mexico, to the San Francisco Bay area in California many years ago—when my husband was 21 years old. They left behind countless relatives. When we visit those relatives and their descendents, we can see the different courses their lives took from those who moved to the United States. Just a few of the influences that have affected the U.S. family and the Mexican family in different ways are the changing international, national, and local political situations; the economies of the two

The family immigrant status is part of the context the child is in.

National Institute on Aging

countries and the local economies; and the changes that occur when one culture bumps up against another one, as is happening in both countries.

Education and socialization always occur in a context, and any specific context is embedded in a web of ever-changing other contexts. There is no such thing as a decontexualized child. To study "the child" without understanding the context is like studying the statue of a cat in order to understand its life. This whole book is about the education and socialization of the child in context. Simply put, the book examines the child in the context of developmental theory, which comes in the context of family, which lies in the context of community. All of these contexts can be thought of environments or settings that hold people, which influence each other and are influenced by culture.

Understanding the bigger picture of the child in context has been the theme of this book through its previous editions. This edition adds a further area of focus and that is on working with the family. Rather than making parent education and involvement just one component and dedicating a chapter to it, this edition is about family-centered care and education. To understand both the child and the family in context, we need an encompassing theory.

LOOKING AT CONTEXT THROUGH ECOLOGICAL THEORY

The history and foundations of family-centered care and education go way back. Something I learned as a student in an early childhood class in 1967 stuck in my mind. "Your client is not the child, but the *family*." The teacher of that class, Lilian Katz,

This book isn't just about parent education and involvement, but rather is about family-centered care and education.

University of Illinois professor and a pioneer in the field, is the one who made that statement. I've never forgotten what she said, but it has taken many years for the field as a whole to begin to understand and embrace that concept. This book is dedicated to not only expanding the understanding, but also to giving specific strategies to the reader about how to take that concept out of the theoretical realm and into the early childhood classroom, child care center, or family child care home.

Bronfenbrenner's Ecological Model

This new slant and organization falls in line with the model that Urie Bronfenbrenner first laid out for us in 1979. When he wrote that there are layers of context, he referred to a set of Russian dolls that are nested inside each other, the smallest one at the core. The organization of the book relates to Bronfenbrenner's layers. Although his layers may have different names, all the components of Bronfenbrenner's model are here in this text. Simply put, what Bronfenbrenner called an ecological model of human development means that every child is at the center of what can be visualized as concentric circles of context set in an overarching system of time, which affects all the contexts and changes them continuously. (See Figure 1.1.)

The microsystems layer, the smallest of the contexts in which the child is embedded, is made up of the environment where the child lives and moves. The people and institutions the child interacts with in that environment make up the microsystems. Examples are immediate family, child care (teachers and peers), and perhaps neighborhood play area, depending on the age of the child; school and religious institutions or spiritual groups may also be part of the system. The younger the child, the smaller the number of microsystems. The microsystems are set in the mesosystems layer, which relates to the interactions the people in the microsystems have with each other—as parents interact with child care providers, for example. The child is not directly involved with the mesosystems, but nevertheless is affected by them. The exosystems layer is a wider context—and though the

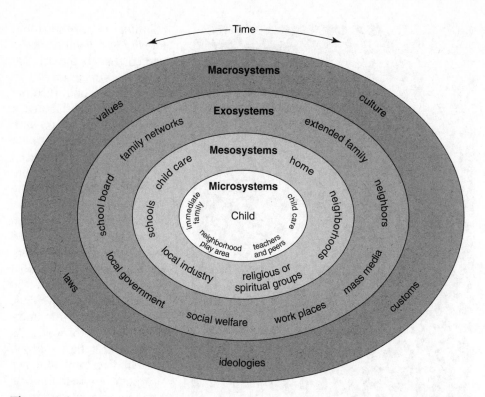

Figure 1.1
Bronfenbrenner's Ecological Model
Source: Gonzalez-Mena, Janet, *The Young Child in the Family and the Community*, Instructor's
Manual 4th Edition, © 2006. Reprinted by permission of Pearson Education, Inc., Upper Saddle
River, NJ.

child may not have direct contact with it, the systems affect the child's development and socialization—as do all the systems. Because the people in the child's
life are affected by the exosystems and mesosystems, the child is also. The exosystems can be thought of as the broader community, including the people, services,
and environments. Examples of what's in the exosystems layer are extended family,
family networks, mass media, workplaces, neighbors, family friends, community
health systems, legal services, and social welfare services. An example of how the
exosystems affect the child shows up when a parent goes to work or gets laid off
from work. The changes in the parent's life impact on the child's life. Another
example of an exosystem affecting the microsystems comes when the family has to
move because the apartment building where they live is scheduled to be torn down
to make room for urban renewal. The outer layer, called the macrosystems,

Urie Bronfenbrenner

contains the attitudes and ideologies, values, laws, and customs of a particular culture or subculture.

The point of the ecological model is that each component interacts with other components, creating a highly complex context in which the child grows up. Another point is that the child isn't just a passive recipient of what goes on in his or her life. The child at the center of Bronfenbrenner's ecological model interacts directly with the people in the microsystems, and the effects of the interaction go both ways. As people affect the child, so the child has an influence on them. Another point is that nothing ever remains static. As a result, the child, systems, and environments are ever changing. Milestones and life events occur as time passes, the child grows, and the contexts change.

IMPLICATIONS FOR EARLY EDUCATION: FAMILY-CENTERED APPROACHES

So understanding the child in context brings up an important question: why is it so common to send children off to child care, preschool, or school and leave the families out of the picture except for parent night and parent/teacher conferences? This book suggests a different approach, a family-centered approach to early care and education. There is a growing movement to change the focus of early childhood education (ECE) from the child (and groups of children) to the family. Part of the reason for this movement is increasing regard for the greater context the family is in, which includes culture, race, ethnicity, and economics among others, all of which influence the family's physical and social location in the neighborhood, community, and greater society (Bloom, Eisenberg, & Eisenberg, 2003; Epstein, 2001; Fitzgerald,

2004; Keyser, 2006; Lee, 2006; Lee & Seiderman, 1998; McGee-Banks, 2003). Leaders in the movement see the importance of including the families in all aspects of their children's care and education.

Family-Centered Defined

What is a family-centered approach? A family-centered approach takes the individual child and the group of children out of the spotlight and instead focuses on the children within their families. That means that parent involvement isn't something the teacher does in addition to the program for children, but that the program includes the family as an integral, inseparable, part of the child's education and socialization. Families, along with their children, *are* the program.

What does a family-centered program look like? Family-centered programs offer a variety of services, services in tune with what the parents as individuals and as a group need and want. But more than just services, they offer partnerships between professionals and families. Collaboration is a key word. The point is for professionals to become allies with families and share power. In a partnership, each partner brings a special set of strengths and skills that enhance the group. Through building relationships and ongoing communication the partnership results in mutual learning as both sides share resources and information with each other. Everyone benefits: the early educators, the families, and the children!

The Benefits of Family-Centered Programs for Children

When parents and teachers work together they enhance children's emotional security, which facilitates development and makes it easier for them to develop and learn. The children also benefit by being understood better—their strengths and needs—as individuals and in their family context. Continuity between home and program can be another benefit as teachers and parents understand each other better. There's a better chance for cultural consistency as a result of the parent-professional partnership or at least an understanding of and respect for cultural differences. Children's identity formation is enhanced when children don't have to experience uncomfortable feelings around the differences between what they learn at school and what they learn at home.

When children see adults modeling healthy, equitable relations in their interactions with each other, they receive a huge benefit. They learn that adults aren't just polite to each other, but have rich, authentic exchanges and even disagreements. Children gain by seeing how those adults solve their disagreements without harming their relationships with each other. If those adults deal with their own biases and increase their ability to communicate across differences, children are watching equity in action, which goes beyond trying to teach children to be fair by using an anti-bias curriculum.

Because positive relationships are important to development, security, and getting along with others, "relationships" is the first item listed in the accreditation standards of the National Association for the Education of Young Children. What better way to encourage relationships than to model them everyday as professionals and adults interact and collaborate.

The Benefits of Family-Centered Programs for Teachers

Early educators who understand the child within his or her family context can do a better job of teaching that child as well as working with the group of children. It makes the job more satisfying as teachers watch children gain in trust and self confidence. Teachers can learn new and effective teaching and guidance strategies as they observe parents and exchange information with them. Cindy Ballenger (1992) is one teacher who gained new insights by observing and coming to understand the approaches the Haitian families she worked with were using. As a result she expanded her guidance strategies. As professionals learn more about other cultures they can enlarge their views and gain knowledge and insights on child development, education, desired outcomes, and approaches related to these views. Families add richness to a program and provide resources to professionals.

As parents learn from teachers, they too can gain insights about their children. Sometimes the close contact with families brings teachers attention, acknowledgment, and appreciation that they might not receive otherwise. Partnership-type relationships can be very rewarding! Through relationships with families teachers can become more a part of the local community, if they aren't part of it already.

The Benefits of Family-Centered Programs for Families

Families today often feel isolated. Gone are the days for many of the old extended family where somebody was home or close by to give support or lend a hand to family members who needed it. A family-centered program can become like an extended family to those who desire such a thing.

When families are not part of their children's education, they have to just hope that what the program provides for their children is the same as what they want. That can be a big problem. Barbara Rogoff, author of *The Cultural Nature of Human Development*, said, "The goals of human development—what is regarded as mature or desirable—vary considerably." So if children are to spend big chunks of their lives throughout their childhood in educational programs, it makes sense that the goals of the program match the goals of the families, or at least don't contradict them. With pressures to conform to outcomes and desired results by policy makers and funding sources, it becomes even more important for parents to be knowledgeable and vocal.

Just as teachers can learn from parents, so can parents learn from teachers who look through a child development framework as they observe the children in the school environment with their peers. This gives parents a broader view than just knowing that child in the context of home and family. Families can gain greater knowledge of resources from the professionals in their children's program.

Mutual Benefits

Family-centered programs can expand everybody's horizons. One benefit for both teachers and parents is that of self-knowledge about their own culture—the beliefs and values that come from their roots and group membership. This benefit occurs whenever teachers and parents run into practices that seem wrong, or at least uncomfortable, and are able to talk to each other nonjudgmentally about their differences so they can come to understand not only their own but the other person's views (Im, Parlakian, & Sanchez, 2007). Barbara Rogoff has advice about how to do that: "We must separate *understanding of the patterns from judgments of their value*. If judgments of value are necessary, as they often are, they will thereby be much better informed if they are suspended long enough to gain some understanding of the patterns involved in one's own familiar ways as well as in the sometimes surprising ways of other communities" (Rogoff, p, 14).

Families, including their children, and professionals gain from the collaborative relationship in several other ways, including:

- Enhanced communication as the groups relate to each other around shared power and decision making
- Supportive relationships leading to networks of mutual support

The community also gains when families and ECE programs work together. These partnerships increase the chances of a better educated population and a more pluralistic society, one that values the richness diversity brings. As families and professionals work at getting together, another ultimate outcome can be equity and social justice growing from mutual understanding and acceptance.

HISTORY OF FAMILY-CENTERED CARE AND EDUCATION

The roots of family-centered care and education go way back. As professionals we've always known that families are important to children, whether they are at home or in early care and education programs. We have research to back us up, some of it from a pioneer, John Bowlby (1969;1973), a researcher noted for his attachment theory. He studied children separated from their parents while in the hospital, which was common practice at the time because children are easier to work with when parents aren't "in the way." Bowlby found that separation from family can be devastating to children's development and mental health, even if the professional care and medical procedures take care of their physical problems. He did the classic work on attachment and hospitalization, which made a difference in how doctors and hospitals treat the parent/child relationship today. Medical personnel no longer exclude parents from their children's presence in the hospital. We know now about attachment and hospitalization; we are still learning about attachment and education.

Instead of the teacher sharing information with families, there is two-way information sharing.

Head Start, which is still going strong today, was born in the Mississippi Freedom Schools. During the War on Poverty of the mid-1960s it became a federally-funded comprehensive preschool and social services program with not only a mandate for parent involvement and education but also built-in devices for parents to have some say in the education of their 4-year-olds. Several generations now have been through Head Start. Today Head Start teachers are sometimes grown-up Head Start children, as are some of the directors.

Urie Bronfenbrenner, mentioned earlier, was co-founder of Head Start. His *Ecology of Human Development* had a big influence on creating family-centered programs. He emphasized that the abstract concept of "the child" doesn't exist (Bronfenbrenner, 1979, 1994; Bronfenbrenner & Morris, 1998). His ideas not only caught hold in Head Start, but expanded the program downward to include infants and toddlers, the idea being not so much to educate the babies but to work with the families, because they are the ones that have the greatest influence on their children's lives.

Pioneer parent educator Ira J. Gordon (1968, 1976) created a program in Florida back in the 1960s involving parents of infants with the goal of improving child outcomes. He studied parent education and involvement and eventually came up with a hierarchy of types of involvement (Olmsted et al, 1980), moving from parents being recipients of information, to learning new skills, to teaching their own children and becoming a classroom volunteer. The two top kinds of involvement are becoming a paid para-professional and, finally, taking on the role of decision maker and policy advisor.

Today you can find elements of these various levels of involvement in many kinds of programs, including Head Start, other kinds of preschools, kindergartens, and primary grades. Some programs involve parents more than other programs.

The special education law PL 94–142, called the Education of All Handicapped Children Act of 1975, mandated parent involvement in planning for the education of the child. Each child identified with a disability or special need must have an Individual Educational Plan (IEP), or if an infant or toddler, an Individualized Family Service Plan (IFSP). A group of professionals along with the parents create these plans. According to the law and the reauthorized Individuals with Disabilities Act (IDEA) in 1990 and 1997, parents must be involved in all aspects of their children's education. PL 108–446 aligned special education with the No Child Left Behind (NCLB) legislation in 2004 and continued the mandate for parent involvement and power so that families disagreeing with a diagnosis or placement can call a hearing.

The "parent as the child's first teacher" is a motto now and a widespread notion throughout early care and education. Parent education materials, classes, and videos are available for new parents to see how important they are to their babies. Preschools involve parents in a variety of ways including volunteering in the classroom. One first-grade teacher has parents come in to the classroom twice a week first thing in the morning to read to their children. Most kindergarten and primary teachers encourage parents to help children with their homework. Also those same teachers usually encourage parents to help their children by finding a quiet place to do their homework and take an interest in school and what their children are learning.

That motto of "parents as the child's first teacher" can also be interpreted in another way in family-centered programs, which emphasize a broad range of parent-support services. Of course parents are welcome to come into the classroom, but they are not mandated to do so. The focus of the support is to help parents with whatever they need rather than telling them how to be involved in their child's education or that they have to take the role of teacher. Some families find that through the kind of support they gain from the program staff and other families in the program, they are better able to organize their lives so they can support their children emotionally, and meet their basic physical needs for nutrition, rest, and exercise. Children whose physical and emotional needs are met have the focus and energy for learning. These are real basics.

Douglas Powell wrote about the family-centered program movement in 1986. He said, "This shift toward family-oriented programs is typical of the direction many programs in the field of early childhood are taking" (1986, p. 50). Powell used Head Start as an example when he wrote about the shift from child-focused programs to family-centered ones. Head Start today, in its many forms, still makes the family the client. In 1998, Powell acknowledged that the movement toward family-centered programs wasn't as widespread as it should be. He illustrated with a metaphor of programs as a piece of fabric made of three colors of thread—one color each for children, staff, and parents. He described the most common pattern as a weaving of the child and staff together; the parents end up in a separate section. Many programs still show this same pattern. The family-centered program would make a different fabric, with the parent threads woven throughout the pattern so that all three colors of thread are integrated. In a family-centered program there is no separate section of the pattern just for parents (Powell,1998, p. 60).

The Epstein Model, based on Gordon's roles for parent involvement, was created by Joyce Epstein (2001), who wrote a handbook called *School, Family, and Community*

Partnerships. The handbook lists the six types of partnerships that reflect Gordon's hierarchy using a little different language and going one step further to include "collaborating with the community."

Here is Epstein's list:

- Parenting
- Communicating school-to-home and home-to-school
- Volunteering
- Helping students learn at home
- Decision making (including families as participants in school decisions, governance and advocacy through PTA/PTO, school councils, committees, and other parent organizations)
- Collaborating with the community

As parents move up the "involvement ladder," they move beyond thinking about just their own children and becoming an advocate for them, to looking at advocating for all children, including ways to improve the program, the school, or the system.

Family-centered care and education is a giant step forward from parent involvement hierarchies. It involves a much larger vision of families being vital parts of their children's care and education.

The National Association for the Education of Young Children (NAEYC) supports family-centered programs. The NAEYC says, "Young children's learning and development are integrally connected to their families. Consequently, to support and promote children's optimal learning and development, programs need to recognize the primacy of children's families, establish relationships with families based on mutual trust and respect, support and involve families in their children's educational growth, and invite families to fully participate in the program" (NAEYC, 2005, p. 11). Earlier the NAEYC also came out with a new book, *From Parents to Partners: Building a Family-Centered Early Childhood Program* (Keyser, 2006). In addition, the NAEYC instituted a project in 2007 called Strengthening Family-Teacher Partnerships, which started with several "training the trainer" institutes.

The Harvard Family Research Project has been and is still aggressively working on linking families to their children's educational programs. When parent involvement takes the form of family support, there is evidence that it can lower stress levels in parents and make their lives easier.

The Parent Services Project started in the 1980s by Ethel Seiderman in California as a mission to strengthen families by having them take leadership in assuring the well-being of children, families, and communities (Lee, 2006; Lee & Seiderman, 1998). The Parent Services Project, or PSP, now provides training, technical assistance, and consultation nationally to help programs and schools engage families. Instead of merely involving families, the approach they take is to provide a wide variety of services that reflect the interests and needs of the families enrolled. Instead of predetermining what will be offered the programs are designed to involve families in deciding, planning, and organizing the activities. As a result programs trained in the

PSP approach find increased parent involvement, leadership, and participation, which strengthens community ties and leads to effective community building (Pope & Seiderman, 2001; Seiderman, 2003).

Child abuse prevention is one of the goals of the Doris Duke Foundation and the Center for the Study of Social Policy (2004). They take the approach of supporting protective factors in families through a project called Strengthening Families Through Early Care and Education (Doris Duke Web site 2007). Parental resilience, social connections, parenting, and child development knowledge are all protective factors in preventing abuse as well as giving support in times of need (Olsen, 2007). Like the Parent Services Project this project sees early care and education professionals as a logical group for working with parents to gain positive results and lower the risk of child abuse. The project is based on a body of research that focuses on protective factors to reduce risks of child abuse. The delivery system comes from early care and education professionals who learn how to support parents, provide resources, and teach coping strategies that will then reduce stress and prevent child abuse.

One of the premises of all these family-centered early care and education programs is that they work better when professionals understand families and involve them in respectful ways. Instead of the teacher just sharing information with families, there is two-way information sharing. This is true for general early care and education programs and also for special education. There is some evidence that parent involvement is a critical factor in early intervention programs. The rationale is that parents spend more time with their children than early interventionists and should take an active role in the interventions, not just turn their children over to the specialists. Parents have many more opportunities to influence their children's learning and development, and involvement in their children's programs expands their knowledge of and skills in specific ways for their individual child (Mahoney & Wiggers, 2007; Turnbull et al, 2000).

Challenges to Creating Partnerships with Families

Responsiveness to families is a theme of this book. It's hard sometimes to be responsive when you think you know more than the family does. Obviously professionals have funds of knowledge from their training, professional education, and experience that most families don't have. Families also have funds of knowledge that professionals don't have. It's the professionals job to acknowledge that fact and to learn from parents as well as teach them. It's more of a sharing of knowledge than it is imparting. It also requires suspending judgments when the professional thinks families are wrong or misguided, even if research backs up the professional. Consider this quote from Asa Hilliard, III (2007):

> The great error in behavioral research, now acknowledged by prestigious scholars, is that in most cases there has been a failure to take context into account. Research tends to proceed as if constructs, methods, instruments, and interpretations in

culturally embedded studies are universal. Nothing could be further from the truth. Most researchers are ill prepared to do research in a culturally plural environment or to deal with hegemony as it relates to culture.

Rogoff sees that the theories of development studied by teachers and human development specialists have a "single developmental trajectory, moving toward a pinnacle that resembles the values of the theorist's own community, indeed of the theorist's own life course (page 18)." Most human development theorists come from a strong literacy background and therefore have held literacy as the hallmark of a successful outcome of development. Piaget, a scientist and thinker, saw the development of reason as the ultimate outcome of development. From these theorists' points of view, it's easy to see societies as primitive when they don't hold these same values or visions.

Hilliard (2004) also has a concern about how the lens of culture is often left out of what he calls mainstream psychology. Though he's looking at the field of psychology rather than human development, the two fields overlap in many places. Hilliard observed that mainstream psychology rarely shows any academic or scientific expertise in culture. In fact, according to Hilliard, many scholars seem to believe that cultural diversity matters are "more political than scientific." He went on to say that there is real resistance among many traditional psychologists to engage in the required scientific study and dialogue about these cultural matters. "Their cultural naiveté is almost legendary." When one looks through a cultural lens, one sees sets of realities that are different from what has been analyzed and studied in the name of psychology and human development.

OTHER LENSES THROUGH WHICH TO LOOK AT FAMILY-CENTERED APPROACHES

Context is important. This book emphasizes going deeper to understand children and families in the context of their environment, their community. Context can be viewed from a number of lenses. One of them is a cross-cultural lens, used by anthropologists, which both Rogoff and Hilliard say should be used by anybody looking at context, especially scholars who create and study developmental and psychological theories. That particular lens was viewed as a challenge in the preceding section. Here we want to look at three more lenses through which to look at children in families and communities.

The Family Systems Theory Lens

Another way to understand context and use your understanding to work with families is family systems theory. I first encountered this theory when I read Virginia Satir's *Peoplemaking* and heard her speak, back in the 1980s. To explain the universality of her theory, she used an analogy of the human body—that any surgeon who studies medicine can operate on any human in the world because the organs are the same. The theory behind family systems theory is that families may be very different in many ways, but they all have some things in common and that is that they are governed by systems. One such system is communication, and another is rules. All families communicate with each other. How and to what extent differs, but communication is a given. All families have rules—what they are and how they are carried out is different for each family.

The lens of family systems theory puts the focus on the way the family works rather than on the behavior of any individual in it. That makes the focus of the family therapist different from that of traditional therapists who work only with individuals. Family members are connected to each other; each one influences the others, and all are influenced by the family system. Understanding those influences and the shifts that take place when changes occur in the family is what guides family therapists. Early educators aren't therapists and shouldn't be doing therapy. Their job isn't to diagnose family problems and fix them. Still, early educators can find family systems theory useful to further their understandings of how the systems work in each family. Think of a framework for understanding in a deeper way.

Even though the systems themselves are the same, they can vary greatly from one family to another in the way they operate. It's also useful to realize that changes, even small ones, can affect the system and the individuals in it. When early educators look at a child through a family system lens, they realize that they can't work on behavior changes in children all by themselves, because those children are part of family systems. I think back to times I've been in teacher meetings where a child's challenging behavior is being discussed. A missing ingredient of these discussions was the family's involvement.

Linda Garris Christian (2006) in her article about family systems and its relevance to early educators lists six systems that are useful to understand when working with families. The systems are: boundaries, roles, rules, hierarchy, climate, and equilibrium. She says that all families have these systems, but they look very different from one family to another.

Take *boundaries* for example, which relate to limits, togetherness, and separateness—what or who is in or out of the family. I remember an exercise from a workshop I attended where the group was asked by the facilitator to think about the family they grew up in. She asked how many grew up in a large family. When participants raised their hands, she then questioned them about how they defined a large family and who was in it. Their answers reflected differences in boundaries. One person counted 50 people in her family. She included blood relatives and close others. Her family might have been called a kinship network by some. Another had an even larger family, and she included people who were no longer alive. Another person who came from a large family numbered six in her family—herself, her parents, and her three siblings. The boundaries in the families of the first two participants were much looser than those of the third participant as determined by the definition of family members—who was included and who was not.

How emotionally and psychologically close family members are to each other is another part of boundaries. In families where the priority is raising children to be more independent than interdependent, the boundaries are different from those families where interdependence is a top priority. Christian uses the term *enmeshed* to label families who are extremely interdependent. I bristled at that word. It seemed judgmental to me. My experience with people I have known who come from families a therapist labeled *enmeshed* is that they emerged from therapy convinced they had "boundary issues" because they weren't closer to the middle of the boundaries continuum. *Disengaged* is the term Christian used for the families on the other end of the continuum. Just thinking about the cross-cultural views of boundaries in my own family gives me pause. If my mother and mother-in-law had studied to be family systems therapists, I'm pretty sure that my mother would have labeled my mother-in-law's family as "enmeshed" and my mother-in-law would have called my mother "disengaged." Having been part of both those families now for a number of years, I think both labels are too harsh. Certainly, putting on a cross-cultural lens makes a difference in how one views family boundaries that don't fit one's own ideas and experiences.

A danger of using the family systems theory is the temptation to play therapist. Another danger is judging other people's family systems, without regard to your own. Obviously early educators are the product of some kind of family systems, and just as we have to understand our own culture, we have to understand our own family systems so we can stop just looking outward. "Know thyself," said Shakespeare. That's the lesson here.

Understanding and working with family systems theory is a much bigger and more complex job than just focusing on caring for and educating the developing child. But taking a family-centered approach is more complicated too. The challenges are great, but the rewards are too.

All these mandates to deal with the huge complexity in the program, the child, the family, and the community may seem overwhelming! I have warned more than once to be cautious. Perhaps my warnings are too strong and early educators will put aside who they are and what they know so they can just focus on opening up their minds to what the families they work with know. So at this point, it needs to be said that that early childhood educators also have the responsibility to share their professional knowledge and personal beliefs with the families. This may be harder in a cross-cultural context and may take more sensitivity than when working with one's "own people." Nevertheless, information sharing has to be a two-way street.

The Whole Child Lens

Early educators learn from families, and families learn from early educators. This issue becomes important when you realize that this book focuses heavily on the social-emotional aspects of development even though school readiness and cognitive development are in the spotlight at present. School readiness is, of course, a concern for everybody, but professionals with a child development background often come at it from a different angle than some other professionals and families by recognizing that social-emotional development is vitally tied to cognitive development.

Way back when I started in this field, I remember the families who came into the program where I taught wanting their children to learn to read. The same is true today. Family members sometime arrive in ECE programs much more focused on their children's intellect than on their feelings and social abilities. Yet research indicates that matters of the heart are the very foundation of mental growth. A book called *Toward a General Theory of Love* (Lewis et al, 2000) gives eloquent scientific explanations for how emotional ties that link children to others create actual changes in the brain structure leading to stability, health, and the ability to think.

Early care and educational professionals study what has been called "the whole child." The child is made of mind, body, and feelings, and one system is vitally tied into the others. Though child development books may tease out the parts and put them in separate chapters, in reality, the child is always a whole. No matter how much you want to promote school readiness, you can't separate the intellect from the emotions.

What part does the body play in school readiness? How often does a parent look into the play yard, see the children having a good time, and think, "how can they learn if all they do is play here?" Carla Hannaford (2005) answers that question in her book *Smart Moves: Why Learning Is Not All in Your Head*. She is clear that children need to move in order to think. The book brings compelling information from the neurosciences about the relationship of body movement to learning. This is the kind of professional information that early educators can share with parents so that families come to understand that care and education in the early years may be different from their own experience in their childhood or their concepts of what school should be like.

ABRAHAM MASLOW'S HIERARCHY OF NEEDS

Another theorist whose model relates to the whole child concept is Abraham Maslow (1954). His hierarchy of needs provides important information for anyone concerned with working with young children and their families. His theory rests on the idea that basic needs must be met for growth to occur. The most basic needs of all are physiological and include air, food, water, and rest. A hungry child is motivated to get food and uses all available energy for that end, energy that well-fed children use for going on to meet higher needs. On the next level up is the need for safety. One way that the safety need can be met in young children is by making their lives predictable. Some children especially find their security in the routines of the day. Change the routine and feelings of safety disappear. Children crying at separation is another expression of safety needs. The next step up is the need for love and belonging, though with the latest information about the importance of relationships to a child's brain development, perhaps this need for relationship is as strong as the need for food, water, air, and rest. Recognition is the next step up in the hierarchy of needs. Self-esteem is part of this level as well as recognition from others. This step has to do with a feeling of self worth. At the top of the pyramid (See Figure 1.2) is self-actualization, which reflects the need to live up to one's potential—be all that one can be. Although originally Maslow worked to define the self-actualized person, later he decided that it's an ongoing process that lasts a lifetime. So he changed the term to the self-*actualizing* person. Meeting all these needs is behind the ability to seek knowledge, learn, and develop. When children consistently come to school, child care, or to early care and education programs hungry, they have less intellectual curiosity and motivation to learn than those whose nutritional needs are met on a regular basis. Head Start figured that out a long time ago and took the responsibility to meet the children's daily nutritional needs. Subsidized school breakfast and lunch programs are based on the same idea for low-income school-age children. This is an example of how the community can meet a child's need, when the family cannot. Another example of meeting a different kind of need is when teachers in a full inclusion program gain the skills needed to

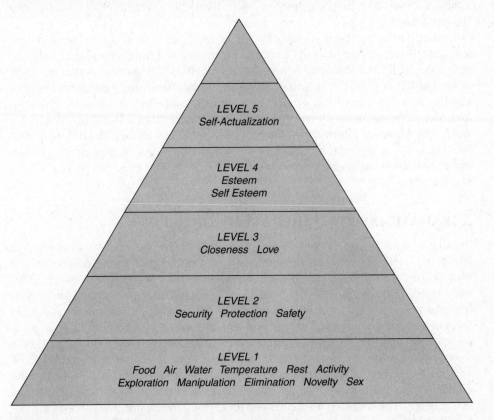

Figure 1.2
Maslow's Hierarchy of Needs

Source: Maslow, Abraham H.; Frager, Robert D.; Fadiman, James, *Motivation and Personality,* 3rd Edition, © 1987. Adapted by permission of Pearson Education, Inc., Upper Saddle River, NJ.

integrate children with special needs into the group of
their typically developing
peers, so everyone has a
sense of belonging.

To truly meet children's
needs in care and education
programs, the family must
be the focus, not just the
child. When you relate to
families in ways that make
them feel understood and
valued you are doing a service to the child. The first
goal is to help families feel
supported by the program.
But the early educator's job
goes beyond understand-

Abraham Maslow

ing, valuing, and supporting—most important of all is for families to have the voice
to say what they need. That makes each program a little different, rather than some
kind of standardized curriculum for parent involvement. It's also very different to
find out what families need than it is to just ask them to support the program's
goals. The idea is to take a collaborative approach (Gonzalez-Mena & Stonehouse,
2008). A collaborative approach means that change not only occurs within the families, but also within the program as it begins to reflect those enrolled rather than
just the predetermined policies and practices (Powell, 1998). The movement for
family-centered programs isn't just about improving child outcomes, though that
may be the focus of some of the leaders in the movement. Other leaders are most
concerned about empowering parents through making programs more collaborative. These leaders come from the perspective of parental rights; some also come
from wanting to respect diversity and promote equity. Certainly, understanding how
social support can lower stress factors and improve parental functioning gives
advocates good reason to push for programs that address parents' needs and create
family-centered programs.

LOOKING BACK AND LOOKING FORWARD

The chapter started with a look at why this book is called the *Child, Family, and
Community* and considered Bronfenbrenner's ecological model as part of the reason:
because children always come in a context. You can't ever consider a child without
thinking of the family in which that child is embedded, which is why family-centered
approaches to early care and education programs are so important. Of course, there
are also challenges, which the chapter also considered. One way of understanding
families is to understand their family systems and how they play out. The chapter

ended with a discussion of the concept called the "whole child," which means that though you can tease out particular domains of growth and development, like physical or mental, everything is always intertwined. That led to a discussion of school readiness and Marlow's hierarchy of needs.

The next chapter continues the idea of the whole child by looking at how the social and emotional influences of attachment affect brain development in infancy, which in turn affects how well the child can think and learn.

FOR DISCUSSION

1. What do you think about working in a family-centered program? Do you have any experience with that approach?

2. What do you see as the benefits and challenges of a family-centered approach?

3. Thinking about your own life using Bronfenbrenner's ecological model, can you draw a picture of the various layers of context in which you grew up?

4. What are your memories of your early care and education? Consider that the term covers programs serving children and families from birth to third grade. To what extent was your family involved in your out-of-home care and education?

5. What is your understanding of Maslow's hierarchy of needs? Do you know someone who you would consider has reached the highest levels?

WEB SITES

The Doris Duke Foundation
http://www.cssp.org/doris_duke/index.html
Highlights projects called Strengthening Families in early care and education programs across the country which are designed to prevent child abuse by building on protective factors.

The Ecological Model of Human Development
http://www.headstartinfo.org/publication/enhancing growth/modl.htm
A Head Start training module to help teachers understand how to use Bronfenbrenner's ecological model of human development to better serve the child and family.

The Harvard Family Project
http://www.gse.harvard.edu/hfrp/
The Harvard Family Research Project (HFRP) is a large, on-going research program with the goal of promoting more effective educational practices, programs and policies. Click on *Family Involvement Makes a Difference* for a large number of resources on family involvement.

National Association for the Education of Young Children (NAEYC)
http://www.naeyc.org
The National Association for the Education of Young Children provides many resources for professionals about family-centered care and education.

Parent Services Project
http://www.parentservices.org/
This program trains early childhood professionals on how to partner with families in ways that develop and strengthen their leadership qualities and roles in educational programs for their children.

Zero to Three
http://www.zerotothree.org/
Zero to Three: National Center for Infants, Toddlers, and Families, designed for parents and professionals, has development a project called PCAN (Preventing Child Abuse and Neglect) teaching infant–toddler care teachers how to partner with parents.

FURTHER READING

Ballenger, C. (1992, Summer). Because you like us: The language of control. *Harvard Educational Review* 62(2), 199–208.

Bloom, P. J., Eisenberg, P., & Eisenberg, E. (2003, Spring/Summer). Reshaping early childhood programs to be more family responsive. *America's Family Support Magazine*, 36–38.

Bronfenbrenner, U. (1979). The ecology of human development: Experiments by nature and design. Cambridge, MA: Harvard University Press.

Bronfenbrenner, U. (1994). Ecological models of human development. In T. Husen and N. Postlethwaite (Eds.), *International Encyclopedia of Education*, Vol. 3, 2nd ed., 1643–1647.

Bronfenbrenner, U., & Morris P. A. (1998). The ecology of developmental processes. In R. M. Lerner (Ed.), *Handbook of child psychology*, Vol. 1. *of Theoretical models of human development*, Ed. W. Damon. New York: Wiley.

Christian, L. G. (2006). Understanding families: Applying family systems theory to early childhood practice. *Young Children* 61(2), 12–20.

Epstein, J. L. (2001). *School, family and community partnerships: Preparing educators and improving schools.* Boulder, CO: Westview Press.

Fitzgerald, D. (2004). *Parent partnership in the early years.* London: Continuum.

Gonzalez-Mena, J., & Stonehouse, A. (2008). *Making links: A collaborative approach to planning and practice in early childhood programs.* New York: Teachers College Press.

Hannaford, C. (2005). *Smart moves: When learning is not all in your head.* Salt Lake City: Great River Books.

Hilliard, A. G. (2004) Assessment equity in a multicultural society. New Horizons for Learning, www.newhorizons.org

Im, J. Parlakian, R., & Sanchez S. (2007). Understanding the influence of culture on caregiving practices . . . From the inside out. *Young Children* 62(5), 65–66.

Keyser, J. (2006) *From parents to partners: Building a family centered early childhood program.* Washington DC: National Association for the Education of Young Children, and St. Paul, MN: Redleaf.

Lee, L. (2006) *Stronger together: Family support and early childhood education.* San Rafael: Parent Services Project.

Lee, L., & Seiderman, E.(1998). *Families matter: The Parent services project.* Cambridge, MA: Harvard Family Research Project.

Lewis, T., Amini, F., & Lannon, R. (2000). *A general theory of love.* New York: Vintage Books.

Mahoney, G., & Wiggers, B. (2007). The role of parents in early intervention. *Children and Schools* 29, (1), 7–15.

McGee-Banks, C. A. (2003). Families and teachers working together for school improvement. In J. A. Banks & C. A. McGee-Banks (Eds.), *Multicultural education: Issues and perspectives* (4th ed., pp. 402–410). New York: Wiley.

Maslow, A. (1954). *Motivation and personality.* New York: Harper and Row.

National Association for the Education of Young Children (2005). *Families and community relationships: A guide to the NAEYC early childhood program standards and related accreditation criteria.* Washington, DC: National Association for Education of Young Children.

Pope, J., & Seiderman, E. (2001, Winter). The childcare connection. *Family Support* 19(4), 24–35.

Powell, D. R. (1998). Research in review. Reweaving parents into the fabric of early childhood programs. *Young Children* 53(5), 60–67.

Rogoff, B. (2003). *The cultural nature of human development*, New York: Oxford University Press.

Seiderman, E. (2003). Putting all the players on the same page: Accessing resources for the child and family. In B. Neugebauer & R. Neugebauer (Eds.), *The art of leadership.* Redmond, WA: Exchange Press

CHAPTER 2

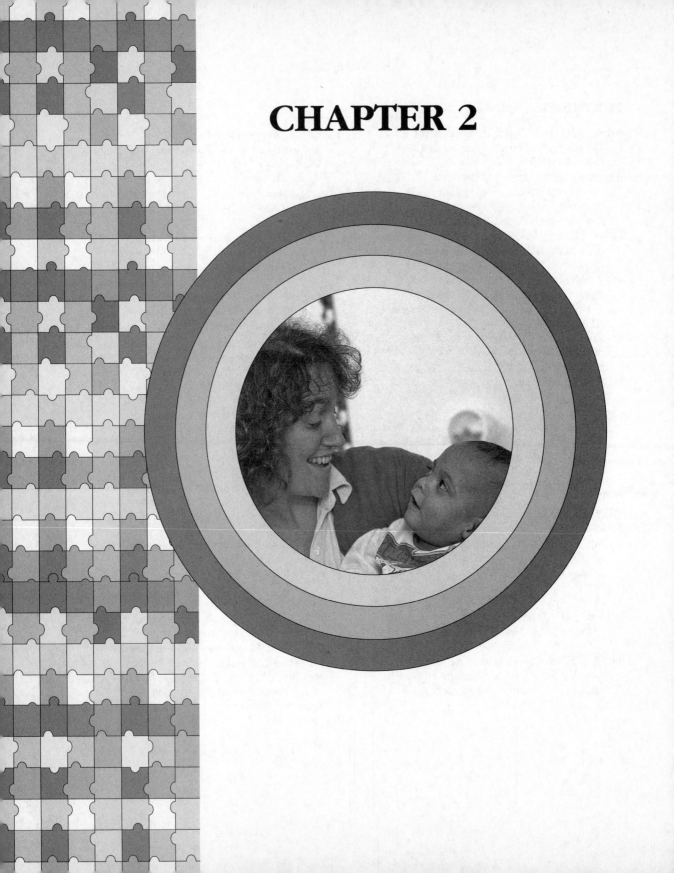

Supporting Families Around Issues of Attachment

In *this chapter you'll discover* . . .

- Why attachment is important
- What helps babies develop trust
- How parents show they are attached to their baby
- How babies show they are attached to their parents
- Your role in attaching to babies and supporting their attachment to family
- How child care affects attachment
- The difference between being an infant-care teacher and being a parent

What is attachment, and why is it important? Why should early childhood educators in general and infant-care teachers in particular be concerned about attachment? Attachment is a lasting emotional relationship that begins to develop in infancy and serves to tie the infant to one or more people in his or her life. It is a two-way process—adults (usually parents or other family members) attach to infants, and infants attach to adults. This two-way process results in a significant relationship. Attachment is a lifelong process that starts in the first year of life and carries throughout the life span. The first early attachment sets the tone for a child's development and defines some of the issues that he or she will carry into adulthood. This chapter focuses on attachment in infancy and the issues and implications for early care and education professionals working with families.

Although attachment is an emotional process that we associate with "the heart," other processes engaging the brain are also involved. Healthy attachment provides the foundation for later intellectual development, according to research being done on the brain. The positive nurturing experiences associated with attachment produce hormones called *neurotransmitters* that give the infant a sense of well-being. This sense of well-being reinforces certain pathways in the brain, which leads to mental growth. On the other hand, children who have attachment issues or worse, no attachment figure(s), lack a sense of security and experience stress, which has a detrimental effect on the brain's development. Bruce Perry (2002; 2006) in his writings and lectures talks about the chemicals that wash over the brain when babies experience some of the results of lack of attachment, like abuse or neglect.

With school readiness receiving so much widespread attention in the early care and education field, some people think the main message from the brain research is that academic teaching should start early. To the contrary, the real message is the important role that social-emotional development plays in intellectual development. In a new journal published by the International Mind, Brain, and Education Society, Immordino-Yang and Damasio (2007) make an excellent case for emotional processes profoundly affecting learning, attention, and memory. Although they focus on neuroscience and education, and not on infants, attachment is the foundation of the emotional processes they write about. They say that feelings provide an "emotional rudder" to guide judgment and action. That's one of the reasons that this book focuses in on social-emotional development throughout and starts right off with attachment the basis for early social-emotional development. It's important for early childhood educators and the families they work with to recognize the role that social-emotional development plays in the lives and development of children.

A short article in *Time* brings this point home further (Park, 2007). In 2006 parents spent $200 million on *Baby Einstein* videos to help their babies get ahead intellectually. Yet in a study done at the University of Washington, researchers found that for every hour babies spent watching the videos, they understood an average of seven fewer words than the babies who had no exposure to the videos. The parents of the video-free babies apparently followed the advice of the American Academy of Pediatrics, which recommends that parents keep babies under two away from screens and just interact with them instead. Those interactions are likely to result in stronger, healthier attachment.

Here's another example of how attachment contributes to cognitive development in infants. When children feel secure, they are freer to explore the environment around them. Watch a group of babies in a playroom. You're bound to see some exploration as the ones who are mobile go looking to see what's there. If these babies get too far from their infant-care teacher or become startled, they head back to touch base, get a little hug, and gather up their courage to move out again. The greatest explorers are usually the ones who are securely attached. According to Ainsworth's research (1977, 1978) secure attachment can be easily seen in the behavior of infants who are separated from their parents and then reunited with them. Attachment is a matter of trust, which is the subject of the next section.

ATTACHMENT AND TRUST

The basis of healthy care and education is social-emotional development and the basis of that is attachment comes from a synchronous relationship, which grows from a number of synchronous interactions. Here's what a synchronous interaction looks like, whether the adult in the scene is the baby's parent, a center-based infant-care teacher, or a family child care provider.

The adult is bent over a 3-month-old baby who is lying on her back in a play area. The adult is expressionless. The baby rounds her mouth and lets out a breathy sound while reaching out her arms. The adult responds by widening her eyes, rounding her own mouth, and imitating the sound. She reaches for the baby's hands and holds them in her own. The baby pulls her hands away, kicks her feet, and widens her own eyes in imitation of the adult. The adult smiles. The baby smiles back. The adult keeps smiling, makes clucking noises, and claps her hands. The baby turns away. "Oh, that was too much for you," responds the adult, quieting her activity. The baby looks back. The adult smiles. The baby smiles, then arches and reaches. "You want up?" the adult asks, reaching out her arms to the child.

These two are "in sync" with each other. The adult is sensitive to the baby's signals and reads the turning away as a need to tune out, not a personal rejection of her. The baby knows how to "light up" the adult's face. The adult knows how to "turn on" the baby. The two are good together. If they are not already attached, they are becoming attached.

The two are "in sync" with each other.

Doris Pfalmer

Babies become attached when people in their lives are sensitive and responsive. That means that they pay attention to the baby's signals and read them accurately, responding readily and appropriately. Adults practice being responsive when they play with babies, as in this scene. They also meet needs by reading babies' cues and responding in a timely fashion with feeding, for example. Both play and meeting needs contribute to the development of attachment.

> *Imagine yourself a very young baby, lying asleep in a crib. You open your eyes—suddenly you're wide awake. You see nothing except a blur of light—there are no objects, no movement within your visual range. You feel a very uncomfortable sensation in your midsection. You squirm around. Changing position doesn't help. Suddenly you feel desperate. The sensation in your midsection takes over your whole body. You squeeze your eyes shut tight and open your mouth wide. Into your ears comes a piercing sound. You don't know that it's your own cry. You only know that something is terribly wrong, and your whole being reacts to it. Your heart pounds, your face burns, and you scream in agony, then gasp for breath, only to start screaming again once you get your lungs full. You're like this for what seems an eternity but is actually less than 2 minutes. You feel something touch you. You open your eyes and find something very distinctive and vaguely familiar in front of the blur of light that was all that was there before. The something moves in a way that makes you feel comfortable. As you pause for breath, you hear another sound—not the high, agonized one of before, but a soft, soothing one. You feel a blanket of pleasure surround you, providing immeasurable relief, and, true to your most cherished hope, you find yourself lifted in the air out of the loneliness—the isolation—and snuggled into a pair of warm arms. You're basking in the glow of the feelings of this, when—wonder of wonders—something familiar touches your cheek. You jerk toward the something, manage to get your mouth around it, and begin sucking. A warm, sweet sensation floods your mouth and you're in heaven.*

Imagine now a different scene where the hungry baby wakes up and doesn't have to signal her needs because the adult is right there with her and feeding occurs immediately, before the baby even cries.

These two scenes illustrate how needs, attachment, and trust all come in a bundle in the beginning of life. The scenes are slightly different. In the first one, the infant wakes up alone and must let the adult know about the need for food and comfort. In the second scene, the infant wakes up in physical contact with the adult, who anticipates the needs before crying occurs.

You may prefer one scene over the other—you may actually feel critical of one of the scenes. However, both of these patterns of relating to the needs of the very young infant lead to a healthy attachment, one that serves both the individual and the culture. It's important to remember that attachment patterns are related to parental values and goals (Chang, 1993; Gonzalez-Mena, 1997, 2004, 2008). Parents rear their children to fit the world as they perceive it. (See Chapter 6 for more on this subject.)

Attachment is vital. It is a means of ensuring survival of the child and also of the species (Bowlby, 2000). It creates the caring (the feeling) that motivates the *action* of giving care. It ensures that nurturing and protection will be provided to the relatively helpless infant. But beyond physical survival, the first attachments provide the basis for all future relationships.

If the infant finds that when needs arise they are met with reasonable promptness, as in the two prior scenes, he or she comes to see the world as a welcoming place. A sense of trust grows from fulfillment and satisfaction in the first year of life. Infants who are left screaming for long periods, gripped in the agony of hunger pangs, come to see the world as an unfriendly place. They find that they can't trust anyone to take care of them. If they give signals and no one responds, they see themselves as powerless and the world as cold and hostile. When these children grow out of infancy, they continue to view the world with distrust.

This early issue of developing trust versus mistrust was originally defined and described by Erik Erikson (1963), who sees life as a series of what he calls *psychosocial dilemmas* to be resolved (see Figure 2.1).

Trust is a lifelong issue for all of us. However, children who develop a sense of distrust in infancy grapple with the issue more intensely than others. Some of these children are left with unresolved trust issues; others successfully deal with the problem if the situation changes and those around them become more responsive and meet their needs more promptly. Children with unresolved trust issues often reach adulthood still seeking the early caregiver who left their needs unmet. Because it is never too late to resolve trust issues, some adults seem continually to choose to connect to people who treat them much as their early caregiver(s) did. They put themselves back into their infant situation, to perhaps give themselves another chance to relive the situation and manage a different outcome. The human being is very resilient! Continually seeking their early caregiver later in life may not be necessary for those children who find a warm, nurturing person to whom to attach in their early care and education program. According to Bruce Perry, a firm, healthy attachment is one way to get children through hard times in their lives with less damage to their brain development and therefore to their social-emotional and cognitive development (Perry, 2006).

Attachment is a powerful process—and it seems that even a little goes a long way. Look at studies of survivor types—children who manage to cope and live a productive life in spite of factors in their early years that work against that. The one thing that all

Child's Stage	Approximate Age	Task		
Infancy	0 – 1	Basic trust	versus	Basic mistrust
Toddlerhood	1 – 3	Autonomy	versus	Shame and doubt
The preschool years	3 – 6	Initiative	versus	Guilt
School age	6 – 10	Industry	versus	Inferiority

Figure 2.1

Erikson's psychosocial stages of development

Source: From Erikson (1963).

these survivor children have in common is a person they could attach to sometime in their first year—even though it might not have been an ideal attachment or a long-lasting one. Emmy Werner, a developmental psychologist, did classic research on resiliency over the last 40 years. Her findings show that attachment in the early years with a caregiver who had predominantly positive interactions with the child acts as a protective factor (Werner, 1984, 1995, 2000; Werner & Smith, 1992). These findings are important for early care and education practitioners to know about, because they focus on the protective factors that can make a difference in children's lives. In fact, you could be the person who makes the difference in a child's life.

Strengthening Families Through Early Care and Education is a research project that has identified exemplary family-support programs which show that staff in child care centers and other early education programs can make a difference. Using a "protective factors" framework, the project documents how exemplary programs reduce abuse and neglect. The idea is that programs can intentionally strengthen families while serving their children. One of the protective factors occurs when staff works to build trusting relationships with parents and offers support to them when they are going through difficult periods. That kind of relationship, which can be a type of attachment, is different from what staff provide to children (www.cssp.org/doris_duke, accessed June 20, 2007).

Attachment may begin prenatally, as parents begin to relate to their visions of the growing fetus.

Blend Images/Superstock Royalty Free

HOW ATTACHMENT OCCURS

There are many different ways of getting attached to infants and older children, depending on the individual and the culture. Although attachment, like love, can't necessarily come on command, there are certain factors in infant programs that make it more likely to occur. It might be easier to describe the factors that work against it. Imagine a large room in an infant center with a number of babies of different ages and adults there to care for them. The adult/child ratio is within the funding standards—one adult to three children. But the size of the group is big, and there is a chaotic feeling in the room. One child just had his second birthday, and one of the infant-care teachers is getting him ready to move to the classroom in the next building where the two-year-olds are housed. He is protesting loudly. Another screaming child is a 9-month-old who is just getting moved up from the baby room today. What's wrong with this picture?

According to Ron Lally (1995) three important factors—group size, primary care, and continuity of care—make a big difference in whether relationships grow between adults and the infants in their care. Group size is important. Babies get lost in large groups. Primary care and continuity of care are two other factors that affect whether children form attachments in out-of-home care. Primary care means that, even if there are six, eight, or nine in the group, each caregiver has primary responsibility for only a small number of children—two or three—four at the most. Continuity of care means that children stay with their small group and their primary caregiver, whenever possible, for several years. They don't move to a new room, new group, and new infant-care teacher whenever they reach a new stage or have a birthday.

These ideas have been tried and tested for the last 60-plus years in Budapest, Hungary, where a pediatrician theorist and researcher named Emmi Pikler started an orphanage for children under three years of age after World War II at the request of the Hungarian government. Pikler was greatly concerned about attachment, and she not only set up the program to support the forming of attachments, but she trained the staff very carefully in exactly how and to what extent to promote this. The program, now called the Pikler Institute, is still running today under the directorship of Pikler's daughter, Anna Tardos, who continues to carry on her mother's research. Ideas from Pikler's approach were brought to the United States back in 1956 by Magda Gerber, who ran parenting groups for years and whose program, Resources for Infant Educators (RIE), is still being carried on.

Pikler's ideas about attachment are useful today to infant-care teachers as well. She stressed in her training that this was a special kind of attachment—one that gave the children enough security to develop well and function optimally, but was not so strong an attachment that moving into an adoptive family—or back to their own— would devastate the children when the ties with the caregiver in the Institute were cut (David & Appell, 2001).

Attachment, according to Pikler, grew during the one-on-one times when the primary caregiver was able to be intimate and uninterrupted with her primary children. Those times come about during the essential activities of daily living, such as feeding, diapering, dressing, bathing, and grooming.

Becoming attached to someone else's baby is delicate business. Earlier I said that you may be the protective factor in a child's life. You may be the one that makes a difference. That's a heady thought and needs some serious consideration. Some people who go into early care and education have a tendency to rescue children from their parents. This is a stage many pass through. It is important to recognize those tendencies in yourself and set them aside. If you look down on parents, you can't support them, and it's your job to be supportive. Watch out that you don't find yourself in competition with the family for the child's affection. Be professional at all times, but realize that professional in this profession means warm and caring. Be close and attentive, but also be aware of keeping an optimum distance in your attachment to a child. Optimal closeness should be the parents' goal, not yours. The child's attachment to the family is and should be a lot closer than your attachment to the child. The child's past, present, and future is in the family, not with you. Your attachment is important, but it's also temporary. If it is too strong, both you and the child will suffer when you separate, as you are bound to do eventually.

ATTACHMENT BEHAVIORS

Attachment can be observed in adults and babies alike. There are certain sets of behaviors that indicate attachment is forming or is already fully established.

Signs of Attachment in Parents

Some parents show signs of attachment right away. They're smitten with their babies. They feel close to their offspring. They find parenting pleasurable—even the hard and frustrating parts. One mother recalls how her whole life changed when her first baby was born. Suddenly she became important to someone. Her baby depended on her. She had a new interest in world news because it seemed important to make the world a safe place for her baby to grow up in (Gonzalez-Mena, 1995). Not all parents go through such a transformative process, but some do.

Some cultural rituals are related to attachment. Giving a name to the baby and calling him or her by that name is a way of acknowledging the child as an individual. Buying possessions for the new baby is also a way of recognizing individuality and personhood. These are so expected that they don't seem to relate to attachment, but when they don't occur, it can be a sign that something is wrong with the attachment. Be careful though about judging across cultures. Attachment behaviors may look quite different.

Signs of Attachment in Infants

Babies take longer to show signs of attachment, although careful research shows that signs exist from birth. Babies just a few hours old can distinguish their mother's smell and her voice, for example (Cernoch & Porter, 1985; DeCasper & Fifer, 1980). Before long, babies begin to act differently around their primary caregiver (who may or may not be the mother). They may be more animated, less fussy, more interested and alert.

Eventually some babies begin to show distress when someone they don't know arrives in their field of vision. The distress may accelerate if the stranger approaches. This stranger anxiety shows that the baby can distinguish between the person(s) he or she is attached to and others.

However, some babies never show stranger anxiety, not because they are not attached but because they have had a secure and trusting life with multiple caregivers (either at home or in child care). If babies skip this milestone, some parents and even some experts become distressed because they think it shows lack of attachment. That's not necessarily true.

For some babies, the next milestone is *separation anxiety*, as the baby protests at being away from the caregiver. (More about this subject appears in the next chapter.)

Attachment behaviors can be seen in situations involving both stranger anxiety and separation anxiety—as the baby looks or moves toward the primary caregiver for comfort and reassurance. Clinging, crying, fussing, whining, and following are all attachment behaviors that can show the emotional bond between the child and someone else. Although they are indicators of attachment, an absence of these behaviors does not necessarily signal a lack of attachment in children with multiple caregivers.

OBSTACLES TO ATTACHMENT

You need to know about these obstacles to attachment so you won't judge parents who don't seem as attached as other parents do. Your job is to help support parents in their attachment to their children. You can do that in several ways.

- Help make parents aware of their child's qualities and uniqueness. Encourage them to observe and to ask about what they see. Delicately point out any positive qualities that they may miss.
- As mentioned before, stay out of any sort of competition with parents. Don't set yourself up as the expert who's good at working with children—especially their child. When a child is acting out in front of the parent, avoid saying things like, "He only acts like that when you're here. He's fine with me."

Optimum attachment often starts before the baby is born, continues after delivery when the baby and family "bond," and then follows a continuous progression from there (Lieberman & Zeanah, 1995). Many families don't start with optimum attachment. What can get in the way? For many reasons, parents may not feel an emotional connection to their baby before or after it is born.

- They may be unhappy about the pregnancy or with each other, and those feelings may influence their feelings for the baby.
- The father may not be in a relationship with the mother—so any feeling for the baby on his part will necessarily be "long distance."
- Even for the mother, the reality of the baby may be fuzzy. It's hard to love someone you can't see or touch or interact with.

Then, at birth, the time may still not be right. The birth itself may not be a pleasant experience, and that unpleasantness can carry over into the period after. Or the birth may be complicated. If the baby or the mother is in any kind of physical distress, medical procedures may take precedence over time alone to "bond" together. For one reason or another, baby and parents often miss out on the initial bonding period. Even if it is arranged so that parents and baby can spend the first hour or so together, there may be worries or disappointments that cast an emotional overlay over the bonding process and prevent the magical happy moment from occurring.

Adoption can present another obstacle to bonding at birth and early attachment. The new parents may not have been a part of the birth or may not have had a period together immediately afterward.

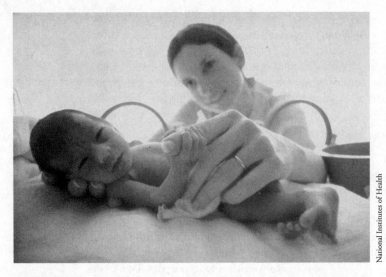

If a baby is very sick and separated from family, attachment may be delayed.

Attachment can proceed very well in spite of all these obstacles to early bonding, as long as the relationship grows and flourishes, preferably in the first year—the earlier the better. If you think back to what you know about your own birth, the chances are that you didn't experience "bonding" immediately there in the delivery room (if you had a hospital birth). Allowing parents and babies time together right after delivery is a relatively new procedure in standard medical practice in this country. Perhaps your life might have been different if your parent(s) had been given a chance to fall in love with you at first sight immediately after your birth. Or perhaps it wouldn't have made a difference.

Attachment, the process of creating a close and lasting relationship, may be delayed for many reasons. If the infant is very sick, parents may unconsciously protect themselves from getting attached by putting an emotional distance between themselves and the baby. Sometimes the difficulty is that, for whatever reason, the baby remains unresponsive to the caregiver's initiations. Some infants are born with disabilities, a circumstance that cuts down on their ability to respond. Others simply don't have the kinds of behaviors that draw adults to them. They're not cute, or cuddly, or smiley. They don't make eye contact. These infants, who don't reward the adults around them, need adults who make a conscious effort to attach. Even mismatches of temperament can delay attachment as the quiet, placid parent gets used to a highly active baby, or the reverse.

If babies experience early lengthy separation, the attachment process can be disrupted. Babies in foster care may be moved around; changing caregivers can disrupt attachment. These delays or disruptions in attachment can influence future life in drastic ways if a sense of basic trust is not established. The child may put up barriers so that no one can get close. The hurt from loss is too great to chance again.

Temperament and Attachment

Temperament can affect attachment in either a negative or positive way, depending on the temperamental match between the infant and adult, whether parent or infant-care teacher. Temperament is built in and can be detected early in a child's life. Genetically determined, temperament becomes obvious as infants show differing levels of activity, emotionality, and sociability that tend to remain the same over time. Thomas, Chess, and Birch (1963), the pioneers in temperament research, categorize babies as "easy," "slow to warm," and "difficult." Their work helps today's parents and caregivers understand how temperament affects behavior and shapes personality. J. Ronald Lally and his colleagues in the WestEd Program for Infant–Toddler Caregivers renamed the categories "fearful," "flexible," and "feisty," which puts them in a more objective light. A good match between parent temperament and child temperament promotes attachment; a mismatch may hinder it. If the two aren't a natural fit, the adult must adjust to the baby rather than expecting the reverse. This is important for you to understand—both when considering your own attachment process with the children you work with and also when working with parents. You can be the one to help a parent understand temperament if a mismatch is getting in the way of attachment between parent and child.

What would a mismatch look like? If an active and intense mother with a high energy level finds herself with a slow, calm, mild baby, she may be disappointed. She may even wonder whether something is wrong with her baby, even though the baby is perfectly fine. If this high-energy mother is not aware of what she is doing, she may overstimulate her baby. She has to learn to read the signs that the baby has had enough. You can help her do that. Some parents keep on after the baby turns away or closes his or her eyes. A serious mismatch occurs when the mother interprets this behavior as bored and continues to try to "wake the baby up and make her more lively."

Or imagine a calm, relaxed father who loves things done on schedule and appreciates predictability in his life. He'll find a mismatch with a highly active, intense baby who never seems able to regulate his rhythms or body needs. Some babies don't keep any sort of routine, even eating at a different time every day. Napping is as unpredictable as appetite and never follows a schedule. If the father of such a baby doesn't accept that his son is different from himself, he may have trouble being sensitive to the child's needs.

Parents who have children whose temperaments don't match their own have to adjust their expectations, accept their babies as is, and learn to understand them. They have to be flexible about how and when they respond. They have to be supersensitive so that they can meet their baby's needs. All that may be hard for a parent whose temperament isn't flexible or sensitive. That may be hard for you too, but hopefully understanding more about temperament will help you.

Developmental Differences

Babies who are born with developmental differences may not have the attachment behaviors that draw adults to them. For example, neurological issues can cause babies not to be cuddly. Some stiffen when held. Some even cry out in pain when held or touched. Others who can't control their facial muscles may not smile or look

Laura Vitale

Learning to cope with feelings of loss; Children who are attached experience feelings of loss when separation occurs.

interested in the same way typically developing babies do. Or eye contact may be missing. A child with a visual impairment, for example, may not use eye contact to establish a relationship. A child with a hearing impairment may not respond to soft talking. In these cases it is important for adults to look for the attachment behaviors the children do exhibit. Adults must be constantly aware of the importance of establishing connections even if the baby's behaviors tend to get in the way. Sometimes outside help is needed to support parents, infant-care teachers, early educators, or family child care providers when attachment isn't occurring in spite of efforts to encourage a close connection. As you gain experience, you may be the one who provides help to the parents.

LEARNING TO COPE WITH FEELINGS OF LOSS

Babies who are attached experience feelings when separation occurs. Separation is the other side of attachment. Each human has the lifelong task of coming to grips with separations and coping with the feelings that occur as people come into and go out of one's life. Each broken relationship, physical departure, or death brings into play all the coping skills learned earlier. The skills for dealing with separation begin to develop in infancy.

You can perhaps get in touch with the power of the feelings surrounding separation by thinking back to a time in your own life when you were apart from someone you cared about. Perhaps it was the first day of school, or a trip to the hospital, or even the first time you were left with a babysitter. It may be a less significant event—but one that sticks in your memory—like the time you took the wrong turn in the grocery store and were "lost" for a minute or two. It might be an even more significant event like the day one of your parents walked out, never to return, or the day your one of them died. All of us have experience with separation, and those experiences start earlier for some than for others.

If you can remember your feelings surrounding these experiences, you can probably get in touch with one or more of the following: panic, fear, anxiety, misgivings, apprehension, qualms, terror, horror, bewilderment, confusion, annoyance, irritation, anger, outrage, fury, wrath, frenzy, desperation, indignity, sadness, loneliness, desertion, and abandonment. The feelings come from the need for security as well as a sense of loss of control over the situation.

The memory of your pain may be intense, or it may have muted over time. Or perhaps you have a fuzziness around the feelings or even an absence of feeling. You may even dredge up a sense of depression when you get in touch with this early separation experience.

There are all kinds of separation experiences in infancy—some that help the child grow to independence, others that leave scars and long-lasting aftereffects. One common separation infants experience comes when they are put into cribs to sleep by themselves. In cultures that place a high priority on independence, this physical separation from the beginning is regarded as important. Learning to sleep alone as an infant is a skill that is valued by many in this country. It's an important step for children coming to see themselves as separate individuals. Some parenting experts are adamant about babies sleeping alone. Some experts, including Ferber (1985), who wrote *Solve Your Child's Sleep Problems*, say that babies can't get a good night's sleep if they have to "interact" all night with someone else.

Ironically, information on sudden infant death syndrome (SIDS, or crib death) indicates that an undisturbed night's sleep may put infants at risk. In cultures where infants are held, jostled, and put to bed with an adult or another child, the rate of SIDS is dramatically lower than in cultures where infants sleep apart from the hustle and bustle of family life in cribs in their own rooms (Grether, Shulman, & Croen, 1990; McKenna, 1992). Of course, that doesn't mean babies should be in bed with someone. Statistics show that placing babies on their backs to sleep makes sleeping alone in a crib safer; the "back-to-sleep" campaign is designed to lower the risk factor of sleeping alone, and it has worked!

Where babies sleep is a cultural issue. Some cultures value sleeping alone and others don't, even if they have the space and means to do so. Some cultures aren't as interested in their children becoming independent individuals as they are in creating a spirit of interdependence and connectedness to others. In many families both in the United States and around the world, infants and toddlers sleep with the mother or both parents until the next baby comes, then move into the bed of siblings or grandparents. Some European Americans have made an attempt to change the way they were raised by instituting what is called the "family bed" (Thevenin, 1987). More recently, trends for "co-sleeping" with the baby are finding support and even products to promote it. Sears and Sears (2001) encourage bed sharing in their book *Attachment Parenting*, though they also say families should decide if it's right for them and their baby. Of course, it's not safe for postpartum mothers who are exhausted or using sedatives to sleep with their babies.

A number of articles and books have been written about getting babies to sleep by themselves, because it isn't as easy to accomplish as it might seem. Many babies comfort themselves while alone in the crib by developing an attachment to a particular object. This process fits right in with being part of an object-oriented culture. Most parents and caregivers are delighted when a child attaches to a favorite blanket or a stuffed animal. Experts see this particular way of self-comforting as a sign that the child has coping skills.

Learning to put oneself to sleep and stay by oneself is a step toward independence and is a valued behavior in many families. It's a healthy sign that infants are able to handle separation.

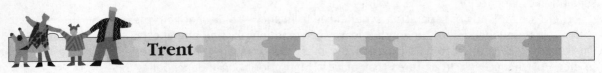

Trent

Trent's mother took drugs when she was pregnant. No one was aware of this problem until the day Trent was born. He arrived in the world full of the harmful substances his mother had ingested, and his first days of life were spent in withdrawal. He suffered and so did the hospital staff who tended him.

"Poor little guy!" said a nurse, as she tried to make him more comfortable.

Getting the drugs out of his system didn't end his problems. Trent was a difficult baby from the beginning. He cried incessantly—it seemed sometimes as if he would never stop. He'd scream and scream until he finally wore himself out; he'd sleep restlessly for a period and then start again. It was hard to be around Trent.

His foster mother, a patient woman, understood how hard life was for Trent just now. Although she had other babies to care for, she spent special time with him, trying to give him the message that he was cared about—that he was loved. It wasn't easy. When an adoptive family came along that knew Trent's history and his problems, she was relieved because she felt he deserved a permanent home and parents—a family of his own who could give him a good deal of time and energy—the time and energy she had were stretched so thin!

Trent's new parents were special people. They didn't go into the adoption expecting to rescue a child and have him be forever grateful to them. They knew something about the kinds of problems that Trent had at the time and the kinds he was likely to have in the future. They were prepared to deal with these problems.

They started out right away to establish an attachment with Trent. It wasn't easy—he wasn't an appealing baby. When his new parents picked him up, he stiffened and shook. He didn't cuddle like lots of babies. He seldom seemed relaxed; in fact, his movements were jerky and uncontrolled. He twitched, jiggled, and shook as he lay in his crib.

Trent didn't like to be touched; often he screamed louder when he was touched than when he wasn't. It was tempting to leave him alone, since picking him up seemed agonizing to him. But his parents knew that leaving him in his crib wasn't the answer, so they did some observing and brainstorming to discover what ways they could pick him up that would cause him the least discomfort. They felt proud when they were able to discover some. It became more rewarding to pick him up.

Trent didn't look at anyone very often. Even when his parents tried to get his attention, he tended to look away. It's hard to develop a relationship with someone who doesn't make eye contact, but they managed. They just kept on trying until the day came that Trent looked his mother right in the eye. What a moment that was for her—worth waiting for. That was the beginning of the development of a series of positive behaviors that made Trent easy to love. On the big day when Trent smiled for the first time, his father grinned back as if his face would split in two. "You're going to be okay, Trent," he said, patting his son.

Since happily-ever-after stories only occur as fairy tales, I have to tell you that Trent did continue to feel the influence of his early drug exposure into his preschool years. But with the help of his parents and their love for him, he was able to cope with the cards that life had dealt him.

VARYING ATTACHMENT PATTERNS

The classic research has been done on attachment between mothers and babies. Although attachment patterns can vary significantly from that one pattern, the early research is still worth understanding.

Bowlby and Ainsworth's Research

John Bowlby was the first to apply to humans the idea that attachment behaviors evolved because they promote survival. He took a psychoanalytic view that attachment of infant to caregiver affects an infant's sense of security and ability to trust.

Mary Ainsworth was a student of John Bowlby, and her research is used widely in assessing attachment of infants and toddlers. She set out to study how securely attached babies are to their mothers (Ainsworth & Bell, 1977; Ainsworth, Blehar, Waters, & Wall, 1978). She used something she called "the Strange Situation," in which a baby is observed in an experimental room with toys designed to entice. The situation involves the mother and a stranger in a series of comings and goings. How the baby reacts to the separation, the stranger, and the reunion is used to judge the type of attachment.

From her research, Ainsworth came up with different types of attachment. If the baby is what Ainsworth called securely attached, he or she uses the mother as a base to move out from and explore the interesting toys in the room. You can see this happening in any setting where there are toys and a baby with enough mobility to get to them. Babies move away from their mothers, checking back periodically to see where they are, and crawling back to get a snuggle, hug, or a bit of comfort when needed. If the mother leaves, securely attached babies usually show some distress, but not always. They show they are delighted to see her when she returns.

Not so with insecurely attached infants. They may show what's called avoidant attachment, resistant attachment, or disorganized/disoriented attachment. Avoidant attachment shows when babies act the same around the stranger as they do around the mother. They seem not to care when the mother leaves the room. When reunited, they are slow to greet the mother and either ignore or avoid her.

Babies who show resistant attachment stay close to the mother before she leaves and do little exploration in a strange place. They get upset when she leaves, but when she comes back they show anger and sometimes behave in a push-pull fashion—for example, alternating between clinging and pushing her away. Sometimes even picking them up fails to comfort them.

Disorganized/disoriented attachment was the product of more recent research (Main & Solomon, 1990; Solomon & George, 1999). This type of insecure attachment shows up as a pattern of confused, contradictory behaviors when reunited with the mother. Sometimes infants look frozen, dazed, and disoriented. Some rock or engage in other repetitive behaviors. Some cry after the mother has managed to get them settled down.

Ainsworth's research provides interesting information, but be careful about judging attachments in families you work with. You're not a researcher, and you can't understand everything about a family based on what you see when they leave their children. One criticism of Ainsworth's way of judging attachment is the unnatural setting. Do babies and mothers behave the same in a laboratory as they do at home or somewhere else?

Another criticism of the Strange Situation as a way of assessing attachment is that it is based on a particular model of mother-child attachment. There are a lot of variations on that model. What if the baby has been in child care and is used to multiple caregivers? Is he really showing insecure attachment if he avoids the mother when she returns, or is he accustomed to having an interesting environment and being separated from his mother? Or what if the baby comes from a large family in which the mother isn't the only caregiver? What if the mother isn't the person the baby is most attached to? What if the baby has two mothers? Or two fathers?

Questions About Classic Attachment Research

Ainsworth and other researchers focused on attachment as it relates to the insular or nuclear family. Today we know better. We can see with our own eyes that, even in the nuclear or insular family, caregiving may be shared between mother and father or between one parent and another relative or child care provider. Under these circumstances, attachment is not just between mother and baby, although often the mother remains the primary attachment.

As mentioned earlier, much of the focus on attachment has been related to the insular or nuclear family with mother, father, and child. This, of course, isn't the only kind of family. Another type of family is the single-parent family. Sometimes the parent(s) and baby are not a unit by themselves but are part of a larger extended family. Stack (1991) describes *kinship networks* as clusters of people who are related through children, marriage, and friendship who come together to provide domestic functions. This domestic network may spread over several households, and changes in individual household composition do not significantly affect cooperative arrangements. The single-parent family that finds itself in this type of network may be thought of as "embedded" rather than alone.

A woman once told me a story about how she had changed her perspective on her family. This person was a single parent with two children, who lived with her parents in their house. She thought of her situation as two families living in one house, until she decided to have a family portrait taken. She included all five family members, deciding for herself that this was one family, rather than two. This story of her family portrait started me thinking about my own family situation as I grew up. My mother, my sister, and I lived most of my childhood in the house of my grandparents. We never had a family portrait taken. We didn't see ourselves as a unit; rather, we were two families—an intact one (my grandparents) and a "broken" one (my mother and her two children). Nowadays, of course, we would call ourselves a single-parent family rather than a broken one, but many would still see us as deprived without a father in the household, rather than enriched because of grandparents and the uncles who lived there for periods during my growing up. I now prefer to think of myself as growing up embedded in my extended family.

Children can acquire secondary attachments in child care in addition to those at home.

The concept of an embedded family is a more positive and realistic one. In an embedded family the attachment might be quite different because of shared caregiving. Certainly that was my experience. My attachment to my grandmothers was as strong as my attachment to my mother. Although we may think of the mother-child dyad as the way "it should be," that's not necessarily so. The child can become attached to several caregivers or to a group rather than to just one or two individuals. When you are used to looking at attachment as an exclusive relationship, you may be concerned about the infant who is attached to multiple caregivers (Zimmerman & McDonald, 1995). However, cultures all over the world raise their children this way. Shared care has advantages over one or even two parents carrying total responsibility for a child's well-being. What a burden that much responsibility can be, especially for a new parent who may have had little previous experience with babies!

Some child care programs function as an extended family, a kinship network, or a family-support system, rather than as just a place to leave children during the day. These programs are able to provide families with the kind of connections they would find in embedded families if they had them. One such family support system is the Parent Services Project, which a visionary child care director, Ethel Seiderman, started in California, and which has now spread nationwide in the United States. The purpose of this project is to help programs recognize that the well-being and sense of significance of parents are of central importance to the child's development. Furthermore, support is important to all families, and social-support networks reduce isolation and promote the well-being of the child, the family, and the community.

JUDGING ATTACHMENT IN A CROSS-CULTURAL SITUATION

When a mother doesn't seem sensitive to the baby's emotional signals, seldom speaks to the baby, and/or never holds the baby in a face-to-face position so adult and baby can make eye contact, it is not clear whether these are functional or dysfunctional behaviors. Do they fit customs and expectations and make sense if viewed in cultural context? Or are they left over from a time when survival was the main issue and many babies died before their first birthday? Or do they have another explanation? For example, in a situation in which the baby is never called by the given name, you may not immediately understand what is going on, unless you are of the same culture and social class as the family you're observing. If you don't thoroughly understand the culture and perhaps even the individual family, you can't make judgments about the way people are raising their children and whether they have a healthy attachment.

Language is another area in which an outsider may misjudge what is happening. European American middle-class families are very vocal, and all this vocalization is part of the attachment process. Watch most middle-class European American parents and you'll see that they talk face-to-face with their babies—chattering away as if the baby understands. They even wait for a response, creating a turn-taking situation that imitates real conversations in which both participants talk. Research (done by European Americans on European Americans for European Americans) shows the value of this kind of behavior, not only for attachment but also for future development. For example, this early emphasis on verbalization makes a difference later in school performance; children with good verbal skills do better academically.

In contrast, some families rarely speak to their infants. What may not be clear to the outsider is how much the family is using *nonverbal* communication that the observer isn't aware of. Because a family doesn't behave the same as a European American middle-class family toward babies doesn't necessarily mean that there is an attachment problem—it may be more a matter of cultural difference.

CHILD CARE AND ATTACHMENT

For many who come from the tradition of mother-child attachment as an exclusive relationship, a crucial question is: What does child care do to attachment? This section focuses on child care rather than the larger picture of early care and education because the concern relates to long hours out of the home. Preschool, kindergarten, and primary school don't cause people to worry about attachment for several reasons. The time factor is one. When children leave home for preschool they aren't gone for as many hours as they may be when in full-day child care. Age is another reason. Children are older when they leave home for preschool, and presumably attachment to family has already occurred. The big worry is when an infant who is still in the beginning stages of attachment spends most of his or her waking hours away from home and family.

From the days of the classic research on orphanages, the term *maternal deprivation* rings in the ears and sends chills down the spine. Horror stories of old-time orphanages come to mind—babies left to themselves in rows of cribs along sterile walls. The picture is heartbreaking. Those babies had no attachment, few interactions, little power to influence anyone in their lives, a feeling that no one cared about them, and a great lack of any kind of sensory stimulation. No wonder many died and the rest were left impaired. More recent orphanage pictures come to us from Romania and China. Not pretty pictures!

Resistance to creating child care for babies has been strong, but when Clinton signed the welfare reform bill and sent mothers of babies out of the home, that resistance melted. Some still worry about group care for babies—and well they should. It takes special knowledge and expertise to do a good job with babies. Now we know you can't just line babies up in cribs, change and feed them on schedule, and expect them to be okay while their family members are working.

Luckily we have better models than those old-time orphanages. From Budapest in Hungary comes a different picture. The children thrive in the Pikler Institute, which was mentioned earlier in this chapter. There attachment has been carefully thought through and fits into a comprehensive approach that has been studied by the World Health Organization. According to their results, children who spent their first three years in this residential care nursery end up as adults who show none of the signs of impairment that children from deprived orphanages show. A key factor is the approach taken to attachment described in a book called *Loczy: An Unusual Approach to Mothering* (David & Appell, 2001).

Effects of Child Care on Attachment

Child care is not an orphanage; the children have families who are raising them. Child care is supplemental to these families, not a replacement for them. A way to look at attachment in out-of-home-child care is this. Children in child care have not just one person who cares about them—a parent—but often two or more. Children usually arrive in child care already firmly attached to their own family and may well acquire a secondary attachment or two in child care.

A look to Israel reassures us that parents and children can remain attached even if the parents never live with their children or are never responsible for their day-to-day care. In some of the kibbutzim in Israel, where communal living was a norm and a value, children were raised from infancy separate from their parents. They visited their parents, but they didn't live with them. Full-time caregivers/teachers, rather than the parents, were in charge of child rearing and education.

There was no lack of attachment between parents and children in the kibbutzim. Attachment looked different because children split their attachment between parents and peer group. However, each child was well aware of his or her identity as a member of his or her own family—and each felt a sense of belonging.

Another question to ask when looking at the effects of child care on attachment to family is: What is the situation of the child's family? Obviously if a family is overwhelmed by stress and the members are not functioning well, and a baby is born into the family at this point, some protective factors may be crucial. The early care and education program can provide these factors. In some situations, as when an over-burdened single parent is able to get the support and referral to services needed, the child care program can literally be a lifesaver.

Such programs exist. Some child care and early education programs in the United States today not only give services to children but also give families the support they need to get on their feet so they, themselves, can provide for their children's needs. These kinds of programs are cost-effective because they deal with attachment and other needs at the beginning rather than trying to fix problems that arise later, which is much more expensive (Pawl, 1995; Raikes, 1996). We could use many more of these kinds of programs! *Prevention* is a key word when looking at early deprivation and attachment problems.

Unfortunately, these kinds of comprehensive programs are too few in number. If the baby in the above example is placed in a child care program in which he never gets to know any of his caregivers and his mother gets little or no support, it's a different story. Attachment may be delayed because caregivers come and go too fast. Not one of the adults gets to know him well enough to read his signals, understand his uniqueness, become fond of him. Child care may save his life yet still not provide for his attachment and trust needs. Because of underfunding, that's the tragedy of the state of many child care programs in the United States today. The turnover rate of caregivers and teachers in underfunded programs is shocking.

You can't know exactly how child care affects attachment without considering countless variables that have to do with the quality of the care and the way the family works. One important aspect of quality care is the partnership between the parents and the program. When child care staff and providers develop a collaborative relationship with the parents that includes more than just parent education and involvement, everybody stands to gain—including the child!

Some parents don't have much choice about using child care for their babies and won't until parental leave becomes a societal policy. It may reassure these parents to know that most studies have shown that babies become attached to their own parents even when child care is begun quite early.

How Caregiver and Parent Roles Differ

Good infant-care teachers have many of the qualities of good parents, and those qualities promote attachment (Katz, 1980). One vital quality is sensitivity. When the infant-care teacher learns to read each infant's signals, he or she can respond appropriately and in a timely fashion, that is, if the staff-child ratio is good. Infants learn that they can give messages. They can influence the people in their world. They have personal power. They become attached. The attachment grows out of the sensitivity and the ability of the infant-care teacher to communicate and also promotes further communication. Infants becomes better at sending signals when someone is trying to read theirs. The infant-care teacher gets better and better at reading signals as he or she grows to know the baby as an individual. A synchronous relationship results.

Good infant-care teachers and good parents have many similar behaviors and goals, but they also have some differences, which Lilian Katz, professor at the University of Illinois and a longtime leader in the field of early childhood education, wrote about. Katz (1980) says that the infant-care teacher's attachment is necessarily short-term, and it's important for him or her to remember that fact. This child care arrangement isn't forever; the infant-care teacher has little control over the future. It's the parents' job to have a vision for the child's future, just as they have the knowledge of the past. It's the parents—the family—who connect the child in time, giving a sense of continuity. The child has a life beyond child care; that's a fact that the infant-care teacher must keep in mind.

Krista Greco/Merrill

The child's attachment to the teacher should always be secondary to that of the family—close enough for security, but not too close.

Parents and infant-care teachers differ in the degree of closeness that's appropriate. The goal of *parental* attachment is to establish *optimum closeness* with the child; the *infant care teacher's* goal is *optimum distance.* The child benefits from attachment to both, but it's a different kind of attachment. The infant-care teacher must put limits on the degree of attachment; after all, the family may move out of town tomorrow. In addition, infant-care teachers usually have other children to consider; they can't allow themselves to get completely wrapped up in just one to the neglect of the others. Strategy Box 2.1 includes a summary of ideas for early educators when keeping their role separate from the roles of parents.

Strategy Box 2.1

Working with Families Around Attachment Issues

- Recognize that the well-being and sense of significance of parents are of central importance to the child's development.
- Work to build a trusting relationship with each family.
- See yourself as a support for families instead of merely being there for their children.

- If policies are in place in an infant center that allow attachment between infant-care teachers and a small number of children, do what you can to promote that attachment. If there are no such policies, discuss with the people in power the need for them.
- Keep in mind that your attachment is secondary to that of the parents. Examine the degree of closeness with each child with a professional eye. Be close enough to help the child feel secure, but not so close that the child turns from family to you.
- Avoid competition with family for the child's affection.

Fairness is another category in which parents and infant-care teachers differ. Parents can be advocates for their own children. They don't have to be fair and consider all the children in the program. It's appropriate for parents to focus on their own children. Infant-care teachers can't afford to favor one child over another, but that doesn't mean that they must treat all the children in their care alike. Similar treatment in the face of differing needs doesn't create fairness.

Attachment in Full-Inclusion Programs

Full-inclusion programs are those where children with developmental differences, disabilities, and particular challenges are placed in child care with their typically developing peers rather than being separated into special programs. Every adult involved in such programs must aim to help all children feel they belong. That means that the children with exceptional needs must be integrated into the group. Unless the adults in the program have the time and skill to facilitate this integration, some children may feel left out. Although this attention to integration is slightly different from the kind of attachment this chapter has focused on so far, it brings up the issue of attachment not just to an adult or two, but also to the group.

The work of Lev Vygotsky has implications for integration. Vygotsky worked at the Institute of Psychology in Moscow where he created what's called sociocultural theory, which emphasizes social interaction as an influence on development and learning. His *zone of proximal*

The goal is to help every child feel he or she belongs.

Anne Vega/Merrill

development, or moving children forward from where they are to where they can be, involves peer interaction (Berk, 2001).

LOOKING BACK AND LOOKING FORWARD

Trust and attachment are lifelong issues. When conditions are right, parents and babies get "hooked" on each other right from the beginning. The relationship that results serves both well. It not only ensures the baby the nurturing and protecting he or she needs at the beginning, but also sets the stage for later relationships. Being attached feels good. It offers security. The job of the early care and education professional is to help support attachment to the family as well as encourage a secondary attachment in the center or family child care home.

Attachment provides the security that the baby needs to move out from the parent and care provider to become a fully functioning individual. That subject is the focus of the next chapter.

FOR DISCUSSION

1. Have you been aware of attachment occurring? Describe the kinds of interactions that encourage attachment that were part of this experience. Was synchrony involved? How did the attachment serve the people who were becoming attached? Tell about that experience.

2. What are your experiences with obstacles to the bonding or attachment process? Did the people involved get over or around these obstacles? How?

3. Discuss separation anxiety. What behaviors indicate the child is trying to keep the attached person from leaving? What emotions might a child display? How can an adult help the child to separate from the person he or she is attached to?

4. Have you had any experience with how child care might affect attachment? What are your ideas or thoughts about this subject?

5. What are your ideas, thoughts, or feelings about working with families around issues of attachment? What experience do you have in supporting parents' attachment to their infant?

WEB SITES

Attachment Disorder Site
http://www.attachmentdisorder.net/
Many resources and additional links here pertain to attachment, attachment disorder, and related issues.

I Am Your Child
http://www.iamyourchild.org/

This site includes the connection between warm interactions leading to attachment and brain development.

Institute for Attachment and Child Development
http://www.instituteforattachment.org/
This Web site identifies issues that transform the lives of families and children with attachment,

behavioral, and emotional disorders and promoting healthy family relationships.

Pikler Institute
http://www.pikler.org/
and
International Pikler Association
http://www.aipl.org
Both Web sites give information on the Pikler approach used at the Pikler Institute, a residential nursery in Budapest, Hungary, an approach which focuses heavily on attachment.

Program for Infant/Toddler Caregivers (PITC)
http://www.pitc.org/
The Program for Infant/Toddler Caregivers supports and promotes quality care for infants and toddlers through resources, information, and training. The site includes information on brain research and implications for infant development.

Resources for Infant Educarers
http://www.rie.org/

Resources for Infant Educarers™ is a nonprofit organization that uses the teachings of Magda Gerber to promote a unique philosophy and methodology in working with infants in ways that respect them as individuals.

Society for Research in Child Development (SRCD)
http://www.srcd.org/psarchive.html
The Society for Research in Child Development Web site contains information summary of many research articles on child development, including several on attachment.

Zero to Three
http://www.zerotothree.org/
Zero to Three: National Center for Infants, Toddlers, and Families is designed for parents and professionals. A leading resource on the first three years of life, its mission is to strengthen and support families, practitioners, and communities to promote the healthy development of babies and toddlers.

FURTHER READING

Berlin, L. J., Ziv, Y., Amaya-Jackson, L., & Greenberg, M. T. (Eds). (2005). *Enhancing early attachments*. New York: Guilford..

Barnard, K., & Brazelton, T. B. (Eds.). (1990). *Touch: The foundation of experience.* New York: Bantam.

Bernhard, J. K., & Gonzalez-Mena, J. (2000). The cultural context of infant-toddler care. In D. Cryer & T. Harms (Eds.), *Research to practice in infant-toddler care* (pp. 237–267). Baltimore: Brookes.

Bhavnagri, N., & Gonzalez-Mena, J. (1997, Fall). The cultural context of caregiving. *Childhood Education* 74(1), 2–8.

Chang, H. N. L., Muckelroy, A., & Pulido-Tobiassen, D. (1996). *Looking in, looking out: Redefining child and early education in a diverse society.* San Francisco: California Tomorrow.

David, M., & Appell, G. (2001 [1973, 1996]). *Loczy: An unusual approach to mothering.* Translated from *Loczy ou le maternage insolite,* by Jean Marie Clark; revised translation by Judit Falk. Budapest: Association Pikler-Loczy for Young Children.

Derman-Sparks, L. (1995). The process of culturally sensitive care. In P. Mangione (Ed.), *Infant/toddler caregiving: A guide to culturally sensitive care* (pp. 40–73). Sacramento: Far West Laboratory and California Department of Education.

Egeland, B., & Farrell Erickson, M. (1999, October–November). Findings from the parent-child project and implications for early intervention. *Zero to Three* 20(2), 3–9.

Gerhardt, S. (2004). *Why love matters: how affection shapes a baby's brain.* London: Routledge.

Gillespie, L. G. (2006, September). Rocking and rolling: Supporting infants, toddlers and their families: Cultivating good relationships with families can make hard times easier! *Young Children* 61(5), 53–55.

Gonzalez-Mena, J. (2004, September). What can an orphanage teach us? Lessons from Budapest. *Young Children* 58(5), 26–30.

Gonzalez-Mena, J. (2006) Caregiving and literacy. In J. Knapp-Philo and S. Rosenkoetter (Eds.) *Learning to Read the World: Language and Literacy in the First Three Years.* Washington DC: Zero to Three.

Gonzalez-Mena, J. (2007). What to do with a fussy baby: A problem-solving approach. *Young Children* 62(5), 20–25.

Gonzalez-Mena, J., & Bernhard, J. K. (1998, Summer). Out-of-home care of infants and toddlers: A call for cultural and linguistic continuity. *Interaction* 12(2), 14–15.

Honig, A. S. (2002). *Secure relationships: Nurturing infant/toddler attachment in early care settings*. Washington, DC: National Association for the Education of Young Children.

Schneider, B. H., Atkinson, L., & Tardif, C. (2001). Child-parent attachment and children's peer relations: A quantitative review. *Developmental Psychology* 37, 86–100.

Stern, D. N. (1990). *Diary of a baby*. New York: Basic Books.

Wittmer, D. S., & Petersen, S. H. (2006). *Infant and toddler development and responsive program planning: A relationship-based approach*. Upper Saddle River, NJ: Merrill/Prentice Hall

CHAPTER 3

Supporting Families with Autonomy-Seeking Youngsters

In this chapter you'll discover . . .

- Why toddlers poke, prod, and bang everything they can get their hands on
- Why some adults teach children interdependence instead of independence
- What toddler behaviors have to do with power issues
- What to do about biting
- How setting limits gives toddlers a sense of power
- How to handle separation problems
- Why those who work with toddlers should partner with parents
- Some strategies for creating partnerships with parents of toddlers

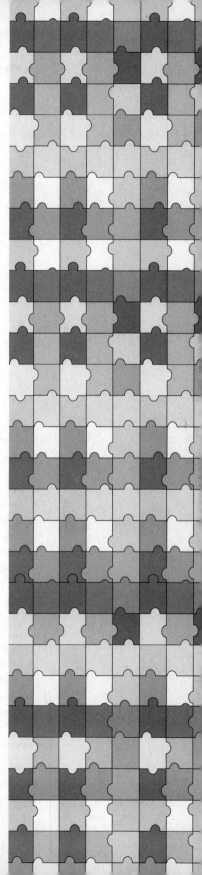

TODDLERS AND AUTONOMY

Sometime around their first birthday, most babies pull themselves to their feet and stagger forward. That first shaky baby step represents a huge developmental leap. The baby is now a toddler, and the central task of his or her life is to become a separate independent being. Erik Erikson (1963) calls this the *stage of autonomy* (see Figure 3.1). Of course, not all babies get up and take steps. Some children with disabilities go through the stage of autonomy without becoming mobile. The term *toddler* doesn't apply to all children, but most of the material in this chapter applies to both typically and atypically developing children sometime before the fourth year of life.

Your job as an early care and education practitioner is to not only appreciate this special stage of life, but to help families also appreciate it. That may be harder than it seems, because the behaviors described in this chapter come from a particular cultural perspectives and are not universally regarded in the same way. For example, the push behind this stage is for children to recognize their power as individuals and learn to assert this power. That isn't the goal of all families (more about that later in the chapter).

In some ways, you may find that the toddler stage is the hardest one for you to find ways to support families whose perception of the child and goals for him or her are different from those advocated in this chapter. But those kinds of challenges are always present when working across cultures. It's important to keep your professional perspective, your personal/cultural perspective, and still allow yourself to open up to each family's perspective. Not an easy job, but nobody ever said working with young children and their families is easy!

Many adults find the way that toddlers carry out this thrust for autonomy to be a headache, and your job is to help support families in ways that reduce the headache. Families sometimes see the behaviors that come along with this push for independence as difficult to manage. The theorists (who generally see things from a perspective that rates independence as a higher priority than interdependence) explain the meaning behind the behaviors and expect adults to understand and put up with the difficulties. The labels put on this stage by some parents (*the terrible twos*) and by

Child's Stage	Approximate Age	Task		
Infancy	0 – 1	Basic trust	versus	Basic mistrust
Toddlerhood	1 – 3	Autonomy	versus	Shame and doubt
The preschool years	3 – 6	Initiative	versus	Guilt
School age	6 – 10	Industry	versus	Inferiority

Figure 3.1

Erikson's psychosocial stages of development

Source: From Erikson (1963).

some experts (*the terrific twos*) reflect the various ways to look at the behaviors of this stage. The words the theorists use to label the process are *seeking autonomy, separating,* and *individuating.* Experts are willing to concede that the behaviors associated with this stage are sometimes "difficult." The words parents commonly use are *stubborn, obstinate,* and sometimes even such loaded terms as *willful, contrary,* and *spoiled.*

SIGNS OF DEVELOPING AUTONOMY

What are the behaviors that indicate a child is becoming an autonomous individual who will one day be self-sufficient and self-reliant? The most notable behaviors are negativity, exploration, self-help skills, and a sense of possession.

Negativity

The first sign of the developing autonomy is when the darling baby who happily opened his mouth for each bite of cereal or strained vegetables suddenly one day clamps his lips shut and turns aside. His meaning is clear. Without a word spoken, this is the beginning of "No!"

The theory says that the child can now begin to see himself as an individual separate from his mother or other object of attachment. He finds power in his difference—he's not the same person as this adult in his life. He finds power, and he uses it.

This is only the beginning. By 2 years of age, this child is likely to be contrary about everything. If his mother likes peas, he hates them. If his father wants to take him for a ride, he balks. He refuses to get into the bathtub, and when he is finally coaxed in, he refuses to get out again. Life becomes a struggle because he is so busy asserting his individuality.

Sometimes toddlers say "no" so much because they hear the word all the time. If parents or caregivers use the word *no* as the primary means of managing behavior, the first *no*'s of their children may be imitations of adults.

However, even if adults use a variety of means of guiding behavior and minimize the number of *no*'s in their child's life, toddlers still learn to say that magic word.

It's important to realize that learning to say no is a vital skill. What would your life be like if you never said no to anything? Do you remember the temptations of your teen years? Do you wish you had learned to say a good strong "No!" earlier? What are your temptations now? Do you find saying no a useful skill in your life today? How much do you remember about your own toddler years? Did the adults who were in your life regard your *no*'s as skill building, or as defiance of their authority? Their perception of you then may influence *your* perception of children in the toddler stage now.

Exploration

Exploration starts in infancy, grows out of attachment, and increases as children move toward autonomy. It may seem ironic that a child who is firmly attached explores more than one who is not. But it makes sense if you think of the attachment as providing a secure base to move out from. In fact, you can even see this phenomenon in action by watching a parent and a young child who are in a strange environment. The child will move out from the parent but will check back regularly. Sometimes it's just a glance; other times she runs back to the parent and clings for a moment before venturing out again.

The other factor in exploration is the freedom to move that the child is given in infancy. The research of Dr. Emmi Pikler indicates that babies who develop their movement skills independent of adults learn that they are capable individuals. Their trust in their own skills make them remarkable explorers (David & Appell, 2001; Gonzalez-Mena, 2004; Pikler, 1971, 1973; Pikler & Tardos, 1968). Babies in the Pikler Institute, a residential nursery in Budapest, are put on their backs where they have the most freedom to use their bodies. They are free of restrictive devices like infant seats, swings, even high chairs. No one puts the babies into positions they can't get into by themselves. Adults don't sit them up, stand them up, or walk them around. As they grow, these babies show an amazing sense of physical security. This same approach is also used by the staff at the Resources for Infant Educarers in Los Angeles, California. Founded by Magda Gerber and known as RIE, the program follows the teachings of Emmi Pikler, who was the teacher of Gerber (Gerber, 1979).

Infants who learn to use their bodies well and who experience adult appeciation of their exploration urges become toddlers who move around a lot when they feel secure. Toddlers, without urging, spontaneously explore the space around them. In my classes I've asked students to observe a toddler in child care and to map the territory the child moves through. The maps that come out of these observations are amazing. A toddler can cover miles in a single day just by trotting back and forth across a room or a play yard.

Toddlers explore with their hands—and use their other senses as well. Given something new, they'll bang it, smell it, try to pull it apart, maybe throw it, and quite often taste it. They are little scientists. They want to know what everything can do—how it works.

Toddlers are "doers" but not "producers." They explore, experiment, and try things out to see what will happen. That means if you give them a toy or an activity that is designed to be used in a certain way, they're sure to try a dozen other ways to use it. They are not interested in outcomes or products. They enjoy the process of exploring and experimenting for its own sake, and they don't need anything to show for it.

Independence and Interdependence

Newborn babies are faced with two major tasks: (1) to become independent individuals, and (2) to establish connections with others. The parents' job is to help their children with these tasks. Most parents focus more on one task than the other. Some even ignore one and leave its accomplishment to chance.

European American parents and researchers focus on *independence* and individuality, which is also the focus of this chapter. Parents from other cultures are more concerned about their children's ability to create and maintain connections. These parents have a different view of practically everything because of their focus on *interdependence,* or mutual dependence, instead of independence.

Parents whose primary goal is to establish and keep connections may have little concern about teaching their children self-help skills. For example, self-feeding may be postponed because feeding is a time in which connections are nourished. They may continue spoon-feeding long past infancy, into toddlerhood and beyond. This practice can get them in trouble if their child enters child care. Teachers may be shocked when a 3-year-old sits down at breakfast the first day and waits to be fed. Parents can be quite surprised and disappointed when they learn of a program's policy on self-help skills.

Although parents who stress independence look down on the idea of "coddling" children, to the parent focused on making connections there's nothing negative about doing things for children. These parents see no reason to keep from prolonging babyhood and continuing the closeness. Their attitude makes sense if you understand their goal. They worry about too much independence, so they try to discourage it. Independent-minded parents have the opposite worry. They fear that if they don't encourage independence, their children will remain dependent on them, maybe forever!

Parents who stress connectedness expect their children to be independent as well, but they believe it will happen naturally. In fact, they worry that the drive for independence is too strong; that's why they have to work so hard to maintain connections.

Self-Help Skills

Another behavior that indicates growing autonomy is the push for self-help skills. How the adults respond to this and to the exploring behavior will determine to some extent the child's adult behavior. Children who aren't allowed to touch or to try things on their own get a message about their own capabilities. When restricted to an extreme, they can lose their curiosity, their willingness to take risks, and their drive to be independent of others and do things for themselves.

Consider the difference between these two scenes:

Hannah has unbuckled herself from her car seat and is demanding that she be allowed to climb out of the car by herself. "Hannah do it!" she proclaims loudly.

She has never done this before and nobody knows if she can do it safely or not. Her father, annoyed by her demands, steps back out of reach and says in a sarcastic tone, "Go ahead, little girl, show me how grown up you are!" True to her father's expectations she falls. Crying, she reaches for her father: He picks her up and comforts her. Brushing away her tears, he tells her that she's too little to do things by herself. He makes it clear that she needs him. Later he tells the story, and the whole family laughs at the little girl who is "too big for her britches." It becomes a family joke—the "Let Hannah do it" joke.

Now let's replay that scene:

Here's Hannah, unbuckled from her car seat, demanding, "Hannah do it!" Her father, instead of trying to prove to her that she is too young, decides to help her find out what she

"Look, I can do it all by myself!"

can do, but he will protect her while she's making the discovery. Instead of being sarcastic and stepping back, he says, "I'm here if you need my help." He stands far enough away that Hannah can maneuver but close enough to help her if she needs it. She does fine until the slick sole of her shoe slips on the door frame. She starts to fall and reaches out a hand. Her father grabs it and restores her balance. She lets go of his hand, holds on to the armrest, and climbs the rest of the way out safely. They both rejoice at her accomplishment. Later her father tells the family proudly, "Hannah climbed out of the car by herself today!"

Consider the difference in the messages of the two scenes. Scene 1: "You're too uppity and you need a good lesson. When you learn it, you'll know that you're too young to try things on your own." In scene 2, the father encouraged self-help but provided the protection needed for Hannah to be successful. The Hannah of scene 2 sees her father as a facilitator of her independence; the Hannah of scene 1 does not.

When independence is a strong cultural priority, the first stirrings of it prompt adults to begin to encourage and facilitate it. However, in some cultures *interdependence* is the priority, and signs of independence may trigger a push on the part of the adult to work harder to promote the cultural goal. For example, in Japan some parents find their children too independent from the start, so they begin right away giving lessons in dependence. The goal is to help children see themselves as connected, not separate. When at about 9 months of age children begin to assert themselves—pushing away the adult hand trying to feed them, for example—the lessons in interdependence intensify. The specific objective is to teach children to accept help graciously, even if they can do it for themselves.

Sometimes adults share responsibility for the same child, and one pushes independence while the other struggles against the same behaviors. These two adults may be parents in a cross-cultural marriage, or teacher and parent. If they are in disagreement about their goals and priorities for the child, they need to sit down and talk about their differences. It's hard on a child to have two conflicting approaches to deal with.

Self-Feeding.   Take, for example, self-feeding. The teacher who values independence encourages self-feeding as soon as the baby grabs for the spoon or can pick up a teething biscuit and get it to her mouth. This caregiver gives the baby her own spoon and lets her help, and before long lets her feed herself—as soon as she can get enough in her mouth to count. Also, she cuts up small bits of appropriate finger foods and makes them available for the child to self-feed. Because what this teacher does is considered developmentally appropriate practice among early childhood practitioners, she won't feel a conflict until she runs into a parent who see things differently.

Some parents have different priorities for toddlers. Self-feeding, in particular, is not a priority for all parents. For some parents, the goal for their children is learning to help others rather than helping oneself. Therefore, they model helping skills by spoon-feeding children into the preschool years. They may justify their actions in a number of ways, including their desire to keep things neat and clean and not waste food, for example. When a teacher and a parent see something like self-feeding from very different perspectives, arguments and angry feelings can result.

It's important as a family-support person that you not get into arguments about your different perspectives, but work on your relationship with the family and practice good communication skills so you can work out differences together. See Strategy Box 3.1 for some ideas about how to work through conflicts.

Toilet Training and Learning.   Toileting toddlers is another area where values of independence and interdependence can collide. Just as no culture produces adults who are unable to feed themselves, no matter how late they start, no culture produces adults unable to toilet themselves. But the approach and the timing are different

Strategy Box 3.1

When Conflicts Arise: Strategies for Working with Families

- In the face of differing ideas about care practices, seek to establish common ground with individual families without simply imposing regulations, rules, and restrictions.
- The first step in looking for common ground is to suspend judgment. Make your goal to talk about the differences and see the family's point of view.
- Develop appreciation for contrasting patterns of care and understand that they need not be mutually exclusive.
- Aim for consensus in the face of conflicts and differences in perception.
- If you are feeling highly emotional about a particular issue, do some self-reflection to understand why this is a particular "hot button" for you. Gaining insights into your personal issues may help you better understand the family's perspective.

depending on whether you believe in *toilet training* or *toilet learning*, which can be related to whether your stress is independence or interdependence.

When most professionals discuss toilet learning, they consider it from the independence perspective. Their advice is to watch for signs of readiness, which fall into three general categories: physical, intellectual, and emotional. P*hysical readiness* means the ability to hold on and let go. A first sign is when children go for longer and longer periods with a dry diaper. Physical readiness also is determined by children's ability to handle their own clothing—pulling down pants, for example. A sign of *intellectual readiness* is when children tell the adult *after* eliminating or indicate in other ways that they are aware and can communicate what is happening with their own body. *Emotional readiness* comes when children show a willingness to use a potty or a toilet instead of diapers. The timing for these signs varies with each individual, but in general they seldom appear before the second birthday.

An adult with a priority of interdependence may look at toileting from an entirely different point of view. This person won't wait for a child to reach the age of 2 but may start when the child is as young as a few months; some may even start at birth, as they try to "catch" the baby and hold him or her over a potty. Readiness takes on a whole different meaning when the goal is interdependence. This approach emphasizes the training aspect rather than the learning aspect of toileting. It involves a conditioned reflex.

Interestingly enough, a new trend toward early toilet training shows the idea is growing. Instead of being "old fashioned" it's becoming the latest thing. An article in *Twins* Magazine by Kahwaty (March/April 2006) explains not only how to train a baby, but how to train two of them at once. The article points out that the United States is a "diaper culture" so babies using potties is a "foreign idea." The trend even has a name—Infant potty training (IPT) or elimination communication (EC)—and at least one Web site (diaperfreebaby.com).

Professionals in the United States frown on training children during the first year, partly because in the past this approach has sometimes been associated with using harsh methods. It is important to recognize that toilet training differences can be cultural—or not—and that harshness is not necessarily a part of the process. The *Twins* article warns against using either rewards or punishment, or even showing disappointment if the methods aren't successful. The article stresses that the adult should be relaxed and not have an opinion about whether the child goes or not.

Here's how toilet training using a conditioning method works. Timing is crucial. Sometimes the adult can predict based on the baby's regularity. "Time to hold her over the potty," says the adult periodically. Also, the adult learns to read subtle body messages that indicate the baby is about to wet or defecate. The baby learns to let the adult know, and the adult trains the baby to let go at a signal—usually a shoosh or a whistling sound. It's truly amazing to a teacher whose only experience is with toddlers to see how young babies with the help of an adult can manage dry, clean diapers most of the time.

"It's the adult who's trained, not the baby!" is a common reaction to this interdependence approach. Teachers who use the learning approach rather than the training approach are sometimes critical of those who train—and vice versa—yet each method works well for the adults and children who are using it. Both approaches eventually result in fully trained children who are able to handle all of their own toileting.

Toilet training or learning can become difficult when the child perceives that his or her autonomy is being usurped and who then fights back. Some children even feel that the adult is depriving them of something that is rightfully theirs—their body products! The resulting power struggle can be ugly and its effects long-lasting. Some children with an unfortunate toileting history may be left with big control issues that pop up in a variety of arenas. But don't assume that every family who believes in toilet training before the first year uses harshness or force.

When a difference between pottying methods becomes apparent, it is important for the early educator to set aside assumptions and judgments and talk about the differences until each party understands the other.

Working with parents around differences in ideas about toilet training can be difficult and cause conflicts. Review Strategy Box 3.1 for ideas on approaching a conflict with a family. And always keep the relationship in mind when you enter a conversation about differences. Your first priority should be to keep the relationship intact, if you already have one, or to build a relationship if this family is just starting the program. Listen to them!

A Sense of Possession

It is important to note that not all cultures are object-oriented to the same extent and that not all regard personal possessions as important. In a culture that does prize possessions, a sense of ownership and its counterpart—a willingness to share—become important developmental steps. What many adults of this culture don't realize is that the one must come before the other. Without a firm sense of possession, children can't understand the concept of sharing.

There's quite a difference between the infant who

Frank Gonzalez-Mena

An effective way to intervene in this situation is to protect both children from getting hurt and to reflect their feelings by saying what you see in a nonjudgmental way.

doesn't have a sense of possession and the toddler who does. Most of us have seen babies receiving gifts that they have no feeling for or interest in. The adults have the concept of ownership—the baby doesn't. That picture is a contrast to the toddler holding a toy as far out of reach as possible and screaming "Me! Mine!" at an advancing playmate.

The immediate adult inclination is to rush in with a lesson on sharing. However, it's a little too soon for the lesson to be truly effective. This toddler is just beginning to get the concept of ownership. She is starting to see herself as a person with possessions. She needs to grasp that idea fully before she can understand the idea of sharing. She'll just harbor a grudge if you take the toy away and insist that she share it. Anger and grudges are not involved in the true spirit of sharing, which is the lesson most adults want to get across when they teach the behavior.

At this point the conflict between the two children over a toy is more a momentary power issue than anything else, and there are feelings on both sides. An effective way to intervene in this situation is to reflect the feelings of both parties rather than to discuss issues of sharing or fairness. If you get good at handling these kinds of conflicts, you provide a good model for parents who might get more heavy handed about resolving the situation. For example, here's an example of an adult using the approach just described to help Olivia and Jacob, both 2-year-olds, with their feelings:

> *Olivia is triumphantly holding a rag doll in her arms. Jacob is standing near her, crying his eyes out. An adult is squatting beside them.*
>
> *"You both want that same doll, and Olivia has it," says the adult.*
>
> *Jacob sits down on the floor and screams in response to the adult intervention.*
>
> *"I see how unhappy you are, Jacob," says the adult.*
>
> *Olivia flaunts the doll in front of Jacob's face, saying again, firmly, "Mine!"*
>
> *Jacob grabs for the doll, connects, and jerks it away. Olivia is the one screaming now.*
>
> *"Jacob has the doll now," says the adult, announcing the action rather than making any judgment about it. Then the adult reflects the feelings. "You don't like it when he grabs things from you. You can tell him 'No!'"*
>
> *Olivia screams "No!" at Jacob's departing back. A moment later Jacob drops the doll to pick up a cloth book that is lying at his feet. Olivia starts for the dropped doll, then changes her mind and grabs a page of the book, yelling, "Mine!" Jacob starts to cry.*
>
> *The adult says, "You don't like that, Jacob! You don't like it when she grabs things. Tell her 'No!'"*

And so it goes. Now look at these two a couple of years later:

> *They are painting side by side at an easel. Olivia reaches for the brush that Jacob has in his hand—the one that goes in the green paint. "That's mine," says Jacob firmly.*
>
> *"No, it's not, it's the school's," says Olivia, "and I need it."*
>
> *"I'm using it," says Jacob.*
>
> *Olivia continues to reach for the brush and grabs hold of it so Jacob can't paint.*
>
> *"Stop that!" says Jacob.*
>
> *"I need the brush!" insists Olivia.*

"Can't you wait until I'm through?" asks Jacob.

"No," says Olivia.

"I have an idea," says Jacob. "There's another green brush on the other side of the easel. Let's get that one."

Olivia lets go long enough for him to reach to the other side and retrieve the brush and the paint container. "Here," he says, handing it to her.

"Thanks," she replies.

Later in the same year, at the same easel, Olivia asks Jacob for the brush he is using. He says to her, "I'm almost finished. You can have it in a minute." She waits until he is finished, uses it, and then gives it back to him.

These two have learned the behaviors of sharing and also the spirit. They have experienced the benefits. They understand the concept of possession and ownership. In cultures where private ownership is not an issue and personal possessions do not play a large part in people's lives, this sequence might be very different.

DEALING WITH ISSUES OF POWER AND CONTROL

The behaviors discussed—saying no, exploring the world, learning self-help skills, and gaining a sense of possession—all have to do with issues of power and control. Just as the *infant* came to experience a sense of power through signaling his needs and satisfying them by means of the adults around him, so does the *toddler* need to experience a sense of power through these typical toddler behaviors.

An adult can do much to facilitate this empowerment and the controls that need to go with it to keep the toddler and others safe and secure.

Set Up a Developmentally Appropriate Environment

Not all families have the kind of living conditions that allow them to set up a developmentally appropriate environment, but when they see the one in the early care and education program, they may get ideas about how to make their living situation a bit more developmentally appropriate. Such an environment provides freedom for exploration with few prohibitions. Think of the difference between a toddler in a playroom set up for her, versus spending an hour in his great aunt's living room, trying to keep her hands off all the precious and fragile treasures sitting around on display. Yes, toddlers need to learn that there are some things they can't touch, but if parents understand the toddlers' need to explore and manipulate objects, they can limit this lesson to a few times when it's important and spend the rest of the time teaching them that there are many things in the world that they *can* touch.

When toddlers spend their time in an environment that is appropriate for their age, they are freer to explore. They won't be faced with so many *no's*. If they don't have to hear the word *no*, they may decrease their own usage of the word. It is worth encouraging parents to think about what kind of environment says "Yes!" to toddlers, and then arranging things so that where toddlers spend their time affirms their developmental needs. At this stage they touch, explore, try things out, and use their bodies to learn about the world. Their natural inclination is to climb, push, poke, prod, and perform a huge variety of other movements. They need a safe place to do all this—a place where they feel empowered rather than prohibited. Often parents can see the advantages of a developmentally appropriate environment without your needing to point it out to them.

Appreciate Play

Children gain power through playing. They play with themselves, other people, and objects. Why do they play? Jones & Cooper (2006) wrote a book called *Playing to Get Smart*, which is the answer to that question. A baby who discovers her hand in the first year of life (called *hand regard*) is playing with herself. She stares at her hand, wiggles her fingers, and turns the hand around to get a different perspective on it. Some children find their own bodies endlessly fascinating. Later this same child will take a crayon in her hand and enjoy the feeling of circling her arm round and round. She doesn't care if the marks are on paper or on the wall, which is where they'll be if no one is monitoring her. The marks aren't the point of interest—the body movement is. Eventually the marks themselves become fascinating as she watches herself create them.

Children also play with people. They play with adults and with each other. Although the classic research by Parten (1932) labeled toddlers as mainly playing *parallel* to each other rather than *with* each other, a short period of observation in a child care program shows this isn't always so. An example of parallel play as described and named by Parten is in the sandbox when two 2-year-olds sit side by side, each shoveling sand and talking, but not paying obvious attention to each other. It may seem as though each is living in his own world, but when you listen you see that they are influenced by each other's play. They may not interact, but one picks up on what the other is saying or doing and

Provide a developmentally appropriate environment for youngsters.

Laura Zahner

incorporates it into his own play. Children today who are in child care or in other situations where they have peers in their daily lives go beyond parallel play into true interaction. They talk to each other, carrying on a back-and-forth conversation. If you have a chance to observe with family members, get them to talk about the good things they are seeing that relate to the benefits of play.

Children play with things. Anything within reach becomes a toy, as children reach out to learn about their world and the objects in it. They use all their senses. It may not seem important to adults to know how things taste and to discover textures with their tongues. For babies, however, mouthing is a natural way to learn about any object they can get their lips around. That's why it is so important that young children be in a safe environment where they won't get hurt in their explorations. As they grow, their exploration of objects becomes more sophisticated, and they learn how things work and what they can do. In a consumer-oriented culture many adults place a high priority on toys and see them as educational. Even newborns are given toys and encouraged to touch, look, and hold them.

The typical child care program today relies on toys and other objects as part of their curriculum, and many programs have an abundance of things in their environment. These things may be recognizable commercially manufactured toys, or they may be "found objects" such as margarine tubs, egg cartons, and lids from frozen orange juice containers. Art supplies and materials include such items as wood scraps from a carpenter shop and homemade play dough consisting of flour, water, and salt. Construction materials made for children are also usually present in early childhood programs, ranging from wooden blocks to small plastic pieces that link together. Although not literally objects, sand and water are considered educational materials in most programs. You might want to consider the messages you give with your choice of toys. The temptation for many families is to shower their young children with toys. The marketing of toys often emphasizes their educational value but almost none of those claims has research behind it. Consider that found items and simple substances (such as sand and water—just mentioned) give children more opportunities to explore and interact with the play materials. Again, parents can learn from you, just by observing.

Play has roots in imitation. From birth babies imitate what they see. If someone sticks his tongue out, even a newborn baby is likely to do the same. The adult is usually delighted at the baby's response to almost anything he does, and so begins a give-and-take sequence of playful interaction. The socialization aspects of this kind of play are obvious. The child is learning to take turns, which will become useful later when the baby has enough language to take part in real conversations. At the beginning the conversations are nonverbal and playful.

At first babies only imitate when they can see what they are imitating. By about age 2, the typically developing child has moved from imitating only things he sees to playing pretend in creative and imaginative ways. Jean Piaget (1954, 1962), a pioneer in explaining cognitive development, had an explanation for the growing ability to pretend. The Swiss theorist and researcher explained that the shift occurs when children are able to make "internal representations" of things, actions, behaviors, and patterns. Piaget's stages of cognitive development have guided several generations of early childhood educators to understand more about how the intellect unfolds. The term *internal representations* means the child can hold images in her mind, and it is this ability that allows her to pretend. Using imagination, a block becomes a telephone and the child calls Daddy at work. Imaginary coffee comes out of toy coffee pots, and play dough rolled and molded becomes food. Although none of this may look *intellectual*, it is indeed an aspect of cognitive development. It is also vitally connected to self-development and socialization. This may not be information that is important to pass on to parents, but it is good for early educators to have a grasp of the unfolding of play and an appreciation of the benefits.

In his book *The Power of Play* (2007), David Elkind, child development expert, makes a strong case for spontaneous, imaginative activities rather than passive electronic entertainment and "educational" toys, games, and activities. He worries that free time and lazy periods of unstructured play are endangered species.

Encourage Self-Help Skills

Encourage children to do for themselves what they are capable of; don't do for them what they can do for themselves. This bit of advice comes from an author with a cultural priority on independence and may not apply to those from cultures who see early independence as a threat to interdependence. When independence is a priority, teaching self-help skills as a way of empowerment starts in infancy as the adult includes the child as a full partner in caregiving routines. For instance, diapering is a teamwork affair, and the baby is treated as a whole person worthy of respect, not just as a bottom that must be tended to while the top half is being entertained with something else.

This attitude of teamwork makes the toddler feel a little less rebellious because the adult is sometimes seen as a partner rather than as an adversary. It isn't a cure-all for rebellion, of course, because the struggle to defy the adult is a mark of the toddler stage.

When children are old enough to eat solid foods, giving finger food allows them to practice getting food to their mouths, even if they still need to be spoon fed. And before long they will want to take over completely. That means the adults have to put up with messy eating for awhile until children develop the skills to eat neatly. Children can learn to dress themselves at an early age if encouraged to do so. The learning process starts with undressing. Even a baby can pull off a sock that is sticking out from her toe. Setting it up so it is easy for her is encouraging self-help skills. Putting up with a less than perfect performance is also encouraging. Perfectionism on the part of the adult tends to discourage young children's self-help skills. It may be hard to explain that to parents with perfectionist tendencies, but you can demonstrate it without making it a huge issue. Remember that modeling is a powerful teaching tool, with adults as well as with children.

Give Choices

Help toddlers feel powerful by laying out options instead of giving a single directive. Instead of saying, "Get in that bathtub now!" offer an alternative such as, "Do you want to take a bath before supper or after?" When after supper comes and the child still balks, you can say, "After you get in, you can choose between the boats or the blocks to play with." And if the child still balks and it's time for a showdown, you can still give a choice: "Do you want to climb in by yourself, or should I put you in?" This way the child still feels empowered, and you are able to do what you perceive he needs to do. You're not being wishy-washy. The child *will* take a bath, but he has some choices about when, with what, and how he will enter the bathtub.

This is a culturally specific approach based on the concept of life as a series of choices. When you regard learning to make choices as important, you give children practice when they are young so that as they grow up they have had experience with making choices and living with the consequences. In cultures that don't see life in this same way and don't regard learning to make choices as important, giving toddlers choices doesn't make as much sense.

Speaking of choices, a family-centered program also gives choices to families— what kind of support they need, what kinds of activities they want to engage in, and how they want to be involved are just some examples. Giving families choices is an important part of the Parent Services Project. Lee (2006) discusses the approach of family-centered care, which finds out what the famiies want rather than giving them what the program perceives they need. When teachers try to help by putting on programs that are poorly attended by families, that's a clue that those families were not included in the decision making. When parents decide for themselves what parent involvement means, the program has much more success. Parents can even run their own activities rather than having staff put them on for them. Some activities can be a joint effort of staff and parents. One way to increase parent involvement is to offer a menu of services based on what families say they want and need.

Provide Control

Provide the control toddlers need. Here are two scenes that illustrate that principle. Let's go back to Olivia and Jacob, the 2-year-olds. In this first scene the adult doesn't provide control for Olivia. Watch what happens. Let's call this adult, A.

They are playing happily and the phone rings. The adult, A., turns her back to answer it, and Jacob grabs the toy Olivia has in her hand. Olivia, who hasn't learned to express her feelings in words yet (though the adults have been working on that) expresses her anger and frustration by sinking her sharp little baby teeth into Jacob's arm. Jacob lets out a yell, and A. comes running. She scolds Olivia, telling her it isn't nice to bite, then puts her in a time-out chair. Olivia keeps getting up, so A. continually puts her back, scolding her each time. Finally she hugs her, lets her up, and warns her not to bite again.

Later that afternoon, when Olivia is tired and a little lonely for her mother and A. is busy with another child, Olivia walks up to Jacob and bites his arm again. She remembers the stir it caused this morning, and she enjoys a repeat performance this afternoon. However, she feels vaguely uncomfortable because she knows that she should control that urge.

Contrast that scene with this one. This provider is called B.

Olivia and Jacob are playing together when the doorbell rings. B. knows that Olivia has the urge to bite when she gets frustrated, so rather than taking the chance of leaving her alone with Jacob for even a minute, she takes Olivia with her to open the door.

Later that morning, when Olivia and Jacob are playing together, Olivia gets frustrated. She makes a move toward Jacob's arm; before she can connect, B.'s hand covers her mouth gently. "I know you are unhappy, but I won't let you bite Jacob," she says in a clear tone that doesn't imply judgment—just fact. "You can bite this teething ring," she adds, "or this plastic toy." She offers the choice. Olivia grabs the teething ring and bites down hard. "You really are upset," affirms B.

Adult B. wisely provides the control that Olivia lacks at this age. She prevents the biting from occurring instead of dealing with it afterward in a way that rewards Olivia with extra attention.

Of course, it isn't realistic to assume that an adult will be there 100 percent of the time. Even with careful vigilance, Olivia might get her teeth into Jacob sometime. If that were to happen, B. would then deal with the situation as a failure to control on her part—not as badness on Olivia's part. After all, Olivia is using her mouth to express her feelings in the only way she knows how. She lacks control—the control that it's up to the adult to provide.

If the bite occurs, B. responds in much the same way she responded over the toy-grabbing incident earlier in this chapter. She approaches both children, modeling gentleness by touching them both lightly and lovingly. She says, "That really hurts, Jacob." To Olivia she says, "Jacob is unhappy because you hurt him." As she says the words, she touches gently the red place on Jacob's arm. Then she touches the same place on Olivia's arm. After the demonstration of gentleness and the words indicating the feelings, she deals with any first aid needed. She is careful not to give either child a great deal of the kind of extra attention that hooks children on either the victim or the aggressor role. She doesn't turn her back on Olivia and say, "Oh, poor little Jacob, let's put some ice on that bite—poor baby," because she knows that ignoring Olivia may make Jacob feel it's worth it to get bitten in order to enjoy this lavish sympathy. And Olivia is not left with the uncomfortable feeling of being ignored while realizing that she doesn't have the control she needs to keep from hurting someone. Being out of control is as scary for the child experiencing it as it is for the victim.

The adult B. approach provides excellent modeling for parents. It may require some explanation for parents to really understand what she is doing and why, Of course, there isn't always time to explain everything you do, but squeezing time in to talk to parents is an important part of the early educator's job.

Set Limits

Setting limits and enforcing them also empowers children by giving them freedom within those limits. You can think of limits as a fence around a pasture. The horse is free to graze within the fence. Without the fence his freedom would have to be limited by a rope, by vigilance, or by training—none of which gives the freedom of the fence.

Limits for toddlers work the same way. The limits may be environmental boundaries, such as a barricade across the stairs, a lock on the toilet lid, or a gate on the driveway. Or they may be human boundaries, such as consistently taking a child off a counter he insists on climbing up on, stopping a child from throwing toys, or holding a kicking child who threatens to hurt others.

Children will test limits until they find that they hold. The child locked out of the bathroom pounds on the door, jiggles the doorknob, and tries to poke something into the keyhole. He gives up when the physical barrier holds. Human boundaries are the same way. The child may continue to climb on the counter, and if the adult gives up and quits stopping him, he gets the message that this isn't a real limit—it doesn't hold if he's persistent enough. If the child is allowed to throw toys sometimes, he doesn't know there's a limit. His test shows that it doesn't hold up. It's hard to have the patience to watch a child continually test the limits. It's tempting to just give in— but that makes it worse the next time. It's good for parents to watch how you handle setting limits. It is quite possible that as children many parents got a spanking when they pushed a limit, and they may think that this is the only way to handle limit testing. With your patience and skill, however, you can show them another way that eventually works. Notice that in this section and the previous one, alternatives to time out and spanking were demonstrated. Some family members have a limited repertory when it comes to guiding behavior. You can open their eyes to a wider variety of approaches to take.

It also helps if you understand that to empower a child and provide security at the same time, it is necessary to set limits and hold to them. Because toddlers are persistent and are still discovering things about the world, you can also expect those limits to be tested until the toddler is satisfied that they're firm. The testing makes sense if you understand what's going on. If you don't, it seems as if the child is just trying to make you unhappy with his persistently unacceptable behavior. Don't get unhappy— just outpersist him! Show parents what you are doing and explain if necessary.

Janice and Emily

Janice is 17 and has an 18-month-old, Emily, who is driving her crazy. Janice has just started in a young parent program that allows her to continue her high school education. Emily is taken care of at the school in a portable building that has been set up for infants and toddlers. Although Emily protests at being left in the morning, which really bothers Janice, she quickly becomes contented while playing with the other babies. Janice misses her, so she pops in briefly between her classes—which almost always results in another crying spell when she has to leave again. That annoys Janice. Why can't she just come and go without all this fuss!

Whenever she is around Emily, the child clings to her, making it impossible for her to even walk from one place to another. Janice doesn't like this.

Janice also doesn't like it when the child care teachers assure her that Emily was fine all day and didn't miss her at all. That doesn't feel good. And she doesn't like the way Emily is beginning to hang around one of the teachers and even hugs her good-bye when they leave at the end of the day. Janice wonders whether Emily still loves her when she shows affection toward the teacher.

Some of Emily's other behaviors bother Janice as well. She doesn't like the defiant look Emily gets in her eye when Janice tells her to do something. That makes Janice feel angry, and she gets just as stubborn as Emily has become.

Sometimes she feels like hitting Emily, but she talks about that feeling in her parenting class, where she is learning a variety of ways to guide Emily's behavior. Somehow talking about hitting helps her control herself, so she doesn't do it. She's seen another child in the center whose mother got carried away with spanking and ended up abusing her daughter. It was pretty awful, both how the child looked and what happened to her mother. She ended up losing her baby. Janice couldn't stand to lose Emily, and she cries at the thought that she might ever hurt her. So she is careful to never spank her, no matter what.

Another thing that bothers Janice is how dirty Emily gets. She insists on doing things for herself—like feeding herself. She isn't very neat! And the child care staff doesn't seem to understand how important it is to Janice that Emily look like a sweet little doll. They let her feed herself, which means that often her clothes get messed up. Sometimes Janice comes in and finds Emily in the center's old beat-up clothes, because they ran out of changes for her. Janice doesn't like seeing her like this.

And the sand! Can't they understand how hard it is for Janice when Emily gets sand in her hair? It seems that whenever they go out in the yard, Emily ends up with her head full of sand. It's a lot of trouble to wash that out and redo her hair. Besides, Emily *hates* to have her hair washed and puts up quite a fight.

This is all so different from when Emily was younger and she used to just lie around and laugh and look cute. It was a lot easier then. But this is a different stage, and it isn't so easy!

Janice knew that none of this would be easy when she decided to keep Emily. She had lots of warnings about the life of a teen mother. But with her family's support and the help of the center staff, she's making it. And Emily is an important part of her life!

COPING WITH LOSS AND SEPARATION

Separation issues start in infancy and continue into toddlerhood and beyond; they are never handled once and for all. The infant who has learned to sleep alone may well become the toddler who, because new fears arise, balks at going to bed and staying there. Even though a toddler copes very well with separation and independence during waking periods, she may resist sleep because she must give up the control she has. Lack of control can be very scary because it means that coping mechanisms don't work in the same way as they do during waking periods. In addition, dreams, which can also create fear, enter in. Parents and child care teachers who recognize this fact will be more understanding when children develop sleeping problems at home or react badly to sleeping away from home.

Taking Separation in Small Steps

It is easier for children if they first experience separation in small steps. Sleeping alone is one of these steps, though all families don't agree with babies sleeping by themselves. Having a babysitter or being away from the person(s) they are attached to for short periods are other examples of steps of separation. Taking these steps may be questioned by some families who are not anxious for the children to learn to separate from them at a young age; however, the reality of child care and other early education programs for very young children is that they will experience separation.

With a succession of periods away from the parent(s), either at home or away from home, children come to trust that the attachment holds and that they will be reunited.

Be aware of the dangers of giving children more to cope with than they can handle. If parents feel a need to take an extended vacation away from their child, they should realize the possible effects of a prolonged separation during the toddler period. Obviously, if the child has someone else he or she is attached to, the effects of such a separation won't be as serious as if the only person or two people in the world the child feels close to suddenly disappear for a few weeks. Such an interruption in attachment can be devastating to the child's sense of trust.

Some sudden and prolonged separations can't be helped, of course. If the child must undergo an extensive hospitalization, he or she will get through it better if parents stay at the hospital with the child or at least visit frequently. Visiting isn't the perfect solution because of the continual anguish of painful good-byes; it's better if a parent can stay with the child. When this isn't possible, visiting is preferable to nothing, even though parents may be tempted to cut down on their visits because of the pain their departures cause the child. But children who feel deserted can experience depression, according to the research of John Bowlby (2000a, 2000b), who studied the effects of long-term separations in childhood.

Entering Child Care

When a separation such as going into child care is on the horizon, it's best to prepare the child (Balaban, 2006; McCracken, 1986). Imagine being the child of a mother who has been with you day and night for the first two years. Your mother suddenly decides to go back to work, and one day she drives you to a strange place and leaves you there for the entire day. How would you feel?

It's far gentler if you can get families to visit beforehand and to keep the first experiences short, so the child gets to know the place and the people. Being left for only an hour or so in the beginning, the child learns that the parent will return after a time. If the day is gradually lengthened, the child gets used to it and it's not such a shock.

Helping Children Adjust.   Some children walk right into child care without batting an eye. They're so intrigued with the new setting that they forget their fears. Other children cling and suffer greatly. In this case it helps if the parent can let the child make the decision to separate rather than peeling him off and walking out the door, leaving him screaming.

One program has a room for the use of parents whose children hesitate to leave them. The doorway just beyond the "separation room" is open and is filled with the sounds and sights of children playing, which serve to entice the child to leave the parent's side. Parents are asked to be patient about the separation process, and they're given some help and support to make it a healthy coping experience for both parent and child. Of course, everyone doesn't have the option of a slow departure. However, if this approach is proposed and the program promotes it, more families might find ways to ease their children into the new situations and relieve some of the separation upset.

When the good-byes come, it helps to make things predictable. Some parents prefer to sneak out and miss the protests from the child. When they do that—leave the child playing without saying good-bye—trust issues arise. Instead of feeling secure, the child is left with the feeling of never knowing when the parent is there or gone. How can the child feel any power in the world if there's no way to predict what will happen? Saying good-bye may bring tears and protests, but it's the open, honest way of helping the child understand what's happening. It may be hard to explain that to families, but it's worth it.

Accepting Feelings.   When strong feelings are a part of the good-byes, it's important to acknowledge and accept the feelings rather than distracting the child from them. If the early educator has left-over issues of separation and loss from childhood, it may be very hard for him or her to deal with the child's feelings. It's just too painful. If that's your problem, it's important to recognize how your own unresolved issues may be influencing your ability to deal with a child in the throes of a separation. Separation experiences remain

Jim Darter

Some children walk right into child care without any fear. Other children are less brave about the new situation.

with us—especially the unexpressed and unresolved feelings. Bringing these to awareness can help us cope with them in ways that are healthy for us and allow us to be available to the child who needs us.

Many adults who find separation painful because of their own experiences do whatever they can to distract the child and not acknowledge what he or she is feeling. Far better to put the child's feelings into words: "You're upset that your mother left you." It's also important to emit a sense of confidence that the child will be all right and that she will be reunited with the loved one. Don't go overboard, however. If you constantly reassure the child, she'll begin to wonder whether you're reassuring yourself because what you're saying is not true. Better to be empathetic about the feelings and reassuring without discounting them. Your confidence and empathetic acceptance of the child's feelings not only help the child, but give the parent some assurance as well that you know what you are doing and everything will be okay.

It's also important to recognize that parents may have strong feelings about separation. It may hurt to leave their child with someone else. They may feel guilty. Some parents prolong good-byes because of their own feelings of ambiguity. These slow departures can be torture to everyone, especially if the child has shown willingness to be left but has second thoughts because of the way the parent is dragging his or her feet. In these situations, teachers sometimes have to help parents see how the child's feelings are affected by their reluctance to leave. Teachers need to support parents and accept their feelings in the same way they do with children, without supporting detrimental actions such as agonizing, lingering departures.

Helping Children Cope. Some children are comforted and reassured by what's called a *transition object*—some kind of comfort device, such as a stuffed animal or a favorite blanket. Having something from home that they're attached to provides a link between home and child care. Leaving something of the parents at child care can help, too. One child was comforted when his mother left her purse (she carried her wallet with her) because he figured if she forgot to come back for him, she'd at least remember her purse. He knew how important it was to her. Many parents are already aware of the value of transition objects to help separation—though they may not call them that.

Some children are comforted and reassured by what's called a "transition object" such as this boy's blanket.

Providing something to do that's compelling and interesting is a good technique for helping the child cope with feelings of loss. Often the child will migrate to an interesting activity or a friendly person after the pain of arrival is beginning to pass. Don't hurry this process of moving to an activity or other person, however. Give time for the feelings. There's a fine line between helping children cope with feelings and distracting them from those feelings. It is important that the feelings be accepted and acknowledged. It may also help the parent to know what you are doing and how you are using particular activities or play objects to help the child make the transition. It's always good to explain the problem with distraction, because some families may have never thought about the problem of moving a child away from what he or she is feeling.

In addition, allow the child to play out the feelings. Often you can see children over among the dolls or out in the sandbox, working through what's on their minds. This is a healthy way to deal with feelings that may be hard to express directly in words. You can also point out to parents what's happening—or listen while they point it out to you. The parent may have a greater understanding of the experience the child is playing out than you do.

PARTNERING WITH PARENTS OF TODDLERS

Just as you have been seeing examples of early educators partnering with toddlers, so have you been provided examples of how to partner with parents. See Strategy Box 3.2 for more ideas of how to work with parents in a partnership way.

While you are broadening your perspective in order to understand each family and their child's behavior, there are also lots of opportunities to help a parent

Strategy Box 3.2

Creating Partnerships with Families

- Work hard to create and maintain a relationship with each family. Part of it is everyday behavior—greeting them by name every time you see them. Squeeze in conversations wherever you can.
- Recognize that demonstration is a strong teacher. This chapter offered examples of how early educators can model behaviors for families to give them insights and expand their repertory of guidance approaches.
- Recognize that you can also learn from observing. If you encourage the parents to demonstrate for you how they do things, you may also gain insights and expand your knowledge and skills.
- Find ways to share power with the families even though you may have many barriers in the way, such as funding requirements, regulations, and other kinds of mandates.

broaden his or her perspective too. Take the parent who thinks her child's personality is warped because the child is displaying a good deal of defiance and other kinds of negative behavior. You can offer up the information that you have about the stage of autonomy and that may help the parent see the behaviors in a slightly different light. If this is a first-time parent, she may not realize that children aren't toddlers forever. You can lend perspective the parent may not have. On the other hand, you may wonder why this child crawled under the table and refused to come out when the nurse came to give eye exams. The parent might tell you something you didn't know about the child's medical history and the painful procedures he had to go through for a long time. Maybe you didn't know that he had been hospitalized periodically. With this knowledge the extreme reaction makes more sense.

LOOKING BACK AND LOOKING FORWARD

This chapter explored the variety of behaviors that accompany the task of developing autonomy. Each section offered ideas of how to work with parents around the issues that arise in this stage of development. We looked at exploration and self-help skills, and examined ways of handling behavior that is difficult, ways of empowering children, and helping children cope with separation and loss. Cultural conflicts were a recurring theme in this chapter, but we also pointed out that not everything that seems cultural is. For example, toilet training infants may be cultural, but it is also a growing trend among middle-class European-Americans who themselves grew up in a "diaper culture." In this chapter, we also took a quick look at the value of play, which is carried on as an important theme in the next chapter.

FOR DISCUSSION

1. Do you agree that negativity, exploration, self-help skills, and a sense of possession are indeed signs of developing autonomy? What are some examples? Can you think of other signs?

2. Have you ever known a family that valued interdependence over independence? Which parts of this chapter would not pertain to them? Which parts would?

3. How much do you help a child who is struggling to do something on his or her own? What experience do you have in teaching self-help skills? Do you agree that children should be given opportunities to do things on their own, or do you feel better about helping children, especially when they are struggling? Which was stressed more when you were growing up—independence or interdependence?

4. How does typical toddler behavior relate to power issues? Can you give an example of how an adult can empower a toddler? Does everyone agree that toddlers need to feel powerful? How are power and autonomy related?

5. Saying good-bye can be hard for some children. What experience do you have with helping children cope with separation issues? What advice would you have for a parent who is leaving his or her child in child care for the first time? What advice would you have for the teacher/caregiver or family child care provider of that child?

WEB SITES

Child Development Institute
http://www.childdevelopmentinfo.com/parenting/helping_children_cope_with_separation.shtml
This Web site has an article on helping children cope with separation and loss of all sorts, but focusing particularly on death.

Early Head Start National Resource Center
http://www.ehsnrc.org/
The Early Head Start National Resource Center Web site contains a database of all the Early Head Start Program sites as well as valuable tips and strategies for trainers and many full-text documents on a range of infant- and toddler-related topics.

National Association for the Education of Young Children (NAEYC)
http://www.naeyc.org
The National Association for the Education of Young Children has a number of resources available for parents and professionals including books and journals, one of which is called *Young Children*.

National Center on Birth Defects and Developmental Disabilities (NCBDDD)
http://www.cdc.gov/ncbddd/default.htm
This Web site identifies issues that promote the health of babies, children, and adults and enhance the potential for full, productive living. Through its Child Development Studies Section, CDC has initiated Legacy for Children™, including emotional development, temperament, attachment, and autonomy.

Pikler Institute
http://www.pikler.org
and
International Pikler Association
http://www.aipl.org
Both Web sites give information on the Pikler approach used at the Pikler Institute, a residential nursery in Budapest, Hungary.

Program for Infant/Toddler Caregivers (PITC)
http://www.pitc.org
The Program for Infant/Toddler Caregivers supports and promotes quality care for infants and toddlers through resources, information, and training. The site includes information on brain research and implications for infant development.

Resources for Infant Educarers™
http://www.rie.org/
Resources for Infant Educarers is a nonprofit organization that uses the teachings of Magda Gerber to promote a unique philosophy and methodology in working with infants and toddlers in ways that respect them as individuals.

Zero to Three
http://www.zerotothree.org/
Zero to Three: National Center for Infants, Toddlers, and Families is for parents and professionals. A leading resource on the first three years of life, the group has as its mission to strengthen and support families, practitioners, and communities to promote the healthy development of babies and toddlers.

FURTHER READING

Balaban, N. (2006). *Everyday goodbyes: A guide to the separation process*. New York: Teachers College Press.
Gerber, M. (1979). *The RIE manual*. Los Angeles: Resources for Infant Educarers.

Gillespie, L. G. (2006, September). Rocking and rolling: Supporting infants, toddlers and their families: Cultivating good relationships with families can make hard times easier! *Young Children* 61(5), 53–55.

Gonzalez-Mena, J. (2000, July). In the spirit of partnership: High maintenance parent or cultural difference? *Exchange* 134, 40–42.

Gonzalez-Mena, J. (2008). *Diversity in early care and education: Honoring Differences*. New York: McGraw-Hill.

Gonzalez-Mena, J. (2004, September). What can an orphanage teach us? Lessons from Budapest. *Young Children* 59(5), 26–30.

Gray, H. (2004, September). "You go away and you come back": Supporting separations and reunions in an infant/toddler classroom. *Young Children* 59(5), 100–107.

Harmon, C. (1996, May). In the beginning: Helping parents and children separate. *Young Children* 51(4), 72.

Im, J., Parlakian, R., & Sanchez, S. (2007, September). Rocking and rolling: Supporting infants, toddlers, and their families. Understanding the influence of culture on caregiving practices . . . from the inside out. *Young Children* 62 (5) 65–66.

Szanton, E. S. (2001, January). For America's infants and toddlers, are important values threatened by our zeal to "teach"? *Young Children* 56(1), 15–21.

Wittmer, D. S., & Peteresen, S. H. (2006). *Infant and toddler development and responsive program planning: A relationship-based approach*. Upper Saddle River, NJ: Prentice Hall.

CHAPTER 4

Sharing Views of Initiative with Families

In this chapter you'll discover . . .

- How guilt helps or harms children and what determines which it does
- What children get out of playing and how to share that information with parents
- The difference between a child with high energy and one who is hyperactive
- Whether all shy children are shy for the same reason
- How some children learn to be aggressive and what families and teachers can do about it
- Some considerations for supporting play in children with special needs

The United States is built on individual initiative, which has a high value for many in this country. When does initiative begin to develop? What factors facilitate its development? How do adults socialize children to have initiative?

According to Erik Erikson (1963), initiative is the developmental task of the 3- to 6-year-old. The child of preschool or kindergarten age, whether in a program or at home, is usually bursting with initiative. Sometimes the behavior behind these urges gets the child into trouble, especially around adults who don't understand developmental ages and stages. Early educators, including kindergarten teachers, can help families appreciate how children learn initiative.

What does initiative look like? Take a look at Briana, a 4-year-old who shows initiative.

WHAT INITIATIVE LOOKS LIKE IN A 4-YEAR-OLD

Briana runs in the door of her child care center, leaving behind her mother, who is still coming up the steps. She flings a hasty "Hi" at the teacher seated by the door, glances at the interesting "science" display set out to capture the interest of the arriving children, tosses her coat at a hook on the rack by the door, and runs into the classroom with her teacher on her heels.

"Whoa," says her teacher good-naturedly. "Let's go back and do that again." She gently guides Briana back toward her coat on the floor, where her mother waits. Briana kisses her mother good-bye and then starts to take off again. Her teacher grabs her as she goes by. She patiently reminds her again to hang up her coat, which Briana does hastily. Then, released from the teacher's grasp, the lively girl takes off again into the classroom at a fast clip. She heads straight for the art table, which is set up with wood scraps and glue. She elbows her way into a spot at the table, finds an interesting assortment of wood within reach, and begins applying glue to various pieces, which she stacks one on another. She works busily for quite a while, absorbed in what she is doing. After her flighty entrance, the focused attention is quite a contrast. At last she looks up from her project. Turning to a boy sitting next to her, she remarks, "I'm making a house."

He answers, "I'm making a spaceship. See how it launches?" He waves his creation in the air several times. Briana ducks and then turns to the boy on the other side of her. "My mommy's gonna have a baby, and I'm making her a bed," says Briana. The boy ignores her, concentrating on his gluing. Briana goes back to work on her project, concentrating her whole attention on the wood in front of her.

"I need scissors," says Briana to the teacher, who is seated at the end of the table. "I need to put something here," she says, indicating a spot on her wood project. The teacher looks interested and says, "You know where the scissors are."

Briana gets up with her creation in her hand and dances to a nearby table set up with scissors, crayons, various kinds of paper, hole punches, and tape. She sits down at the table and carefully chooses a piece of yellow paper. She painstakingly cuts the paper into an irregular shape, folds it in half, and glues it on a piece of wood sticking out at right angles from the central core of her work. It takes her about 10 minutes to complete this task. She gets up to leave and then turns back to the table, picks up the paper scraps she left there, and hurriedly glues them on too. Then she grabs a pencil, writes a B on the paper, then another B, and then a third. She then "flies" her sculpture over to the art table and passes it under the nose of her teacher, saying, "I wrote my name on my art."

She gives her teacher a hug. The teacher hugs her back. "I see," is the response. Then, "If you're finished, put your art in your cubby."

Briana flies her sculpture to a row of lockers by the coat rack, pokes it inside one of them, and takes off running to the dramatic play area. She ignores the children already there and pulls out a frilly smock from a box of clothes, puts it on, pats it down the front, looks in the mirror, and turns away satisfied. She flounces over to the little table, sits down, picks up a small empty teacup, and pretends to drink.

"You can't play," announces a girl already seated at the table. Briana ignores her and continues slurping noisily into the cup. Then she gets up and takes the cup and the pot with her to the sink, where she swishes them around in the soapy water she finds there. She stands there for a long time, relishing the sensory experience. "Let's play house," suggests a boy, thrusting his hands into the soapy water.

"OK," agrees Briana. "I'll be the mom," she says.

"I'm the mom," says the girl who told her she couldn't play.

"Then I'll be the *other* mom," says Briana, squeezing a sponge out and carrying it over to wipe off the table. "You're my baby," she announces to the boy, who immediately falls to the ground and clings to her foot, clawing at her legs and making a whimpering sound.

"Stop being bad!" Briana scolds him in a harsh voice. "Bad baby, bad, bad, bad!" she screams angrily. The boy cries louder. A teacher passing by smiles at them and continues on her way.

"Pretend I have to spank you," Briana tells the boy. He responds by crying even louder.

She gives him a couple of dramatic whacks, which only connect lightly. He screams in agony. Then she gives him a third whack, which accidentally lands hard.

"Hey, stop that! You hurt me." The boy jumps to his feet, and his voice becomes his own. He looks mad.

A quick look of surprise, a touch of fear, then remorse comes across Briana's face. She hastily retreats to where four children are lying on cushions looking at books. She flings herself to the ground and takes a book out of the hand of the only child within reach.

"Don't!" protests the child, reaching to grab it back. Briana holds up a hand as if to slap her, then slowly lowers it. She turns two pages of the book carefully and deliberately, then tosses it back toward the waiting child, gets up, and leaves.

Seeing the door open, she runs toward it, snatching off the smock and dropping it on the floor as she runs. She stops, looking around to see whether a teacher has spotted the smock on the floor. No teacher is around. Briana hesitates. Then she goes back, picks up the smock, and takes it over to the box where she found it. She dumps it in and hurries back to the open door. She pauses in the doorway for a moment, glancing around. Then she shouts "Sarah!" joyfully and runs down the ramp into the play yard.

ANALYZING INITIATIVE IN A 4-YEAR-OLD

Let's examine that scene in terms of initiative. Can you see it? If you were watching this scene with a parent, could you explain what's good about Brianna's behavior? Suppose the parent is comparing what she is watching with her own experience as a child in school. She might be quite critical of what she sees in this scene. Here are some ways to explain that scene in terms of developmental appropriateness. Though Briana and the other children are learning, this is preschool, not school. It is appropriate for 4-year-olds. The environment is set up for free choice, and Briana knows how to take advantage of that. She finds lots of things to do—hands-on kinds of activities, sensory experiences, ways to use her imagination. She is able to move around, socialize, and finally choose to go outdoors and hook up with her friend. The teacher is facilitating learning rather than structuring learning. There will be a group time later in the morning, but even that looks different from either kindergarten or the primary grades.

Let's focus on Briana's initiative. Because Briana is 4 years old, she is able to use her fertile imagination quite effectively, and she can solve problems. She is also becoming increasingly more competent in her physical abilities and communication skills. Her attention span has lengthened, and she can spend long periods in concentrated focus. She's active, curious, and energetic. A phrase that describes Briana is *get-up-and-go*. She's got it!

What does she do with all this energy and newly developed ability? She uses it to make decisions about what she wants to do. She is so interested in everything that you could almost describe her as in an "attack mode." It's not a negative kind of attacking but a thrusting kind of energy that propels her toward activities and materials that seem to draw her. Briana needs no motivation from her teachers to get involved. She has her own inner motivation.

Much of what Briana undertakes is spontaneous, but that doesn't mean that she is incapable of planning and executing a plan. For example, she had something definite in mind when she asked the teacher for scissors at the wood-gluing table. The teacher, understanding the value of encouraging initiative, responded in a positive way instead of restricting Briana to what was available on the table for that particular project. Briana also had something definite in mind when she scanned the play yard, found Sarah, and headed over to play with her.

It's important to note that some children are as active as Briana but lack her ability to focus attention and concentrate on any one thing. They don't plan out what they want to do but impulsively rush from one thing to another, perhaps destroying things in their path. These children may not yet have learned to channel their energy. Or perhaps they are overstimulated by too many choices or too much going on around them. Because these children are displaying a different kind of high energy, some adults may think of them as hyperactive. Indeed the word *hyper* is now commonly used for children who move a good deal and have trouble being still. Although there is a condition known as an *attention deficit/hyperactivity disorder* (ADHD) (Barkley, 1997) there is some controversy over diagnosing and treating children as young as 3 or 4.

Julie and ADHD

Julie is a 7-year-old who has just been diagnosed as having an attention deficit/hyperactivity disorder (ADHD). In a way, her mother, Shannon, is glad to get the diagnosis because it confirms her idea that Julie is not "bad." She has been worried about her for a long time. It seems as though Julie was born kicking. She was an irritable baby who cried a lot. She seemed to sleep very little. She was in constant motion and she hasn't slowed down yet. Once she got on her feet, life got even harder, if that was possible. Julie was into everything. She never sat still for a minute. Shannon compared her with a neighbor child, Hannah, and saw that Julie was very different. By age 4, Hannah would sit for periods of time looking at books or drawing with crayons. Julie never did that. When she looked at a book, she flipped through at a rapid rate, threw the book down, grabbed another one, threw it down, and was off to something else in the space of less than a minute. In fact, none of Julie's activities lasted more than a minute. What was wrong?

Shannon decided to send Julie to preschool, but that didn't help much. Although it gave Shannon a few hours of peace each day, the reports from school kept her in a constant state of tension. Every week it was something new. "What can we do about Julie's behavior?" the teachers kept asking. "She's so impulsive that she constantly makes decisions that result in unfortunate consequences. But she doesn't seem to learn from her mistakes. She just keeps jumping into things and making rash decisions." Shannon felt discouraged that they called her in for her ideas and opinions. Why didn't they know how to handle Julie? They were the trained experts!

When the school called a meeting and the teachers and Shannon sat down and did some brainstorming, things improved. They all shared ideas and information about what worked best at home and what worked best at school for Julie. One of the problems was that preschool was so stimulating. There was just so much to do that Julie was overwhelmed with the number of choices. She ended up constantly running around and not doing anything. Also, the room tended to be noisy and sometimes a little chaotic when all the children were inside. Julie reacted to the high energy level of the classroom by losing what little control she had.

At home two things captured her attention: television, sometimes, and video games, almost always.

Things didn't improve by kindergarten, and first grade was a nightmare. When the school finally suggested that testing Julie might be in order, Shannon felt relieved. When she got the results, she felt even more relieved. She is now involved with a team of experts who are creating an Individual Education Plan (IEP) for Julie. Shannon is pleased to see that she is a full member of the team. They listen to what she has to say, so she also listens to what they have to say. One of the decisions Shannon is faced with is whether or not to medicate Julie. That's where she is right now. She has joined a parent support group and is discussing the pending decision. She discovers there are lots of arguments on either side.

DEVELOPMENTAL CONFLICTS

With all the energy and activity that this stage of initiative brings with it, Briana is bound to run into trouble—at least occasionally. How she handles adult guidance and corrections has to do with her stage of development.

Autonomy Versus Shame and Doubt

As a toddler, Briana learned about getting into trouble. In her constant search for autonomy, 2-year-old Briana got into trouble all the time. She learned to look for one of her parents or her family child care provider when she did something she knew was wrong. She responded to their reactions by showing shame for what she had done. If they weren't watching, however, and she didn't get caught, she didn't show signs of remorse.

Erikson defines the major task for toddlerhood as working out the conflict between autonomy and shame or *doubt*. Briana has done that and come out with a sense of what she can do that is not greatly overshadowed by a sense of shame. She has managed a positive resolution for this dilemma.

Initiative Versus Guilt

Briana has now moved into Erikson's next stage, which signifies a new dilemma— that of initiative versus guilt (see Figure 4.1). She's a big girl with a beginning sense of responsibility *and* a budding conscience. She has taken the watchful eye of her parents and teachers inside herself and can now begin to judge her own behavior. She can feel the kind of guilt whose nagging warns her when she's about to violate some behavior standard and gives her a sense of remorse when she carries out the action anyway. Her guilt is useful because it helps keep her in control sometimes. It guides her toward positive and acceptable behavior.

Briana now has an internal government that dictates the ideals and standards of behavior that are requirements of society. Her government is a benevolent one.

Child's Stage	Approximate Age	Task		
Infancy	0 – 1	Basic trust	versus	Basic mistrust
Toddlerhood	1 – 3	Autonomy	versus	Shame and doubt
The preschool years	3 – 6	Initiative	versus	Guilt
School age	6 – 10	Industry	versus	Inferiority

Figure 4.1
Erikson's psychosocial stages of development
Source: Erikson (1963).

Her guilt serves as a little warning sign when her parents or teachers aren't present. She needed reminding to hang up her coat, but she knew not to leave the smock lying on the floor. She stopped herself from hitting the child who was trying to grab the book back.

Briana's guilt is not expected to always control her actions. She still needs adults close by to help her control herself when she can't manage. They do this without making too big a fuss, knowing that Briana has the beginning of control within her.

Briana's guilt is only a small sign—a signaling device. It's not a battering ram hitting her over the head or an acid eating away her insides.

Not all children are as fortunate as Briana. Some are governed by an inner tyranny. They judge themselves so harshly to enforce the standards of those around them that they lose their initiative. They're afraid to act. Their energy is sapped by the overkill methods of their inner government.

This situation happens when adults go overboard and use heavy-handed punishment, accusations, threats, or torments on young children. Children who grow up in this atmosphere develop an exaggerated sense of guilt, and they torture themselves even for trivial offenses. One of the benefits of being a family-centered program where teachers and parents get to know each other and spend time together is that parents who use inappropriate discipline can learn gentler, healthier ways of managing their children's behavior. Although it may be tempting to just tell them—and lay a guilt trip on them—there are more effective ways. Modeling has been mentioned throughout this chapter and in the previous ones. When families see strategies working, they may begin to use them themselves. Also when they begin to understand the stages of development children go through, that can help too. Some parents learn best by reading—and the program should have a parent lending library. A DVD library is a good idea too. Some parents learn best by discussion with other parents, and teachers too. Observation is a good learning tool for parents and teachers alike.

What's perhaps most notable about the stage of initiative is the way children work their imaginations and use fantasy.

IMAGINATION AND FANTASY

What's perhaps most notable about the stage of initiative is the way children work their imaginations and how they use fantasy. By the preschool years, pretend play has become far more complex than the simple imitation of infancy (Berk, 1994; Jones & Cooper, 2006; Jones & Reynolds, 1992; Van Hoorn, Nourot, Scales, & Alward, 2007). The toddler shows the beginnings of the complexity by using objects to stand for other objects (a plastic banana or block for a telephone). By age 4, the imagination soars! What was Briana doing when she was playing house? She was doing just what adults do with dreams and daydreams. She was experiencing hopes and fears by dealing with the past symbolically and rehearsing for the future. She tried on roles and feelings in the same way she tried on dress-up clothes. Fantasy play gives Briana practice in interacting with others while in these roles. She also uses fantasy play to express fears and anger and to discover ways to adjust to painful situations. If parents observe fantasy play, you can discuss together what the child is getting out of it. With the parents' knowledge of what goes on in the rest of the child's life, he or she can give you ideas about what you're seeing that you couldn't get otherwise.

THE VALUE OF PLAY OF ALL SORTS

Play is an arena where children learn new skills and practice old ones, both physical and social. Through play they challenge themselves to new levels of mastery. They gain competence in all areas of development—increasing language, social skills, and physical skills, for example. Briana not only practices such important skills as eye-hand coordination but also at times uses her whole body to improve balance and coordination.

David Elkind, long an advocate for play, says in his book, *The Power of Play*, "One legacy of our Puritan heritage is a lingering ambivalence toward child play." The parent or program that buys "educational" toys can justify play as educational, but there is little research that shows toys marketed as educational really are. Elkind makes the case that it's of more benefit to children to use their imagination in an environment that lends itself to exploration, initiative, and active engagement with objects, materials, and other children. It's important that teachers don't buy the consumer-oriented mindset that marketers are trying so hard to sell. Teachers can give a different message to parents and counteract some of the hard-sell coming from advertising.

Play provides for cognitive development in ways that educational toys don't necessarily address. Cognitive development is tied in with physical and social interactions in the preschool years as children are constructing a view of the world

Play provides for cognitive development, which is tied in with physical and social interactions.

and discovering concepts. So when parents see their children running around, playing outdoors, seemingly doing nothing constructive, a teacher should be there to help the parents look deeper at what's really happening. Teachers can give parents the message that there's nothing passive about play—even if the body is passive for a time, the mind is busy working. Children at play are active explorers of the environment as they create their own experience and grow to understand it. In this way they participate in their own development.

Through play, children work at problem solving, which involves mental, physical, and social skills. While playing, they can try on pretend solutions and experience how those solutions work. If they make mistakes, those mistakes don't hurt them as they would in real life. They can reverse power roles and be the adult for a change, telling other children what to do. They can even tell adults what to do, if the adults are willing to play along.

Play enables children to sort through conflicts and deal with anxieties, fears, and disturbing feelings in an active, powerful way (Frost, Wortham, & Reifel, 2008). Play provides a safety valve for feelings. When they pretend, children can say or do things that they can't do in reality.

Play makes children feel powerful and gives them a sense of control as they create worlds and manipulate them. Watch children playing with blocks, or dolls and action figures, or even in the sandbox. Think about how they create the worlds they play in. What power!

Children also get a sense of power by facing something difficult and conquering it—like finding a place for a puzzle piece that just won't fit anywhere or climbing higher on the jungle gym than they've ever climbed before. Think back to

Teachers can help families appreciate the value of play as a way of learning. One way to do that is to observe with the parents when their children are playing and share some of the benefits children are deriving from the experience.

your own childhood. Think of a time when you were challenged in play. What was your feeling as you overcame obstacles (including perhaps your own fear) and met the challenge?

Helping families understand the value of play is a big challenge for preschool teachers and also for kindergarten teachers who have a play-based curriculum. Play may look very unorganized and frivolous to parents. You need to be able to make a good case for play as learning. Hopefully this chapter will help you do that. See Strategy Box 4.1 for ideas on working with parents around issues of play.

HOW THE ENVIRONMENT CONTRIBUTES TO A SENSE OF INITIATIVE

The environment reflects whether the adults in charge of it regard developing a sense of initiative to be of value. Individual initiative, like independence, is not a universal priority. In some cultures, individual initiative is less important than going along with

Strategy Box 4.1

Helping Families Appreciate Play

- Observe with the parents when their children are playing so that you can see the child through their eyes and give parents input on what you see.
- Help families appreciate the value of play as a way of learning and developing in all the domains of development: mind, body, and feelings.
- Have parents help you understand how to adapt the learning environment so that it is accessible to the special needs of their particular child.

the group spirit. Initiative may only count when it obviously serves the group rather than the individual alone. So as you read about how the environment setup relates to the value of initiative, realize that what you are reading reflects the value behind it. When families have a different set of priorities, instead of arguing your side, try creating a dialogue so you can understand more about where they are coming from. Everyone stands to gain when communication comes in the form of a dialogue.

If initiative is a value, then the environment in which children spend most of their time will be set up to give them a range of options so that they can choose how to spend their time.

Suppose that initiative is a value; then the environment in which children spend most of their time will be set up to give them a range of options so they can choose how to spend that time. We saw such an environment in the Briana scene. Not only will there be choices of developmentally appropriate activities, toys, and materials, but these items will be enticingly arranged to attract attention and draw children to them.

Not all adults see giving children choices as valuable. Some people expect children to adapt to what is and to entertain themselves in the environment of adults, rather than selecting from a number of options that have been provided for them. They disagree with the notion of a child-oriented environment isolated from the real world of adults (Mistry, 1995; Rogoff, 2003). Some adults do not believe in creating learning situations to teach their children; they put their children in adult-oriented environments and expect them to learn by observation, not from playing in an environment specially set up for them. For an example of this different view of what children need and are capable of, see the following "Perspectives on Child Rearing."

Perspectives on Child Rearing

A preschool teacher enjoying a sunny afternoon in San Francisco sat on a bench watching two street musicians playing music from the Andes for a crowd in Ghiradelli Square. She noticed their daughter, who appeared to be about 4 years old, sitting on a bench next to where the parents were playing. The child sat quietly on the bench until her parents took a break. She had no toys and nothing to do. She seemed to be able to content herself with people watching and listening to the music. When her parents took a break, she moved over to be with them. She hung around listening to what they were saying and periodically taking short excursions to look in shop windows around the perimeters of the plaza. She was never gone too long but kept coming back to where her parents were. She never demanded their attention while they were talking. When they went back to playing music, she went back to sitting. She never left or distracted them in any way while they were working. She was obviously well trained.

The little girl was a contrast to two little boys, about 2 and 4 years old, who were also entertaining themselves as their parents stood watching the performance. They had toys with them that they played with. When they got tired of the toys, they started running around the plaza, with one parent trailing after them. To the preschool teacher the boys' behavior was more to be expected than the girl's behavior, not because of gender but because of age. The teacher marveled at the ability of the girl to sit on the bench. She wondered what would happen if this child went off to child care or to a preschool where active play was considered vital to development. Would the philosophy of the preschool upset the situation the parents had created so they could earn their living? Would the girl get bored with sitting (she never looked bored that afternoon)?

Dimensions of Play Environments

Elizabeth Jones and Elizabeth Prescott (1978) at Pacific Oaks College in Pasadena, California, looked at children's play environments in terms of what they call *dimensions*. To create an optimum environment for the kind of play that enhances initiative, Jones and Prescott advocate a balance of these dimensions: soft/hard, open/closed, intrusion/exclusion, high mobility/low mobility, and simple/complex.

Balancing the *soft/hard* dimension means that the environment is both responsive and resistant. Softness in play environments comes from things like rugs, stuffed animals, cozy furniture, grass, sand, play dough, water, soft balls, pads, and laps, to name a few. Hardness comes in the form of vinyl floors, plastic and wooden toys and furniture, and concrete.

The *open/closed* dimension has to do with choices. Low, open shelves displaying toys to choose from are an example of openness. Some closed storage is also appropriate, so that the number of choices are manageable. Closed storage also gives a sense of order and avoids a cluttered feeling. Maintaining a balance between open and closed is important.

The open/closed dimension also has to do with whether there is one right way to use a toy or material (e.g., a puzzle, a form board, graduated stacking rings) or whether the toy or material encourages all kinds of exploration. A doll, finger paint, and play dough are open; so is water play. Children need both open and closed toys, materials, and equipment.

The environment should provide for both optimum *intrusion* and optimum *exclusion*, or *seclusion*. Desirable intrusion comes as the children have access to the greater world beyond their play space—for example, through windows that allow them to see what is happening outside but protect them from dangers and noise. Desirable intrusion also occurs as visitors come into the play environment.

Seclusion should be provided so children can get away by themselves. Think of the hideaways you had as a young child. Given a little freedom, children will find these kinds of places for themselves; however, in a child care center or home, they sometimes need to be provided. Lofts, large cardboard boxes, and tables covered with sheets provide semi-enclosed private spaces in which children can make "nests" to hide from the world.

A balanced play environment provides for both *high-* and *low-mobility* activities. Children need quiet and still activities as well as opportunities to move around freely and engage in vigorous movement.

Although parents don't necessarily need to be given all of this information about the design of the environment, it is helpful for you to have it in case they have questions. The information in the next paragraph, however, is very relevant to parents and should be communicated.

We all know that young children can be satisfied with the simplest things. A baby can be fascinated with something that an adult wouldn't give more than a glance. This fact relates to the *simple/complex* dimension of the child care environment. As children grow older, they need complexity, which they often provide for themselves by combining simple toys with other materials. Watch a child who finds sand, water, and utensils conveniently close to each other. The park designers may never have thought of how that drinking fountain close to the sandbox would be used, but the 4-year-old who finds an empty soda can is almost certain to think of using it to carry water to the sand. Complexity presents increased possibilities for action. Preschool and child care teachers know this, so they put a dripping hose in the sandbox on warm days and give the children scoops, buckets, cups, spoons, and a variety of other implements to use. They know that attention span lengthens when children find or create complexity in the environment. The more complex a material or toy (or combination of materials and toys), the more interesting it is. Blocks are fun. Blocks with small figures and wheel toys are even more fun! Some parents may resist the idea of messy play. You can explain the importance of sensory experiences, but also listen to their ideas about what children do and don't need. And always respect their perspective.

HOW ADULTS CONTRIBUTE TO CHILDREN'S INITIATIVE

Adults contribute to the development of children's sense of initiative in several ways. They are responsible for setting up the environments for children's play. As just stated, the kind of environment they set up determines to some extent whether initiative is a value. Adults are the ones who must guide and control children's behavior in these environments. How they do that also contributes to a sense of initiative. Discipline methods that encourage children to continue to explore, try things out, and solve problems contribute to their growing initiative. Methods that squelch children's interest, inhibit their behavior, and make them afraid to try things because they might make a mistake take away their confidence in themselves and work against bringing out each child's own initiative. In addition, adults encourage initiative in children by modeling it themselves. (Chapter 7 examines this subject at length.) As mentioned earlier, all parents may not want to encourage individual initiative. Sometimes they will agree to disagree and feel okay about the fact that what goes on in the program is different from what they do at home. Other times you may need to have a deeper discussion about differing perspectives on individual initiative.

SPECIAL CONSIDERATIONS FOR CHILDREN WITH DISABILITIES

Some children arrive in a play environment with less initiative and motivation to play than others. It may be that they have not been encouraged to play and explore. Or children who are medically fragile may have parents who concentrate more on keeping them safe and healthy than on encouraging them to play. Or it may be that the child is interested, but has little or no access to the toys, materials, and activities. It's up to the adult to ensure that all children have access, including those with disabilities and other challenges.

Sometimes providing access is as simple as restructuring the environment so that a child in a wheelchair, for example, can move around. Putting toys within reach of a nonambulatory child is another practical strategy. Or positioning a child so he feels secure enough to use his hands and arms to explore and manipulate will enable a child who has a disability to more fully experience his environment. Close attention to what interests each child can guide the teacher when selecting toys and materials to make available. Also being aware of what playthings will build on a child's strengths is important when setting up the environment. Toys and materials that are responsive—that the child can have an effect on—are usually winners. Some toys that are already available can be adapted so they are easier to use. One teacher glued tongue depressors to the pages of a cardboard book to make the pages less difficult to turn for a child with cerebral palsy. One way to figure out how to modify the environment is for teachers to put themselves at the level of the child in question and look around. For example, a child lying on his back may be looking directly into a bright ceiling light.

Families can be helpful in thinking with you about how to organize or adapt the environment for their child's special needs. They often have access to experts who can be helpful too. Don't try to figure it out by yourself, or just with the help of other early educators. Use the families and their resources. Work together to discover the adaptations that are appropriate for each child.

Children who have attention deficit disorders may be distracted in a play space where there is too much going on. The way their brains are wired seems to give them the urge to seek novelty, and everything attracts their attention (Jensen, 1998). The early childhood educator can simplify the environment, but it isn't enough just to create an appropriate play environment and then expect children with certain challenges to automatically start playing with their typically developing peers. Special strategies are necessary to support interactions with other children and promote skill development (Chandler, 1998). One such strategy is to slow down the pace for those who need it and allow plenty of time to react. Some children need the slow pace to help them focus. Others need help to refocus. For example, giving plenty of time for a reaction can be a help to children with Down syndrome, who need the extra time to change the focus of their attention. Asking a question and expecting an immediate response, for example, doesn't work as well as pausing after the question and just waiting quietly for the child to absorb it before expecting a response.

Again, you don't have to discover all this for yourself. Engage the families in helping you understand their children. Share information that you have and listen to what they know. Teamwork is critical here for making the environment work for every child in it.

A child with language delays can benefit when the other children see the teacher responding to communication attempts and building on the skills the child has. Modeling has a strong effect, and other children pick up on what the teacher is doing and do it also.

Children with autism benefit from playing with their peers who are more accomplished players. Their ability to play increases with the support of the teacher in an integrated setting where the environment and the learning plan focus on play. Their imagination increases as well (Wolfberg, 1999).

In some cases you may have more information than the parents if they haven't seen their child around other children. Share what you know. Collaborate with the parents to make your programs a good experience for each and every child.

Vygotsky's sociocultural theory has implications for including children with special needs in programs with their typically developing peers. As mentioned in Chapter 1, Vygotsky used the term *zone of proximal development* to describe how social interactions increase understanding. Certainly in a play environment there are lots of opportunities for children to help one another move forward in their understanding and skill building (Vygotsky, 1967).

THE SHY CHILD

Some children seem to lack get-up-and-go. Even though they have no developmental differences, challenges, or disabilities, they seem to lack initiative. They may be labeled *shy*, or perhaps they are looked at as withdrawn.

Let's look at one of these children:

Dakota has always been the quietest child in the preschool she attends. She hangs out on the fringes of things and seldom talks or even smiles. When someone talks to her, she lowers her eyes and stares at her shoes. She follows the routine of the program but never really joins in with anything that is going on. She's so quiet that sometimes she's almost invisible.

What could be going on with Dakota? The place to start answering this question is with the family. What is their take on their daughter? Is she the same way at home as she is at school? Certainly this conversation should be held without indicating that the teachers think something is wrong with Dakota. An exchange of information is what will be helpful. In this situation what the teachers finally figured out was Dakota fit a particular pattern that they had already discovered in other children.

Here's the pattern. Some children are born extra cautious. This trait may even be in their genes. They don't enjoy putting themselves out in the world, taking risks, trying new things. Sometimes this trait doesn't really hinder them, because it's more a matter of timing than a deficiency. Some children are observers; they learn a good deal by watching for long periods before they try something themselves. When they do try something, they make rapid progress because of their careful observations. They may be thought of as being slow to warm up. Other children jump in with both feet without giving a thought to the consequences. If these more impulsive children are successful in their endeavors, they may be valued for their speed and compared with children like Dakota. (*Bright* and *quick* are sometimes thought to be synonymous with *intelligent*.) Thus, Dakota's slow, cautious way of doing things may be undervalued in some settings. That wasn't the case in either the family or in the school in this situation with Dakota. The teachers decided along with input from the family that though Dakota may look as though she lacks initiative, it's really a matter of timing more than initiative. An unfamiliar environment slows her down even more. Dakota at home with a sibling or a playmate is much more secure and outgoing, She doesn't look so shy and cautious. Shyness and caution are situational with Dakota.

The teachers at Dakota's school have discovered that pushing her doesn't do any good. She's very resistant to joining an activity until she decides on her own to do so. She has the ability to absorb by watching—far more ability than any of her teachers, who at first worried that she must be bored, because they were projecting their own needs onto her. She isn't bored. In fact, they discovered that she was getting much more out of preschool than anyone realized, but she was doing it in her own way. The teachers, with the family's input, decided to be patient with Dakota and to respect her style. They also, when they could, arranged for her to be in smaller groups and play alone with one or two children rather than always urging her to join into large-group activities.

The teachers have discovered that this quiet, cautious child has grown into something of a leader in the class. The other children are drawn to Dakota and are influenced by her. In fact, the day doesn't truly begin until Dakota arrives. The teachers were really surprised when they discovered that Dakota's quiet presence now influences the activities in the classroom. They shared their findings with the parents, and invited them to come observe their daughter's new-found leadership role.

Factors other than those that influence Dakota may be at work on another child who exhibits similar behavior. Take Brandi, for example:

Brandi is shy and cautious for entirely different reasons—she has a history of abuse and attachment issues. As a result, she has a great deal of trouble separating from her foster mother, who delivers her to school. She cries loudly and must be peeled off, so that the foster mother, who has other children to deliver to another school, can leave. Once Brandi quits crying, she goes into mourning. She stands by the art table with one finger in her mouth and her eyes staring vacantly. The teachers have decided that she isn't even really "there" most of the time. She stares into space. She sits in circle time silently. She doesn't seem to have learned a single song (compared with Dakota, who never sings at school but at home can go through every word of every verse, complete with hand movements). Brandi is withdrawn, and it isn't just that she has a slower pace than most children. She has a problem. In fact, this child might well have been born quick, lively, and a willing risk taker, but her life circumstances have beaten her into the child she is now—one who needs more help than her teachers alone can give her. Under ideal circumstances, Brandi's teachers, foster parents, and biological family are working with social workers and therapists to help her family get back together, help her resolve her attachment issues, and heal the raw scars of her abuse. If all goes well and everyone cooperates, Brandi will get her life back together and her spark will come back. She'll be the child she really is rather than the child she has become.

The vital difference between Dakota and Brandi is that Dakota is the child she is and Brandi is not—she's been damaged.

A LOOK AT AGGRESSION

Let's examine the subject of aggression in the preschool-age child—where it comes from and what to do about it.

We'll start with Cory. He's a 4-year-old who attends an all-day preschool in which he is one of a group of 30 children. He gives his teachers a lot of trouble because he seems always to be hurting someone. Someone is constantly having to deal with the aftermath of his aggressive behavior. What's going on with Cory?

Causes of Aggression

It's not easy to say what's going on with Cory. There are many possible reasons for his aggressive behavior—some simple and fairly easy to solve, and some much more complex. It could be simple—Cory has just not learned any other way to behave. In that case, he needs to be taught. Or it could be that Cory was rewarded for this behavior in the past and is continuing to be rewarded for it, so he continues his aggressive behavior. It could also be that Cory's behavior is the result of bottled-up emotions. Maybe something is going on at home, and he's feeling very upset by it. He's letting off steam at school. His behavior might even stem from a physical source—either his own body chemistry or influences of the environment interacting with his physical makeup. Or his aggression can come from an extreme defensiveness. The following sections explore these sources of aggression more closely.

Learned Aggression.   Children can learn aggression from watching others get what they want through aggressive means. They may see this on television or in their own homes or neighborhoods. They can even learn it at preschool from watching classmates. They can, of course, also learn it from firsthand experience.

Laura Zahner

Vigorous physical activity can serve as an outlet for strong feelings.

For example, a child wants a toy. She grabs it from another child, and pushes him when he fights back. She has the toy—she gets her reward. Or, if adult attention is the reward she's looking for, she gets that attention when the adult marches across the room, grabs the toy out of her hand, and holds her arm tight while squatting down to look her in the eye and give her a good, long scolding. She gets even more attention when she is marched over to apologize. Her final rewards come when she is placed in a time-out chair and brought back every time she gets up. She has the adult's full attention—including eye contact, touch, and a long stream of words. She can get the adult to notice her even from clear across the room simply by her behavior. If she still wants more reward, all she has to do is push one of the adult's buttons. Spitting will probably do it. A "bad word" will usually do it, too.

If this child has learned this way of getting attention, the solution is to give her the attention she needs in other ways, and to make her "unlearn" the ingrained behaviors. Behavior modification is the answer. The adult must unlink the behavior and the reward by withdrawing attention rather than pouring it on. This is not easy to do while keeping everyone safe. Sometimes it is a matter of providing physical control while giving the least attention possible. Other times just ignoring the behavior will eventually make it go away. However, if this is a longtime pattern, it will probably get worse before it gets better, until the child learns that the attention she so desperately needs will come, but is linked to a different kind of behavior.

The problem is that most adults who have to deal with this kind of aggression in a child are sorely tempted to turn to punishment; they want to hurt the child either physically or emotionally. What they may not realize is that hurting children doesn't work. You don't make a child less aggressive by hurting her—you make her more aggressive. Way back in 1975, Barclay Martin reviewed 27 studies on the effects of harsh punishment and concluded that children were likely to store up frustration from being punished and vent it later, using the violence that was used on them. The message regarding avoiding using aggression to deal with aggression is still valid today.

Power may be behind the child's need for aggression. Power issues are never solved by being overpowered, which is the message behind punishment.

Aggression as the Result of Bottled-Up Feelings.   Some children react to tension with aggression. Their feelings are bottled up inside them, and even a little incident can "uncork" them. What "pours out" is more than the provoking incident calls for. That's a clue to tension as a cause of aggression. Any little frustration can cause "the top to blow off the bottle." When tension is behind the aggression, it is best to work on the source of the tension. However, that may be a job for a social worker and a therapist. If you're Cory's teacher, for example, you don't have the opportunity to work on his home tensions, and you're not a trained therapist. What you *can* do is reduce frustration for him at school. You can also give him outlets for his angry feelings. Some examples of outlets are as follows:

1. Vigorous physical activity can serve as an outlet—for example, running, jumping, and climbing.

2. Aggressive activities are also beneficial—for example, pounding punching bags, digging in the dirt, hammering nails, and even tearing paper.

3. Soothing sensory activities can help calm the aggressive child—activities like water play, clay work, and finger paint. Cornstarch and water available as a paste to play in is a wonderfully soothing sensory activity.

4. Art and music activities also serve as outlets for emotional expression. Many children paint picture after picture, covering every inch of the easel paper with paint. From the looks on their faces, you can tell that they are finding the activity soothing.

Physical Influences on Aggression.   Teachers *can* work on the problem of physical influences on aggression. For example, Cory's diet may be terrible. Perhaps some parent education is in order. Careful observation can determine whether low blood sugar is influencing his behavior. Is he particularly aggressive when he's hungry? Steps can be taken to remedy that situation, both with a change of diet and with increased high-protein snacks. If physical problems are suspected, a visit to the doctor is in order.

It's easy to see how environment can influence behavior. If Cory is part of a group of 30 children and they spend much time together in one classroom, he may well be overstimulated, which can easily result in a lack of control on his part. Crowding is a clear cause of aggression in animals. I think we, as a society, try to ignore this problem in people because crowding is a part of our daily lives and we just expect children to adjust to it.

Other environmental influences can be heat, lighting, and environmental pollution. Even weather can make a difference. If you've ever been with a group of children on a windy day, you know how it can affect their behavior.

Extreme Defensiveness.   According to Selma Fraiberg (1959) in her classic book, *The Magic Years*, some children imagine danger everywhere and interpret every little action of playmates as threatening to themselves. They are defensive to an extreme. Out of their fear, they attack first, rather than waiting to be attacked and then striking back. They need help to change their perspective and come to see the world as a nonthreatening place. Their worldview may be due to attachment or abuse issues, in which case those are the areas in which they need help. That help may need to come from a trained therapist rather than a layperson, though teachers may carry out whatever program the therapist suggests. All by themselves, the teachers probably can't solve the problem of Cory's aggression if that problem comes from damage inflicted on him.

No matter what the cause behind the aggression, it's important to be working together with the family to discover what to do about it. Teamwork makes a big difference. Imagine how hard it is on a child to find one approach to aggression being taken at home and an entirely different one being used at school. Sometimes just teaming isn't enough—outside expertise is needed. It's also important to recognize when a situation is beyond the ability of the teacher and parents to solve by themselves. In that case they can work together to find the outside resources needed for assistance and support.

TEACHING YOUNG CHILDREN PROBLEM-SOLVING SKILLS

The roots of violence start in the first years of life as children who don't know how to solve problems turn to aggression. You can spot children in preschool who are at risk for becoming violent teens. They are the 4-year-olds who solve all their social problems physically. If they want a truck, they grab it and then sock the little kid who had it first. If accidentally bumped, they shove the offender back harder.

Of course, all children who grab, hit, and shove won't become violent teens. After all, this is normal behavior for young children. Some will outgrow it, but others won't. Instead they will develop deeply ingrained ways of approaching problems, which can lead directly from preschool aggression to teenage violence.

Four weaknesses in problem-solving skills are exhibited by teenage offenders:

1. They make assumptions about a situation and neglect to get further information.
2. They seldom give anyone the benefit of the doubt, but see everyone as a potential adversary. They think people are "out to get them."
3. They have a narrow vision of alternative solutions and rely mainly on violence.
4. They fail to consider consequences when they lash out.

Adults can help young children develop problem-solving skills before the weakness becomes ingrained. They can help children clarify situations, consider consequences, and explore alternatives to aggression.

To help, the adult must be on the spot when difficulties arise between children. It's important to intervene before the action gets physical. For example, as the 4-year-old grabs for the truck in the other child's hands, the adult can stop him and say, "You really want the truck. I wonder what you can do besides grabbing it." If the child's response shows he can't think of anything but grabbing, the adult can list some other ideas.

This is not a natural approach for most adults, especially when the tendency is to meet child aggression with adult aggression. That's where training comes in. Teachers can learn to take this approach and model it for parents. Aggression can also be the subject of a parent meeting. Certainly most families are interested in both how to keep their children safe from the aggression of other children and/or manage the aggression they find in their own children. Skillful intervention by adults is a skill well worth learning.

It's important that adults not be critical or judgmental when they intervene. This approach is about talking it through, not giving lectures on being nice. Tone of voice and attitude are all-important as the adult guides the talking. The goal is for the children to begin to see the other's perspective and consider alternative solutions.

Four qualities are important when helping children talk to each other in a conflict situation:

1. Firmness should come through—"I won't let you grab or hurt."

2. Empathy also should come through—"I know how much you want that truck."

3. A problem-solving attitude rather than a power play must be part of the exchange—"He might give it to you if you ask him."

4. Persistence is critical—"Well, asking didn't work. I wonder what else you could try."

The objective is not to solve the problem in a particular way for the child but to help him discover his own alternatives to violence.

Adults often short-circuit this kind of learning by putting children in time-out. Or they solve the problem themselves: "He had it first; give it back to him." "If you're going to fight over that toy, you can't play with it." Those adult actions don't teach the problem-solving skills so necessary for the future.

Skillful intervention makes a difference. We can teach children nonviolence in the preschool years. Of course, teaching alone won't eliminate violence. Other factors come into play. If the child sees violence at home, on the streets, or on TV, the modeling effect comes in. Or if the child is a victim of abuse, the likelihood of his becoming a perpetrator is increased.

Safe Start is a nationwide program designed to deal with the roots of violence through prevention and intervention. Supported by the Ounce of Prevention Fund, a public/private partnership based in Chicago and built on decades of research on child development, this program is a most promising approach to reducing violence through focusing on children ages birth to 5. Brain research points to the impact of early emotional experiences on brain development, altering both structure and brain chemistry. Early experiences set up patterns of response that can last a lifetime. The program stresses prevention approaches that include helping adults understand how to teach children self-control. Adults in the program learn how to set limits, discourage unacceptable behavior, model appropriate behavior, and reduce the risk factors for violence. Early intervention includes quality early childhood education programs for children, including specialized teacher training in violence prevention. Safe Start approaches are making a lasting difference.[1]

---

[1]Safe Start puts out a six-page brochure called "Safe Start: How Early Experiences Can Help Reduce Violence," an Ounce of Prevention Fund paper by Theresa Hawley (2000). It can be obtained from the Ounce of Prevention Fund, 122 S. Michigan Ave., Suite 2050, Chicago, IL 60603–6198; (312) 922–3863.

There is no single simple solution to violence. If we are to create a peaceful world to live in, we must take a many-pronged approach. A good prong to start with is to help children learn effective nonviolent problem solving in the early years.

EMPOWERING THE PRESCHOOL-AGE CHILD

Adults often believe that to manage children's behavior and set them on the right path, they must dominate them by overpowering them. Trying to *over*power children often leads straight to power struggles, which are the antithesis of *empowering* children. Children miss out whether they win or lose the power struggle. If they win, they discover that they can dominate an adult, which is frightening. Young children know that they need adults, and they want someone to look up to, to protect and support them. It shakes their confidence in the adult to learn that they are stronger than the larger, more experienced adult. If children lose the power struggle, it takes them down a notch or two rather than convincing them of their own power. Power struggles are to be avoided rather than encouraged if you are working on empowerment.

To explore empowerment further, think of a time you felt powerful as a child. Avoid focusing on those times when you were overpowering someone; concentrate instead on personal power that gave you the feeling of being able to be yourself and of having some effect on the world or the people in it. Focus on this feeling. Isn't this a feeling you would like children to have?

Empowered children feel as if they can be themselves and have an effect on the world.

When I ask students to give examples of times they felt powerful as a child, they come up with a variety of situations in which they demonstrated effectiveness. Sometimes the situation has to do with carrying out some responsibility; some remember a time when they were particularly competent at something; others remember a moment of strength or courage—particularly in relationship to being challenged and conquering their fear. Some felt powerful because of their affiliations—the support people in their lives. Some people got a sense of their own power simply from being able to make choices—even when the consequences weren't what they expected.

One way that children in preschool gain a feeling of power is by "dressing up" and trying on powerful roles. They do this by itself or in conjunction with creating their own world and then playing. That puts them in the role of creator—a very powerful position indeed.

Pearson Education Corporate Digital Archive

Even something as simple as physically changing perspective makes children feel powerful. One young woman remembered spending time as a child squatting on the top of the refrigerator, looking down from her vantage point at the world and the people beneath her. Another had a secret hideout on the garage roof, under the shelter of a tall spreading tree.

One less than desirable way that children gain power is by misbehaving and making adults angry. Only when you watch a scene of a little child sending an adult into a frenzy do you realize what a feeling of power the child must get from this reaction. It's a little like being the person who pushes the button that sends a rocket into space. Wow! It's also a bit frightening to feel so powerful.

Sometimes a child in a preschool situation will cause a good deal of trouble. This child manages to affect everyone around him. It gets so that everyone breathes a sigh of relief on the days he is absent

Children gain feelings of power by trying on powerful roles.

because things are so different. Children who behave like this are often so needy for power that they get it in the only way they know how—by making a big impact on the environment, including the people in it.

If you recognize power as a legitimate need, it seems reasonable to find ways to empower children so that they won't need to manipulate or disrupt to feel a sense of their own power. The following are some ways that adults can empower children:

* *Teach children effective language and how to use it.* Even very young children can learn to hold up a hand and firmly say "Stop!" to someone threatening them. They won't need to hit or shove once they learn to use the power of words. They can learn to express feelings. They can learn to argue their point. They can become effective language users. (More information on this subject is given in Chapter 8.) Remember, though, that some cultures have a different view of teaching children to express their feelings. The goal is group peace and harmony over individual expression of feelings. It is important to recognize this difference when working with children who come from these cultures.
* *Give children the support they need while they are coming to feel their personal power.* Don't let them continually be victimized until their personal power becomes so trampled that it threatens to disappear from sight altogether. Use your personal power *for* them so they can come to use their own eventually. Don't rescue them. Instead,

When children learn how to use language effectively they have less need to hit or shove. They can argue their point and express their feelings with out resorting to physical action.

teach them ways to protect themselves—with your support at first; later they can do it without your support.

• *Teach them problem-solving skills* (see Chapter 8).

• *Help children tune in on their uniqueness and appreciate their differences.* Help each child become more fully who he or she really is rather than trying to cast him or her into some preset mold. Do remember, however, that not all cultures see uniqueness and individuality as a value. Some emphasize downplaying any characteristics that make one stand apart from the group.

The idea of empowering children in general, and these suggestions in particular, may be very uncomfortable for some families. That's why you have to use your best communication skills to share these ideas. But don't just talk, also listen. Communication is a two-way street. If you open up to new ideas from the families you work with, you'll expand your view and know more about what to do with each particular child in each particular family. Strategy Box 4.2 gives further ideas about how to work with families around the behaviors of their children in the stage of initiative.

We can't leave the preschool-age child without a discussion of early learning. The scene with Briana showed a developmentally appropriate preschool setting with activities and approaches that encouraged initiative. Unfortunately, everyone doesn't understand the value of such a program. Many well-meaning adults take the position that academics rather than play should be the focus of the preschool curriculum. They base their view on the facts that the early years are important ones and that most young children are equipped with a good memory and a willingness to please. A response to this view is: Just because children *can* do something doesn't mean that they *ought* to.[2]

When children are pushed to engage in rote learning or to perform for adults, their initiative can be squashed. Their need to please the powerful others in their lives conflicts with their own inner motivation. The need to please often wins out, and children take to heart the message that adult-directed learning is more valuable than child-directed activity.

[2]I've heard Lilian Katz, early childhood education professor at the University of Illinois, make this statement a number of times.

Strategy Box 4.2

Sharing Approaches When Working with Children in the Initiative Stage

- Don't just teach parents, learn from them. They know more about their child than you do. They see the child in different contexts; you mainly see the child in the context of the early care and education program setting.
- Find out parents' views of the theme of this chapter: encouraging children to take initiative. The subject may be something they never thought of before. Or it may be quite a familiar subject. On the other hand, it may not fit their cultural background and will need to be discussed so that you understand where they are coming from.
- Be sure that families know that you are a mandated reporter for abuse. Define the difference between abuse and punishment. Also, help them see the disadvantages of punishment both physical and psychological.
- Demonstrate the many alternatives to punishment explained in this chapter.
- Recognize when you and the parents need outside help for working with their child.

LOOKING BACK AND LOOKING FORWARD

This chapter focused on the preschool-age child, who, according to Erik Erikson, has the task of developing a sense of initiative and grappling with feelings of guilt when faced with social restrictions. We examined how adults provide for initiative in children by setting up an appropriate environment and by their own actions. We also looked at shy and aggressive children and explored the roots of these behaviors, as well as ways to respond to them. A major part of this chapter concerned how to work with parents in a partnership around the behaviors that come with the stage of initiative. The chapter ended with an examination of personal power and how to encourage it in children.

The next chapter continues with the subject of personal power and looks at it from the view of school-age children and working with their families.

FOR DISCUSSION

1. The chapter gives the perspective of a culture that values independence, initiative, and individuality. What might be the perspective of a culture that instead puts a priority on interdependence, obedience, and putting the group before one's own needs, urges, wishes, and desires?

2. Consider Briana. Remember how she pretends to spank a boy. If you were the teacher, how would you know that it was just "pretend"? Would you stop that

behavior? How would you describe a child who had a high level of initiative but was different from Briana?

3. How do you react to the idea of an "internal government"? Do you believe it is better for children to always have someone in authority watching them and taking charge of their behavior?

4. Analyze the environment you're in right now in terms of the five dimensions named by Elizabeth Jones and Elizabeth Prescott. Is it an appropriate environment for 3- to 6-year-old children to play in? Why or why not?

5. What is your opinion of the expectations that the street musicians ("Perspectives on Child Rearing," pp. 87–88) have of their daughter? Are the parents' expectations hampering her development? How much play time do children need? Does it harm them to put the good of the parents over their own urges to play and run around all the time? Remember, these are cultural questions. Different perspectives give different answers. If you talk with someone who disagrees with you, try to create a dialogue instead of a debate or argument.

6. How easy would it be for you to talk to parents about the subjects dealt with in this chapter? To what do you attribute you level of comfort or discomfort?

WEB SITES

ADHD Information Library
http://www.newideas.net
The ADD ADHD Information Library explains what ADD/ADHD is, treatment options, resources for parents, and classroom interventions. Many additional links are found here.

Afraid to Ask
http://www.afraidtoask.com/ADHD/index.html
This site contains information related to signs and symptoms of ADHD, treatment, and common questions, with additional resources listed.

Children's Defense Fund (CDF)
http://www.childrensdefense.org
The mission of the Children's Defense Fund is to ensure every child a healthy start, a head start, a fair start, a safe start, and a moral start in life.

Dr. Green
http://www.drgreene.com/21_1021.html
This site has information on attention deficit/ hyperactivity disorder (ADHD).

Illinois Early Learning Project
http://www.illinoisearlylearning.org/tipsheets/ importanceofplay.htm

This is a link to a tip sheet on why young children need to play.

National Association for the Education of Young Children (NAEYC)
http://www.naeyc.org
The National Association for the Education of Young Children has a number of resources available for parents and professionals including books and journals, one of which is called *Young Children*.

National Association for Family Child Care (NAFCC)
http://www.nafcc.org
The National Association for Family Child Care is devoted to promoting quality and professionalism in family child care homes.

National Network for Child Care (NNCC)
http://www.nncc.org/
Cooperative Extensions System's National Network for Child Care has resources on infant/toddler care, nutrition, quality child care, child abuse, and child development for parents and professionals.

Perpetual Preschool
http://www.perpetualpreschool.com

Ideas for working with young children are provided for early childhood educators, as well as ideas and links for fantasy play.

Public Broadcasting Service/Whole Child Program (PBS)

http://www.pbs.org/wholechild/providers/play.html
PBS offers tips for child care providers about supporting creativity through play.

White Hutchinson Leisure & Learning Group

http://www.whitehutchinson.com/children/articles/benefits.shtml
Benefits for children of play in nature in play gardens or naturalized playgrounds are described here.

FURTHER READING

Bergen, D. (Ed.). (1998). *Play as a medium for learning and development.* Portsmouth, NH: Heinemann.

Bronson, M. B. (2000, March). Research in review: Recognizing and supporting the development of self-regulation in young children. *Young Children* 55(2), 32–36.

Duckworth, E. (2001). *"Tell me more": Listening to learners.* New York: Teachers College Press.

Edmiaston, R., Dolezal, V., Doolittle, S., Erickson, C., & Merritt, S. (2000). Developing individualized education programs for children in inclusive settings: A developmental framework. *Young Children* 55(4), 36–41.

Eggers-Pierola, C. (2005). Connections & Commitments. Reflecting Latino values in early childhood programs. Portsmouth, NH: Heinemann.

Elkind, D. (2007). *The power of play.* Cambridge, MA: Da Capo Press.

Ferguson, C. J. & Dettore, E. (2007). *To play or not to play: Is it really a question?* Olney, MD: Association for Childhood Education International.

Frost, J., Wortham, S., & Reifel, S. (2008). *Play and Child Development* (3rd ed.) Upper Saddle River, NJ: Merrill/Prentice Hall.

Holland, P. (2003). *We don't play with guns here: War, weapon, and superhero play in the early years.* Philadelphia: Open University Press.

Hyson, M. (2004). *The emotional development of young children* (2nd ed.). New York: Teachers College Press.

Jones, E. & Cooper, R. (2006). *Playing to get smart.* New York: Teachers College Press.

Kern, P., & Wakeford, L. (2007, September). Supporting outdoor play for young children: The zone model of playground supervision. *Young Children* 62(5), 20–25.

Kostelnik, M., Onaga, E., Rohde, B., & Whiren, A. (2002). *Children with special needs: Lessons for early childhood professionals.* New York: Teachers College Press.

Noonan, M. J., & McCormick, L. (2006). *Young children with disabilities in natural environments.* Baltimore: Brookes.

Pellegrini, A. D. & Smith, P. K. (Eds). (2005). *The nature of play.* New York: Guilford.

Sandall, S. R. (2003, May). Play modifications for children with disabilities. *Young Children* 58(3), 54–55.

Stinger, D. G., Golinkoff, R. M., & Hirsh-Pasek, K. (Eds.) (2006). *Play = Learning: How play motivates and enhances children's cognitive and social-emotional growth.* New York: Oxford University Press.

Van Hoorn, J., Nourot, P., Scales, B., & Alward, K. (2007). *Play at the center of the curriculum* (4th ed.). Upper Saddle River, NJ: Merrill/Prentice Hall.

Wolfson-Steinberg, L. (2000, May). "Teacher! He hit me!" "She pushed me!" Where does it start? How can it stop? *Young Children* 55(3), 38–42.

CHAPTER 5

Working with Families of School-Age Children

In *this chapter you'll discover* . . .

- How family-centered kindergartens can help ease the transition into "real school"
- Where in Erikson's stages the kindergarten and primary child fit
- What's happening to recess in many schools
- How parent-teacher partnerships work in schools and after-school programs
- How children learn morals and values
- The power of adult attention and the use of affirmations
- A close look at praise
- Resilience in children
- Ways of working with parents to teach children prosocial behaviors

It's the first day of kindergarten for Daniel. He's been to preschool and now he is in "real school." He's 5 years old and he's a little scared. His mother senses his fear—an unsettled feeling that wasn't eased by the orientation the week before. She too is having some qualms. This is nothing like the small, informal setting of the preschool and its cozy play yard with grass, dirt, and a tricycle path circling a little play house. This is school and it's big and hard—in more senses than one. Out beyond the kindergarten room is a playground with crowds of screaming children running around. Mother and son reach the door. A bell rings and the screaming crowd heads toward the building. The mother says good-bye and opens the door. She leans over for a kiss, but Daniel, looking embarrassed, turns away, walks inside, and the door shuts behind him. That closed door makes Daniel's mother want to weep. Her son is growing up. He doesn't need her like he used to. She feels shut out of his life. She turns and walks away.

That's one scenario—here's another. Emily and her younger sister, Samantha, have never been apart from each other since Samantha was born. Both their parents work so the two of them have been together in child care their whole lives. Today their mother drops Samantha off at the family care home. She and Emily go in to get Samantha settled and then it's time for them to leave. It's Emily's first day at kindergarten. Emily and Samantha were both excited last night, but now that the reality is upon them, it's a different story. Samantha protests loudly and holds on to her mother, trying to keep her from going out the door. She hasn't done that for years! Emily looks worried but walks out bravely. In the car, she looks upset and puts her thumb in her mouth. She hasn't sucked her thumb since she was 8 weeks old! Both girls seem to recognize this is a big transition in their lives—not just a one-time event but the beginning of a separation that will be ongoing. School lasts a very long time. Although neither of them fully comprehends that they'll be grown up before they are finished with school and that they will never be in the same classroom together again, they do both sense that beginning today things will not be the same. Imagine their great relief when in the afternoon the child care provider goes to the school to pick up Emily along with the other school-age children in her home. The reunion of the two sisters is something to behold!

Starting school is a major transition in the lives of children and their families, an event full of challenges even when the teachers do a great deal to ease everyone into the new setting and situation. For Emily, the transition was a little easier because she didn't have to change child care arrangements. Family child care programs usually

Starting school is a major transition in the lives of children and of their families

Anthony Magnacca/Merrill

have mixed age groups and provide what is sometimes called "surround care" or before- and after-school care. Children who are leaving home for the first time, as well as those 4- and 5-year-olds in early care and education programs who have "graduated" into kindergarten, face a whole new program both in kindergarten and in surround care or after-school care. Those children have a tremendous transition to deal with.

Think about the kinds of ways that teachers and school-age care staff can help parents and their children feel more comfortable. In Daniel's case, the kindergarten teacher had an orientation the week before for new children and their families. They saw the classroom, tried out the desks, learned where things were and how the schedule worked. The stories of both Daniel and Emily are true; unfortunately, neither child entered a family-centered school. Let's imagine now that the kindergarten, at least, was family-centered. In a family-centered school, how might the children and their families have been more prepared for this big step forward?

A FAMILY-CENTERED APPROACH TO KINDERGARTEN

In a family-centered program the teacher sees the importance of creating a relationship with each family, so instead of one big orientation, he or she meets with each family individually or in small groups over a period of time. Some families might even have a home visit before school starts.

In a family-centered program, the relationship starts even earlier than the first meeting before the start of the new school year. Teachers often send out invitations to families, encouraging them to visit the program in action before the end of the last school year. Some families accept the invitation. Some also get to spend time in the school-age child care center at the school.

At first meetings, there are always forms to fill out. But in a family-centered program, completing school forms is not the main purpose of the meeting. Teachers often send out forms ahead, and many families bring the form to the meeting already filled out. The purpose of the first meeting is for teachers and families to make connections to each other. On page 108 is a sample of the kind of form that helps get connections started (see Figure 5.1).

In families where either the child or the parents are worried about separation, the subject is discussed. Parents' feelings about separation are acknowledged, and the teacher, the parents, and the child all brainstorm together about how to ease the separation. Teachers know what a big step it is to send children to school for the first time—even for those parents who have had previous experience with early care and education programs.

Family-centered programs try to stagger the entry so all children don't start at the same time. That's not always possible, but when it is, it helps children ease in. Together with the teacher the family decides if a family member should come in and stay with the child until he is comfortable, or if it is best that they stay out of the classroom until the child gets used to being there on his own.

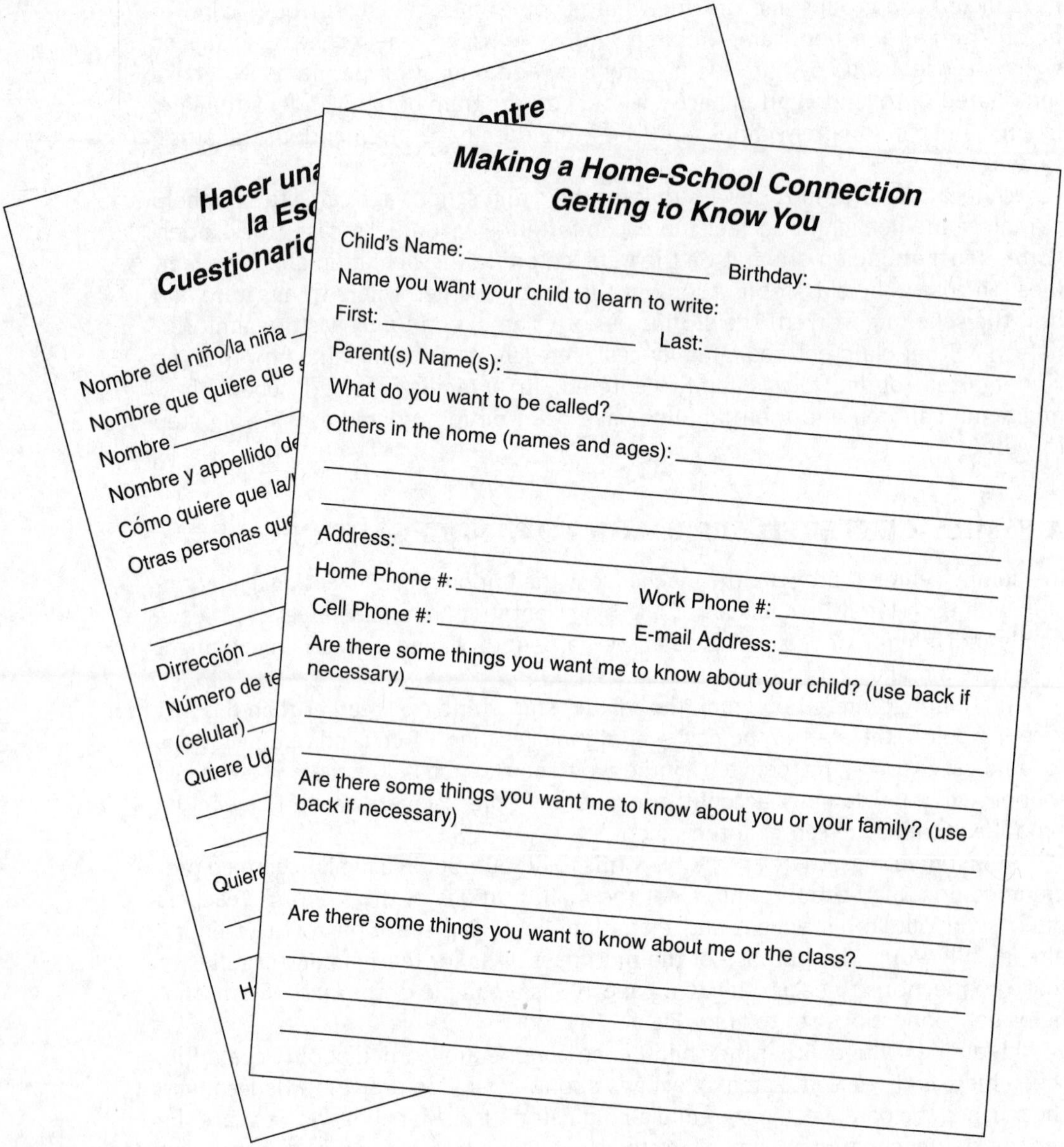
Hacer una ... entre la Esc... Cuestionari...
Nombre del niño/la niña
Nombre que quiere que s...
Nombre
Nombre y appellido de...
Cómo quiere que la/...
Otras personas que...
Dirrección
Número de te...
(celular)
Quiere Ud...
Quiere...
H...

Making a Home-School Connection
Getting to Know You

Child's Name: ______ Birthday: ______
Name you want your child to learn to write:
First: ______ Last: ______
Parent(s) Name(s): ______
What do you want to be called? ______
Others in the home (names and ages): ______
______
______
Address: ______
Home Phone #: ______ Work Phone #: ______
Cell Phone #: ______ E-mail Address: ______
Are there some things you want me to know about your child? (use back if necessary) ______
______
______
Are there some things you want me to know about you or your family? (use back if necessary) ______
______
______
Are there some things you want to know about me or the class? ______
______
______
______

Figure 5.1

ERIKSON'S STAGES OF DEVELOPMENT

Starting "real school" comes at a time when children's development is in transition—they are growing out of one stage of development and into another. The change of stages doesn't come at the same age for every child, and this definitely isn't the first transition phase of their lives. Children start-ing kindergarten have already moved through Erikson's first stage, where trust is the major focus. That transition happens during the first year, more or less. Children ready to start kindergarten still have trust issues, but how much those issues domi-nate their lives depends on how they resolved what Erikson saw as the psychoso-cial conflict all children go through. These children have also moved through Erikson's second stage—that of autonomy, as they have worked on resolving the issues involved with developing an identity that gives them the ability to see themselves as separate people with wants and likes, and the power to say no! Erikson's third stage, the stage of initiative, occurs during what some call the "play years." It usually starts around the age of 3 and ends around 6. That means most children are still in the stage of initiative when they enter kindergarten. Chil-dren in the "play years" may find school a shocking experience as they discover that

Patrick White/Merrill

Somewhere between the ages of 6 or 8 children can begin to do what Piaget called operations *in their heads. Think of operations as mental actions on the environment.*

play doesn't have the prominence in "real school" that it had in their preschool or child care program, though the after-school program, if they are enrolled in it, may ease the shock a bit if it provides more play time. Children are in transition in kindergarten, leav-ing the stage of initiative and headed straight for the stage of industry, which comes in around the age of 6 or 7. By third grade most children have both feet firmly planted in the stage of industry. See Figure 5.2 for Erikson's stages of psychosocial development.

The stage of industry brings with it the urge to master many skills and become competent. Children who have reached this stage want to know how things work. School can be an important factor in this stage as the world of learning opens up beyond what it was in the earlier years. Peers become even more important also. Families and teachers appreciate children's urge for industry and mastery and find their role in enhancing these urges rewarding.

At the same time that children are getting ready to leave kindergarten, they are moving to a more advanced stage of intellectual skills, according to Piaget (1952) At age 2 children move beyond the sensorimotor stage, where thought is connected to the body and senses. After age 2 they are into the stage of preoperational thought, where they can use symbols and words and have some reasoning skills, but they are still deceived by their senses and go by perceptions instead of reason. When children enter school they are moving toward the concrete operational stage but aren't there yet. They still use some magical thinking and lack organization in their thinking processes.

Child's Stage	Approximate Age	Task		
Infancy	0 – 1	Basic trust	versus	Basic mistrust
Toddlerhood	1 – 3	Autonomy	versus	Shame and doubt
The preschool years	3 – 6	Initiative	versus	Guilt
School age	6 – 10	Industry	versus	Inferiority

Figure 5.2
Erikson's psychosocial stages of development
Source: Erikson (1963).

Somewhere between the ages of 6 and 8 children can begin to do operations in their heads. Think of operations as mental actions on the environment. Before this stage, children have to do everything physically, but now they are able to use their heads. The most successful schools are the ones that recognize that children don't all move forward at the same rate in either psychosocial development or cognitive development. Sensitive teachers meet each child where he or she is and move that child forward. It's not easy to respond to individual differences today with No Child Left Behind (NCLB) in place—the federal program that has the goal of getting every child up to grade level. Since grade level is an average, that's like saying all children should be of average height rather than recognizing some will be shorter and some taller, which is what makes average height, average. Expecting every child to be at grade level is a little like Garrison Keeler saying that where he comes from all the children are above average.

For most children, school comes at just the right time for their psychosocial and cognitive stages. For others the school and the child may not fit each other. Unfortunately most schools expect the child to be ready for them. Another way of looking at children' education, however, is that schools should be ready for each child who comes, even if he or she isn't yet as developed as some of the other children. In schools where developmentally appropriate practice is the foundation for the educational approach, it's more likely that the program is set up to take differences into consideration. The more teachers know about development, the better job they can do. Also, having knowledge about ages and stages lets the teacher add to families' knowledge.

Children enrolled in surround-care programs or after school programs may find relief from the stress of trying to keep up with the others. That doesn't mean that school-age care programs don't have to deal with homework. In all settings, sensitive staff who understand developmental issues and children's needs, individually and as a group, can do much to support a child's academic progress in understanding ways. They also can partner with parents in ways that help the child and the family, as well as the program.

A collaborative relationship is the kind that family-centered programs aim for—a relationship in which families and teachers are partners. In a partnership both sides can pool their specialized information and skills in order to see the whole picture. For example, families know their own child best, but they may not have a deep grasp of child development. The teacher has experience with more children than the family and has training and education in working with children. So as the family members share what they know about their own child, the teacher can share knowledge of child development and help the parents see how their child is moving though the stages. Parents can also see that these stages apply beyond their own child and are pertinent to all children.

DIFFERENCES FAMILIES NOTICE BETWEEN SCHOOL AND PRESCHOOL

There are many educational theories, but from a family's point of view two approaches in particular may seem at the forefront because they often differ greatly between preschool and elementary school. The two educational philosophies involve the constructivist philosophy to learning and the role of recess, or play time.

Constructivist Approach

Many preschools take a constructivist approach, which takes developmental stages into consideration and helps children at each stage "construct" knowledge (Chaille 2008). The learner is active and the teacher is more of a facilitator who sets up a rich environment and then helps each child take full advantage of it. It's the opposite from pouring knowledge into the child. "Teaching is not telling" is a motto of the constructivists. Many preschool teachers are constructivists whether they use that term or not.

School is less likely to be taught by constructivists, for a lot of reasons, one of which is the federal legislation called No Child Left Behind (NCLB), mentioned previously. The effect of this legislation is governmental pressure to teach academics and to use sanctions when children don't perform up to par on the tests designed to measure academic abilities. "Back to the Basics" used to be the term used for this movement toward academics and away from what was sometimes called the "discovery learning" that constructivists promoted. With children's test scores threatening, teachers may be forced to use more skill drill and memorization than they would otherwise. Some teachers are complaining that what children learn for the tests goes into their short-term memory instead of long-term memory and is soon forgotten. But many educators don't see that they have a choice.

Role of Recess

Something else that preschool families can't fail to notice when their children enter elementary school is recess, or the lack thereof. In most preschools and child care programs, outdoor play involves a lot more than a 10-minute break to go outside and run around. The time spent outside is not just a time to exercise because children need a break from learning. Rather, the outdoor program takes place as an extension of the educational environment.

Dan Floss/Merrill

Parents used to preschool may be surprised when the school recess is a break from learning and so different from the outdoor-learning experiences in preschool. Some schools don't even have recess any more.

Recess in public schools, however, has become an endangered species. Back in the 1980s children got three recesses a day to play outdoors, plus an hour for lunch. The trend now is to cut back on recess or eliminate it all together. According to Anne Marie Chaker (2006) in "Rethinking Recess," because of the pressure for academic accountability and the standardized tests to measure it as a result of No Child Left Behind (NCLB), schools are cutting back on playtime; however, there is no research to indicate that children do better academically without recess than they do with periodic recesses throughout the day. On the contrary, according to the American Academy of Pediatrics (2006), "Play is integral to the academic environment . . . It has been shown to help children adjust to the school setting and even to enhance children's learning readiness, learning behaviors, and problem-solving skills."

Some families are doing something to bring back recess. An article in *Mothering* (Gross-Loh 2007) says that only three states require elementary schools to hold recess, according to a study by the Centers for Disease Control and Prevention. This article includes a section on how to be a recess advocate and suggests advocates join forces with other parents and interested teachers to keep recess alive where it exists and to bring it back where it has disappeared. Start locally, says the article, and if you don't get results, go higher to the media or to state-level groups such as the PTA.

Though public school teachers are under many constraints, joining with families to create family-centered programs gives them some advantages the other programs don't have. For one things they can better meet the educational and socialization needs of the children if they know what the parents' expectations are. The parents whose children have been in early care and education programs before they reach public school may be used to being included in planning; they may know how to take a supportive role and would be happy to continue the experiences they have had in previous programs. They may be more vocal about their perspectives on learning than parents who have no earlier experience with care and education programs. Teachers in family-centered programs may find families have widely diverse expectations. The goal should be to respect all families' perspectives and help them respect each other's. That may be difficult but it's worthwhile.

HOW DO YOU FIND OUT WHAT FAMILIES WANT FOR THEIR CHILDREN?

The key to understanding each family is becoming a good communicator and implementing a number of approaches that encourage communication whether you are a kindergarten teacher, primary teacher or school-age care staff member.

Finding time to communicate is usually a problem. Teachers and parents have to look for opportunities to have both casual conversations before and after school and planned ones as well. Phone calls and e-mails are one way to keep in touch regularly. Scheduled opportunities such as meetings and conferences are also standard practice. Be sure that meetings are scheduled at times that accommodate all families. Scheduling conferences only in the afternoon eliminates anyone who can't take time off work to attend. Be sure to have interpreters if you don't speak the home language of the families and they don't speak yours.

Written communication is also important. Of course, make sure any written communication is translated into the languages represented in your classroom. On page 114 is a sample of a letter from a first-grade teacher to parents (see Figure 5.3). Although this sample letter is a one-way communication designed to inform, it's also an invitation for the parents to communicate with the teacher as well. This teacher is showing that she is open to listening, and she even gives her home phone number! This kind of letter or announcement is a useful communication from school to home. Some programs also have regular two-way written communication— for example, a journal that goes home and comes back regularly, or a journal that stays in the classroom and whoever wants to write in it can— parents, teachers, children. Interactive bulletin boards are another means of two-way written communication.

The key to understanding each family is becoming a good communicator and implementing a number of approaches that encourage communication. Finding time to communicate is usually a problem. Teachers have to look for opportunities to have both casual conversations as well as planned meetings.

Anne Vega/Merrill

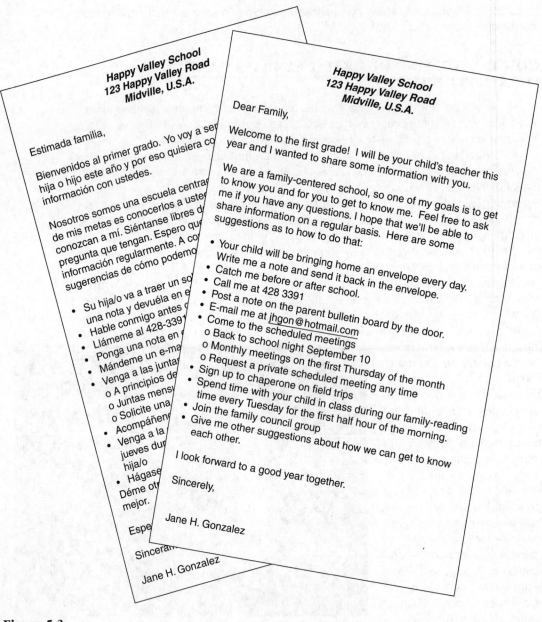

Happy Valley School
123 Happy Valley Road
Midville, U.S.A.

Dear Family,

Welcome to the first grade! I will be your child's teacher this year and I wanted to share some information with you.

We are a family-centered school, so one of my goals is to get to know you and for you to get to know me. Feel free to ask me if you have any questions. I hope that we'll be able to share information on a regular basis. Here are some suggestions as to how to do that:

- Your child will be bringing home an envelope every day. Write me a note and send it back in the envelope.
- Catch me before or after school.
- Call me at 428 3391
- Post a note on the parent bulletin board by the door.
- E-mail me at jhgon@hotmail.com
- Come to the scheduled meetings
  - o Back to school night September 10
  - o Monthly meetings on the first Thursday of the month
  - o Request a private scheduled meeting any time
- Sign up to chaperone on field trips
- Spend time with your child in class during our family-reading time every Tuesday for the first half hour of the morning.
- Join the family council group
- Give me other suggestions about how we can get to know each other.

I look forward to a good year together.

Sincerely,

Jane H. Gonzalez

Happy Valley School
123 Happy Valley Road
Midville, U.S.A.

Estimada familia,

Bienvenidos al primer grado. Yo voy a ser hija o hijo este año y por eso quisiera co información con ustedes.

Nosotros somos una escuela centra de mis metas es conocerlos a uste conozcan a mí. Siéntanse libres d pregunta que tengan. Espero que información regularmente. A co sugerencias de cómo podemo

- Su hija/o va a traer un so una nota y devuéla en e
- Hable conmigo antes c
- Llámeme al 428-339
- Ponga una nota en
- Mándeme un e-ma
- Venga a las junta
  - o A principios de
  - o Juntas mens
  - o Solicite una
- Acompáñen
- Venga a la jueves du hija/o
- Hágase
Déme ot mejor.

Espe

Sincer

Jane H. Gonzalez

Figure 5.3

One area of education that is often minimized in schools is development and learning in the social-emotional domain, including learning to be a moral person with values. The next section lumps those subject under *prosocial skills* and looks at how schools, child care, and families can partner to support children's healthy socialization.

TEACHING PROSOCIAL SKILLS

How do children come to know what's important in life and set their goals accordingly? How do children come to know right from wrong? Although the two questions are in many ways the same, the answer to the first question mostly concerns values; the answer to the second mostly concerns morals.

Teachers and families may not agree on including this area of education in the curriculum, and some individuals may find problems with some aspects of it. The question may come up right away: whose morals and whose values? In a diverse society such as the United States there is bound to be some disagreement, but the differing opinions can make for interesting discussions with families as you bring the subject to them. Discussing the subject gives opportunities for all parties to practice respect for each other. One way to frame the discussion is to look for universal values. Another way to frame it is to use the 11 strategies for teaching prosocial development on pages 127–129 at the end of this chapter and to see if there is agreement on some of the ideas.

Where do we get our values? Our values begin to come to us in our cribs (or our parents' bed) when we are infants. Values are absorbed along with the breast milk or the formula we drink. They come hand in hand with our culture. They are the *shoulds* and *shouldn'ts* that guide our footsteps through life and the beliefs we feel compelled to stand up for. They tell us what to respect and what to oppose.

Some values are simply absorbed in infancy; others come later in the form of little lessons. "Don't hurt the caterpillar" may reflect a value of life. "Be gentle with your brother" may reflect a value of peace and harmony. "Don't let people push you around" may reflect a value of self-assertion. "Work hard at school" may reflect a value of attaining individual success or of being an asset to your family. As children grow, they continually define, appraise, and, sometimes, modify their values. In cultures that value independence, children are expected to do some deep soul-searching at some point, usually in adolescence. They are expected to examine the set of values they've grown up with and come to their own conclusions about whether to embrace those values or to redefine them and come up with their own set. Upset as parents may be at the possibility that their children will reject their values, these parents aren't entirely surprised, because the culture expects people to make up their own minds about values. After all, independence is a value—independence of thought as well as of action. Interestingly enough, after the teen years, even offspring who swung far from their parents' values usually come back to them later in life.

Parents from cultures that value interdependence may be far less tolerant if their children threaten to deviate from the set of values the family embraces. The younger generation is not supposed to question the older one. Deciding values is not an individual matter for children—or for adults either, for that matter.

LOOKING AT THE DECISION-MAKING PROCESS AS A WAY OF EXPLORING MORALS

We—children and grown-ups alike—deal with morals and values with every decision we make. Each time we are forced to choose an action (and each action is a choice, whether we realize it or not), we go through a process of determining whether we're making the right decision. The impulsive person puts less thought into decisions than the more considered one; however, unless the person is reacting from reflexes alone, there is a flash of thought behind each decision.

If you could tune in on the flash, you'd find some of the following questions:

- Will I be punished if I decide to do this (either by my own bad feelings or by someone else in a physical or emotional way)?
- Will I be rewarded? (Will I gain some benefit, including feeling good about doing this?)
- Will this action or decision make someone whom I care about happy—thus making *me* happy (another form of reward)?
- Is there a rule (or a law) that requires or forbids it? And if I break the law and get caught, what is the punishment? And if I break the law and don't get caught, how will I feel?
- Is this what I would want someone else to do? (This calls into play the Golden Rule: "Do unto others as you would have others do unto you.")
- What's the right thing to do? (Using my highest reasoning abilities—is this the best decision, most right, highest good, or least bad thing to do?)
- Who might be hurt by my decision or action?

We don't always ask these questions consciously, but on some level they govern our decisions. We're more aware of that fact when the decision concerns a situation where there is a good deal at stake. The questions above came from the work of two researchers, Lawrence Kohlberg (1976) and Carol Gilligan (1982). Kohlberg, an early researcher on moral decision making, followed the work of Jean Piaget and saw a pattern of

Nell Noddings says that moral development comes from creating the kinds of caring relationships that support moral ways of life. Noddings calls the attentiveness that characterize these relationships engrossment, which she describes as acutely receptive.

Eyewire Collection/Getty Images—Photodisc

organization of moral thought, which he laid out in progressive stages that linked to Piaget's cognitive stages. Kohlberg described children in the early years as determining what's right and what's wrong by whether they are rewarded or punished. Later they move to being motivated to obey rules in order to uphold a social order. Kohlberg's final stages of development involve a personal commitment to an abstract hierarchy of principles. In Kohlberg's scheme, intellectual development—specifically the ability to reason—is vitally linked to moral development. It is, however, important to note that Kohlberg did his research on men and boys.

Children don't worry about theory or stages. Their decision making is usually quick and unconscious. We can help children be more thoughtful about moral dilemmas they face by bringing the questions into the open and examining them. We can also be more thoughtful ourselves about what is motivating children to make the decisions they do. If you look at the questions listed earlier, it is possible to determine, from Kohlberg's view, which ones are most likely to be of importance to younger children. Most children under the age of 7 are able to think only in concrete terms, according to Piaget. Although they may feel emotions related to such abstract concepts as love, honesty, and justice, they don't think or reason about them. They do, however, have a sense of what's fair and what's unfair from their point of view. Instead of using sophisticated cognitive processes, young children are more likely to make judgments about right and wrong actions based on their experiences with the reactions of those around them. They consider the possibility of punishment or reward when trying to decide on the "right thing to do."

Carol Gilligan's work has focused most on the last of the questions posed in our list: "Who might be hurt by my decision or action?" From her work has come what is called an *ethic of caring*. Gilligan sees moral decision making as coming from a concern about acting so that the people one cares about will be hurt the least by one's decision. Although Gilligan's work reflects the moral decision making of women and girls, she assures us that males also use the same types of decision-making processes.

Another researcher, Nel Noddings, has written many books and articles about the ethic of caring. In *The Challenge to Care in Schools* (2005), she takes the early childhood principles espoused in this book out of preschool and puts them into the K–8 system. Another of her books—*Educating Moral People: A Caring Alternative to Character Education* (2002)—deals directly with how to develop morals in children using the ethic of caring. She says that moral development comes from creating conditions and relationships that support moral ways of life rather than teaching children to be virtuous, which is the approach taken by those who use character education. Caring relationships are what count. Caring relationships involve a particular kind of attention from the carer to the cared-for. Noddings calls this attentiveness *engrossment*, which she describes as acutely receptive. Engrossment involves the carer directing motivational energy toward the needs of the cared-for. Another requirement of a caring relationship is that the caring must be detected and received. The response of the cared-for is then received back by the carer in further moments of engrossment.

This information has implications for teachers and care providers. The National Association for the Education of Young Children (NAEYC) recognizes the importance of relationships—placing "relationships" in the number 1 place in their program standards.

Care is not a word often found in teacher education materials, except in programs for infants and very young children. Yet caring relationships are a vital part of teaching, with implications for the parent-teacher relationship. The more teachers and providers can support parents, the more likely they are to enhance the caring relationships those parents have with their children. Support and care breed more support and care.

Caring must be genuine and not just a means of coercion or emotional manipulation to get the parent or child to behave in ways the teacher deems acceptable. Caring relationships have received a good deal of attention from those who train adults to work with babies. Both Magda Gerber (1998) and Emmi Pikler (David & Appell, 2001; Gonzalez-Mena, 2004) have provided living examples of what Noddings calls *caring relationships*. At the Pikler Institute in Budapest, one can observe caregivers interacting with babies in genuinely caring ways. The caregivers are trained in a practical and effective approach based on an ethic of caring, which makes a huge difference in outcomes of children who spend their first years in an institution. Magda Gerber's work, based on an attitude of respect, also demonstrates caring relationships. Her work can be seen wherever her Resources for Infant Educarers (RIE) Associates are at work, in Los Angeles and elsewhere. Noddings notes how care and trust come together so that positive behavior is more a result of the relationship than of the many manipulative techniques so often used by educators. Following an ethic of care, according to Noddings, is more likely to produce caring, moral people than just teaching them to be good. Diane Carlebach and Beverly Tate (2002) assert that using an approach based on Gerber's work creates *peaceful* people and leads to caring communities.

How can teachers and families together direct children down the path of prosocial behavior? Here's one way, as illustrated by a story I heard once—reported to be an Native American story. A grandfather sharing his wisdom with his grandson told him this: "Everybody has two wolves inside—wolves that battle with each other. One is an evil wolf who is full of anger, envy, jealousy, sorry, regret, greed, arrogance, self pity, guilt, resentment, inferiority, lies, false pride, superiority, and ego. The other wolf is good. It is joy, peace, love, hope, serenity, humility, kindness, benevolence, empathy, generosity, truth, compassion and faith." The grandson listened carefully, then a quizzical look came across his face. "Grandfather," he said, "which one wins the battle?" Grandfather looked at him knowingly and responded with only four words, "The one you feed." A very wise grandfather. He knew the power of attention. What you pay attention to feeds off that attention.

THE POWER OF ADULT ATTENTION

When I was getting my teaching credential I observed children in a first-grade classroom. I learned a lot from that experience, but one thing really sticks in my mind—a boy named Ralph. His was the first name I learned in that class of 30 children. I heard the teacher say his name just seconds after I arrived in the classeoom, and she continued to say his name at least an average of every five minutes throughout my observation period. "Ralph, please sit down." "Ralph, stop it!" "Ralph, don't push other children." Sometimes she just said "Ralph!" when she saw him doing something he wasn't supposed to. When he was sitting quietly listening, or doing his seat work, or getting along with other children, he never heard his name called. He definitely knew how to get the teacher's attention. He had the teacher's focus on him more than any other child. His behavior was working for him. It wasn't evil behavior, but still, the teacher was feeding the wrong wolf in Ralph.

I saw another example of the power of attention while I was observing one of my early-childhood practicum students working in an after-school program. It was snack time and the pitcher of milk on the snack table was empty. One child picked up his empty glass, held it out and said gruffly to the teacher, "More milk!" Right about the same time another child said, "Please, can I have more milk?" The teacher immediately responded to the second, ignoring the first, who quickly changed his tone and words to sound more like the other child who got such a quick response from the teacher.

So the message is: pay attention to children who exhibit the prosocial behaviors you're looking for. Notice how gently the big kids help the younger ones. Remark on how nicely Ty is waiting for his turn. You're a good model for parents when you begin to use the power of your attention.

Here's another story about the power of attention. Ana is a family child care provider whose home gets busy after school with the children who come to her. Two of those children have a good deal of trouble getting along with each other. Ugly squabbles constantly break out when they are together. Ana's usual method is to respond to them when they are arguing. She has taught them not to hit each other, but she can't seem to keep them from yelling at each other. She spends a good deal of her time settling their disputes.

Ana talks about these two to her neighbor, Irene, who is a teacher's aide in a nearby elementary school and is enrolled in an early childhood class at the local college. Irene tells her what she recently learned about the principle that when you pay attention to behavior, it tends to continue; when you ignore the same behavior, it tends to disappear. "What you stroke is what you get," says Irene, quoting from the book she is reading for her class, written by Jean Illsley Clarke (1998), who is an expert on strokes and affirmations. She suggests that Ana start ignoring the arguing. She does. It gets worse.

Ana complains to Irene that the suggestion didn't work. "I ignored them and ignored them and they kept right on fighting."

"Maybe," says Irene, "you took away the attention you were giving them for arguing without replacing it with attention for something else."

"What do you mean?" asks Ana.

"You have to pay attention to them when they *aren't* arguing."

"Oh," says Ana.

She tries that approach. Whenever the two are playing nicely together she remarks about how well they are getting along. It isn't easy to do this, because she's not used to it, but she makes a conscious effort. When a squabble breaks out, she leaves the room and starts washing dishes. Sometimes the squabble follows her, but she makes a point of ignoring the angry voices.

Ana doesn't feel entirely comfortable about this approach. It seems dishonest and unnatural to her. Children ought to be good without her making this special effort. After all, cooperative behavior is what's expected. It shouldn't get special notice. It should be the norm. When she was growing up, her mother didn't have to put up with this kind of annoyance. All she had to do was look at her children and the squabbles stopped. She wishes that would work for her, but it doesn't. She begins to notice, however, that the squabbles aren't true disagreements, anyway, but are bids for her attention. She continues to use the approach of paying attention to the positive behavior and ignoring the rest.

It works! Of course, the children still have their disagreements, but not so constantly anymore. Furthermore, Ana has gotten to know the children better and has even grown closer to them since she's not so annoyed at the continual bickering. Ana has learned about the power of attention.

WHAT ARE AFFIRMATIONS?

Ana also learned about affirmations from Irene. *Affirmations* give messages that validate the person as an individual who has needs and rights. Affirmations are positive messages about expectations. They encourage children to be who they are. They can come in the form of being interested in individuals and expressing appreciation to each one.

Ana knew something about affirmations, though she didn't call them that. Being interested and expressing appreciation was something she did naturally, something she learned from her own parents. She wasn't sure about using affirmations on purpose to help the children feel good about themselves so they wouldn't have such a need to squabble with each other. Ana especially had trouble with the idea that with affirmations she was validating the children as *individuals*. Of course, she recognized that each was a separate person, but what she wanted to emphasize in her family child care home was their *connections* rather than their separateness. She wanted them to focus less on themselves and more on others.

Ana brought up her concern to Irene one evening when the children had gone home. "I don't want them to think about their own needs" was how Ana put it. "That makes them selfish. They should put other people first," said Ana.

"But until your own needs are met, how can you think of other people?" asked Irene. "Think of this example," she went on. "When you fly, the flight attendant instructs you that in case of a loss of cabin pressure, you must put your own oxygen mask on before you help other people."

"I think that's an extreme example," Ana responded.

"Maybe, but I think it applies. And it points out that your own needs are important *in order for you to help other people*. Isn't that what your goal is—that your children not be selfish?"

"I see what you mean," said Ana.

The two didn't resolve this issue because Irene tended to *always focus on individuals* when she thought about young children and families, and Ana tended to *avoid focusing on the individual*. Irene seemed to emphasize separateness. Ana liked to emphasize relatedness, embeddedness. But they understood that they disagreed on this issue and were friendly about it. There is more about this subject in relation to family systems in Chapters 1, 11, and 13.

Affirmations can also be used to let children (or adults) know how they *can be* while accepting how they *are* at the present moment. Irene, who understood how this principle worked, used it in the classroom where she was a teacher's aide. One example: she avoided labeling any child as "shy." When one parent talked to her about her son's shyness, Irene shared what she had observed and made it clear that she saw the boy as cautious and careful, putting a little different light on the behavior. Irene used affirmations with this boy, letting him know that he was fine the way he was. If he was slower to accept a new person or situation than other children were, she let him know that was all right too. She affirmed his need to feel safe. She also affirmed the individuality of his pace. It usually took him awhile to warm up and she didn't hurry him. On the other hand, Irene encouraged him to take a few risks, recognizing his potential as a person who could eventually come out of his protective shell and become more able to explore freely. All this was discussed with the teacher and the parents. Everyone agreed with Irene's approaches.

When thinking about strokes and affirmations, it is important to look at both in a cultural context. This chapter, because it is in line with my own cultural background and also my training to be a teacher, focuses on independence and individuality to some extent. It's what I know best. The idea is to help children feel good about themselves. In some cultures the focus is on downplaying individuality, keeping the child firmly embedded in the group, teaching humility instead of pride, and putting others before self. As you saw with Ana, strokes and affirmations seemed strange and in opposition to the goals of her family growing up and her situation as a family child care provider.

Also, in some families direct communication is not valued. Subjects may be talked around instead of directly addressed. Indirect communication, in the form of behavior (including body language), is more valued than what is put into words. In fact, in these families, the kinds of statements used in this chapter to illustrate strokes and affirmations may be regarded as uncomfortable or manipulative. When parents want their children to do something, they just tell them to do it, and the children have respect for their parents, so they do it. Those parents don't need to make their children feel good about themselves. The children feel good just being part of the family and fulfilling their role as son or daughter.

These are two very different approaches to child rearing that seem to be oppositional in some ways. The fact that they are different doesn't mean that one way is right and the other is wrong. It means that there are differences, and differences must be acknowledged, accepted, and honored. When people who have diverse perspectives come together, they have opportunities to learn from each other. That is a strong message in this book. We share what we know and believe in with others and remain open to what others have to share with us. So with all that in mind, let's look further at strokes and other forms of positive adult attention.

Children's Response to Positive Adult Attention

Does giving positive adult attention always work? No. There's nothing that *always* works all the time, in every situation, with every child. How children respond to positive affirmations and strokes depends on their previous experience, which relates to their opinions of themselves and their reality about how the world is. Some children feel validated by affirmations; others don't. Some children accept the positive strokes they are given; others ignore or reject them.

Why would that be? These patterns have their roots in early experience. Imagine a baby who is ignored most of the time. He knows at some deep level that he needs attention and, because he is an infant, the strokes he needs are physical as well as social. He needs physical care given in a way that tells him he is cared about. Strokes in one sense of the word relate to physical touch and in another sense of the word mean caring personal attention. The baby needs strokes or he'll die. Because he is an infant, he can't get attention except by crying, and even then his cries are often ignored. He does get fed and changed often enough to keep him alive, but he doesn't receive his full quota of warm caring strokes—either physical ones or in the form of adults paying attention to him. So when he gets old enough to create a ruckus, he does that. He soon learns that some behaviors bring adults to him. If the behavior is unacceptable enough, they even lavish attention on him—not affection, but attention. It's not positive attention that he receives. He is yelled at, scolded, even punished. But because he is so desperate for strokes—so needing attention of any kind—he accepts these negative responses. He comes to expect them, and when he's old enough to think about such things, he even may regard negative strokes as his due—somehow convincing himself, consciously or unconsciously, that he deserves them.

That attitude, that concept of reality, is what makes it so hard to get through to a child who is used to getting negative strokes. Positive strokes are ignored. Affirmations go in one ear and out the other. They don't relate to the child's reality.

Imagine a child, Michael, who comes from that type of situation early in life and is finally removed from the home, passed through several foster homes, and finally adopted at age 4. He now arrives in kindergarten at the age of 5. The teacher, aide, and parent volunteers are kind and loving to him, but he doesn't accept that kind of attention. They tell him what a good job he is doing on his art project; he throws it to the ground and stomps on it. He refuses to accept positive strokes. He seems to *need* the negative ones. And he is an expert at getting them. He hurts other children. He destroys their things and laughs about it. He constantly butts heads with the adults. He acts like a general all-round menace.

It is tempting to label this child based on his behavior. He has a knack for making adults very angry. The teacher and aide begin to resent all the time they spend trying to manage his behavior. He spends a lot of time in the principal's office. No one feels like giving him positive strokes anymore. "That just doesn't work," they all agree.

The parents feel equally helpless in the face of Michael's negative behavior. They know what is going on at school; it's much like what goes on at home. They are taking a parenting class and getting some counseling, but they haven't yet been successful at making a difference in Michael's behavior. They remember the first conversation they had with Michael's teacher about his challenging behavior. See Strategy Box 5.1 for the process the teacher used to communicate with the parents about concerns about Michael.

Strategy Box 5.1

Working with Michael's Family to Explore Ways to Support His Development and Learning

* After making some careful observations of specific incidents involving Michael, the teacher recorded what she saw objectively, so she could be clear and nonjudgmental about Michael's behavior before meeting with the parents.
* She met with the family in a place where they could have privacy and not be overheard or interrupted. She invited any family members the parents thought they should bring along. They came by themselves.
* She let them know that the purpose of the meeting was to find ways to better support their child's development.
* The discussion started with the teacher asking how they, his parents, saw Michael. They shared their views and then the teacher shared her observations. When they compared notes they found there was consistency— what the parents saw at home related to what was happening at school—they felt they were all on the same page.
* The teacher shared her perceptions of Michael's strengths and asked his parents to do the same.
* The teacher shared her concerns, using examples from her observations and the parents shared theirs. They spent the rest of the meeting brainstorming approaches to take with Michael.

Michael might sound like a child with a disability or mental health issues. Perhaps he is, but nobody yet is willing to take the step forward to get a diagnosis. They may feel helpless, but at the same time still hopeful that they can work together and help him improve his feelings about himself and the behavior that goes with them.

There is another child in the class who has been identified as a child with special needs; she has a whole team of professionals, along with the teacher and her parents, who have worked together to create a plan for her education. The plan is called an IEP— an Individualized Education Plan—and was the result of a series of discussions among the team until they came to an agreement about what was needed for this particular child.

An IEP might be in Michael's future but is not part of the discussion at this time. For now, Michael's parents and his teacher are working together to figure out what to do about Michael, but in a less formal system than if he enters the special education system.

Michael is a tough nut to crack, but his behavior makes sense when you understand his history. He is getting his strokes in the only way he knows how. His reality is that he is "bad," and therefore he believes deep down that he deserves the negative attention he gets. The positive strokes he gets from the school and at home are brushed off. They are not part of his reality. They don't belong to him.

The adults in his life frustrate him because he can't get the same intense reaction to his behavior that he used to get from his birth mother and from the people she lived with before he was removed from the home. The teachers don't show their anger as passionately as the people he lived with in his first years. They don't hurt him the way he was used to being hurt. He doesn't understand the reality of the environments he is in now.

What to do about Michael? The abuse and neglect that still have such a hold on him lie back in his past. Now it is up to the people in his life to help Michael control his unacceptable behavior, learn some prosocial behaviors, and come to feel better about himself.

Here's what they finally come up with as a group—teacher, family, and principal. In spite of the failure of their past efforts, they all continue to focus on the positive aspects of Michael's personality. They search for tiny bits of acceptable behavior. Sometimes they joke that they need a microscope to do this searching, but they discover that when they look hard enough they can find positive behaviors—brief though they may be. Every scrap of positive behavior from Michael brings immediate adult attention—hugs, smiles, words.

They also begin to see Michael in a new light. Instead of a difficult child, they see the behavior for what it is, patterns that he has learned in response to his early environment. The patterns are working against him now, rather than for him, but they can be understood as adaptive behaviors. They discuss how he could be if he overcame his behavior issues and learned to feel good about himself. Once they even took some time at one of their meetings to visualize this new Michael. They closed their eyes and "saw" the potential that lies beneath the difficult behavior.

When the teacher and aide are with Michael, they manage his behavior without rejecting him. It isn't easy. In fact, they really need an extra staff person to do this job properly, but they are able to use the daily parent volunteer to help out so they can do whatever is necessary to focus more fully on Michael.

Little by little they are managing to disconfirm Michael's perception of himself as a "bad person." They're changing his attitude by changing his behavior. They take a prevention approach—physically stopping him before he performs a malicious act.

When they first started this approach, they called in an extra aide so they had plenty of people in the classroom, thus releasing the regular aide to "track" Michael—to keep a constant eye on him. That meant that even when the aide went on a break, someone else was assigned to take over, so that Michael was never unobserved during any part of the first few days of the new approach. He was "tracked" during recess as well as in the classroom. His behavior began to improve—so much so that they were able to reduce the "tracking" to difficult parts of the day. This way they could dispense with the extra aide. The principal agreed to come in sometimes when they needed augmented staffing. Eventually they needed to track Michael only during transition periods, such as arrival and departure times as well as before and after recess, which were always bad times for Michael.

Of course, prevention doesn't always work. Sometimes the adults slip and accidentally let Michael do something unacceptable. The other day, for example, while the teacher was tying another child's shoelace, Michael grabbed a shovel from a boy who was digging in the sandbox. When the child protested and tried to get the shovel back, Michael kicked him, and he was continuing to kick when the teacher grabbed him.

The teacher's response was to separate Michael from the other children. He took him inside. The teacher stayed with him—not to scold him and tell him how badly he'd behaved (Michael already knew that) but to let him know that someone will provide the control that he still lacks and that he is supported and cared about.

The idea is to not allow Michael to make others reject him, which is what used to happen regularly. He still hasn't made friends among the children, but he's beginning to form an attachment to the regular aide—and that's helping to build trust and to give him a sense of the pleasures of closeness with another person. The Michael who's been locked away inside is starting to emerge.

With Michael, remediation must be done. He must be "reprogrammed." Children usually don't need to be reprogrammed when the adults in their lives pay attention from the beginning to what messages they're giving and strive to emphasize positive ones. Messages, of course, don't come just from words. They come from actions as well—even little actions such as facial expressions, gestures, and body language.

Not all children who come from an unfortunate background like Michael's have his same needs. Take Jay, for example, another 5-year-old in the same kindergarten.

Jay is what's called a "resilient child." Remember Emmy Werner (1984, 1995, 2000), the developmental psychologist mentioned in Chapter 1, who did a long-term study on resilience? Jay is like the children Werner described, those who tend to have the ability from infancy on to elicit positive responses from people; who have established a close bond with at least one caregiver during the first year of life; who have a perspective that allows them to use their experiences constructively; who take an active approach toward solving problems; and who have a view of life as meaningful.

Jay was shuffled from relative to relative after his mother left him in the arms of his grandmother the day he was born. His grandmother was able to keep him until he was 15 months old, but then she had a stroke and Jay went to live with his aunt. He's only seen his mother twice in his young life, once last Christmas when she came to visit and once when he was $2\frac{1}{2}$; and he went to visit her—in prison.

When Jay arrived in kindergarten, he had lived in four different homes and had been removed from the last one because of an abusive situation. You'd never know all this to look at Jay. He's a sunshiny kind of child who beams at anyone who notices him, and he's very good at getting people to notice him. There's something about Jay that attracts people to him, children as well as adults. His special friend in kindergarten is the custodian, and Jay can often be found at recess hanging out with him.

In spite of his difficult home life, Jay seems to have managed to get enough positive strokes when he most needed them—during the first year or so of his life. That period with his grandmother seems to have helped him develop an attitude that he's a person worthy of positive attention. As a 4-year-old, he seeks it—*and* he knows how to get it and use it. (See Chapter 12 for more on the subject of resilient children.)

Notice that in all this discussion of affirmations and positive strokes, the word *praise* was never used. Many teachers, when thinking about helping children develop prosocial skills, tend to zero in on praise. Praise can work, but it has some side effects. It takes some skill to use praise effectively. Let's look a little more closely.

Observe children who have been used to a good deal of praise. Watch them turn to adults after every little accomplishment. "Look at me, Teacher," they say, either verbally or nonverbally. For example, Alexis stands at the easel painting a picture. When she finishes it, she takes it down and carefully carries it over to show the teacher who is busy working with a small group. She waits impatiently for awhile, then seeks out the aide and shows it to her. The aide makes a comment, which Alexis barely hears because just then she notices the teacher is getting up from the group. Alexis rushes over and puts the picture in the teacher's face and waits for a response. The teacher looks at it and remarks about the use of color and moves on to something else. Alexis sees the easel is still free, so she lays her picture out to dry and starts on a new picture. She finishes this one in a hurry and goes through the same routine of seeking praise for her accomplishment. Is she really painting for her own pleasure, or is she just producing paint on paper because she's trying to get praise from the adults in the room?

You can see this behavior starting in infancy as a baby puts one block on another and looks immediately for an adult to clap, smile, or say something. One common response is "good boy!" This is the kind of response someone who was just learning about *behavior modification* might give. Behavior mod, as it is called, is a particular approach for changing behavior based on behaviorist theory. The idea is that a verbal reward, called *reinforcement*, will increase the behavior. The baby will be encouraged to try something like this again.

But let's look more closely at that kind of reward. Calling a child a "good boy" when he performs can backfire. What if he tries and tries and doesn't accomplish the feat? Is he a "bad boy"? Or what if he doesn't try at all? Anyone who believes strongly in a positive approach wouldn't tell him that he's a bad boy, but the absence of the label of "good" can easily be interpreted by a child as its opposite. When adults do use both "bad boy" and "good boy" (or "good girl"/"bad girl") to give feedback on behavior, there is a real danger that the children will label themselves in those same terms. As children try to live up to their labels, they limit their options and potential. It's best to avoid global judgments that reflect on the child's worth as a person when using praise to motivate.

The teacher might say "Good job!"—making a nonspecific reference to the behavior (rather than a global judgment of the child). Even better, the teacher might say "Good stacking!" or "Good painting!"—specifically labeling the skill and the outcome. Or the teacher might focus instead on the process—the effort put in: "You worked hard to get that block to stay on top"; "You put a lot of effort into making that picture" (see Gartell, 2007).

Instead of words, the teacher might give a passing smile or a little pat (nonverbal stroke). But let's go a step further and think about how to give encouragement instead of praise. What can you say that will keep a child working on whatever it is—doing it for himself rather than you? The interactions demonstrating praise could be improved if they were designed to move children forward on their own rather than making them dependent on the adult's praise.

All the examples mentioned so far are examples of *extrinsic rewards*—they come from someone else. However, children need to also learn intrinsic rewards—to tune in on their own sense of satisfaction.

One way the teacher and aide can do that for the kindergarten painter is to say, "You must feel good about that picture. It looks like you put a lot of work into it." This statement helps the child tune in on the good feelings of accomplishment. The child learns eventually to stroke herself by bringing this good feeling to her conscious awareness. This approach takes the focus off the outside reward and puts it inside, where it does the most good of all.

Watch a group of children in a classroom or on the playground with adults nearby supervising. Notice that some accomplish great feats and never look to an adult. Others look for attention for each little success, no matter how small. Some adults are that way too, but it doesn't show the way it shows in children.

TEACHING MORALS BY PROMOTING PROSOCIAL DEVELOPMENT

How do teachers, child care staff, and parents promote prosocial development in the children they rear or care for? It helps to be clear about which prosocial behaviors are important to you. This could be a good exercise for a parent meeting. Start by asking the families to make a list of some behaviors they want to encourage in children. Their lists will probably include such items as sharing, nonviolent conflict resolution, consideration for others, sensitivity to feelings, cooperation, involvement with and responsibility to others, kindness, reverence for life, and respect for self, others, and the earth (nature). Many people will probably have these values on their list regardless of whether they are from a culture emphasizing independence or interdependence.

Then ask the families to brainstorm ways to encourage those behaviors that they value in children.

Here are my ideas. See if you can add some of your own.

1. *Model them yourself.*   If you want children to share, they need to see you share. If respect is important, they need to see you being respectful. Modeling is the most

powerful way to convey your messages. You'll see your own behaviors reflected in the children around you. If honesty is a value, be honest. If cooperation is important to you, show yourself to be cooperative—don't just expect it from children.

2. *Explain why you are setting limits.* Say "I can't let you run in the classroom; you might get hurt or hurt someone," rather than "The rule is no running indoors!" Children need to know the effects of their behaviors. They need to know the reasoning behind your prohibitions.

Todd Yarington/Merrill

Encourage cooperation by finding ways to get children to work and play together. Let children do seatwork in small groups. Have them do projects that call for cooperation. Every picture doesn't have to be individually drawn—how about painting a mural? Collage can be a group effort.

3. *Encourage cooperation by finding ways to get children to work and play together.* Let children do seatwork in small groups. Have them do projects that call for cooperation. Every picture doesn't have to be individually drawn—how about painting a mural? Collage can be a group effort.

4. *Take a problem-solving approach when dealing with conflicts, rather than a power stance.* Help children talk to one another, explain their feelings, and brainstorm solutions. Don't rescue them from the conflict or cut the conflict short by deciding the outcome for them. Let them talk it through. If they don't have the words, provide the words for them. (Chapter 8 deals with this subject at length.)

5. *Avoid punishment as a way of disciplining.* Although punishment may suppress some behaviors, it doesn't eliminate them—they go underground. Benching a child at recess for restlessness in the classroom, doesn't make the restlessness go away. It just prevents the child from getting the movement and exercise he needs to settle down and concentrate. Besides, punishment doesn't teach prosocial behaviors—it models antisocial ones. (See Chapter 7 for ideas of ways to guide behavior without punishing.)

6. *Examine your power relations with children.* Do you *overpower* them rather than *empower* them? Don't rob them of opportunities to develop skills and to experience their own competence by doing things for them or to them. Use your power, your superior size and skills, to bring out their own sense of power—their sense of themselves—who they are and what they can do. Empowered people have less need to use force and violent means of solving problems than do people who feel powerless. When you find yourself in power struggles, take a close look at why the parties concerned need to feel power. Take steps to empower them (and yourself, if you are one of the parties).

7. *Avoid using competition to motivate.* If you value competition, you probably think that starting early to teach children to compete with each other won't hurt. But it does. Even though we live in a competitive society, we do a disservice to children if we start too young to teach them about competition. Young children are still figuring out who they are. Even though you may see competition as a motivation device, you may be setting up comparisons that damage self-esteem and relationships. Avoid questions such as "Who is the fastest?" or "Who is the neatest?" or "Who got the most right?" or "Who is the best drawer?" Also don't always play games that have win-lose outcomes. No young child can afford to be stuck with the label "loser"! Losers have poor self-images, and they behave according to their labels. Though some children in this age group like competitive games, balance them with noncompetitive ones as well. Many games require cooperation—choose some of those.

8. *Help children appreciate the world they live in and the people they share it with.* Adults can do this best by feeling the sense of wonder children feel and encouraging the awe they experience at the beauty and mystery of nature. It's vital to help children perceive their connection to the earth and to all the earth's creatures, including other humans.

9. *Give choices.* Only by experiencing the effects of their own actions on the world around them can children understand how things work. When they are faced with choosing from alternatives, they get practice in becoming good decision makers.

10. *Teach children to solve conflicts without violence.* Conflict is natural and is to be expected, but violence is never an appropriate response to conflict. Especially never use violence as a last resort, because the message then is that when all else fails, you can always fall back on violence. Do allow children their violent *feelings*—it's healthier to feel them than to deny them. Make it clear, however, that children won't be allowed to act on those feelings. Teach a number of ways to express those feelings in ways that do no harm. (See Chapter 8 for further explanation.)

11. *Teach children to be peacemakers.* Peacemaking is a vital part of moral education. Peace is not an absence of tension or conflict. Creating peace is an active process of balancing opposing forces and dealing with conflicts and tensions. True peace cannot be imposed. Peacemaking requires resourcefulness in using a number of skills, including confrontation, debate, dialogue, and negotiation. The goal of peacemakers is to bring conflicts to the surface and to respect differences while resolving or managing those conflicts in ways that preserve the self-esteem of everyone involved. Children learn both the philosophy and the skills of peacemaking from the adults around them who daily help them settle the numerous disputes that occur in the natural course of life, both at home and in early childhood programs.

LOOKING BACK AND LOOKING FORWARD

This chapter focused on school-age children. Starting with a discussion of the transition from preschool to kindergarten, we compared a family-centered approach to one that is focused mainly on the children. The kindergarten through primary age child is in a transition between Erikson's stage of initiative and that of industry. Many children reach third grade before they complete the transition. What might a family coming from preschool find different in school? Preschool is often more about "discovery learning," and the outdoors is usually considered a learning environment, whereas there are constraints on primary teachers to teach in a different way and to use outdoor time as recess, if there is outdoor time at all. The after-school child care program may help make the transition easier because many of those programs are more like the early care and education programs the child experienced before going into kindergarten. This chapter also looked at how parent-teacher partnerships work in schools and how parents can become advocates for children and programs. A chunk of the chapter focused on how children learn morals, values, and prosocial behaviors, and the part that affirmations play in guiding children on the right track. A look at resilience was part of this chapter also. This chapter is a great lead-in to the next one on understanding and supporting families goals, values, and culture.

FOR DISCUSSION

1. What are your memories of starting school? How do they compare with Daniel's and Emily's. Do you also have memories of after-school child care?

2. What do you remember about being in Erikson's stage of industry? Do you know any children in that stage today? How are they like or different from you?

3. How might the parent-teacher partnerships in the primary grades be like the ones in preschool or child care? How might they be different?

4. What was your reaction to the section about the power of adult attention and the use of affirmations? What are your experiences with using praise to motivate children?

5. What do you know about resilience in children? Have you known a resilient child? What do you think helped that child become resilient?

6. What was your reaction to the list of ways to teach prosocial behaviors? Did some resonate more than others? Were there any that you disagreed with?

WEB SITES

Council for Exceptional Children
http://www.cec.Sped.org
Has a teaching and learning section that includes current topics of interest, and research based practice. Site also includes articles, discussions, and a variety of resources.

Education Week
www.edweek.org
Web site for teachers gives news, issues, opinions, and resources.

The Harvard Family Project
http://www.gse.harvard.edu/hfrp/
The Harvard Family Research Project (HFRP) is a large, on-going research program with the goal of promoting more effective educational practices, programs, and policies. Click on *Family Involvement Makes a Difference* for a large number of resources on family involvement.

Marc Sheehan's Special Education/Exceptionality Page
http://www.halcyon.com/marcs/sped.html
This very helpful site contains many Internet links to special education-related sites.

Mental Health Net (MHNET)
http://www.mentalhelp.net/psyhelp/chap3/
This site presents 9 articles for understanding Kohlberg's and others' stages of moral development. Enter *Kohlberg* in the search area.

National Association for the Education of Young Children (NAEYC)
http://www.naeyc.org

The National Association for the Education of Young Children has a number of resources available for parents and professionals including books and journals, one of which is called *Young Children*.

National Network for Child Care (NNCC)
http://www.nncc.org/
The National Network for Child Care is an Internet source of over 1,000 publications and resources related to children. Publications are research based and reviewed. This site includes articles, resources, and links on various subjects such as public policy/advocacy, health and safety, child abuse, diversity, and more.

Parent Services Project
http://www.parentservices.org/
This program trains early childhood professionals on how to partner with families in ways that develop and strengthen their leadership qualities and roles in educational programs for their children.

Resilience in Action
http://www.resiliency.com/htm/research.htm
From research to practice. Resources for understanding protective factors related to resilience in human development.

Understanding Resilience in School Children
http://cmcd.coe.uh.edu/article/resilience.html
An article that looks at successes in inner city school children instead of focusing in failures. Explores studies showing factors in resilience.

FURTHER READING

Allen, P. G. (1998). *Off the reservation*. Boston: Beacon.

Axtmann, A., & Dettwiler, A. (2005). *The visit: Observation, reflection, synthesis for training and relationship building*. Baltimore: Brookes.

Billman, J. (1992, September). The Native American curriculum: Attempting alternatives to tepees and headbands. *Young Children, 47*(6), 22–25.

Butterfield, P. M., Martin, C. A., & Prairie, A. P. (2004). *Emotional connections: How relationships guide early learning*. Washington, DC: Zero to Three.

Cajete, G. (1994). *Look to the mountain: An ecology of indigenous education*. Durango, CO: Kivaki.

Chaille. C. (2008). *Constructivism across the curriculum in early childhood classrooms: Big ideas as inspiration*. Boston, MA: Allyn & Bacon/Pearson Education.

Clarke, J. I. (1998) *Self-esteem a family affair*. Minneapolis: Winston.

Delpit, L., & Dowdy, J. K. (2002). *The skin that we speak: Thoughts on language and culture in the classroom*. New York: New Press.

Derman-Sparks, L., & Ramsey, P. G. (2006). *What if all the kids are white? Engaging white children and their famiies in anti-bias/multicultural education*. New York: Teachers College Press.

Diffily, D., & Sassman, C. (2006) *Positive teacher talk for better classroom management: Grades K–2*. New York: Scholastic.

Fadiman, A. (1997). *The spirit catches you and you fall down: A Hmong child, her American doctors, and the collision of two cultures*. New York: Noonday.

Gartell, D. (2007 May) You worked really hard on your picture! Guiding with encouragement. *Young Children, 62*(3), 58–59.

Greenfield, P. M., Quiroz, B., Rothstein-Fisch, C., & Trumbull, E. (2001). *Bridging cultures between home and school*. Mahwah, NJ: Erlbaum.

Grieshaber, S., & Cannella, G. S. (2001). *Embracing identities in early childhood education: Diversity and possibilities*. New York: Teachers College Press.

hooks, b. (2003). *Rock my soul: Black people and self-esteem*. New York: Atria.

Kawagley, A. O. (1995). *A Yupiaz worldview: A pathway to ecology and spirit*. Prospect Heights, IL: Waveland.

Kern, P., and Wakeford, L. (2007, September). Supporting outdoor play for young children: The zone model of playground supervision. *Young Children, 62* (5), 20–25.

Landy, S. (2002). *Pathways to competence: Encouraging healthy social and emotional development in young children*. Baltimore: Brookes.

Marshall, H. H. (2000, November). Cultural influences on the development of self-concept. *Young Children, 56*(6), 19–22.

Martinez, F. (2005) Early care and education for Hispanic children. *Childhood Education, 81*(3), 174–176

Morrison, J. W. (2001, Spring). Supporting biracial children's identity development. *Childhood Education, 77*(3), 134–138.

Noddings, N. (2002). *Educating moral people: A caring alternative to character education*. New York: Teachers College Press.

Noddings, N. (2005). *The challenge to care in schools*. New York: Teachers College Press.

Noonan, M. J., & McCormick, L. (2006). *Young children with disabilities in natural environments*. Baltimore: Brookes.

Pulido-Tobiassen, D., & Gonzalez-Mena, J. (1998). A *place to begin: Working with parents on issues of diversity*. Oakland: California Tomorrow.

Rael, J. (1993). *Being and vibration*. Tulsa: Council Oak Books.

Rhodes, M., Enz, B., and LaCount, M. (2006, January). Leaps and bounds: Preparing parents for kindergarten. *Young Children 61*(1), 50–51.

Rogoff, B. (2003). *The cultural nature of human development*. New York: Oxford University Press.

Tedla, E. (1995). *Sankofa: African thought and education*. New York: Lang.

Valdes, G. (1996). *Con respeto: Bridging the distances between culturally diverse families and schools*. New York: Teachers College Press.

Werner, E. E. (2000, February–March). The power of protective factors in the early years. *Zero to Three, 20*(4), 3–5.

CHAPTER 6

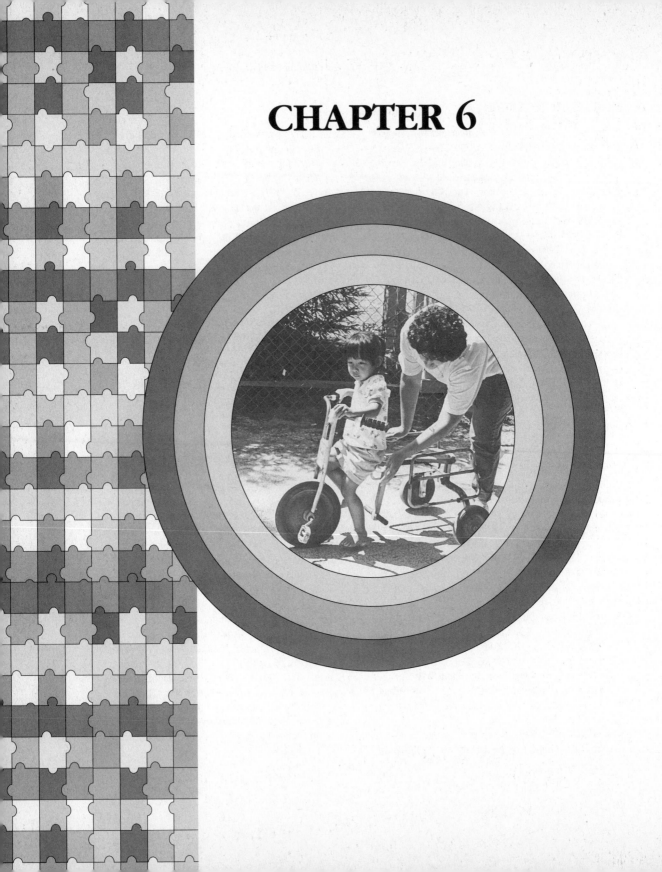

Understanding Families' Goals, Values, and Culture

In *this chapter you'll discover* . . .

- Why a salad bowl is pluralistic and a melting pot is not
- The goals for a pluralistic society
- How unconscious culture is
- Two contrasting cultural patterns that affect child rearing
- Why one parent teaches her child pride while another criticizes her child for being proud
- How to work through conflicts between early educators and families
- A particular way of approaching problems, called "RERUN"

A worthwhile exercise for all parents, caregivers, and teachers is to examine their values, see how they relate to their goals, and decide whether what they are doing with their children is in tune with what they believe in. Take, for example, a family who highly values peace. Their goal is that each child be raised to always pursue nonviolent solutions to problems. If a parent in this family spanks as a means of controlling behavior, the child-rearing practice is out of tune with the value and the goal.

Anyone who works with families and their children—as an infant care teacher, family child care provider, center-based staff, director, preschool teacher, kindergarten teacher, or primary teacher—should understand the values and goals the families have for their children. They should examine the policies of their program plus their own behaviors to see whether what they are doing with the children, or with the families, is in harmony with what the families want for their children.

Recognizing that cultural learning starts at birth and is mostly nonverbal, it is imperative that those who work with families familiarize themselves with cultural differences. The ideal is that families and the agencies that work with them are involved in a joint process to ensure that each child will remain a full member of his or her own family and culture through a steady developmental progress toward cultural competence. That's not to say that cultures never change, but being part of a changing culture is different from living outside it and lacking the feeling of belonging. Children may well become bicultural eventually through attendance in early care and education programs and through schooling; however, taking on another culture should be adding to what they already have. It's detrimental when children lose the original culture of the family unless it is the family's explicit desire that they do so.

Preserving diversity is a vital issue for all of us in the United States and the world beyond. It's not just that it's nice to be nice or even that it's good to be fair. Kindness is important and so is equity, especially when one group dominates another. It's not just because of the shifting demographics. Preserving diversity is a way to save us all!

Look at the biological argument. The rain forest that disappears today may well contain a plant that holds the cure for a disease that doesn't yet exist or that we haven't discovered (Rogoff, 2003). As variety in the grain supply is more and more determined by the profit in selling certain seeds and not in others, globalization occurs and diversity disappears. When a devastating disease comes along that wipes out the world's grain supply, there's nothing to replace it. Native grasses with immunities no longer exist and the world goes hungry.

Look at the cultural argument. In the name of unity through uniformity, making everyone in America "American" by putting them in a melting pot moves them away from their culture of origin. Whether intended or not by the society at large, the result is the loss of the original culture. In other words, the process tends to be a subtractive one—one culture replacing another rather than an additive one resulting in a bicultural person. Cultures disappear every day in this country as the last person of that culture who speaks the language dies. When that happens, the survival of all of us becomes riskier. We face an uncertain future, one in which we can't even conceive of the problems that will arise. As cultural diversity diminishes, the solutions to those problems may disappear. For example, Native American wisdom has allowed some cultures to continue for countless thousands of years and should not be looked down on as primitive, but should be held in high regard as containing potential solutions we need now and in the future (Brody, 2001). We have a lot to learn about preserving the environment and alternative approaches to medicine and healing.

We find better, more effective solutions when we have a diverse team working on a problem. Differing worldviews and life experiences bring more opportunities for new and creative ways of looking at things in a new light, which offers a wider range of solutions.

This view of preserving diversity is based on cultural pluralism as a value. *Cultural pluralism* is the label for the idea that groups should be allowed, even encouraged, to hold on to what gives them their unique identities while maintaining their membership in the larger social framework. The old concept of the United States was that of a melting pot, of all cultures blended into one. The new image, for those who believe in cultural pluralism, is of the United States as a salad bowl, where each of the many ingredients retains its own unique identity, but the parts combine into a "delicious" whole.

CULTURAL DIFFERENCES IN GOALS AND VALUES

Our culture affects everything we do, from determining the precise way we move our arms and legs when we walk to deciding the objectives we're moving toward. Culture rules how we position our bodies, how we touch each other, what we regard as mannerly, how we look at the world, how we think, what we see as art, how we sense time and perceive space, what we think is important, and how we set immediate and lifelong goals.

Most people find it hard to talk about their own culture until it bumps up against one that's different. Culture is so much a part of our lives that we don't see it or pay attention to it. Yet it determines our values, which are also so much a part of our lives that they, too, remain invisible most of the time. Values are behind

Cultural learning starts at birth and is mostly nonverbal.

Frank Gonzalez-Mena

everything we do and every decision we make. They guide us in child rearing and working with children.

Everybody is influenced by his or her culture. Sometimes people describe themselves as a mixture or "a mutt" because their ancestors came to the United States from a number of different countries. They explain that they don't have a culture. What they mean is that they don't have one particular heritage that they can put their finger on—but they do have a culture. It may be influenced by several ethnicities in their background, but nonetheless cultural rules are behind their behavior—whether they keep them or break them. Most of those people who think they don't have a culture are part of the dominant culture of the United States, which is uniquely American but highly influenced by its European roots. It's not that the dominant culture has a blandness about it. There are lots of different flavors within the culture, which can be influenced by the part of town or the area of the country where one grew up. Someone from California has only to spend a short time in New England, the South, or the Midwest to begin to taste those flavor differences, even when among people also of the dominant culture. Many people don't grow up in just one place, as is often the case with military families, for example. Living in several different areas of the country adds its own special flavor.

Most people recognize when they meet up with people of their own culture because they find they have things in common and feel comfortable with each other, unless class differences get in the way. Culture, race, ethnicity, class, gender, religion, and sexual orientation, all mix together to make the study of culture difficult and confusing. For this reason instead of continuing to focus on culture alone, I'm going to examine a set of patterns that influence how parents raise their children. This set of patterns has come up in each of the chapters preceding this one, but here the pattern is named and explicitly explained. The pattern has to do with independence and interdependence. Most parents put more emphasis on one or the other, and they set goals for their children based on which one is their top priority (Greenfield, Quiroz, & Raeff, 2000; Greenfield, Quiroz, Rothstein-Fisch, & Trumbull, 2001; Zepeda et al, 2006).

How Do the Goals of Independence and Interdependence Differ?

What do parents who focus on independence actually do that shows their focus? They encourage early self-help skills, for one thing. They expect toddlers to feed themselves and soon after to dress themselves. They teach their children to sleep alone in their own beds. They may take them into their bed for short periods, but their goal is to get the child back to bed. If they "baby" their children, they feel guilty. Families that emphasize independence can be thought of as pattern 1 individuals.

Parents who focus on interdependent relationships are less adamant about babies learning to sleep through the night alone. The idea of "babying" children is viewed in a positive light, not a negative one. Babies and family members tend to have strong connections, so prolonging babyhood makes sense if your goal is *inter*dependence. These parents are more worried about maintaining relationships than creating an independent individual, so they see nothing wrong with coddling children. Families that emphasize interdependence can be thought of as pattern 2 individuals.

Pattern 1 and Pattern 2 parents have completely different ways of meeting their children's needs. Children who grow up in an individualistic home learn that it's each person's job to take care of his or her own needs. But children who grow up in "other-centered" homes learn that the needs of the others are their problem. They still get their needs met, because while they are taking care of others, they are being taken care of. In both kinds of homes, basic needs get met, but the process is different in each.

Of course, most people, no matter how they were raised, do become *both* independent individuals and people who create and maintain relationships. Children accomplish both the major tasks even if their parents only focus on one. Parents expect their children to be both independent and connected, but they work harder on what they believe to be most important. They leave to chance what they are less concerned about or work toward it in random bits and pieces.

CONTRASTING CULTURAL PATTERNS

Because one culture is best seen in contrast to another, I've taken the approach of pointing out cultural patterns that are quite different from each other, rather than listing characteristics of various cultures. These patterns have been introduced earlier but will be expanded on here. It is important to point out that to make a contrast I've exaggerated differences. Although some families may fit neatly into one category or the other, many defy categorization. As you read about pattern 1 and pattern 2 families, you'll probably find that your family fits somewhere between the two. The point is not to fit families into categories but to show contrasts and differences by highlighting them.

Pattern 1 values people as unique individuals, starting at birth. The emphasis is on independence of both thought and action. Members of this culture regard the individual's feelings highly and encourage expression of those feelings. Individuals in this culture are perceived to have personal power, and they are taught assertiveness from an early age. If you're not a pattern 1 person yourself, you probably know some people who are. You probably also realize that there is diversity even among people who all belong to pattern 1. They aren't all alike.

Pattern 2 sees the group as more important than the individual. Individual uniqueness is valued only as it serves the group. Children are taught to blend in, to fit. They learn to see the group as the basic unit and themselves as a part of it, rather than seeing the individual as the basic unit. In other words, the individual is nothing by him- or herself—the individual counts only as a part of the group. Pattern 2 stresses interdependence (mutual dependence) and obedience. Obedience has to do with the group will, which is often expressed by a hierarchy of authority.

The sense of identity of a pattern 2 person comes from membership in the group rather than from personal competence, power, significance, lovability, or virtue.

The behavior of an individual is never just a reflection of him- or herself; instead it reflects on the group and either adds to or detracts from the group identity. Remember, all pattern 2 people are not alike. There is always diversity in any group.

The two patterns differ in their view of the attachment process, which was mentioned in Chapter 1. The pattern 2 person sees early attachment as important—something that must happen to ensure that the baby will be properly cared for. Attachment and separation cannot be divided and are viewed as two parts of a single process that follows a progression leading to later independence from the family of origin. Indeed, the separation part of the process is as important as the attachment part and occurs in stages throughout childhood and then finally culminates in "leaving home" at some point after adolescence. In the pattern 1 culture, after an individual leaves home, he or she is expected to take full charge of his or her own life and no longer look for parental advice or support more than just occasionally.

The pattern 2 person sees attachment differently. The focus is on keeping the child in the family/group rather than on teaching separation skills. Attachment is not such an issue at the beginning because group expectations ensure that each baby will be taken care of properly—if not by the mother, then by another member of the group. It's not up to the individual to be drawn to the baby and therefore give it the care it needs; instead, it's up to the group member to fulfill an expected role that is unquestioned.

Attachment in the pattern 2 culture is a lifetime process; the child is expected to remain unto death a viable member of the family into which he or she is born. Each person in the group is connected to and interdependent on the other members of the group.

How might these themes of individual versus group, attachment versus separation, and independence versus interdependence show up in child-rearing practices? Where might the conflicts lie in a pattern 1 person is the infant care teacher, early educator, family child care provider, kindergarten teacher, or primary teacher of the child in a pattern 2 family?

WHEN FAMILIES AND EARLY EDUCATORS HAVE CONFLICTING GOALS AND VALUES

Consider the differences between an infant program based on pattern 1 and what a baby is used to whose family comes from a pattern 2 culture. The pattern 1 infant care teacher might expect that the parents put their baby daughter to sleep in a crib in a room separate from their bedroom. In fact, if they can afford it, they might give her a room of her own from the beginning. A goal would be to get her to put herself to sleep in her own bed and stay there asleep all night long. Families might vary about when they would expect this to occur—and some would "baby" the child longer than others—but eventually the child is expected to show her ability to manage on her own by sleeping alone.

That's a contrast to pattern 2 parents, who might sleep with their daughter from birth on, never buying her a crib or planning to provide her with a room of her own. They might move her out of the parental bed when another baby comes along, but they most likely would move her into a sibling's bed or perhaps in with her grandmother. Being alone, even when asleep, is not sought after by most members of a pattern 2 culture.

A pattern 1 infant care teacher or early educator may expect to raise each child's self-esteem by emphasizing individuality. The teacher may purposely set out to praise accomplishments—drawing attention to individual behavior. Comments like "You did that all by yourself!" illustrate this emphasis on the individual. Along the same lines, the caregiver or teacher may provide for each child a storage cubby that is decorated with the child's name in bold print and a picture of him or her. The idea is for the child to gain a sense of his or her own personal identity while experiencing private ownership, even in the group situation.

A pattern 2 family may dislike their child being singled out. They would prefer that the early educator point out group accomplishments rather than individual ones. They would like the focus to be on rewarding cooperative efforts instead of individual efforts. A member of a pattern 2 family will likely downplay individual achievement by refusing personal credit when given a compliment. They may be teaching modesty at home to their children and be concerned that at school their child is being taught to "brag" about himself.

Several examples common to preschool and some homes serve to show the difference between a group emphasis and an emphasis on individuals. In one program children use clay to create objects to fire and take home. Another program uses clay to explore and experiment with, and when it is time to clean up, all the clay goes back into the common pot.

In one home each of the four children have their own small box of crayons, so each would have a full set. In another home the parent bought a big box of crayons for his six children to share. A similar example in a preschool shows the same two mindsets. One teacher sorted the crayons and gave each child a paper cup with a variety of colors of crayons in it. Another teacher sorted the crayons by colors and put a cup of each color in the middle of the table. When the first teacher questioned this, the second teacher explained that she wanted the children to interact with each other rather than having a "personal set" of crayons.

One program has a finger paint table where children work together to experience the qualities of the material and then wash off the finger paint when they are finished. Another program has separate pieces of paper, and each child does a finger painting, which, when dried, is hung up on the wall and eventually taken home.

At home, one mother made play dough and colored each of the wads a different color so the children could tell which one was theirs, while another mother made one big batch all of one color. These examples are designed not to show right or wrong but to illustrate differences in perceptions of what children need to learn. They also aren't intended to show pure pattern 1 or 2 programs, only in little ways how diversity works. Many programs and parents combine the two styles.

Other differences show up in ordinary daily routine activities. In a pattern 1 culture, the emphasis is on helping oneself; in a pattern 2 culture, the emphasis is on helping others. This difference shows up in the attitude about training for self-help skills. A pattern 1 parent or infant care teacher is in a hurry for the child to learn to feed himself, for example. When the baby first grabs the spoon, many pattern 1 people will get another spoon and let the baby begin to help. If the baby isn't yet capable of using a spoon, finger food is given so the child gets the idea that he or she can feed independently.

A pattern 2 parent is too busy modeling "helping," in keeping with the goal of interdependence, to worry about teaching the baby to "do it himself." Needless to say, pattern 1 children are able to do things for themselves at a surprisingly young age, and pattern 2 children are able to do things for other children at a surprisingly young age. In some cultures around the world with pattern 2 tendencies, preschool-age children take charge of their younger siblings, doing for the baby what was done for them only a short time before.

Toilet training is another area where the two patterns may conflict. The pattern 1 parent or infant care teacher puts the emphasis on self-help, so he or she doesn't see signs of readiness for toilet training until the child is somewhere around 2 years of age. To this adult, toilet training starts when children are able to control bladder and bowels, handle clothing, and get to the toilet or potty on their own.

A pattern 2 parent has a very different view. With the deemphasis on self-help and the emphasis on interdependence, the adult is part of the child's elimination processes from the beginning. The adult watches from the early months on for signals preceding bowel and bladder activity. When the signals appear, the adult responds immediately. Eventually the two set up a system of signals that allow the adult to get the child bare-bottomed and to the proper place, and then trigger the elimination response. If you've never seen this, I can assure you, it's impressive!

A pattern 2 parent or infant care teacher may view manners as much more important than self-expression. Learning manners reflects the goal of becoming a good group member. Pattern 2 adults may be horrified as they watch a pattern 1 adult encourage children to speak out, say anything they want to adults, express anger, and eat in less than mannerly ways.

To illustrate the difference in the early months, contrast these two approaches. One adult touches a screaming baby lightly on the shoulder and says, "I know you're mad. It's OK to cry!" After reviewing the situation—he's not tired, hungry, or in need of a change—she leaves him alone to express himself, checking in periodically to let him know that he hasn't been deserted. She doesn't try to distract him or lull him with words or touch because she thinks that his expression of emotion is healthy.

Another adult, rocking and lulling, holding the baby tight, says, "There, there, quiet down, it's OK! You're upsetting everyone else. Please don't cry!" She tries to stop the crying, using all the verbal and nonverbal techniques she has. She doesn't regard displays of anger as healthy. She doesn't feel that the baby has the individual right to destroy the peace of the household. She tries to teach him to consider others, even though she understands that he's too young to learn this lesson.

A pattern 1 parent or infant care teacher is understanding when a 4-year-old cries when away from home or parents for the first time. But the expectation is that this child needs to learn to cope with separation and that this experience is good for him.

The crying may go on for awhile, but the adult is confident that the child will gain coping skills and will eventually adjust. The adult sees this period as just one in a long series of separation experiences.

On the other hand, the crying of a pattern 2 child may be considered "bad behavior" because the goal is harmony and equanimity. In their book *Culture and Attachment*, Harwood, Miller, and Irizarry (1995) point out that many Puerto Rican mothers saw crying in this situation as showing a lack of manners. Crying in a pattern 2 child may be devastating to the adults in his life because they don't see that being away from family is in his best interests, even though circumstances have dictated the separation. They may be less willing to look at this situation as good for him. They may have less knowledge about teaching coping strategies or helping with separation because they don't value separation.

A pattern 1 parent or infant care teacher says, "Call me by my first name," in her eagerness to be friendly. She values casualness. The pattern 2 adult, who is more used to respecting titles and lives in a social hierarchy, may be uncomfortable with such informality. She may insist on using the teacher's last name with *Mrs.*, *Ms.*, or *Miss* in front of it. She may even use the title *Teacher* instead of the name and teach her children to do the same. She doesn't see this first-name business as creating closeness but only showing a lack of respect.

WHAT TO DO WHEN CONFLICTS ARISE

Conflicts constantly arise—in families, between parents, and between parents and the professionals who serve them. This subject has been touched on in previous chapters, but here it gets fuller attention. In some cases, but not all, these conflicts have cultural differences at their bases.

In the United States today, the professionals in most areas of expertise, regardless of their home culture, are trained from the perspective of the dominant culture, which has its roots in the immigration of people from Europe who rose to power in government, business, and the professional world. Many of those people don't think of themselves having a culture. When they work with families not of their own culture, they have to figure out how they are different. In the 1960's the term for many people of other cultures, especially if they were people with low-incomes, was "culturally deficient." We've mostly moved beyond accepting labels like that, but sometimes the attitude is still there. A strong message in this book, indeed a mandate, is the importance of being sensitive to, understanding of, and respectful of differences. We must all honor and appreciate diversity if we are to fulfill the dream of a pluralistic society based on equity and social justice.[1]

So that brings us back to the question: What do you do when you are having a cultural conflict with a family? First, become aware that you are in a cultural conflict. Because we all tend to look at any situation from our own point of view, it may

---

[1]Stanley Sue and Thom Moore (1984) make a good case for why the United States should be a pluralistic society; they do a good job of defining and describing such a society.

Scott Cunningham/Merrill

very hard to understand another person's frame of reference, which, of course, is cultural. All of us are ethnocentric—that is, we look out of our own cultural eyes and measure others with our own cultural yardstick. It takes awareness and skill to move from our ethnocentric position.

Dialoguing, as has been mentioned previously, is an approach to problem solving a conflict that is effective at helping the disagreeing parties see each other's point of view. Rather than trying to convince another of one's own viewpoint, people engaged in dialogue try to understand the other perspective. The idea is not to win but to find the best solution for all concerned.

The following list summarizes the differences between an argument and a dialogue:

Dialoguing is an approach to problem solving a conflict that is effective at helping the disagreeing parties see each other's point of view.

- The object of an argument is to win; the object of a dialogue is to gather information.
- The arguer tells; the dialoguer asks.
- The arguer tries to persuade; the dialoguer seeks to learn.
- The arguer tries to convince; the dialoguer wants to discover.
- The arguer sees two opposing views and considers hers the valid or best one; the dialoguer is willing to understand multiple viewpoints.

Most people are better at argument than they are at dialogue. When faced with a conflict or problem, almost nobody considers starting a dialogue. Especially when it is an emotional conflict, many people are likely to jump feet-first into an argument rather than begin a dialogue. When they argue, they are anxious to win, which makes them leap to conclusions.

If you watch people arguing, you can see some types of body language that show each person is trying to convince the other of something. When arguing, many people tend to stand firm and tough when listening—assuming a defensive position. They are anything but open. They seem to be just waiting for their turn. When they talk, they lean forward and make aggressive gestures with their hands. Just by looking at them, even if you can't hear their words, you can tell that they are fighting about something. The body language of someone in a potentially win-lose situation is different from someone who is truly trying to understand another point of view, such as happens when people enter a dialogue. Gestures reflect their attitude—hands, especially. Instead of waving fists or making strong, tense movements, dialoguing people tend to let their hands remain open.

So how does one switch from an argument to a dialogue in the heat of the moment? Start by noticing your body language. Sometimes you can just change your body language, and an energy switch will follow. Then it's a matter of doing one simple thing: listening to the other person. To truly listen, one must suspend judgments and focus on what's being said rather than just gathering ammunition for the next attack. Really hearing someone is extremely simple, but it's not easy.

From then on it's a matter of working through a problem-solving procedure. One procedure for problem solving is called RERUN: the letters stand for reflect, explain, reason, understand, and negotiate.

- *Reflect.*   This is the action of acknowledging what you perceive the other person is thinking or feeling. If you understand where the person is coming from, say, "I think you're looking at it this way . . . ." Or if you perceive that the person is full of emotion, acknowledge your perception: "You really sound upset." Those two openers are invitations for the person to talk some more. People who know that their feelings and thoughts are received and accepted by you are likely to be more open to listening—if not right away, eventually. Reflect also includes self-reflection. If you can get in touch with your own feelings you may gain insights about why you have the perspective you have. Strong feelings may indicate something left over from your childhood that is keeping you from being rational about this conflict.
- *Explain.*   Remember, we have two ears and only one mouth; that's a reminder that we should listen twice as much as we talk. Only after you have listened, listened, and listened again is it time to explain your point of view.
- *Reason.*   Part of the explanation should include the reason you have for your perspective. If you are being entirely honest with yourself, the reason you are in this conflict may not be entirely rationally but may be emotional. That's okay, but recognizing that you have hot buttons that put you in conflicts is the first step to doing something about them.
- *Understand.*   Next comes the hardest part. Tune in to both thoughts and feelings and try to understand the situation from both points of view. You don't have to say anything out loud at this point; just be sure you have clarity. You may have to talk inwardly to yourself to get it. And while you're going inward, make sure you understand yourself as well as the other person. Self-reflection is an important part of the process. When you think you understand, you're ready for the next step.
- *Negotiate.*   Now is the time for the finale. Try brainstorming together until you can find a mutually satisfying solution. Don't give up. Refuse to take an either-or attitude. ("It's either my way or your way, and it can't be both ways.") If you don't get stuck in a dualistic frame of mind, you can probably find a third or fourth solution that is different from or combines both your stances on the matter. Creative negotiators can open up new avenues of action that no one ever thought of before. Bredekamp and Copple (1997) point out that thinking in terms of either one

solution or the other keeps us from communicating across cultures. We need to move into a "both-and" mode. Isaura Barrera, in *Skilled Dialogue* (Barrera & Corso, 2003), calls the move away from dualistic thinking "third space." She says that third space goes beyond compromise and includes both positions. It's not a meeting in the middle, but finding a different space altogether that is big enough to encompass more perspectives and a larger view of truth.

The finale is seldom final. In only the simplest situations do you negotiate an agreement without communication breaking down. When feelings arise, return to the beginning. Go back through the first four (R-E-R-U) parts. You may have to R-E-R-U-N many times before the problem is solved. Be patient.

Strategy Box 6.1 shows how to use the RERUN process with a parent who is concerned that with independence and self-help skills stressed in this program, her

Strategy Box 6.1

Working with a Family Member Using the RERUN Strategy

- Reflect what you perceive the other person might be thinking or feeling. With such words as, it seems like you are uncomfortable with the way we do mealtimes here. Listen carefully to what her response is. Accept what she says without arguing. See if you can keep the conversation going so you truly understand her perspective.
- The reflect component of this RERUN process also includes self reflection. Try to become aware of why you have the particular perspective you have and any emotional issues around it.
- Explain. Only when you have a good idea of the other person's perspective and an awareness of what's behind your own, then is the time to clarify the way your mealtimes work.
- Reason. Give the reason(s) why they are that way. Try hard to do both the explanation and give the reason without being argumentative or defensive. The idea is to create a dialogue so you can continue to discuss your differences without stopping the conversation.
- Understand. When you can see the situation from both points of view and are able to explore it clearly without defensiveness or judgments, then you are ready to see if you and the other person can find common ground. You may have to try looking for different words to use other than the ones you both started out with. This is called reframing. You need to understand in order to reframe.
- Negotiate. Only when you can understand the other person's perspective and you have helped her understand yours can you figure out what to do about your differences. The ultimate negotiation process ends with neither side feeling they had to "give in." Creative negotiators can open up new avenues of action that no one ever thought of before.

child is left to eat on her own. She thinks her child needs more adult help to get the food into her in a neat, clean, non-wasteful manner.

Often, instead of taking time to really work through something, we get impatient and reach into the old hip holster and pull out a power play if we have one. It's unfortunate when that happens because one-upmanship destroys relationships rather than strengthening them. It may take a long time to solve a particular problem when the conflict is deep and serious, but a positive outcome in the form of a solution everyone is satisfied with is worth the time and effort it sometimes takes.

Though the RERUN device seems to consist of distinct steps or a sequence to follow, the elements are more holistic than that. They come as a package and may occur in a different order or all mixed up as one. The fact that the acronym spells *rerun* serves as a reminder that you can repeat the process as often as necessary until the problem is solved—you come to an agreement, or you agree to carry on while disagreeing.

A Cultural Conflict

Helen is a vegetarian. When she put her daughter, Sissy, into child care, she had a talk with the director to explain her dietary beliefs. The director explained to her that the center's food was catered and that the protein was usually a meat dish. She suggested that Sissy be served everything but the meat and that Helen supplement with some kind of protein dish. Helen agreed, and everything went well for awhile.

Then the director moved on and a new director was hired. Sissy moved up from the younger group to the older group, and that meant a new teacher. Helen got busy one morning and forgot to send Sissy's protein dish. No one complained, including Sissy, so before long Helen was dropping her daughter off in the morning without the supplemental food. She assumed that her daughter was getting enough to eat without it.

Then one day Helen took the afternoon off and arrived at lunchtime to pick up her daughter. She was horrified to find Sissy sitting at the table with the other children, chewing happily on a chicken drumstick. She looked around to see who was responsible and found a substitute in charge. She complained to the substitute and then thought the matter was settled.

However, a few weeks later Sissy talked about the fish sticks she had had for lunch. Helen stormed into the center, demanding to see the director.

The director pushed herself back from her desk and its huge pile of paperwork and invited Helen to sit down. Angrily, Helen threw herself into a chair, launching into a bitter tirade. When she finally paused for breath, the director said, with concern in her voice and in her facial expression, "I see how upset you are about this!"

That got Helen going again. When she paused, the director said that she wanted Sissy's teacher in on the discussion and went to get her.

When the three of them sat down together, Helen was calmer. "Why did you feed Sissy meat?" she demanded of the teacher.

"I didn't—only fish. I know she doesn't eat red meat," answered the teacher.

"She doesn't eat any kind of meat," Helen shot back.

The teacher looked surprised. "I didn't realize you considered fish meat."

"And chicken!" added Helen.

"Oh!" responded the teacher, biting her lip. "I'm sorry," she went on. "It's just that Sissy always seems so hungry, like she can't really get full on the fruits and vegetables alone. I feel sorry for her."

The conversation went on—give and take—and slowly the facts and feelings on both sides began to emerge. The teacher's misunderstanding about what Helen considered meat gave way to her feelings about Sissy feeling hungry and left out as the other children enjoyed hamburgers and hot dogs and other foods forbidden to Sissy. She was obviously not committed to vegetarianism herself, and it was hard for her to see why Helen felt so strongly about it. She even questioned whether a vegetarian diet was a properly nutritious one for a child.

Helen in turn confessed that she had some resentment that children with food allergies were carefully monitored and given special consideration, yet no one seemed to care what Sissy ate. She felt the program should individualize more.

For awhile it looked as if these two might never see eye to eye, yet once the feelings got out in the open, the atmosphere began to change. It became obvious that both were concerned about Sissy, and once they realized that they had that in common, they found it wasn't so hard to sort out the problem and solve it. Respect and communication were the keys, they decided; and when the conversation ended, they both left with good feelings about each other.

The suggestions that follow for working on cross-cultural communication are inspired by Louise Derman-Sparks (1989) and her Antibias Task Force. These tips are designed to help facilitate communication in a cultural conflict involving values, goals, and early childhood child-rearing and educational practices.

Build Relationships

People who have good relationships are more likely to work on their conflicts in more healthy ways. Relationships sometimes just happen, but more often, they need to be initiated and then nurtured. Commit yourself to working constantly on the total relationship, not just the conflict.

Know Yourself

Be clear about what you believe in. Be aware of your own values and goals. Check to see whether your behavior reflects your values and goals. If you are in tune with yourself and are clear about what you believe in, you're less likely to present a strong defensive stance in the face of conflict. It is when we feel ambiguous that we come on the strongest.

Work to Bring Differences Out in the Open

Be sensitive to your own discomfort in response to the behavior of others. Tune in on something that bothers you, instead of just ignoring it and hoping it will go away.

Work to identify what specific behaviors of others make you uncomfortable. Try to discover exactly what in yourself creates this discomfort.

You need to be honest with yourself and to do some soul-searching to get your prejudices out in the open. None of us likes to do that, but it's an important part of relationships and clear communication.

While you're looking at yourself, look for signs of discomfort in other people in response to your behavior. When you discover discomfort, talk about it!

Discuss Differences

Discussing differences isn't easy to do. Some people shy away from direct discussion of sensitive areas. Many want to cover up differences because they perceive that recognizing them will complicate the relationship. Others avoid discussion of differences in hopes of promoting equality and harmony. Some have never thought about values until they bump up against a set that is different from their own.

Become an Effective Cross-Cultural Communicator

Learn how to open up communication instead of shutting it down. Work to build a relationship with the person or the people with whom you're in conflict. You'll enhance your chances for conflict management or resolution if a relationship exists. Be patient. These things take time.

Learn about communication styles that are different from yours. Teach your own communication styles. Become aware of body language, voice tone, posture, and position. All of these carry cultural messages that are open to being misinterpreted across cultures. For example, if you're a teacher, and a parent stands too close to you when carrying on a conversation, you may feel that she is pushy or at least strange, whereas she may think she is conveying warmth and friendliness. If a parent is very late to an appointment and then arrives and fails to apologize, you may make assumptions about his priorities or his manners. But he may have a very different time sense from yours and not consider himself late at all. He may have no idea that he has offended you.

If you tend to talk in a high-pitched voice when you are excited, and others interpret your tone of voice as anger, explain to them what you're really feeling. (Pitches and tones carry emotional messages that are culturally based and not the same across cultures.)

Problem Solve

Use a problem-solving approach to conflicts rather than a power approach (if you're the one with the power in the situation). Dialogue. Communicate. Be flexible when you can. Negotiate when possible. (See Chapter 8 for examples of how to use this approach with children.) Notice when you are getting defensive. Defensiveness gets in the way of problem solving. Defensiveness indicates that you have some kind of emotional issue around this conflict. That may be something you need to sort out and understand.

Commit Yourself to Education

Learn about other cultures. Become a student of culture if you are in a cross-cultural situation. You don't have to become an anthropologist, but you can use some of the anthropologist's approaches to studying a culture. Read, but don't believe everything you read. Check it out. Observe and listen. Ask, but don't believe everything you are told. Check it out. You'll hear lots of generalizations about particular cultures. Don't get sucked into promoting more stereotypes! Discuss what you are seeing, hearing, reading, and being told with other people of the culture you are learning about. Be a critical thinker.

HELPING CHILDREN UNDERSTAND AND VALUE CULTURAL PLURALISM

Just as adults are ethnocentric, so are children. Ethnocentrism relates to the egocentrism that young children struggle with as they slowly learn to see the world from more than one point of view. Adults need to help children work through both their ethnocentrism and their egocentrism. Adults can do that only if they have grappled with their own ethnocentrism. It's a matter of getting children to communicate with each other, accept the reality of another as valid, and learn what it's like to walk in another's shoes.

Some books focus on multicultural or antibias education for children. This book has only a small section on that subject, because this book focuses more on the effect of the adults in children's lives. It doesn't do any good to teach children about equity and social justice and then hope they will grow up and make the world a better place. We can't wait. We need to be working on ourselves, so we can be models for children about how to do what we hope they will

Laura Zahner

Sensitivity to, understanding of, and respect for differences are vital.

learn. Giving lessons to children about getting along across cultures won't work if they look around and see that the adults in their lives aren't treating each other with respect. They won't learn about equity if they learn that some people who are doing the same job as other people are getting lower pay. There is lots to be done to reach a greater level of equity and social justice and it's not up to children to do it. It's up to us—the adults!

Some children come from a multicultural background and have firsthand experience with cultural pluralism. They may already be good at crossing cultures. This can be a great benefit for them and for those around them who can use them as models. When we see a person who is comfortable operating out of more than one culture, we gain an idea of how it works.

Here is an example of a bicultural child:

David was born in the United States of a Mexican father and an European-American mother. The family traveled frequently to Mexico and enjoyed extended visits with the father's family. By the time David entered preschool at the age of 4, he was already bilingual and bicultural. He could perform amazing feats, such as making a judgment about which language to speak with someone he met for the first time. He was seldom wrong. He could also switch midstream from English to Spanish when the occasion demanded. For example, if he was playing in the sand with an English-speaking child and a Spanish-speaking child approached, David would speak English with one and Spanish with the other, while playing with both. David fits very well in an all-European-American group or an all-Mexican group or a Mexican-American group. He has chameleon-like qualities. He is a truly bicultural person.

Children have the ability to compartmentalize—that is, to understand that one set of behaviors is appropriate at Grandmother's, another at child care, another at school, and still another at home. Although we, as adults, may try hard to make most of the environments children find themselves in consistent, that's not the way the world works. One set of behaviors is expected in the bank, another at the park. Part of socialization is learning how to behave in each of the many environments in which children find themselves. Learning culturally appropriate behavior is one aspect of this same skill.

LOOKING BACK AND LOOKING FOWARD

This chapter looked at goals and values, from a particular framework. Called pattern 1 and 2, they represent differing priorities not often discussed, but found in families as well as in early care and education programs. Pattern 1 focuses on independence. Pattern 1 people tend to teach children that they are separate individuals. Pattern 2 focuses on interdependence. Pattern 2 people tend to down play individualism and instead have a group orientation. They tend to teach children that connections are the most important part of life. Of course, most families and programs combine elements of both perspectives, but when a strong pattern 1 infant care teacher or early educator meets up with a strong pattern 2 family, conflicts can result. The two patterns can strongly affect child rearing, care, and education practices in both the home and the child care center. This theme has implications for the next chapter which is about guiding the behavior of young children.

FOR DISCUSSION

1. What did you think of the two contrasting patterns in this chapter? Do you or someone you know fit one or the other of these patterns? Which pattern do you think is more likely to emphasize modesty over pride? Why? Which pattern do you think is likely to emphasize manners over honest self-expression? Why?

2. Some people say that to talk about cultural *conflicts* creates a different mindset than if you think of them as cultural bumps or cultural dilemmas. How might different wording change the picture of what is happening when two people or two groups disagree? Can you think of other examples of when a change of vocabulary made a difference?

3. Although the title of one of this chapter's boxes, "A Cultural Conflict," indicates that the difference between the parent and the teacher is a cultural one, nothing in the story shows that the two are of different cultures. Does it matter? Is it important to know whether diversity is related to culture, religion, family traditions, or just individual differences? If yes, how might a teacher respond differently after learning what was at the root of the issue?

4. The cultures in this chapter are not labeled. Does that frustrate you? Why do you think the author chose to deal with patterns rather than particular cultural differences? Why do you find no lists in this book of typical characteristics of the most common cultures in the United States and Canada today?

5. What are some of the factors in children's lives that work against their prosocial development?

WEB SITES

Clearinghouse on Early Education and Parenting (CEEP)
http://ceep.crc.uiuc.edu/
The Clearinghouse on Early Education and Parenting has print and online resources for the worldwide early childhood and parenting communities. Use the search button and type in *Cultural Differences in Child Rearing* and find an abundance of resources.

Early Childhood Care and Development
http://www.ecdgroup.com
This site, Early Childhood Care and Development: International Resources in Support of Young Children (ages 0–8) and Their Families, has resources and a library to expand views of cultural differences.

National Association for Bilingual Education
http://www.nabe.org
An organization for bilingual teachers and English teachers who teach English learners. Dedicated to the pursuit of excellent conditions and education for all English language learners and speakers of more than one language.

National Association for the Education of Young Children (NAEYC)
http://www.naeyc.org
The National Association for the Education of Young Children has focused on cultural differences in journal articles in *Young Children* and other publications to be found on the Web site.

National Association for Multicultural Education

http://www.nameorg.org

Advocates for educational equity and social justice. Two goals are to respect and appreciate cultural diversity and to promote the understanding of unique cultural and ethnic heritage.

Program for Infant/Toddler Caregivers (PITC)

http://www.pitc.org

The Program for Infant/Toddler Care has one of it's 6 cornerstones to honor and respect diversity in families, children, and staff. Culturally responsive care is a goal. Web site has resources to promote that goal.

Webster's World of Cultural Democracy

http://www.wwcd.org/action/ampu/crosscult.html

This article, on the Webster's World of Cultural Democracy Web site, presents six fundamental patterns of cultural difference, respecting differences, and working together and cites guidelines for multicultural collaboration.

WestEd: Culture and Language in Education Research

http://www.wested.org/cle/-

WestEd's CLE department has a goal of enhancing the capacity of learning organizations to provide excellent education for traditionally underserved students.

The World Forum on Early Care and Education Foundation

http://www.worldforumfoundation.org

A collaborative effort to bring early care and education professionals from around the world together. Started by *Exchange* Magazine, as an annual conference, the organization now has expanded to working forums and projects.

Zero to Three

http://www.zerotothree.org

Zero to Three: National Center for Infants, Toddlers, and Families, for parents and professionals, is a leading resource on the first three years of life to promote diversity and the healthy development of babies and toddlers.

FURTHER READING

Akbar, N. (2003). *Akbar papers in African psychology.* Tallahassee: Mind Productions.

Allen, P. G. (1998). *Off the reservation.* Boston: Beacon.

Bandtec Network for Diversity Training. (2003). *Reaching for answers: A workbook on diversity in early childhood education.* Oakland, California: Bandtec Network for Diversity Training. Available at the Bandtec Web site (www.bandtec.org).

Barrera, I., & Corso, R. (2003). *Skilled dialog.* Baltimore: Brookes.

Bhavnagri, N. P., & Gonzalez-Mena, J. (1997, Fall). The cultural context of caregiving. *Childhood Education, 74*(1), 2–8.

Brody, H. (2001). *The other side of Eden: Hunters, farmers, and the shaping of the world.* New York: North Point Press.

Bruno, H. E. (2003, September–October). Hearing parents in every language: An invitation to ECE professionals. *Child Care Information Exchange, 153*, 58–60.

Carlebach, D., & Tate, B. (2002). *Creating caring children: The first three years.* Miami: Peace Education Foundation.

Chang, H. N., & Sakai, L. (1993). *Affirming children's roots: Cultural and linguistic diversity in early care and education.* San Francisco: California Tomorrow.

Chao, R. (1994). Beyond parental control and authoritarian parenting style: Understanding Chinese parenting through the cultural notion of training. *Child Development, 65*, 1111–1119.

Chen, X., Rubin, K., Gen, G., Hastings, P., Chen, H., & Stewart, S. (1998). Child-rearing attitudes and behavioral inhibition in Chinese and Canadian toddlers: A cross-cultural study. *Developmental Psychology, 34*(4), 677–686.

Coll, C. G., Lamberty, G., Jenkins, R., McAdoo, H. P., Crnic, K., Wasik, B., Hanna, G., & Vazquez, H. (1996). An integrative model for the study of developmental competencies in minority children. *Child Development, 67*, 1891–1914.

David, M., & Appell, G. (2001[1973, 1996]). *Loczy: An unusual approach to mothering.* Translated from *Loczy ou le maternage insolite,* by Jean Marie Clark; revised translation by Judit Falk. Budapest: Association Pikler-Loczy for Young Children.

Delpit, L. (1995). *Other people's children: Cultural conflict in the classroom.* New York: New Press.

Delpit, L., & Dowdy, J. K. (2002). *The skin that we speak: Thoughts on language and culture in the classroom.* New York: New Press.

Eggers-Pierola, C. (2002). *Connections and commitments: A Latino-based framework for early childhood educators.* Newton, MA: Educational Development Center.

Ellison, S. (1998). *Don't be so defensive!* Kansas City, MO: Andrews McMeel.

Epstein, J. L. (2006, January). Families, schools, and community partnerships. *Young Children,* 61(1), 40.

Fadiman, A. (1997). *The spirit catches you and you fall down: A Hmong child, her American doctors, and the collision of two cultures.* New York: Noonday.

Fernea, E. W. (1995). *Children in the Muslim Middle East.* Austin: University of Texas Press.

Friend, M., & Cook, L. (2003). *Interactions: Collaboration skills for school professionals* (4th ed.). Boston: Allyn & Bacon.

Garcia, E. E., & McLaughlin, B. (Eds.). (With B. Spokek & O. N. Saracho). (1995). *Meeting the challenge of linguistic and cultural diversity in early childhood education.* New York: Teachers College Press.

Gerber, M. (1998). *Dear parent: Caring for infants with respect.* Los Angeles: Resources for Infant Educarers.

Goldenberg, C., Gallimore, R., & Reese, L. (2003). Cause or effect? A longitudinal study of immigrant Latino parents' aspirations and expectations, and their children's school performance. *American Educational Research Journal,* 38, 547–582.

Gonzalez-Mena, J. (1994, May). Learning to see across a cultural gap. *Child Care Information Exchange,* 97, 65–68.

Gonzalez-Mena, J. (1999, July). Dialogue to understanding across cultures. *Exchange,* 128, 6–8.

Gonzalez-Mena, J. (2008). *Diversity in early care and education.* New York: McGraw-Hill.

Hale, J. (1991, September). The transmission of cultural values to young African American children. *Young Children,* 46(6), 7–15.

Hale, J. E. (1992). An African-American early childhood education program: Visions for children.

In S. A. Kessler & B. B. Swadener (Eds.), *Reconceptualizing the early childhood curriculum: Beginning the dialogue* (pp. 205–224). New York: Teachers College Press.

Hall, E. T. (1977). *Beyond culture.* Garden City, NY: Anchor.

Hall, E. T. (1984). *The dance of life.* Garden City, NY: Anchor/Doubleday.

Harkness, S., & Super, C. M. (Eds.). (1996). *Parents' cultural belief systems.* New York: Guilford.

Hyun, E. (1998). *Making sense of developmentally and culturally appropriate practice (DCAP) in early childhood education.* New York: Lang.

Kagiticibasi, C. (1996). *Family and human development across cultures.* Mahwah, NJ: Erlbaum.

Kendall, F. (1996). *Diversity in the classroom.* New York: Teachers College Press.

Knight, G. P., Bernal, M. E., & Carlo, G. (1995). Socialization and the development of co-operative, competitive, and individualistic behaviors among Mexican American children. In E. E. Garcia & B. McLaughlin (Eds.), *Meeting the challenge of linguistic and cultural diversity in early childhood education* (pp. 85–102). New York: Teachers College Press.

Kochman, T. (1981). *Black and white: Styles in conflict.* Chicago: University of Chicago Press.

Lee, L. (1997, July). Working with non-English-speaking families. *Exchange,* 116, 57–58.

Lewis, C. C. (1995). *Educating hearts and minds: Reflections on Japanese preschool and elementary education.* New York: Cambridge University Press.

Lubeck, S. (1996). Deconstructing "child development knowledge" and "teacher preparation." *Early Childhood Research Quarterly,* 11(2), 147–168.

Makin, L., Campbell, J., & Diaz, C. J. (1995). *One childhood, many languages.* Pymble, Australia: HarperEducational.

Mallory, B. L., & New, R. S. (Eds.). (1994). *Diversity and developmentally appropriate practices: Challenges for early childhood education.* New York: Teachers College Press.

Morelli, G., Rogoff, B., & Oppenheim, D. (1992, July). Cultural variation in infants' sleeping arrangements: Questions of independence. *Developmental Psychology,* 28 (4), 604–619.

National Association for the Education of Young Children. (1996, January). Linguistic and cultural diversity position paper. *Young Children*, 51 (2), 4–12.

Patterson, K., Grenny, J., McMillan, R., Switzer, A., & Covey, S. R. (2002). *Crucial conversations: Tools for talking when the stakes are high*. New York: McGraw-Hill.

Payne, R. K. (2003). *A framework for understanding poverty*. Highlands, TX: Aha Process.

Poussaint, A. F. (2006 January). Understanding and involving African American parents. *Young Children*, 61(1), 48.

Powers, J. (2006 January). Six fundamentals for creating relationships with families. *Young Children*, 61 (1), 28.

Raeff, C., Greenfield, P. M., & Quiroz, B. (2000, Spring). Conceptualizing interpersonal relationships in the cultural contexts of individualism and collectivism. *New Directions for Child and Adolescent Development*, 87, 59–74.

Reese, L. (2002). Parental strategies in contrasting cultural settings: Families in Mexico and El Norte. *Anthropology & Education Quarterly*, 33, 30–59.

Rogoff, B. (2003). *The cultural nature of human development*. New York: Oxford University Press.

Rogoff, B., Stott, F., & Bowman, B. (1996). Child development knowledge: A slippery base for practice. *Early Childhood Research Quarterly*, 11 (2), 1169–1184.

Rothstein-Fisch, C. (2003). *Readings for bridging cultures: Teacher education module*. Mahwah, NJ: Erlbaum.

Russell, J. A., & Yik, M. S. M. (1996). Emotion among the Chinese. In M. H. Bond (Ed.), *The handbook of Chinese psychology* (pp. 166–188). Hong Kong: Oxford University Press.

Small, M. (1998). *Our babies, ourselves: How biology and culture shape the way we parent*. New York: Anchor.

Some, S. (2000). *The spirit of intimacy: Ancient African teachings in the ways of relationships*. New York: HarperCollins/Quill.

Stipek, D. (1998). Differences between Americans and Chinese in the circumstances evoking pride, shame, and guilt. *Journal of Cross-Cultural Psychology*, 29(5), 616–629.

Tan, A. L. (2004). *Chinese American children and families: A guide for educators and service providers*. Onley, MD: Association for Childhood Education International.

Tobaissen, D. P., & Gonzalez-Mena, J. (1998). *A place to begin: Working with parents on issues of diversity*. Oakland: California Tomorrow.

Trumbull, E., Rothstein-Fisch, C., & Greenfield, P. M., (2000). *Bridging cultures in our schools: New approaches that work*. Knowledge Brief. San Francisco: WestEd.

White, E. (Qoyawayma, P.). (1992). *No turning back: A Hopi woman's struggle to live in two worlds*. Albuquerque, NM: University of New Mexico Press.

Wu, D. (1996). Chinese childhood socialization. In M. H. Bond (Ed.), *The handbook of Chinese psychology* (pp. 143–154). Hong Kong: Oxford University Press.

CHAPTER 7

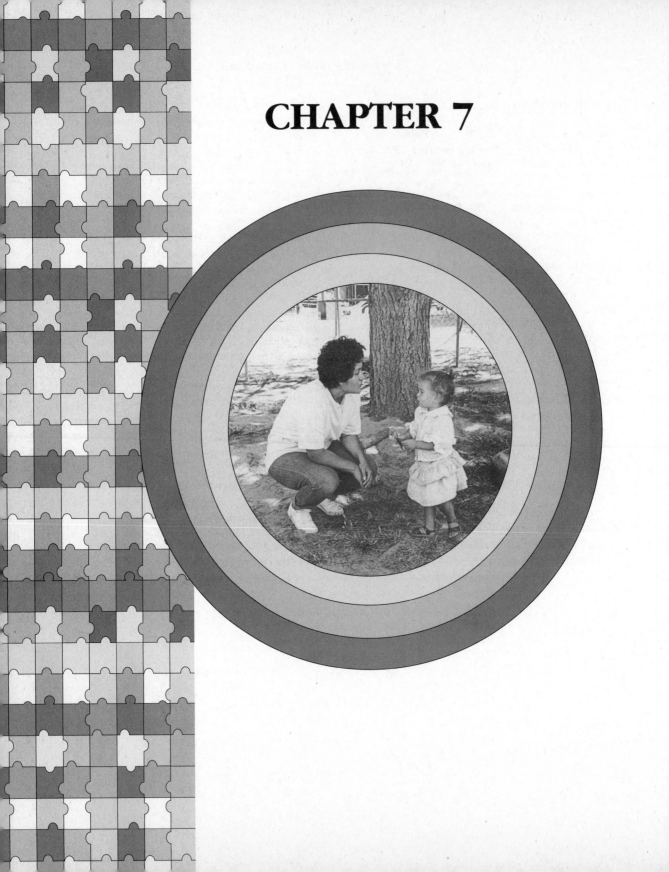

Working with Families on Guidance Issues

In *this chapter you'll discover* . . .

- ◆ Ideas about guidance and discipline you might not have thought about before
- ◆ Suggestions of ways to work with parents around guidance and discipline approaches
- ◆ Ways to prevent children's misbehavior
- ◆ How to respond positively to children's negative behavior
- ◆ The difference between using punishment and consequences with children
- ◆ When time-out is useful and when it's not
- ◆ Why you might want to ignore children's unacceptable behavior sometimes

How do you work with families around the behavior of their children in ways that are comfortable for everybody? Guidance is a hot topic with lots of emotions attached to it. Sometimes those emotions are because of the adults' own childhoods, sometimes because of cultural differences, and sometimes because people haven't thought through their approaches to guidance.

Individuals and groups have differing ideas about basic human nature, and their ideas influence their approaches to dealing with what they deem as unacceptable behavior in children. I illustrate this in classes and workshops by saying we are going to talk about human nature, focusing on the child. I then create an imaginary line and ask participants to place themselves on it. At one end the child is represented as a flower—at the other end as a tree. I explain the flower end by saying the child is like a seed. When planted in good soil and nurtured, it grows. The potential of a beautiful flower is in the seed and all it that is necessary is for it to get its needs met. On the other end is the tree. It also has its potential built-in and must have its needs met to grow; however, to have a tall, straight, shade-giving tree you must clip and prune. If it just grows wild it can look very different—crooked or ugly with crowded limbs that encroach on each other. "As the twig is pruned so grows the tree," is an old saying that relates to this end of the continuum.

To make the metaphors more dramatic, I sometimes point to the flower and say that a baby is like an angel—full of good. Inside is a benevolent guiding force and with love and nurturing the baby will grow up fine. At the other end is a devil baby—born bad—ready for trouble. The guiding force inside is very different from the angel baby.

When participants place themselves on imaginary line of the continuum, most cluster toward the middle, though some are out toward the ends. People toward the flower/angel end are usually those who have taken child development classes and are well trained in early childhood education. They say that the baby *unfolds* in the way he or she was designed to unfold. It's a natural process and a beautiful one, like a rosebud opening. They may have been influenced by the very word *development*, which means unfold. People at the other end of the spectrum have a different view and are usually cynical about the rosy picture painted at the opposite end. They also see a driving force from within, but one that puts temptations and obstacles in the way of positive growth. It, too, is a natural process—but one that needs constant monitoring and intervention if it is to result in a desirable end product. Children are not naturally born pure and good; they cannot be allowed just to unfold according to their human nature. The words vary with the person's philosophical stance or religious background, but what is clear is that the child's sense of direction is not always toward the good. If the child is to turn out okay, he or she needs a good firm adult hand to stay on the right path. Some say that it's more natural to be bad than it is to be good. *Sin* is a word that comes up in this discussion.

Once in a while there's a participant who refuses to stand on the continuum at all and protests that there is no basic human nature, natural unfolding, or driving force. What counts is how the environment shapes a person. This person explains that the way to get the child to behave the way you want is through careful attention to and manipulation of the rewards the child receives. This is a "behaviorist" view and it is detached from such concepts as "bad" and "good." Behaviors are more likely to be seen as acceptable or unacceptable rather than branded with moral judgments.

All of these views are simplistic. In reality, development is more dynamic and involves a much more complex picture. Children grow and change through a complicated process composed of many interacting elements, some that can be controlled and others that cannot. Keep that in mind as you read through this chapter on guidance. A *dynamic* theoretical view of growth and development makes it clear that behavior is the result of the interplay of the child (and his or her individual genetic makeup) with culture, developmental stage, environmental input, and the natural inclination to imitate or model after others. The perspective on which this chapter is based takes into consideration the dynamic interplay of all these forces. It also urges you to understand that not everybody has the same perspective and to honor differences.

DEFINING THE WORD DISCIPLINE

Discipline is a loaded word. For years, early childhood experts tried to remove it from the vocabulary of teachers, caregivers, and parents, substituting the word *guidance* instead. But too many parents and educators were uncomfortable with what they considered the lack of discipline being advocated by the experts (*guidance* just didn't do it); so the word has refused to die.

Why did the experts want to change the word *discipline* to *guidance*? It has to do with the associations connected with each word. *Guidance* has a more positive tone to it. To many people, *discipline* means punishment, and punishment means pain or at least humiliation. But it doesn't have to be that way! If you look up the word in the dictionary you find that discipline and disciple come from the same root word. Think of two people walking along a path—a big person and a little one—a master and a disciple. Discipline might mean punishment to some, but it can also mean guiding and managing behavior, not through punishment but by being attached to a more experienced partner. This partner is someone who is wiser, knows more, and has lived longer than the child. Eventually children internalize the master or the older partner and take charge of themselves. This development of *inner controls*, or self-discipline, is the goal of disciplining children.

That is one way of looking at what children need in the way of guidance. I and many others in the field of early childhood education come from a culture that emphasizes independence and individuality, so it is important to internalize the control. There are other cultural views. For example, in some cultures, as mentioned in previous chapters, the emphasis is not on individuality but on being part of the group. Although the partner image may still work, it works in a different way. The idea of "inner controls" at an early age may not be a priority, according to Janice Hale (1986), a longtime advocate for cultural sensitivity to African American children. Hale says that discipline in many African American families depends on what she calls an "external locus of control." She describes how adults in the black community play a social-control role by creating a network of people who firmly correct behavior and report misbehavior to the parent. Therefore, parents are at the center of this social-control network. For the child, this means that he or she is always under the surveillance of adults. The significant feature of the control system is that it seems to operate externally to the child. Therefore, the child seems to develop an external locus of control.

Hale sees a conflict for children when teachers give children responsibility for their own behavior. She says that in schools where adults often behave as if they expect children to monitor themselves without outside help, the children's behavior may be labeled as problematic. The adults aren't functioning in the ways children expect, so the system the children are used to is not present to guide their behavior.

Snowden (1984) also writes about cultural differences between African American and European American child rearing. Like Hale, Snowden explains how in many African American families responsibility for the control of children's behavior is in the hands of an extensive network of adults. Snowden sees this approach as one of extended parenting, which ensures that children's behavior receives closer monitoring and results in more immediate sanctions than is the norm in the dominant culture. Children feel free to actively explore and take on assertive styles, because they know someone will be there to stop them when they go too far. But most adults in charge of educational programs for children, including school, don't have the same direct and straightforward control over children's behavior. They expect children to be passive and immobile, which many African American children are not. According to Snowden, the cultural conflict is clearly drawn.

Some of these examples relate to different ideas about authority, about how authority figures should behave and how children should relate to authority (Phillips 1995). When authority figures behave in ways that aren't familiar to children, the children can feel confused. Some children are used to firm, strict, and sometimes physical guidance, and without it they keep testing the limits. They may even come to the conclusion that the teacher doesn't care what they do. These children can end up labeled as problem children (Hale, 1986; Gonzalez-Mena & Shareef, 2005). Ideas about discipline and guidance get extremely complex when they intersect with culture and oppression. Some groups of people who are targets of racism have to protect their children from the oppressive practices of racist individuals and institutions. Their methods of guidance and discipline may be different from those of groups for whom oppression is just a word. Ideas about what's best for children can vary greatly and be influenced by history and experience, not just by culture alone.

Ballenger (1992, 1999) describes her work with Haitian preschool teachers and Haitian children. She sees a system of guidance that does stress inner controls, but not the way this chapter has described them. Children are not encouraged to reason out behavior choices. They aren't expected to learn from consequences of those choices. In the system Ballenger describes, children are taught to be good by appealing to their emotional connections to family and teachers.

Sandoval and De La Roza (1986) discuss the way extended family and inter-dependent network orientation work to provide external controls in the Hispanic community. They describe how the mother constantly gives directives to young children, even when they are not misbehaving. It is a way of letting them know that they are constantly being watched and that her "protective eyes" are on them. These constant directives given in public are ways to let others engage in the social control of the children. Anyone who sees children getting into trouble is expected to stop them and treat them as if they were their own.

We can learn from each other, but only if we become aware of what we are doing and begin to discuss our behavior with people who are different from ourselves. Eggers-Pierola (2005) gives advice about how to have these discussions with Latino families. One of the advantages for children in early childhood education programs is that parents can learn from each other and from the early educators.

One approach to guidance that some learn when they become early childhood educators or when they enter early childhood programs as parents is called a *consequences approach*. Often used in early childhood programs, the approach is consid-ered an empowering one. Children are allowed to make *choices* about their behavior, within limits. Sometimes those choices lead to uncomfortable or undesirable *consequences*. The choices and the consequences are controlled by the adult so that they don't involve any real risk or harm for the child. But some consequences can still be emotionally painful. It may seem as if using a consequences approach is the same as using punishment, but it is not. Suffering the consequences of your own choices feels different from being punished because someone bigger or more powerful than you decides to punish. Punishment, the time-honored approach to teaching children acceptable behavior, has some side effects that parents, teachers, caregivers, and family child care providers should be aware of.

PROBLEMS WITH USING PUNISHMENT TO TEACH

One problem with punishment is the negativity that accompanies it. Often the adult uses punishment to get even, which triggers a spirit of retaliation on the part of the child. This starts a vicious circle that ends only when one or the other triumphs, sometimes leaving quite a path of destruction in the wake of the conflict. Children who are frequently punished become more devious, not more cooperative. They respond to the hurt, loss, or penalty (the punishment) with anger, resentment, and defiance. Thus, punishment prevents the building of good relationships that are the basis of effective discipline and causes resentment and the urge to strike back.

Children who are punished for trying things out and making mistakes in the process can become inhibited in their development of autonomy and initiative. The urge to explore and experiment is squelched when punishment hangs over a child's head. Learning is reduced. Of course, childhood urges are strong, and many survive in spite of what adults may do to discourage them. However, it is important to under-stand how punishing young children can affect their later development. Children can come to see new situations as potentially "troublemaking" rather than as opportunities to use their initiative to find out more about the world around them. When those children become adults they may be afraid to try anything new because they were punished for mistakes as children.

When punishments hurt, the teachable moment is lost. Children are most open to learning right after they've done something wrong or made a mistake. That's the time for helping them see what went wrong. If they are wrapped up in pain (physical or psychological), they can't concentrate on the "lesson" the adult has in mind and may instead learn some other lesson that wasn't even intended.

Physical punishment is not an option in an educational setting, but for those adults who still use it at home, it can be especially problematic because it models aggression. Parents who are trying to keep their children from hurting others or using violence to solve problems work against their own goals when they use physical punishment. The message the children get is that it is OK to hurt people if you are bigger and have a good reason.

Worst of all, physical punishment can lead to child abuse when adults go further than they intend to. When a parent first starts using physical punishment, the result of even a little is often resentment. Just as modern germs build up resistance to medicine, so does the resentful child become resistant to punishment. The parent finds it takes more and more punishment to get the same effect. Some children are willing to take a lot, so the parent continues to escalate. It's a vicious cycle. Some parents end up abusing their children when they get caught up in this ugly pattern.

A question someone asked me that has stayed with me for a long time is this: When you are faced with a child's misbehavior, are you more interested in changing the behavior or in winning, controlling, coming out ahead, and making the child suffer? Helping parents look at their own motives can be a valuable first step to helping them look at their guidance methods. When we accept people as they are, we give them permission to look deeper and consider changing. When we push people to change, they tend to resist. That's something I've tried always to remember when working with families, children, or anybody else.

GUIDELINES FOR DISCIPLINING YOUNG CHILDREN

Here are some general guidelines I've found useful for disciplining young children. If you pass them on to families, and are open to discussion, you might learn something more about the family. If you model these behaviors, the message is even stronger than the written word. Maybe families will want to discuss what they see you doing. You might even get into a dialogue with them and expand your view. Everybody stands to gain from discussions about guidance.

- *Communicate with children what you are doing and why.* Don't reason at length, but provide reasons. If you do this, children will eventually do their own reasoning.
- *Check communication to see whether it is clear.* If it is not, you may discover that you have ambiguous feelings about the situation. If you've called the children in for lunch, for example, and they aren't coming in, maybe something is going on. Was breakfast

late and nobody is really hungry, but you're trying to keep to the schedule? Maybe the children are picking up on your ambiguity and that's why they aren't responding to you. An example I've dealt with as a parent educator is when children won't go to bed at night. It doesn't take a whole lot of discussion to realize that some parents who have been away all day have very ambiguous feelings about putting the children to bed. Children feel the ambiguity and are less likely to do as they are told than when the parent is very clear and certain.

- *Trust children*. Misbehavior often comes as a result of children being thwarted in having their needs met. Look closely at any pattern of misbehavior, and take the attitude that this behavior is trying to communicate something. Trust the child to know what he or she needs, even though on the surface the behavior may look just plain troublesome or contrary. Just because he or she seems to be "out to get you" doesn't mean that there aren't needs behind the behaviors.

Build good relationships. Discipline is more effective if it comes from a loving place.

- *Trust yourself*.   You also have needs. You can only make good choices about guiding and disciplining children when your own needs are met. When your needs clash with children's needs, strive to find a balance, so that no one's needs are neglected. Convey the message to children that everyone's needs are important—theirs and yours, too.
- *Build good relationships*.   Whatever approach you take to discipline will be more effective if it comes from a loving place. Remember in Chapter 5 how Nel Noddings's (2002) approach to creating moral people is to focus on the caring relationship. Her ethic of care involves close, positive, caring relationships. When adults come from a place of genuine caring, guidance and discipine measures work much better than when they are used as mere techniques by an adult without any relationship with the child.

What follows are 14 concrete examples of ways to guide behavior. You may find these useful yourself, or you may want to pass them on to families. You could use them to create workshops for parents on the subject of guidance. Those kinds of workshops are usually well attended. .

Discipline as Preventing Unacceptable Behavior

Start with prevention. The following sections present seven things to do *before* the unacceptable behavior occurs. Though they may not seem like guidance techniques, they are effective ways to guide behavior. The first two have to do with the environment, the third with modeling, the fourth and fifth with redirection and control, the sixth with feelings, and the seventh with needs.

Child Abuse: A Story

Carla is dealing with the consequences of abusing her child. Right now she is in a group session with other abusing parents, listening to their stories. She's surprised that some of the themes are the same as hers, though the details are different.

As she listens to the others, she involuntarily goes back to the moment before she threw Cody against the wall, fracturing his skull. She gets a sick feeling in her stomach as the memory floods her.

She had reached the end of her rope that evening—she knew it then and she knows it now. "How much do you think I can take?" she had screamed at Cody, who was standing over a broken plate he had just thrown down from the counter in anger. She remembered the series of incidents that had led up to this confrontation better than she remembered what happened afterward. It had been a bad day!

The problem was that she was so alone. Since Cody's father had left her, she found herself with fewer and fewer social contacts. She knew she needed friends, but it was so hard to make them with two children to support and raise. They took up all her time. And they drove her crazy sometimes. Like that awful rainy Saturday when Cody ended up breaking the plate.

As the other parents in the circle continued talking, it became obvious that being isolated was a theme for most of them. Another problem for Carla was that Cody was so immature. She had told him time and again that now that his father was gone he was the man of the house. But he just didn't live up to any of her expectations. Sure, he was only 4, but still . . . .

Carla didn't know it yet, but this was another common characteristic of parents who abuse their children. They don't understand developmental stages and often have unrealistic expectations for their children. Carla will learn about this subject from the class she is enrolled in.

She will also learn some techniques for guiding and controlling her children's behavior in positive ways. She knows she needs those techniques. Discipline has always left her feeling helpless. She only knows what she learned from her own parents, who used belittling, sarcasm, and, above all, beating on Carla when she was little.

Carla never thought of herself as an abused child. She figured that all children were punished in the same way she was. She knew that she had more scars than some of her childhood friends, but she accepted that as a fact. She never considered that she could question her parents' methods, and indeed she couldn't—she just would have been beaten harder for talking back.

It's not that her parents didn't love her—Carla knows that they did. In her mind they showed their love by hitting her; in fact, they even told her that. In Carla's experience, love and hurt were linked together.

Carla knows now that she *must stop* abusing Cody. No matter what problems she has, there's no excuse for not controlling herself—she knows that now. She also knows that she's not alone anymore. She's getting help, in the form of education, therapy, and, above all, support. Things will be different now, and eventually Cody and his sister Candace will be back home again.

Carla breathes a sigh of relief as she sits back in her chair, ready to talk. It's her turn now. The group looks at her expectantly.

"I have lots of feelings," she starts out.

---

1. Set Up an Appropriate Environment.   The younger the child the more he or she needs freedom to move, things to explore, and something to do. For example, you can predict unacceptable behavior when you have a toddler for any length of time in a fancy restaurant, an elegant living room, or a department store. You are more likely to find acceptable behavior when children are in an environment that is age-appropriate as well as suited to their needs and interests.

2. Let the Environment Provide the Limits.   Fence off dangerous areas from young children. Most communities have laws about swimming pools, but they don't expect rules alone to prevent drownings. The same approach could be used in the home or early care and education programs. Put breakables out of reach. Lock doors to rooms that are off limits to children.

This principle works beyond childhood. Freeways and throughways are good examples of how the environment provides the limits. Most are designed so you *can't* go off the on-ramp. Center dividers make it difficult, if not impossible, to cross into oncoming traffic. The safety principles used by highway designers are a good model to keep in mind as you design or help families understand appropriate environments for children.

Frank Gonzalez-Mena

Set up an appropriate environment. The younger the child, the more he or she needs freedom to move, things to explore, and something to do.

3. Model Appropriate Behavior.   Model gentleness in the face of aggression. Model courtesy, kindness, sensitivity, sharing, and caring. It works! You may be surprised how much children pick up. If you yell at children to stop yelling, or if you're aggressive in response to aggression, they'll follow your actions instead of your words. Modeling is powerful. It works, either for you or against you. As mentioned throughout this book, modeling also works as a way of working with parents as well. What they see you doing, they may pick up on and start doing themselves—especially when they see it works. Modeling for parents is one of the best ways of expanding their ideas of guidance and discipline.

4. Redirect Energy.   Much unacceptable behavior is just exuberance. It doesn't need to be curtailed; it just needs to be redirected. Find ways to turn potentially unacceptable actions into acceptable ones. Provide time outdoors for a child who wants to run, for example. If exuberance becomes overstimulation, try some calming activities—water play is a good one for the younger child. Playing with "goop" (a mixture of cornstarch and water) will calm almost anyone. Baths are a time-honored calming device.

5. Provide Physical Control When Needed.   For the very young child, physical guidance may prevent problems. Stop the hitting hand by gently but firmly taking hold of it, unless you're sure words alone will trigger the control that the child needs to stop his or her own hand. Words may work fine, but don't depend on them by themselves, especially with toddlers. Back up words by providing the physical control that the child may lack. Eventually you can use words alone; perhaps just a look will do it. But they need to know you really mean it—which you show by consistently providing gentle physical control when needed.

To provide this physical kind of guidance, the adult needs to be nearby when trouble threatens. There's a rule of thumb for interaction distance that early childhood teachers have been using for years. You can pass it on to families. Here it is: Speak to a child from the distance of 1 foot for each year. When you ask a 2-year-old at 2 feet to control his hitting hand, you're close enough to reach out and control it for him if necessary. Children can hear you shout from across the room, but most won't listen. It takes your close physical presence to be sure that any words they might not want to hear will register.

6. Teach Appropriate Expression of Feelings.   Feelings are important and should be not only allowed and accepted but also appreciated—by yourself and by children. Children need to learn how to express their feelings in ways that don't harm themselves, anyone else, or the things around them. Teach them to say, "I'm angry!" Teach them to accept the feelings even if they don't show them or act on them. Again, it is important to acknowledge that this acceptance of individual feelings comes from a culture that focuses on individuals. People from cultures that do not focus on individuality might not feel comfortable following this advice. In some cultures, group harmony is more important than individual expression of feelings. Jerome Kagan, a researcher concerned with cultural differences, says about the cultures of Java, Japan, and China that respect for the feelings of elders and of authority "demands that each person not only suppress anger but, in addition, be ready to withhold complete honesty about personal feelings in order to avoid hurting another. This pragmatic view of honesty is regarded as a quality characteristic of the most mature adult and is not given the derogatory labels of insincerity or hypocrisy" (1984, pp. 244–245). When two people with different views about expressing feelings are responsible for the same child (as parents or as early childhood professional coworkers, or professional and parent), they need to talk about their differences and decide how to work together for the good of the child.

7. Meet Needs.   A good deal of undesirable behavior can be prevented when children (and adults, too) are feeling satisfied because their needs are met. Basic needs such as food, rest, and exercise come first; but beyond the basics lie higher needs such as security, protection, love, and closeness. Abraham Maslow, a psychologist, emphasized the importance of recognizing needs in his book *Motivation and Personality* (1970). When any needs are unmet, discipline problems can result.

Guidance as Responding to Unacceptable Behavior

When unacceptable behavior occurs in spite of your efforts to prevent it, an appro-priate and effective response is in order. The responses that follow are all positive approaches. Jane Nelsen (2001), famous for her books on discipline, says not to make children feel bad about themselves in order to motivate them to behave better. In fact, negative approaches usually work at cross purposes. Children who feel bad about themselves are less likely to behave in acceptable ways unless they are dominated by fear. If you rule by fear, you can damage relationships, an important requirement for positive guidance.

The following sections offer seven effective and healthy ways to respond to unacceptable behavior. They include giving feedback, allowing consequences, using time-out, rewarding some behaviors and ignoring others, teaching desired behaviors, and meeting needs.

8. Give Feedback.   If the problem belongs to the children involved and you can keep your feelings out of it, the best kind of feedback is "sports announcing." For example, when children are fighting over a toy, you can step in and narrate what you see, express the feelings you pick up, and get the children to talk to one another. This kind of sports announcing leads to problem solving on the part of the children.

If, on the other hand, you have strong feelings because your needs are being trampled on, state them in a sentence that starts with I and contains a feeling word. These "I-messages" were first described by Thomas Gordon (2000), a doctor who has had great influence on parents and early childhood educators and parents with his book *Parent Effectiveness Training* (called PET for short). When using an I-message, the sentence should also encapsulate the behavior in question. For example, if children are screaming their lungs out and it bothers you, say, "I feel nervous [upset, tired] when I hear you scream." Feedback is different from judgmental criticism or blame.

Of course, families from a culture that does not value individual expression of feelings, an approach such as the one suggested here, may feel uncomfortable. Having a discussion about their perspective—if you can listen and not try to persuade—might be profitable to all parties concerned.

9. Allow Children to Experience the Consequences of Their Actions.   *Natural* consequences don't have to be arranged, according to Rudolf Dreikurs, who coauthored a classic book some years ago called *Children: The Challenge* (Dreikurs & Soltz, 1964). Variations of that book and its offspring have now been read by several generations of parents. Using natural consequences is a matter of stepping back and not rescuing a child from a decision he or she has made. When a child chooses not to wear a sweater when going out to play, the natural consequence is to feel cold. Next time the child will consider the consequences of going outside without a sweater if he is allowed to feel the cold.

Logical consequences (Dreikurs & Loren, 1990) are set up by adults and reflect the reality of the social world. Logical consequences are a direct result of the child's own actions. When children leave their clothes on the floor instead of in the hamper, the clothes don't get washed. If the child can't be trusted not to go into the street, he or she is taken into the house. Children talk during story time and the adult stops reading. The child who spills the milk sponges it up. These are all logical consequences.

As stated earlier, consequences are different from punishment, even though they may cause anguish, because they are related to the child's own actions. They are reasonable, not arbitrary. Adults must be respectful when allowing or applying consequences. If adults are angry or harsh, consequences become punishment.

As a teacher, you can get in difficulties with families for using the consequences approach, partly because it involves letting children make their own decisions—an approach that fits better with an independent/individualistic perspective than with a interdependent, holistic perspective. If you model it while parents are observing, it would be good to ask their opinion. Or discuss the approach beforehand and be sure parents understand. Using consequences to teach may feel cold and uncaring to people from cultures where the adult role is warm and protective and where constant close connections are valued. In her work with Haitian children and teachers, Ballenger (1992, 1999) discovered how uncomfortable they were with the consequences approach. It's hard for some adults to stand back knowing that a child will not like living with a choice he or she is about to make. They feel compelled to protect children from making decisions when the consequences will be unpleasant.

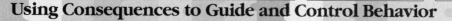

Using Consequences to Guide and Control Behavior

Jean is a mother who decided not to use punishment on her 5-year-old, Trevor, anymore. She had learned about using consequences as a discipline method and was ready to try it. She had the perfect opportunity the day she got tired of trying to get Trevor to put his dishes in the dishwasher after eating.

Trevor was very lazy about this—lazy to the point of stubbornness. Up to now Jean would remind him, time after time, but he'd "forget." She began to feel like a nag. She finally got so frustrated that she resorted to threatening him, but that didn't work either. Nothing worked!

Of course, nothing worked because Trevor knew that if he waited long enough, his mother would put the dishes away for him. Besides, it didn't really matter to him if a few dirty dishes were left lying around. His next meal always arrived right on schedule. The only consequence for leaving dishes on the table was that they magically disappeared eventually anyway. Finally, Jean decided she needed to get more creative about how to handle this problem, which she recognized as *her* problem. She decided that using a "consequences approach" would make it Trevor's problem as well.

She started by asking herself what the ultimate consequence of not putting dirty dishes in the dishwasher would be. She visualized a house full of molding dishes—it looked terrible. Would he mind that? She wasn't sure. Then she visualized an empty cupboard—no dishes for the next meal. That's the ultimate consequence. Even if the dirty house didn't affect him, the empty cupboard would if he didn't find his next meal, all hot and delicious, waiting for him on a clean plate.

So Jean explained to Trevor that she wouldn't remind or nag him anymore about dirty dishes, but she wouldn't put them away, either. She didn't. He didn't, either. By bedtime the first day the place was a dump, but Trevor didn't seem to mind.

Jean was discouraged. She thought she'd see results quicker. How long was this going to take, anyway, she asked herself, looking at the smeared glasses, sticky plates, and crusted forks lying here and there around the kitchen and the family room.

She had a brainstorm. "I'll hurry up the process by adding to the problem," she told her sister, whom she called for moral support. "I'll just quit putting my dishes away, too."

"Do you think it will work?" her sister asked.

"Yes," replied Jean enthusiastically.

That night Jean left a plate on the coffee table, with a dirty glass beside it. The next morning she left her coffee cup on the newspaper by her rocking chair, her cereal bowl and juice glass on the table, and an empty water glass on the television—next to the two empty glasses Trevor had left there the previous day.

It didn't take long. They never got to the point of the bare cupboard. Trevor didn't like the mess once it got really ugly. He picked up his dishes, Jean picked up hers, and that was the end of it.

So how was this different from punishment? For one thing, Jean didn't inflict it on Trevor. She merely quit doing what hadn't worked before and let his own actions show him what the problem was. He learned a lesson about the benefits of household order without being punished. Jean was a bystander—not a moralizer, judge, or jury. She even managed to refrain from saying, "I hope you learned your lesson."

---

10. Use Time-Out appropriately.   Time-out (sitting apart, being sent to another room or to a certain place in the same room) was discussed previously as sometimes culturally inappropriate. Here it is looked at as appropriate if done in a certain way with certain children. Time-out can be punishing if done in a punishing way (as can any of the approaches listed here). Time-out used appropriately gives some children who need it a chance to gain control of themselves. This only works when the child is truly "out of control." And it works best with children from families who have a more individualistic orientation. This use of time-out gives adults a chance to become an ally, a helper to the child. The attitude the adult conveys is "I see that you can't control yourself in this situation, so I am going to help you by taking you out of it and getting you into a peaceful, less stimulating situation." This is very different from a punishing attitude, in which the adult is viewed as an adversary rather than as a partner. Time-out should be followed up with a problem-solving session between the child and the caregiver.

Unfortunately, time-out is overused by some adults, who respond to every misbehavior by sending the child off to sit in a chair. It is also abused. Instead of being a positive means of discipline, time-out often takes the place of the old-fashioned stool and dunce cap, which was an old-fashioned shaming device.

Here again cultural differences come into play. As mentioned earlier, if an adult is from a culture where interconnections are stressed more than individuality, time-out may seem like an extreme punishment. Being cut off from the group is called "shunning" by some and is regarded as a very serious sanction. In some groups, time-out as a way of managing children's misbehavior is avoided because even when done kindly and in the child's best interests it feels excessive. Children should not be shunned through time-out or any other device.

Pay special attention to children who are not misbehaving.

11. Reward Desired Behavior. Notice when children are "being good." Pay special attention when children are being kind, courteous, sensitive, and helpful. Naturally, these are the times when we are tempted to ignore children because they aren't causing any problems. This is the behavior we expect, so why should we go out of our way to make a fuss over it? Some families feel strongly that expected behavior should not get special attention. That's not the way of behaviorist learning theory, which points out the power of the reward—even if it's only adult attention. Behavior that's rewarded tends to continue. Behavior that's ignored tends to disappear. Be careful about going overboard, however. Constant gushing praise doesn't work. In his book *Punished by Rewards*, Kohn (1999) wrote about how, when we try to manipulate children's behavior through using incentives, side effects arise and our good intentions backfire. In a subsequent book, called *Unconditional Parenting: Moving From Rewards and Punishments to Love and Reasoning* (2004), Kohn gives the same message to parents. Citing hundreds of studies, he makes it clear that the more we use rewards to get children to do what we want, the more they lose interest in doing it. Children don't perform as well and they aren't as creative when we entice them to do something by dangling a reward in front of their noses.

It's not manipulative to be honest and sincere. Use your powers of observation to notice behavior that deserves noticing. For example, if you view a child treating a younger child in a gentle manner, you could say, "I see that you're being very careful when you touch Ty." Just regular manners work, too: "I appreciate it when you help me set the table." "Thanks for putting away the tricycle."

12. Ignore Misbehavior That Is Designed to Attract Attention.   Everyone needs attention—it's like a life-giving substance. When children don't get the attention they need through positive behaviors, they develop negative ones that are hard to ignore. If the message behind these behaviors is "I'm here, notice me," the only way to change the behaviors is to ignore them, and then give the needed attention at times when the child is acting acceptably. Walk out of the room when a child is trying on purpose to annoy you. Turn your back on arguing that is designed to get your attention (much arguing among children is for that very purpose). Of course, don't leave children alone if they might hurt each other.

13. Teach Prosocial Behavior.   Don't just teach what *not to do* through the aforementioned approaches. Take a proactive stance and teach what *to do* as well. Indirect

A good deal of undesirable behavior can be prevented when children are feeling satisfied because their needs are met.

Jim Darter

teaching comes about through the already mentioned devices of modeling and rewarding. Direct teaching comes about through talking. Avoid lectures. Instead, use stories and role-plays, and even actually practice prosocial behavior by trying it out in little dramas or puppet shows.

14. Meet Needs.   Children often behave in unacceptable ways because they are needy. Respond to behaviors from that source by meeting the needs. Don't yell at a boy who is fussing because he's hungry; feed him. Don't give feedback to a tired girl who is out of control; put her to bed. Don't prevent restless children from wiggling; take them someplace where they can get the wiggles out. Of course you can't always meet each child's needs immediately, and it doesn't hurt them to learn to wait a bit—but not too long! Do what you can to control the truly unacceptable behavior, and put up with behavior that is only expressing feelings about having to wait.

What One Town Did About Child Abuse

Awhile back, in a medium-sized town in a northern California valley, a baby died as the result of abuse. A group of citizens, led by one individual, decided to do something about child abuse. This was about the time that national awareness was beginning to grow, as emergency room doctors questioned where all those mysterious bruises and broken bones were coming from. It was the same time that psychotherapists were hearing adult stories of early beatings. Each person who dredged up these memories was convinced that he or she was a unique case. No one realized that child abuse was so widespread.

Now, of course, we have one glaring statistic after another showing that for many children, growing up is very dangerous business. As a nation we decided to change the statistics, and we passed laws prohibiting child abuse.

The laws were not enough for this particular group of citizens, who wanted to *prevent* abuse in their community, not just punish it. This motivation on their part coincided with some funding set aside for prevention, intervention, and treatment of child abuse. The group went to work.

First they established a hotline for parents to call, just to talk, when they felt as though they might not be able to control themselves. Then they began to educate the community about child abuse and about using the hotline. What they and the community were surprised to discover was that child abuse crosses all economic, cultural, and racial lines. No one is immune. We're all at risk for "losing it" and hurting our children.

These citizens and others soon discovered that what parents needed was a variety of support services. Some needed parenting information and skills; some needed relief child care; some needed a job; some needed a place to live; and some just needed relief from the many stresses in their lives that led them to take out their frustrations on their children. The picture was much bigger than anyone had ever suspected.

Today many of these services are in place, but many more are needed. The original citizen group went on to establish a variety of types of services: relief child care, an after-school "phone friend" for children who come home to an empty house, parent support and education groups, an emergency aid fund, and support services for children in foster care. They also provided part-time temporary home service, where parent aides go into the home to help with household and child management through support and role modeling.

A good deal of energy has gone into changing things for children and their parents in this community. The group continues to provide community education by making speakers available and through a regular newsletter. Through its 25-year history, this organization has remained overwhelmingly a volunteer group, with a ratio of more than four volunteers to each paid staff member. Volunteer training is an ongoing focus as new recruits become involved and old volunteers change from one program to another within the organization. The funding now comes from a variety of federal, state, and local sources.

Working with families around guidance and discipline approaches can be rewarding, because it's a subject most families are interested in. See Strategy Box 7.1 for ideas about how to use some of the information in this chapter to expand parents' ideas around discipline. If you give a workshop on discipline, families may come to you as the authority but then may resist what you tell them because it doesn't fit their ideas of what children need. The best approach to take is to have open discussions in which everyone is free to express their ideas. That means the atmosphere must be one of respect and acceptance.

Alan Pence, a noted early childhood expert from the University of Victoria in British Columbia, talked about what happened when educators and First Nations people met to create an early childhood curriculum. The two groups each came

Strategy Box 7.1

Working with Families Around Ideas of Guidance and Discipline

◆ Set aside judgments. When two groups or two people have different perspectives on guiding children's behavior, instead of judging right or wrong, early educators must first try to understand those differences and where they come from. Are they cultural, familial, individual, or do they come from something else?

◆ At the same time be clear about your bottom line. Doing harm to children is wrong. But to judge what is truly harmful and not in the best interests of a child, family, or community requires a deep understanding of the perspective of the person or family you are working with and the meanings behind their behaviors. At the same time, you have a legal mandate to report child abuse. Don't be so open minded that you seem to be condoning abuse.

- ◆ Try to avoid making families feel defensive. Do what you can to keep yourself from feeling defensive.
- ◆ Try to get to a deeper understanding. Try reframing contradictions. Move from dualistic, exclusive perceptions of reality and try integrating the complementary aspects of diverse beliefs into a new whole concept.
- ◆ Challenge yourself and your beliefs. Step outside your norms. Open yourself to discovering from families something you weren't aware of.

---

with different sets of knowledge and experience. He says, "In the space between these two sets of knowledge was the opportunity to envision and generate something new, something that had not been articulated before" (Pence, 2004, p. 32). Pence and his colleagues have created an early education approach called the "Generative Curriculum," which they first introduced in Canada (Ball & Pence 1999; Dahlberg, Moss, & Pence, 1999). Training is now being offered in 10 sub-Saharan countries through an online course offered by the Early Childhood Development Virtual University (based at the University of Victoria in Canada). One of the exciting parts of the Generative Curriculum is that those who use it are able to make a positive use of the tensions that arise when differing perspectives collide.

So my advice is this: when you are in a situation in which differing perspectives are headed toward an argument, try using those tensions in a creative manner. Teach yourself and the families you work with to play what Jones and Cooper (2005) call "the believing game." They suggest that trying to imagine another person's perspective requires suspending reality — playing pretend. They point out that when we encounter people who don't believe what we believe, "We can sneer at them, or fight them, or pretend they're invisible . . . Or we can accept the challenge to 'embrace contraries'" (p. 23). You'll be surprised what you can learn when you embrace contraries!

LOOKING BACK AND LOOKING FORWARD

This chapter discussed contrasting perspectives on guidance and helped early educators know what to do when working with families who don't understand or agree with the approaches suggested in this chapter. A theme of this chapter is to communicate with children about what you are doing and why and do the same with parents. Create situations where you can have formal and informal discussions with families about different ways of looking at guidance. The chapter outlines several approaches to guidance—half of them preventing situations where guidance is required and the other half responding after something has happened requiring guidance.

Because feelings and problem solving play such a prominent part in matters of discipline, the next chapter focuses specifically on those subjects.

FOR DISCUSSION

1. How do you feel about using the word *guidance* instead of *discipline*? What associations do you have with each word? Do you prefer one word over the other when talking with parents?

2. Discuss how the environment can be used to curb behavior and restrict a child from doing something dangerous or unacceptable. What is an example of learning from experiencing a consequence? Is your example a logical or a natural consequence?

3. Can you explain the difference between a consequence and punishment? What are some problems with using punishment to teach? Have you ever experienced any of these problems yourself?

4. Give examples of three prosocial behaviors you would want to teach young children. Have you ever taught these behaviors? If yes, how? Would you use this particular discussion question when working with parents? If yes, why? If no, why not?

WEB SITES

Child Development Institute
http://www.childdevelopmentinfo.com/
Find child development information here, including 27 articles on discipline.

Clearinghouse on Early Education and Parenting (CEEP)
http://ceep.crc.uiuc.edu/
The Clearinghouse on Early Education and Parenting has print and online resources for the worldwide early childhood and parenting communities. CEEP also offers access to the archive of ERIC/EECE materials at
http://ceep.crc.uiuc.edu/eecearchive/index.html

National Association for the Education of Young Children (NAEYC)
http://www.naeyc.org/
The National Association for the Education of Young Children has a number of resources available for parents and professionals including books and journals, one of which is called *Young Children* which has a number of articles on guidance.

National Network for Child Care (NNCC)
http://www.nncc.org/
NNCC is an Internet source of over 1,000 research-based and reviewed publications and resources related to child care.

Parent Center
http://www.parentcenter.babycenter.com/preschooler/ptoilet/index
This Web site is an online resource center of articles for parents of children 2–8.

Positive Discipline
http://www.positivediscipline.com/
This site features articles relating to disciplining and teaching children appropriate behavior. It includes resources for parents and teachers, such as online workshops, information, and additional links.

Prevent Abuse Now
http://www.prevent-abuse-now.com/
Child protection and abuse prevention information is offered, with additional links.

FURTHER READING

Ballenger, C. (1999). *Teaching other people's children.* New York: Teachers College Press.

Baumrind, D. (1996). Parenting: The discipline controversy revisited. *Family Relations, 45*(4), 405–414.

Bell, S. H., Carr, V. W., Denno, D., Johnson, L. J., & Phillips, L. R. (2004). *Challenging behaviors in early childhood settings: Creating a place for all children.* Baltimore: Brookes.

Brault, L., & Brault, T. (2005). *Children with challenging behavior: Strategies for reflective thinking.* Phoenix, AZ: CPG Publishing.

Bronson, M. B. (2000, March). Research in review: Recognizing and supporting the development of self-regulation in young children. *Young Children, 55*(2), 32–36.

Charney, R. S. (2002). *Teaching children to care: Classroom management for ethical and academic growth.* Greenfield, MA: Northeast Foundation for Children.

Diaz, R. M., Neal, C. J., & Amaya-Williams, M. (1996). *The social origins of self-regulation: Vygotsky and Education.* Cambridge: Cambridge University Press.

Drifte, C. (2004). *Encouraging positive behavior in the early years: A practical guide.* London: Paul Chapman Publishing.

Duncan, T., Temple, K. M., & Smith, T. M. (2000, Summer). Reinforcement in developmentally appropriate early childhood classrooms. *Childhood Education, 76*(4), 194–203.

Elicker, J., & Fortner-Wood, C. (1995, November). Adult-child relationships in early childhood programs. *Young Children, 51*(1), 69–78.

Fox, L., Dunlap, G., Hemmeter, M. L., Joseph, G. E., & Strain, P. S. (2003, July). The teaching pyramid: A model for supporting social competence and preventing challenging behavior in young children. *Young Children, 58*(4), 48–52.

Fox, L., & Little, N. (2001). Starting early: School-wide behavior support in a community preschool. *Journal of Positive Behavior Intervention, 3,* 251–254.

Gartrell, D. (2002). Replacing time-out: Part two—Using guidance to maintain an encouraging classroom. *Young Children, 57*(2), 36–43.

Gonzalez-Mena, J. (2008). *Diversity in early care and education: Honoring differences* (5th ed.). New York: McGraw-Hill.

Gonzalez-Mena, J., & Shareef, I. (2005 November). Discussing diverse perspectives on guidance. *Young Children, 60*(6), 34–38.

Goodman, J. F., & Balamore, U. (2003). *Teaching goodness: Engaging the moral and academic promise of young children.* Boston: Allyn & Bacon.

Howes, C., & Ritchie, S. (2002). *A matter of trust.* New York: Teachers College Press.

Hyson, M. (2004). *The emotional development of young children* (2nd ed.). New York: Teachers College Press.

Lee, L. (Ed.). (2006). *Stronger together. Family support and early childhood education.* San Rafael, CA: Parent Services Project, Inc.

Kaiser, B., & Rasminsky, J. (2003). *Challenging behavior in young children: Understanding, preventing and responding effectively.* Boston: Allyn & Bacon.

Kohn, A. (2004). *Unconditional parenting: Moving from rewards and punishment to love and reasoning.* New York: Atria.

Kranowitz, C. S. (1998). *The out of sync child: Recognizing and coping with sensory integration dysfunction.* New York: Paragee.

Lillard, A., & Curenton, S. (1999, September). Research in review: Do young children understand what others feel, want, and know? *Young Children, 54*(5), 52–57.

Marion, M. (2007). *Guidance of Young Children* (7th ed.). Upper Saddle River, NJ: Merrill/Prentice Hall.

McLoyd, V. C., Hill, N. E., & Dodge, K. A. (Eds). (2005). *African American family life.* New York: Guilford.

Nelsen, J. (Ed.). (2001). *Positive discipline: A teacher's a–z guide* (2nd ed.). Rocklin, CA: Prima.

Reynolds, E. (2001) *Guiding young children: A problem-solving approach.* New York: McGraw-Hill.

Rightmyer, E. C. (2003, July). Democratic discipline: Children creating solutions. *Young Children, 58*(4), 38–44.

Sandall, S., & Ostrosky, M. (1999). *Young exceptional children: Practical ideas for addressing challenging behaviors*. Denver: Division for Early Childhood of the Council for Exceptional Children.

Schreiber, M. E. (1999, July). Time-outs for toddlers: Is our goal punishment or education? *Young Children, 54*(4), 22–25.

Segal, M., Masi, W., & Leiderman, R. (2001). *In time and with love: Caring for infants and toddlers with special needs*. New York: New Market Press.

Siccone, F., & Lopez, L. (2000). *Educating the heart: Lessons to build respect and responsibility*. Boston: Allyn & Bacon.

Wien, C. A. (2004, January). "From policing to participation: Overturning the rules and creating amiable classrooms. *Young Children, 59*(1), 34–40.

Wolfson-Steinberg, L. (2000, May). "Teacher! He hit me!" "She pushed me!" Where does it start? How can it stop? *Young Children, 55*(3), 38–42.

CHAPTER 8

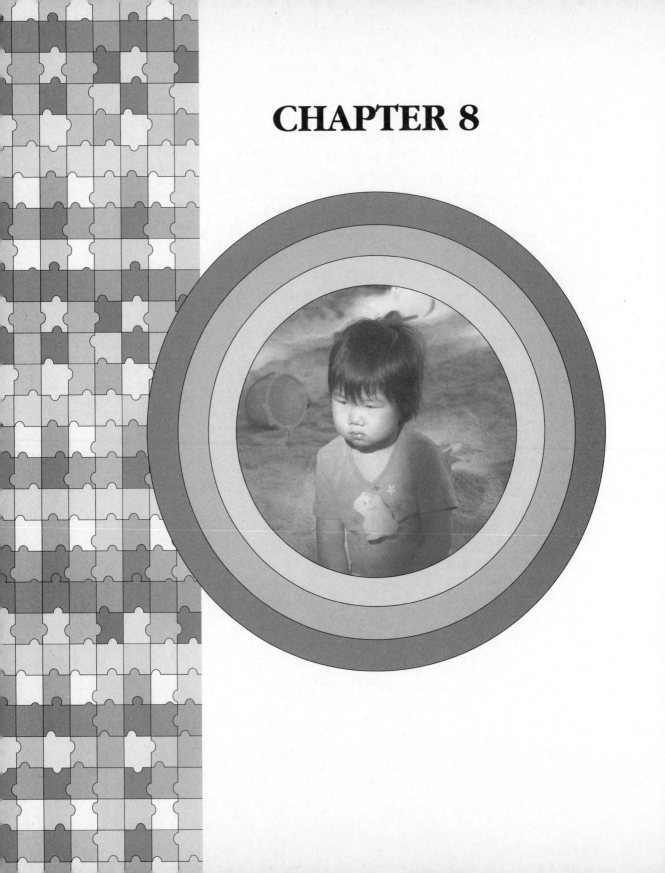

Working with Families on Addressing Feelings and Problem Solving

In this chapter you'll discover . . .

- How children can be helped to cope with fear and anger
- The difference between expressing and acting on feelings
- How adults give children clues about what to feel in certain situations
- Why sometimes you shouldn't give children clues about what to feel
- How to look at feelings and problem solving from several points of view
- What kind of parent is neither permissive nor authoritarian

A job both early educators and families have to do is help children cope with their feelings and also help them learn problem-solving skills. This chapter is divided into two parts, each representing one of those two subjects. These two may seem to be unrelated, but consider that emotions carry energy and energy is what is needed for problem solving, especially in difficult situations. When adults and children alike learn to harness the emotional energy that comes with, for instance, anger, they can live much healthier lives. This is a lesson that is hard to learn for most of us because it's not a subject that's taught in school or even in most families. It's also fairly unusual even in a book like this one. I'll start with feelings and then go on to problem solving.

FEELINGS

The perspective this chapter takes is that early educators need to encourage children to feel their feelings, to decide whether and how to express and act on them, and, above all, to decide how to cope with them. Feelings are an important aspect of education and social-emotional development. Children need to accept, sort out, identify, label, integrate, and appropriately express their feelings. Not all families will agree with this way of helping children with their feelings, so handling disagreements about different ways of looking at feelings is also a part of this chapter. From one perspective, the greatest task of all is helping children become socialized while fully experiencing their feelings. Part of the socialization process involves learning to know in each instance whether to express feelings or not, and if expressing them is acceptable, then how to express them appropriately becomes the next decision. The ultimate decision is whether to act on the feelings and, if acting is the right thing to do, how to act in socially appropriate ways. These are enormous lessons to learn, and children need adult help to learn them in culturally relevant ways.

Obviously children learn a lot about feelings at home by observing their family members. They also learn from the response they get when they express feelings. Some families have clear ideas about what they want their children to learn about feelings, but not all children grow up with adults who help them with the emotional aspects of development. Some adults demonstrate lopsided emotional development. We all know adults who reached maturity skilled in some areas of feelings but unpracticed and unskilled in others. A person may be good at expressing anger and self-assertion and dealing with power relationships but lack the abilities that lead to intimacy and closeness; this individual is less able to be sensitive, nurturing, loving, tender, vulnerable. Another person may be skilled in the nurturing mode but lacking in self-assertion and fearful of his or her own power. These people may hold in their anger, fearing it as they would an untamed animal. They keep it all inside by tying it down, locking it in, because, in their minds, if this vicious animal gets loose it will commit unspeakably violent acts as it rages out of control. This perception of anger as a wild, vicious animal hides deep within many tender, nurturing people. Sometimes two people with opposite styles get together and parent a child—so the child see the whole range of emotions but split between two parents.

Then there are the adults who see themselves as a mind walking around in a body; they avoid feelings altogether whenever possible. Many of these adults are so afraid of their feelings that they spend years denying them and teach children to do likewise.

The point of starting this chapter by looking at adult feelings is that children learn about feelings from the adults in their lives. When adults set effective examples and provide modeling of what to do with feelings, children grow up with much more awareness and coping skills than when adults provide restricted models.

It's not up to the early educator to teach parents what to do with their feelings. It is important, though, to understand how much the teaching you do with the children matches what they are learning at home. If there is a serious mismatch, you must talk about it with the family and figure out together what to do about it.

Using Anger

Marcie is a 35-year-old stepmother who has recently discovered how to use anger. As a child, she was taught to hide her feelings. She learned early that strong emotion bothered the adults in her life. "Mad is bad" was a motto of her family. She still hears her own mother's voice inside her head telling her "Don't be angry!" and "Oh, just don't think about it!"

And that's just what she learned to do—forget about what was bothering her. But just willing to forget isn't enough. She had to learn some distraction techniques. Those techniques worked well, and she learned to stuff her feelings deep down inside, hiding them even from herself. One technique she used was "intellectualizing": getting out of her feelings and into her head. But avoiding her feelings caused stewing. Grown-up, Marcie is a master stewer. When she's upset, the simmering is practically audible.

Take the other day when her stepdaughter, Serena, screamed at her, "You can't tell me what to do! You're not my mother!" Marcie felt a surge of anger rising, but as was her practice, she stuffed it down inside herself and calmly responded to the 5-year-old in a reasonable voice.

The same thing happened during dinner when Serena complained about the food, only picked at her plate, got up from the table, and 15 minutes later asked for a snack. Marcie handled the situation well, but she was silent and sullen the rest of the evening. When her husband asked her what was wrong, she said, "Oh, nothing. Just tired."

But the problem with stewing is that the stuffed anger builds up until it eventually boils over. Then the rage comes pouring out unexpectedly.

That happened on the weekend. Marcie was still stewing when she emptied out Serena's dirty clothes basket and at the bottom, all wrinkled and smelling of dirty socks, was the little 100 percent cotton outfit that Marcie had hand-washed and ironed for Serena the week before. Furious that Serena had put it in the dirty clothes without once wearing it, Marcie stomped into the living room where Serena was lying on the floor watching TV. "What's this doing in the dirty clothes?" she screamed at her startled stepdaughter.

"You told me to pick up everything on the floor. And that was on the floor," sassed Serena.

Marcie's reason left her. She began to rage. When she finally finished, she was exhausted and heartsick with guilt. She was extra nice to Serena to make up for her own lack of control. This pattern was familiar to both Marcie and Serena: to stuff anger, stew for a long period, suddenly rage, then feel guilty and try to make it up to Serena.

Marcie knows she needs to learn to break that pattern, so at the suggestion of Serena's teacher, she signed up for a parenting class. She's learned that she can recognize anger when it arises and that she can turn off the voices of her parents that tell her to ignore what she's feeling. She can stay with the feeling and fully experience it instead of distracting herself by becoming "intellectual" about it. An important lesson she has learned in the class is that she can still *think* while she's *feeling*, but she must be careful to accept and acknowledge the feelings.

Marcie knows now that whenever she can focus on her anger, she can get a clarity that doesn't come when she's busy distracting and stuffing. The teacher told the class that unfelt feelings can be damaging—physically and psychologically. Felt feelings, and the emotional energy they bring, can be used constructively. Marcie's goal is to use her feelings to improve her relationship with Serena. She knows now that her tension can be released periodically instead of being buried and then exploding. The tension from the anger can be turned into positive energy that would be useful for solving problems.

Marcie is learning to operate out of new patterns. She's learning to feel her anger and use its energy. The bystander might not notice the difference. Marcie still often decides *not* to express her anger directly to Serena. But now she acknowledges the feelings to herself and experiences them fully. She's replaced the models in her life who were so busy avoiding emotions with ones who make good decisions about feeling, those who express and act on their feelings.

Marcie does look happier and more relaxed now that she has learned that anger brings important energy that can be used for problem solving. Serena looks more relaxed too, since Marcie has begun to move away from the stuffing, stewing, and boiling-over pattern.

Because this chapter takes the perspective that feelings are important and should be not only allowed and accepted but also appreciated—by yourself and by children, it is important to recognize that this view is alien to some cultures. Families from some cultures don't have the same goal of teaching children to label or express their feelings. The acceptance of individual feelings comes from a culture that focuses on individuals. People from cultures that do not focus on individuality might feel uncomfortable following the advice in this chapter. In some cultures, where the parenting priority is interdependence, group harmony is much more important than individual expression of feelings. Jerome Kagan, a researcher concerned with cultural differences, says about the cultures of Java, Japan, and China that respect for the feelings of elders and of authority "demands that each person not only suppress anger but, in addition, be ready to withhold complete honesty about personal feelings in order to avoid hurting another. This pragmatic view of honesty is regarded as a quality characteristic of the most mature adult and is not given the derogatory labels of insincerity or hypocrisy" (1984, pp. 244–245).

If you are a person for whom the information in this chapter fits and makes sense, it's important that you recognize the families who disagree with this perspective. When two people with different views about expressing feelings are responsible for the same child, they need to talk about their differences and decide how to work together for the good of the child. Remember that at least half of communication is listening, so see what you can understand about the parents' perspective. You are bound to learn something that goes beyond the information in this chapter.

Even if you and families have different perspectives about accepting feelings it's still useful to consider the benefits of *redirection*. Redirection is one way to handle children's anger as you guide a child from hitting another child to hitting a pillow or pounding clay. Art, music, dance, and physical exercise are classic ways of expressing feelings that should be available to children. You don't have to make a point of the feelings themselves. Also you don't have to provide anything elaborate. Simple experiences in art, music, movement, and dance work fine. And getting children outdoors to physically use the energy that comes up with anger can be very helpful. On the other hand, some children can get rid of a lot of anger simply through tearing paper into very small bits and throwing them into the wastebasket.

WHAT ARE FEELINGS?

Let's look at the word *emotion*, which is what is meant by *feelings*. *Emotion* comes from the Latin word *emovere*, which means "to move out from, stir up, excite." So feelings indicate a stirred-up state of the individual. It is important to remember that the experience of this stirred-up state is subjective. The only way one can know about another's feelings is through communication (verbal and nonverbal), but the communication is not the feeling.

Feelings are complex subjective experiences that are different from but involve the physical and mental aspects of the self. That definition of feelings is derived from Greenspan and Greenspan (1985) in their book, *First Feelings: Milestones in the Emotional Development of Your Baby and Child*. Feelings can be felt, expressed, acted on, and thought about, but each of those experiences of feelings is different.

All Feelings Are Positive

If you made a long list of all the feelings you have ever experienced, it would be tempting to divide them into positive and negative feelings. However, all feelings have value and are useful, even the ones we wish would go away. They serve a purpose. Feelings are a reaction to experience; they help us define and organize experience. They give us direction for action. They give us cause for expression. Some of the greatest works of art, music, and dance have come from feelings—and not always pleasant ones.

LEARNING FEELINGS

Feelings come naturally. From the beginning, in some cultures, adults teach the labels for those feelings. Children come to understand concepts of emotional states; eventually they can think about feeling.

This labeling starts in infancy, when the adult begins to label the child's emotional state: "That loud noise scared you!" or "I see how unhappy you are that your mommy isn't here to feed you yet." Labeling feelings is part of the socialization process.

The socialization process is also involved in feeding children cultural information about feelings and their expression. There is a fine line between the kind of cultural explaining, shaping, and molding of feelings that adults do to socialize children and manipulating them with value judgments that cut them off from their true experience.

Placing values on feelings—teaching children *what* to feel and *what not* to feel— can do great harm. Rogers (1980) wrote about this subject long ago in his book, *A Way of Being*. He wrote about how infants trust their experience. When they are hungry they want food. They are in touch with their deepest needs. But if as they grow their parents begin to tell them what to feel or not feel, they come to distrust their own experience. It's even worse if the parents connect love to the issue of feelings, saying things such as "If you feel that way I won't love you." Doing so can cut children off from their feelings. Adults have a tremendous responsibility for children's emotional development.

How do adults teach children what to feel? One way is through something quite innocent, called *social referencing*.

Surprise! Children play with feelings.

Doris Pfalmer

Social Referencing

Have you ever noticed how a young child who is faced with an uncertain situation will turn to a parent, infant care teacher, preschool teacher, or family child care provider for clues about how to react? This is very helpful; the adult can calm fears. Consider this example: The child is approached by Uncle Mario, a large man with a big beard and glasses. This child has never seen a human who looks like this before. He turns to the trusted adult for cues. The adult smiles, puts an arm around him, and walks confidently toward Uncle Mario, talking to the man as if she trusts him implicitly. Every child won't take the adult's cues, but some will, and what had been a scary situation becomes an ordinary one—the meeting of a new relative. That's social referencing.

Anyone who has been around young children very much knows that when a young child falls down, she will often look to her parent or other adult to see how she is supposed to feel. That's social referencing.

Adults use social referencing to calm children's fears, warn them of danger, help them like a new food, even infect them with joy. Children constantly receive unspoken messages about how to react to situations through adult facial expressions, body language, posture, and even muscle tone. They eventually build up what can be thought of as *cultural scripts* about how to respond to specific situations.

Most children have some tendency toward being influenced in their feelings by important people in their lives. That means

Children "try on" feelings like they try on dress-up clothes.

adults must be very careful about wielding this influence, or they'll put children out of touch with their real feelings. They'll cut them off from their true experience.

As an early childhood teacher, recognize the power of social referencing and use it wisely. When a child looks to you for your reaction to something, decide whether it is beneficial to give it to him in that situation. Know that you can remain neutral and let the child decide for himself how to react. *After* he decides, a supportive verbal or nonverbal response from you is appropriate.

Remaining neutral eliminates the possibility of a mistaken response. Consider these two examples of an adult mistake in influencing children's feelings: A toddler falls down. The adult acts as if everything is all right, but the child is hurt. The adult response discounts the child's feeling and makes him question his own reality. Or, conversely, if the adult makes a big fuss over what was only a little hurt, the child learns to ignore reality and exaggerate feelings to get attention.

Some parents may appreciate observing you when you are using social referencing wisely. They see you remaining neutral at times when you are trying not to influence a child's feelings. That may be a new idea to them.

Social referencing naturally starts in infancy, when babies look to adults to help them understand and interpret the world. The toddler also uses social referencing, but

Lloyd Lemmerman/Merrill

Adults influence children's feelings through something called social referencing.

this approach should begin to fade in the preschool years. If it doesn't, its continuing presence may indicate a problem.

The outcome of the overuse of social referencing shows in the joke about the henpecked husband who, when offered a choice of custard for desert, asks his wife, "Dear, do I like custard?" But it involves more than simple likes and dislikes; it's a matter of a power differential. Take the example of the slave who when asked, "How's the weather?" looks at the master's face rather than out the window to answer. No one wants children to grow up with a slave mentality, unable to express their own feelings and relate to their own perceptions in the face of powerful others.

Cultural Scripts

All these warnings aside, it is important to recognize that feelings are influenced by cultural scripts that dictate the proper feelings for each occasion. Scripts can be specific to individual families or cultures, telling their members what they are supposed to feel and how to convey it. These scripts are useful in telling us what someone is likely to feel under certain circumstances. We know what emotion is "called for," for example, when someone close dies. Part of the socialization process is to learn these cultural scripts that dictate the correct emotional response to a situation. Even if we don't feel the way the script dictates, it is important to recognize that, in the eyes of others, the definition of *sane* or *normal* depends to some extent on knowing the cultural script.

One advantage of cultural scripts is that we get clues about how another person of our culture feels, even if they don't tell us. But a disadvantage, of course, is that though the unwritten script tells us how someone is *supposed to feel*, there is no guarantee that a person *will feel* as expected. And, of course, our own script may not help us understand a person from another culture unless we know the script of that person's culture as well as our own.

Scripts differ greatly from culture to culture. For example, there is an enormous difference about when it is OK to get angry and express oneself. As has already been mentioned, in cultures such as the European American culture, which stresses individuality, everyone is encouraged to express feelings. The idea is that a person will function better as a group member if he or she enjoys the mental health that comes from expressing feelings. Good early childhood practice requires that adults accept all feelings as valid and convey that message to children, as well as teaching them appropriate expression of those feelings. The adult's job is to teach the child to recognize and express all feelings, especially anger.

Anger gets a lot of attention in European American culture. Some therapists, parents, and early childhood practitioners see the importance of allowing a child to express anger thoroughly, even to the point of raging. The idea is for the child to experience the feeling fully, to "work it through." These people see raging as a process that should not be interrupted until it is finished; otherwise, the unexpressed feelings may remain unfelt and go underground, popping up again and again as a "leftover" instead of arising as a feeling that is clearly connected to the immediate situation and not to the past. These adults may also assure the child that it is all right to feel whatever it is that he or she is feeling. They seek to prove to the child that expression of strong feelings won't result in abandonment. Of course, not all European Americans deal with anger in the same way. There is great variety in the European American culture.

Some European Americans and also people of other cultures don't have the same view of feelings and their expressions as described in the prior paragraph. They are more concerned about group harmony than about individual expression of feelings, particularly anger. They don't see unexpressed feelings as dangerous to either individual mental health or the group.

Lee (1959) says of the Hopi, "It is his duty to be happy, for the sake of the group, and a mind in conflict and full of anxiety brings disruption, ill-being, to the social unit" (p. 21). And Trinh Ngoc Dung (1984) says that in Vietnamese families, "children are taught at an early age to control their emotions" (p. 12).

Although some may feel that the mandate of these cultures is to repress feelings, a situation that is regarded as unhealthy in white, Northern European-derived American culture, others view this approach in a more positive way. For example, in his book *Americans and Chinese*, Hsu (1970) compares the

> prominence of emotions in the American way of life . . . with the tendency of the Chinese to underplay all matters of the heart . . . . Being individual-centered, the American moves toward social and psychological isolation. His happiness tends to be unqualified ecstasy just as his sorrow is likely to mean unbearable misery. A strong emotionality is inevitable since the emotions are concentrated in one individual.
>
> Being more situation-centered, the Chinese is inclined to be socially or psychologically dependent on others, for this situation-centered individual is tied closer to his world and his fellow men. His happiness and his sorrow tend to be mild since they are shared. (p. 10)

The Importance of Accepting Feelings

In spite of cultural differences in how you teach children to express feelings, it is important that children be allowed to *feel* them. The first 2 years of life are important in socializing a child to feel or not feel. Children suffer when adults refuse to accept their feelings. Feelings are important to spontaneity, to being in touch with one's experience, and to mental health. We *need* our feelings to develop in healthy ways.

Letting Go of Responsibility

Julie, mother of 4-year-old Alexa, felt shattered when she learned that a friend's teenage son had committed suicide. "I can't believe it," she lamented to another friend, Laura. "She's such a good mother!" All Julie's own hopes and fears about how her parenting skills would ensure her daughter's happiness had come tumbling down around her ears.

"Being a good mother is no guarantee of anything," Laura spouted without thinking. She wanted to comfort Julie, but her words only made matters worse.

A tear rolled down Julie's cheek as she said, "I've always thought if you tried hard and were a good parent, you'd have control over how your children turned out. But this tragedy ruined that theory." She was weeping openly now—tears for her friend and tears for herself.

As the conversation continued, Julie realized she was feeling fiercely protective of her own Alexa. She kept trying to figure out how to keep her happy so that she'd never lose her. What good were parenting skills if they didn't guarantee the happiness and well-being of your child?

Laura wasn't able to comfort her because Julie had learned a cruel lesson about life: Even good parents suffer tragic disappointments and losses because of their children's decisions.

Parents can control (or at least try to control) what *they* do, but they can't control how their children receive, perceive, or react to what they do. They can love their children, but they can't ensure that they feel loved. They can't control their children's personal perspective on things. They can't control the decisions they make about how to act based on those perspectives.

A major task of most parents is to let go. Though the first obvious letting go comes at birth when the cord is cut, letting go continues throughout life, a snip at a time. The most important letting go, and perhaps the hardest, is relinquishing the responsibility for the child's happiness.

Of course a parent's job is to meet children's needs, and that job logically *should* lead to happiness. It sometimes happens that way, but not always, because life isn't logical and because cause and effect are never simple or clear-cut in human development.

As the child gets older, the parent's ability and responsibility for meeting needs diminish, and the child takes over the job. The parent no longer has the same degree of control of creating well-being or bringing about happiness (assuming he or she was able to do it in the first place). This is a hard realization for parents to swallow. Of course all parents want their children to be happy, but they can't *make* them happy!

Parents can only do the best they can—improve their parenting skills and take care of themselves and their children. They'll have their expectations and hopes, of course, but they must realize that too many factors are involved for them to take direct responsibility for their children's feelings and the decisions (even life-and-death ones) that result from those feelings.

Even if it were possible to control the feelings and decisions of others, would that be good? Think what loss of freedom that outside control would mean. Imagine feeling the way your parents wanted you to or turning out exactly as they intended!

Teaching Children Healthy Expressions of Feelings

Acceptable expression of feelings is culturally determined. The perspective I am basing this chapter on is what I have learned from being a professional early educator. Some I learned in classes and workshops, some from experience, some from reading. It isn't the way I was raised, but it does fit my middle-class European American culture best. I know from experience and what I've learned from colleagues and families that this typical "early childhood perspective" doesn't fit everyone. So I am trying to be forthright and honest when I say that this chapter is written from one perspective. The strategies for working with parents are designed to make sure that interactions with parents help the early educator who has this perspective expand beyond it.

I will start by stressing the differences among three things: the feelings themselves, the expression of those feelings, and the actions based on those feelings. It is never inappropriate to *feel* whatever one feels. That message should be given to children loud and clear. However, it is sometimes inappropriate to express those feelings, and part of the socialization process is to understand when it is appropriate to express feelings and when it is not. Maturity is in part determined by being able to make good decisions in this area. Deciding when to act on feelings also takes some maturity. Because of all the energy feelings bring forth, the urge is to act each time. However, the young child learns soon enough that getting mad and slugging someone is not a socially acceptable action around most adults. Grabbing what you want has side effects, and taking a bite out of someone because you love them does not get a loving response.

It takes some children awhile to learn these lessons. It is wise to be both kind and patient while the child is learning to control the actions brought forth by feelings and to find appropriate ways to express them. Susan Isaacs, a pioneer in early childhood education, gave advice in

Adults have different ideas about how to express feelings appropriately. They may not all agree that what this child is doing is acceptable.

Michael Newman/PhotoEdit Inc.

1930 to a parent, and that advice was still valid 55 years from when she wrote her book (Smith, 1985) and continues to be valid today. She assured the parent that determination, obstinacy, and outbursts of temper are very normal and that it takes patience to socialize children. Often adults respond to these behaviors by getting upset. Isaacs explains that it is better to ignore these difficult behaviors than to display adult emotion, because that can make things worse. When adults get upset, the power that gives the child makes it likely that it will happen again. Or the adult getting upset may cause the child to be afraid. It helps to realize that the child has to learn to accept adult ways and desires and has to also learn to control his or her own behavior. We can't expect perfection, but we can help the child work toward more and more control, reasonableness, and friendly agreement. Isaacs is clear that teaching by spanking doesn't work because the child can't see the difference between the adult behavior and his own violence. Ruling by fear only increases obstinacy. Adults should avoid unnecessary demands and pick only a few issues, making sure they are ones they can follow through on. When the adult gives lots of choices on smaller matters, it is easier to be friendly and understanding.

It may be hard to follow Isaacs's advice in the heat of the moment, but it is worth having patience as a goal. While being patient, you can be teaching words to express the feelings and help the child move to more acceptable behaviors. When children begin to label feelings, you know they have now conceptualized them, bringing intellectual processes in to help with the emotional ones. Once the mind comes into play, it isn't long until you see the child using "pretend" to help him further understand and cope with feelings. Now the child's mind and body are working in concert with feelings, thus helping the child integrate.

What are some appropriate ways for young children to express their feelings? Many adults encourage direct verbalization and teach children to say, "I'm mad because you took my toy" or "I'm unhappy because my mommy had to go to work." They also teach children to say to each other, "I don't want you to do that" or "I don't like it when you hit me. It hurts."

Many adults agree in this approach—teaching one child to talk to another in a direct way. However, not everyone is comfortable with teaching children to talk so directly to adults. Some feel it is disrespectful for children to tell an adult they are mad at him or her. They are even more uncomfortable if the child translates "I'm mad at you" into "I hate you!" Other adults accept this form of expression, perhaps disregarding the actual words and responding to the feeling behind them. It is common for an adult trained in early childhood education to reflect back the angry feeling by saying something such as "You're really mad at me right now."

Whatever ways of expressing feelings are acceptable to the adults in the child's life, those are the ways that should be taught to the child. Imagine how a parent who is very concerned that his child show a certain kind of respect to adults would feel if he walked into the classroom just in time to hear his child scream "I hate you" at the teacher. Although the teacher may find nothing wrong with this way of expressing anger, it is important to take the parents' perspective into consideration and find some way to accept their feelings and teach another mode of expression.

Examples of ways of expressing feelings that are acceptable to some adults and not to others are as follows:

* Yelling and screaming
* Stating negative wishes or imagining violent happenings (e.g., "I hope your new toy breaks" "Maybe you'll break your leg" or "I wish my baby brother would die")
* Taking out anger symbolically on toys or other objects (e.g., spanking dolls or pounding pillows)

Most adults agree that name-calling and using obscenities are not appropriate ways for young children to express feelings. It's important, though, to realize that to a young child "bad words" have little meaning except that children know certain words hold power for adults. However, if you listen to young children trying to wield power over *each other*, they don't use adult words. They call each other "baby" or say, "I won't like you anymore." Those expressions have more meaning and carry more weight than all the four-letter words they may have ever learned.

TEACHING CHILDREN TO COPE WITH FEELINGS

Developing Self-Calming Skills

One of the greatest skills an adult working or living with young children can have is the ability to calm an upset child. Of course, the optimum is for children to learn to calm themselves, and for that reason adults should respect their attempts to do so. For example, when the crying infant finds a soothing thumb and pops it in, the adult should rejoice and not try to distract or substitute something else. The thumb is an example of a very effective self-soothing device.

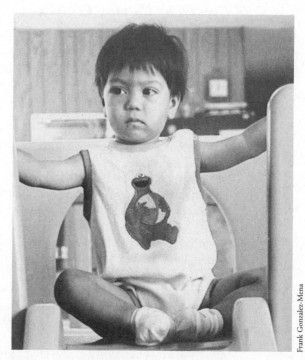

If infants are to learn self-calming techniques, the adult must not jump up and respond to each little whimper or tiny demand. Timing is important; it takes skill to create a response gap that is just long enough to allow children to discover ways to meet their own needs. If the adult waits too long, children feel neglected; they may go beyond the place where they can calm themselves. Once the child gets overly excited and chaos sets in, the adult needs to be on hand to stop the momentum and

It is never inappropriate to feel what one feels.

help the child get reorganized. Sometimes this is merely a matter of being present and allowing the child to pick up your calm rhythms. Some adults have the natural instinct of tuning into the child's rhythms, flowing with them until the two are in tune, then slowing the combined rhythm until the child is once more relaxed and calm. Thoman and Browder (1987) give specifics about how this can be done with a baby. They start by advising the adult to find a quiet, softly lit room and relax completely while holding the baby: "Breathe deeply. Feel all your muscles unwind . . . . Now tune in to your baby. Listen to his breathing. Feel his breathing against your chest. At first, try to match your breathing to your baby's breathing, so you're inhaling and exhaling in unison. Then slowly make your breathing deeper" (pp. 181–182). They say that as the adult changes his or her breathing, the baby's breathing will change to match it.

This approach can be used with some children who are no longer babies. Some children are able to use the adult closeness to bring down their energy level and become calm. Something similar can even be used with a group of children. Some infant-care teachers and early educators know how to go with the flow of energy and then bring it down to a less chaotic level. There's usually an ideal time to intervene. Determining this ideal time is a skill adults who live and work with young children can acquire through experience.

Coping by Playing Pretend

Playing pretend is a way that children experience feelings in a way that they can control. In a sense, they *practice* emotions through playing. They're in charge of the environment and of themselves, which puts them in a very powerful position—often the opposite of their position when they are overcome by a feeling in real life.

Adults who understand how important pretend play is to emotional development encourage children to engage in it. They give them props to get them started. (That's what the "housekeeping corner" and all the "dress-up clothes" are about in a child care center.) When children don't automatically show interest in playing pretend, adults can get them started by playing with them. Adults who see the value of time spent pretending provide opportunities, space, and materials to stimulate imagination. They also provide encouragement.

Two early childhood experts, Susan Isaacs and Vivian Paley, working 50 years apart, have important ideas about the use of what is called *dramatic play*. Isaacs (Smith, 1985) says that through what she calls "imaginative play, children symbolize and externalize their inner drama and conflicts and work through them to gain relief from pressures." She explains that through creating make-believe situations, children practice predicting or hypothesizing what might happen and play it out. Children free themselves from the here and now of the concrete world by acting as if something were true. They not only revisit the past but project into the future through playing pretend.

Paley (1988) talks about the kind of pretend play she sees daily in her classroom of preschoolers. She says, "Whatever else is going on in this network of melodrama, the themes are vast and wondrous. Images of good and evil, birth and death, parent and child, move in and out of the real and the pretend. There is no small talk. The listener is submerged in philosophical position papers, a virtual recapitulation of life's enigmas" (p. 6).

As children create their own worlds through pretend play, they gain a sense of power. They transform reality and practice mastery over it. No wonder pretend play is appealing. In addition to personal power, children also gain communication skills. Through play with, for example, small figures, they deal with several levels of communication as the figures themselves interact, and the players who control them also interact. Children engaged in this type of play practice negotiation and cooperation in real life and on a pretend level. They can get very sophisticated at expressing feelings through this medium.

As an early educator you should thoroughly acquaint yourself with the benefits of play so you can help families appreciate it. It takes some skill to observe with a parent and point out the benefits without talking down or lecturing the parent. You don't want to flaunt your knowledge, but you do want to expand the families' view of play. Of course, not all families devalue play as an important activity in children's lives; many, however, have gotten the message that the early years are learning years, and they may not see play as a worthy way of learning.

Coping with Simultaneous Feelings

It would be easier to teach children to accept, express, and cope with their feelings if all feelings came singly. However, almost no feelings come as a single, pure and simple unit of emotion. Often, two feelings come simultaneously. For example, I feel sad that my dog has died, but I'm greatly relieved that his suffering is over; or I'm delighted about my contract to write a new book, but I'm worried about my ability to do it. Adults recognize mixed feelings. Having simultaneous feelings can be an advantage because we can focus on one to help us cope with the other.

However, it is a different story for young children, who can only focus on one feeling at a time; they aren't aware of mixed feelings (Harter & Buddin, 1987). We adults can help them begin to experience more than one feeling by verbalizing for them when we perceive they might have mixed feelings (e.g., "You're happy to stay overnight with your friend, but you're scared about being away from home"). Experiencing simultaneous feelings may take some time, since it only comes as the result of increasing maturity.

Coping with Fear

Uncomfortable as they may feel, fears are useful. They protect and help keep children out of danger. A problem is that sometimes fears get in a child's way of fully experiencing the world. They can limit explorations and discourage healthy

Adults can help children deal with fear by taking them seriously and not discounting their feelings.

risk taking, the things that give children a fuller life and help them expand their experience and knowledge.

Adults can help children deal with fears by doing the following:

• *Taking them seriously.* What may not seem significant to an adult may be terrifying to a young child. It is important for the early educator to be reassuring without discounting the feeling. Children need their feelings validated, even when the adult is convinced that there is no danger present.

• *Modeling.* Children can learn fears from other people. They can also learn to not be afraid by watching others interact with the object of their fear. The child who is afraid of dogs may be reassured when both an adult and another child pet the dog in a friendly, trusting way.

• *Playing out fears.* Sometimes the early educator can find ways for the child to experience something in a safe environment that he or she is afraid of. Sometimes children will do this on their own through pretend play, either in a dramatic play setting or with small figures. Another example of playing out fears is when an adult encourages a toddler to play with a small amount of water in a dishpan or sink to help cope with bathtub fears.

Dowrick (1986), in his book *Social Survival for Children*, describes how he trains children in relaxation and helps them visualize themselves feeling brave in situations that scare them. He also talks about alleviating fear in children through helping them perform in graduated small steps following a carefully established hierarchy.

Dowrick gives an example of such a hierarchy: A 5-year-old child greatly feared doctors yet needed to go to the dentist. The first step was to help him pretend to be a doctor with another child as patient. That was followed by getting him to play patient with another child as doctor. When he was comfortable with that, he was talked into allowing an adult "doctor" to pretend to inspect the inside of his throat. When he was finally able to allow a "pretend" adult doctor to put dental instruments in his mouth, he was ready for his visit to the real dentist. Each step of the play was recorded on videotape and then edited and reviewed by the child. Watching himself in repeated experiences in a benign environment strengthened his coping responses—a kind of self-modeling. In addition, the child was taught relaxation techniques, using positive imagery.

Many early childhood practitioners also use a technique of having children help other children cope with fears. The teacher sends a gentle, outgoing child over to interact with the fearful child who is hanging back from participating in activities. Some early educators have a real talent for linking up one child with another for the good of both. Some go so far as to suggest to parents that so-and-so might be a good friend to invite over. The friendships that result from these linkages sometimes last for years.

Adults "Being Put Up Against Themselves"

It is hard for adults who grew up without fully experiencing their feelings to be around children who are able and willing to do so. A crying child can touch sore spots deep within adults who then react from their own pain as much as from the child's. Marjory Keenan (1996), an infant–toddler caregiver, calls this phenomenon "putting one up against oneself" as she tells her story of trying to contend with the lengthy separation agonies of three little girls in her care.

Marjory was professional—warm, caring, and supportive of these girls in their grief. She helped them write daily letters to their mommies telling them they were missed. But nothing worked for long to relieve them of the need to chant pitifully, "I want my mama." It took Marjory two months to finally face her own deep pain of her mother's death when she was just a little younger than these children. She realized what was happening one day in her classroom when the chanting started again. Marjory found herself thinking, "Shut up! You have a mommy, and your mommy always comes and gets you." Marjory's mommy never came back again, and the 2-year-old inside of her was reacting. Marjory's feelings finally resurfaced when the three little girls "put her up against herself" with their nearly nonstop lamenting.

"The girls in my class were not consciously trying to upset me," Marjory says. "They were only expressing their true feelings of loss, and these were mirroring my deep pain. The more I listened to the child within me, the less my lamenters irritated me. I began to realize that they were speaking the words that I could only feel internally." (Keenan, 1996, p. 75)

Coping with Anger

Sometimes anger carries good, clean, strong energy. Children can learn to use that energy to express themselves, to protect themselves, and, when needs or wants conflict, to work toward problem-solving solutions. The ultimate in problem solving is when the child is able to satisfy the need, thereby eliminating the source of the anger without tearing down or intentionally hurting other people. Anger can give extra strength or insight on how to get needs met and to aid this problem solving process.

Teaching young children to express angry feelings without hurting anyone or anything is a goal for early educators. They help children learn these skills by doing the following:

• *Accepting and labeling the feeling.*   "I see how angry you are." "It really makes you mad when she grabs your doll!"

• *Redirecting the energy and helping the child get it out.*   "I know you feel like biting your sister, but bite this washcloth instead." "Why don't you go out and run around the play yard three times and see if you still feel so mad."

• *Calming the energy; soothing the chaos.*   "I see how upset you are right now. Do you want to sit on my lap and rock a little?" (for the younger child). Or for the older child, a neck massage might help or a suggestion to "try messing around with this goop and see if it makes you feel better." (Time-honored substances for "messing around" are mud and its substitutes—wet clay, cornstarch and water, play dough. Water alone is a great soother in a water-play table, a tub, or a sink.)

• *Avoiding a reward for anger.*   Some adults respond to a child's display of anger with so much attention that the behavior is reinforced. If a powerless child can achieve a powerful feeling by displaying anger, she is bound to continue to use the same approach unless someone helps her experience power in a different way.

• *Teaching problem solving.*   When children learn to solve problems by communicating in a give-and-take negotiating kind of way, they feel less frustrated and have less need to try to get their way by using anger.

Adults can help children experience, express, think about, and cope with feelings.

PROBLEM SOLVING

Problems are an important part of life. They are the way children learn, from infancy on. Problem solving is a reasonable way to cope with feelings that arise from problems. The feelings provide energy and motivation to do something. Problems provide challenges that keep life interesting. When teachers see problem solving as a skill that children can benefit from knowing, they can help parents understand problems, and problem solving, in that way too.

Using the RERUN Problem-Solving Process with a Child

Chapter 6 introduced a problem-solving process called RERUN. The elements are reflect, explain, reason, understand, and negotiate. In that chapter the process was explained as a way to solve cross-cultural disagreements with adults. Here is advice about how to use that same process with a child.

When you encounter a problem to solve, start by checking your own position. Are you clear about the problem? Do you know for sure what you want? Ambiguity on your part will change the whole situation.

I'll use an example from my own life of something I'm very clear about—young children running into the street. Since I have five children, I've been through this situation many times. I never take chances. I know there's a problem if my child is close to a street and can't be trusted to stay out of it. Let's say my 3-year-old has been playing in the front yard with a toy truck. I have been watching him, because he is on the verge of understanding street safety. But just now he rolled the truck down the driveway and has started down after it. I'm not going to take a chance. I move fast and grab him before he goes into the street. Then I go through the RERUN sequence. Here's how it works:

- *Reflect.* As my child squirms and protests, I let him know that his feelings are received and accepted. I reflect them back with such words as, "I see how unhappy you are about being stopped."
- *Explain.* I help my child understand the situation: "I can't let you run in the street."
- *Reason.* I give the reason for my prohibition: "You might get hurt."
- *Understand.* I tune in to feelings—both mine and my child's. I try to understand the situation from both points of view. I don't have to say anything out loud at this point, I just need to be sure I have clarity. I may have to talk to myself to get it.
- *Negotiate.* Since a 3-year-old can talk, I can discuss the problem, and together we can look for a mutually satisfying solution. If he had been 2, I would have just given two alternatives: "You can stay up here on the porch, or you can play in the backyard." I might do that with a 3-year-old too, if the talk turned into game playing and we weren't working toward a solution.

I try hard not to talk every situation to death. Notice the few words used in this RERUN sequence. The negotiations are the only part that need more than a brief phrase.

With an older child and a less drastic problem, the negotiations can get quite lengthy, but I try to recognize when I'm getting involved in a game. When negotiations are breaking down, I return to the beginning and go through the parts again. I may have to RERUN several times before the problem is solved.

PROBLEM SOLVING AS A CULTURAL ISSUE

Cynthia Ballenger (1992, 1999), has been observing the differences between European American culture and Haitian culture for many years. She points out some major differences in child-handling techniques between Haitian and North American preschool teachers. North American teachers focus on the individual child, the feelings, the situation, and the problem. They like to help the child look at consequences and make choices. The teacher remains rather emotionally unattached during the process of problem solving, as I was in the RERUN example just explained. Good or bad behavior is not usually mentioned during a problem-solving process.

Haitian teachers, on the other hand, clearly distinguish bad behavior. They emphasize group values and the responsibility of the child to the group. Children's feelings are not a focus during this discussion; the discussion is about emotional ties and adult expectation. There's no feeling of detachment as there is when North American teachers are helping a child problem solve a situation. Haitian teachers don't talk about consequences but rather good and bad behaviors, which relate to respect and obedience. Haitian teachers do not use a detached and individualistic problem-solving technique, like North American teachers, but put emphasis on shared values in a moral community.

In spite of the fact that this chapter is about feelings and problem solving, it's important to realize there are other cultural perspectives on how to handle feelings and problems. You may be more comfortable with the North American way that Ballenger describes. Or the Haitian way may resonate with you even if you aren't Haitian. Don't think of "right" and "wrong" when you compare these two approaches with managing young children's behavior; think of "different." Much of the material in this chapter may be new to families. Strategy Box 8.1 gives some ideas about how to share it with them.

PROBLEM SOLVING AND PARENTING STYLES

How parents respond to seeing teachers working on problem solving with children could be a cross-cultural issue, but it could also be affected by parenting styles, regardless of culture. Three parenting styles were named some time ago by Diana Baumrind (1971, 1986) who did some classic research visiting families in their homes in the late afternoon just before dinner—a time that is stressful in most families with young children. The three parenting styles she named are the *authoritarian approach*, the *permissive approach*, and the *authoritative approach*.

The Authoritarian Approach

The authoritarian approach is the "do-as-I-say" way of relating to children. Authoritarians see their power as inherent in their position. In conflicts, they see win-lose solutions—and it's important that they win. That's the way they keep their authority.

The strict authoritarian parent demands uncompromising obedience. Rules are established and infractions punished. Parental needs and desires come before child needs and desires. Authoritarian parents may have a good deal of self-respect but may not show respect for the child, in ways recognized by adults not of the authoritarian school of thought.

Strategy Box 8.1

Working with Families Around Issues of Feelings and Problem Solving

* Open up conversations with families to discover their perspectives on feelings and problem solving. Be prepared for the fact that feelings are cultural issues and families may have strong ideas about their place in human relationships.
* Create opportunities for conversations when an issue comes up with a particular family. Such opportunities occur in some programs at the beginning and end of the day when families drop off and pick up their children. They can also be scheduled meetings.
* Put on regular meetings to discuss a wide range of subjects, including perspectives on feelings and ideas about problem solving. Try to figure out what prevents some families from attending these meetings and address the problems, whether scheduling, transportation, or child care.
* Create an atmosphere at meetings that feels both welcoming and comfortable. Make sure the families get to know each other. Make each meeting interactive.
* Consider using a "Transformative Education" model instead of a traditional "Parent Education" model for your meetings. Transformative education is defined by a two way flow of information and knowledge rather than one-way delivery system. In transformative education two people or two groups come together and interact in such a way that both are transformed by the experience.

Authoritarian parenting has a bad reputation with many early educators. From an outsider, one who doesn't believe in an authoritarian approach, authoritarian behaviors may feel very uncomfortable; however, for some families it is the appropriate approach and their children find security in knowing that their parents are in charge. They may take the parents' strictness and demands for obedience as a sign of love.

The authoritarian parent is unlikely to embrace the problem-solving approach, if there are negotiations or choices involved.

The Permissive Approach

Permissive parents seek to have little control over their children. These parents may take the role of guides and friends—being warm and involved with their children—or they may be less interested and involved and more lackadaisical. In an extreme permissive approach, it may seem as if parents just lie back, and let their children walk all over them. Parental needs take a backseat to child needs. In a win-lose conflict, the children win because the adult doesn't take any power into his own hands. He grants all the power to the children.

From the view of someone who is uncomfortable with permissiveness it looks as though the permissive parents fail to display self-respect because they let their children win conflicts with them. They find the children dissatisfied and perhaps uncomfortable if they seem to be out of control and have few or no limits set by their parents. They say that it doesn't feel good to treat people like doormats, even when they invite you to do so. The permissive parent may resist the structure of a problem solving approach, though it is unlikely that even very permissive parents would let their children run in the street. However, Barbara Rogoff in her book, *The Cultural Nature of Human Development* (2003), has many examples of parents from other cultures trusting their young children to do things, like handle machetes and knives, that would be horrifying to most adults in the United States.

The Authoritative Approach

Neither authoritarian styles nor permissive ones are ideal according to Baumrind's research and those who have followed after her. From Baumrind emerges the "right approach"—the authoritative approach. Authoritative parents listen to children's justifications and requests and make decisions that take into consideration the needs of the child. They provide limits and control when necessary. They believe in mutual respect.

Authoritative parents derive their authority from the fact of their experience, size, and ability. They know that they have lived in the world longer than their children and have expertise their children don't have. They see their role as using reason to guide, protect, and facilitate development.

Authoritative parents have firm standards but employ a flexible approach. They are apt to use what's been called a win-win approach to parenting. They are concerned about their children's needs and also about their own needs. When the two clash, they don't sacrifice one for the other but look for solutions in which both their needs and their children's are met. Resolution leaves both parties satisfied. Children of authoritative parents are thought to be self-reliant, independent, socially responsible, and explorative.

An important device for the win-win parenting used by authoritative parents is the problem-solving process.

A DEEPER LOOK AT THE THREE PARENTING STYLES

The research on the three types of parenting styles was done on European Americans and applies to European Americans. However, Ruth Chao (1994) at UCLA questions the validity for Chinese parenting. She raises a paradox. Authoritarian styles of child rearing predict low achievement in school, yet Chinese children who are raised by authoritarian parents do well in school. Chao proposes that the concept of authority is ethnocentric and does not explain important facets of Chinese child rearing.

Authoritarian child rearing in the United States was handed down from puritanical beginnings, which advocated harsh treatment of children. This view of authoritarianism in child rearing lasted two centuries. It wasn't until World War II that Americans became more permissive. The history of authority in China is very different. Authority in China is not harsh but gentle, coming as it does from a Confucian tradition related not to predestination but to social harmony.

Though authoritarian-style child rearing is equated with distance and harshness in European American tradition, in China it is equated with closeness, both physical and emotional. (The child sleeps with the mother, for example.) The mother is greatly involved in promoting success in the child and is the main caretaker. That situation contrasts with a European American view of independence and individuality.

Training is another concept that differs culturally. To some European American parents, training involves something militaristic, rigid, and strict. The word has negative connotations. Chinese parents regard training as positive—an act of love.

This chapter is bound to give you much to think about when working with families. Though there is quite a bit of agreement in the field about various approaches to working with children, families don't necessarily fit neatly into the research that guides the field. That may leave the early educator confused and maybe upset. But that's exactly what this chapter has been about—coping with feelings and using problem-solving approaches to figure out what to do.

LOOKING BACK AND LOOKING FORWARD

This chapter explored feelings and some of the ways adults can help children experience, express, think about, and cope with feelings. Feelings can provide useful energy for problem solving, a subject also examined in this chapter. How the idea of problem solving is viewed by families can sometimes be influenced by their parenting style. Three such styles, based on some classic research, were explained along with some of the issues that are taken by people who question the research. All of the material in this chapter could easily lead to fascinating cross-cultural discussions when the focus is on working with parents.

When people have a problem-solving attitude, they may feel empowered. Empowered people are more likely to see themselves as capable, feel good about themselves, and have high self-esteem, which is the subject of the next chapter.

FOR DISCUSSION

1. How does social referencing work? Can you give an example? When is social referencing useful and when is it not? Why would you not want to use social referencing when responding to a toddler who has just taken a spill?

2. Can you give an example of a cultural script? Do you have any cultural scripts? What are they?

3. Which of the three parenting approaches mentioned in the chapter do you prefer and why? How were you raised? How do you think the way you were raised affects you now?

4. Make up a scene involving the RERUN process of problem solving.

WEB SITES

American Psychological Association (APA)
http://www.apa.org/pubinfo/anger.html
This page explains what anger is, how it is expressed, anger management, cognitive restructuring, and more.

Children Today
http://childrentoday.com/resources/articles/parent.htm
Do you know your parenting style? Take a quiz based on Diana Baumrind's research.

Development Psychology
http://www.devpsy.org/teaching/parent/baumrind_styles.html
A collection of resources about Diana Baumrind's observed parenting styles, this page includes excerpts from her original work on the topic, further information, and a related role-playing activity.

Good Beginnings Alliance
http://www.goodbeginnings.org/childrencope.htm
This group helps children cope with fears by supporting them through threatening world events. Web site has good strategies for helping children cope with fears in general.

Jeanne Beckman
http://www.jeannebeckman.com/page35.html
This site provides information on the effects of media violence on fears in children and what parents can do.

National Network for Child Care (NNCC)
http://www.nncc.org/Guidance/dc31_cope.anger.html
This link describes specific ways children cope with anger and teaches appropriate ways of expressing feelings.

Parenting Toolbox
http://www.parentingtoolbox.com/hand/violence.html
This is an article about talking to children about anger and violence.

A Place of Our Own
http://www.aplaceofourown.org/question_detail.phd?id=63
Expert and practitioner advice is offered about how preschool-type activities can present situations where children use problem-solving skills, which supports cognitive development.

Purdue University Extension
http://www.ces.purdue.edu/terrorism/helpingchildren.html
This article discusses how to recognize stress in children, reduce it and help them cope with it.

Royal College of Psychiatrists
http://www.rcpsych.ac.uk/info/mhgu/newmhgu13.htm
Helps adults cope with worries and anxieties in children, including phobias.

FURTHER READING

Barkley, R. A. (1997). ADHD *and the nature of self-control*. New York: Guilford.

Berk, L. E. (1994, November). Vygotsky's theory: The importance of make-believe play. *Young Children*, 50(1), 30–39.

Bronson, M. B. (2000, March). Research in review: Recognizing and supporting the development of self-regulation in young children. *Young Children*, 55(2), 32–36.

Bruno, H. E. (2007, September). Gossip-free zones: Problem solving to prevent power struggles. *Young Children, 62*(5), 26–32.

Butterfield, P. M., Martin, C. A., & Prairie, A. P. (2004). *Emotional connections: How relationships guide early learning.* Washington, DC: Zero to Three.

Clyman, R. B., Emde, R. N., Kempe, J. E., & Harmon, R. J. (1986). Social referencing and social looking among 12-month-old infants. In T. B. Brazelton & M. W. Yogman (Eds.), *Affective development in infancy* (pp. 75–94). Norwood, NJ: Ablex.

Crary, E. (1990). *Kids can cooperate: A practical guide to teaching problem solving.* Seattle: Parenting Press.

David, M., & Appell, G. (2001 [1973, 1996]). *Loczy: An unusual approach to mothering.* Translated from *Loczy ou le maternage insolite,* by Jean Marie Clark; revised translation by Judit Falk. Budapest: Association Pikler-Loczy for Young Children.

Eisenberg, N. (Ed.). (1998). *Handbook of child psychology: Vol. 3. Social, emotional, and personality development* (5th ed.). New York: Wiley.

Fraiberg, S. (1959). *The magic years: Understanding and handling the problems of early childhood.* New York: Scribner's.

Furman, R. A. (1995, January). Helping children cope with stress and deal with feelings. *Young Children, 50*(2), 33–51.

Goleman, D. (2000). *Working with emotional intelligence.* New York: Bantam.

Gonzalez-Mena, J. (2007). What to do with a fussy baby: A problem-solving approach. *Young Children, 62*(5), 20–25.

Greenspan, S. I. (1999). *Building healthy minds.* Cambridge, MA: Perseus.

Greenspan, S. I., & Wieder, S. (1998). *The child with special needs: Encouraging intellectual and emotional growth.* Reading, MA: Perseus.

Hyson, M. (2004). *The emotional development of young children* (2nd ed.). New York: Teachers College Press.

Kitayama, S., Markus, H. R., & Matsumoto, H. (1995). Culture, self, and emotion: A cultural perspective on "self-conscious" emotions. In J. Tangney & K. Fisher (Eds.), *Self-conscious emotions: The psychology of shame, guilt, embarrassment and pride* (pp. 439–463). New York: Guilford.

Klein, M. D., & Chen, D. (2001). *Working with children from culturally diverse backgrounds.* Albany, NY: Delmar.

Kuebli, J. (1994). Research in review: Young children's understanding of everyday emotions. *Young Children, 49*(3), 36–47.

Lieberman, A. F. (1993). *The emotional life of the toddler.* New York: Free Press.

Lillard, A., & Curenton, S. (1999, September). Research in review: Do young children understand what others feel, want, and know? *Young Children, 54*(4), 52–57.

Marion, M. (1997, November). Research in review: Understanding and managing anger. *Young Children, 52*(7), 62–67.

Okagaki, L., & Diamond, K. E. (2000, May). Responding to cultural and linguistic differences in the beliefs and practices of families with young children. *Young Children, 55*(3), 74–80.

Petersen, S., Bair, K., & Sullivan, A. (2004). Emotional well-being and mental health services: Lessons learned by Early Head Start Region VIII programs. *Zero to Three, 24*(6), 47–53.

Reynolds, E. (2001) *Guiding young children: A problem-solving approach.* New York: McGraw-Hill.

Rogoff, B. (2003) *The cultural nature of human development.* Cambridge, MA: Oxford University Press.

Simons, B. (2000, January). A more tender separation. *Young Children, 55*(1), 30.

Vance, E., & Weaver, P. J. (2003, July). Words to describe feelings. *Young Children, 58*(4), 45.

Van Hoorn, J., Nourot, P., Scales, B., & Alward, K. (2007). *Play at the center of the curriculum* (4th ed.). Upper Saddle River, NJ: Merrill/Prentice Hall.

CHAPTER 9

Working with Families to Support Self-Esteem

In this chapter you'll discover . . .

- Some ways to promote self-esteem
- What happens when the media stereotype in negative ways
- Why always being positive is not a way to raise children's self-esteem
- How "scaffolding" a child's learning works toward the development of self-esteem
- How *affirmations* can be used to communicate positive messages that focus on strengths and help to build relationships with families
- How cultural differences can affect the way parents perceive self-esteem
- How a self-fulfilling prophecy works

Much attention is focused these days on promoting self-esteem in children because a link is seen among achievement, behavior, positive growth patterns, and high self-esteem. This chapter looks at working with families around the development of self-esteem.

PORTRAIT OF A PERSON WITH HIGH SELF-ESTEEM

What does a person with high self-esteem look like? On the surface, this seems like a fairly simple question to answer. Without much thought it's easy to come up with a portrait that's something like this:

> People with high self-esteem have self-confidence that shows in the way they dress, groom themselves, walk, and talk. People with high self-esteem are secure and happy. They're outgoing, energetic, brave, strong, and proud. They're also motivated, successful, independent, and assertive.

That description is a typical one produced by students of mainstream cultural backgrounds. But in a class where the students are diverse, and comfortable enough to speak up, the items on the list come into question, as the students discover that the traits listed are not particularly indicative of high self-esteem but rather reflect a cultural ideal.

If you think of a specific person who seems to have high self-esteem, the picture changes, even if that person is of the mainstream culture. The person is not likely to be a walking example of this list of culturally specific ideal traits. Rather, the person is more likely to be himself or herself. And if you compare that person with another who also has high self-esteem, the two may be very different from each other because the second person is also likely to be himself or herself, a unique individual.

High-self-esteem people aren't necessarily happy, though we would like to think that happiness comes from boosting self-esteem. Often people who are themselves and feel good about who they are run into problems when they are in circumstances that challenge their ability to express who they are and have their needs met. A person in a refugee camp may have high self-esteem but probably won't be too happy. More is said about this later in the chapter, but here let me just point out that part of being who you are has to do with feeling your feelings, which means that you'll have a wide range of emotions—not just constant sunshiny happiness.

High-self-esteem people also aren't necessarily talented, good-looking, strong, or financially successful. If they were, ordinary people wouldn't have much of a chance, and people with disabilities would have even less of a chance. Just look around you and you'll discover that a person's looks, abilities, possessions, or wealth aren't necessarily related to self-esteem. Some of the best-looking people in the world feel inferior. They either think they're not *really* good-looking, or they worry that all they have is their looks, which are destined to fade. If they feel significant or powerful based on looks alone, they're in trouble.

Actually, if you scratch the surface of people who seem to have high self-esteem, you'll find that some are covering up perceived inadequacies. People are often the opposite of what they seem. The extremely assertive person may be hiding a shy, scared child underneath. The paragon of virtue may have a core of hidden vices. Judging self-esteem in others isn't easy! There's lots of room for error. People just aren't always what they seem.

So instead of trying to judge the degree of self-esteem in adults, let's look at where it comes from in childhood. Let's start with some definitions.

DEFINITION OF SELF-ESTEEM

What is self-esteem, anyway? Self-esteem is a valuing process and results from an ongoing self-appraisal in which traits and abilities are acknowledged and evaluated. Self-esteem is made up of *self-image*—the pictures we carry of ourselves—and *self-concept*—the ideas we have about ourselves.

High self-esteem comes when, after a realistic appraisal of pluses and minuses, a person decides that she has more positive attributes than negative ones. High self-esteem means that a person feels good about herself—she holds herself in esteem. Overall, she likes herself, warts and all. Low self-esteem means that a person lacks a global sense of self-worth.

This concept of self-esteem or self-worth is entirely tied to culture. For example, in a culture that values independence and individuality, the perception is that infants are born unable to differentiate themselves from the rest of the world. It is the family's job to help the infant learn to draw boundaries and discover her separateness. She must come to see herself as an individual, an independent human being. When she does, she feels successful. Another family from a different culture sees the infant as separate and independent to start with. That family wants to blur the boundaries and deemphasize the independence. Jerome Kagan, in his book *The Nature of the Child* (1984), says, "The Japanese, who prize close interdependence between child and adult . . . believe they must tempt the infant into a dependent role . . . in order to encourage the mutual bonding necessary for adult life" (p. 29). Self-esteem in a family that emphasizes separateness will look different from a family that deemphasizes separateness.

When a family promotes self-assurance, self-help, competence, and being "special," self-esteem rises if the individual is proud to perceive herself as being in possession of those traits. However, in some cultures the proud, independent, self-assured individual who stands out in a crowd will be given strong messages about the importance of fitting in, belonging, and putting others first. Culture makes a difference in one's view of what comprises self-esteem. In some cultures the very notion of holding oneself in esteem is abhorrent, and pride is a no-no. Instead, humility and humbleness are valued (Greenfield, Quiroz, Rothstein-Fisch, 2001; Rogoff, 2003). People in these cultures find other ways of feeling worthy. Conflicting cultural messages can tear down self-esteem. Although some people can rise above cultural messages and continue to feel good about themselves, others can't. Self-esteem isn't simply deciding that you're great just as you are and giving that message to the world.

Children from any culture can sometimes have an exaggerated sense of their own power, one that doesn't reflect self-esteem at all but rather their stage of cognitive development. Take, for example, the 3-year-old who feels angry about having been dethroned by a baby sister. He makes ugly wishes concerning the baby. Then the baby gets sick—or worse, *dies*—and the 3-year-old thinks he caused the tragedy by willing it. The child's misconceptions aren't caused by the degree of his self-esteem but rather by thinking himself capable of willing things to happen. He lacks logic at this age.

Self-perception must relate to reality to create true self-esteem. Exaggerated misperceptions that aren't stage-related, as in this example, are delusions. A picture that appeared on the cover of *Newsweek* on February 17, 1992, depicts this problem: An ugly, skinny, weak, flabby, sickly looking man stands in front of the mirror, and the reflection he sees is the opposite of what he is. The mirror shows a strong, well-built, handsome, self-assured man, whom we can assume to be talented and intelligent as well. Nothing in the reflection is the same as the man creating it—nothing relates to reality. That's not self-esteem!

If, in the name of promoting self-esteem, you try to fool a child by painting him a false picture of himself, it won't work. (If it did, it wouldn't be healthy, anyway.) Take a child who is miserably aware of his lack of ability, feels unloved, has little power to control anything in his life, and is behaving in unacceptable ways. You can't raise this child's self-esteem by telling him that none of what he is experiencing is true. He simply won't believe you. If there is no reality to back up what you're saying, you're wasting your breath. Even if you point out his good traits, if he's focused on what he perceives to be his bad traits, he won't pay attention.

It's harder to change someone's self-esteem than it seems. In fact, only when the person himself decides to change his perceptions will he allow someone else to be effective in helping him. *Building self-esteem involves a collaboration, not a deception.* The goal is to help the child build a sense of self that is both valued and true.

DIMENSIONS OF SELF-ESTEEM

According to Stanley Coopersmith (1967), a pioneer researcher in this area, self-esteem has at least four dimensions: significance, competence, power, and virtue. Other researchers use similar ideas but employ different words. Susan Harter (1983), for example, uses the words *acceptance*, *power and control*, *moral virtue*, and *competence*. Your self-esteem depends on what you value, which is likely to be influenced by what your family and culture values for you (which may depend on gender) and where you perceive that you fall in each category. Let's take a look at each of these dimensions in turn.

Significance

Significance has to do with a feeling of being loved and cared about, the feeling that you matter to someone. You can't instill this feeling in a child. You can try to influence it with words and deeds, with nurturing and protection, with caring, and with meeting needs, but you can't ensure that the messages you send are the ones the child will receive. A feeling of significance, the feeling that you are important because you are cared about, is a choice the individual makes.

It is vital to understand that children are active participants in the development of their sense of self. No matter what hand fate deals, it's not the events themselves that determine self-esteem—it's how the child reacts to those events. Obviously some children are born into more fortunate circumstances than others, yet there are children who have everything going for them who don't feel good about themselves. Other children are just the opposite. They manage to emerge from a series of traumas with self-esteem intact and, indeed, growing. These children seem to be able to use

Significance has to do with a feeling of being loved and cared about.

adverse circumstances to their own advantage. They grow and learn from their experiences and come out stronger than ever. They seem to take the negative and twist it around to have a positive effect.

Competence

You can influence *competence* in a child by helping him become increasingly skilled in a number of areas. But whether the child *feels* competent depends on whether he compares himself with someone who is more competent than he is. It's a decision the child makes, not one that you make, though you can influence his decision by making comparisons yourself or demanding perfection. If competence is particularly important to him, he may experience lower self-esteem, even though he is highly competent, simply because he doesn't see himself as competent *enough*. There's a discrepancy between where he thinks he should be (or wants to be) and where he is. He doesn't meet his own standards (which may or may not have come from his family or his culture).

Power

Let's look at *power*, the third dimension of self-esteem. Feeling that you have some control over being who you are, making things happen in the world, having an effect on the people and events in your life, and living your life satisfactorily give a sense of power. If power is of major importance to you, having a feeling of it can raise your self-esteem. Notice that power is not defined here as having control over other people—it's not a matter of *overpowering*, but power in the pure sense of the word: personal power, which reflects the root meaning of the word—"to be able." Power has to do with effectiveness.

Virtue

Virtue is the fourth dimension of self-esteem. Being good is important to some people. Their self-esteem relates to how much of a gap there is between how good they perceive themselves to be and how good they want or need to be. Virtue is not a supreme value to everyone.

THE ROLE OF BELIEFS AND EXPECTATIONS IN SELF-ESTEEM

So suppose that self-esteem depends on two things: the dimensions that are of utmost importance to the individual, and the gap between where this person perceives herself to be and where she wants to (or feels she should) be. Take the housewife who sees herself as good and loved (excels on the scales of virtue and significance) yet values only power and competence, where she sees herself sadly lacking. In this case her self-esteem may be quite low.

The housewife is a contrast to, for example, a monk who values virtue above all and derives his self-esteem from being obedient to his faith. He doesn't care about power, competence, or significance. These are extreme examples, granted, but they make the point. A discrepancy between where you are and where you want to be on the scale(s) most valuable to you is what counts in self-esteem.

Although self-esteem eventually becomes established and relatively stable over time, it's not forever fixed and static. For one thing, it changes as children develop. If we look at Erikson's (1963) stages of development in view of the dimensions described here, we see that different periods of development have different emphases. For example, power is a particularly strong issue for 2-year-olds, who are in Erikson's stage of autonomy. Competence comes into focus in the school-age years when children enter Erikson's stage of industry versus inferiority (see Figure 9.1). Industry, as Erikson uses the term, is about developing areas of competence.

Self-esteem also changes when circumstances change. It can even change instantly. The child who is competent at many things, active, and talkative at home may become quiet and hide his competence when he enters school for the first time. A severe trauma can also make a difference in the child's feelings about himself. Creating and maintaining self-esteem is a lifelong process—it gets shaped and reshaped.

Self-esteem brings with it self-confidence, which is a vital trait for development. What a child *believes* he can or cannot do sometimes influences what he *can* or *cannot* do. Children who perceive that they lack competence, for instance, may not try something because they've had bad experiences in the past, or simply because they have

Child's Stage	Approximate Age		Task	
Infancy	0 – 1	Basic trust	versus	Basic mistrust
Toddlerhood	1 – 3	Autonomy	versus	Shame and doubt
The preschool years	3 – 6	Initiative	versus	Guilt
School age	6 – 10	Industry	versus	Inferiority

Figure 9.1
Erikson's psychosocial stages of development
Source: Erikson (1963).

no confidence in themselves. What we *believe* influences our behavior greatly. Our beliefs create a self-fulfilling prophecy. What we expect is what we get, for no other reason than that we expect it.

Past experience can play a big part in raising or lowering expectations. The research on learned helplessness is eye-opening. Dogs who were shocked when they tried to get out of their cages learned to stay in even after the shocks stopped and the cages were left open. They were free to leave, but they didn't perceive it that way. They continued to act on past experience even though the circumstances of the present were different. Their perceptions didn't relate to reality (Seligman, 1975).

Picture this cartoon: A man stands in a cage, gripping bars in both hands with his face pressed up against them. But those two bars are the only ones holding him in the cage—there are no other bars. His perceptions are what are trapping him, not the reality of the situation. Perceptions make up self-esteem, including wrong perceptions.

WHERE DOES SELF-ESTEEM COME FROM?

Self-esteem, along with self-identity, comes from early experiences and continues up through the school years into adolescence and adulthood. Children define themselves partly by looking at the images that they see reflected in the people around them (Briggs, 1975; Lally, 1995). If they develop close attachments with people who love and value them, the reflection they see is positive, and they're likely to have positive feelings about themselves. They decide that they are lovable. If they create an impact on the world—starting as babies when they cry and are responded to in ways that meet their needs—they develop a sense of self-efficacy, which they then include in their self-definition. If they develop a wide variety of competencies that are well received by those around them, they are likely to decide that they are competent. If they learn acceptable ways to behave and are given recognition for their good behavior, they are likely to decide that they are virtuous. Put all together, the child who sees

Children define themselves partly by looking at the images they see reflected in the people around them.

more positive reflections of himself is likely to develop a global sense of self-worth, or self-esteem.

So it seems as though a child who has someone who cares about him and meets his needs and creates positive reflections will likely develop a healthy sense of self-worth. But what if the outside world gives you a different set of messages because of your color, your gender, your ethnicity, or your physical/mental abilities? What if the reflections you see in the eyes of those outside your home depict you as somehow inferior? What if you go to the movies or watch TV and you see people like you either not pictured at all or pictured in negative ways? What will all that do to your self-esteem?

What if the people and/or institutions you encounter outside your home give you differential treatment and act as if you are inferior? Furthermore, what if those people or institutions create insensitive or even assaultive environments, and you find yourself in those environments?

Under these circumstances, can the positive messages you get from home counteract the negative ones you get from outside? Maybe. Some parents provide their children with lessons on how to survive and stand up to racism, sexism, or ableism, which is discrimination or prejudice against individuals with disabilities. Their children go out into the world with a protective shield that can help them maintain their self-esteem even when they are bombarded with negative messages. Surely what children get at home from these aware parents will make them stronger and probably more able to withstand the negative images thrust on them. But what about children who go out into the world with self-esteem already a bit damaged? What happens to them when they enter an insensitive or assaultive environment outside the home? The results can be devastating.

PROMOTING SELF-ESTEEM

This section examines some general ways to promote self-esteem, including some that are specific to changing the negative messages just mentioned above to positive ones.

The first step is to get rid of critical attitudes, labeling, and name calling. Even in the name of socializing a child, *you can't make him feel better about himself by making him feel bad about himself.* That doesn't mean to move right to "La-La Land," where everything is sweetness and light and nothing connects to reality. Of course children misbehave, make adults angry, and act in less than loving ways. They need guidance and protection. They need honest feedback. But the form in which you guide, protect, and give honest feedback matters.

Give More Honest Feedback and Encouragement Than Praise

Some adults, in the name of building self-esteem, vow always to be positive and to praise children at every possible opportunity. They replace honest feedback with constant overblown praise. Praise is no cure for low self-esteem. All it does is create a need for the child to look to the adult for a judgment of everything he does. Children need coaches, not cheerleaders (Curry & Johnson, 1990). If you overdo praise, your words become meaningless. For example, if you say "Great job!" about every little thing, it becomes an empty phrase. It's more effective and less damaging to use encouragement instead of praise. Call attention to children's legitimate successes, but don't butter them up with heavy judgments. Compare past performances with present ones, but not with those of other children—"You picked up more blocks this time than last time," rather than "You're the best block-picker-upper I've ever seen." Better yet, explain why this behavior is valuable (Hitz & Driscoll, 1988). There's more on the subject of praise in Chapter 5.

Give Children Opportunities to Experience Success

Even more important than just talking is to give children many chances to experience success of all sorts. Challenge them so that when success comes they've worked for it—it didn't just arrive on a platter. Do this by creating a manageable, yet challenging, environment that is appropriate to their age and stage of development. The book *Developmentally Appropriate Practice in Early Childhood Programs Serving Children from Birth Through Age 8,* by Sue

Give honest feedback and encouragement.

Bredekamp and Carol Copple (1997, 2006), gives many ideas about how to respond to children appropriately.

When adults give children a helping hand, they also help them experience success. Lev Vygotsky (1978) came up with the term *assisted performance* to describe this helping hand. He suggested that other children can be the ones who provide the helping hand, not just adults. Others now use the term *scaffolding*. Scaffolding is a process that can be viewed as similar to the temporary structure one puts up to paint a building. In other words, the adult provides the support the child needs, allowing him to problem solve at new levels. The scaffolding helps the child experience success, which encourages the child to challenge himself further, thereby meeting with the possibility of new success. Scaffolding, because it is temporary, can be built for a specific need on each occasion and can easily be remodeled to serve changing needs.

Travis

Travis is 4 years old, and he's big for his age. His size alone commands attention, but his behavior commands even more. He pushes kids around every chance he gets. He walks with a swagger and with a challenge on his face. "Just try to get the better of me," his expression seems to say. He's also loud and sometimes unruly. What he wants, he wants *now*—and he lets everybody know it.

One day at the staff meeting, one of his teachers confessed her discomfort about Travis and his attitude. "I don't like him very much," she said in a quiet voice. "I try, but his behavior just gets in the way of the warm feelings I *want* to have for him. It seems like self-esteem is just oozing out all over him, and I don't like that."

The rest of the staff was silent for a moment, amazed at her confession. Then her coteacher spoke up. "I don't see Travis as a high-self-esteem child," he said cautiously. "Sure, he acts like he's got all the confidence in the world, but I think he's just making up for what he thinks he lacks."

"What do you mean?" asked the first teacher.

"Well, his bullying, for instance. When kids bully, it's not a mark of high self-esteem. Rather, it's a mark of low self-esteem. Kids who feel good about themselves—who they are and their capabilities—don't have to push other kids around."

"What else makes you think that Travis doesn't feel good about himself?" asked the first teacher. "I always thought that he felt *too* good about himself."

"The way he avoids doing anything that would show he's not as capable as the other kids. I think that because of his size people always expect more out of him than he can manage. It must be hard for him. I know I keep forgetting that he's not as old as he looks. So, if it's a problem for me, it's probably a problem for other people too."

"I've noticed that," acknowledged another teacher. "He puts a lot of energy into avoiding things. But he's so loud about his demands that we pay attention to those and not to the fact that he rarely gets involved in much of anything."

"I wonder if he has picked up my negative feelings," worried the first teacher. "It won't help him much to be around someone who admits she doesn't like him."

"I like him," said her coteacher. "But he probably doesn't know it because I'm always dealing with his negative behavior. That's when he gets attention from me. I think I'll work on changing that situation."

"I wonder how we can help him have more positive experiences in our program," mused the first teacher out loud. "Maybe we can gently move him toward activities that particularly interest him. I saw him trying to fold a paper airplane yesterday. Maybe I can get him to help me set up a project of paper airplanes for all the kids. That might give him some recognition."

"We could focus more on giving him some social skills, so he can quit bullying," was another suggestion.

"I wonder what would happen if we used the video camera and showed him what he looks like when he bullies," another colleague offered. "Or maybe that would be too threatening at this point."

"I think what he needs is a friend," said another. "I've noticed he seems drawn to Paul. Maybe we could encourage that relationship."

"Well," said the first teacher, "I'm glad I brought the subject up. I see Travis differently now, and I'm already beginning to like him better!"

Optimum challenge and risk taking is the secret to development, to learning, and to skill building. Scaffolding supports children so they have experiences with positive results when challenged to take a risk. When children encounter a problem or an obstacle and are about to get stuck in the problem-solving process, instead of rescuing them, adults can provide help—not heaps of help but the smallest amount necessary. In this way adults can facilitate the continuation of the problem-solving process. They provide the missing link in the chain that allows children to move forward toward solutions. Thus, children's success is eventually their own, not the adult's. Experiencing personal success in the face of obstacles gives children messages about their abilities, about their self-worth.

Look at the following scenario, which illustrates scaffolding:

Dashinique wants to try out for the school play but has to choose a scene, and she can't make up her mind. An adult helps her sort out the possible contenders and then offers to listen to her try the part in each scene to see which works best. The answer becomes obvious to both of them as Dashinique acts out each scene. But then comes the second problem. Dashinique is scared of the tryout. She can speak her lines fine, but the thought of standing up in front of people makes her nervous. Again the adult helps by gathering some people to listen to her say her lines so she can practice in front of them and get used to being watched. It works. By the day of the tryouts, Dashinique has gained self-confidence and does well in spite of a few leftover nerves. Dashinique gets the part, and her success is her own. She only had a small bit of help (but lots of support and encouragement).

The next situation shows the difference between scaffolding and "rescuing," in which adults provide too much help:

> *Brandon and Shelby are having an argument over who gets to use the glue gun to finish the craft projects they are both working on. Brandon had it first, but Shelby grabbed it and is holding it out of Brandon's reach when an adult comes up to the table. The adult could rescue Brandon by taking the glue gun from Shelby, but instead he helps the two sort out the situation. He starts by merely saying what he sees: "Brandon wants the glue gun." He waits to see what happens. Shelby answers, "Yeah, but I need it." Brandon cuts in, "I had it first." Shelby responds, "But you were just holding it—you weren't using it." Brandon turns to the adult, "Make her give it to me—I had it first! It isn't fair!" Shelby responds, "I really need it. If I don't hold down this piece the whole thing is going to fall apart." "Well…," says Brandon, "I could let you use it for a minute if that's all you want to do. But next time don't grab!" he says emphatically. No longer needed, the adult walks off, and the two continue to work on their projects. Think about what the children learn and how they feel when they solve a problem themselves rather than depending on adults to fix it.*

Most of us are tempted to take care of problems quickly when the solution is something we can deliver. When an adult sees a toddler fall, the urge is to pick him up and set him back on his feet. If the same person saw an adult fall, he would be more likely to come over and ask some questions and see what was needed at the moment. Maybe getting back on his feet isn't the best solution. Even without medical training, most of us know that it is better if the person can get back on his own feet after a fall. It's a test to see whether there is an injury. But with a child we tend to think differently. Why? Does it make us feel powerful? Does it feel good to help someone less capable than we are? Why are we more likely to use a scaffolding approach in a situation involving an adult and just fix the problem for a child? Scaffolding is appropriate for both children and adults. Rescuing doesn't promote self-esteem. It's more important to build real skills and remark about them than it is to try to boost self-esteem through empty words and pretending to be excited about nonexistent successes.

While you're thinking about skill building, consider all skills. Social skills are as important as physical and intellectual ones. When a child doesn't have a clue as to the effect of his or her behaviors on others, help that child come to see what is effective and what is not. Teach the skills the child may lack.

CHILDREN LEARN FROM FAILURE

One of the best feedback devices we have is failure. When we try something and it doesn't work, that's clear feedback. Of course, children need an array of positive experiences every day of their lives. However, in the name of success we sometimes go overboard in protecting children from failure, thus cutting them off from valuable learning experiences.

The problem with failure is that it often comes accompanied with heavy value judgments, spoken or unspoken. For example, many of us were called "dummy," or something comparable, as children when we made a mistake. It's hard not to pass on that kind of response to children when they make mistakes if that is the way we were treated. However, if children are to learn from mistakes as well as emerge from failure with an intact sense of self-worth, it is important that adults be supportive rather than critical. After all, a mistake is just that. We all make them, and we all stand to learn from them.

CELEBRATING DIFFERENCES: AN ANTIBIAS APPROACH

How adults react to differences in people affects how children react to differences, which influences self-esteem. Louise Derman-Sparks (1989) and her antibias curriculum task force have brought awareness of issues of bias that were hidden from many until recently.

The tendency in early childhood education and mainstream cultural child rearing has been to be blind to both privilege and injustice. The motto of many is that "Children are children," by which they mean differences such as skin color and gender don't matter (although the expression "Boys will be boys" dispels the gender-blindness myth). Many people who are "blind" to differences are those who don't carry the bruises and scars left by unfortunate remarks and by the biased behavior of those who promote stereotypes and practice unfair treatment. Conscious and unconscious racism, classism, sexism, and ableism are areas of bias still with us in spite of the fact that many assume that the way to equity is to ignore differences.

Instead of disregarding differences, we should celebrate them. "Celebrate differences"—what does that mean? A loving attempt to do just that occurs regularly, as well-meaning adults bring "culture" into children's lives in order to teach them about people who are different from themselves. I remember a Japanese "tea party" put on in the classroom of one of my children. I attended as a parent guest and happened to sit next to a Japanese parent, who was also a guest. She was aghast at what she saw. "There's nothing Japanese about this!" she whispered to me, insulted by the whole proceeding. What had happened was that the teacher, based on what she had read and on her own ideas, had created a strange conglomeration of stereotypes and fantasy, which she believed was promoting cultural knowledge in the children.

Michael Dorris, in an article titled "Why I'm Not

Teach children to respond positively and appropriately to differences.

Thankful for Thanksgiving" (1978), writes about this phenomenon as it occurs with Native American children who may know nothing about their own heritage other than the mistaken stereotypes they encounter everywhere. Stereotypes of fighting savages come televised year-round from sports arenas across the country. Thanksgiving arrives every year, and cute little savages come out of the woodwork and get pinned on the bulletin boards, complete with feathers and tomahawks. Throughout the rest of the year, children are told not to act like "wild Indians" (a stereotype) but to sit quietly "Indian-style" (another stereotype) and sing songs that are deeply insulting to Native Americans, such as "Ten Little Indians" (dehumanizing). How can Native American children get a sense of who they are and of their worth if their culture is so stereotyped, devalued, and misrepresented?

Many mistakes and insults occur in the name of "celebrating differences." What is largely unrecognized or at least little discussed is that differences are connected with privilege and power. Differences carry values. It shouldn't be that way, but it is; and until that fact is recognized, there is little hope for change. That's where the antibias approach comes in. Adults must begin to recognize that value messages, both spoken and unspoken, are constantly sent and received about color, language, gender, and differences in physical abilities. Once adults become aware of the messages, they can begin to intercept them and change things. They can stop teaching children to ignore differences and instead teach them to respond positively and appropriately to differences.

Bias Can Hurt

Although bias is natural, it can be bad for children and bad for adults. It's obviously bad for those who are the target of bias. It not only harms self-esteem but sucks energy from the developmental process. It hurts to feel inferior. To be disempowered influences your life course.

But bias is also bad for those who are regarded as superior. When you see others as beneath you, you're out of touch with reality. It's dehumanizing to act superior and to enjoy unearned privilege, even when you are not aware of what's happening (Derman-Sparks, 1989; Howard, 1999).

It may seem easier to just pretend we're all alike in the name of equality. It may be easier to say to someone who is a different color than you are, "I don't think of you as different from me." But we're not all alike, and to pretend we are is to ignore the truth. That kind of ignorance can be very insulting. If you are a woman, how would you like it if a man said to you, "I never think of you as female," meaning that remark as a compliment. Personally, I would be shocked if someone looked at me and didn't see me as a female. If you are a man, reverse the situation. Can you imagine yourself without your maleness? What if someone thought it was a compliment to you to remain ignorant of the fact that you are a male? How would you feel?

People want others to respond to who they are—not some blind, misguided version of who they should be. They want to be valued for who they are. For example, we would all be very uncomfortable around those who pretend to be "gender-blind," if, indeed, such a thing is even possible. But adults pretend to be "color-blind" all the time in the name of equity. *Discriminating* on the basis of skin color is immoral. *Recognizing differences* in skin color is not, as long as you don't present one color as better than another.

People with disabilities also face these same problems, and any antibias approach should include them as well. Children need to learn to appreciate people for who they are and respond respectfully. With the push now for including children with disabilities into early care and education programs with their typically developing peers, children have opportunities to get to know people who don't have the same abilities that they have. And it also means that adults have to ensure that all children are treated fairly and with respect. They have to teach all children to get along with each other in the face of what may be big differences in ability. It's good learning for citizenship in a diverse society.

So, how can you teach children to respond positively in the face of differences if they've been taught to be blind to them? How can they respond positively if they've been exposed to biased attitudes and behaviors?

Start by modeling *antibias* behaviors. Become aware that the white able-bodied male is the norm in the society, and then try to get beyond that. Acknowledge the existence and experience of others by creating an antibias environment; expose children to pictures, books, and experiences of adults and children both like themselves and unlike themselves.

Point out stereotypes in the media when they occur. For example, when a book or a TV program shows weak, helpless women in limited roles, remark about the fact that women can be strong, intelligent people capable of doing many things.

Make it clear that bias is unacceptable. Children understand the concept of fair and unfair. Bias is definitely not fair. It is only fair that people of all races, religions, cultures, and physical abilities be treated with equal respect. It is only fair that both genders be allowed and indeed encouraged to expand beyond the limits of narrow gender roles. It is not fair to exclude someone from playing because of skin color, gender, or ability. Children need to understand that biased behavior is unacceptable.

Cultural Differences and Self-Esteem

Who am I? Each of us continues to explore that question throughout our lifetime. The answer we come up with and the value judgment we make about that answer make up our self-esteem.

As children grow, they develop an idea of themselves. This idea influences the behavior of the actual self—the one that operates in the world. The actual self in turn influences the self-concept, which continues to influence behavior. Thus, the actual self and the self-concept are forever tied together, and self-esteem grows from the interaction of the two.

Self-esteem is culturally based and depends on the basic concept of what makes up a person. As stated earlier, one culture looks at each person as a unique, potentially self-sufficient individual; another deemphasizes individuality and regards each person as an inseparable part of a greater whole. How parents focus their socialization efforts depends on which view they take.

Laura Zahner

Who am I? Each of us continues to explore that question throughout our lifetime. The answer we come up with, and the value judgment we make about that answer, make up our self-esteem.

An example that illustrates this point is how two people answer the question "Who are you?" As one talks about herself, she points out her personal characteristics and lists her roles and her accomplishments. She is emphasizing her individuality. The other one answers it by explaining her family lineage. She explains herself by pointing out relationships and ignoring individual accomplishments. A native Hawaiian person explained to me how hard it was to fill out an application for the university that asked her to list her achievements. "That's not who I am," she said. Instead she wanted to explain all the people she was related to in her family, including her ancestors.

Parents whose goal is individualism see their baby arriving in the world connected and dependent. The responsibility of the parent then is to help the baby learn that he or she is separate and apart. So those parents concentrate their efforts on autonomy, stressing self-help skills as the baby is ready. "I can do it all by myself" is music to their ears.

Parents who are more concerned about their children's ability to maintain connections have a different goal. They perceive an independent streak in their baby and see that independence as getting in the way of the close lifelong relationship to family that is their goal. So they focus on showing the baby in every way that dependence is a value and relates to connections—the greatest value. They know that some independence is inevitable, but they want to be sure that the baby is forever connected before he discovers autonomy. These parents focus on interdependence instead of independence. They are more likely to help the baby and young child than to teach self-help skills. They are not eager for the young child to brag, "I can do it all by myself."

How you build self-esteem in the early years is influenced by your view of the individual. However, realize that both views are valid, and they are not mutually exclusive. It isn't an either-or situation. When two people disagree about which is most important—individuality or group embeddedness—it's a matter of *where* they are placing the emphasis and *when* they see independence as an issue. It isn't independence versus interdependence. We all need both to survive. It is a matter of timing. One person may see the importance of *early* independence and its relationship to later getting along in a group. Another may perceive that only through subduing early independent urges can the child be truly part of the group, which will *later* lead to his or her developing or finding the *individual* skills, feelings, dreams, and desires that contribute to furthering group goals.

A valid goal of self-esteem is to enable children to stand on their own two feet as well as to stand together—indeed, lean on each other. It is important to get and give support and to feel good about it.

A True Story from the Author

When I was a new teacher faced with the job of educating parents, I had great enthusiasm for sharing all that I had learned in my teacher training, plus what I knew from experience. My energy was boundless, matched only by my zeal.

I will never forget trying to explain the concept of self-esteem to Teresa, a Mexican immigrant mother. Teresa kept insisting that there was no such concept in Spanish. I didn't give up. I kept trying to explain it to her. She stood there the whole time with a blank look on her face. She wasn't getting it. Finally she said in complete bewilderment, "*Self-esteem* doesn't make any sense at all. You can't esteem yourself; you can only esteem others."

I've been thinking about that exchange for 25 years. She didn't get what I was saying, but I didn't get what she was saying, either.

I've become less zealous in my parent education efforts as I've gotten older. I am much more willing to accept parents as they are; and if they want to "get better," I'll help—but only when I know what they perceive their weaknesses to be. Mainly I just support them in the good things they are doing. I don't decide where they need to improve; that's their decision. I help parents sort out what isn't working for them rather than tell them what I think and give advice. My motto is: The less advice the better.

But I still try to teach concepts. Although self-esteem is one concept I haven't given up on, I've broadened my view of what I mean when I define self-esteem. I include the fact that though the concept fits European American culture, it probably doesn't fit everybody in the same way.

That's why I am not surprised when my students and I don't agree on what the term *self-esteem* means. For example, a student described a child who thought only of himself, never of others. He had a fierce temper and got out of control when he didn't get his way. He even hit his parents. His parents' efforts to guide his behavior didn't work. This boy didn't get along with anybody and didn't have any friends either.

The student concluded that the child's problem was his self-esteem; he had too much of it. That isn't the way I see self-esteem. You can't get too much. When you have a good strong sense of self-worth, you are more able to see others as being worthy too. That's the point. Esteem breeds esteem.

Maybe it was just a translation problem with this student. Like Teresa, this student was a Spanish-speaker. However, I suspect that it wasn't a simple language difference. I believe our mismatch went deeper than that.

I decided to start with language as the path to understanding. I looked in my husband's huge Spanish-English dictionary. It had 196 entries under *self* in English and only 13 entries in Spanish. The concept of "self" is different in Spanish, and that difference influences the way people feel about the term *self-esteem*.

My experience with some parents, especially those from cultures where interdependence is more important than independence, is that focusing on "self" is a negative thing to do. To them, any word that has *self* connected to it is suspicious. They don't want to raise "self-ish" children. They want to raise children who put others first and think of themselves last.

I didn't understand that when I was trying to teach Teresa about self-esteem. I did understand it when I read my student's self-esteem paper, and so I put less effort into trying to teach her my way of looking at self-esteem and more into trying to understand her way.

Values show through misunderstandings. Every day I live I discover new ways of conceiving reality. The older I get the less I try to change people in general and parents in particular, and the more I try to tune in on their realities.

This chapter so far has focused on self-esteem, what it is and how to build it in children. It also took a good look at some cultural issues around the concept of self-esteem. Now it's time to focus on relating to families when it comes to focusing on self-esteem in children. The approach I am taking is to look at *affirmations* as a way of building relationships with families.

Chapter 5 had a whole section on affirmations—those positive messages that validate the person or the family. Affirmations encourage people to be who they are. Telling parents you appreciate them says you have positive feelings about their existence. Affirmations focus on strengths and encourage parents to see how they *can be* while accepting how they *are* at the present. Affirmations can create self-fulfilling prophecies that have a positive effect.

An interesting experiment done on children back in the 1960s shows the power of expectations. (Rosenthal and Jacobson, 1987). In this study, teachers were shown a list of children who were expected to have a "growth spurt" within the school year. In reality the students were randomly selected. But guess what! Those selected students did show remarkable improvement, while the others didn't. What adults believe about children and what they *expect* from them tends to come true, as they send children messages, both verbal and nonverbal. Those messages, even the ones sent unconsciously, influence children's behavior and performance.

Think about how this study might apply to adults as well. If you regard each parent in a positive light and focus on strengths instead of deficits, you not only strengthen the relationship between the two of you, but you also support that parent in being the best he or she can be.

It has been said that you can't give something that you don't have. Self-esteem falls into that category. There is a direct relationship between the amount of self-esteem adults have and their ability to enhance the self-esteem of the children in their lives.

It's worth noting that the messages we give as adults are strongly influenced by the ones we've been given as children. Often we are unaware of the connection. We don't even know that messages we carry with us are left over from our childhood. One way to get in touch with those messages is to become aware of the voices floating around in your head—the ones that praise, criticize, and tell you how you should act. These voices create what's been called a *life script*. They have influenced you to be who you are. Once you understand the concept of the influence of early messages, you can use this concept to guide you in responding to children and their families in positive ways rather than haphazardly giving out messages that may be negative.

Changing Negative Messages to Positive Ones

If you're walking around with mostly negative messages in your head, it will be hard for you to give out the positive messages that children need. So I have a suggestion: Get rid of those negative messages you're carrying around with you.

One way to do that is to become aware of the voices and to write down their messages—all of them, the negative ones and the positive ones. If you write each one on a separate slip of paper, eventually you'll have an array of messages. Once you have collected at least 10, sit down and sort them out. Put the negative ones in one pile, the positive ones in another, and any that are a mixture in a third pile. Then take the mixture pile and rewrite those messages so they have a positive effect in your life. Put them in the positive pile. Now take the negative messages and see whether you can rewrite some of those as well. Perhaps you can't. Set aside those you can't rewrite and put the rewritten ones in the positive pile.

Now it's time to deal with the negative messages you're stuck with. Start by spreading them out in front of you. Take fresh slips of paper and write down some positive messages—ones you'd like to hear. Write one for each of the negative messages in front of you.

Once you have replaced those negative messages with some positive ones, pick up each negative piece of paper, tear it up, and throw it away! Make a big deal out of this act of discarding. As you tear up the paper, think about the conscious choice you have made not to listen to that message anymore. Although we can't program other people, we *can* reprogram ourselves!

Imagine yourself as you can be without those negative messages telling you how you are, directing your actions, and creating your personality. Put a picture in your mind of the *new you* acting in accordance with the stack of positive messages you have at your fingertips. Carry that picture with you. Accept it as true. Review the positive messages regularly. Take charge of your life! You can make choices about who you are and how you act. This exercise was inspired by Clarke in her book *Self Esteem: A Family Affair* [1998]. If you found that it worked for you, consider using it with the parents you work with. See Strategy Box 9.1 for more strategies for working with parents around issues of self-esteem.

While you are supporting children and parents to be the best they can be, also work on yourself. And while you are doing that, figure out ways to nurture yourself—and encourage parents to do the same. One way is to give nurturing and then leave the room for reciprocation. (I'll scratch your back if you scratch mine.) If reciprocation

Strategy Box 9.1

Working with Families Around Issues of Self-Esteem

- Seek to understand each family's view of self-esteem and determine whether your program is giving contradictory messages to children. It's important to be open to differences and to figure out what to do about them in collaboration with families.
- Practice giving affirmations to parents as a means of supporting their strengths and building relationships along those lines. Don't use this as a mere technique, but put your heart into it.
- Be aware of the power of self-fulfilling prophecies for children and for parents. Make sure you take a positive view of everyone in your program, children and adults alike.
- If you have trouble giving positive messages because of your own negative messages from your early years, try the activity suggested on page 221. If it works for you, try it at a parent meeting.

isn't forthcoming, ask for it. This is risky business, because if you ask, you might be turned down. However, asking is still a good approach, because unless we tell others our needs, they'll never know about them. When my last son was born 13 weeks early and was hovering between life and death in intensive care, friends said, "What can we do for you?" My first response was, "Oh, nothing." But then I thought about it and said, "Feed us." And they did. Every day when we came home from our lengthy and frustrating visits at the hospital, there was a cardboard box on our doorstep with a full meal inside it. What a blessing! Without our friends we would have lived on fast food and snacks. Not only the nourishment was important to us, but also the message that we were cared about—cared for. We needed that during that period!

We all need affirmations all the time, not just during crisis periods. Let's learn to give them so we can get them, and to get them so we can give them.

LOOKING BACK AND LOOKING FORWARD

We all ask ourselves the question "Who am I?" periodically, beginning in infancy when we must learn to distinguish ourselves from the environment around us. As we answer that question, we become more and more aware of ourselves as individuals. We learn about our personal power.

The answer to "Who am I?" reflects our *idea* of ourselves—our *self-concept*. How we *see* ourselves reflects our *self-image*, which is related to *self-concept*. How we *feel* about our self-concept and self-image reflects our *self-esteem*. Children are in a malleable state; and their self-esteem is, to some extent, in the hands of the adults in their lives. Those adults need to see the importance of keeping self-esteem intact so that children can grow to their fullest potential.

Working with parents around issues of self-esteem can be complex, especially across cultures. An important approach to working with parents is to support them by focusing on their strengths. Using affirmations is a particular way of recognizing parents as people and nurturing their strengths. This chapter ended with a look at how early educators can nurture themselves and provide models for parents.

Throughout the chapters so far, little distinction has been made between the socialization process for boys and for girls. The next chapter examines that subject at length, including why it is important to be aware of differentiation in stroking patterns.

FOR DISCUSSION

1. How much does self-esteem show? Is it easy to tell who has high self-esteem and who doesn't? The text says that people aren't always what they seem. Do you believe that statement? Has that been your experience? Do you have some examples to back up your opinion?

2. Building self-esteem in a child involves a collaboration, not a deception. What does that sentence mean? What are some ways to collaborate with a child to help build self-esteem? What are some ways to help a child change a bad feeling about herself to a good feeling?

3. No matter what hand fate deals, it's not the events themselves that determine self-esteem; it's how the individual reacts to those events. Explain. Do you agree? If that is the case, how can adults help children who consistently have reactions that indicate low self-esteem?

4. What effect do bias and stereotyping have on self-esteem? Do you think that children in target groups for bias automatically have low self-esteem? Why or why not?

5. How do labels relate to self-fulfilling prophecy? Can you give examples from your own experience?

6. What are some perspectives that may differ greatly from the information presented in this chapter? Can you explain at least one?

WEB SITES

About Self-Esteem in Children
http://www.cyberparent.com/esteem/
Some of the subject include: Listening and self-esteem; the language of self-esteem; the relationship of discipline to self-esteem.

Kidshealth
http://www.kidshealth.org/parent/emotions/feelings/self_esteem.html

How healthy self-esteem helps children face challenges, conflicts and resist negative pressures. How to foster self-esteem in infants and young children.

National Association for the Education of Young Children (NAEYC)
http://www.naeyc.org
The National Association for the Education of Young Children has a number of resources available for

parents and professionals including books and journals, one of which is called *Young Children* which regularly has articles on building self-esteem in children.

National Association for Self-Esteem
http://www.self-esteem-nase.org
The National Association for Self-Esteem Web site outlines the history, aims, and objectives of this organization and gives information about its programs.

National Network for Child Care
http://www.nncc.org/Guidance/self.esteem.html
The important people in children's lives affect their self-esteem—that includes child care providers and parents. This Web site tells why self-esteem is important and how to support it.

Parenting Web
http://www.parentingweb.com/dev_edu/
selfesteem.htm
This site has information on self-esteem and young children.

Psychology and You Newsletter
http://www.homestead.com/selfhelpsolutions/build.
html
This site describes things parents and teachers can do to help improve self-esteem.

Shyness Institute
http://www.shyness.com/
This site is for people seeking information and services for shyness.

FURTHER READING

Akbar, N. (1985). *The community of self*. Tallahassee: Mind Productions.

Allen, P. G. (1998). *Off the reservation*. Boston: Beacon.

Billman, J. (1992, September). The Native American curriculum: Attempting alternatives to tepees and headbands. *Young Children, 47*(6), 22–25.

Butterfield, P. M., Martin, C. A., & Prairie, A. P. (2004). *Emotional connections: How relationships guide early learning*. Washington, DC: Zero to Three.

Cajete, G. (1994). *Look to the mountain: An ecology of indigenous education*. Durango, CO: Kivaki.

Chang, H. N. L., Muckelroy, A., & Pulido-Tobiassen, D. (1996). *Looking in, looking out: Redefining child and early education in a diverse society*. San Francisco: California Tomorrow.

Chu, G. (1985). The changing concept of self in contemporary China. In A. J. Marsella, G. DeVos, & F L. K. Hsu (Eds.), *Culture and self: Asian and Western perspectives* (pp. 252–277). New York: Tavistock.

Coll, C. G., Lamberty, G., Jenkins, R., McAdoo, H. P., Crnic, K., Wasik, B., Garcia, H., & Vazquez, H. (1996). An integrative model for the study of developmental competencies in minority children. *Child Development, 67*, 1891–1914.

Council on Interracial Books for Children. *Ten quick ways to analyze children's books for racism and sexism*. (1986). New York.

Delpit, L., & Dowdy, J. K. (2002). *The skin that we speak: Thoughts on language and culture in the classroom*. New York: New Press.

Egertson, H. A. (2006, November). Of primary interest. In praise of butterflies: Linking self-esteem and learning. *Young Children, 61*(6), 58–60.

Eggers-Pierola, C. (2005). *Connections & Commitments: Reflecting Latino values in early childhood programs*. Portsmouth, NH: Heinemann.

Epstein, J. L. (2006, January). Families, Schools, and Community Partnerships. *Young Children, 61*(1), 40.

Fadiman, A. (1997). *The spirit catches you and you fall down: A Hmong child, her American doctors, and the collision of two cultures*. New York: Noonday.

Fernea, E. W. (1995). *Children in the Muslim Middle East*. Austin: University of Texas Press.

Greenfield, P. M., Quiroz, B., Rothstein-Fisch, C., & Trumbull, E. (2001). *Bridging cultures between home and school*. Mahwah, NJ: Erlbaum.

Grieshaber, S., & Cannella, G. S. (2001). *Embracing identities in early childhood education: Diversity and possibilities*. New York: Teachers College Press.

Harwood, R. L., Miller, J. G., & Irizarry, N. L. (1995). *Culture and attachment: Perceptions of the child in context*. New York: Guilford.

hooks, b. (2003). *Rock my soul: Black people and self-esteem*. New York: Atria.

Hopson, D. P., & Hopson, D. S. (1990). *Different and wonderful: Raising black children in a race-conscious society*. New York, NY:

Kawagley, A. O. (1995). A Yupiaz worldview: A pathway to ecology and spirit. Prospect Heights, IL: Waveland.

Kendall, F. E. (1996). *Diversity in the classroom: A multicultural approach to the education of young children.* New York: Teachers College Press.

Kitayama, S., Markus, H. R., & Matsumoto, H. (1995). Culture, self, and emotion: A cultural perspective on "self-conscious" emotions. In J. Tangney & K. Fisher (Eds.), *Self-conscious emotions: The psychology of shame, guilt, embarrassment, and pride* (pp. 439–463). New York: Guilford.

Knight, P., Bernal, M. E., & Carlo, G. (1995). Socialization and the development of cooperative, competitive, and individualistic behaviors among Mexican American children. In E. E. Garcia & B. McLaughlin (Eds.), *Meeting the challenge of linguistic and cultural diversity in early childhood education* (pp. 85–102). New York: Teachers College Press.

Landy, S. (2002). *Pathways to competence: Encouraging healthy social and emotional development in young children.* Baltimore: Brookes.

Marshall, H. H. (2000, November). Cultural influences on the development of self-concept. *Young Children, 56*(6), pp. 19–22.

Mintzer, D., Als, H., Tronic, E. Z., & Brazelton, T. B. (1984). Parenting an infant with a birth defect: The regulation of self-esteem. *Psychoanalytic Study of the Child, 39,* 561–589.

Morrison, J. W. (2001, Spring). Supporting biracial children's identity development. *Childhood Education, 77*(3), 134–138.

Noddings, N. (2002). *Educating moral people: A caring alternative to character education.* New York: Teachers College Press.

Phillips, C. B. (1995). Culture: A process that empowers. In P. Mangione (Ed.), *Infant/toddler caregiving: A guide to culturally sensitive care.* Sacramento: Far West Laboratory and California Department of Education.

Pulido-Tobiassen, D., & Gonzalez-Mena, J. (1998). *A place to begin: Working with parents on issues of diversity.* Oakland: California Tomorrow.

Rael, J. (1993). *Being and vibration.* Tulsa: Council Oak Books.

Rashid, H. M. (1984, January). Promoting biculturalism in young African-American children. *Young Children, 39*(2) 13–23.

Rogoff, B. (2003). *The cultural nature of human development.* New York: Oxford University Press.

Ross, A. C. (Ehanamani). (1989). *Mitakuye oyasin: We are all related.* Denver: Wichoni Waste.

Stipek, D. (1998). Differences between Americans and Chinese in the circumstances evoking pride, shame, and guilt. *Journal of Cross-Cultural Psychology, 29*(5), 616–629.

Tedla, E. (1995). *Sankofa: African thought and education.* New York: Lang.

Valdes, G. (1996). *Con respeto: Bridging the distances between culturally diverse families and schools.* New York: Teachers College Press.

Wardle, F. (1987). Are you sensitive to interracial children's special identity needs? *Young Children, 42*(2), 53–59.

Werner, E. E. (1995, June). Resilience in development. *Current Directions in Psychological Science, 4*(3), 81–85.

CHAPTER 10

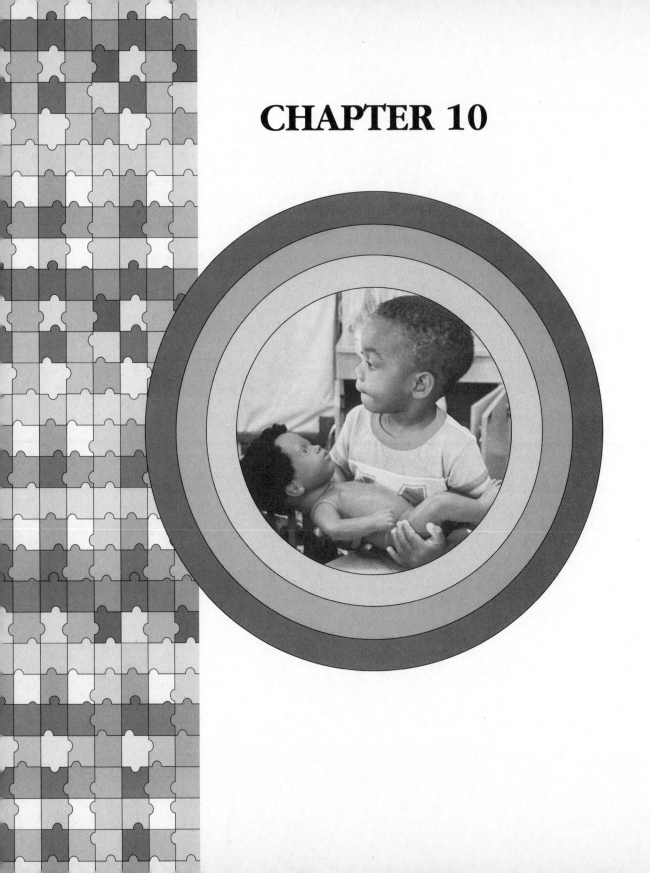

Working with Families Around Gender Issues

In this chapter you'll discover . . .

- How toys help define gender roles
- What girls may miss out on if they never play with blocks
- How to make boys feel comfortable expanding their "dramatic play"
- Another term for *fireman*
- The connection between language and power
- How children learn gender roles by imitating adults
- Some ideas about addressing gender equity issues with families

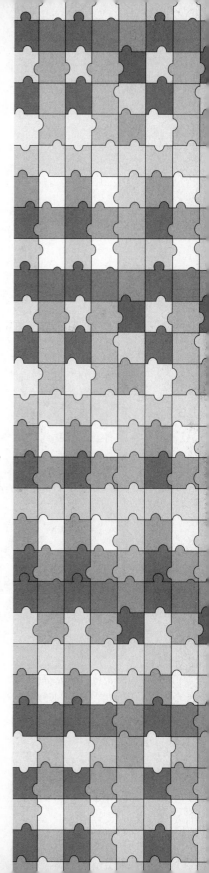

WHY THINK ABOUT TEACHING GENDER ROLES?

We live with many misconceptions concerning gender roles.[1] It may seem as though gender roles come automatically when children are born—and to some extent that is true. Shaping the gender role may even start prenatally because many parents know the sex of their baby *before* birth. What many people don't think about when they accept traditional gender roles as a given is how narrow and confining these roles can be to children, who grow into adults molded into a role they may not fit at all. Many don't consider how unfair, to both men and women, traditional gender roles can be. The unfairness shows up when we look backward at history to a time when women were clearly considered inferior to men and therefore had few rights as citizens. It's hard to believe that people are still alive today who remember the time when women in the United States couldn't vote. It may be startling to realize that although the women's rights movement started in 1838, it wasn't until 82 years later that women gained the right to vote. And the right was won only for some women. Others, because of the color of their skin or their lack of education, faced literacy and education taxes, intimidation, and violence at the polls. These women were kept from voting for almost half a century longer, until the passage of the 1964 Voting Rights Act and its 1974 amendments.

Imagine having no say in your government just because you happened to be born female instead of male, dark-skinned instead of light-skinned, or poor and uneducated instead of comfortable and educated. Also imagine, if you can, a woman being considered her husband's property along with his children and cattle. We think those times are long gone in the United

Getty Images—Stockbyte

Shaping the gender role can start prenatally when parents know the sex of their baby. Imagine what is in these packages if everybody already knows it's a girl.

---

[1]Sometimes a differentiation is made between *sex* and *gender*—*sex* meaning the biological fact of being male or female, and *gender* referring to the person's identification as male or female through a socialization process. Usually sex and gender roles coincide, but in some cases a child of one sex may be socialized to be the opposite gender (Money & Ehrhardt, 1973).

States, but remember, each generation is socialized into gender roles, and all the steps toward equity between the sexes could disappear if we don't continue to think carefully about how we socialize boys and girls. We must continue to guard against children's lives being shaped by restrictive gender roles, myths about a child's capabilities based on gender, and laws, both written and unwritten, that work against gender equality.

THE WOMEN OF TODAY

Every U.S. citizen—male and female—can vote now, but life's still no bed of roses for many. Many African American, Hispanic American, Native American, Asian American, and immigrant women are still undereducated and work in hard jobs for low wages while trying to care for their families (as do growing numbers of European American women who are single parents). Women

Women who manage to work their way into jobs that have traditionally been men's have to be "superwomen."

still earn less for equal work than men do. Barriers still exist for women who are exploring nontraditional jobs and who are struggling to reach higher in the business world. In many arenas the "glass ceiling" that keeps women at a lower level than men is still in place. Although women have worked their way into most professions, it is still a little surprising when flying to hear a woman's voice from the cockpit say, "This is your captain speaking."

Women who manage to work their way into jobs that have traditionally been men's have to be "superwomen." It's not easy for them to succeed with so many expectations put on them. It used to be that success came only if women acted like men when they competed in the traditional masculine arena. Now women are exploring new ways to do their jobs, using their feminine perspective, styles, systems, and skills. But sometimes they are punished for their femininity.

Yes, times have changed. The old riddle doesn't work anymore—you know the one about the father and son who were in an accident and the father was killed? When they brought the injured boy in for surgery, the brain surgeon took one look, paled, and turned away, saying, "I can't operate on him—that's my son!" It used to be that people wondered how the father could be the brain surgeon if he was dead. (You knew the answer is that the brain surgeon was the boy's *mother*, didn't you?)

Broader roles mean that mothers of young children are less likely to be criticized when they take jobs outside the home. Broader roles mean that some men feel freer to participate more fully in parenting their children; many men are now choosing to be full-time, stay-at-home parents. Men can also now enter more traditional women's fields such as nursing. However, when the average citizen meets a man and a woman dressed in green scrubs in a hospital corridor, the assumption still is that the man is the doctor and the woman the nurse.

Will we continue to move forward to eliminate the institutionalized oppression of women, to broaden gender roles, and to create an increasing range of opportunities for all individuals? This is an unanswered question. Whether women and men are fully able to be who they are and do what they choose depends on how the next generations of children are raised. We can't just sit back and assume that men and women already are or will one day be freed from confining gender roles. Gender roles are learned by every generation. A danger of complacency exists as the younger generations accept as normal what feminists have worked so hard for. How easy it would be to lose the gains isn't clear, but it should be a worry.

GENDER EQUITY AND CHILD REARING

Many forces work to confine children in narrow gender roles, prune back their potential, and limit their opportunities. It may seem like steady progress was made in the last half of the 20th century toward broadening gender roles, but when comparing a 1975 study of children's bedrooms (Rheingold & Cook) with one done in 1990 (Pomerleau, Bolduc, Malcuit, & Cossette), little difference showed. Researchers looked at the bedrooms of children from 1 month to 6 years of age. They carefully recorded the toys, decorations, and furniture and found many more action-oriented toys—machines and vehicles, war-related toys, and sports equipment—in boys' rooms as compared to dolls and more family-focused toys in girls' rooms. Even the curtains and bedspreads were a contrast. Fifteen years didn't make any difference.

In a 1999 study, Parke & Brott found that parents were still dressing their children in ways that clearly distinguished the boys from the girls. Is this a way to make sure that everyone knows what gender the child is? Do clothes shape gender roles? Certainly baby girls in dresses can't crawl the way boys in pants can. Is that a gender socialization message about being more or less active?

Consider how television pounds out the message that some clothes and toys are for girls and others are for boys. This advertising works against what nonsexist parents work for. The Family Lifestyles Project, which started in the 1970s, studied the socialization of children in families that emphasized gender role equality (Eiduson, Kornfein, Zimmerman, & Weisner, 1988). Weisner and Wilson-Mitchell (1990) assessed the children over a 3-year period and found them broader in their selection of activities and interests than a comparison group. Without a strong plan beyond just buying trucks for their girls and dolls for their boys, parents run up against their children's opinions once children learn from TV which toys are for whom.

Toys and Gender Roles

Toys play an important part in defining gender roles. If parents buy girls dolls, dollhouses, high-heeled shoes, and makeup, they give one set of messages. If they buy boys chemistry sets, tool kits, doctor's bags, building blocks, and wheel toys, they give another set of messages. Children learn roles and skills from playing; the toys they have to some extent determine which roles and skills they learn.

Visit a child care program and examine the environment, specifically the block area and the dramatic play corner. Vivian Paley (1984) deals with this subject at length in her informative, easy-to-read book *Boys and Girls: Superheroes in the Doll Corner*. Though the book is not new, the superhero play hasn't changed. Only the names of the heroes, and the few heroines, change regularly. No more He-Man or Teenage Super Ninja Turtles. Superman is still around, and Spiderman is big. While you are looking into the dramatic play area, notice whether more girls are there or boys. Check out the block area. Is that where you find the boys? If this is the case, examine the factors that might contribute to this situation. Sometimes the adults in the program subtly encourage this kind of gender differentiation. Notice the way the environment is set up. If the dramatic play area is a traditional "housekeeping" corner with frilly girls' clothes, shoes, and purses, most boys won't be attracted. If a variety of male or non-gender-specific hats, shoes, ties, and accessories are added, that can help. What helps most of all is adding a little water to the play sink, and maybe some soap suds and sponges.

Because boys tend to dominate block play in many programs, some teachers have tried a variety of approaches to encourage girls to go into the area also. One technique is to arrange the environment so that the blocks are close to the dolls or to put a dollhouse in with the blocks. Another idea is to put up "girls only" signs occasionally to give the message that this is valuable play for both sexes.

Why does it matter if boys never play house and girls never play blocks? It doesn't, if in other areas of their lives they are getting the skills they miss out on by avoiding these two activities. Dramatic play gives boys a chance to be nurturers, to experience domestic relations, to feel comfortable trying on a variety of emotions. Blocks give girls experience in spatial relations. They learn mathematical concepts as they build things. Ordinary wooden "kindergarten" blocks, called by some *unit blocks*, represent multiples of the basic square that is found in the set. Block play contributes a good deal to the concrete experience behind math knowledge, and gives the player experiences with principles of physics as well. Frank Lloyd Wright attributed his success as an architect to the set of blocks his mother brought home from a kindergarten conference in Europe back before anyone in the United States had heard of giving children blocks to play with.

It isn't just where children play or what they play with. It's also with whom they play. Young children tend to separate themselves by gender. One kindergarten teacher, Stacey Zeitlin (1997), describes how she purposely matched up boys and girls for a science activity. She made a conscious decision not to let the children select their own partners, as she usually did, but assigned them each a partner of the opposite sex. She was worried how it would work, because the children liked to team up with their same-gender best friends during activities like this one. Surprisingly, it worked very well, and she saw how it broke down gender barriers. Children who had never spent time together before spent the rest of the day together. Some continued to seek out their partners as playmates the rest of the year. Zeitlin is now committed to reducing the self- and peer-imposed gender segregation that she sees children practicing.

All of this information has implications for families. Of course, gender role differentiation and segregation may be something some families value. It's important not to just try to "educate" parents out of their beliefs, but to understand how the beliefs fit into their culture. At the same time it doesn't hurt to put equity issues on the table for discussion. Parents who take note of some of the practices you are using may learn from them, come to support those practices, and even take them home besides. Parent group discussions that are respectful of differences and disagreement can be useful for helping parents examine their practices around arranging play dates, buying toys, setting up a nonsexist environment, and encouraging broader gender roles.

The Power of Language

Language has an influence on gender role development. Language shapes perceptions. The terms *firemen*, *policemen*, and *chairmen* give the impression that these jobs are filled by men and that it's an exception when there's a "woman policeman." Better to make these titles non-gender-specific. That can be accomplished by using the terms *firefighter*, *police officer*, and *chair* or *chairperson*. Children will get the message that either gender may fill these roles.

Some titles are already non-gender-specific—for example, *teacher*, *doctor*, and *president*. However, children may consider them as gender-specific because of their own experience. There's the story of the English girl who asked her mother, "What are they going to call the new prime minister now that Mrs. Thatcher's gone?"

"By his name, of course," answered the mother.

"But what's his *title*?" persisted the child.

"Prime minister," answered the mother.

"But that's a woman's title!" said the child.

Once when I was talking about language and gender to a group of parents, one of them, a woman from Iran, pointed out to me that my language (English) is more gender oriented than hers. I was surprised and asked to hear more about that. She then said that, as English speakers, we mention gender every time we talk about a child, since we use either "he or she," or just "he." She then went on to say that in her language the same word encompasses both genders.

Interruption as an Indicator of Power and Importance.   Studies of "conversational politics" have found that people use language to show their power, as one person exerts control over another. For example, men tend to interrupt women more than the reverse. Interruption is an important indicator of relative power and importance. Children learn these interruption patterns early from the people around them. People can become aware of these patterns and can stop using them. It's not easy to do when you're an involved party, but it's possible. It's easier to look for the patterns when they occur between boys and girls and then intervene, insisting that the girls get their say. Empowerment of girls in such ways is important if there is to be gender equity. It's also important to empower boys to be free to be gentle and caring.

Using Language That Is Direct and Informative.   Teachers can also help empower girls (and boys too) by teaching them to use assertive language. To do this, teachers need to model such language themselves. Pay attention to how often you end a sentence with a question that dilutes the message. For example, "I want you to sit down in your car seat, OK?" or "It's time for lunch—will you come in now?" Those ways of talking are fine if the child truly has a choice. If not, the statement needs to be clear about what's to be done.

Teachers can model assertive language by cutting down the number of times they hedge with phrases such as *sort of* and *I guess*. They can also quit being ultrapolite. For example, "Your shoes are sort of muddy. It'd be really nice if you took them off before you walk into the classroom. I'd sure appreciate it." That way of talking is very courteous, but it depends on the goodwill of the listener to be effective. When being polite gives the message that the speaker is powerless, it's a good idea to find more assertive ways to speak. It's more powerful for a person to say what she means—to be direct and informative. That's what a lot of men do, and that's why they are more likely to be listened to than women. For example, a direct way to deal with the muddy shoes is this: "Please take off your muddy shoes. They'll dirty the floor." Or: "Muddy shoes belong on the mat by the door." Or if necessary: "If you walk on the floor, you're going to have to clean up the mud from your shoes."

This whole subject becomes much more complicated when working across language groups. I'm speaking from the point-of-view of an English-speaking person. Vocabulary, interruptions, and assertive language are different in each language. What I say here may not apply at all to people who speak other languages. It would be interesting to explore this subject further with parent groups. I am well aware that I miss the emotional content of conversations when I'm listening to some languages. I know a German speaker and a Russian speaker who not only sound assertive about everything they say but also a bit angry. It took me awhile to realize I was misinterpreting the pitch of their voices, which gave a very different message than the same pitch in English.

USING MODELING TO TEACH

As the preceding section indicated, modeling is an important method of teaching gender roles. Children imitate the important people in their lives, so when girls see their mother act helpless in the face of a flat tire or their female preschool teachers wait for a man to appear on the scene to unclog toilets or fix the broken handle on the cupboard, they pick up silent messages about women's capabilities. When a boy sees his father hand his mother a needle and thread and a shirt with a missing button, he gets a silent message about men's capabilities; when a boy sees his male teacher turn a child who needs comforting over to a female teacher, the boy gets a message about the role of men in the classroom. Of course, all these people in the examples may have very good reasons for their actions, but the point is that, with enough of these types of genderized examples, children take away a message about their own gender roles.

What makes all this more difficult is that children often see power differential that is determined by gender. In a program where the tasks are shared, children get a broader idea of capabilities as well as appropriateness.

A good deal of modeling comes from television. I tend to notice whenever an old woman is the "bad guy." Powerful elderly females as evil is a stereotype that has been with us for centuries. The witch hunts of the past show how such a negative stereotype can be used to oppress, even kill. Some older feminists facing the negative stereotype of being feminine and old have decided to redefine themselves as "crones"—the old woman as powerful, knowledgeable, and wise, but not evil.

Another problem created by the media is the sexualization of girls. Seeing constant sexy images of women and now even girls is harmful according to the American Psychological Association's 2007 Report on the Sexualization of Girls. Sexualization equates attractiveness with sex appeal and leads to a range of physical and mental health problems in girls and women, including low-self esteem, depression, and high-risk sexual behavior. To combat this problem families and teachers can join advocacy groups and press to make changes. The APA recommends the development of educational media literacy programs in public schools. It also recommends that parents look at media with kids and discuss what they are seeing, while pointing out that becoming sex objects is not a great way to feel valued. Parents should point daughters to better, more positive images of females.

Books can leave strong stereotypical images. In early readers, Dick was always busy fixing something, while Mother, Jane, and Sally stood helplessly looking on. Dick and Father were active in a variety of ways. Mother, Jane, and Sally were passive, except in the kitchen. It seems as though times should have changed by now, but as late as 1986, when books read to kindergartners were analyzed, the main character was male more than 70 percent of the time. In 1996 females in books were more passive and dependent than their more active and assertive male counterparts. Women were shown engaged in a narrower range of occupations than men (Turner-Bowker, 1996). Still today it is easy to see that children's books are more often about boys than girls, male animals instead of female ones. You can also easily find females being dependent more often than independent and as poor damsels needing help.

Help families become aware of media messages. In one educational program, whenever the teachers bought new books for the classroom they made the books available to parents first and asked them to comment on them. They pasted a sheet of paper inside the front cover and had parents write their comments so other parents could see them. That way families had a broader view of each book than just what they thought or what the teachers thought about the books.

DIFFERENTIAL SOCIALIZATION

Adults socialize girls and boys differently, which results in females ending up in subservient roles. How does this happen? Besides modeling, how else do children learn gender roles and develop a gender identity? Why do many boys gain confidence, competence, mastery, and assertiveness, while many girls come to see themselves as lacking those qualities? Why do many girls fail to identify themselves as strong, responsible, and powerful?

Gender Roles and Cultural Differences

Two parents meet outside the door of the child care center where they have just arrived to pick up their children at the end of the day. They know each other slightly and feel a connection because they are of the same culture, although one was born in the United States and the other in the "old country." Both speak English, but they are more comfortable talking to each other in their own language, which is what they are doing now:

"How did you like the last parent meeting?" inquires Parent A, making conversation.

"Well, to tell the truth, it upset me," answers Parent B.

"Oh?" responds Parent A.

"All that talk about letting boys act like girls and encouraging girls to be powerful bothered me a lot. I just don't think that's appropriate!"

"Yes, I know what you mean . . .," says Parent A.

"I can't stand the thought of my son playing house and wearing dresses. That makes me sick to my stomach. And they let him do that if he wants to."

"Does he want to?"

"How do I know? I'm not there!"

"It does seem kind of strange to me, too, but I don't think it hurts anything." Parent A leans casually against the stair rail.

Parent B stands, nervously rubbing her arms as if she is cold. She looks distressed.

"But the worst thing of all is that the teacher told me to send my daughter in pants and sneakers. She says that she's afraid to get dirty and that it's hard for her to run and climb with a dress and good shoes on. I guess she thinks I want her to look ugly, get dirty, and run around like a wild person!"

Parent A touches her friend's arm. "That really bothers you."

"Yes! That's not proper behavior for a girl! Do you think it is?"

"Well," says Parent A slowly, brushing her hair back from her face, while carefully considering her words, "I don't really like my daughter to get dirty, but I have to admit that what the teacher said is convincing."

"What's convincing? All that garbage about sexism?"

The two parents stop talking in their own language and switch to English as another parent arrives at the bottom of the steps. They greet her and move over to let her go up the steps and into the child care center.

"Yes, sexism and oppression!" continues Parent A, as if there had been no interruption.

Parent B replies passionately, "I don't see that my daughter is restricted in her development. She's going to grow into a woman. She has to know how women act in our culture. She has to fit in. She'll never get a decent husband if she starts acting like the other girls in this country. I don't want her to be like them. I don't want her to lose her culture."

"I know what you mean," says Parent A slowly. "But I've been thinking about whether women's inferior status is something we should just accept because that's the way it's always been."

"Oh, you're as bad as they are!" snorts Parent B angrily, stepping backward on the stair. "I thought you would understand."

"I *do* understand," comes the answer, "but at the same time I'm confused. I just don't know what I think."

"Well, I do. And I warn you, if you listen to them, you'll end up like them. You'll be melted right into the melting pot! How would you like that?"

"I don't know," answers Parent A, looking doubtful as she slowly turns and walks to the door of the center. "But I think," she says, pausing and turning around to watch Parent B climb up the rest of the steps, "that ensuring that my daughter grows up with a sense of her self-worth as a person is a good idea. I don't think oppression has to be part of our culture."

"I disagree that women who dress and act the way they are supposed to are oppressed. That's ridiculous. Look at me. Am I oppressed?" Parent B is at the door now, too.

"I'm beginning to understand what you mean about losing our culture. I don't want that to happen. I can be American and still be part of my culture. That's important to me. Let's talk more later," says Parent A, opening the door and stepping back to let her friend walk through first.

Differential Treatment from Parents

Differential treatment starts at birth, when parents perceive their daughters to be more fragile than their sons (Weitzman, 1979). Fathers play rough and tumble more with their sons and talk to them in ways that indicate toughness, like "Hi, Tiger!" (Parke, 2002). From early on, many parents encourage their sons to be active, assertive, and strong, and they protect their girls. They do more touching and talking to girls; they stress independence, self-reliance, and achievement-related skills to their boys. Although some parents make an effort to support egalitarian roles, they tend to start when their children are older, and not at the beginning (Ruble & Martin, 1998). When children leave babyhood, if the differential treatment continues into toddlerhood and beyond, eventually, lo and behold, the boys have a tendency to be active, clever, assertive, and aggressive doers, and the girls often turn out to be sweet, dependent, verbal, and social. Whatever natural inclinations children might have been born with can be diminished or magnified by the socialization process.

Differential Treatment in Preschool

This same differential treatment continues when the children leave home for child care or preschool. In 1973, Serbin, O'Leary, Kent, and Tolnick looked at how preschool teachers treated girls and boys. They found that teachers paid attention to boys' disruptive behavior, which reinforced it; the attention acted as a reward and encouraged the behavior to continue. Girls, on the other hand, received attention only when they stood or played near the teacher. Direct reinforcement, even when it is unintended, is a powerful way to influence behavior.

Things haven't changed much from the early 1970s. Observe for yourself how adults in group care spend a lot of time looking over the heads of the girls who hang around them (being dependent and getting attention for it) to notice the boys, who are throwing blocks, hitting each other, or climbing the fence of the play yard. The untrained adult will yell at the boys. The trained one will leave the cluster of girls and go over and handle the problem with the boys in some professional way—often touching them, getting down to their level, and making eye contact while he or she describes the unacceptable behavior and explains why it must stop. Both the yelling and the more professional intervention strategies are rewarding. They say to the boys, "I'm paying attention to you." The attention and the behavior that preceded it become solidly linked. Many boys never learn any other ways of getting the teacher to notice them. And many of the girls never break out of the "be-dependent-to-get-noticed" pattern.

Clothes can limit activity. Certainly this child will have a hard time climbing trees in this outfit.

While you are observing, notice how adults make conversation with young children. I'm sure you'll discover that girls are often noticed for their appearance. Child care and preschool staff, plus parents of other children, make remarks such as "Oh, you got your hair cut—it looks very pretty" and "I see you got new shoes!" and "What a nice design on your shirt." Those same adults are more likely to notice boys' abilities. They say things like "How strong you are to lift that heavy piece of wood" and "I saw you climb all the way up to the top of the jungle gym!" and "How clever you are. You figured out how to make that work!"

Differential Treatment in Elementary School

Some patterns similar to those that Serbin and her colleagues found in preschool-age children were reported by Thorne (1993), who looked at children in elementary school. Thorne reports that boys control much more space on the playground than girls do—up to 10 times more. The girls play closer to the building and remain near

Doris Pfalmer

Broaden all children's interests and skills.

adult aides who watch over them and protect them. Boys invade girls' space more often than the reverse. And boys are more likely to define girls as "polluting" or "contaminated" in the old game of "cooties." Thorne also noticed that though boys and girls segregate themselves, when they are mixed together by adults, boys and girls interact in more relaxed ways. When adults are the ones who organized the mix, it legitimizes the togetherness and removes the risk of teasing.

While all this is going on in early childhood programs, at home parents tend to give help to their daughters more than to their sons (and the girls ask for help more often, which is not surprising, because they are rewarded for doing so). Girls are also more likely to be criticized for touching, handling, and manipulating objects, and for active play. In other words, girls are taught to be dependent and quiet, even passive, at home and at school, and boys are encouraged to figure things out for themselves and to be active in their play. Some families may not realize these patterns and be grateful when they begin to see and understand them. Other families have put those patterns into effect on purpose. Educating them out of these patterns isn't wise, at least until you understand the family's culture and learn how those patterns do or don't work for them to achieve their goals for their children. You always have to understand the context of behaviors before you judge them.

Socialization of girls has been of interest to feminists for years because of

Barbara Schwartz/Merrill

Young children tend to separate themselves by gender. Gender-conscious teachers can pair up boys and girls in order to break down gender barriers.

what happens when no thought is given to equity. But what about the boys? Who worries about their socialization? Those are questions that many people are asking. Two popular books published in the late 1990s do what they can to answer those questions. One is called *Real Boys*, by William Pollack (1998), and the other is *The Wonder of Boys*, by Michael Gurian (1997). Both address the issues that lead boys to act the way they do. Both books also look at how adults can shape boys into men and move beyond myths and stereotypes about masculinity.

THE ROLE OF BIOLOGY IN CREATING DIFFERENCES BETWEEN BOYS AND GIRLS

When we look at the socialization of males and females, it seems as if boys and girls simply learn their respective roles and that's all there is to it. It's important to recognize, however, that while learning is taking place, physiology is also contributing to male-female differences. Exposure to hormones during pregnancy, genetic influences, and other biological factors can influence the development of sexual identity and roles. There is a dispute about the degree to which differences are learned and the degree to which physiology influences how children see themselves and what skills they develop. We're still working on answering that question. Science swings back and forth on this issue: some research seems to show that many of the differences between males and females are biologically determined, while other research emphasizes the role of differential socialization.

A piece of research reported in the Science and Technology section of *The Economist* (2007) comes out on the side of socialization. The article explains a test called "odd man out," which is designed to rate people's ability to spot unusual objects that appear in their field of vision. Men had a 68 percent success rate while women had a 55 percent success rate. So the researchers took it a step further and had one group of volunteers spend 10 hours playing a video game described as "an action-packed, shoot-'em-up" game. The control group played a calm, non-action-packed video game called "Ballance" for 10 hours. When retested on the odd-man-out test, both sexes who played the action-packed game improved their scores but the women's improvement was greater and brought them up to the same average score as the men. The gains lasted too—after five months these women scored the same as the men. The Ballance players showed no improvement in their ability to spot unusual objects.

Research in the 1960s and 1970s also supported socialization. Money and Ehrhardt (1973), who did some rather startling research then, were convinced that they had proven that babies are born gender-neutral and can be assigned one gender or the other without harmful effect. These gender assignments were done to children with ambiguous external genitalia. Sometimes the assignments were wrong. Hormonal corrections were made at puberty when the mistake was discovered, so that the child could continue in the previously assigned gender role to which he or she had been socialized. Other times the assignments were made when something went wrong with a circumcision and a boy would then be castrated and raised as a girl. The research seemed to show that gender roles are more learned than they are natural. In other words, in spite of the fact that genetically the child was a boy, being socialized as a girl made him exhibit typically female behavior.

The case of a person named "Joan" disputed this research. In an article called "A Boy Without a Penis," Gorman (1997) tells the story of Joan, named by researchers Milton Diamond and Keith Sigmundson in a follow-up study that looked at the long-term effects of assigning gender. The baby, a male, was surgically made into a female after a botched circumcision destroyed the penis. The article relates the agonies Joan went through rebelling against the gender assignment she was given. She knew she was a boy, but no one would confirm that. In 1977 at the age of 14, Joan decided she had only two options, to commit suicide or live life as a male. When she confronted her father with her decision, he finally told her the truth, and a sex change operation eventually gave her a body to go with her identity. To what extent are gender roles learned and to what extent are they natural? No one has the final answer to that question yet.

How does growing up in a family with same-sex parents affect gender roles and the sexual orienation of the children? Studies suggest that what children learn about gender roles in heterosexual families isn't significantly different from what children learn in gay and lesbian families. Further, there is no evidence to suggest that children reared in same-sex families are more likely to develop a gay or lesbian sexual orientation. Their gender-role behavior and sexual orientation are similar to children reared in heterosexual households.

No matter what is discovered about gender roles and sexual orientation, we still have equity issues to consider. We know that the adults in young children's lives have a great influence over their gender role socialization and their attitudes about same-sex families. What are some ways that these adults can help children accept each other and honor the family that each comes from? How can adults empower both boys and girls? How can they promote equality of development for both sexes? With stereotypes still such a part of all of our lives, how can adults counteract stereotypes and help boys learn that they can express feelings and be nurturing, and help girls learn to be independent, assertive, and capable problem solvers? What can adults do to enable each child to fulfill his or her own potential rather than grow up bound by restrictive gender roles?

Sexism in Stroking

Jennifer is a single parent, mother of a 4-year-old boy, Zach, and a daughter, Jade, who is 2½. Jennifer knows about the importance of strokes and affirmations, and she gives them regularly. Here are some examples:

She regularly tells her daughter how nice she looks. She is pleased to note that her little girl is already beginning to take an interest in her own appearance. She notices when her daughter plays nicely with her baby doll, when she pets the cat gently. Lately she's been amazed to see that her daughter is trying to help her do things around the house. Small as she is, she works to make the bed, tries to unload the dish drainer, and wants to fold clothes. Jennifer is very happy about these behaviors and, naturally, wants them to continue, so she praises her daughter when she shows a willingness to help. Once when Jennifer was feeling very down about losing her job, Jade caught her with a tear rolling down her cheek. She left the room and came back dragging her own precious "blankey," which she tenderly gave her mother to help her feel better. Jennifer was really touched by this gesture and she told Jade that.

Zach is his mom's "big boy." He feels that he is the "man of the house" and that he needs to be responsible. Of course he slips now and then, but his mother still loves him greatly—accepting his need to play instead of being grown-up. She thinks his loud manner and his rough play are appropriate, even when they bother her a little. She's proud of the way he figures things out. "You have a good head on your shoulders!" she tells him regularly. She's pleased that he spends so much time playing with the construction toys she's bought him. He creates truly amazing structures and machines. She talks to him about what he'll be when he grows up and how happy she'll be if they can figure out a way to get him into a good college. She has great hopes and aspirations for her son.

When Jade does something well, Jennifer says, "You angel!" When Zach does something well, Jennifer points out what was so good about how he did it. She's more specific with Zach than with Jade.

Anything wrong with this picture? Jennifer is using strokes and affirmations effectively, but she is selective. She is stroking her daughter for some qualities and her son for others. Her children respond accordingly. Her daughter is becoming more and more interested in her appearance and in nurturing others, and her son is coming to see himself as a "doer" and as a capable problem solver who can use his head. Imagine the messages they are receiving about their futures. Will Jade come to see herself as someone beyond an angel who pleases others and makes them happy both by her appearance and by her nurturing actions? Will Zach learn to be a nurturer? How will Zach, the doer, relate to his family when he is grown? Will he go beyond providing the financial support that will come from the brilliant career he's being programmed for?

What Jennifer needs to do is to help her daughter also see herself as a "doer," not just a helper. She needs to catch Jade "thinking." Girls need to know that they are "smart" and capable just as much as boys do. It wouldn't hurt to talk to Jade about college, too, even though the event is far in the future. She could also encourage Jade to play with a wide range of toys, not just those advertised for girls.

Zach needs to see himself as a nurturer as well as a problem solver. His heart should be as big and strong as his head and body. Jennifer can help him do this by finding nurturing men to expose him to, by making it clear that nurturing is appropriate for boys, and by stroking him for any nurturing he might do.

This little family is a reminder of the strokes and affirmations explained in chapter 5. Strokes and affirmations have to be used wisely.

So how do you work with families around issues of gender equity? Such work can be very touchy. See Strategy Box 10.1 for ideas.

Strategy Box 10.1

Working with Families Around the Subject of Gender Equity

- Probably the place to start is by finding out how each family perceives the gender equity issues around which this chapter is based. This could be a very hot topic. Hone your facilitation skills!
- When you put equity issues on the table for discussion, parents who agree may have already noticed some of the practices and may have taken them home to try themselves. In that case you can pat yourself on the back for doing parent education. But don't try to "educate" parents out of their beliefs if they have some serious disagreements with the material in this chapter. Try instead to see their perspective and understand how it fits into their family culture.
- Help families become aware of media messages. For example you can create discussions around the gender role messages that children see on TV. Or ask parents to bring in a children's book and rate it on stereotypical images and messages about gender.
- Share the research in this chapter about gender differentiation in child rearing; discuss the research with families and note their reaction to it. Be sure you and everyone else honors diverse perspectives.
- Try using the guidelines on this page to create discussions with parent groups. Be sure you are open to their perspectives and feelings. Help parents respect each others' differences.

GUIDELINES FOR PARENTS AND EARLY CHILDHOOD EDUCATORS

Here are some guidelines for teaching young children about gender equity:

- *Help children develop awareness of sexist stereotypes.*   Point out such stereotypes in pictures, in books, and on TV. Look for stereotypes in commercials as well as in regular programs and movies.
- *Create a nonsexist environment.*   Find books and pictures that show all kinds of families, including single-parent families (not just single mothers), gay and lesbian families, and extended families, for starters. These books and pictures should show men and women doing similar activities and include examples of women and men in nontraditional occupations. Invite visitors who are in nontraditional jobs to the home, child care, or preschool to talk about their work. (Or visit these workers at their workplaces.) Expand children's awareness beyond narrow views and stereotypical gender roles.
- *Watch your own behavior.*   Do you treat girls differently from boys? What do you notice about each gender? What do you remark about? Do you give both sexes equal physical freedom? Do you allow both to express feelings? Do you encourage

both to seek help at times and to be independent as well? Be observant of yourself and catch the ways you may be promoting narrow gender roles. When children ask about the difference between boys and girls, stick to anatomical differences and avoid mentioning dress, behavior, or personality traits.

Teach an antibias attitude to young children and give them the skills they need to challenge sexism.

• *Teach an antibias attitude to young children and give them the skills they need to challenge sexism.* Teach children to recognize injustice and to speak out against it. When Brandon says to Lindsay, "You can't come in our fort. Only boys are allowed," help her speak up and say, "That's not fair!" If he tries to exclude her on the basis of her behavior, the situation is different. For example, if he says, "You can't come in because last time you grabbed all the toys," she's getting feedback about something she can change. She can't, however, change the fact of being a girl, so for him to exclude her for that reason is unfair discrimination. Children need to learn to speak up for their own rights. Teach them to do that.

• *Help all children develop empathy.*   Notice when children of both genders are sensitive to the feelings of another. Pay attention to behaviors that show caring for another person. Model empathy yourself.

• *Help all children become problem solvers, in both the physical and the social worlds.*   Teach children to troubleshoot. Help them extend their perspective to include many possibilities. Help them learn to negotiate.

• *Broaden children's views of themselves and their capabilities.*   Entice them to develop skills they've been avoiding. Find ways to get the girls that need to be out in the yard more into activities that increase their strength, courage, and dexterity. Figure out a way to get the boys who never sit down at tables, given the choice, involved in activities that take eye-hand coordination and require careful manual skills. Some boys who avoid traditional preschool art projects will glue wood scrap sculptures or take apart an old radio.

• *Notice how clothes get in the way, especially girls' clothes, and determine activities accordingly.*   The crawling baby is hampered if she's in a dress or has lots of ruffles and flounces on her clothes. The slippery shoes of the preschooler keep her from running or climbing. Light-colored pants get stained knees if a girl crawls around on the grass or in the dirt. Will this situation cause problems for her, and serve to restrict her activities?

♦ *Last, but definitely not least, check out your own attitudes.* If you see the male of the species as more important, more deserving of power, worthy of a higher status, you need an attitude adjustment. Until you deal with that attitude problem, you'd better watch yourself carefully when you are around young children. You can't promote equity if down deep you don't believe in it! That's a strong statement, and one that may get me in trouble for including it in a book that claims to be sensitive to cultural differences. But in some cultures gender roles are strictly defined. That may fit the culture and the people in it just fine. The problem for me is when one sex is in power and the other is in a powerless position. I have been told that because I'm judging from outside the culture, I don't really understand the power relationships between the sexes. I have to admit that is a possibility. Still when oppression exists and I'm told it's cultural, I am in a double bind, because I feel it is important to accept and honor differences; *however*, I must also stand up against oppression.

LOOKING BACK AND LOOKING FORWARD

This chapter examined how socialization—in the home, in the early care and education program, and in the outside world as represented by the media—plays a role in creating differences between boys and girls. We discussed the importance of gender equity, focusing on how to avoid stereotypes by looking at the influence of toys and play materials, and adult models. In the next chapter the theme is continued, as we look at various stresses in families, stresses that often relate to the feminization of poverty and the inferior status of women.

FOR DISCUSSION

1. What part does TV play in limiting children's concept of gender roles? Give specific examples. What can be done about any limitations that you perceive?

2. What part does language play in carrying out inequities? How does language influence children's ideas of their capabilities? What can be done to broaden children's views?

3. What if children are exposed to limited models of men's and women's roles? How can children learn about gender equity?

4. Brainstorm some ideas about how to empower both boys and girls.

5. What are some cultural views that are different from the gender equity goals promoted in this chapter?

WEB SITES

American Association of University Women (AAUW)
http://www.aauw.org/
This organization promotes education and equity for women and girls and includes research on gender issues related to girls.

Beyond Title IX
http://www.maec.org/beyond.html
Information about gender equity issues in schools includes gender bias in teacher student interaction and gender differences in learning styles.

An Educators' Guide to Gender Bias Issues
http://www.ed.uiuc.edu/wp/access/gender.html
The technology gender gap and gender bias—
evidence that such a thing exists and what to do
about it. Includes a list of resources.

Gender.Org Web Site
http://www.gender.org.uk/
Click on About Gender for a balanced account on
human gender and sex differences. Many issues of
gender are addressed such as gender roles, gender
identity, and gender in education.

Healthy Place
http://www.healthyplace.com/Communities/Eating_
Disorders/children_parents_6.asp
Addresses self-esteem issues in girls as a way of
preventing eating disorders. Includes a checklist for
parents.

Love Our Children
http://loveourchildrenusa.org/parent_
teachgirlselfesteem.php

Teaching daughters self-esteem. A parenting Web site
designed to keep children safe and strengthen families.

National Network for Child Care (NNCC)
http://www.nncc.org/
The National Network for Child Care is an Internet
source of over 1,000 research-based and reviewed
publications and resources related to children. This
site includes articles, resources, and links on
various subjects.

**National Association for the Education of Young
Children (NAEYC)**
http://www.naeyc.org/
The National Association for the Education of
Young Children has a men in child care interest
forum that meets regularly at conferences and has
growing numbers of members who are concerned
about the small number of men in the profession.
The Web site also has a number of resources
available for parents and professionals including
books and journals, one of which is called *Young
Children*.

FURTHER READING

American Psychological Association. (2007). Report
of the APA Task Force on the Sexualization of
Girls. www.apa.org/pi/wpo/sexualization.html

Chow, E. N., Wilkinson, D., & Zinn, B. (1996).
Common bonds, different voices. Newbury Park,
CA: Sage.

Collins, P. H. (1990). *Black feminist thought: Knowledge,
consciousness, and the politics of empowerment*. Boston:
Unwin Hyman.

Cox, A. J. (2006). *Boys of few words. Raising our sons to
communicate and connect*. New York: Guilford.

Derman-Sparks, L., & the ABC Task Force. (1989).
*Antibias curriculum: Tools for empowering young chil-
dren*. Washington, DC: National Association for
the Education of Young Children.

Faludi, S. (1991). *Backlash: The undeclared war against
American women*. New York: Crown.

French, M. (1992). *The war against women*. New York:
Summit.

Gallas, K. (1998). *Sometimes I can be anything: Power,
gender, and identity in a primary classroom*. New York:
Teachers College Press.

Kenway, J., Willis, S., Backmore, J., & Rennie, L.
(1998). *Answering back*. St. Leonards, Australia:
Allen & Unwin.

MacNaughton, G. (2000). *Rethinking gender in early
childhood education*. St. Leonards, Australia: Allen
& Unwin.

Neighbors, H. W., & Jackson, J. S. (Eds.). (1996). *Mental
health in black America*. Newbury Park, CA: Sage.

Parke, R. D. (2002). Fatherhood. In M. Bornstein
(Ed.), *Handbook of parenting* (2nd ed.). Mahwah,
NJ: Erlbaum.

Patterson, C. J. (2002). Lesbian and gay parenthood.
In M. H. Bornstein (Ed.), *Handbook of parenting*
(2nd ed.). Mahwah, NJ: Erlbaum.

Powlishta, K. K. (1995, July). Gender segregation
among children: Understanding the "cootie"
phenomenon. *Young Children*, 50(4), 61–69.

Ruble, D. N., & Martin, C. L. (1998). Gender development. In W. Damon (Gen. Ed.) & N. Eisenberg
(Vol. Ed.), *Handbook of child psychology* (Vol. 3,
pp. 933–1016). New York: Wiley.

Sheldon, A. (1990, January). Kings are royaler than
queens: Language and socialization. *Young
Children*, 45(2), 4–9.

Turner-Bowker, D. M. (1996). Gender stereotyped
description in children's picture books: Does
"Curious Jane" exist in literature? *Sex Roles*, 35,
461–488.

CHAPTER 11

Stress and Success in Family Life

In *this chapter you'll discover* . . .

- The characteristics of a successful family
- The stories of six families and the stresses they face
- Why stress is sometimes good for us
- Some factors that are common to resilient children
- How "protective factors" can counteract the effects of stress

So far in this book we have looked at how to work with families around issues related to children's development, education, and socialization. This chapter puts the spotlight on the families themselves—their lives outside the times you see them. Obviously children are influenced by much more than the time spent in early care and education programs. They live their lives 7 days a week, round the clock, whereas they are in the early education environment only a limited number of hours. Although some children spend 8 to 10 hours a day, 5 days a week, in out-of-home programs, many children are in their educational setting as few as 15 hours a week. But even the children who spend long hours away from their families are more affected by being part of their families than anything else. Early educators need to take the family setting into consideration if they are truly to understand the child and support the family in a collaborative kind of way. So this chapter looks closely at various families and their stresses and successes.

What is meant by the word *family*? Close your eyes and imagine a family. Does this family fit your *concept* of a family? Look around at symbols of families. Think of the logos of agencies that serve families. What is the image conveyed by most? The images I usually see are a male, a female, and one or two children. Perhaps the balance and symmetry cause this type of family to be chosen as a logo—it's visually attractive. Or perhaps we're still living in the aftermath of the *Leave It to Beaver* tradition. Whatever the reason, many of us carry in our heads an image that doesn't apply to a large number of families in the United States today.

What are some of the many different ways a family can vary from the mother-father-child model? Each family can have more children or fewer. It can involve a marriage or not. The members can be all the same gender. Its members can vary greatly in age—by more than just two generations. It can include a number of people who are not related but are living under the same roof. It can include people who are related by blood or marriage along with those who are not related and who do not live under the same roof. (This kind of family is called a *kinship network*.) Its members can share the same bloodlines or name, or both, or neither. Its members can share the same history or not. The family can be *blended*—that is, composed of individuals coming together as a couple who each have children of their own. The blended family can live all together or not. The family can be composed of people who have traditional relationships to each other but were not born into them. Children may come into the family from outside—through adoption, fostering, or less formal arrangements.

There are numerous traditional names for these varying kinds of families. They include nuclear, insular, extended, embedded, single-parent, step, blended, adoptive, foster, communal, kinship networks, gay, and lesbian.

Families can vary infinitely in their makeup. Each variation has an effect on the socialization of any children in them. Families may originate through interracial or interreligious unions. Families may have members who are differently abled. Families may come about through marriages or affiliations that cross generational lines.

Though the forms of families may vary greatly, virtually all families experience stress—and always have. Stress is nothing new to family life, though it may seem now with the times changing so rapidly that we are under more stress than in the past. Certainly family structure is changing, and that alone can create stress in those who think back with longing to what they consider the good old days. This chapter looks at the kinds of stresses that affect families today. It also looks at what makes for successful families. The overarching question is: what can early educators do to support families so they have less stress and more success?

It's important to take into account the strengths of families in stress who manage to socialize their children successfully. What enables these families to function effectively under difficult or demanding circumstances? Why do some families remain organized and supportive of each other under extreme pressures? Early childhood educators need to learn how to promote that same kind of togetherness in families that lack it. They need to understand more about the effects of classism, racism, and sexism, as well as cultural and ethnic biases.

You can't take families out of their cultural context. The early childhood profession needs to focus less on universals and more on understanding a variety of cultural patterns of child rearing as they relate to care, education, and socialization. It's important to recognize that the cultural imperatives of families determine which competencies it is appropriate to foster in children. It is important to understand how educational and socialization techniques, plus child-rearing practices work to promote the survival of any given culture, even though to a critical eye outside the culture some techniques may look undesirable. Early childhood professionals must avoid equating cultural survival with what may seem to be harmful practices and family breakdown.

There's a lot of talk today about the family breaking down. When a family is not functioning well, raising children is difficult and there's cause to be concerned. However, the definition of *functional family* varies from culture to culture. It's tempting to see a family as dysfunctional when its patterns or structure are different from your image of what they should be, but family structure alone doesn't tell you how well the family functions. It only tells you that it's different from what has been regarded as a traditional family.

For too long society, researchers, and the media have been thinking of the two-parent, middle-class family and their birth children as the standard by which all other families are to be judged. For too long those families that differed were thought not to measure up and were labeled as lacking or deprived. It's time to give legitimacy to cultural differences and alternative lifestyles.

A good start is to get rid of the term *broken family*, which sounds as if something is wrong, when in reality the so-called broken family may be quite functional. You can't tell by family structure whether a family functions in healthy ways. The single-parent family in apartment A may be quite functional compared with the two-parent, *intact*, but highly dysfunctional family in apartment B next door.

You have to be very careful about making generalizations about family structures. For example, some African American family structures have been portrayed as deficient. Stereotypes of domineering mothers, absent fathers, disorganized families plagued with abuse and neglect sometimes overshadow the reality of families that don't fit what is sometimes thought of as the ideal structure.

It's time to quit looking at differences as deficits and view them instead as legit-imate forms in themselves. Families of all types and sizes are fully capable of producing healthy children and providing a support system for all of the people who comprise the family. You can't judge a family's degree of functionality by its structure, patterns, or makeup.

Instead of automatically labeling some family structures as deficient and looking at them as social problems, it's time that we started to see their strengths. We should be supporting diversity in family structure. When we, as a society, come from a point of view that the family is breaking down, rather than changing in form, we put all of our resources into looking at the causes of the breakdown. We already know some-thing about what causes stress in families. We know that you can't separate the way families function from the social, economic, and political realities that influence their lives.

SUCCESSFUL FAMILIES

A successful family is one that functions in healthy ways; it supports and nurtures its members so that everyone's needs are met. Although happiness and satisfaction may come periodically to members of successful families, those aren't the only emotions they experience; they feel a wide range of emotions and are free and able to express them when appropriate. A successful family isn't a perennial sunshine family. It has its ups and downs, just as its individual members do.

There is much talk about dysfunctional families these days. Many people have dis-covered that some of the ways they were reared weren't good for them—their families were abusive, created codependencies, and taught family members to ignore their own needs. The statistics vary, but it has been said that up to 98 percent of us grew up in dysfunctional families. Yet if 98 percent of us are raised in a particular way, that way must be *normal*—a word often equated with *right* and *good*. So where does that leave us as far as dysfunctional families are concerned?

Because the family prepares its members for society, we'd better look beyond the family to see what this high rate of dysfunction is about. A quick look will show that the so-called dysfunctional family is not so out of tune with the present society, which nurtures a system in which some have power over others and not everyone's needs are met. Power, both in the society and in the family, is often wielded like a sword rather than radiated like light. Privilege and hierarchy, sanctioned by the soci-etal system, often squelch our ability to be who we really are; they take our personal power from us. The dysfunctional family reflects the dysfunctional parts of society.

The theme of the strong dominating the weak is pervasive both in the family and in the society. If we take that theme to extreme, we see that world peace in the past has depended on the strongest nations stockpiling enough weapons to stop each other from making war. That's the ultimate in the power approach to getting along with others. No wonder families have been hard-pressed to help their members grow in healthy, sane ways to become who they really are as unique people—each able to radiate the power inside.

We're beginning to change our approach—but change doesn't happen in an easy, linear way. It is often accompanied by periods of uncomfortable chaos, when things seem to get worse instead of better.

Many who desire this change are beginning to create their own scripts instead of living by the old myths of power in which the strong overcome the weak, one race dominates another, and men control the lives of women. Many are altering the themes that have been handed down for generations.

Families are starting to rear their children for the emerging society—one in which it will be possible to raise children without abusing them and to be both connected and autonomous, one in which the dominator model gives way to a true equity model. Parents are learning how to use their power *for* or *with* their children instead of overpowering and dominating them. They are learning to *empower* their children—that is, to allow them to experience personal power, which gives them the feeling of being able to be themselves and of having some effect on the world or the people in it. People who are empowered don't need to overpower or manipulate others. They are free to experience being who they really are—to fulfill their unique potential; they will resist being cast into some preset mold.

No matter how much things change, all family systems will continue to have some degree of dysfunction, or they wouldn't be of human origin. We'll never live in a perfect world, but we can improve it by focusing on what kinds of traits make for successful families—the traits that will allow each member to function effectively within the family and in the society beyond. What are these traits?

When you focus more on families' successes than on their stresses, you can then work with them from a strength-based perspective. Strategies related to a strength-based approaches can be found in Strategy Box 11.1.

TRAITS OF SUCCESSFUL FAMILIES

Healthy involvement with each other is one trait of a successful family. Its members feel attachment to each other. They care. They don't just fulfill a social role; they have a deep sense of commitment. They give time and attention to the family. They don't get overinvolved in activities that exclude the family.

People in successful families recognize the signs of unhealthy *codependence*, in which one person encourages and enables another to lean too heavily on him or her, creating bonds that trap both of them. People in successful families understand the importance of independence and healthy *interdependence*. They know how to get their needs met in a relationship that allows the other person to get his or her needs met as well. They know how to take care of others without making them overly dependent on that care. They understand mutual nurturing. One way to look at this trait of successful families is using what Christian (2006), writing about family systems theory, calls boundaries, which relate to togetherness and separateness. A family that values individual decision-making, openness to new ideas, and separate identities for each member over close connections and conformity has a different set of boundaries in their system from the one that emphasizes togetherness and sees each member's

Strategy Box 11.1

Working with Families from a Strength-Based Perspective

- The first goal in working with any family is to form a relationship with that family. That means building the relationship is a top priority any time that you communicate with them.
- Look for every family's strengths and focus on those. When you communicate with the family, remember their strengths, which will help you have faith that they can answer many of their own questions and solve a number of their own problems. Don't be the "expert," instead be a supporter and facilitator who helps put them in touch with their own expertise.
- When you have problems finding strengths, examine your own attitudes and look at the stereotypes you hold. Self-awareness on your part is essential if you are to move beyond your biases and stereotypes so you can get to know this particular family and discover their strengths.
- Acknowledge the family's strengths to its members. Notice the skills they use with their children and mention those. Affirmations work with adults just like they do with children by emphasizing positives.

identity as closely tied to the family. The problem is if you're from the first family you may see the members of the other family as enmeshed. If you from the second family you may see the first family as disengaged. It's very hard to determine which families are dysfunctional without understanding how their systems serve them.

Successful families tend to build and maintain self-esteem in their members instead of continually tearing it down. They know how to discipline children and to guide and control behavior in ways that leave self-esteem intact. Virginia Satir, who wrote *Peoplemaking*, found in her practice as a family therapist that developing a feeling of self-worth is one of the primary traits of successful family systems. In Chapter 9, we discussed self-esteem, which is another word for self-worth, and we explored issues relating to cross-cultural perspectives on self-esteem. What looks like parental behaviors that tear down self-esteem from one family's perspective may not look the same at all from another family's perspective. It's very hard to judge across cultures. That's why the early care and education workforce needs to reflect the diversity of the society!

Successful families know how to communicate effectively. Communication is another of Virginia Satir's family systems. Effective communication means that family members can both give and receive feedback. They have some skill at resolving conflicts in ways that do not neglect anyone's needs. They use problem-solving methods to deal with even small issues when they arise. They know how to cope with problems that can't be solved. They know how to express feelings in healthy ways as is appropriate to their culture. They know how to give and get culturally appropriate strokes or recognition. Communication styles are greatly influenced by culture. Some cultures put much more emphasis on words than others. The ones who use the most words are called *low context* cultures. They are a contrast to ones that use fewer words; they are called *high context cultures*. The mainstream culture of the United States is a low context culture, while the Chinese culture is a high context culture, because the meaning of communication comes from the context rather than words. Learning the traditions is a task of childhood—so children grow up to share the context and don't need words to communicate (Hall, 1981).

Successful families know how to protect their members, providing a secure environment within the home. Though a safe home is a haven from the outside world, it is also important that family members connect to the greater society. Therefore, two important family functions—protection and connection—seem to be opposites, but in reality they balance one another. Virginia Satir says one way of looking at family systems is to understand how every person in the family links to society. The degree of function is determined by how they link and what the results are.

The early care and education program can provide a helpful link to the society—and for some families it's their first experience with societal institutions related to schooling and education. That's another benefit of family-centered early care and education. The link can be more than a very loose one, and parents can become vitally involved in their children's education.

Successful families have rules that work for each member and for the family as a whole. "Rules are sets of standards, laws, or traditions that tell us how to live in relation to each other" (Christian, p 16). Some families are clear about their rules and put them into words. Other families' rules are buried in the cultural context. When a couple gets married they sometimes discover rules they didn't know they had. They have to work to figure out what to do about contrasting rules. Rules can be about very large things, like how do adults and children talk to elders and who gets served first. When I grew up I wasn't aware of any family rules about who got served first. There may have been some rules, but apparently I never broke them. My husband's family though, had very strict rules, which I discovered one night after a party. I remember that a decision was made in the kitchen to serve all the children first and get them out of the way before the adults sat down to eat. One elderly grandmother was upset to watch the children eat when the older people should have been served first. She didn't say anything at the time, but the look on her face showed her disapproval. Afterwards she complained about the children being fed before the adults. She had a strong rule in her family about that.

Rules that seem big to some can seem small to others—like taking off shoes when entering a house. If you don't have the rule, it may seem like a foolish and even annoying rule. If you do have the rule, it may be a very important one to you.

Parents and elders in successful families know how to pass on values to the next generation, through modeling, discussion, teaching, and problem solving. They also know how to accept differences when value conflicts arise.

So what does a successful family look like? Do they all have fulfilling jobs, live in nice houses, drive "newish" cars, and live stress-free lives? Of course not. Successful families come in all sizes, shapes, configurations, and financial conditions. Circumstances contribute to success, of course, but they aren't the sole determiners. If they were, rich people in good physical health would automatically be better at creating successful families than sick poor people, but that just isn't the way it works, is it?

No family is 100 percent successful. All families are in process. Think of success as a path—a path where no one gets to the final destination (just as no one reaches human perfection). Some start out on this path farther behind than others.

Compare two families. The first is made up of a couple who both came from stable families where their needs were fairly well met. When they had children, they tended to create the kind of home life they both experienced as children. They have their problems, of course, but they seem to take things in stride. They work at their marriage, at their individual development, and at their parenting. They had good models in their parents for this work. They are on the path of success.

The second family is composed of a couple who came from less stable homes. They are also working at their marriage, at their individual development, and at their parenting, but they have to work harder because they haven't had the firsthand experience that the first couple had. They've had to come to the realization that their own upbringing was lacking—which means that they've had to *learn* healthy ways of dealing with their children. It didn't just come to them naturally. They are also on the path to success, but it's a rockier road for them, with numerous barricades to climb over and potholes to fall into.

What the two families have in common is that they have a vision of success. They are both on the path, moving toward their vision—and they are determined to make progress.

Let's take a look now at six families who, in spite of a number of pressures in their lives, are also struggling along the path to become successful families. Some are much farther along than others, but stress is a theme in all of their lives. Let's see what kind of stresses they are coping with. One thing that these six families have in common is that all are enrolled in the same early care and education program.

Sara's Family

Meet Sara. She was a teen parent when she had Ty four years ago; now she is 20. Ty and his 2-year-old brother, Kyle, are both in the center because Sara is in nursing school at the local community college.

Sara has had a hard time of it since she became a mother at 16. She lived with her mother for the first couple of years, but they argued over how she was raising Ty, and Sara left to join the homeless population of her city. She and Ty lived for awhile in her car until the poor old auto quit running, sat in one place too long, and got towed. Then she lived under a bridge between the highway and the river. Pregnant again (as the result of being raped), hungry, and desperate, she finally found a social worker in an agency that hooked her up to some of the services available in her community (more about this in the next chapter).

Now Sara is in nursing school, and life is better, but it still isn't easy. She has financial aid and a place to live, but she's going crazy trying to go to school all day, study all night, and raise her boys at the same time. They reflect her stress and they have stresses of their own. Ty seems to have an attention deficit problem; although the teachers in the center are working with him, he moves from one activity to another so fast that it's hard to keep track of him. He never seems to settle on any one thing and becomes frustrated very easily when he tries to do something. The result is that he throws regular tantrums.

Then there's Kyle. He appears to be a very sweet child, cuddling up to the teachers whenever he gets a chance. But his brother beats on him, which is starting to make him aggressive toward other children. He has to be watched all the time because he bites. The staff is thinking of putting him in one of the satellite family child care homes available to the center because the stimulation of the center seems to be too much for him to handle.

Sara is learning about communication, discipline, and family relations from a parenting class and from her therapist. She doesn't feel very successful as a family head, but she is moving in the right direction. When she looks at her past, she sees that she has come a long way. She has hopes for the future.

Roberto's Family

The second family is Roberto's. His 4-year-old daughter, Lupe, is in the local Head Start program in the morning, and she comes to the center in the afternoon. Roberto transports her from one program to the other when his old pickup is running and he's not working. Otherwise, his wife, Maria Elena, who takes classes in English as a second language at the adult school, uses the bus to pick up Lupe and deliver her to the center. Maria Elena takes their baby, Paco, with her in the morning to class, where they have child care, but she brings Paco to the center in the afternoon while she cleans houses to support the family. Roberto does odd jobs when he can get them and has been looking for steady work for some time.

Lupe has a hearing loss, and the teachers in the center keep telling Maria Elena and Roberto that they must take her to see a specialist. But they went once and there were so many papers to fill out, none of which they understood, and no one was there to translate for them—so they walked out and haven't gone back. The center staff is working to find them a translator so they can get the help that Lupe needs, but so far they haven't found one. Maria Elena is very worried about Lupe, and so is Roberto, but he is hesitant to put his name on any kind of papers that might bring him to the attention of the government. He just doesn't trust what might happen once the government becomes aware of him and his family. It was bad enough signing up for Head Start and for child care, but at least those papers were in Spanish and he knew what he was signing. He didn't have to depend on someone with limited Spanish trying to explain them to him. His neighbor tells him he's being paranoid about this, but Roberto's family has had some bad experiences with government officials, and he doesn't want to repeat them. Roberto is wary!

Roberto has never even thought of whether his is a "successful" family or not. He's too involved in the daily struggle for survival.

He is anxious that his family live according to the traditions he grew up with, but he sees all of them being changed as the different cultures rub up against each

other. He resists that change, but at the same time he appreciates what he and
Maria Elena are learning about child rearing from their involvement with Head Start
and the child care center. They are beginning to examine some of the "givens" of
their own upbringing and thinking about whether they contribute to the goals they
have for their children. They are most anxious to retain their culture and be the best
parents they can be!

Junior's Family

The most vocal member of the third family is 12-month-old Junior. He cries all the time.
The staff at the child care center tries hard to comfort him, but what works with other
children doesn't work with Junior. The whole family—refugees from their homeland—are
obviously suffering from having had to flee, but the loudest sufferer is Junior. The center
staff has never had a baby in the program who has been so unhappy for so long. He cries
all day, every day, except for the periods when he sleeps.

The staff doesn't know too much about Junior's family, except that they live with
a number of relatives in a small house that they're pooling their money to buy.
Although the house is crowded in the evenings and on weekends, there's no one
home during the day to care for little Junior. Everyone's out working. Great-Grandma
used to take care of him, but she's sick now and can barely care for herself. Perhaps
he misses her, and that's why he cries so much.

Language must be a problem for Junior, too. No one in the center knows more than
a word or two of his language, and that must be very scary for him. And he doesn't stop
crying long enough to listen to English.

The staff has tried to find out about Junior's diet, but his mother is very vague.
She doesn't speak English too well, so she leaves things like food decisions up to
them. The center provides the food for the children, but the staff is anxious to
respond to any special cultural or family food preferences. They just can't find out
from Junior's family what those might be.

Like Roberto's family, Junior's family is also rubbing up against other cultures, but
they are so busy surviving in the new country, with its different cultures and different languages, that they are in culture shock. They are still reacting to what is new and strange to
them, and they are not yet able to take in any benefits from the broadened experience.

Michael's Family

The fourth family has one child enrolled in the child care center. Three-year-old
Michael is a quiet boy with long dark eyelashes that sweep down on his cheeks
when he lowers his eyes, which he does a good deal of the time. He is cautious and
slow to warm up to people, but his slightly withdrawn manner has captured the
hearts of the staff.

Michael's parents, Margaret and Beth, are a lesbian couple. Although the child
comes every day, the staff has barely talked to his parents. They seem to move in and
out of the center like shadows. Margaret usually brings Michael. She is friendly to

staff but always in a hurry. Because the staff members have mixed feelings about this couple, several are rather glad the two women are so unobtrusive and seemingly unwilling to engage in conversation. However, one staff member has strong feelings about the bias this family may be experiencing in the center. She wants to change the atmosphere and be sure that the parents and the child feel comfortable and accepted. She has begun to introduce the subject of antibias regularly at staff meetings, and this has brought forth some discomfort among the staff. At the last meeting she pointed out that although the program is committed to "celebrating diversity," there is no physical evidence in the center that lesbian and gay couples are considered normal families. Pictures abound (on the walls and in books) that show all kinds of family configurations, except same-sex parents. No books in the center show gay or lesbian families.

"What can we do to make school more comfortable for and accepting of Michael and his family?" was the teacher's question to the rest of the staff.

"Good question," responded one teacher. "This is something we should talk about. I'm concerned about Michael," she added emphatically.

"I'*m* concerned about his parents as well!" said the first teacher, equally emphatically. "What can we do to raise their comfort level?"

The staff is still working on this question, because they are in conflict with each other about what should be done. They can't even agree about the idea of bringing in books and pictures of families like Michael's. Some feel strongly that it's an equity issue they are discussing; others are taking a moral or religious stance. In the meantime, it's easy to see the discomfort level rise in Michael and his parents as they pick up unspoken messages from various staff members.

Although Michael's parents have many traits of the successful family, they are unable to benefit from what the staff might have to offer them to increase their knowledge of child development and family relations because of limited communication.

Courtney's Family

Courtney's family commands a good deal of staff attention for all sorts of reasons. Courtney, the mother, has been married before, and two of her four children are in the program. Roland, her 4-year-old, was abused by his father, and the family lives in fear that one day the father will arrive at school, claim his son, and take off with him. The staff has been warned of the situation and is aware of the restraining order that gives them the authority to refuse to let the father take Roland. Roland, after all his bad experiences, is fearful of men—and he doesn't get along with the other children, either.

Courtney, Roland's mother, a European American, is married to Richard, who is Native American. They have their own child, a 2½ year old named Soleil. Roland's half-sister looks more like her father than her mother, and her beauty is remarkable—literally. Adults passing through the center stop to discuss what a lovely child she is.

Soleil is remarkable in other ways too. She is intellectually mature far beyond her years, but socially she's still a baby. She confuses adults, who don't know what to think of her. They marvel at the way she is teaching herself to read but become distressed by the fact that she kicks, screams, and even bites when a child refuses to give her a toy that she wants to play with.

Courtney is in a drug recovery program and has just decided to continue her education. She wants to become a lawyer. Richard works in construction and is going to college part-time to become a history teacher. He has very strong feelings about his heritage, which the teachers found out about last Thanksgiving when they put up pictures of Pilgrims and Indians on the walls.

One of the teachers was just stapling the last picture up when Richard arrived with Roland and Soleil. He stopped, stared intensely at the picture, then turned abruptly to the teacher and said, "I'm sorry, but it's offensive to me that you're using caricatures of my people as decorations. It feels as if you're making fun of my culture."

The teacher stopped, stapler in hand, shocked by his words. "I don't understand. Thanksgiving stands for friendship and love. That's what these pictures are about— brotherhood—people helping people."

"Maybe that's the way you see it," explained Richard, "but what I see is that you're celebrating a day that marks the beginning of the genocide of my people. I don't want my children to have any part of such a celebration." He left the room abruptly, taking the children with him.

Later, during nap time, the other teachers were shocked to hear such a different version of the happy holiday they had always celebrated. But they took the pictures down and agreed to stress the harvest aspects of Thanksgiving rather than give it a "historical slant."

Richard heard about this through Courtney, who brought the children back later in the day. When he arrived the next morning, children in hand, he remarked about the missing pictures to Roland's teacher and expressed his gratitude about the staff's willingness to see his point of view and make some changes in their celebration. As a cross-cultural family, Courtney and Richard are exploring where their concepts of a successful family coincide and where they collide.

The Jackson Family

Holidays are a big issue for the sixth family—the Jacksons—as well. They have three children in the program and are pleased with everything but the celebration of what they consider Christian holidays. At a recent parent meeting, they got caught in the middle of an argument between two groups of parents. It started when Mrs. Jackson asked the staff to downplay religious celebrations. "I don't want my children to learn someone else's religion," she remarked. "We'll teach our religion at home, so please leave religious observances out of the program."

One parent answered her by insisting that Christmas had nothing to do with religion. Two other parents rose to their feet, arguing loudly that it was a terrible shame that Christ had been removed from Christmas and that there ought to be more religion in the center rather than less.

When the director finally got the parents calmed down, Mrs. Jackson spoke up once again, this time about dietary differences. She was concerned that her children were being fed food that violated the dietary restrictions of her religion.

She spoke politely and with great concern. The director asked her to make an appointment for another time to discuss the problem.

Mrs. Jackson arrived the next day at the agreed-on time and found the director in her office waiting for her. The two had met here earlier: Before the family came into the program, they had several discussions about whether the oldest Jackson child, who has spina bifida, could be accommodated in his wheelchair. Several modifications to the environment were required, which Mr. Jackson worked on with the help of Sara and Richard, who both have carpentry skills.

Mrs. Jackson and the director expected to have a good talk this time, because they had gotten along well in the past. Mrs. Jackson expressed her feelings that the teachers were not watching what her children ate, and the director promised to do all she could to make sure that the Jackson children were carefully monitored at meal and snack times. She also asked Mrs. Jackson if she would be willing to do a cooking activity with the 4-year-old group and teach them how to make one of the special dishes of her culture. She agreed, and that was the beginning of her involvement in the program.

At present Mrs. Jackson is working night and day on a big fund-raiser for a climbing structure for the play yard. She's finding it very satisfying to use her talent, skills, and connections in the community to benefit the program and the children, some of whom, she realizes, are severely financially deprived. She has involved a number of other parents, and they are getting to know and appreciate each other in ways that only come from working together toward a common cause—something they could never have done by just attending parent meetings.

The Jacksons have a lot going for them as a successful family. But, like the rest of the families, they still have a way to go.

Comparing the Six Families

These six families have varying concepts, images, and dreams of what a successful family is. They all have many stresses in their lives. Their successes include varying degrees of the following:

- Commitment
- Attachment to each other
- Individual independence and group interdependence
- Ability to give and receive nurturing
- Ability to get needs met
- Coping skills
- Methods of building self-esteem
- Effective communication
- Ability to pass on culture, goals, and values

Their stresses include the following:

- Poverty
- Special needs of their children
- Problems with substance abuse
- Divorce and custody issues
- Stepfamilies and blended families
- Lack of support
- Communication difficulties
- Inaccessible resources
- Bias issues

Besides being in the process of building toward success and experiencing stress, what else do all of these families have in common? They're in the same child care program. They love their children and want the best for them, although they have different ways of showing their love and different ideas about what "the best" is and how to achieve it.

How are they different? They represent different cultures and traditions, different family structures (with different degrees of outside acceptance of those family structures), and different degrees of being part of the mainstream culture of the center. They also differ in their ability to handle the stress in their lives.

Real-Life Families: Some Statistics

According to the Children's Defense Fund (2004), the teen birth rates are going down. In 1990, 59.9 out of 1,000 females aged 15 to 19 gave birth to babies, while in 2002 the rate was 43. That's good news; however, the number of children raised in poverty is growing. In 2002, one in six children lived in a poverty-level family, as defined by an annual income below the government poverty level (Children's Defense Fund, 2004). In 2005 it was reported that the number of children living in extreme poverty increased 20 percent from 2000 to 2004. Extreme poverty means that families have to get by on $29 a day (Children's Defense Fund, 2005). Poverty makes meeting needs difficult, if not impossible. The Children's Defense Fund keeps track of the statistics affecting children. Here are some more from the Children's Defense Fund, (2005):

- 37 million people in the United States are poor. Of these 13 million are children.
- Poverty in the United States is more prevalent now than in the 1960s and 1970s and has escalated rapidly since 2000.
- There are 1.8 million poor children living in female-headed families with no income from either work or welfare.

And more information about poverty and children from the Children's Defense Fund, (2004):

- A child from France, Canada, Germany, Britain, or Spain is less likely to be poor than an American child.
- An American child is 5 to 8 times as likely to be poor as a child in Sweden, Norway, or Finland.
- Many members of poor families work but don't receive enough payment to rise above the poverty level.
- Many families above the poverty level don't make enough to afford food and rent.
- Poverty affects children's health, which affects education.

It is interesting that President Lyndon B. Johnson's War on Poverty began more than 40 years ago, yet children are still the largest group of poor people in the United States. We are the richest nation on earth—first in GDP (gross domestic product) among industrialized nations. We have the greatest number of millionaires and billionaires and are way ahead in health technology, yet we have so many children living in poverty.

It's not that we don't know what to do to keep poverty factors from affecting child outcomes. We have found antipoverty policies that work. Two different projects provide examples of ways to make a difference in outcomes for children. An antipoverty experiment called the New Hope Project in Milwaukee, Wisconsin, showed that a child's outcome can be affected by society's support. The project provided an above-poverty income, health insurance, and child care. As a result children's literacy test scores improved, and children showed more positive social behavior five years later. Another study, the Minnesota Family Investment Program, also found that supplementing the income of poverty families resulted in a measurable difference in outcomes for their children. The results included improvements in children's behavior and school performance (Children's Defense Fund 2004).

Now think about the six families under stress in this chapter. Although poverty was a big factor in the majority of the six families, they had other stresses as well. All families have stress. Stress is part of life. When stress eats on people and overwhelms them, it has harmful effects, but stress doesn't have to be bad.

STRESS AS A POSITIVE FORCE

When the six families and the child care staff at the center to which they are all connected think about what to do to help their children, they can start by recognizing that stress isn't necessarily bad. We all need some stress in our lives. Stress can be a growth factor. A physical example of how stress is useful can be seen in the way a baby's bones form to enable the child to walk. The leg bones that connect to the hip socket have a different shape in the newborn than in the child about to walk. What makes the shape change to accommodate walking? Stress—the stress of weight being put on them. A similar example relates to old age. The older woman at risk for osteoporosis babies her bones by never exercising and creates the very condition she's trying to avoid—her bones grow weak and brittle. Her bones need some stress to help keep them strong.

Frank Gonzalez-Mena

Stress isn't necessarily bad—we all need some stress in our lives. Stress can be a growth factor.

Of course, too much stress isn't any better than too little. Again an example from physiology: Look at the sports injuries of children who overuse their pitching arms, for example. Irreparable damage occurs from too much stress.

What is too much stress for one family, or for one person, may be optimum stress for another. Some people are knocked down by seemingly minor setbacks; others manage much harder situations. Still others seem to take on adversity as a challenge and grow from it.

When I was first learning about child development, I took a trip to the high country above the California desert. There I observed a natural phenomenon that I have never forgotten: the bristle-cone pine. I saw this gnarled, ancient tree, bowed by the wind and stunted by lack of water and the thin air and soil of its habitat, as the perfect symbol for the benefits of stress. Instead of weakening under adverse conditions, these trees grow stronger than other plant life in less stressful situations. Using their adversity to the maximum, these trees survive longer than any other living thing on earth. Somehow they take the hardships life has to offer and use them to their own advantage. Some children do that too.

We know that poverty, abuse, neglect, being shuffled around, lack of attachment, and not getting needs met can adversely affect children's lives. Obviously it is better for children to get what they need, be raised by people who care for them, have a stable home life, and meet loving acceptance inside and outside the home rather than having to live with abuse, neglect, bias, and discrimination. Yet we all know about "resilient children"—those children who, in spite of much hardship, manage to turn out with healthy personalities and find success and happiness in life.

WHAT WE CAN LEARN FROM STUDIES OF RESILIENT CHILDREN

Studies by Werner (1984, 1995; Werner & Smith, 1992) and others (Luthar, Cicchetti, & Becker, 2000) show that there are some protective factors and personality traits that are common to *resilient children*—children who have the psychological strength to recover from misfortune or who emerge intact from a history of severe distress. One vital factor that the children had in common was a sense of connectedness to someone in the early years. These children found attachment, usually in the first year (not necessarily to a parent). Many of the children whose parents were not able to meet their needs found or recruited surrogate parents, inside or outside the home. Werner uses the term *recruited* to indicate that attachment wasn't just by chance, that the children had more than a passive role. From this recruited attachment, the resilient children received enough attention and nurturing early on to gain a sense of trust. Their lives may have been marked by abandonment, either physical or emotional or both, but at some period

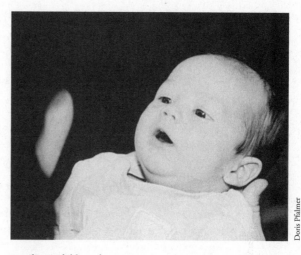

Resilient children have experienced a sense of connectedness at some point in their lives.

they found someone to believe in them and care about them. Even if they were shuffled from family to family, never belonging anywhere, they found sources of support. They made connections, and those connections seem to have provided enough to keep the children going in positive directions.

One reason these resilient children were able to make connections was that they had the ability to elicit positive responses from others. Even at a very young age, they were somehow able to gain other people's positive attention.

These children were problem solvers, taking an active approach toward negotiating, communicating, and grappling with the obstacles that life presented to them. They had not only the willingness but also the skills to take an active rather than a passive role.

Another important commonality these resilient children had was that at some point during their lives they found themselves needed by someone else. They had responsibility thrust on them. They were required to help another person—a younger sibling, for example. Relating to someone else's helplessness gave them a sense of their own power.

Most important of all, perhaps, these children had a tendency to perceive their experiences constructively and each held a positive vision of a meaningful life. In spite of their hardships, life made sense. In other words, their attitude made all the difference in the world.

Interestingly enough, it wasn't just the resilient children identified by the study who were able to get over their unfortunate beginnings and move on to lead healthy, fulfilling lives. The other participants in the study—the ones who didn't have the above factors going for them—also were able to work beyond their early childhood problems. It took them longer, but by their 30s and 40s, most were living meaningful lives.

What can adults who live or work with children and have responsibility for their education and socialization learn from this research? How can children from families in stress be helped to be less vulnerable and, indeed, resilient? How can children grow up in stressful conditions such as poverty, family strife, instability, disabilities, bias, abuse, and neglect and not be harmed in their development? How can we help them grow in positive ways?

The key is to balance the stressful life events with protective factors. The stress must be decreased or the number of protective factors increased or, when possible, both. The protective factors are those just mentioned—a sense of connection, sources of support, skills for solving problems and for eliciting positive responses from others, and, above all, a positive attitude toward life and a feeling that it will all work out somehow.

HELPING ALL CHILDREN BECOME RESILIENT CHILDREN

How does that information translate into adult behavior? What are some guidelines for parents, teachers, caregivers, family child care providers, and others who work with children and families in stress?

1. *Provide support for the child and for the family.*   Encourage connections; help build networks. Children and families need all the support they can get—both formal and informal. The Parent Services Project (PSP), mentioned in Chapter 1, was started in California by Ethel Seiderman and is now nationwide. PSP specifically addresses this need for support for families by child care programs (Lee & Seiderman, 1998; Links, Beggs, & Seiderman, 1997). The idea behind PSP is that by supporting the family you make the family more able to support the child. One of PSP's guiding principles is that support is important to all families and that social-support networks reduce isolation and promote the well-being of the child, the family, and the community.

2. *Teach the skills necessary for making connections and gaining support.*   Teach children social skills. Teach them ways to initiate contact and maintain it. This means being there with them while they are playing with peers to guide them toward effective ways to enter play and resolve the issues that come up while playing. Reinforce contacts with peers and adults. They'll learn better if they start early (even in infancy) and have a chance to practice with small numbers of people. Encourage families to focus on positive discipline techniques (see Chapter 7). Model prosocial behaviors, then pay attention to and reward such behaviors.

3. *Teach problem solving* (see Chapter 8).   Crockenberg (1992) observed 95 mothers using negotiation with their 2-year-olds to get them to pick up toys. Crockenberg came up with some interesting conclusions. The effective strategies combined a directive with an explanation, persuasion, or accommodation. That way the mothers gave the message that their wishes were important but also the child's wishes were important. By using this approach, the mothers conveyed information to their children about the way conflicts with others can be resolved. When parents adopt negotiation as an approach to resolving conflicts, they teach their children long-term relationship skills that they can apply to peers.

4. *Give children responsibilities*. Require them to help out. Hook them up to someone who is less capable than they are and needs them. When chores are shared, children gain a sense of being important and belonging. In China, real work is brought into child care centers to be done by the children and then sent back to the factory where it originated. Making real contributions is important. In families with several children, often older children help care for

Help all children become resilient by teaching them problem solving.

younger ones. In child care centers where children are separated into groups by age, caring for each other can take the place of caring for someone younger. Also plants and animals require care, which can be done by children. In family child care and in other settings where there are mixed age groups, adults can give older children responsibilities for children younger than themselves.

5. *Most of all, provide role models*. Children and families need to see people they can identify with doing all the things just mentioned—finding support, demonstrating social skills and the ability to make connections, using problem-solving skills, and taking responsibility. For early childhood institutions, finding positive role models for children becomes part of the recruitment and hiring process. Training helps, too. In addition, children need role models who have faith that things will work out and that life has meaning. If adults don't have it, they must be seeking it. No one can tell another person just how to do that seeking. Certainly spiritual traditions and religious institutions are a possible path. Therapy can help, too.

I don't mean to downplay the effect that stressful conditions have on children's education and socialization by painting too positive a picture. Neither do I mean to overemphasize resiliency. I just want to point out some obvious changes that could make a difference in some families' lives so that unnecessary stress can be eliminated and children don't need to be "superresilient."

To end on a cheery note, here's what Galinsky (1989) says: "Things can be hard, but they don't have to do us in. It isn't whether good or bad things happen to you; it's how you handle them that matters" (pp. 2–3). She talks about how important it is to teach parents and their children to face problems, practice generating multiple solutions, figure out how to change what can be changed, and learn to cope with what can't. It's a matter of taking a can-do attitude and engaging in continuous problem solving. It's also a matter of getting together as a society to face the conditions that create ever-growing poverty and changing them.

School Success Linked to What Goes on at Home

It's not social class, family structure, parent's marital status, ethnic background, or the amount of money a family has that makes a difference in how well children eventually will do in school. What counts most is what goes on at home.

Parents can be poor, unmarried, and undereducated and still manage to groom their young children for a successful school career. It may be harder if one is poor, unmarried, and undereducated, but it is possible.

How do families manage to create early childhood experiences that result in future school success? They do it in a number of ways—including the way they relate to the children, the kind of home life they provide for them, and what they teach them.

First, children must be protected. Families who groom their children for future success in school know how to protect them, keeping them from physical and psychological harm. They set limits. They monitor whereabouts and behavior.

These families see their children as capable and hold a vision of the future that includes the child as an able student. They encourage learning of all sorts by the ways they relate to their children, how they talk to them, and the activities they provide.

They teach their children social skills, defining appropriate behavior for them. They give them feedback to increase their sensitivity to others. They do this in a warm and nurturing way, creating an emotionally supportive environment that emphasizes decision making.

They help their children learn to express themselves. They give them chances to develop a sense of responsibility and learn both leadership and follower skills. They encourage them to concentrate, focus, be attentive, and follow through. Most of all, they respect their children and themselves.

LOOKING BACK AND LOOKING FORWARD

This chapter started by examining traits of successful families and went on to look at a lot of problems. It may seem that the situations of some of the families portrayed are fairly bad. Yet, they are not hopeless, and each is working on acquiring more and more of the traits of successful families outlined at the beginning. Some arrived at the center already knowing about these traits; others are learning them from each other and from the center staff. In addition, each of the families is connected to some of the many community resources that address the variety of difficulties they are having. The next chapter looks at the community resources available to help families meet challenges, to alleviate some of their stress, and to support them in their coping.

FOR DISCUSSION

1. Give examples of three of the traits of successful families that are present in a family that you know.

2. Have you ever known a family like one of the families in this chapter? How was the family the same as the one in the chapter? How was it different?

3. Have you ever known a resilient child? What do you think made this child resilient? Did this child share the common protective factors and personality traits described in the chapter?

4. Give examples of some things you could do to help all children become resilient.

5. Think of an example of how the following sentence plays out in someone's life: "It isn't whether good or bad things happen to you; it's how you handle them that matters."

WEB SITES

Adolescent Substance Abuse and Recovery Resources
http://www.winternet.com/~webpage/adolrecovery.html
This is a resource for adolescent substance abuse and recovery, with links to other informative sites.

Alcoholics Anonymous (AA)
http://www.aa.org/
Information on Alcoholics Anonymous for the general public and professionals appears here. Information in English, Spanish, and French.

Child and Family Resiliency Research Programme
http://www.quasar.ualberta.ca/cfrrp/cfrrp.html
This group uses a multidisciplinary approach to building successful families with varied challenges.

Division for Early Childhood
http://www.dec-sped.org
Links are provided here to early intervention for children with special needs.

Making Lemonade
http://www.makinglemonade.com/
This is a resource for single parents, with additional sites listed for information on children and parenting, schools, and divorce.

National Center for Children in Poverty (NCCP)
http://www.nccp.org/
The National Center for Children in Poverty helps identify and promote strategies that prevent child poverty in the United States and that improve the lives of low-income children and families.

Parents Action for Children
http://store.parentsactionstore.org/prostores/servlet/-strse-template/aboutus/Page
Rob Reiner's video series for parents about implications of brain search for child rearing (in Spanish and English). A new series now available for foster parents about the mental health resources available for the children. Has contact information about how to provide the videos to your community.

FURTHER READING

Akbar, N. (2003). *Akbar papers in African psychology*. Tallahassee, FL: Mind Productions.

Alderete-Baker, E. (1998). *Internalized achievement-related motives of Native American women*. Unpublished doctoral dissertation.

Allen, P. G. (1998). *Off the reservation*. Boston: Beacon.

Beaglehole, R. (1983). Validating all families. *Interracial Books for Children Bulletin*, 14(7, 8), 24–26.

Bell, D. (1992). *Faces at the bottom of the well: The permanence of racism*. New York: Basic Books.

Bernhard, J. K., Freire, M., Torres, F., & Nirdosh, S. (1998, Spring–Summer). Latin Americans in a Canadian primary school: Perspectives of parents, teachers, and children on cultural identity and academic achievement. *Canadian Journal of Regional Science, 19*(3), 217–237.

Blimes, J. (2004). *Beyond behavior management: The six life skills children need to thrive in today's world.* St. Paul, MN: Redleaf Press.

Brown, J. L., & Pollitt, E. (1996, February). Malnutrition, poverty, and intellectual development. *Scientific American, 274*(2), 38–43.

Casper, V. (2003, January). Very young children in lesbian- and gay-headed families: Moving beyond acceptance. *Zero to Three, 23*(3), 18–26.

Children's Defense Fund. (2004). *The state of America's children 2004.* Washington, DC: Children's Defense Fund.

Chow, E. N., Wilkinson, D., & Zinn, B. (1996). *Common bonds, different voices.* Newbury Park, CA: Sage.

Clark, K. E., & Ladd, G. W. (2000). Connectedness and autonomy support in parent-child relationships: Links to children's socio-emotional orientation and peer relationships. *Developmental Psychology, 36,* 485–498.

Clay, J. W. (1990). Working with lesbian and gay parents and their children. *Young Children, 45*(3), 31–35.

Coll, C. G., Lamberty, G., Jenkins, R., McAdoo, H. P., Crnic, K., Wasik, B., Hanna, G., & Vazquez, H. (1996). An integrative model for the study of developmental competencies in minority children. *Child Development, 67,* 1891–1914.

Comer, J. P., & Poussaint, A. E. (1992). *Raising black children.* New York: Plume.

Cummins, J. (1996). *Negotiating identities: Education for empowerment in a diverse society.* Ontario, CA: California Association for Bilingual Education.

DeJong, L. (2003, March). Using Erikson to work more effectively with teenage parents. *Young Children, 58*(2), 87–95.

Delpit, L. (1995). *Other people's children: Cultural conflict in the classroom.* New York: New Press.

Dorris, M. (1978). Why I'm *not* thankful for Thanksgiving. *Interracial Books for Children Bulletin, 9*(7), 6–9.

Fadiman, A. (1997). *The spirit catches you and you fall down: A Hmong child, her American doctors, and the collision of two cultures.* New York: Noonday.

Fernea, E. W. (1995). *Children in the Muslim Middle East.* Austin: University of Texas Press.

Gonzalez-Mena, J. (1997, July). Cross-cultural conferences. *Exchange, 116,* 55–57.

Harkness, S., & Super, C. M. (Eds.). (1996). *Parents' cultural belief systems.* New York: Guilford.

Harwood, R. L., Miller, J. G., & Irizarry, N. L. (1995). *Culture and attachment: Perceptions of the child in context.* New York: Guilford.

Hildebrand, V., Phenice, L. A., Gray, M. M., & Hines, R. P. (2008). *Knowing and serving diverse families.* Upper Saddle River, NJ: Merrill/Prentice Hall.

Huntsinger, C. S., Huntsinger, P. R., Ching, W.-D., & Lee, C.-B. (2000, November). Understanding cultural contexts fosters sensitive caregiving of Chinese American children. *Young Children, 55*(6), 7–15.

Kagiticibasi, C. (1996). *Family and human development across cultures.* Mahwah, NJ: Erlbaum.

Keyser, J. (2006) *From parents to partners: Building a family centered early childhood program.* Washington, DC: National Association for the Education of Young Children and St. Paul, MN: Redleaf.

Korfmacher, J., & Marchi, I. (2002, November). The helping relationship in a teen parenting program. *Zero to Three, 21*(2), 21–26.

Landau, S., & McAninch, C. (1993, May). Young children with attention deficits. *Young Children, 48*(4), 49–58.

Lee, L. (Ed). (2006). *Stronger Together. Family support and early childhood education.* San Rafael, CA: Parent Services Project, Inc.

Lee, L. (1997, July). Working with non-English-speaking families. *Exchange, 116,* 57–58.

Luthar, S. S., Cichetti, D., & Becker, B. (2000). The construct of resilience: A critical evaluation and guidelines for future work. *Child Development, 71,* 543–562.

McLoyd, V. (1990). The impact of economic hardship on black families and children: Psychological distress, parenting, and socioemotional development. *Child Development, 61,* 311–346.

Moore, E. K., & McKinley, M. K. (1972). Parent involvement/control in child development programs. In D. N. McFadden (Ed.), *Early childhood development programs and services: Planning for action* (pp. 77–82). Washington, DC: National Association for the Education of Young Children.

Morrison, J. W. (2001, Spring). Supporting biracial children's identity development. *Childhood Education, 77*(3), 134–138.

National Association for the Education of Young Children (2005). *Families and community relationships: A guide to the NAEYC early childhood program standards and related accreditation criteria.* Washington, DC: National Association for Education of Young Children.

Neighbors, H. W., & Jackson, J. S. (Eds.). (1996). *Mental health in black America.* Newbury Park, CA: Sage.

Odom, S. L., Teferra, T., & Kaul, S. (2004, September). An overview of international approaches to early intervention for young children with special needs and their families. *Young Children, 59*(5), 38–43.

Okagaki, L., & Diamond, K. (2000, May). Responding to cultural and linguistic differences in the beliefs and practices of families with young children. *Young Children, 55*(3), 74–80.

Payne, R. K. (2003). *A framework for understanding poverty.* Highlands, TX: Aha Process.

Randolph, S. M., & Koblinsky, S. A. (2001, August/September). The sociocultural context of infant mental health in African American families. *Zero to Three, 22*(1), 29–37.

Rogoff, B. (1990). *Apprenticeship in thinking.* New York: Oxford University Press.

Rogoff, B., Stott, F., & Bowman, B. (1996). Child development knowledge: A slippery base for practice. *Early Childhood Research Quarterly, 11*(2), 169–184.

Seploch, H. (2004, September). Family ties: Partnerships for learning: Conferencing with families. *Young Children, 58*(5), 96–100.

Soto, L. D. (1991, January). Understanding bilingual/bicultural young children. *Young Children, 46*(2), 30–35.

Swick, K. (2004). *Empowering parents, families, schools, and communities during the early childhood years.* Champaign, IL: Stipes.

Tobaissen, D. P., & Gonzalez-Mena, J. (1998). *A place to begin: Working with parents on issues of diversity.* Oakland: California Tomorrow.

Valdes, G. (1996). *Con respeto: Bridging the distances between culturally diverse families and schools.* New York: Teachers College Press.

CHAPTER 12

Early Care and Education Programs as Community Resources

In this chapter you'll discover . . .

- Why early care and education programs can be considered child rearing
- Three things that influence quality in early care and education programs
- Some arguments about breaking large centers into small groups
- Some ideas about bridging the gap between early care and education programs and home
- How to help parents gain a sense of community in early care and education programs
- Some roadblocks to respect between parents and teachers

The last chapter looked at six different families who were all participating in early care and education programs at the same center. This chapter gives an overview of the different kinds of early care and education programs and their benefits to children and families. It also looks at some of the issues around providing full-time child care to working families.

Early care and education programs are difficult to explain to anyone who hasn't experienced them. They go by different names, serve different age groups, and occur in a variety of settings. The first three years of elementary school, the primary grades 1–3, fall under the category "of early care and education" because developmentally the children are more like their younger peers. They make a developmental shift around the time they leave third grade into what has been called "the age of reason." By fourth grade most children are cognitively ready for what can be thought of as more traditional schooling. The developmental perspective is that children have different needs in each stage of development. (Chapters 2–5 focused on working with parents during each of the various developmental stages.)

Kindergarten is in a category by itself because it isn't quite school, but it isn't preschool either. Kindergarten was started in the United States because some wise educators saw the need for a transition for children instead of sending them from home directly to school. Kindergarten was designed to ease children into the routines and behavior expected of them when they entered first grade. Kindergarten now seems to be more of a first grade, and preschool has become the transition period.

Child care for school-age children is also in a category by itself and has the unique feature of often including children who are no longer in their "early years." A variety of programs support families who need to have a safe environment and supervision for their school-age children during the hours they work, when their children are not in school. In addition to having educational, developmental, and caring elements, school-age care also has important socialization functions as children learn to get along in groups of their peers in less structured programs than school usually offers. School-age care often comes in the form of "surround care" where children leave home before school, spend an hour or more in child care in mixed age groups, then go to a classroom where the children are all the same age. After school they go back to the child care program. During school holidays and summer vacations, surround care becomes full-day care to meet the needs of working parents. These programs take place in a variety of settings including homes with family child care providers. If programs are run by schools, they are often in portable buildings on the school grounds, or sometimes in a multipurpose room. Some school-age programs are stand-alone programs that serve only children from kindergarten up. They may be privately owned or publicly funded. They may be in their own building or in a rented space. Other school-age programs are part of a comprehensive child care program serving children from birth to 12 years of age. Usually in those programs, the younger children are separated by age, while those in the school-age population are put together in mixed age groups.

The most well known of the early care and education programs is the preschool program. The term *preschool* is confusing because it brings up different pictures for different people. Preschool merely means "before school." Another term for it is prekindergarten, or pre-k. In the past, the preschool program was commonly called *nursery school*, which is the term I prefer because it emphases the nurturing part. I was on a campaign for awhile to spread the term *nurtury* since nursery school is so old fashioned. But with all the push for readiness and academics, I missed out, so now I just use preschool, even though it annoys me that early care and education programs have to be *pre* anything. It seems to me that they are an institution in their own right—just as children are children—not preadults.

So what does the term *preschool* encompass? It includes half-day programs such as Head Start and other compensatory programs for low-income children. When I first entered the early care and education field in the 1960s preschools were half-day programs for stay-at-home mothers, who were mostly middle-class housewives. Head Start was begun for a whole different segment of the population. Day care, as full-day programs were called then, was for single mothers who worked, or families with two working parents. Some were run by school districts, and some still are.

Infant–toddler programs were separate and apart—and to some extent they still are. Back in the 60s when I was a preschool teacher, I worked in a parent involvement program. The children were in preschool, the parents in English as a Second Language classes, and the babies were in a "nursery" with a group of untrained volunteers "watching" them. The first programs for infants with trained staff were early intervention programs for children with special needs. Infant care for working families was mainly done by family child care providers.

That's another form of early care and education: family child care. Those programs were, and still are, conducted in private homes by the people who live there and represent the largest service providers for working parents in the United States. Over the years these programs have become part of the regulating system. In many states the programs are licensed, and in some the individuals working in them are trained as well. States vary a great deal in how much attention is paid by government workers, funders, and policy makers to family child care providers.

Though family child care may be looked down on by those early educators who consider themselves more professional, family child care programs have a lot going for them. As a consumer of family child care, I've always been aware of the advantages. Usually parents have more choices when it comes to family child care programs. Homes, necessarily (and often by regulation), have smaller groups of children than programs outside the home. Providers can develop personal relationships easier with children and their families. Continuity of care, an important component of children's early experiences, is more likely to be available in family child care. That means that children can stay in the same home from infancy until the time they don't need the service any more. Of course that doesn't always happen, but it's possible, whereas in most out-of-home programs children change classrooms, teachers, and sometimes groups every year or even more often.

In the days when I started in the field preschool and child care were separate entities, and preschool was considered educational while child care was considered custodial. That doesn't necessarily represent reality, but rather the image many people both inside the field and outside it carried in their heads about the distinction of the two. Some still see the two as separate, but others, such as myself, have been working hard to help everyone see the link between care and education and to quit separating programs by types.

In Australia, where I have traveled quite a bit, a simple descriptive title distinguishes the two. Children go to "sessional programs" or to "long-day programs," and the whole field is called children's services, which connects everything rather nicely. We, in the United States, are still working at these connections.

The reality is that if staff is well trained, if the groups are appropriate sizes for the ages of the children, and if the environment is set up appropriately to promote development, learning, and caring, any program can provide both care and education—whether the program is part-day in a school following an academic calendar or all day, year round, and whether it is in a separate facility or in someone's home. Good quality care and education don't just happen accidentally—there are lot of people and organizations working hard to make sure that every child has the opportunity to be in a setting that provides both good care and education. We're not there yet, but we're working on it.

Making the link between care and education hasn't been easy. What has helped is that Nell Noddings, a Stanford professor has written several books making a good case for always having a connection between care and education all the way up through the university. She wrote a book called *The Challenge to Care in Schools* (2005) in which she described how public schools, from kindergarten up can have a caring curriculum that is educational. She sees a caring curriculum as vital to moral development, a hot topic among families and educators these days. As I read her book, I was anxious to tell her that she was describing what we already do in early care and education programs. So I wrote her a "fan" letter and got a very nice reply! I've never written a fan letter in my life.

Universal pre-k, sometimes called preschool for all (or PFA) is a movement that is gaining momentum. Advocates want to assure that every four year old has a chance to attend a free half-day preschool. Though universal pre-k looks different in different states, that's the main push behind it. Some states have already succeeded in instituting the change, while others are still investigating it. According to ExhangeEveryDay (an online child care newsletter delivered through e-mail June 12, 2007) all but 11 states are in various stages of at least discussing universal pre-k. According to Morgan and Nadig (2007) there is no standard way to institute universal pre-k. Some states are creating a class before kindergarten in the public school system, while others are considering free education for 4-year-olds in a variety of settings. Still others are targeting low-income famlies for free education for their 4-year-olds. There are different ways to look at universal pre-k at this stage of the game (see Figure 12.1).

As the number of child care and education programs continues to increase, many are asking the question: Who is rearing America's children, and how are they being reared? That is an increasingly compelling question. It was a nonquestion just a generation or two ago, because America's children were mostly reared by their own

Universal pre-k is a good idea. If kindergarten is to become first grade, each child still needs a transitional year. It's good to start children in school early, especially low-income children.

Universal pre-k is a good idea. All families should enjoy what middle-class families have—access to preschool programs

Universal pre-k is not a good idea. The real need is for full-day programs that have both good care and education. With all the money and attention going into universal pre-k, what are working parents going to do? Universal pre-k requires before and after care. It would be better to use the money to upgrade and expand the existing child care programs

Figure 12.1
Some Ways to Look at Universal Pre-K

parents, or by specific substitutes whom the parents designated. Child rearing belonged to the family. Business, education, and government mostly stayed out of the picture, except for a brief period during World War II and except for protective and remedial reasons.

Today the picture has changed. The number of single-parent families in which the parent trains or works outside the home is steadily rising. And in a majority of two-parent families, both parents work outside the home (see Figure 12.2). Child rearing is now shared, as families use an array of early care and education services. Furthermore, business and government have become part of the picture.

According to the 2005 American Communities Survey, conducted by the U.S. Census Bureau, in 2005 there were:

7,493,881 mothers with children under 6
4,830,391 mothers with children under 6 in the labor force

This means that

64% of mothers with children under 6 were in the labor force.

There were:

19,114,058 mothers with children ages 6–17
14,464,528 mothers with children ages 6–17 in the labor force

This means that

76% mothers with children ages 6–17 were in the labor force

Figure 12.2
Mothers in the Workforce

The Child Care Center Licensing Study of the Children's Foundation in Washington, D.C., indicates that there were 117,284 regulated child care centers in the 50 states, District of Columbia, Puerto Rico, and the Virgin Islands. This is an overall increase of 26 percent since their 1991 study (see www.childrensfoundation.net).

Who is raising America's children? Perhaps you are or will be—either as a parent or as a professional in the field of early care and education. As the need for services expands and programs struggle to keep up with the need, more and more early educators, such as child care workers, teachers, caregivers, infant care teachers, family day care providers, in-home care providers, and nannies, supplement parent care.

EARLY CARE AND EDUCATION PROGRAMS AS CHILD-REARING ENVIRONMENTS

Why does this text keep equating early care and education with child rearing? After all, the United States doesn't have a communal child-rearing system in which children are taken out of the home and socialized into a model consisting of a single set of ideals. We don't believe in social or political indoctrination for our children. Child rearing is an individual matter of individual families and always has been. As a society, Americans agree to disagree. Diversity has always been a key theme as well as a strong point of America's people. Families want to rear their children in their own way. However, these days individuals and families must look outside themselves for supplements to what they can provide. They can no longer do all the child rearing themselves.

Anne Vega/Merrill

You can't park your children like your car. Children need to be in an environment where they can grow and learn.

But is child care really child rearing? Yes. You can drive your car to work, park it in a garage, and come back and pick it up in the afternoon, and, except for a new layer of dust, it is almost always in the same condition you left it in. You can even leave your car at home in the garage, take the bus or the train to work, and come back and find it just as you left it.

But you can't park children. Wherever children are, they are growing and learning, being changed by their experiences. They are being reared. How they are being reared is a big question. They can be reared in accordance with parental expectations and values, or they can be reared in ways that are quite contradictory.

The challenge for our society in these times is to offer enough choices so that parents can find programs in tune with what they want and need for their children. The choices could include both nonparental care solutions such as out-of-home early care and education or in-home care, as well as creative alternatives that allow working parents a greater role in caring for their own children. Flextime, one of these alternatives, allows parents to stagger their work schedules to be with their children, thereby doing the child rearing mostly themselves. Part-time work also allows more parental involvement in child rearing; job sharing is one way to become a part-time worker. In some countries, workers are subsidized to stay home with their children instead of working a full day or a full workweek. Flexible benefits plans and flexible leave and transfer policies can also be creative alternatives that allow parents to spend more time with their children.

Worthy Wages and Quality Care

Kayla is in a quality child care center with a stable staff who know her well and can provide just the kind of care and education she needs. Staff members are sensitive and well trained, and they have the time and energy to arrange the environment in appropriate ways and to set out a variety of interesting and worthwhile activities that promote growth and development. They are there to guide, protect, and teach Kayla by relating to her on an individual basis and by supporting her development in numerous ways. Kayla is happy in her school, and her mother is happy that she is there. But what about the teachers?

If the teachers are happy, it's because they love teaching and work in a well-funded program in which they are paid what they deserve, have a good benefit package, and have adequate support through staff and other resources. Or perhaps they are happy because they have other sources of income and have figured out how to scrounge up the resources they need. Or they may get so many rewards from teaching that money isn't an issue with them. Many good teachers remain in the field despite the low pay.

However, in most child care programs, the staff is underpaid, and if any of them are the sole support for their families, they have a hard time managing on a child care teacher's wages. Child care teachers' wages reflect their status, which, according to the Bureau of Labor statistics, is equated with parking lot attendants. Some refuse to leave the field, even though they are being paid less than prison guards and animal tenders. These dedicated souls are helping to rear the nation's children—rearing these children at the point of their lives when they are very impressionable.

What does it mean to children and families that child care teachers are underpaid and undervalued? It means a lot. It means that many people will never even consider going into the field—people who have a lot to offer children. It means that anyone who isn't totally dedicated to the profession and wants to make an adequate living will look elsewhere. It means that few men, especially those who don't have a partner who can supplement their income, will look to child care as a career option. This limits the field drastically.

The problem of low status and salary is reflected in the turnover rate (Whitebook & Sakai, 2004). Many people enter the field only to leave it in a short time, when they find the demands of the job too much and the pay too little. One-third to one-half of the people working in child care are new every year. That means that children see their teachers constantly changing—continually coming and going. As soon as they get to know and trust someone, that person leaves. Eventually children stop developing relationships with their child care teachers—it's just too painful to keep saying good-bye for good.

That's not good for children.

Quality is tied to status, salaries, and training. Who is going to spend the money for training if the status and salaries are so low?

We are in a crisis situation. We have a great need, as a nation, for early care and education programs. Working in the early childhood education field can lead to a very satisfying career. Yet the money for quality programs just isn't there. Most parents couldn't possibly afford what quality care costs. They need subsidies. A few parents get some subsidies from the government; others get them from employers. But an enormous number receive their subsidies from the teachers who are willing to work for so little pay. That's not the ordinary way to look at subsidizing child care, but it is one way. Don't you think that it is time things changed?

AFFORDABILITY AND AVAILABILITY

Two A words loom up when we look at requirements for early care and education, especially those for working families: *affordability* and *availability*. When we, as a society, work to create both affordable and widespread early care and education programs that meet families' needs for child care, quality often gets lost. We get into a double bind when we deal with both quality and cost: Most parents can't afford to pay what quality programs really cost. In 48 states, the cost of center-based child care for a 4-year-old is greater than tuition at a 4-year public college (Children's Defense Fund, 2004). If you consider that one-third of the families with young children earn less than $25,000 a year, according to the Children's Defense Fund, you can see that child care costs are beyond what these families can afford. Even when both parents are working, if they work at minimum-wage jobs, together they make less than $25,000 a year. How can they pay for full-day early care and education on their salary?

Child care professionals come out worse than that. They can't afford child care unless it is provided free where they work. Their average salary is far less than other educators and service workers, according to Whitebook and Sakai (2004). The families who need care most can't afford it, yet as a society we can't afford not to pay it, especially for low-income families. Quality costs, but it saves in the long run. Studies show that risk factors associated with cognitive delay and other developmental problems can be lessened by early intervention in the form of quality early care and education programs that meet the needs for child care (Illig, 1998; Karoly, 1998). Furthermore, quality early care and education programs can cut the crime rate. A report prepared by an expert panel convened by Fight Crime: Invest in Kids shows that 989 children who had been enrolled in government-funded child-parent centers as 3- and 4-year-olds cut the risk of problems with the law in their teens. Half as many of the children in the program had arrests in their teens as a similar group not included in the program (Brazelton, Zigler, Sherman, Bratton, & Sanders, 1999).

The North Carolina Abecedarian Project showed that early childhood education can make a critical difference in the later success of poor children. This project was a carefully controlled research design project in which children who had an individualized prescription of educational activities and games as a part of their daily routine tested higher in cognitive test scores up to age 21, achieved higher levels in reading and math, completed more years of education, and were more likely to attend college than children not in the program (Campell, Pungello, Miller-Johnson, Burchinal, & Ramey, 2000).

A study of Head Start called FACES (U.S. Department of Health and Human Services, 2003) showed that the program narrowed the gap between the performances of children from poverty-level families and their higher income peers. Low-income Head Start children showed significant improvement in social skills, emotional development, and behavior, which was linked to their cognitive development. Parent participation in educational activities with their children was positively correlated with children's behavior and early literacy skills. A different study found that Early Head Start, the program that serves infants and toddlers, also has significant benefits and impacts social-emotional development as well as children's cognitive and language development at age 3.

As a society we haven't yet learned the lesson that quality costs but pays off. We aren't willing to pay what child care really costs. We say we can't afford it. As a result, early care and education programs, including child care in the United States, aren't as good as they could be.

Status and Salaries

The Status and salaries of child care teachers are two problems related to quality and cost that haven't been solved yet. Child care teachers are still underpaid, and a majority receive no benefits. Their salaries put them at the poverty level, and their status puts them in the same category as parking lot attendants. Not a pretty picture! The National Center for the Early Childhood Workforce in Washington, D.C., has been addressing this issue for a number of years. The pattern goes like this: The lower the salary, the higher the turnover rate. The greater the turnover, the lower the quality of services and the more likely for the children to have poor developmental outcomes. In a program with a high turnover rate, the less likely that children will experience responsive care-giving and sensitive interactions (Whitebook & Sakai, 2004).

Imagine the children in a program with a high turnover rate. They are constantly disrupted by changes in their routines. High turnover means that rules switch as teachers come and go. It means that just as the children get to know a teacher, he or

Doris Pfalmer

Child care is a necessity for many families.

she disappears suddenly and is replaced by a new person. Separation issues don't get resolved. The consistency of the stable environment that children need to flourish is a sought-after vision but seldom a reality.

We need to find ways to solve these problems. It isn't just up to families and early educators to work toward solutions. Indeed, as mentioned earlier, many parents are paying more than they can afford now. A low-income family can pay as much as 26 percent of the family budget for child care. And teachers, by working for poverty wages, are subsidizing child care themselves. No, it's not up to parents and teachers to solve this problem alone. It is in the public interest to help also. Children are the future of America.

Even without platitudes, you can look at the situation from a very personal point of view. When you reach retirement age, you will be dependent on a strong, healthy, productive workforce to keep the society and the economy going. You won't be able to sit back and enjoy the fruits of your own labor if there is no one to carry on.

Even more personally, imagine yourself in a retirement home being cared for by men and women whose own upbringing left much to be desired. If today's society allows its future citizens to be neglected at home or warehoused in an institutional setting, how well will they treat you if and when you need their care in your old age?

THE STATE OF CHILD CARE IN AMERICA TODAY

The picture of child care is sad. We still have a long way to go. We aren't yet close to creating a system that fills the need and provides quality care. When President Bill Clinton signed away the traditional welfare system in 1996 and changed it to Temporary Aid to Needy Families (TANF), all of a sudden the need for child care increased dramatically, as former welfare recipients became trainees, and their children, including babies, needed a place to go. Although infants had been trickling into child care for some time, all of a sudden they came pouring into the system at a rate programs couldn't keep up with. This situation meant that for TANF to work, child care had to expand, which called for more funding to keep up with the demand and more training dollars to increase the child care workforce. We still haven't met the current need, and a large number of children are in inadequate settings. Families of all income levels still have problems finding quality care, but the problems are worse for low-income families. These families have more at stake also because the consequences of inadequate care plus lack of effective educational approaches tend to be more severe for children of low-income families.

Our system of child care is notable for its diversity, which is both a strength and a challenge. Creating a seamless system that meets the needs of all children and all families is still a distant dream that we are only just beginning to realize. Unlike some smaller European countries, there is no single policy or program that can address the child care needs of all families and children. No single entity or organization can provide child care for the nation, but rather the responsibility for meeting the nation's child care needs has to be widely shared among individuals, families, voluntary organizations, employers, communities, and government at all levels.

LOOKING AT QUALITY

Defining, measuring, and monitoring the quality of child care are very hard tasks, because to some extent the definition of quality is highly subjective and personal. However, the classic study done in the 1970s—the National Day Care Study (Ruopp, Travers, Glantz, & Coelen, 1979)—came up with three variables that influence quality: *group size*, *caregiver-child ratio*, and *caregiver qualifications*. This study helped justify and substantiate the laws and regulations governing child care. It also helped back up the National Association for the Education of Young Children's (NAEYC) accreditation criteria, which are now contained in a major instrument to assess quality across the nation. There are 10 NAEYC program standards (found at www.naeyc.org), organized

into four focus groups. The first group of standards focuses on children, on what is needed to support their development and learning. The other three groups focus on what is needed to create and maintain excellence in programs and relate to teachers, family and community partnerships, and leadership and administration (see Table 12.1).

Although we continue to move forward as a profession, in many places in the United States child care remains unregulated—and

Frank Gonzalez-Mena

Group size is a variable that influences quality.

Table 12.1
NAEYC Accreditation Standards

Focus Area:	Children
Program Standard 1:	Relationships
Program Standard 2:	Curriculum
Program Standard 3:	Teaching
Program Standard 4:	Assessment
Program Standard 5:	Health
Focus Area:	**Teaching Staff**
Program Standard 6:	Teachers
Focus Area:	**Family and Community Partnerships**
Program Standard 7:	Families
Program Standard 8:	Communities
Focus Area:	**Leadership and Administration**
Program Standard 9:	Physical Environment
Program Standard 10:	Leadership and Management

even where it is regulated, laws and regulations provide only a bottom line (i.e., they define *minimum* standards). Various national and state professional organizations have provided more optimum guidelines, including a book of standards from NAEYC called *Developmentally Appropriate Practice* (Bredekamp & Copple, 1997) and an updated introductory version called *Basics of Developmentally Appropriate Practice: An Introduction for Teachers of Children 3–6* (Copple, 2006).

ADULT-CHILD INTERACTIONS IN CHILD CARE AND EARLY EDUCATION SETTINGS

When looking for high-quality settings, an important question to ask is: What is the quality of adult-child interactions, regardless of the program model? Taking into account that the first program standard of NAEYC's accreditation model relates to relationships, let's look at adult-child interactions with that in mind.

Most early educators and many parents today would agree that children should spend their days actively involved in exploring and learning about the world and each other. A helpful adult close by is essential for providing resources, input, and guidance. Is that what happens in most child care programs? According to researchers Susan Kontos and Amanda Wilcox-Herzog, academics have only just begun to study how interactions take place and what kind are related to what outcomes in children. In an article titled "Teachers' Interactions with Children: Why Are They So Important?" (1997), Kontos and Wilcox-Herzog examine the research on interactions to see whether they could confirm that interactions foster relationships that promote development. They found that because children outnumber adults, the frequency of interactions is not high (31 percent of the children in one study received no individual attention) even though the adults studied spent 71 percent of their time interacting with children. Thus, because adults are necessarily spread thin—especially in center-based care—it is important that they become aware of how they distribute their attention. They must also be conscious of the quality of the interactions. Adult-child ratio and group size affect interactions. Smaller groups and good ratios allow adults to have more sensitive, responsive interactions with children. In programs with less than optimum ratios and group sizes, adults are much more likely to use pressure to seek compliance by issuing demands, giving orders, quoting rules, even ridiculing and making threats. In homes and in smaller centers, or in large centers where attention is paid to group size and ratios, adult input is more likely to be facilitative—encouraging, helping, and suggesting, rather than demanding. Kontos and Wilcox-Herzog conclude that it is possible to see a connection between sensitive, involved adult interactions with children and enhanced development. The effect of positive relationships shows in cognitive, socio-emotional, and language development. From warm, sensitive interactions where adults are nurturing, accepting, and respectful, responsive relationships grow that encourage the development of autonomy and initiative, which, according to Erik Erikson (1963), is vital to healthy development in the early years.

A goal should be to break centers into smaller, self-contained groups. Group size is a vital factor to quality. Way back in 1979, the National Day Care Study (Ruopp et al., 1979) showed that group size has more effect than any other factor on teacher and child behavior and on intellectual development. Yet regulations about group size are still not universal.

Another indicator of quality centers around the question of what place the families have in the program. In extremely child-centered programs, family members may feel unwelcome, especially if they arrive with younger siblings in tow. This book is advocating for family-centered programs where families feel welcome in many ways, including among others:

- Space for them to be comfortable, with provisions for children not enrolled
- Staff that greets them warmly and finds time to talk to them

Quality care provides a safe, healthy, nurturing learning environment designed to meet the needs—physical, emotional, intellectual—of the individual and the group.

Frank Gonzalez-Mena

+ Communication in many forms coming on a regular basis
+ Opportunities to not only give input to the program, but also become part of decision-making bodies and processes

To summarize: A quality care and education program provides a safe, healthy, and nurturing learning environment designed to meet the needs—physical, emotional, intellectual—of the individuals and the group. In other words, it combines care and education. Meeting the needs of the families enrolled is also a part of the program; the focus is not just on the children alone. This environment can be in schools, centers, or family child care homes. Good care and education, like good child rearing, enhances each child's development as a unique and powerful person who is capable of cooperating with others and living in a group situation. The goal is to establish a sense of being an individual while incorporating a growing sense of community. This happens most easily with a stable, consistent, trained staff, available at least some of the time to interact with children one-on-one and in small groups. Another contributing factor is plenty of play time during which the child is actively engaged with peers and practices decision making, problem solving, and resolving conflict. Quality care and education can occur in a variety of environments, including home and center settings.

Quality care programs put families at the center of the attention along with their children and do not focus just on children alone. One way to bring families into the picture is to create a sense of community in the program. Strategy Box 12.1 gives some ideas about how to give families a sense of belonging to the program and to each other.

Strategy Box 12.1

Working with Families to Create a Sense of Community

+ Creating a sense of community among the people involved in your program is an important goal when working with families. Start by trying to create a sense of belonging from the beginning by finding out names right away. Check out pronounciation so you get it right.
+ Introduce everyone who is part of the program to everyone else.
+ Put up a picture board of staff with something written about each person.
+ Consider a picture board of families, also.
+ Introduce families to each other and help them become resources to each other, such as when families share in carpooling.
+ Find out what special interests or skills family members have.
+ Make the environment welcoming to everybody.
+ Think of meetings as a way to get to know each other better, no matter what the purpose of the meeting is. Get people to interact with each other.

INCLUDING EVERYBODY: CHILDREN WITH SPECIAL NEEDS

In the past, children with special needs often ended up in special education programs rather than in child care programs designed for everybody's children. Since 1992, when the Americans with Disabilities Act (ADA) was passed, the mandate is to provide people who have disabilities with access to all community services, including child care. Then, in 1997 came the Individuals with Disabilities Education Act (IDEA) amendments, which state: "To the maximum extent appropriate, children with disabilities . . . are educated with children who are not disabled." Children with disabilities are to be cared for and educated in a "natural environment," which means an environment where their typically developing peers are to be found. Furthermore, each child must have an individualized education program (IEP), which includes, among other things, a statement of the child's present levels of educational performance, measurable annual goals, short-term objectives, program modifications, or supports.

What is the definition of "a child with special needs"? A child with special needs is one who requires specialized care because of physical, emotional, or health reasons. The kinds of disabilities vary greatly, from physical challenges to developmental differences to illness. They may include communication disabilities, developmental disabilities and delays, emotional and/or behavioral disabilities, visual and hearing impairments, exceptional health needs, learning disabilities, and/or physical challenges. Some children have a combination of several conditions.

How do parents who have children with special needs approach putting their children into child care that is not designated as special education? Some have great hesitation. What if the adults in the program don't pay close enough attention to their child? What if their child gets lost in the crowd? Most parents have this concern, but when the child has special needs the anxiety may be greatly heightened because of certain risk factors. What if the disability is severe allergic reactions and nobody is paying close enough attention to notice that the child is being served milk or is eating peanuts or is playing around the garden where bees are in abundance? What if the program staff members have informed the family that increasing self-help skills are a major goal of their program, and the family worries that because the child is so physically challenged he will be neglected in the name of making him more independent? Of course, cultural differences enter in here, too. If a family sees dependence as a blessing, not a curse, the parents may not be as eager for their children to learn self-help skills as a family that wants to maximize independence.

Professional early educators recognize that caring for and educating a child with special needs does take extra watchfulness and thoughtfulness. It helps, though, when they remember that a child with special needs is more similar to than different from other children. These children need what all children need: a safe, nurturing environment with adults who respect them and know how to meet their needs. They need chances to explore, to make choices, and to be supported. They benefit from an individualized approach and also from being included in a group.

How can early educators possibly know all about every condition of every child who might end up in a program designed that is primarily for typically developing children? That is a question often asked by practitioners who are faced with providing care and education for a child with a disability they know little about.

PARTNERING WITH PARENTS

One way to find out about a child is to observe that child. "The child is the teacher," is something that Magda Gerber, infant expert and founder of Resources for Infant Educarers (RIE), used to say all the time. Through observations and interactions the early educator can learn a good deal, but not everything. He or she also needs resources. The first and most important resource is the family of the child. When programs take a parents-as-partners approach, they can learn more about all children in their care, including those with special needs. The family knows their child better than anyone else. If the child has been identified as having special needs, the family has already become part of the system of resources and support. The professional early educator can find out from the family what they have been told, what agencies and individuals are working with the child, and who can help the child care program meet the child's special needs. Also, the early educator can share observations with the family and other professionals and ask them what strategies and ideas work at home. Working closely with the family is essential. Connecting with the resources and supports they have is useful, too. Chapter 13 explores community resources, including those for families with a child with special needs. There are many ways to find help and support from agencies in the community.

Sometimes a child comes into a program without being identified as having special needs, but early childhood professionals have concerns about the child. Professionals with training and experience in development may notice that a particular child isn't following a typical pattern. It may be hard for that professional to put a finger on his or her concerns, but if there is a nagging feeling, it is important for the professional to begin to observe closely. That means writing down what is observed and keeping a record. Writing each observation as objectively as possible and recording the date can show progress or lack of progress as well as provide useful information about the child's developmental differences. Patterns may begin to emerge as the professional notices that the child often seems "stuck," can't remember things, or can't seem to get involved in anything. It may be that the child doesn't get along with other children, or has a low energy level, or seems confused often. Perhaps the difficulty has to do with the program, and a change or two makes all the difference. But sometimes what the professional does to help fails to make a difference. After making specific observations and writing down the details, the professional may decide that this child needs more specialized help. Talking to the family about the professional's concern is the next step.

Suggesting to a family that something is going on with their child is a delicate matter and needs to be carefully thought out by the professional before setting up a meeting. Having a positive attitude and approach makes a difference. Having specific information with details about observed behavior gives a clearer, more objective picture than just pointing out problems the child may be having. Using neutral language is a key to keeping things positive, which means avoiding labels and negative judgments but discussing behavior and skills in terms of what has actually been observed. Sharing observations about strengths and areas of weakness to see how well the professional's observations match with the family's observations gives a more complete picture. When early childhood professionals use language families understand, they reduce any possible power differential and open up communication. When they speak in terms of developmental ranges rather than comparing the child to other children, they do the child and the family a service. The point of the meeting should be to share information, gain a clearer picture, and figure out together what has worked, what has not worked, and what is to be done to optimize development for the child. Perhaps further resources are needed. Pooling information about resources is useful.

How do family members feel when called to such a meeting? For some it may be a relief to know that what they have been noticing that has caused them concern is validated by a professional. Others feel a wide range of emotions. Typical reactions are tears, denial, guilt, fear, blame, and anger. Parents may feel they are failures or their child is a failure. If communication has occurred all along, the content of the meeting will be less of a surprise or shock than if this is the first conversation the early childhood educator has had with the parents. Having time to talk and sort things out, including feelings, gives parents the opportunity to cope with what may be painful news. Sometimes it takes awhile for the information to sink in, and parents are unable to hear what is said at such a meeting. If the parents have heard and understood, having an idea what to do next can be helpful, too. Perhaps more observations are in order. Or parents may want to contact their pediatrician or local school district about an evaluation and resources.

QUESTIONS CONCERNING CONTINUITY BETWEEN CHILD CARE AND HOME

How much should the early care and education program reflect the methods, approaches, and values of the parents? If special needs are involved, should there be continuity between what goes on at home and what happens in the child care program? When what happens at home is different from what happens at the center, the two settings may provide a balance. For example, if the family loves taking care of a child who can do very little for herself, the program can provide more opportunities for the child to try out self-help skills. In such a situation, teaching the self-help skills has to be done skillfully and sensitively if the child is to feel safe and secure away from those who constantly do everything for her.

What about value differences? The subject of values was discussed in Chapter 6; however, it is important to consider the following two additional questions as well:

• Is *continuity between home and program always valuable*? A look at a cross-cultural example gives one view. In China today, couples are allowed to have only one child. Yet China is very family-oriented, so all the energy that went into the many children of the large families of the past is focused today on a single child. As a result, this child gets a good deal of attention—"spoiling," if you will—from two parents and four grandparents. Six adults are all vitally concerned with this one small child. So child care is set up to purposely counteract this effect. Child-adult ratios are large, so that adults cannot focus very much time on any one child. Group expectations are heavy—the child must learn to be a good group member. Although learning to be a good group member happened easily at home in the old days of big families, it doesn't happen at home as easily now. So the child is learning this lesson at child care. Child care is set up to create a gap between home and program—one is designed to counterbalance the other (Tobin, Wu, & Davidson, 1989).

• *Is the ideal to aim for racial and cultural similarities between caregivers and children or to aim for diversity?*   The advantage in similarity is that when children see adults of the same race as themselves, they identify with these people. When children of color see adults of their race in positions of authority and competence, they have models, which can be valuable for their self-esteem.

When consistency exists between family and program, cultural competence is more likely. All children, no matter what race, culture, or ethnicity, should be in settings that increase their cultural competence. An example of when continuity and consistency is important is when a child is in danger of losing home language and culture. For some children, being in a program where their language is spoken and where they can continue to relate daily on a close basis with people of their culture can make a big difference in helping them to keep their identity intact and to continue to develop in their own language. In infancy such continuity can be especially important because infants aren't born members of their culture but must learn to be culturally competent. If they don't get enough waking hours of exposure to their own people and language, the consequences can be negative.

That's not to say that cultural continuity is vital in every situation. For some children there are advantages of experiencing interracial, multicultural staff and children in their child care settings. They can learn early to respond in positive ways to diversity. Children in America today need to learn to adapt to people who are different from themselves.

Choosing Child Care: Debbie and Walt

Debbie is a physical therapist in her middle 30s. She and her husband, Walt, delayed having children, but now they have 18-month-old Evan. Debbie took a 6-month leave when Evan was born, but when it came time to go back to work, she had such strong feelings about leaving him that she and Walt worked out a time-share plan. She went back to work half-time, and he rearranged his work schedule so that he could be home when she wasn't. So far they haven't had to use child care. But now they've decided that their city apartment isn't the right place for Evan to grow up, so they're in the market for a house. In addition, Walt, who has two teenage children from his first marriage, is feeling some pressure because his oldest daughter is applying to expensive colleges. It's time for Debbie to go back to work full-time. She is looking for child care. Here's her story.

Debbie started by calling a friend at work, who recommended the child care center that she uses. Debbie went over right away. She was appalled at what she saw. The place seemed like a madhouse—furniture overturned, paper on the floor, children everywhere yelling and screaming. Debbie couldn't imagine her precious little Evan here! A harried-looking teacher showed her around but was interrupted every 10 seconds by some squabble or a child demanding something. After 10 minutes the teacher handed Debbie a fistful of papers, told her that all the information she needed was on them, and left her standing wide-eyed by the door. She made a fast exit, depositing the papers in the trash can in the parking lot.

Next Debbie checked the phone book. At random, she picked another place, close to her work. She was astonished to find this center just the opposite of the first one. She arrived to find the children waiting in line to go outside. Although they were talking quietly and wiggling just a bit, they were not unruly. The room was immaculate, a little cold, and on the bare side. Debbie tried to imagine exuberant Evan in this setting. She couldn't. She left without talking to anyone.

The next place Debbie tried was down the street from her apartment. "At last!" she thought as she stepped inside a pleasant, well-lit room alive with healthy child activity. She liked what she saw—clusters of children playing busily, adults on the floor with them. "Good energy here," she concluded. But when she talked to the director, she discovered that this center took only low-income children, and even for them it had a waiting list with 100 names on it. She left, disappointed.

"Your turn," she told Walt when she got home that night. "I'm just too discouraged."

By the end of a week she and Walt had learned a lot about child care. They found a local resource and referral agency that gave them information about centers as well as family child care providers—people who use their own homes for child care.

By the end of two weeks, they had visited a number of centers and family child care homes and found two that suited them that had openings. They sat down to make a decision.

First Walt brought up an earlier discussion about in-home care. "Are you sure you don't want to reconsider looking for someone to come here? If we could find someone it would be easier."

"Yes, it would be easier, but I want Evan to be with other children. I can't imagine him here all day every day by himself with someone who isn't me or you."

"So what will it be, Mrs. Watson's house or the River Street Center?" asked Walt, ready to settle this question. "They both have pros and cons. The center is more convenient and cheaper. It's warm and homelike. I like the way they plan curriculum around the children's interests. The staff seems stable—I asked each how long he or she had been there and was impressed at the low turnover rate. What do you think?"

"Well," Debbie said slowly, "I liked the center, too, but I wonder how Evan would fit in with those kids. They are so much older than he is."

"Mrs. Watson has a 5-year-old and a 4-year-old," said Walt.

"Yes, but the group is so small that the older kids are an asset rather than a liability. I don't worry that he will get lost in a crowd of big kids."

"But Mrs. Watson's is twice as far away."

"True, but I really like the fact that he'd be sort of part of a family. He has so many years to be in school, I'd rather he experience family life at this point. And when he's older he could go to the preschool down the block from Mrs. Watson, so he could have a larger group experience before he goes to kindergarten."

"I think you've made up your mind."

"I guess I have. What about you?"

"I think Mrs. Watson's house is great! Let's call her."

PARENT–PROFESSIONAL PARTNERSHIPS

An important aspect of child rearing is *care*—the feeling and the function. We can't legislate the feeling, only the function. But we can make it more likely that the feeling will follow if we have well trained, well paid, recognized staff and providers who are not overworked or burned out. This means that, as a society, we have to place a value on child care and on those who provide it.

This book has emphasized family-centered care throughout. In this section we'll look at child care in particular because with this shared care arrangement, a focus on the family is even more vital than in half-day preschools, kindergarten, and the primary grades. Child care is more of a child-rearing environment than school is. Child care workers and parents—who together equal the full picture of child rearing—must be partners. Many parents today can't do it alone. But a child care system can't do it alone, either, no matter how good it is. What parents give is passionate feeling, highly personalized, that comes with a history and a future. Watch a power struggle between a parent and a child, and you'll see emotion seldom seen between two other people. Although providers and teachers are often critical of the passionate exchanges they witness from time to time, it is important to recognize that that's what parenting is about. It's about connectedness, which results in intense interactions. Parenting is passionate business—the anger as well as the love. Parenting is a long-term affair—much longer (excluding certain circumstances) than any child care arrangement. The parents provide the continuity through the child's life as he or she passes from program to program or from child care to school. Child care and teachers and providers come and go, but children need continuity in their lives, and it's up to the parents to provide it.

Parent and caregiver are partners in child rearing. Therefore, it is vital that they appreciate, respect, and support each other.

Roadblocks to Mutual Appreciation, Respect, and Support

What gets in the way of this mutual appreciation, respect, and support? One roadblock on the part of some early educators—even those not in full-day care programs—is the "savior complex." I remember my own period of being a savior. I was a beginner, and I thought I knew everything. And besides, I had a great desire to rescue children from their parents—especially the parents I didn't like much or understand very well. I went even further—I saw myself saving the world through the work I was doing with young children. Can you imagine how it must have felt to be a parent trying to communicate with me way up on my high horse?

Child care professionals and parents together equal the full picture of child rearing. A good many parents today can't do it alone. But a child care system can't do it alone, either, no matter how good it is. Parents and teachers have to be partners.

Another roadblock I've encountered in others I've worked with is anger and resentment. Tune in on the following scene, which takes place in the living room of a modest home:

> The sun is still just a hint in the eastern sky as the doorbell rings. A family child care provider in her bathrobe, who has barely managed to get her hair combed at this early hour, rushes to the door, followed by her fussing baby, who keeps raising his arms to be picked up. She is greeted by a mother who is dressed in a lovely print dress with jacket and jewelry to match. Hiding behind the woman is a sniffling toddler who is wiping her nose on the sleeve of her pajamas. After a rapid exchange of greetings, the mother explains briefly that she will be late tonight because she is taking an important client to dinner. She says a quick good-bye and then turns on her high heels and leaves.
>
> The provider closes the door with a slight slam and leans up against it for a moment before she faces the two needy children who are both fussing at her. Although reminding herself that she made a conscious decision to stay home while her own child is a baby, she is nevertheless resentful of the nice clothes, jewelry, and makeup, as well as the freedom to attend power lunches and client dinners. All of that is totally unrelated to her own day of picking up messes, wiping noses, and changing diapers.
>
> Meanwhile, in the car at the curb, the mother sits for a moment trying to rid herself of the distress she feels at leaving her daughter like this. She wonders whether the sniffles are the beginning of an illness. She wishes she could be there to watch her daughter closely and take care of her. She's resentful that the provider can be in her bathrobe at this hour and not have to worry about makeup or clothes. She starts up her car, thinking about how nice it would be to have all day to play with children instead of dealing with clients and coworkers in a dog-eat-dog world.

Neither woman in this scenario really wants to trade places with the other, but they both harbor resentments. Consider how these resentments might influence communication between the two. Imagine how the provider will feel tonight if the mother arrives later than she promised. Imagine how the mother will feel if the provider calls in the afternoon and says the child has a fever and must go home regardless of the important dinner scheduled. Will either one feel very understanding? Probably not, with all that resentment that was brewing earlier in the day.

A major issue between parents and child care workers is competition—of all kinds but especially competition for the child's affection. Because children are likely to be attached to both their parents and their providers, the competition is often intensified. Although in most cases child care workers remain only secondary attachments for children, parents can feel quite insecure about what they perceive as the threat of being replaced as number one in their child's eyes. It is up to both parents and providers to be aware of the feelings generated by this situation and to learn to respect and relate to each other in supportive ways. Acknowledging the feelings is a first step. Working on the relationship is also a positive approach to take. Setting out purposely to strengthen the relationship is accomplished most easily when all parties involved remind themselves that the child's welfare is at stake.

We have a model for sharing the care of a child: the extended family so prevalent in many cultures. In this model, the child experiences several simultaneous attachments instead of an exclusive one with the parent alone. There may be a single primary attachment, but the child who grows up in an extended family is likely to be parented by more than one person.

Choosing Child Care: Roberto

Roberto is a single parent and a physical therapist who works with Debbie, the mother in our earlier case study. Roberto has custody of his 4-year-old daughter, Mercedes. Now he is looking for child care, as Debbie had done previously.

When Mercedes was born, Roberto's mother, Barbara, offered to care for her on a daily basis. The arrangement worked out very well until just recently. Barbara inherited some money, and she's gotten the travel itch. This itch came at a convenient time, because Roberto was just thinking that Mercedes needed to expand her horizons a bit. Not that she didn't get what she needed in her grandmother's home, but Roberto wants her in a program with teachers and other children.

Roberto started his child care search about six months after Debbie did. He felt a good deal of pressure from Debbie to check out Mrs. Watson's, where Evan was so comfortably settled, so he did. He liked what he saw, but it wasn't what he wanted for Mercedes. Mrs. Watson was warm and kind, and obviously knew how to provide developmentally appropriate activities for the children in her care. She was also motherly to Roberto, but he bristled at that. "I don't need another mother," he told himself.

It was easy to decide against Mrs. Watson's family child care home. What Roberto wanted for Mercedes was a center.

He visited a number of places, including the ones that Debbie had gone to. Roberto wasn't as appalled as Debbie was at the variety of programs he found.

Roberto knew what he wanted. It's just a matter of finding it, he told himself. He wanted a place where Mercedes could experience children and teachers of other cultures—one where teachers were trained to treat 4-year-olds as 4-year-olds and provide a rich variety of creative activities. It was hard for Barbara to open her house to easel painting, clay and play dough, carpentry, and other messy kinds of projects.

Barbara and Roberto have discussed this subject before. They are in agreement. "Those are the kinds of experiences a child care center should provide—ones it's hard to set up for at home," Roberto told Barbara.

Barbara agreed. "It will be nice for Mercedes to be with other children, too, instead of all by herself with just me."

Roberto found several programs that he liked. The one he liked best was in a church. He worried at first that they might teach religion there but was assured that the program was only renting the Sunday school rooms, and it wasn't affiliated with the church itself.

What Roberto particularly liked about this program was the racial mix of the staff and the atmosphere. He made a couple of visits and was pleased to see the variety of creative activities, including a sensory table and water play, available for the children. When he brought Mercedes to visit, some children were finger painting. Mercedes dived right in and was soon up to her elbows in oozing reds and yellows. She was having a glorious time smearing paint around. No one got upset that she went beyond the paper a couple of times.

Mercedes loved circle time and was the first to grab some streamers and start dancing to the music. She beamed as the teacher sang her name in a good-morning song. There wasn't anything that Mercedes didn't love.

"This is the place for us," Roberto told the teacher as he walked out the door, Mercedes in tow, protesting.

"Can't I just stay a few more minutes?" his daughter begged.

"You can come back tomorrow and spend all day!" Roberto answered.

LOOKING BACK AND LOOKING FORWARD

The United States has a long way to go as a society to solving the many problems of raising children, but we are at least becoming aware of the problems. A key term in child rearing today is *shared care*. We'll make great strides when parents and early care and education teachers and providers become true partners, and when all the adults concerned with a child come to respect, appreciate, and support each other. We know now that children can grow and develop in a variety of settings, including their own homes, family child care homes, and in other kinds of early

Frank Gonzalez-Mena

Children can grow and develop in a variety of settings, including their own homes, family child care homes, and other early care and education program settings.

care and education environments. The key word in any setting is *quality*.

We know, too, that early care and education programs, including Head Start, preschool, and child care, and school can break the cycle of poverty and disadvantage. However, not all programs that serve young children are equally effective. Programs that manage to break the cycle have particular characteristics: They are small, flexible, and interdisciplinary. They often provide more than just early childhood education and child care; they also deliver comprehensive services to meet the child's needs in the family, and the family's needs in the community.

It is taking a long time for this society to make children a national priority. The federal child care bill passed at the beginning of the 1990s, the continued funding of Head Start, and the federal and state dollars increasing child care capacities during the welfare reform period were all steps in the right direction.

This chapter took a look at the whole range of early care and education programs and put a focus on child care as a child-rearing setting. The next chapter looks at other resources the community has to offer in addition to early care and education programs.

FOR DISCUSSION

1. Do you agree that children are actually "reared" in early care and education programs? Can you give the view of someone who agrees? Can you give the view of someone who disagrees?

2. What do you think makes up quality care and education? Explain your answer.

3. What are some ways that families and teachers can come together to create a sense of community in the early care and education program?

4. What do you think about trying to match teachers to children's cultural and language background?

5. What did you think of the scene on page 291, in which both the provider and the parent felt resentment? What solution do you see to this problem? How can the provider and parent communicate better and cope with their feelings?

WEB SITES

Center for the Child Care Workforce (CCW)
http://www.ccw.org
The Center for the Child Care Workforce advocates for increased status and wages for early childhood professionals.

Child Care Aware
http://www.childcareaware.org/
This is a resource for finding names and phone numbers of child care and referral agencies in the United States, with additional tips for parents looking for child care.

Child Care Information Exchange
http://ccie.com
Many resources for directors of child care and other early care and information programs including a daily short e-mail column called ExchangeEveryDay which shares research, gives information, and discusses hot topics of interest to ECE professionals.

Children's Defense Fund (CDF)
http://www.childrensdefense.org
The mission of the Children's Defense Fund is to ensure every child a healthy start, a head start, a fair start, a safe start, and a moral start in life.

Division for Early Childhood
http://www.dec-sped.org/
Early intervention-related links are here, as is information dealing with policy, research, and services.

Marc Sheehan's Special Education/ Exceptionality Page
http://www.halcyon.com/marcs/sped.html
This very helpful site contains many Internet links to special education-related sites.

National Association of Child Care Resource and Referral Agencies (NACCRRA)
http://www.naccrra.net
The NACCRRA is a national network of community-based child care resource and referral agencies that provides a common ground where families, child care providers, and communities can share information about quality child care. The "news" section is up to date and very informative.

National Association for the Education of Young Children (NAEYC)
http://www.naeyc.org
The National Association for the Education of Young Children has a number of resources available for parents and professionals including books and journals, one of which is called *Young Children*.

National Association for Family Child Care (NAFCC)
http://www.nafcc.org
The National Association for Family Child Care is devoted to promoting quality and professionalism in family child care homes.

National Network for Child Care (NNCC)
http://www.nncc.org/
The National Network for Child Care is an Internet source of over 1,000 publications and resources related to children. Publications are research based and reviewed. This site includes articles, resources, and links on various subjects such as public policy/advocacy, health and safety, child abuse, diversity, and more.

Program for Infant/Toddler Caregivers (PITC)
http://www.pitc.org
The Program for Infant/Toddler Caregivers supports and promotes quality care for infants and toddlers through resources, information, and training. This site includes information on culturally relevant care.

Zero to Three
http://www.zerotothree.org
Zero to Three: National Center for Infants, Toddlers, and Families, for parents and professionals, is a leading resource on the first three years of life to promote diversity and the healthy development of babies and toddlers.

FURTHER READING

Bernhard, J. K., & Gonzalez-Mena, J. (2000). The cultural context of infant–toddler care. In D. Cryer & T. Harms (Eds.), *Infants and toddlers in out-of-home care* (pp. 237–267). Baltimore: Brookes.

Butterfield, P. M. (2002, February–March). Child care is rich in routines. *Zero to Three*, 22(4), 29–32.
Chang, H. N. L., Muckelroy, A., & Pulido-Tobiassen, D. (1996). *Looking in, looking out: Redefining child and*

early education in a diverse society. San Francisco: California Tomorrow.

Cleveland, G., & Krashinsky, M. (2003). *Fact and fantasy: Eight myths about early childhood education and care.* Toronto, Canada: Childcare Resource and Research Unit, University of Toronto.

Dombro, A. L. and Lerner, C. (2006, January). Sharing the care of infants and toddlers. *Young Children,* 61(1), 29–33.

Edmiaston, R., Dolezal, V., Doolittle, S., Erickson, C., & Merritt, S. (2000). Developing individualized education programs for children in inclusive settings: A developmental framework. *Young Children,* 55(4), 36–41.

Fromberg, D. P., & Bergen, D. (Eds). (2006). *Play from birth to twelve: Contexts, perspectives, and meanings* (2nd ed.). New York: Routledge, Taylor & Francis Group.

Gonzalez-Mena, J., (2000, July). In the spirit of partnership: High maintenance parent or cultural difference? *Exchange,* 134, 40–42.

Gonzalez-Mena, J. (2007). *50 Early strategies for working and communicating with diverse families.* Upper Saddle River, NJ: Merrill/Prentice Hall.

Gonzalez-Mena, J. (2008). *Diversity in early care and education: Honoring differences* (5th ed.). New York: McGraw-Hill.

Gonzalez-Mena, J., & Eyer, D. (2007) *Infants, toddlers, and caregivers.* New York: McGraw-Hill.

Gonzalez-Mena, J., & Stonehouse, A. (2000, January). Responding in the spirit of partnership: The high maintenance parent. *Child Care Information Exchange,* 131, 10–12.

Gonzalez-Mena, J., & Stonehouse, A. (2008). Making links: A collaborative approach to planning and practice in early childhood programs. New York: Teachers College Press.

Greenman, J. (2003). Places for childhood include parents, too. In B. & R. Neugebauer, (Eds.), *The art of leadership.* Redmond, WA: Child Care Information Exchange.

Greenough, W., Emde, R. N., Gunnar, M., Massinga, R., & Shonkoff, J. P. (2001, April–May). The impact of the caregiving environment on young children's development: Different ways of knowing. *Zero to Three,* 21(5), 16–24.

Jablon, J. R., Dombro, A. L. & Dichtelmiller, M. L. (2007). *The power of observation for birth through eight.* Washington, DC: Teaching Strategies, Inc.

Jacobs, G., & Crowley, K. (2007). *Play, projects and preschool standards: Nurturing children's sense of wonder and joy in learning.* Thousand Oaks, CA: Corwin Press.

Kontos, S. (1992). *Family day care: Out of the shadows and into the limelight.* Washington, DC: National Association for the Education of Young Children.

Kostelnik, M., Onaga, E., Rohde, B., & Whiren, A. (2002). *Children with special needs: Lessons for early childhood professionals.* New York: Teachers College Press.

Lee, L. (2002). *Serving families: A handbook on the principles and strategies of the parent services project approach.* San Rafael, CA: Parent Services Project.

Lombardi, J. (2003). *Time to care: Redesigning child care to promote education, support families and build communities.* Philadelphia: Temple University Press.

Moore, E. K. (1995, May). Mediocre care: Double jeopardy for black children. *Young Children,* 50(4), 47.

Noddings, N. (2002). *Educating moral people: A caring alternative to character education.* New York: Teachers College Press.

Noddings, N. (2005). *The Challenge to Care in Schools.* New York: Teachers College Press.

Phipps, P. A. (2003). Working with angry parents—Taking a customer service approach. In B. & R. Neugebauer (Eds.), *The art of leadership.* Redmond, WA: Child Care Information Exchange.

Schweinhart, L. (1995, May). The United States needs better child care. *Young Children,* 50(4), 48.

Segal, M., Masi, W., & Leiderman, R. (2001). *In time and with love: Caring for infants and toddlers with special needs.* New York: New Market Press.

Shonkoff, J. P., & Phillips, D. (2001, April–May). From neurons to neighborhoods: The science of early childhood development—An introduction. *Zero to Three,* 21(5), 4–7.

Stonehouse, A., & Gonzalez-Mena, J. (2004). *Making links: A collaborative approach to planning and practice in early childhood.* Sydney, Australia: Pademelon Press.

Szanton, E. S. (2001, January). For America's infants and toddlers, are important values threatened by our zeal to "teach"? *Young Children,* 56(1), 15–21.

Tobiassen, D. P., & Gonzalez-Mena, J. (1998). *A place to begin: Working with parents on issues of diversity*. Oakland: California Tomorrow.

Whitebook, M., & Sakai, L. (2004). *By a thread: How child care centers hold onto teachers, how teachers build lasting careers*. Kalamazoo, MI: Upjohn Institute for Employment Research.

Wong-Fillmore, L. (1991). When learning a second language means losing the first. *Early Childhood Research Quarterly, 6*, 323–346.

Zigler, E. F., Finn-Stevenson, M., & Hall, N. W. (2003). *The first three years and beyond: Brain development and social policy*. New Haven, CT: Yale University Press.

CHAPTER 13

Other Community Resources

In *this chapter you'll discover* . . .

- What isolation can do to a family
- Ideas about how to help families expand their social networks and use community resources
- Why families need more support now than ever before
- How the six families introduced earlier in this book use and contribute to community resources
- How to help families access community resources

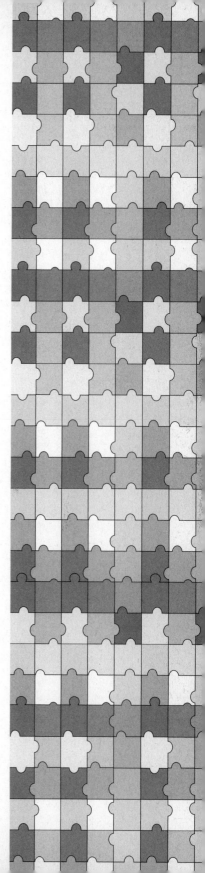

The preceding chapter examined early care and education as a community resource. It gave an overview of the kinds of programs available to the six families who first appeared in Chapter 11. This chapter explores what other contributions the community makes to support families in their struggles toward success.. We'll examine how the community and the institutions and people in it support the family and help it function.

Since this book focuses on working with parents around the education and socialization of children in early care and education programs, you may wonder what "community resources" have to do with that subject. For families to educate and socialize their children in healthy ways, many have needs that exceed their resources. Of course, the early care and education programs are important resources, and many families depend on them. But other needs arise too. Families are never entirely self-sufficient; that's why they live in communities. All depend on their community and the resources in it. Some families are able to seek out those resources more easily than others. It is important for early educators who work with children and families to understand what the resources are and how to access them, so they can advise families.

SOCIAL NETWORKS

Some families already see themselves as part of a larger social network, and they know both how to contribute to and make use of this network. This is the sign of one aspect of a healthy family system, according to family therapist and author Virginia Satir (Satir, 1972). Healthy families do not isolate themselves from the outside community if they can help it. They have a broad perspective that includes the world beyond the family, and they use feedback from that world. They are able to give and receive help from the outside social network.

Each family system has its own set of boundaries. For example, some families don't seek help or support from the larger community. They prefer to see themselves as self-sufficient and regard outside support of any kind as a sign of weakness. Others find support in their personal family or kinship networks but hesitate to use the formal institutions that have been set up to help them, either because they don't feel comfortable accepting help from an outside source or perhaps because they have just never considered it. Many families have no idea what is available in their communities. Some of these families get along fine; others experience a feeling of isolation.

Isolation has a number of negative effects on families. It limits role models for children. It can lead to a sense of hopelessness. And it can even lead to child abuse. When working with families, early educators can help families get together with each other. Those families that are engaged in large social networks can be models for those who are more isolated. The early care program itself can provide the catalyst for bringing families into a new social network—that of the center, school, or family child care program. See Strategy Box 13.1 for ideas on how to do this.

Strategy Box 13.1

Four Ways to Help Families Expand Their Social Networks by Connecting with Other Families in the Center

- ◆ Make contact information available to each family member. Of course, be sure to have permission from every family to be included on the list.
- ◆ Make every meeting interactive. Use icebreakers to get people to know each other.
- ◆ For those family members who exclude themselves, make a special effort to introduce them personally to other families in the program.
- ◆ Notice which children seem to be connecting with each other. Sometimes families appreciate a little encouragement to get their children together outside of the regular school hours of the program.

Developing a Broad Base of Support

In healthy families each member has a broad base of support and knows how to get strokes from people outside the immediate family. Without such a broad base of support, undue pressure falls on those within the family; if those who usually give strokes are unable to do so, the individual is left depleted.

How does one know if his or her support base is broad enough? An exercise called "stroke pie" can tell you. Strokes are behaviors that show recognition, appreciation, and support. They can be pats on the back or just simple acknowledgments. Think of the people in your life who give you strokes and provide support for you. Then draw a circle and make a pie-shaped wedge for each person. Make the size of the wedge correspond to the amount of support you receive from that person. Take a look at

In healthy families, each member has a broad base of support and knows how to get strokes from people outside the immediate family.

PH College

your stroke pie. Do you have a number of different wedges of varying sizes, or do you have mainly just one or two big wedges? If you are getting more than 25 percent of your support from just one person, you are at risk for stroke deprivation if that person leaves even temporarily, or is for some reason unable to support you. By the way, did you put your own name on a wedge of your stroke pie? You should be a source of your own strokes If you have just a limited number of wedges in your pie, you may be overly dependent on a few people for support. That's a sign that you need to broaden your base of support. You can do this exercise at a parent meeting to help make families aware of when they need a larger base of support. You can help families broaden their base by connecting them with other families in the program. Refer back to Strategy Box 13.1 for ideas on how to do that.

Here are sample stroke pies of two people, Kim and Jennifer:

Kim assigned three-quarters of the pie to her boyfriend and the remaining quarter-slice to her mother. Then came the day that her mother discovered she had cancer, which was about the time the boyfriend found someone else. Kim's strokes disappeared all at once, and she had no one to turn to for support.

Jennifer used to be in that position, too: She was dependent on her husband for most of her strokes, with a few coming from her sister. But when she became a parent and discovered that she needed to give out more strokes than she got back, she knew she'd better broaden her base of support. She purposely developed a close relationship with two mothers she had met in her Lamaze class and another mother she met in the park. She not only started swapping child care with these women but also used them for information and for nurturing, too.

Four years after Jennifer's son was born, her stroke pie looked very different from the way it had looked when she first became a mother. Her pie was now divided into 19 pieces, with friends, relatives, neighbors, her son, parents at her son's school, office mates, members of her parenting support group, and two jogging buddies all represented by slices. Her husband's huge slice was cut down to less than a quarter of the pie, and their relationship was blossoming since she had quit depending on him and her sister so heavily to meet all her emotional needs.

Jennifer created a social network for herself. Each individual and each family has a stroke pie that comprises their social network. Each looks slightly different.

Forms Social Networks May Take

In some families, individual members have their own social networks. In others, the family shares a network that consists of individuals and groups that comprise what can be thought of as a greater family, or an extended family. Again, I'm talking about boundaries in family systems this is an example of different kinds of boundaries. Some families are attached to a number of people beyond their own relatives in formal and informal ways. In a Mexican family, for example, this attachment may include, besides relatives, *compadres*—the children's godparents. *Compadres* are more than friends; they have a special kind of family relationship even though they may not have blood ties. Other families have special friends who are considered "aunts and uncles" to the younger generation. They are like family but are not blood relatives.

For some families, the neighborhood where they live may be the most important part of the social network. Neighbors can become a close-knit group that serves as a mutual aid society—sharing resources, providing guidance for children, and contributing to the social life of its members through periodic gatherings and celebrations of all sorts. Although these kinds of neighborhoods still exist in some places, they are becoming more scarce as the American population increases in mobility and at the same time isolates itself from those who live nearby.

For some families, a religious institution or spiritual practice group serves the same functions as the close-knit neighborhood described earlier, providing friendship, a social life, mutual aid, social services, support, counseling, and education, along with worship services, celebrations, and/or spiritual guidance.

Community Institutions That Serve Families

Other formal and informal groups and institutions with specialized functions make up a part of the social network of the community. Some of them have been around since the country began, such as police and fire departments; others are just now in the process of developing in response to changing needs. Public libraries are long-time institutions that provide a variety of services to families, services that have expanded way beyond books, especially with the development of computer technology, which continues to expand ways of communicating and gaining knowledge.

Three ongoing trends illustrate the need for formal and informal support for families: the increasing numbers of mothers of infants and young children in the workforce; the growing challenge for low-income families to attain economic self-sufficiency; and the feminization of poverty.

- *Employed mothers.* More mothers than ever before are working. Adding to the trend are the changes in the welfare system, which means that mothers of children of infants are a fast-growing group in the labor force. Many of these women are single heads of families and are the only source of financial support for their families. The response to this current trend by the greater society has been to provide outside child care in a number of forms. Government, schools, employers, churches, corporations, and individuals are getting involved in the child care scene.

- *Economic challenges*. Growing numbers of families today find themselves in acute economic distress. Because parents are unable to work for a variety of reasons or are working for wages that keep the family mired down in the bog of poverty, children are greatly influenced by lack of money, food, and even shelter. The community response to this problem is lagging far behind the need, as witnessed by the number of homeless in many communities.

- *The feminization of poverty.* Someone once said that most women are just one husband away from poverty. Look around you. Who are most in need of financial help? Women. One in five children are in poverty; of those children, 9 out of 10 live in female-headed households. A generation ago most poor people were old. That has changed now as a result of a local, state, and national response to conditions and problems of the elderly. The composition of the new poverty group is different, and community response has been slow, unfortunately.

FAMILIES USING COMMUNITY RESOURCES

Let's take a look now at how the families introduced in Chapter 11 reflect these trends and how they connect with the social networks outside themselves. Notice how each family uses and contributes to the community resources available.

Sara's Family

Remember Sara? She's the 20-year-old with two sons—Ty and Kyle—who is in nursing school at a community college. She went through a very difficult period, being home-less for awhile. But by now she's an expert in the resources her community has to offer. She's tied into the financial aid program at her college, which gives her support. She also receives child care in an on-campus subsidized program for low-income students, which is funded by the state. She gives back to these two community resources by serving on the advisory committee of the financial aid program and by contributing volunteer time to the child care center. She was asked to help with fund-raising for the center but made a decision to take care of herself and her sons by declining. She knows that fund-raising can be very time-consuming, and with her studies and her family, time is at a premium right now.

When Sara was pregnant the first time, she received assistance from WIC (Women, Infants, and Children), a federally funded nutrition program designed to help ensure that children get the nourishment they need through the prenatal period and into the first year of life.

Ty was born prematurely, which made life even harder for a time. Going to a support group for awhile for "preemie" parents helped Sara get through this period. The group, which was hosted by her local hospital, was led by a social worker and funded by a special foundation grant.

By the time of her second pregnancy (which resulted from being raped while she was homeless), the WIC funding had been cut in half, and she could no longer get into the program, which was unfortunate because she and Ty often didn't have food. She worried about her unborn baby a lot during that period. Kyle too was born prematurely, and by then the funding for the preemie support group had also been cut, so she was on her own. But she did finally get into a teen parent program that enabled her to finish high school. Now she has moved on to college with a plan and hope for her future through the vocational program she is in.

When Sara first went on the Temporary Assistance to Needy Families (TANF) program, she lived in terror that someone would decide that she was neglecting her children and take them away from her. She had seen this happen to several women during her homeless period. She couldn't bear the thought of losing Ty and Kyle, so she was very cautious whenever she discussed anything with her social worker. She felt she had to protect herself. It took her a long time to decide that the worker understood her situation, saw her as a good mother, and wasn't about to report her for neglect to Child Protective Services, which is the government agency in her county that handles child abuse cases.

Recently Sara has discovered a food co-op where, by paying a small amount to join and volunteering a few hours a week, she can get a good deal of food at very reasonable rates. She's also discovered that she can get family counseling services, which the child care center recommended because of Ty's attention deficit problem and Kyle's aggressive behavior (you may remember that he bites). The director of the child care program is also talking about referring both boys to a special education preschool program run by the county office of education. Sara is hesitant about taking the next steps for this service because she hates the thought of changing programs. Besides, the hours of the special ed program don't fit her school schedule very well, and she'd still need child care. Transportation would be a problem, and she doesn't want her boys shuffled back and forth from one program to another, so she's dragging her feet on following up her investigation of what could be done further for her children. What she doesn't know is that there is a strong movement to include children with special needs in programs with their typically developing peers. It's possible that Sara can get her boys the special services that they may need without moving them to another program.

Because of her low-income status, Sara is entitled to health benefits from the government, but she sometimes has a hard time finding a doctor who will see her and the boys.

Sara has been in a lot worse shape in the past than she is now. She remembers eating once a week at a community dinner for the homeless, served in a church by a local women's service group. Sara had very mixed feelings about being there. She couldn't help being grateful, of course, but she felt strangely alienated from everyone there, not only from the other homeless people but also from the good-hearted women who donated their time, energy, and casseroles. She hates being on the receiving end of charity!

Christmas has always brought up the same awful feelings, and it still does, even now. It's great that the community rallies once a year to provide gifts for her boys and a turkey for her table, but every year she has those same mixed feelings of gratitude, shame, and anger. She'll be glad when she gets through school and can support herself. Then she'll be the one doing the giving for a change. She can hardly wait.

Roberto's Family

Roberto's family, if you remember, is composed of Roberto; his wife, Maria Elena; his 4-year-old daughter, Lupe; and baby Paco. Roberto at first resisted signing up for any community resources because he was too proud; besides, he was suspicious of anything connected to any government. But one day he found himself persuaded to send his daughter to Head Start, a federally funded preschool program for low-income children. He discovered early on that with Head Start comes a community aide, who helps the family get connected to other services that they need, many of which are provided right at school for the children, such as vision and hearing screening. The hearing screening proved to be a problem because they discovered that Lupe has a hearing deficit, and now the family is expected to do something about it. Roberto is convinced that the hearing problem would have gone away on its own if it hadn't been discovered. Roberto and Maria Elena went to the place the school told them to go, but there were many papers to fill out and no one spoke their language, so they left. Now Roberto feels very uncomfortable every time he gets a notice from school urging him to follow up on the referral they gave him.

While Roberto was still getting used to all the changes in his life that came as the result of enrolling Lupe in Head Start, Maria Elena announced that she wanted to take classes in English as a second language at the adult school. "I won't have time to drive you," Roberto told her firmly, convinced that that would end the matter.

"I can take the bus," said Maria Elena.

"And who will take care of Paco?" asked Roberto.

"They have child care at the school," Maria Elena shot back.

Roberto was stunned. This had all been worked out without him. What would happen to him if his family didn't need him any more? He felt shaken.

He needed to talk to somebody, so he went first to his *compadre*, Juan, godfather of Lupe, and told him how he felt. Just talking about it made him feel better. Then he went to his priest and talked some more. The priest suggested counseling, but Roberto thought that counseling would show the world that something was wrong with him, and that was exactly the problem he wished to avoid. He felt that enough was wrong with him because of what was happening in his family; he certainly didn't want to announce to the world that he was weak and needed help. The priest made another suggestion, however, that Roberto followed up on. He told him about a clinic that might help with Lupe's problem. It was a community effort run by bilingual volunteers, so he would at least be able to talk to someone in his own language—someone who knew something about medicine. Roberto felt much better when he came home from talking to the priest. Maria Elena noticed the difference and gave him a big hug when he came in the door.

Junior's Family

Remember Junior? He's the 12-month-old who has been crying so hard at the child care center. His family fled from their homeland and are still trying to settle in. Junior used to be at home with his great grandma, but now she is sick and he's in child care. This family is still in a survival mode, while experiencing culture shock and language difficulties.

The members of this refugee family are so busy working that they haven't had time to find out about any resources in their community except for child care; and that isn't working out too well, because Junior cries all the time he's there. The family has been relocated several times, and Junior seems to be expressing the suffering all of them feel. Being crowded is nothing new to this family; they've always lived in close quarters with the extended family in one residence. Their house is packed most of the time. They have to eat in shifts, but they work in shifts, too, so that comes out all right.

One thing they're glad of is that Junior doesn't cry at home the way he does at the center. It's not that crying babies haven't always been part of their lives, but now Great-Grandma is sick, and they worry about disturbing her. Oh, yes, they do use a community resource—a home health nurse who comes in to look after Great-Grandma. Although they were suspicious at first of medical care that they didn't understand, they decided it wouldn't be such a bad idea to learn about how things work in this country. The only problem is that language creates terrible barriers, and they don't understand as much as they want to. They often wonder what the nurse is doing and what the various medications are for, but they have to wait until the oldest cousin, who understands English, gets home to find out. Even then things don't always make sense because the approach to health care in this country is so different.

There have been some scary misunderstandings about health matters—like the time Great-Grandma had a reaction to some medication, and they had to take her to the hospital emergency room. That was a horrible experience because they had no idea what was going on. And when they put her in the hospital for two days, it was very frustrating because the medical staff wouldn't let the family take care of her. In fact, they were asked to leave. They didn't understand this at all!

The family is very lonely at times when they think of their native country, but they are learning to make this country home. They know how to support each other, pooling resources and knowledge, which helps a lot. They aren't used to getting outside help, so that's something new to them. They are learning English rapidly and soon will have an expanded view of the community they live in and what is available to them.

Michael's Family

Michael, a 3-year-old, is the son of a lesbian couple. Michael and his parents are isolated from many of the social networks that support other families. Michael's parents don't want to be isolated, but they have had bad experiences in the past when they reached out and found themselves rejected. They have their own group of friends, and they find closeness and community there. In some ways they are like Junior's refugee family, who necessarily looks close to home for support.

In other ways they are not like Junior's family, because the institutions that they deal with don't recognize them as a family. This became clear and evident the day that Michael fell and needed stitches. Margaret, his birth mother, was at work in another town and couldn't get to the hospital right away. Beth, his other mother, had to hold the crying Michael in the emergency room—no treatment could be started until Margaret arrived to sign permission papers. Beth had no recognized legal connection to Michael.

Having their relationship not regarded as valid or legal by community agencies was nothing new to Michael's parents. They had had previous difficulties not experienced by heterosexual married couples—like not being able to get a loan to buy a house and being refused job-related medical benefits. They also had had countless difficulties living in a neighborhood where some neighbors didn't like them even though they had never gotten to know them. But the incident in the hospital emergency room hurt the most because it involved Michael.

Beth and Margaret aren't without friends. They both have jobs, and each has found personal friends and support systems at work. But these systems don't help the family much, because except for a few individuals, the work friends don't know about the rest of the family.

Margaret, especially, feels isolated at work because of the secret she keeps from her friends and associates there. But in her last job she was more open, and she ended up feeling a lot more isolated than she does now. She finally left that job because she couldn't stand it anymore.

Both Margaret and Beth worry about their son and what will happen when he is old enough to understand what outsiders say about the family. They feel very protective of him and of each other and sometimes feel as though they live in a little cocoon separate from the rest of the world. They don't really want to live that way, but they wish they could keep the cocoon for Michael. They know, however, that soon he's going to grow beyond their protection and will be on his own in what feels to them like a cold and cruel outside world.

Margaret is secure about her relationship to Beth, but she suffers from the reaction she gets from so many who find out about it. In the past, she felt angry a lot of the time, and she knew she needed help in coping with the anger. She finally found a therapist to talk to. It took a long time, because she looked for someone who would really understood her and could help without judging her family composition. She is surprised that being open and honest with a professional therapist can be so helpful. She's urging Beth, who has the same angry feelings about the way she's treated, to talk with someone, too. However, Beth hesitates, feeling that going into therapy means she's admitting that something is wrong with her.

Things are a little better now, because Beth has found a teacher at Michael's center who is accepting and friendly. She feels relieved that at least one outsider isn't cold and cruel.

Courtney's Family

Courtney's family consists of her second husband, Richard; 4-year-old Roland, from Courtney's first marriage; and 2½-year-old Soleil, who is Courtney and Richard's daughter. Roland's two older brothers are also part of this family, but they live with Courtney's parents.

This family has been involved with the legal system for some time; there were issues with both drug abuse and then child abuse during Courtney's first marriage. Now the family lives in fear of the boys' father returning to heap more abuse on previously abused little Roland. There's a restraining order to keep the father from coming near the boys, but Courtney still worries.

Courtney is just about to graduate from a drug rehabilitation program and is very proud of herself for being clean. She has turned her life around and is enrolled in college, the first step toward becoming a lawyer. She has strong feelings about making the legal system work better for everybody.

Richard also has strong feelings about the system. He is a Native American who, though born outside the reservation, has spent periods of his life going back to connect with his roots. He finds the tribal system and the religion of his people appealing, in contrast to impersonal institutions. He knows what real community is—people linked in emotional, social, and spiritual ways, people who provide mutual help and support. Richard's dream is to become a history teacher and to help the next generation see that change is necessary if this country (and, indeed, the planet) is to survive.

Courtney, like Sara, went through a difficult time in the past, which resulted in her being connected with a number of social service institutions—some which seemed to be supportive of her and some that regarded her as "the enemy."

Courtney remembers a very difficult period when she was told that if she didn't leave her boys' father because of the abuse he poured on them, she would lose her children. She felt extremely helpless at that point, and if it hadn't been for a local women's shelter, she never would have been able to take such a big step. When she finally left the shelter and struck out on her own, she was still threatened with the loss of her children because she couldn't provide decent housing for them. The only place she could afford that would rent to her was very run-down. Luckily, there was a new program in her community that was designed to help families overcome obstacles like hers. A social worker from this program, instead of removing her children to foster care, came out with tools to show her how to fix the broken windows, replace the screens, and repair the plumbing, so that she and her children would have a safe place to live. This same social worker gave Courtney some skills for guiding her children's behavior and got her into the rehabilitation program that turned her life around. Courtney is very grateful for the community resources that she sees as saving her life and helping her keep her children.

The Jackson Family

The Jackson family is different from some of the other families because they haven't been through a hard time. They're a stable family, clear about their identity, values, and lifestyle. They're not looking for changes as much as trying to keep things the way they are. Like Margaret and Beth, Michael's parents, the

Jacksons' problems arise from being different from, and therefore misunderstood by, the greater community.

Because the Jacksons are not in crisis, they are not looking for the same kind of support as some of the other families examined so far. The community resources they use and enjoy are those of their own group—the religious and cultural groups they belong to—and those of the greater community, resources such as the library, recreation programs and facilities, museums, and other institutions that enhance the quality of their lives and the lives of the other families described in this chapter. The Jacksons appreciate music and plays, and they support the local groups that provide them. This family has no need for general assistance, food programs, housing support, social services, child abuse programs, or legal agencies, at least at present.

It's not that this is a perfect family; they have their problems, too. Their child, who was born with spina bifida, a debilitating condition caused by a birth defect involving the spine, needs specialized services that they get from the school district. Taking care of him used to take up most of Mrs. Jackson's time, but now that he has enrolled in the school, she has more time to herself. Unfortunately, she is feeling isolated at home, and she's thinking of looking for friends outside her religious community. She had hoped to find a friendly group when she moved into the neighborhood she lives in. In her old neighborhood the women got together regularly and talked over coffee. In this one, however, the neighbors don't seem to want to get to know each other. The women are gone during the day and seem to be busy in the evenings and on weekends. Mrs. Jackson invited her next-door neighbors over when she first moved in, but although they were polite and pleasant, they never reciprocated, and now they just talk once in a while across the driveway.

Now, however, Mrs. Jackson has gotten involved with fund-raising at her son's school, and she's beginning to feel connected to a group. She likes the women who are working with her, and she hopes to continue enjoying their company after the fund-raiser is over.

Mrs. Jackson is also involved in a new project. Her father, who has lived by himself since his wife died, is growing more and more feeble, and the Jacksons recently decided that he should move in with them. Mrs. Jackson is busy investigating what kinds of services are available to help them out. She has discovered the senior center near the library, where her father can enjoy company, take part in various classes and activities, and have a hot lunch on the days she works. She's feeling good about how this move will work out. It will be nice to have her father with her—and good for the children to know their grandfather better.

CONNECTIONS TO THE COMMUNITY

Each of these families has connections to the community beyond their own doors, yet each perceives that community in a slightly different way. Each uses the services of agencies and informal groups. Some give back as much as they receive; others either aren't in a position to reciprocate or don't yet understand the give-and-take aspects of community living. Many of the families we've examined live with multiple stresses in their lives. Some find the support and services they need; others feel the need for more. Some are denied access to available resources.

Let's look at a summary of the kinds of institutions and programs available in varying degrees to most of these families.

A Summary of Community Resources

Though none of these families have needed police or fire protection lately, they all know that these two community services are available at the touch of the telephone push-buttons. They also know about the community resources that are available to enhance the quality of their lives—the parks and recreation department, the library, the local museum, and the 2-year community college, all of which have regular programs for adults and children.

Child care programs, Head Start and other early education programs, and schools, both public and private, provide education to all members of the family. Local hospitals and the county health department provide preventive care and health maintenance to varying degrees, including some perinatal services and a variety of health education programs. They also, of course, provide services for the sick.

Welfare, a big community resource designed to support people with children, underwent a major change in the 1990s. Welfare in the form of Aid to Families with Dependent Children (AFDC) became Temporary Assistance for Needy Families (TANF) in 1996 and has stricter requirements than the old system. Also, there is a time limitation. Training institutions are full of former welfare recipients getting themselves qualified for the job market. These changes in the system and new challenges to families have created more need for child care than ever before— especially for infant care.

Some other community resources are designed to support families in times of emergency and stress, such as child abuse prevention programs, which offer telephone hotlines, parent education services, and respite child care. Mental

Some community resources are available only to eligible families, but many, such as local libraries, are available to all.

health programs that offer therapeutic services and counseling programs are designed as short-term crisis intervention, and some provide long-term help to individuals and families as well. These programs periodically experience reduced funding, which makes them less effective at times. Families who can afford to pay for services continue, of course, to find them available. Substance abuse programs run by both professionals and volunteers also help people get on their feet and live satisfying and productive lives.

Most communities have a variety of support groups. Support groups can be both formal and informal and can respond to any number of needs: general parenting groups, women's and men's support groups, substance abuse, codependency, Overeaters Anonymous—you name it, there's a support group somewhere for it. Mrs. Jackson has even found a spina bifida support group that is attended by parents whose children were born with this condition. She found it through a local family resource network designed to offer support, information, referral, advocacy, and training to families in her community who have children with special needs.

Finding Community Resources

How do you find out what resources are available in your community? A simple way is to start with the phone book; some have a special section right in front. Or the library may have a listing. In some communities, a local organization such as Head Start or a child care resource and referral agency puts together and updates lists of resources that are available to families.

Of course, anyone who knows how to use a computer and surf the Internet can find countless resources right on the computer screen. For those without a computer, the local library can provide not only the computer but also some support and technical assistance to use the system.

Word of mouth is the way many families find out about the individuals and institutions that can serve them. If a family is connected to a child care center, the chances are someone on staff knows what's available for specific problems. In turn, families can help expand the teachers' knowledge of what's available in the community. Some programs have a rack of brochures from local community resources. Others put together lists of them and keep those lists updated.

Some families enter "the system" because of a crisis or a problem. That's the way they 't introduced to the world of accessible resources in their community. In some cities and s, a crisis center is available 24 hours a day to serve those who are in serious trauma, atever reason. Some communities also have women's shelters where the abused and 'dren can find refuge. Public health and mental health systems are usually also able to crisis situations.

often serve as counselors and advisers to individuals and families. They can nts to appropriate community resources for their particular problem.

It's not always easy to find just what you need—in fact, it is sometimes downright difficult. However, with persistence, you'll usually locate whatever there might be. Unfortunately, most communities lack the full range of resources that they need, and many families are left with solving their own problems or looking for help or support from relatives, friends, and neighbors.

Strategy Box 13.2 gives some ideas of how early educators can help families find the services they might need.

Availability of Community Resources

Although the list of community resources may be lengthy, not all are available in all communities. Even those communities that have a variety may not make them available to all families. What are some of the factors that determine availability of community resources?

Funding is one factor—often there's not enough to go around, or it's stretched so thin that no one program can do a good job of helping and supporting families.

Strategy Box 13.2

Helping Families Access Services in the Community

* At least one person in the program or school should become knowledgable about potential resources that might help families, such as federal earned income tax credit; state income and other tax credits; food stamps; child support income enforcement; child-related resources like health benefits; Medicaid or state child health insurance programs; and child care subsidies.
* When a program or school includes children with identified disabilities, make sure someone on the staff knows about early intervention of special education services. Parents can help inform the program.
* Team up with community organizations such as domestic violence, mental health, and substance abuse agencies to address prevention and treatment issues for vulnerable families.
* Consider expanding the mission of your program to become a human service center in your community.
* Increase advocacy along with parents and other groups at both state and local levels to improve funding for services that need expanding.

Lack of funding results in declining services and increased competition for limited resources.

Some programs serve a specific population, and families must qualify to be eligible to receive services. Furthermore, some families qualify for services but have no access to them because of lack of transportation or language barriers. (Or perhaps they don't even realize that such services exist.)

When families do connect with services available to them, they may find the services inappropriate to their need—sometimes because of cultural insensitivity on the part of the service providers. Lack of respect may be a factor when there's a mismatch between services and the families they are designed to serve. When clients are looked down on by the people who serve them, it's often because the agency is using a deficit model to define the people who come to them for help. This model may be quite out of tune with the reality of cultural or class differences.

Each of the community resources that families deal with has a spoken or unspoken set of goals and values. When these goals and values are in tune with those of the family, a match is made, and the chances are better that the support or intervention will be effective. Some goals and values are conscious, written into the agency; some are misinterpreted by outsiders, and some are unintended.

For example, one medium-sized town has two agencies serving pregnant women. One is Planned Parenthood, whose purpose is to offer a variety of services as well as counseling that allows women to make decisions that are right for them about family planning. Planned Parenthood is not just for pregnant women; it has a wide range of services for both men and women. It offers abortion as one of several options for pregnant women to consider.

On the other side of town is a group called Birthright, whose goal is to help pregnant women opt against abortion. They provide counseling and support to women who might otherwise find it difficult to have their babies, doing what they can to make it more attractive to continue the pregnancy than to end it. These two agencies, which serve the same population, have contrasting goals and values and are clear about their differences.

Usually an agency's goals are not so clear, and often families don't look beyond the offer of services to understand the agency's goals or value system anyway. Of course, they can find the agency's goals by examining incorporation papers, mission statements, or patterns of board policies. However, families do not usually set out to investigate the goals and value systems of the agency where they seek help or support. They may become aware of a lack of communication, a mismatch, or a lack of respect, which signals a goal or value conflict, but most of us don't even clarify our own goals or values very often, let alone compare them with those of an agency. However, goals and values do make a difference if we are to serve our community and be served by it. Goals and values are themes in the two chapters that follow.

LOOKING BACK AND LOOKING FORWARD

In this chapter, we looked at how the community supports families and provides resources through informal and formal social networks, institutions, and agencies. Examples of how six different families use the resources made up a good portion of the chapter. We ended with a look at goals and values, which are themes in the two chapters that follow.

FOR DISCUSSION

1. What do you know about the negative effects that isolation can have on families?

2. Name some social networks that you are acquainted with.

3. Give examples of how the families in this chapter might both use and contribute to community resources. Choose examples that haven't been mentioned in the chapter.

4. What would you tell a family about how to find the community resources they might need?

5. Do you know someone who needed a community resource, but it wasn't available to that person? Why wasn't it available? Do you know someone who used an agency that didn't fit their culture or their needs?

WEB SITES

Campaign for the Civic Mission of Schools
www.civicmissionofschools.org
Promotes strong community partnership components for K-12 classrooms and includes civic education.

Center of School, Family, and Community Partnerships
www.csos.jhu.edu/p2000/center.htm
Helps families, educators and community members work together to improve schools, strengthen families, and enhance student learning and development.

Marc Sheehan's Special Education/Exceptionality Page
http://www.halcyon.com/marcs/sped.html
A helpful site from which to research, this page contains many Internet links to special education-related sites.

National Association for the Education of Young Children
http://www.naeyc.org/members

The National Association for the Education of Young Children has created online communities on their Web site of members who share a common interest, which provide networking opportunities.

National Child Care Information Center (NCCIC)
www.nccic.org
Click on Popular Topics and next of Partnerships to find information about and links to community partnerships.

National Network for Child Care
http://www.nncc.org/
The National Network for Child Care is an Internet source of over 1,000 research-based and reviewed publications and resources related to children. This site includes articles, resources, and links on various subjects such as public policy/advocacy, health and safety, child abuse, diversity, and more.

FURTHER READING

Akbar, N. (2003). *Akbar papers in African psychology.* Tallahassee, FL: Mind Productions.

Bernstein, B. (1991). Since the Moynihan report. In R. Staples (Ed.), *The black family: Essays and studies* (4th ed., p. 24). Belmont, CA: Wadsworth.

Bennett, R. (2006, January). Future teachers forge family connections. *Young Children, 61*(1), 22–28.

Children's Defense Fund. (2004). *The state of America's children* 2004. Washington, DC: Children's Defense Fund.

Clark, K. E., & Ladd, G. W. (2000). Connectedness and autonomy support in parent-child relationships: Links to children's socio-emotional orientation and peer relationships. *Developmental Psychology, 36,* 485–498.

Duncan, G. O., & Brooks-Gunn, J. (2000). Family parenting, welfare reform, and child development. *Child Development, 71,* 188–195.

Dunst, C., Trivette, C., & Deal, A. (1988). *Enabling and empowering families.* Cambridge, MA: Brookline.

Edwards, P. A., & Jones Young, L. S. (1992, May). Beyond parents: Family, community, and school involvement. *Phi Delta Kappan, 73*(9), 72–80.

Families USA. (1999). *Losing health insurance: The unintended consequences of welfare reform.* Washington, DC: Families USA.

Fernea, E. W. (1995). *Children in the Muslim Middle East.* Austin: University of Texas Press.

Golden, O. (2000). The federal response to child abuse and neglect. *American Psychologist, 55,* 1050–1053.

Hale, J. E. (1992). An African-American early childhood education program: Visions for children. In S. A. Kessler & B. B. Swadener (Eds.), *Reconceptualizing the early childhood curriculum: Beginning the dialogue* (pp. 205–224). New York: Teachers College Press.

Hernandez, D., & Charney, E. (Eds.). (1998). *From generation to generation: The health and well-being of children in immigrant families.* Washington, DC: National Academy Press.

Ispa, J. M., Thornburg, K. R., & Fine, M. A. (2006). *Keepin' on: The everyday struggles of young families in poverty.* Baltimore: Brookes.

Karoly, L. A., & Greenwood, P. W. (1998). *Investing in our children: What we know and don't know about the costs and benefits of early childhood interventions.* Santa Monica, CA: Rand.

Kilgo, J. L. (Ed.). (2006). *Transdisciplinary teaming in early intervention/early childhood special education: Navigating together with families and children.* Association for Childhood Education International.

Lyons, J. D., & Russell, S. D. (1998). *Child care subsidy: The costs of waiting.* Chapel Hill, NC: Day Care Services Association.

Neighbors, H. W., & Jackson, J. S. (Eds.). (1996). *Mental health in black America.* Newbury Park, CA: Sage.

Parke, R. D., & O'Neil, R. (2000). The influence of significant others on learning about relationships: From family to friends. In R. S. L. Mills & S. Duck (Eds.), *The developmental psychology of personal relationships* (pp. 15–47). New York: Wiley.

Payne, R. K. (2003). *A framework for understanding poverty.* Highlands, TX: Aha Process.

Porter, K., & Primus, W. (1999). *Recent changes in the impact of the safety net on child poverty.* Washington, DC: Center on Budget and Policy Priorities.

Ritchie, S., & Willer, B. (2005) *Families and community relationships.* Washington, DC: National Association for the Education of Young Children.

Ross, A. C. (Ehanamani). (1989). *Mitakuye Oyasin: We are all related.* Denver: Wichoni Waste.

Saracho, O., & Spodek, B (Eds.). (2005). Contemporary perspectives on families, communities, and schools for young children. Greenwich, CT: Information Age Publishing.

Tan, A. L. (2004). *Chinese American children and families: A guide for educators and service providers.* Onley, MD: Association for Childhood Education International.

Tedla, E. (1995). *Sankofa: African thought and education.* New York: Lang.

United Nations Children's Fund. (2000). *The state of the world's children* 2000. New York: United Nations Children's Fund.

U.S. Department of Health and Human Services. (1999). *Eliminating racial and ethnic disparities in health: Overview.* Available on the Department of Health and Human Services Web site. (http://raceandhealth.hhs.gov/sidebars/sbinitOver.htm).

U.S. Substance Abuse and Mental Health Services Administration. (1999). *Summary findings from the 1998 National Household Survey on drug abuse.* Rockville, MD: U.S. Department of Health and Human Services.

Werner, E. E. (1995, June). Resilience in development. *Current Directions in Psychological Science,* 4(3), 81–85.

Werner, E. E., & Smith, R. S. (1992). *Overcoming the odds: High risk children from birth to adulthood.* Ithaca, NY: Cornell University Press.

Whirlpool Foundation. (1995). *Women: The new providers.* New York: Families and Work Institute.

White, E. (Qoyawayma, P.). (1992). *No turning back: A Hopi woman's struggle to live in two worlds.* Albuquerque: University of New Mexico Press.

CHAPTER 14

Societal Influences on Children and Families

In this chapter you'll discover . . .

- How bias affects young children
- That social class isn't as invisible as it seems
- The effect of school "tracking"
- Some things about kindergarten readiness that you probably never thought of
- How to decide by looking at a classroom whether the teacher celebrates diversity
- The influences of peer groups
- Some problems with expecting television to socialize children

The family is the first and major socializing agent, and as such it has responsibility for early socialization patterns. As the child grows and moves outside his or her home, other agents in the community come into play. In the past, outside agents were fewer; relatives, neighbors, religious institutions, and informal community networks shared a good deal of responsibility for socialization. Peers also played a part. Today television is usually the first socializing agent outside the family, with child care a close second. Later, school comes into the picture, with after-school activities and perhaps, eventually, clubs such as Boy Scouts or Girl Scouts. Peers are important as the child grows and become a strong socializing force. The socialization process today is shared. Other institutions such as hospitals, government agencies, and service industries may also come into the picture. These organizations have taken over many of the activities that were once the function of the family, the extended family or kinship network, and neighbors, all of whom used to make up the informal community.

This chapter looks at four major socializing agents: the family, the school, the peer group, and television.

SOCIALIZATION AND THE FAMILY

Because this book is devoted almost entirely to the family, you may be wondering why the family is also included here in these last two chapters, on the community. Because the family is such an important educational and socializing agent, family-related issues appear and reappear throughout the whole book. In this chapter, we look at the family's place in, and its interface with, society, and we examine the influence of the community on the family and therefore on the child.

All families belong to subcultures and networks that reflect their social class position, ethnic group membership, and, possibly, their kinship. These subcultures and networks influence the ways in which families socialize their children. The language the parents use, and sometimes insist that their children use, influences to some extent their ties to one group or another. "Speak Spanish," demands a mother who sees her children drifting away from their roots to dissolve into mainstream America. "Speak English," demands another, who sees language as a way to carry out her upward-bound goals. "Don't say *ain't*," admonishes another because she feels that's what uneducated people say, knowing that language helps people fit into the right group. "Gettin' kinda uppity, ain't ya?" asks another mother, who feels alienated by her son's new way of speaking when he comes back from college for the first visit home. She sees language as a divider.

In addition to social class and ethnic group, families are sometimes tied to other families through occupations or interests, which also affect children's socialization. The family that plays music together, for example, influences the socialization of their children differently from, say, a family that plays sports together. The experiences of the children in those two families may be quite different from the children of workaholic parents who are tied to their corporate "family."

Many families have a primary focus of attention; it may be religious activities, or school achievement, or even income opportunities. Some parents actively mold their children to their own interests by constantly involving them in specific activities. The family whose members devote themselves to nature and to ecology issues, for example, may be quite critical of a family that includes a nightclub comedian and his singer wife who spend most of their work and leisure time in bars at night in smoke-filled rooms, or a family that owns the manufacturing plant in town that has been suspected of polluting the environment. Parents also mold perceptions indirectly by the ways in which they evaluate others; children come to see which types of individuals their family prefers to associate with and who should be avoided.

Status—that is, the family's position in society—affects socialization and can in turn affect where children find themselves when they grow up. Children of wealthy families have a different set of experiences and expectations than, for example, children of poverty-level families. Consider the difference between a child born into a Beverly Hills family with two parents, four cars, and a pile of money compared with a child who was born in jail and who is sent to live with her grandmother in a run-down trailer park near the railroad tracks while her mother finishes serving a term for dealing drugs. Which child is most likely to grow up defining her choices as the "sky's the limit"?

The family not only gives the child status but also makes him or her aware of the status of others. Family members teach, whether consciously or not, whom to copy and whom not to copy. The message about the status of outsiders is clear in some families—who is considered "above" and who "below."

The "goodies" that society has to offer are more available to some children than to others. For some, privilege is a major socializing force; for others, privilege's counterparts—bias and discrimination—play that role.

The Issue of Bias

Bias is everywhere, and we've all felt its effects, though some of us are targeted more than others. We feel bias because of our gender, social class, skin color, ethnic background, the way we talk, our body type or physical condition, mental capabilities, age, sexual orientation, the amount of money or education our family has, or our family configuration, to name just a few of the factors.

Bias hurts everybody—especially children. It hurts those who are its targets because these children must put energy into struggling against the negative messages that they receive—energy that could be used for development. In addition, bias hurts them because they find their opportunities limited; doors are shut to them.

Bias also hurts those who are not targets but who believe that they and others like them are superior. This belief not only dehumanizes them but also distorts their reality. Bias is bad for everybody!

We need to become aware of our areas of privilege and how bias works. We need to become sensitized to help ourselves and others think critically and to speak up in the face of bias. The key is empowerment. Members of target groups must be empowered to develop a strong self- and group identity so they can stand up in the face of attack. Members of nontarget groups must also develop a strong self-identity, but without a feeling of superiority. Each individual must be free, and indeed encouraged, to develop to his or her full and unique potential.

Classism.   Let's look more closely at one area of bias—social class—by examining children from two families who are targets for classism.

The first child is Max, whose family is working class and proud of it. His father, Joe, is a truck driver, and his mother, Mary, is an assembly-line worker in a factory. Max lives with his parents and his two sisters, Sonia and Sally, in a modest house located in a working-class neighborhood that is at the bottom of the hill from a new upscale housing development. The school district drew new boundaries when they built the school for this area, and they included Max's neighborhood in the attendance area, so every day Max's sisters walk him to kindergarten before they go off to their own classrooms in the new elementary school they now attend.

The family is having some problems with what's happening as a result of the contact between their children and the children on the hill. Clothes are one of the problems. The girls feel they need different clothes from what they have always worn. Designer labels have become important to them. They complain that the kids won't like them if they don't dress right. Designer labels aren't an issue for Max. In fact, the rule is that children have to wear old clothes to preschool so they can experience all the sensory activities that the school offers (which tend to be messy).

The issue for Max is T-shirts. The program is doing fund-raising, and they want the families to buy the school T-shirt, which will then be worn on T-shirt Day. All the other kids have them, but the shirts cost a lot. T-shirts aren't the only fund-raising project going on. It seems that papers are always coming home from school announcing something to buy, sell, or donate to. For free public education, there seem to be a lot of expenses, like field trips that require the price of an admission ticket to go to plays or get in the museum. And the parties the children get invited to are expensive, too. Each one requires a present and usually transportation, which presents difficulties. Sometimes specialized equipment is needed, such as roller skates or sleeping bags for slumber parties.

Lately the parties have slowed down for Max and his sisters. That situation is good for the pocketbook but bad for the children's morale. They have begun to feel that they aren't good enough to associate with their classmates; they are starting to believe that that's why they aren't getting invited to parties. At the first open house at school, their parents began to understand their feelings. No one was warm or welcoming to them. When the parents started up a conversation with one couple in the preschool group about the building of the school, the man started complaining about how the school opening had been delayed because of a strike. He made it clear that he thought unions were the root of the economic problems in the United States. Joe told him that he was a union member and that was the end of the conversation. Joe and Mary remembered the old school where everyone was more like them and they felt at home. Here they feel out of place, and they wonder whether the other parents and the teachers are looking down on them.

Is what they are feeling real or just their imagination? It is hard to tell. Maybe some of both. Whether imagination or not, Joe and Mary have vowed to help their children feel good about who they are; they are determined to do what they can to help their children see that money doesn't buy happiness.

The other family we will examine has a different story. Peter, who is 4-years-old, was born into a middle-class family. However, soon after Peter's birth, his father left his mother. Daddy came back just long enough to make a baby brother before departing for good, leaving Peter's mother with two boys to raise. The family slipped into poverty practically overnight.

Although Peter's mother was raised with the values, expectations, and behaviors of the middle class, she has began to change as the effects of poverty mold her. She is unable to keep up with her previous lifestyle. When she was single and after she was first married, she used to enjoy lunch out with her friends; now her lunch hour is full of errands and appointments, and, anyway, she doesn't have the money to squander on a nice lunch. She struggles hard to remain on her former level, but try as she might, she is pulled down. She is beginning to feel strange around people who have so much more money than she does. She also feels strange around the other mothers whose children are in Peter's Head Start class. She doesn't seem to belong anywhere anymore.

She remembers how she and her friends used to criticize poor people who didn't keep their kids clean. "It doesn't cost anything to keep clean," she used to say. But she has discovered that it does. She has to go to the laundromat to do the laundry; that costs plenty—in money, time, and energy. And since her water heater broke, even bathing the boys is harder. She has called the landlord three times already to get it fixed, but she still had to go without hot water for four days.

The last straw came when she popped back into the child care center to leave the diaper bag she'd forgotten to drop off and found Peter's little brother being scrubbed down in the sink. She knew then that she'd crossed the line and had become one of the people she used to frown on. She remembers a conversation with a teacher friend about how some kids arrive at school so dirty and smelly that you just want to give them a good scrubbing. Now her own child had become one of them. She was embarrassed to tears—and angry as well. How dare they bathe her baby without her permission? He wasn't *that* dirty. She'd heated water on the stove and given him a sponge bath that very morning!

We don't know whether this mother is really experiencing a biased attitude. We don't know why the teacher was washing the child or how she felt about it. She perhaps thought she was doing the mother and the child a favor, but the mother perceived the action as an insult, maybe because she had once been on the other side of classism.

Being newly poor Peter's mother has experienced both sides of the poverty line. Some families have never been on the upside of it. They come from a long tradition of poverty and have never known anything else. They are used to people looking down on them and perhaps even blaming them for their poverty.

For some Americans, social class is hard to see, because we, as a society, deny the existence of such a thing. For a long period, the middle and upper classes were even able to pretend that social class didn't exist because they didn't see poor people before their very eyes. All that is rapidly changing; poverty shows everywhere. Poor people aren't tucked away on the other side of town anymore. They're apt to be downtown and even in the parking lots of shopping malls, holding up signs that say "Will work for food."

Social classes exist even though they aren't the permanent, set-in-stone phenomena we see in other countries. We still don't commonly call them *social classes*, though. Sociologists speak of "socioeconomic levels." Whatever you call them, there are differences in the experiences of the children who are raised at each level.

Social class is one factor in socialization and race is another; however, they are often lumped together. Social class may be ignored entirely, for example, when comparing cultural differences of African Americans and European Americans. Often poverty-level African Americans are compared with middle-class European Americans without acknowledging that there are class differences. It's important to be aware that there are poverty-level people and middle-class people in all cultural groups—and you can't just be blind to social-class differences.

Let's turn now to racism, which is another important factor in the education and socialization of children.

Racism.   Those who have experienced racism don't have to read about it to understand it. If you haven't experienced it, it's hard to understand to what extent it exists and what it feels like. It's easier for those who aren't a target of racism to understand it in terms of its counterpart, *privilege*.

Privilege can be thought of as an "invisible package of unearned assets," which it's possible to cash in on whenever it pleases the person carrying the privilege. Most of those who have it are quite unaware of their privilege; they regard it as the way things are. Those who don't have privilege are very aware of its lack. Privilege shows more in its absence than in its presence.

Let's look at the privileges that a 4-year-old white, middle-class child, Lindsay, enjoys because of her skin color:

> Lindsay doesn't have to represent "her people," who, in fact, are seldom lumped into one skin color category. If she arrives at preschool dirty, it's an individual family matter or perhaps attributed to her social class, but it doesn't reflect on white people in general. She can wear secondhand clothes. She can pick her nose or even use bad words, and it's her family that's reflected, not the white race. If her family gets her to school late, no one attributes it to either their genes or their culture. If she arrives at school tired, the teachers may blame the parent, but not anyone else. Lindsay's family has the privilege of representing only themselves, not reflecting or living in the reflection of stereotypes of a group of other people with their same skin color.
>
> Lindsay lives in the best neighborhood her family can afford; though money is, of course, a factor, it is not the major factor. They have the privilege of choosing where they want to live within their price range, and they made that choice assuming that their neighbors would display good or at least neutral feelings toward them. If they have alienated their neighbors, it's more likely because of something they've done rather than because of who they are.

Lindsay will come to see herself and her family as "normal," if she hasn't already. She sees herself and her people represented on television and in books, magazines, and newspapers. She easily finds the food her family eats in the local supermarket. Lindsay's mother can take her any-place she likes to get her hair cut and feel reassured that someone there will know how to cut it. When Lindsay is older and learns about history, she'll be shown that her people (or at least the males) made this country what it is.

Lindsay's mother doesn't worry about educating her children to detect racism. She doesn't even consider teaching them how to operate when racism is present or how to protect themselves from it.

Angelica and her twin brother, Mario, who go to Lindsay's preschool, have a different experience:

Angelica and Mario's mother is well aware of the possibility of racist attitudes toward her children. One of the antiracist strategies their mother uses is to send them to school fashion-ably dressed. The teachers sent Angelica home with a parent handbook the first day, with the sentence highlighted that said, "Please send your child in old play clothes." After a week, one teacher stopped the three of them as they were leaving and complained that it was hard for Angelica and Mario to participate in all the many and varied messy activities because of their clothing. She asked that they come in old clothes that didn't matter. The mother listened, but the next day Angelica arrived dressed in a new fancy dress and her brother in a starched shirt and a pair of slacks. The teachers never understood why their message didn't get through. If they had been able to have a heart-to-heart talk with this mother they would have discovered that she sees her children's appearances as reflecting on their family. She wants her children to look well cared for. She doesn't want her children to fit into any stereotypes that racists may have of her people. Although racists are everywhere, if Angelica and Mario are well dressed and look well cared for, it will be harder for some people to see them as inferior to other children. She is also well aware that clothes and grooming won't matter to a real racist who will only see skin color.

For Janice, the issue is hair:

Janice is the parent education coordinator at a fairly large child care center. One of the parents she has concerns about is Betsy, who is the adoptive mother of Lacy, an African American 5-year-old. Betsy doesn't know how to take care of her daughter's hair, and it bothers Janice a lot. She sends her in the morning looking uncombed. After nap time, she wakes up looking even worse. Janice has taken to combing Lacy's hair twice a day, on arrival and after nap. Lacy loves it! Janice keeps meaning to ask Betsy for a conference to explain to her some of the things she doesn't know about her daughter's hair. She also wants her to understand that an African American child can't afford to look as if nobody cares about her, even if it's not true. People will judge her, and her people!

These three stories show some of the factors that affect socialization. The child's race, family income level, and circumstances influence how others respond to him or her on a personal level.

The stories also provide examples of the problems that can arise when teachers and parents aren't partners. For early childhood programs to be positive socializing agents, the partnership model must be in place. Throughout this book the theme of parent-professional partnerships has been stressed. These stories show the sad effects when the teacher operates out of a one-way model where the teacher is in charge and the parent is the recipient of the teacher's knowledge and expertise. What's lacking in that model is the teacher's awareness and acceptance of the funds of knowledge families already possess when they bring their children to the program.

While personal racist attitudes affect children's socialization, there's another even more powerful type of racism that affects us all. That is the institutionalized racism that is built into the systems of our country that grew out of its history. If you think back to what you know about the early history of the United States, the preamble to the constitution, for example, it sounds wonderful—a country where all men are equal. You may be tempted to update that phrase and make it all people are equal, but that wasn't the original intention. The country's government was founded by white men and continues to be dominated by that same group of people. And it wasn't just any white man—it was property owners. They made laws that worked in their own favor. Today when you hear about corporations having "glass ceilings," that's an indication that only some people can rise to the top. The ceiling stops the "others." Only when we refuse to let this happen, only when we examine issues of equity and social justice at the deepest levels of our societal systems, can we eventually get rid of institutionalized racism. Since the beginning of our country, groups of people have worked to dismantle the built-in racism. They have made a difference, but there is still plenty of work to do.

A child's race, family income level, and circumstances can determine the kind of formal education that the child is likely to receive. We've already examined child care and early education in other chapters. Now we turn our focus to the public school system.

SCHOOLS AS SOCIALIZING AGENTS

This whole book focuses on the socialization of young children and the ways in which early care and education programs serve as socializing agents. This section explores subjects that haven't been covered elsewhere, such as public school expectations of behaviors and mismatches that occur when children arrive with behaviors that work elsewhere but not in school. Antibias curriculum is another aspect of school as a socializing agent that is discussed in this section, as well as the effects of testing on socialization. A large part of this section focuses on a huge issue in early childhood education that has an effect on socialization: kindergarten readiness. The readiness approaches become problematic when they are more concerned with the intellect and particularly academic skills without regard to the role that social-emotional development plays in "getting children ready." Socialization is affected when those pushing a narrow aspect of readiness fail to understand the implications of focusing on just one aspect of development and disregarding the others.

Some children arrive in kindergarten less ready to grapple with the kindergarten curriculum than other children. Sometimes this is merely a matter of developmental differences; in many cases, however, the different in readiness relate to other factors.

Some children, for example, enjoy a variety of early experiences that fit nicely into what they need for kindergarten. Other children's early experiences are different; for them, kindergarten presents an alien world. As a result of these differing experiences, children are sometimes labeled and separated into groups by their "abilities" (this is called *tracking*). If children are tracked and labeled early, their educational course is set, sometimes for life. That means some are given the message that they're learners—winners in the race called school. They

Schools are socializing agents.

tend to take the ball and run with it; they're successful. Others learn early that they're "slow," which they translate to mean "stupid"; they're losers. Once tracking begins, the educational opportunities become limited for some and expanded for others.

Getting into Kindergarten

Even getting into kindergarten may be an issue facing families who send their 5-year-olds off to public school. Public school administrators and teachers are under a great deal of pressure to provide accountability to government funding sources. Those who pay the bills want to be sure they're getting their money's worth. The way they determine accountability is through test scores, so testing has finally reached clear down to kindergarten and even into preschool. Two examples of accountability through testing are in Head Start and in No Child Left Behind (NCLB). As this edition is being written, changes are on the horizon in both arenas.

As a parent volunteer in my son's elementary school, I have seen the effects of testing on 5-year-olds. The day I helped with the standardized achievement tests in kindergarten stands out in my memory. The children were told not to be nervous and that this was nothing to worry about—a contradictory message because everything about the atmosphere that day said, "This is *very important*." In addition, the parents had been sent a notice to be sure that the children got a good night's sleep and a hearty breakfast every day during the week of the testing. So in some cases, the atmosphere both at home and in the classroom conveyed the message that tension existed around these events—that they were different from what the children usually experienced in kindergarten. Even though the children were told not to be nervous (which in itself makes one suspicious enough to be nervous), two cried, one threw up, and one had to go home with a headache. These events alone were enough to influence the test scores, not only of the afflicted group but also of the group not showing any symptoms.

Ready to Learn

A narrow and simplistic view of what "ready to learn" means focuses on teaching academics to young children. This view ignores the huge societal changes that need to come about to ensure that all children have an equal chance for academic achievement in school. To truly have an equal chance for school success we need to eradicate poverty, give everybody health-care benefits, ensure enough nutrious food, and provide decent housing. Focusing on early academics is a cheaper but far less effective road to school success than what the brain research indicates. Good health and social-emotional stability in the early years of life are the real road to later achievement. Cognitive development is vitally tied to the social-emotional realm of development (Lally, 1998; Shore, 1997; Zigler, Finn-Stevenson, & Hall, 2003). Instead of working toward a decent life for every child, the major societal approach is to use standardized tests to see who is behind in academic skills and then use remediation devices to catch them up. It will take a few years to discover that this band-aid approach won't work to take care of the wounds too many children in this country suffer in their early years.

It may not take years to discover the other problems inherent in basing educational systems solely around standardized tests. Testing works as a stratifying tool through cultural bias. Teachers, in order to raise their class test scores, find themselves "teaching to the test," which means they minimize problem solving and creativity in their classroom activities. The tests dictate what children need to know regardless of their knowledge, experiences, and cultural differences.

Kindergarten readiness, a hot topic among politicians, is also a hot topic among parents. With that in mind, let's look at how kindergarten readiness goes far beyond learning the ABC's and starts way back in infancy. Here are some general indicators that early childhood educators agree show that children are prepared to enter kindergarten:

1. *Children who are ready for kindergarten are those who feel good about themselves.* The problem is that much of the discipline used makes children feel bad about themselves. Children don't feel good about themselves by being made to feel bad. Discipline should not only leave self-esteem intact but should also actually raise it when adults use modeling, guidance, and feedback. Communication is an important part of discipline; adults should discuss feelings and behavior instead of criticizing the child. Adults who understand the importance of communication separate the child from the behavior, saying things like "I won't let you hit your sister—it hurts her" instead of "Stop that, you bad boy!"

2. *Children who are ready for kindergarten are those who gain knowledge from mistakes.* Some of the best lessons come from things that don't work. It's easy to take the lesson out of a mistake by rescuing children so they don't learn about consequences of

their actions. Or the opposite situation occurs when the adult reacts to a mistake with harsh punishment. When children become fearful of mistakes, they quit risking. Reasonable risks are good learning devices. The child who avoids them misses out on a lot of important lessons.

3. *Children who are ready for kindergarten can communicate.* They have lots of experience in talking and listening. They know how to carry on a conversation. A conversation means not just talking but listening and responding appropriately as well. Adults should start emphasizing communication early. Even infants enjoy conversations and taking turns "talking." They also play with language. As children grow older, keeping a playful attitude toward language helps encourage it.

4. *Children who are ready for kindergarten can weigh alternatives and make sound choices.* Visualizing alternatives and their consequences is an important life skill. Children who arrive in kindergarten with plenty of opportunities to practice this skill come better prepared. When the "prepared child" gets hit by another child, she asks herself, "What are some ways I can react, and what are the consequences of each?" The child without the ability to visualize alternatives just lashes back without thinking. Aggression in the face of aggression is a poor choice. Some children never learn that, unfortunately. Some children have no ability to imagine any response other than hitting.

5. *Children who are ready for kindergarten can concentrate and focus.* If they can't do that, the problem may be too much television. It might seem as though children develop a long attention span from watching television, because they are willing to sit and stare at it for hours. But turn it off and what happens? They don't know how to entertain themselves. We add to the problem by overscheduling their time. Children don't develop long attention spans when they are never allowed to just play for long periods, never free to follow their inclinations to get involved in something of their own choice, never encouraged to work at length on some project they are interested in (Elkind, 2007). Adults tend to interrupt children, hurry them up, get them going on the next event. Preschool programs can contribute to the problem if they keep children on a tight schedule, move them rapidly from one activity to another, and never give them a chance to work at length or in depth on anything.

The effect of linking accountability to achievement as proved by testing is to make teachers anxious to have only the most teachable children in their classrooms. Say a child enters in September who isn't ready to buckle down and do whatever the teacher, the school, the district, or the state considers kindergarten work (which more and more reflects the test items that will appear during the spring testing period). This child wants to play, and his motivation is so strong that it takes all the teacher's behavioral management techniques and more to get him to settle down to "seat work" for even a few minutes a day. It's easy to say this child isn't ready for kindergarten. And it's even easier to decide to determine readiness *before* the child enters and settles into the class. Therefore, some schools now have screening tests to decide who can come into kindergarten and who can't.

On the surface, that approach may make sense, but dig down just a little. Think about the child who has been at home with an overburdened parent for five years—a parent who doesn't have the time or the resources to contribute to his informal education. Is he better off spending another year in the same environment? Not that home can't be a rich and wonderful learning environment—it can, but by age 5 many children are ready to move out from home a little. In another case, the school may kindly advise the parent that the child needs preschool, but there is no money for a private one and no access to any other kind. Why can't this child go to the free public kindergarten that's offered conveniently close to home? Why can't the kindergarten *provide what he needs* rather than requiring him to fit a predetermined curriculum?

Think about the child who has been in preschool and has outgrown it. For three years he's participated in all the wonderful activities his preschool offered; he's taken part in a variety of field trips and many cognitive and socialization experiences. He's done it all, and now he's ready to move on. But he didn't "pass the kindergarten test," as his parents put it, so now they are trying to talk the preschool into enrolling him for a fourth year.

Think about the parents in an upwardly mobile family who consider education the key to their child's success and who are absolutely devastated to learn, as they put it, that "he flunked kindergarten before he even got in." Their expectations are shattered as they see the child they once considered bright defined, in their own minds, as "dull."

Classroom Behavior

Kindergarten readiness is one issue that closely linked to another—that of classroom behavior. Most public school classroom teachers depend on parents to send their children to school with ingrained behaviors that allow them to perform according to the rules and enable them to learn in the style the school sees as appropriate to the group size and the ratio of children to teachers. Some parents manage to comply with this expectation. And some children, even in spite of their parents or their home life, are willing and able to conform to what school requires. But other children aren't or can't. Expected school behavior may be quite alien to what's needed by some children at home and in the neighborhood where they live. Social skills taught at home may not work in school.

Consider the streetwise inner-city child who has learned, even by the age of 5, to survive by interpersonal skills that allow him to manipulate people and situations. He gets little chance to use those skills in school—except out of the teacher's sight during recess. Interaction during class time is strictly controlled, and certain expectations are enforced according to a set of rules. He comes to school self-reliant and independent, but his manner borders on defiance and that attitude gets him in trouble. He's also aggressive. He knows he can solve problems through physical action, but at school he finds he's expected to use words alone. "Fight back and don't tattle" is the rule at home. School rules are different: "Don't ever touch anybody; tell the teacher if you have a problem." The child who has incorporated the rule from home is going to have problems in school, starting right away in kindergarten.

It may seem reasonable to try to give this family a new set of child-rearing practices to help their child do well in school and eventually rise out of the circumstances the family is in—if not immediately, at least by the next generation. But the truth is that it's not easy to change child-rearing practices. And an outsider taking on such a task is taking on a good deal of responsibility unless he or she clearly understands how the child-rearing practices serve the culture, the family, and the child. In addition, it is quite difficult to get people to change how they are raising their children unless they have a special reason for wanting to change. Changes in child rearing tend to come *after* social and economic changes have come about.

In the meantime, this little streetwise child has a problem. If he conforms to classroom expectations, learns the rules, and takes them home to apply them, they won't work in the same way they do at school. Some children are flexible enough to learn a new set of skills and apply them where they work while keeping the old set for the times when the new set doesn't work. However, other children never adjust to the school environment.

Not all children who don't fit valued classroom behavior are physical and aggressive. Take the girl who finds herself in a classroom where self-direction, initiative, independence, and competitiveness are the skills stressed. These skills are the ones seen as functional to the higher-level, higher-paying, middle-class occupations and social positions. But the girl doesn't see the connection and perhaps has no expectations of growing up to work a high-level job anyway. She only knows that while the teacher is urging her to be special, to do well, to stand alone, to stick out, and to be a winner, all she wants is to fit in and be loved. She doesn't want more stars on her star chart than anyone else. She doesn't want to sit isolated and do her own seat work without talking or looking at someone else's paper. She wants hugs and attention from the teacher. She wants to sit on her lap at story time. She wants to socialize with her classmates. She wants the same warm group feelings that she gets at home. She wants to be a part of things, not separate and individual and alone.

This girl won't get in trouble like the little boy in the first example. She'll be thought of as sweet but probably not too bright (though she may, in fact, be quite intelligent). Eventually she will fade into the background and become invisible like the other children who don't give the teacher problems. Feeling that she doesn't fit in, she may give up on education early and find something else to do with her life. Or, less likely, she'll figure out how to learn even under the alien conditions of the classroom and end up going all the way through college as an invisible person, doing very well, but not drawing attention to herself (McKenna & Ortiz, 1988).

Responding to Diversity

When children arrive at school, they may or may not find a cultural environment that reflects themselves or the diversity of the American population. The school environment reflects the attitudes of the people who create it. If the teacher sees only the dominant culture as valuable and therefore worth recognizing, the classroom will show only white faces in the pictures on the walls, will acknowledge the heroes and holidays of dominant culture only, and will contain only books written for, by, and about dominant culture people.

Sometimes teachers who have this attitude don't realize the limitations of what they offer to children. If they are European Americans, they might not understand any culture but their own, which they naturally see as normal and right—the only way. Such culture-blind teachers may claim to be color-blind. In their attempt not to be bigoted, they ignore differences, thinking that noticing them shows prejudices.

Other teachers regard differences as important and take an ethnic studies approach toward acknowledging them. They accept and promote differences in an attempt to increase understanding and acceptance of them. Taking a "multicultural tourist" approach, these teachers may emphasize ethnic holidays, serve ethnic foods, and teach about customs, history, art, or artifacts of assorted cultures. This approach can make some children feel accepted who wouldn't otherwise feel that way, as well as broaden the view and experience of all the children in the classroom. A difficulty is that studying cultures in bits and pieces tends to trivialize or exoticize them. A multicultural tourist approach may also focus more on foreign cultures than on how those cultures have evolved when transplanted to the United States. This approach represents an add-on to the curriculum, rather than a change in it. The classroom reflects the multi-cultural tourist curriculum by having pictures displayed and books available that show, for example, African tribespeople, Balinese dancers, and Chinese New Year's celebrations. A typical theme for December in a multicultural tourist curriculum is "Christmas Around the World" or the broader "December Holidays," showing celebrations of Hanukkah, Christmas, the Santa Lucia Festival of Lights, and Kwanzaa.

Some teachers approach diversity in the classroom by looking at commonalties in the everyday world rather than just celebrations. "We're all ethnic and cultural beings—same and different at the same time" is the message. This approach may take the theme that we all have needs, but how we meet those needs varies. Teachers may have their children study, for example, ways of carrying babies or kinds of grains eaten by various cultures. Studying breads from around the world as a theme is an example of approaching diversity from the we're-the-same-but-different angle.

Other teachers—more and more since Derman-Sparks's book, *Antibias Curriculum*, came out in 1989—see the importance of changing their whole curriculum to reflect an attitude of respect and dignity toward differences. An antibias approach aims at true integration and equity, regarding empowerment as an issue. Teachers who use this approach teach their children to be sensitive to realities different from their own as well as to think critically about injustice. Antibias is not just a cognitive approach; it includes feelings and actions, too. A full antibias curriculum includes promoting equity for all aspects of human diversity—culture, race, ethnicity, gender, sexual orientation, ability, and age.

Inequity and Schools

How well children are educated and how good their school experience is for them depends on many factors, not the least of which is how many resources are available at the school they attend. Kozol (1991) wrote an eye-opening book called *Savage Inequalities* about the discrepancies between the funding of inner-city schools in poor districts and schools in richer districts. In a nutshell, his message is that many children are being cheated out of a decent education—they don't have a chance.

Inner-city children tend to arrive in kindergarten to find an overburdened teacher trying to handle too many children in a decaying classroom that is badly in need of repair. Equipment, if there is any, is run-down; materials and books are minimal. Children who live in the suburbs have a different experience. They arrive in kindergarten to find much better conditions, even though now, in these hard times, few schools enjoy an abundance of economic resources. Even so, some of the wealthier districts have twice the funding per child of poorer dis-tricts in the same geographic region. In addition, parents in those wealthier schools get heavily involved in serious fund-raising to augment the tax-based income. Parents who know how to fund-raise and have con-nections to wealth have moved far beyond little bake sales. We have great discrepan-cies in our public school system in America today. It's quite likely that the child of wealthy or even middle-class parents will get a much better education than the child of poor parents.

THE PEER GROUP AS AN AGENT OF SOCIALIZATION

Although the peer group is not as important for younger children as for older ones, it is nevertheless an influence. Who makes up the peer group for young children? Kids in the apartment complex, on the block, and in school or child care become friends and playmates. Sometimes the composition of the peer group is controlled by parents as they arrange to get their children together with other children by making play dates. The formal or informal play group is an example of this kind of peer group. Other times children form their own peer group.

Children don't play in groups at first, though they may interact a good deal with whomever is around. If you watch toddlers

Peers are a socializing force.

Frank Gonzalez-Mena

in a group situation, such as in an early care and education program, you find that they often play side by side—aware of each other but not interacting very often. One child might influence the content and actions of the another's play, but each remains headed in his or her own direction, carrying on a private conversation and individually involved with toys or materials. Then you see that more and more often these pairs of children begin to interact. Soon the pairs become threesomes, and the peer group begins to form, eventually becoming a solid group with activities, norms, interests, rules, traditions, expressions, and gestures of its own. The peer group becomes a subculture.

Children's choices of playmates are sometimes affected by gender. Children under age 7 may be willing to choose playmates of either gender, but most have a tendency to prefer those of their own gender. By elementary school this influence of gender on choice of playmates becomes notable (Maccoby, 1998).

To see the peer group influence, watch how something called *behavior contagion* works in a preschool classroom. One child starts screaming excitedly over something. In a few minutes the whole room is screaming and racing around after the leader who started it. Or one child starts swinging belly down on the swings, and soon all the swinging children have flipped over to prone positions.

Communication among peers can involve a very sophisticated set of signals. Watch a couple of 4-year-olds playing with action figures in a sandbox. Each knows what's pretend and what's not. Adults may not be so sure. When angry noises are heard from a distance, the protective adult may rush over to see what's happening only to discover that the children are just pretending. The children know it's pretend, but the adult wasn't sure—it sounded so real!

Usually adults don't teach children how to play pretend. Children learn informally from each other how to choose and sort out roles and characters, how to determine the direction the action will take, and how to signal when something is pretend and not real. They agree on all this as they go along, usually in a manner that's so smooth it's hard for outside observers to notice. David Elkind is worried that playing pretend is disappearing because of television and video games. Children don't seem to use their imaginations like they used to (Elkind, 2007).

Functions of the Peer Group

The peer group functions so that children learn to give and take as equals. That's a different lesson from relating to parents or teachers. The peer group has its own system of modifying behavior through rewards and punishments, which mostly come in the form of acceptance and rejection: "If you don't play nice, I won't invite you to my birthday party!"

Learning to get along with others who are your age and status is important. Developing relationships of one's own choosing is also important and is different from learning to get along with the people who just happen to be in your life because of the family you were born into.

The peer group also teaches a set of lessons that children don't get from adults; some of these lessons lie in areas that are sensitive and taboo. Much sex education comes from peers—whether parents and teachers like it or not.

The peer group serves as a step in developing independence, as children move out from their parents and family into a new set of circumstances. The group is centered around its own concerns and not necessarily bound by adult norms. It has its own hierarchy.

Another function of the peer group is to place the child in history. We don't recognize ourselves as members of a particular generation until we grow up and look at the generation coming up behind us. It is through the contrast that we identify ourselves as a generation of peers.

Adults can help children get along with their peers. Both teachers and parents can model desirable behavior, reinforce children when they display it, and coach children in social skills. Parents have a big influence on their children's peer relationships (Parke & O'Neil, 2000). A close attachment in infancy helps children develop social competency (Schneider, Atkinson, & Tardif, 2001). When parents interact with their children in ways that promote positive social behavior that takes feelings into account, the children tend to do the same with peers. When parents are negative and controlling in their interactions, such behavior can transfer to their children's interactions with peers and can make them less successful socially (Clark & Ladd, 2000).

THE MEDIA AS AN INFLUENCE ON SOCIALIZATION

Mass media—newspapers, magazines, comic books, radio, video games, movies, and especially television—present a very different form of socialization than any other, because they offer no opportunity for interaction. Television is an influence on children from a very young age and affects their cognitive and social development (Elkind, 2007; Wright et al., 2001).

Television is the medium with the greatest socialization effect, surpassing all the other media by far in its influence on the young child. The very fact that television is not an interactive agent is greatly significant to the development of young children. While watching, children have the feeling that they're interacting, but they're not. That's one of the disadvantages of television as a socializer—it satisfies social needs to some extent, but doesn't give children the social skills (or the real-life practice in those skills) that allow them to function effectively with people. Since the average child watches 3 to 4 hours of television a day, the time left for playing with others and learning social skills is drastically reduced. Even infants average about an hour and a half of television viewing a day between the time they are born and age 2 (Wright et al., 2001).

Of course, parents can control the time their children spend watching television, but many don't. They can monitor the selection of programs, but some allow their children to watch whatever happens to be on. Some parents don't consider how they can use television to teach decision making. They don't make children aware that when one program ends they can either weigh the various merits of the next offerings or turn the set off. Some children, especially those with a remote control in hand, flick through the channels periodically, randomly stopping at whatever catches their interest at the moment. That's very different from critically examining options and

Television is a passive form of socialization and replaces real interactions in many young children's lives.

consciously deciding on one. This is where parent education could be effective. Some parents who grew up with television themselves haven't given much thought to the effects of that medium, and how to decrease these effects.

Children learn through watching television. Some of the things they learn are beneficial; others are not. They learn about the world and the ways of the society. They learn something about occupations, for example, getting an idea about what a nurse does, what a doctor does, and how the two relate to each other. They learn about the institutions of the society—what goes on in court, for example. They learn the language to go with these roles and settings—and they learn some language you'd rather they didn't know!

Children also learn about current themes and issues, both from newscasts and dramas—issues such as kidnapping, the homeless, and the spread of AIDS. Most of these issues and themes are not happy ones, and many are very frightening, especially when children watch programs that are intended for adults.

Children learn more than facts from television; they also get a good daily dose of stereotypes and a lot of misleading information about their world. Most of all, they get a big helping of violence and another of commercial advertising.

Television and Young Children

The following list of television guidelines may seem drastic and unrealistic, but television has a powerful impact on children, so drastic measures to counteract it are called for.

1. *Don't expose infants to television.* Don't use television as entertainment, and don't get in the habit of using it as a babysitter, no matter how tempting it is to do so. Infants are distracted by the disconnected noise and movement of television. They don't need distractions; they need personal interactions with people and objects in the real world. With the 24-hour television channel just for infants, it may seem as if some research says that television is educational for babies. There is no such research!

2. *Examine your own television habits.* If you are addicted to the tube, the chances are any children around you while you are watching will also become addicted. Deal with your own addiction and take precautions so that children don't become TV addicts.

3. *One way to avoid the risk of addiction in children is to avoid exposing them to television altogether.* Children grow up just fine with no TV. If you decide you want children exposed, do it with caution and awareness. Don't turn the TV on and flip channels. Using a TV guide, make a conscious decision about what program to watch, turn the set on to watch it, and then turn it off when it is over.

4. *Sit with children while they watch television.* Then you are there to handle feelings, explain what needs explaining, clarify any confusion, and clear up misconceptions. You are also there to turn off the set when the program is over.

5. *Whatever you do, don't let children fill their time with television.* Active play should be the major pastime of the early years, not uninvolved visual entertainment.

These guidelines have been used by adults with good success. If you grew up with TV in your life and have never been without it, consider trying two weeks without TV; you'll find it makes a positive difference in your life, once you get over your withdrawal symptoms. Getting loose from the clutches of the tube will also make a positive difference in young children's lives.

Using these guidelines, educators could set up meetings with parents to discuss television and its effects on children. Some of the parents might be interested in trying the two weeks without TV approach. Some parents probably have already made wise decisions about their children's television viewing, and these parents can be important parts of this discussion. From this discussion, an advocacy movement might develop, which is discussed later in this chapter and also in Chapter 15.

Commercial Advertising

What's wrong with commercials? They're compelling, eye-catching, and more interesting than a lot of programming. What's wrong is that they create artificial needs in children (and, indeed, in all of us). They are as manipulative as they can be, coaxing us, practically forcing us, in subtle ways, to go out and buy, buy, buy. They teach consumerism very effectively.

If you want to see how effective television commercials are, stand in the cereal aisle of a grocery store for just 10 minutes and watch the interactions between parents and children. None of the child's biological signals related to nutritional needs are in play in the cereal aisle. In fact, even if the shelves were rearranged so the most nutritious cereals with the least additives were at children's eye level, little hands would be reaching and pointing at the familiar sugar-filled cereal boxes they know so well from television. In one study, children indicated that they had successfully influenced their parents' buying decisions (Tinsley, 2002).

Helping parents discuss the effects of advertising on children can give them new views of how consumerism manipulates us all. Some parents have already thought a lot about this and can be resources to other parents who are just beginning to think about it.

Violence

Turn on the television set during prime time, and, unless you select your programs carefully, you're likely to see an act of violence within five minutes and several more not too long afterward. Saturday morning is even worse. Eight of 10 programs contain violence, with prime-time programs averaging five violent acts per hour and Saturday morning cartoons averaging about 20 per hour. The average child in the United States has seen 8,000 murders and 100,000 other violent acts during childhood (Bushman & Anderson, 2001). The American Psychological Association, the American Academy of Pediatrics, and other major associations warn parents to keep their children away from mass media violence. Video programs, televison programs, and the nightly news all contain content that's not good for children. Why so much violence and sex? Those things are interesting—and interest sells products—so we get exposed to a good deal of it. The question is: What does all this do to children?

For one thing, research shows that viewing violence influences children in a way that makes them more likely to become violent (Anderson et al., 2003; Singer & Singer, 2005). Watching violence eventually desensitizes us all. If it didn't, how could people sit and eat a meal while watching people in living color be tortured, mutilated, shot, and even blown sky-high before their very eyes? That's enough to turn one's stomach, yet children get used to it by watching television, DVDs, and playing video games.

Years of studies show that television watching and aggression go together. Children who watch more television are more aggressive. However, it's hard to tell whether television *causes* the aggression or whether children who are more aggressive just tend to watch more television. However, some experimental studies show that children who are exposed to a violent televised episode are more aggressive when they are put immediately into a real-life anger-provoking situation. These children show more physical aggression than children who watch something nonviolent before being put into the same situation. In a classic study by Bandura and Walters (1963), children modeled the behavior of adults they saw on films punching an inflated "knock-down" figure. Many other studies since have shown similar results.

Television viewing of violence and real-life violence are connected. A long-term study followed 300 boys for 30 years. The boys who watched more TV violence at age 8 were involved in more espousal violence and more criminal violence by age 32 (Huesmann & Miller, 1994).

One way to discover the effects of television on children is to study a group of children who have not been exposed to television and then observe them after television comes into their lives. Such a study was done in northern Canada in a remote place where television hadn't yet penetrated. Then, when television was introduced, researchers were able to make comparisons. They found that violent behavior increased in both boys and girls (Hirsch, 1997).

If we want to confront violence in our society, we must pay attention to these kinds of studies. We must regard television as the dangerous device it is and bring it under conscious control. We must not let it continue to influence children in negative ways. The children slouched in front of sets today are the ones who grow up to be tomorrow's citizens. What kinds of citizens will they be?

This is not just a concern for families, but also for the community, for the society. Violence affects all of us. There was a time when the society took charge of protecting children from the media. The Federal Communications Commission (FCC) put regulations into effect in the 1930s, regulations that were strengthened enough by the 1960s to protect the first of the television generations. These regulations allowed intervention in cases where children were exposed to commercial exploitation or other forms of abuse by the media. The idea was to ensure that television provided for social good, rather than increasing social ills. When the FCC deregulated television, that protection disappeared; the protection is now left up to families, many of whom are not aware of the problems with unmonitored TV watching by children. It's time now to reinstate those regulations. We allow other regulating bodies to protect our children from unhealthy influences. It's time to allow the FCC to continue to do the good work they started. When children watch TV violence they see that violence is acceptable, and some of them begin to use violence themselves as a way to solve problems and deal with conflict (Bushman & Huesmann, 2001). Television is a strong social force. It needs to be used in growth-enhancing ways (Carlsson-Paige & Levin, 1990). If you have a parent or group of parents in your program who are emotional about this subject of mass media, maybe they can become advocates (if they aren't already) and help change things.

Television is a powerful teaching tool because it is in virtually every home across the nation. Whether you're focusing on the negative or the positive effects, or both, it's easy to see that television viewing influences the knowledge, behavior, and attitudes of children. If the lessons are to be beneficial, the positive aspects of the medium must be emphasized and attention must be paid to the negative, because unmonitored watching can teach racial and gender stereotypes, ideas about sexual relationships, and aggressive sexual behavior (Signorelli & Morgan, 2001), as well as general aggression and violence—all while commercially exploiting young children. When adults concern themselves with what children are watching and for how long, TV can be a teaching tool. The tool works best when adults watch with children, explaining to the children what they don't understand and putting a moral light on what children watch. To be an effective early teacher, television must increase developmentally appropriate and growth-enhancing options for children. In addition, parents must become aware of its potential—both good and harmful. A strong campaign of parent education is needed. Imagine the good that could come of a national conference on children's television that could provide opportunities for media representatives to talk with children's advocates, educators, parents, and sponsors about television strategies to work for the good of children and society (Boyer, 1991). See Strategy Box 14.1 for ideas about how to encourage parents to become advocates.

Strategy Box 14.1

Encouraging Parents in the Role as Advocate

- Encourage parents to be advocates for their own children. Each child should have his or her own family as a champion!
- When a parent stands up for his or her own child, appreciate that behavior. Yes, it's a kind of bias, but it's a healthy kind. Support parents in their role as advocate.
- When a family's advocacy efforts conflict with your perspective or program policy and practice, remember to keep their perspective in mind. Remind yourself that it's good for them to advocate for their child.
- Be flexible. Acknowledge that there are whole realms of possibilities in addition to what you do or what you believe in.
- Recognize that advocating for one's own child is a preliminary step to becoming an advocate for the group and from there advocating for all children. Children need advocates. They can't advocate for themselves.

To summarize, television influences the socialization of children in a number of ways. It replaces active involvement with the world and the people in it, giving children little chance to learn and practice a variety of social skills. The average young child who watches four hours of television a day misses out on his or her full share of early *active* learning. Television also replaces real needs with artificial ones that are created by product manufacturers and distributors to get children to want, want, want. And it affects children's behavior through the sheer quantity of violence that is portrayed.

Television has benefits, too, especially when adults concern themselves with what children are watching and for how long. It can be a teaching tool when adults watch with children, explaining what they don't understand and putting it into a moral context.

Whether you're focusing on the negative or the positive effects, or both, it's easy to see that television viewing influences the knowledge, behavior, and attitudes of children.

LOOKING BACK AND LOOKING FORWARD

This chapter looked at four major socializing agents: the family, the school, the peer group, and television. Throughout this chapter and the preceding ones, a number of societal issues concerning the socialization of the young child were mentioned. A beginning discussion of advocacy was included here under the subject of television. The next chapter wraps up the book by exploring how public policy relates to these issues and how to be advocate.

FOR DISCUSSION

1. What other socializing agents can you think of besides the four discussed in the chapter?

2. Give an example of how the status of the family affects the child's socialization. Give an example of how being the target of bias can affect socialization.

3. How can a family's income level affect the way its children are socialized?

4. Do you know someone who was "tracked" in school? How did that experience affect that person?

5. How are children expected to behave in kindergarten? Do you know a child who doesn't behave that way? Why doesn't he or she? How might that behavior affect that child's kindergarten performance?

6. What would you expect to find on the walls of a kindergarten room where the teacher had an antibias curriculum?

7. What are your feelings, ideas, and experiences in relation to television and young children? How do they relate to what the chapter said about television? What do children learn from watching TV?

WEB SITES

American Academy of Pediatrics (AAP)
http://www.aap.org/
This site contains information regarding health and safety issues for young children.

Center for Law and Social Policy
www.clasp.org
Part of their work focuses on early care and education promotes policies that support child development and the needs of low-income working parents on expanding availability of resources for child care and early education initiatives.

Connect for Kids
http://www.connectforkids.org/
Run by the Benton Foundation, this child advocacy group offers information on various issues concerning children.

Future of Children
http://www.futureofchildren.org/
The Future of Children seeks to promote effective policies and programs for children by providing policymakers, service providers, and the media with timely, objective information based on the best available research.

Healthy School Communities Program
www.healthyschoolcommunities.org
Works to refocus public discussion about education from an academic to a whole child approach that includes strong collaborations between schools and local community organizations.

Kids Health
http://kidshealth.org/parent/positve/family/tv_affects_child.html
This page provides information for parents about how television affects children.

Limit TV, Inc.
http://www.limitv.org/
Lots of information is here about the harmful effects of excessive television watching on children and ways to address the problem.

Media Literacy Online Project
http://interact.uoregon.edu/MediaLit/mlr/home/
This group's goal is to provide information and research related to the influence of media on children, youth, and adults. The webpage lists many resources on the subject.

National Center for Children in Poverty (NCCP)
http://www.nccp.org/
Located at the Columbia School of Public
Health, this center offers media resources,
publishes a newsletter, does research on child
care and early education, and has information
on child poverty.

National Institute on Media and the Family
http://www.mediafamily.org/
This organization conducts research on the
media's impact on the family and provides some
interesting statistics. Discusses how to use media
wisely.

National Network for Child Care (NNCC)
http://www.nncc.org/
The National Network for Child Care is an Internet
source of over 1,000 research-based and reviewed

publications and resources related to children.
This site includes articles, resources, and links
on various subjects such as public policy/
advocacy, health and safety, child abuse,
diversity, and more.

University of Michigan Health System
http://www.med.umich.edu/1libr/yourchild/tv.htm
Information is provided here about specific effects
on children (based on research) of commercial
advertising, violence, stereotyping. Television can
affect brain development and contribute to sleep
problems, behavior problems, and obesity.

World Health Organization (WHO)
http://www.who.int/
The World Health Organization delivers information
on health topics such as diseases and environmental
health hazards.

FURTHER READING

Boutte, G. S., LaPoint, S., & Davis, B. (1993,
November). Racial issues in education: Real or
imagined? *Young Children*, 49(1), 19–23.

Bushman, B. J., & Anderson, C. A. (2001). Media
violence and the American public: Scientific
facts versus media misinformation. *American
Psychologist*, 56, 466–489.

Bushman, D., & Huesmann, L. R. (2001). Effects of
televised violence on aggression. In D. Singer &
J. Singer (Eds.), *Handbook of children and the media*.
Thousand Oaks, CA: Sage.

Byrnes, D. A., & Kiger, G. (Eds.). (2005). *Common bonds:
Anti-bias teaching in a diverse society*, 3rd ed Olney, MD:
Association for Childhood Education International.

Clark, L., DeWolf, S., & Clark, C. (1992). Teaching
teachers to avoid having culturally assaultive
classrooms. *Young Children*, 47(5), 4–9.

Derman-Sparks, L., & Ramsey, P. G. (2006). *What if all
the kids are white? Anti-bias/Multicultural education
with young children and families*. New York: Teachers
College Press.

Lally, J. R. (1998, May). Brain research, infant
learning, and child care curriculum. *Child Care
Information Exchange*, 121, 46–48.

Maccoby, E. E. (1998). *The two sexes*. Cambridge, MA:
Harvard University Press.

National Research Council and Institute of
Medicine. (2000). *From neurons to neighborhoods:
The science of early childhood development*. Board
on Children, Youth, and Families, Commission
on Behavioral and Social Sciences and
Education. Washington, DC: National
Academy Press.

Parke, R. D., & O'Neil, R. (2000). The influence of
significant others on learning about relationships: From family to friends. In R. S. L. Mills
& S. Duck (Eds.), *The developmental psychology of
personal relationships* (pp. 15–47). New York:
Wiley.

Schneider, B. H., Atkinson, L., & Tardif, C. (2001).
Child-parent attachment and children's peer
relations: A quantitative review. *Developmental
Psychology*, 37, 86–100.

Shonkoff, J. P., & Phillips, D. (2001, April–May). From
neurons to neighborhoods: The science of early
childhood development—An introduction. *Zero
to Three*, 21(5), 4–7.

Shore, R. (1997). *Rethinking the brain: New insights in
early development*. New York: Families and Work
Institute.

Signorielli, N., & Morgan, M. (2001). Television
and the family: The cultivation perspective. In

J. Bryant & J. A. Bryant (Eds.), *Television and the American family* (2nd ed., pp. 333–351). Mahwah, NJ: Erlbaum.

Tinsley, B. R. (2002). *How children learn to be healthy.* New York: Cambridge University Press.

Wright, J. C., Huston, A. C., Murphy, K. C., St. Peters, M., Pinon, M., Scantlin, R., & Kotler, J. (2001). The relations of early television viewing to school readiness and vocabulary of children from low-income families: The early window project. *Child Development, 72,* 1347–1366.

Zigler, E. F., Finn-Stevenson, M., & Hall, N. W (2003). *The first three years and beyond: Brain development and social policy.* New Haven: Yale University Press.

Zillmann, D., Bryant, J., Huston, A. C. (Eds.). (1994). *Media, children, and the family: Social scientific psychodynamic, and clinical perspectives.* Hillsdale, NJ: Erlbaum.

CHAPTER 15

Social Policy Issues

In this chapter you'll discover . . .

- More about "ready to learn" and "no child left behind"
- What health and nutrition have to do with children's success in kindergarten
- The effects of poverty on the lives of children and families
- A proposed "children's movement"
- The directions in which child care policy should move
- How "prevention" is more cost-effective than "remediation"
- How to be an advocate for children
- The terrible effects of violence on children and families
- The role of the early educator as a peacemaker

This book has looked at the ways in which families and their early childhood education partners educate and socialize children within a community context. Along the way we examined various obstacles that interfere with the rights of all children to an effective education and healthy socialization process, obstacles that include poverty, lack of access to quality education and child care, and the media.

What can we do, as a society, to address these issues? What can the community do to ensure that all children get an equal chance to develop high self-esteem and fulfill themselves in this society? How can we help all children "make it"? This chapter examines social policy issues that relate to these questions.

WHO IS RESPONSIBLE FOR AMERICA'S CHILDREN?

An underlying social policy on which this nation was founded is that families are responsible for their own children. However, it is becoming clearer and clearer that, although families must still take primary responsibility for their children, many families are not, at present, able to be completely self-sufficient. It's not that these families care any less about their children than more self-sufficient families do; it's just that they find themselves in circumstances that prevent them from being able to meet all their children's needs. The question is: If families can't meet their own children's needs, how much will the society take over the responsibility for those unmet needs?

The future of our country depends on providing for the needs of America's children—all of our children. If we've reached a place in our economic, political, social, and moral history where masses of children are neglected, it's time for us, as individuals and as a society, to change that situation.

What's keeping us from putting forth a giant effort to meet the needs of America's children—of *our* children? One often unspoken theory behind the society's reluctance as a whole to put forth monumental effort to improve the lives of all its citizens is the idea that we each get what we deserve. This perspective justifies leaving things as they are. Those who are society's successes, the top of the heap, are given credit for their ability to work hard and be rewarded; the people who fall to the bottom are seen as not having tried hard enough. The view is that the people who live on the crumbs at the bottom of the barrel were born with the same chances of getting the whole contents of the barrel as everyone else. On the surface that may seem to be true. After all, this is America, land of opportunity, home of the free. But let's look at whether all babies are, in fact, born with the same opportunities.

Does Every Child Get an Equal Start?

Let's examine the situations of three pregnant women who live 20 miles apart from each other: the first, a 16-year-old who lives with her mother and two sisters in a run-down two-room apartment in a gang-ridden neighborhood at the edge of a decaying industrial section of a large city; the second, a 25-year-old who lives with her jobless husband in a small duplex in the older part of a suburban area; and the third, a 28-year-old who lives with her executive husband in a single-family home, surrounded by grass and flowers on a pleasant tree-lined street in a newer development in the sprawling part of the outer suburbs.

The 16-year-old's baby starts out already behind because of her mother's age, physical condition, and situation, which includes lack of prenatal care, poor diet, the stress of living in poverty, and the industrial pollution of the neighborhood. The second woman's baby also starts out behind because when her husband lost his job, they lost their insurance and medical benefits, so she's not getting prenatal care either. In addition, she supports the family by working in a child care center for minimum wage, which barely pays the rent, let alone utilities and food. This family is sometimes hungry. The wife receives no benefits from her job, except for sick leave, which she has used up because of frequent illness from being exposed to the numerous childhood illnesses common at the child care center at which she works. She worries constantly about the family's financial condition, about her husband, who is deeply depressed, and most of all about her baby. The third woman's unborn

Laura Vitale

What's keeping us from putting forth a giant effort to meet the needs of our children?

baby gets all she needs before she is born, including good food, plenty of prenatal monitoring, and a relatively healthy and peaceful environment.

Which of these babies will even be alive at the end of the first year? The chances are excellent that one will, but the other two face the risk of dying before their first birthday. According to Shames (1991) in *Outside the Dream: Child Poverty in America*, the United States ranked 19th in the industrialized world in the infant mortality rate—which is the number of babies who die before their first birthday. By comparison, 14 years later, the United States dropped even further, ranking 25th in infant mortality rate. The drop was not just because the other nations are making gains on the United States. It's also because in 2002 the infant mortality rate in this country rose for the first time in more than 40 years, from 6.8 deaths per 1,000 births to 7.0 per 1,000 (*The Children's Defense Fund Year Book: State of America's Children* 2005). How could that be, with all our technology and scientific advances, including new vaccines, organ transplants, cancer treatments, and improvements in neonatal intensive care?

True, we have technology for sick and premature babies. We save lives, especially in dramatic cases. But the poverty factor enters in. Babies born in many families still die before their first birthday. To assess the situation, you have to look closer at the statistics. Throughout the Children's Defense Fund Yearbook (2004), statistics are given showing the differences between the lives of children of one group compared to others. For example, black infants die at more than twice the rate of white infants (p.180). Are all children, then, born with equal opportunities in the United States?

What about when these three babies reach kindergarten? What are their relative chances of entering public school "ready to learn," as the saying goes—or "ready to succeed in public school," which is a better way to put it? Their chances aren't good if you consider health risks. As a nation we seem to be going backward as far as health goes. According to the Children's Defense Fund (2005), for the first time in United States history, the projected life expectancy for children may be less than that of their parents. States have been cutting back on Medicaid coverage for children, and enrollment in the State Children's Health Insurance Program decreased in 2003. A record 45 million adults are uninsured, an increase of 1.4 percent for the period between 2000 to 2003. Maybe you think that children who are uninsured have parents who aren't working, but listen to this! Almost two thirds of all uninsured children have at least one parent who works full-time throughout the year! Employment does not guarantee health benefits.

What about early care and education programs? Those can help children succeed when they reach public school. But again, according to the Children's Defense Fund, low-income children are much less likely than their higher-income peers to have access to early childhood programs. Though three out of four mothers with children under the age of 18 participate in the labor force (compared to just under half in 1975) only one in seven of the 15 million children eligible for federal child care assistance actually receive it. More than three million children eligible for Head Start and Early Head Start are not served. Which of the babies of the three pregnant women is most likely to arrive at kindergarten prepared? Any guesses?

READY TO LEARN: A GOAL FOR ALL OF AMERICA'S CHILDREN

Ready to learn—what does that mean? In the preceding chapter it was pointed out that readiness is far more than teaching 4-year-olds across the nation their ABC's. Readiness means that children must get their basic needs met—food, shelter, health care, security, and peace in the family. They need to know how to make connections with others, cooperate, get along, and feel good about themselves and others. Socialization is an important part of learning, and learning is an important part of socialization. All children need a variety of early experiences that enrich their minds, tickle their curiosity, fill their hearts, and enliven their spirit. They need adults in their lives who understand developmentally appropriate practices and cultural sensitivity and encourage them to embrace learning joyfully.

Let's look again at this issue of "ready to learn," which was a goal put forth in the early 1990s by President George H. Bush and agreed on by the governors of all 50 states. The goal was stated: By the year 2000, every child in America should start school ready to learn. Did we reach that goal? When George W. Bush took over the White House, his motto was No Child Left Behind. Another worthy goal, but although numerous programs are in full swing across the nation today, indications are that we haven't yet come close to the point that all children start kindergarten on an equal footing and that no children are left behind. Why not?

First, what does "ready to learn" mean, anyway? Anyone who has studied infancy and learning knows that babies are born ready to learn. If we couldn't tell by observation, we now have impressive brain research to back up what a lot of people knew before technology got so advanced (see Shore's 2003 book, *Rethinking the Brain: New Insights into Early Development*). Babies have a lot of learning to do, even in their first year, and in most cases, they come fully equipped to do that learning. What happens early in life can get in the way though. Bruce Perry (2006) had studied the effects on the brain of the stress in the lives of children from infancy on. The actual structures of the brain can be changed by unfortunate events during infancy, or even by witnessing unfortunate events. The brains of those children may be less able to learn than children who had no early ongoing trauma in their lives. So it was a bit naive of Bush (the elder) to think that learning starts in kindergarten and of George W. to think that all it takes to get children up to par is to put pressure on teachers. Besides, education programs designed to ensure that no child is left behind are severely underfunded, and one-size-fits all education policies have the effect of discriminating against poor and minority students and have proven to play a significant role in promoting school failure and an increased dropout rate (Children's Defense Fund, 2005).

Rob Reiner, Hollywood producer and entertainer, is an example of what one person can do if he or she has enough motivation and connections. He wasn't thinking "kindergarten" when he put together a huge campaign to bring the results of the brain research to parents and early educators in this country in the late 1990s. An early effort of his was a television special called "I Am Your Child" that showed an array of Hollywood stars telling the nation's parents, early childhood educators, and policy makers that the first years last forever. What happens in those early years makes all the difference. Later that same year, Reiner passed out 7,000 free copies of a videotape with the same theme to participants at the National Association for Education of Young Children annual conference in Anaheim, California. The campaign has continued and has expanded. For instance, in 1998 Rob Reiner's campaign supported an initiative on the ballot in California (called Prop 10) to place a 50-cent tax on cigarettes, a tax that would go to promoting child development in the early years. The voters passed the tax. Today councils in every county in the state have what is called First Five programs, which use their share of the tax money to support the healthy development of children five years of age and under. We don't have to look only to government to make things happen. It's remarkable what a private citizen can do to make a difference.

So the "ready to learn" campaign took avenues beyond what former President Bush and the governors had in mind in the 1990s. And it all started long before anybody was looking at the face of the new millennium and before George H. Bush had the idea. Early childhood educators have been working for 100 years to make things better for children and families. Their work came to public attention in the 1960s when Head Start began its project of trying to enhance the lives and learning of young children growing up in poverty.

Head Start

Head Start was originally conceived as a quick catch-up summer school program that would teach low-income children in a few weeks what they needed to know to start kindergarten. But once it was determined that you can't make up for five years of poverty with a six-week preschool program, Head Start expanded far beyond its original beginnings.

Head Start has been successful in its efforts to meet many of the needs of the population it serves. As an early childhood program that goes beyond educating children, Head Start has had a comprehensive approach designed to provide services that address a variety of family needs. These services have made a difference in the lives of young children and their families. Head Start continued to evolve to do an even better job by expanding and modifying its program to meet even more needs. An original weakness was that Head Start didn't have models that responded to the needs of teen parents and working parents. That changed over the years, and Head Start was doing a great job of meeting these needs—but, unfortunately, changes and funding cuts have put Head Start into turmoil. The program served 912,000 children in 2003, but that represents only 3 out of 5 eligible children (Children's Defense Fund, 2004). Originally conceived as a prekindergarten program for 4-year-olds, Head Start has moved downward to serve families of younger-aged children. Early Head Start grants are now being used to provide services to infants and toddlers, pregnant women, expectant fathers, parents, and guardians. The goal is to help families fulfill parental roles and move forward toward economic independence while providing for their children's physical, social, emotional, and intellectual development.

Head Start's purpose has always been to involve low-income families in the solutions to their own problems by empowering them politically and economically, instead of just offering them services. From the beginning, Head Start was not just a preschool, but a comprehensive program, though everytime its funding comes up for renewal, there's a call to cut it back to a narrow preschool focus. It is imperative that Head Start retain its family focus because the strength of the family directly relates to their children's future. To make a difference, a program like Head Start can't just deal with children; it has to include the whole family.

Head Start is a national effort, aimed to be locally responsive and locally controlled. If the federal government doesn't provide full Head Start services to each community, the model could be adopted by communities who want to start their own Head Start programs.

Child Care

With the focus now on preschool for all, as mentioned in Chapter 12, child care gets less attention; resources that could be going to child care programs are now being eyed for universal preschool programs. Remember that all programs for young children can be educational—it doesn't matter if children spend all day there because their parents are working, or if they go just half day. The problem is that with so much attention and funding, or potential funding, on the "preschool for all" movement child care gets neglected, which makes the educational aspects of child care programs more of a challenge. As a society we ought to be looking at the needs of all children, whether their parents work or not, instead of focusing on just one segment of the under-five population—the nation's four-year-olds.

In fact, if we, as a nation, were looking at where to put money for young children where it would do the most good, infants would be the place to start. There's plenty of research that shows that what happens in the very first year or two of life sets the stage for the rest of the lifetime. That's when the brain has the most potential for development and also the greatest vulnerability. But, of course, we don't want to start schools for babies. We want to put together a variety of top quality programs for babies whose families work and for babies whose families don't work. Of course, those programs should be family-centered, whether the parents are in the labor force or not. Furthermore, all families should have access to all the outside services they need, including health and nutrition services, mental health and social services, special education experts, and respite care for families who need it after hours. Use your imagination—pretend that every family has full support of all the resources in the community. Imagine what that would look like. Imagine how those children would arrive in kindergarten? If we had such a thing, no child truly would be left behind.

It is time for this society to consider young children as a national priority. We have a peace movement, a civil rights movement, a women's movement, and an ecology movement. We need a children's movement. The Federal Child Care bill, which was passed at the beginning of the 1990s, is a step in the right direction. A demonstration at the nation's capital on June 1, 1996, was another step. The "I Stand for Children" demonstration drew people from across the country to stand in the Capital Mall and show by their presence their concern for the nation's children. The theme has been taken up by local communities since then, and each June 1 different events signal the Stand for Children theme around the country. Clinton's White House Conference on Children in the mid-1990s was the first of its kind and helped bring further attention to the nation's responsibility to its children. George W. Bush, along with wife, Laura, held a somewhat similar White House Conference when he first got into office, gathering early childhood leaders from around the country to listen to his ideas about what he had in mind for the field.

Culturally Responsive Care

Changing demographics present a challenge to child care programs: Educators must now more than ever before discover how to deliver *culturally responsive care*. A report from California Tomorrow (Chang, Muckelroy, & Pulido-Tobiassen, 1996) proposes five core principles for care in a diverse society:

1. Principle 1 involves adults' understanding how racism impacts the development of children's self-identity and their attitudes toward others.
2. Principle 2 advocates building on the culture of the families and promoting cross-cultural understanding among children in child care.
3. Principle 3 relates to preserving children's home language and encouraging all children in child care to learn a second language.
4. Principle 4 has to do with child care staff working with families to nurture the well-being of children.
5. Principle 5 involves child care staff engaging in ongoing dialogue with families as well as self-reflection about diversity.

In addition to the five principles, professional development, recruitment and retention of a diverse workforce, ongoing research, and dissemination of research results to parents are all essential to the kind of care that promotes children's healthy development in a diverse society.

This report relates directly to the National Association for the Education of Young Children's (NAEYC) 1996 position statement "Responding to Linguistic and Cultural Diversity: Recommendations for Effective Early Childhood Education." Both organizations—California Tomorrow and the NAEYC—have as a goal to build support for equal access to high-quality educational programs that recognize and promote all aspects of children's development and learning, enabling all children to become competent, successful, and socially responsible adults.

Diversity is growing in the United States. According to Washington and Andrews (1998) in their book *Children of 2010*, Los Angeles alone has 100 ethnic groups who speak 70 languages. By 2010 children of color will represent the majority of young people in California, Florida, New York, and Texas. These are the states that will account for one third of the nation's youth. At some point in the twenty-first century, no single racial or ethnic group will constitute a majority of the U.S. population. That phenomenon already occurred in California in 2003.

In the future, we, as a society, must offer enough choices so that parents can find early care and education in tune with what they want and need for their children.

Stopping funding cuts and expanding services by providing more programs aren't the only answers. The choices must include programs that allow parents to be with their own children, as well as a wide variety of systems that provide for education and care by others. Creative alternatives in the workplace that allow working parents a greater role in caring for their own children include flextime, which allows parents to stagger work schedules; part-time work; job sharing; parent subsidies, which allow parents to be at home more with their children; flexible benefits plans; and flexible leave policies.

We need more high-quality early care and education programs of all types; we haven't come close to meeting the need. Children from low-income families frequently lack the opportunity to enroll in early care and education programs. Only 40.4 percent of children from low-income families were in early care and education programs, compared to 68.3 percent of families with income over $75,000. In addition, waiting lists reflect the need for child care assistance. In California 280,000 children are on waiting lists, with 48,000 in Texas and 46,960 in Florida (Children's Defense Fund, 2004). We need more child care, but we can't just have *more*—we need to have *better* child care. Cuts to quality initiatives reflect how states are scaling back efforts to improve quality in early care and education programs, including some cuts that involve basic health and safety. For example, Oklahoma's cuts included reducing provider education funding, grants for quality improvement, and fire code compliance (Children's Defense Fund, 2004).

We have to upgrade the training, status, and salaries of child care teachers, who are grossly underpaid, putting them in the ranks of the poor. Children suffer from burned-out teachers and high turnover rates. Quality child care makes a difference. We can't promote economic independence for families without also promoting good child care. Child care is a means to family preservation and a key component in school readiness. Indeed, child care is often seen as the answer to problems of the economy, a means of addressing the miseries of poverty, and a strong tool for eradicating bias in the next generation, besides providing general early education for young children.

The problem is that poorly funded child care doesn't live up to all the dreams we have for it. Quality is a major issue. Without quality, child care doesn't do its job. It is hard to have quality when no one wants to pay the cost, including the government. Certainly most families can't pay what child care truly costs, if early care and education professionals were paid at the rate of other professionals.

Early childhood programs, such as Head Start, and quality child care can help break the cycle of poverty and disadvantage by helping the parents and by preparing the next generation to take full advantage of educational and training opportunities. The Children's Defense Fund (2005) sees education as the path out of poverty. Seventy percent of financially secure post-secondary students graduated from college, compared to 47 percent of low-income students. Students from low-income families drop out of school six times more often than those from wealthy families. Good and widely available early care and education programs can make a difference in these statistics.

The most effective programs do far more than merely deliver early childhood education and care for children. To meet children's needs, they provide comprehensive services to the whole family. They connect the family to the greater community. An example of such a program is the Parent Services Project (PSP), mentioned in Chapters 1 and 12, which was started by Ethel Seiderman (Lee & Seiderman, 1998; Links, Beggs, & Seiderman, 1997). This project serves as a model of how child care can go far beyond just providing care for children by also supporting families.

MOVING TOWARD FULL-INCLUSION PROGRAMS

The United States Congress has been passing legislation since 1975 designed to move children with special needs out of isolation and into programs that serve their typically developing peers. The Individuals with Disabilities Education Act (IDEA) of 1990 has supported what's called "inclusion"—that is, integrating cildren with special needs into early care and education programs of all sorts, including center-based care, family child care, and infant-toddler programs. Inclusion programs encourage children with disabilities to reach higher levels of achievement and develop a broader range of social skills. It exposes them earlier to the larger world that they will live in as adults. All children benefit when children with special needs are integrated into classrooms with their typically developing peers. They can't just be thrown together, however. Care must be taken to be sure everyone's needs are met and the children with special needs are helped to feel that they belong. That takes training of teachers, caregivers, and family child care providers.

For example, children with disabilities may need support when it comes to making use of a rich environment. Materials should be selected to fit all children's capabilities, including those with special needs. Accessibility is important too. It doesn't do any good to put children in a rich environment if they can't get to what they're interested in.

Some children need to be taught how to use an environment set up for learning through play. It helps if a teacher is nearby observing and commenting, modeling, and even making suggestions. Judging how a play environment is working depends on observing how children are using it. All children should be using the toys, materials, and activities creatively and to the best of their abilities. They should be able to make choices and use the materials as independently as they can. The degree of engagement can vary widely, but should be an indication of how the environment is working.

ECONOMIC DEVELOPMENT

You can't just take the child out of the family and provide education and child care without looking at the factors that influence what the child goes home to. Poverty is a big influence on family life and therefore on children's early development, which affects their ability to learn when they reach kindergarten age. According to *Children of 2010*, over 20 percent of U.S. children are being raised below the poverty level—the highest percentage of all NATO nations. Children under six of years of age are more likely to be poor than any other age group of Americans.

Money can't buy happiness, so it isn't just poverty that causes problems. But there is a correlation between poverty and stress on families and children, according to the Children's Defense Fund (2005). The lack of services and treatment for parents' mental health and substance abuse problems can create family crisis. It is estimated that 9 percent of the children in the United States live with at least one parent who abuses alcohol or drugs. Families are the fastest growing segment of the homeless population, now accounting to 40 percent of the nation's homeless. Imagine the stress on families to be living on the street!

A key to alleviating poverty is jobs—jobs with benefits that pay enough to live on. Increased employment can be enhanced by community involvement in identifying available jobs, improving access by reducing discrimination and other barriers, improving training, and developing job search and interview skills in underemployed people.

Who is going to do all that? We all must. No single approach will eliminate poverty in America. It will take a massive effort on the part of government at all levels, educational institutions, corporations, foundations, communities, and individuals.

ADEQUATE HEALTH SERVICES AND NUTRITION FOR ALL

Let's go back to our discussion of the three pregnant women at the beginning of the chapter. The point of those vignettes is that good health and nutrition are vitally linked to later achievement. To enter kindergarten equally prepared, every child must have a healthy birth, adequate pre- and postnatal care and nutrition, and medical protection and care in the early years.

Adequate nutrition starting before birth is a must for healthy development. WIC (Women, Infants, and Children), a federal nutrition program already in place, can accomplish this goal. Unfortunately, WIC doesn't reach everyone who is eligible for the services. Since 2000, the food stamp program has increased by 20 percent and now reaches 10.6 million children. Still, only 54 percent of eligible people receive benefits (Children's Defense Fund, 2005).

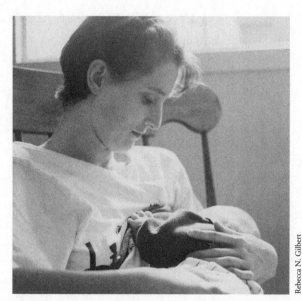

Health-care delivery has been a patchwork system involving federal, state, and private sectors. Unfortunately, this system does not meet the need. For health care to be available to all, each sector of the society must commit to finding ways to make it accessible and affordable to everyone who needs it. After welfare reform occurred and

Good health and nutrition are vitally linked to readiness to learn. To enter kindergarten ready to learn, every child must have a healthy birth, adequate nutrition, and medical protection and care in the early years.

Rebecca N. Gilbert

Aid to Families with Dependent Children (AFDC) was replaced by Temporary Assistance to Needy Families (TANF), the numbers of children without health care rose. Attempts to correct that situation are continuing to be made.

Public health insurance should be expanded to all poor families. Additional community and migrant health centers should be established to serve the medically underserved. The National Health Service Corps, which provides scholarships and loan repayments to health professionals, should be adequately funded. The childhood vaccination program should be augmented to serve all infants and preschoolers who now go unprotected. Community health centers should receive adequate financial support for maternal and child health programs. Employers should offer subsidized health insurance with dependent coverage to all employees regardless of pay level. Plans should fully cover cost-effective services such as prenatal care and preventive care for children. In addition, employer wellness policies should support families by providing adequate sick and family leave. Employers can also provide increased onsite health education.

But just providing services is not enough. Families must take responsibility to seek out and use the services that are available. Some may need to be educated about how to use medical care services. That's where the early care and education program comes in. Much can be done to help parents seek out what is available to them. See Chapter 12.

TAKING A PREVENTIVE APPROACH

With all of the examples, given in this chapter of effective programs and services for families, it sounds as if a lot is being done at this point. However, what is being done is a drop in the bucket compared with the need. Unfortunately, a good many of the services mentioned respond to emergency situations rather than preventing them in the first place. Here's a little parable to illustrate the point:

> Once there was a kindly man walking by a river. He looked out into the strong current and saw a young child struggling in the swirling waters. He threw off his shoes and plunged into the swiftly moving water. It took all the strength he had, but he finally managed to pull the child from the grip of the river, drag him up on the bank, and give him CPR. The child was saved! But lo and behold, the man looked up from the child he had just rescued and saw another child in the water. Again he raced into the river, fought hard, and managed to save this child too. But the same thing happened. He looked up in time to see yet another child struggling in the swift current. Dead tired, he dragged himself once more to the river and plunged in. He continued in this manner until he collapsed from exhaustion and was no longer able to save any more children. That was the end of his rescue mission. Sadly enough, he had been so busy saving children that he was never able to leave long enough to walk upstream to stop whoever was throwing the children into the river in the first place!

This parable shows how our society operates in regard to children at this point. Instead of taking adequate prevention measures, we allow children to flounder in dangerous waters, and then we try to rescue them. It would be much more economical and energy-effective to walk upstream and stop them from being thrown in! It's cheaper and better to prevent damage than to repair it.

A common problem of the rescue approach is that children too often must be rescued from their own parents because they don't get adequate care. That kind of rescuing can be disastrous. Children placed in foster care must deal with the emotional effects of separation and are often left with lifelong scars. Many children could remain at home if there were more programs that focused on strengthening families rather than on removing children. The Doris Duke Foundation is an example of a program that has taken just such an approach. See Chapters 1 and 2.

The costs of taking children from their families are enormous. Besides the emotional costs, there are financial burdens that taxpayers must shoulder. It costs much more to provide foster care than it would to give families what they need to keep their children home. Happily, there has been a recent trend for keeping families together. This trend is reflected in the proposals of the Children's Defense Fund group, which is continually making recommendations for systemic reforms aimed at keeping families intact.

Here are three recommendations that would prevent the society from having to rescue floundering children:

1. Create in every community a network of comprehensive services to strengthen families and give them the tools they need to support and nurture their children.

2. Make family preservation services and other specialized community-based treatment available to all families in crisis.

3. Improve the quality of out-of-home placements so that special needs are met and children are returned to families or adopted as appropriate.

ADVOCACY

Marian Wright Edelman, the founder of the Children's Defense Fund, gives this advice: "If you see a need, don't ask, 'Why doesn't somebody do something?' Ask, 'Why don't I do something?'" That's good advice for all of us. Anyone who cares about America's future must become an advocate for making the world a better place for children and families. Here are some ways to do that as an early educator. This is also good advice for families you work with.

1. *Get involved!*   Start by informing yourself about the status of children and families in your neighborhood, community, state, and nation. Use your own eyes. Visit local programs that serve low-income children and see the effects of poverty. Read. Get a current copy of *The State of America's Children*, published regularly by the Children's Defense Fund (122 C Street NW, Washington, DC, 20001; [202] 628–8787).

2. *Speak out for children!*   Inform others through speaking to religious groups, at candidate forums, and to community groups. Write a letter to the editor of your local newspaper.

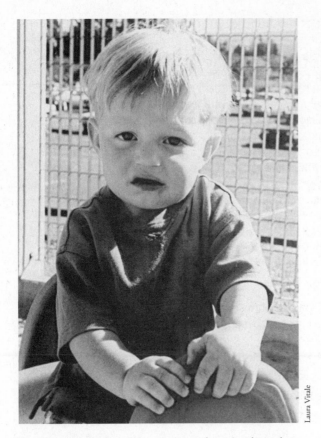

Laura Vitale

Speak out for children. They can't speak out for themselves.

3. *Do something this week to help children.* If you're not already involved, volunteer at a Head Start program, a child care program, or a school. If you are already busy during the day or don't want to work directly with children, offer your services as a fund-raiser. Every program needs more money than it has, and most are involved in varying degrees of fund-raising efforts. If you want to feel good, take a look at a director's face when you arrive in his or her office and offer to help with fund-raising.

4. *Be a role model for your community.* Don't wait around for someone else to take the reins. If you show you care, others are likely to follow your example.

5. *Register and vote.* Elect candidates who keep children and families a priority.

6. *Understand how public policies make a difference.* Public policies, though they may be conceived of on a national, state, or more local level, influence our lives and those of our children. Policies are decisions about goals and objectives, which become plans of action, translating eventually into programs.

The part of the advocate in helping create policy involves the following steps (adapted from Goffin & Lombardi, 1989):

1. Identify a problem that requires action.
2. Convince someone to accept responsibility for helping to solve the problem. This someone may be the government.
3. Develop and propose acceptable solutions to the problem.
4. Monitor the implementation of the solution.
5. Evaluate the program.

It's important to hold your leaders accountable. One way to do this is to keep track of how lawmakers vote on issues of importance to children and their families. Goffin and Washington (2007) give a lot more information about how to be an advocate for children and families.

In Chapter 14 were strategies about how to encourage parents to advocate for their own children and eventually become advocates for all children. Strategy Box 15.1

Strategy Box 15.1

Strategies for Involving Yourself and the Families in Advocacy Efforts

♦ Learn about the families in your community. If you aren't in touch with low-income families, visit a program that serves them. Get a broader view by reading the most current copy of *The State of America's Children*. Share what you learn with families you work with and find out what they already know.

♦ Understand how public policies affect children and families. Educate yourself about the pros and cons of pending legislation. Educate the families in your program and learn from them as well.

♦ Help create legislation when a need arises. Join a group that knows how to do this, or find out how to do it and create the group yourself.

♦ Stand up for children—together with their families. Make your positions known. Contact your legislators. Create letter-writing and e-mail campaigns and petitions. Visit your local lawmaker's office. Go to your state capitol. Go to Washington, D.C., if necessary. Make yourselves known. Make yourselves visible and heard.

♦ Join groups that advocate for children. Many voices are louder than just a few.

♦ Educate yourself about the candidates who make families and children a priority and then cast your vote. Let them and others know why you are voting for them.

takes the next steps and gives strategies for getting together with families in advocating for all children.

VIOLENCE AND ITS EFFECT ON CHILDREN AND FAMILIES

One issue that hasn't been covered yet in this book is the effect of violent conflict in the community on children and families. Some families have come to the United States fleeing from violence in their own countries—from war, blood feuds, oppressive dictators, ethnic cleansing—horror stories none of us like to think about. These refugee families may settle in relatively safe and secure communities but still feel the effects of their previous experiences. And not all families in the United States live in safe communities. Those who are living in communities where rival gangs fight for territory, or where crime and drugs run rampant, also have to deal with violence. Then there is violence in the home that has nothing to do with the neighborhood where the home is situated. Domestic disputes that turn violent can happen anywhere. The aftereffects of violence continue to disrupt the lives of children and their families.

What are some of the specific effects of violence on young children? Some children are direct casualties of violence, but all children suffer physically and emotionally if they are exposed to violence, even by witnessing it. One effect is fear, which is intensified when children hear about violence and see reports in the media. Children need help with their feelings. If they aren't able to explore and express their feelings, those feelings stay hidden inside and eat away at them. The adults in their lives who have also experienced the same violence may be so tender themselves that they may have a hard time allowing children to work through their feelings. With no adult help or support, children can't begin to understand or make any sense out of what is going on. One way they try to work through their fears is through play, but how many early educators allow children to reenact violent scenes? Most are uncomfortable with even pretend violence, though children are drawn to that kind of play—even those who haven't experienced violence first-hand.

Children who have been exposed to violence can experience post-traumatic stress syndrome, which often goes unrecognized. Without help, or at least guidance and support, children's world views become distorted, setting them up for continuing the conflict and violence in the next generation (Connolly et al., 2007).

Families also feel the effects of violent conflict. Some have to deal with the terrible stress that comes when a family member is killed or injured. Children are caught in the stress and feelings of the adults. Because male members of families are most likely to be directly involved in the violence, some families end up without any adult males, which makes it harder for the family to survive and leads to a lack of role models for male children. Families are sometimes displaced as a result of violent conflict and that puts additional stress as they end up economically deprived and with physical and mental health issues. Children's lives are disrupted by such moves as they face separation issues, and even a sense of their cultural identity and feeling of belonging (Connolly et al., 2007).

Communities are also disrupted by violence, especially if there are opposing violent factions in the community whose fights can destroy any sense of togetherness and feelings of trust and safety. Deep divisions can result and communities can literally disintegrate from within.

So the question is: What can early educators do to support families and children in such situations? One answer is to provide the very best early education programs that we can. We have to provide ongoing support to families and get them together so they can support each other. The environments we create must be places where children can safely explore physically and also explore their feelings with trained adults there to help when needed. The relationships we create with children must be the kind that facilitate their social and emotional competence. Where possible, getting children in touch with nature can be a great source of healing. Obviously, early educators need skills to do all this—skills that go way beyond their training in getting children ready for academics by promoting early literacy and numeracy. Further, early educators need skills that help them work with adults as well as children. It's a big order, but it's worth it!

The final question is, what can early education do to make local communities and the world a more peaceful place?

There are many ways to work for a more peaceful world. Strategy Box 15.2 has some specific close-up and personal strategies early educators can use in their work with children and families.

Teach children to be peacemakers.

Doris Pfalmer

Strategy Box 15.2

Strategies for Working with Families and Their Children Around Peacemaking

* Continually explore the idea of moving from a dominator model to an equity one. Another way of putting this idea is always looking for a win-win solution to problems and teach others to do the same. Peace isn't won, it's made.
* Create effective partnerships with families in which power and decision making are shared.
* Become a model for others by solving problems and working through conflicts without using one-upmanship and power plays.
* Teach children to resolve conflicts and deal with issues without using aggression.
* Remember the Martin Luther King, Jr. mandate: "pursue peaceful ends through peaceful means."

This whole book has been about peacemaking—about coming together—families and professionals. This book has been about healing the split so the fabric is whole—not a fractured fabric with teachers and children in one section and families in another. Remember what Douglas Powell wrote about how the typical early childhood education fabric weaves the child and teacher strands together, but the families threads occur in a whole separate part of the design (see Chapter 1). We must integrate the families into the whole pattern—not just create a separate part called parent involvement. And when the parts are integrated, there will still be disagreements, conflicts, and issues, but peacemaking includes knowing how to resolve those by using problem-solving methods to figure out what to do when there is disagreement.

Peace isn't won, it is made. Peace never comes once and for all. You have to continually work at it. Whenever there are two people or two groups who interact, there is the potential for conflict. It isn't about just "making nice" but about understanding how to see beyond one's own perspective, how to honor and respect differences, how to find common ground and come to agreements. This is not easy. It takes time and energy. But we have to stop using a dominator model where one person or group uses what's called one-upmanship to gain control over the other. We need to firmly implant an equity model in our minds and hearts and always work toward peaceful settlements of any problems. We teach children to do that. We can do that ourselves as well.

"One day we must come to .see that peace is not merely a distant goal we seek, but that it is a means by which we arrive at that goal. We must pursue peaceful ends through peaceful means."—Dr. Martin Luther King Jr.

LOOKING BACK AND LOOKING FORWARD

This chapter examined how we, as a society, can use the social policy we have, as well as instituting new policies, to upgrade the lives of the children of this nation by paying attention to the challenges that face their families. It examined the issue of who is responsible for America's children, concluding that we all are.

We, as a society, need to make our children a top priority. We need a children's movement in order to ensure that all children have their needs met. We could put an enormous effort into upgrading the quality of children's lives by strengthening their families, providing for their needs, and making available rich early experiences that engage their minds and bring joy, spirit, and curiosity to their lives.

We, as an American community, can work toward making a greater contribution to the socialization processes of our children. We can look for ways to give all children the opportunities necessary to build a healthy sense of self. We can keep the view that all children deserve an equal chance to fulfill themselves in a peaceful society and world. We can practice peacemaking ourselves and teach it to children.

It won't be easy, but what better way to use our energy to prepare for the future of the United States than through caring for its children?

FOR DISCUSSION

1. What are your ideas, feelings, and experiences related to equal opportunity for children? Does Head Start contribute to equality of opportunity? If yes, how? What are your ideas about getting the nation's children "ready to learn"? What are your ideas about "leaving no child behind"?

2. What are your experiences with the health-care system, and how do you think it affects young children?

3. If you were to make recommendations to create or improve on our national child care system, what would those recommendations be? What could child care programs do to support parents that they aren't doing now? What would parents need in order to be able to do what you suggest?

4. Have you ever been involved in advocating for children? If yes, what are your experiences? If no, how might you become involved?

5. What are your ideas about and experiences with peacemaking?

WEB SITES

Center for Law and Social Policy
www.clasp.org
Part of their work focuses on early care and education and promotes policies that support child development and the needs of low-income working parents on expanding availability of resources for child care and early education initiatives.

Children's Defense Fund
http://www.childrensdefense.org/
The Children's Defense Fund educates the nation about the needs of children and encourages preventive investment before they get sick or into trouble, drop out of school, or suffer family breakdown. Its site contains resources and information about the organization's goals and their programs.

Connect for Kids
http://www.connectforkids.org/
Run by the Benton Foundation, this organization promotes advocacy related to various issues concerning children.

Future of Children
http://www.futureofchildren.org/
The Future of Children seeks to promote effective policies and programs for children by providing policy makers, service providers, and the media with timely, objective information based on the best available research.

National Association of Child Care Resource and Referral Agencies (NACCRRA)
www.naccrra.net
Works toward increasing the quality and availability of child care through advocacy work.

National Association for the Education of Young Children
http://www.naeyc.org/
The National Association for the Education of Young Children sets standards and policy for the profession of early childhood care and education.

National Head Start Association (NHSA)
http://www.nhsa.org/
The National Head Start Association provides services for impoverished children 0–5 years of age

and their families. Its site contains research and resource information, including the history and goals of the organization.

Stand for Children
http://www.stand.org/
The Stand for Children organization is committed to building a voice strong enough to give all children an opportunity to grow up healthy, educated, and safe.

Zero to Three
http://www.zerotothree.org/
This nonprofit organization aims to promote the healthy development of infants and toddlers. Its site delivers information on current research pertaining to infants and toddlers.

FURTHER READING

Campell, F. A., & Ramey, C. T. (1994). Effects of early intervention on intellectual and academic achievement: A follow-up study of children from low-income families. *Child Development*, 65, 684–698.

Children's Defense Fund. (2004). *The state of America's children* 2004. Washington, DC: Children's Defense Fund.

Compton-Lilly, C. (2004) *Confronting racism, poverty, and power. Classroom strategies to change the world.* Portsmouth, NH: Heinemann.

Cook, R. E., Klien, M. D., Tessier, A. *Adapting early childhood curricula for children with special needs* (7th ed.). Upper Saddle River, NJ: Merrill/Prentice Hall.

Dahlberg, G., Moss, P., & Pence, A. (1999). *Beyond quality in early childhood education and care.* London: Falmer.

Dubow, E. F., & Ippolito, M. F. (1994). Effects of poverty and home environment on changes in the academic and behavioral adjustment of elementary school–age children. *Journal of Clinical Child Psychology*, 23, 401–412.

Galinsky, E., & Bond, J. T. (2000). Supporting families as primary caregivers: The role of the workplace. In D. Cryer & T. Harms (Eds.), *Infants and toddlers in out-of-home care.* Baltimore: Brookes.

Gonzalez-Mena, J. (2001). Cross-cultural infant care and issues of equity and social justice. *Contemporary Issues in Early Childhood*, 2(3). Available online at the Web site of Symposium Journals, a division of wwwords Ltd. (www.wwwords.co.uk/ciec).

Liaw, F., Meisels, S. J., & Brooks-Gunn, J. (1995). The effects of experience of early intervention on low birth weight, premature children: The

infant health and development program. *Early Childhood Research Quarterly*, 10, 405–431.

Lombardi, J. (2003). *Time to care: Redesigning child care to promote education, support families, and build communities.* Philadelphia: Temple University Press.

Love, J., Raikes, H., Paulsell, D., & Kisker, E. E. (2000). New directions for studying quality in programs for infants and toddlers. In D. Cryer & T. Harms (Eds.), *Infants and toddlers in out-of-home care* (pp. 117–162). Baltimore: Brookes.

McLoyd, V. (1998). Socioeconomic disadvantage and child development. *American Psychologist*, 53(2), 185–204.

Meisels, S., & Atkins-Burnett, S. (2004, January). Public policy viewpoint: The Head Start national reporting system: A critique. *Young Children*, 59(1), 64–66.

Moddings, N. (2002). *Starting at home: Care and social policy.* Berkeley: University of California Press.

Nieto, S. (2000). *Affirming diversity: The sociopolitical context of multicultural education* (3rd ed.). New York: Addison Wesley Longman.

Odom, S. (Ed.). (2002). *Widening the circle: Including children with disabilities in preschool programs.* New York: Teachers College Press.

Raver, C. C., & Zigler, E. F. (2004, January). Public policy viewpoint: Another step back? Assessing readiness in Head Start. *Young Children*, 59(1), 58–62.

St. Pierre, R. G., Layzer, J. I., Goodson, B. D., & Bernstein, L. (1997). *National impact evaluation of the comprehensive child development program*: *Final report*. Cambridge, MA: ABT Associates.

Thaxton, S. M. (2003). Grandparents as parents—Understanding the issues. In B. & R. Neugebauer, eds., *The art of leadership* (pp.323–325). Redmond, WA: Child Care Information Exchange.

Zigler, E. F., Finn-Stevenson, M., & Hall, N. W. (2003). *The first three years and beyond: Brain development and social policy*. New Haven: Yale University Press.

Zigler, E., & Styfoco, S. J. (2004). *The Head Start debates*. Baltimore: Brookes.

NAEYC: Where We Stand

Many Languages, Many Cultures: Respecting and Responding to Diversity

Adapted from the 1995 position statement *Responding to Linguistic and Cultural Diversity: Recommendations for Effective Early Childhood Education.*

Young children and their families reflect a great and rapidly increasing diversity of language and culture. NAEYC's recommendations emphasize that early childhood programs are responsible for creating a welcoming environment that respects diversity, supports children's ties to their families and community, and promotes both second-language acquisition and preservation of children's home languages and cultural identities. Linguistic and cultural diversity is an asset, not a deficit, for young children.

RECOMMENDATIONS FOR WORKING WITH FAMILIES

* **Actively involve families in the early learning program.**
Links between school, home, and community are important for all young children, but forging them can be challenging when families and program staff differ in culture and language. Ties to the community, respectful relationships with families, and encouragement of active, culturally meaningful family involvement are essential.

> Twenty-eight percent of Head Start children speak a home language other than English.

* **Help all families realize the cognitive advantages of a child knowing more than one language, and provide them with strategies to support, maintain, and preserve home-language learning.**
Families may think that speaking to their children only in English will help them learn the language faster. But home-language preservation benefits children's cognitive development, and families with limited English proficiency provide stronger language models when they emphasize their home language.

* **Convince families that their home's cultural values and norms are honored.**
Continuity between home and the early childhood setting supports children's social, emotional, cognitive, and language development. Though not always identical, practices at home and in school should be complementary.

RECOMMENDATIONS FOR WORKING WITH YOUNG CHILDREN

By 2050, Hispanic and African American children under age five will outnumber non-Hispanic Whites in the United States.

- **Ensure that children remain cognitively, linguistically, and emotionally connected to their home language and culture.** Children's positive development requires maintaining close ties to their family and community. If home language and culture are supported, children, families, and communities stay securely connected.

Screening and Assessment of Young English Language Learners

As an expansion of its position statement on curriculum, assessment, and program evaluation, and in response to needs in the field, NAEYC has developed recommendations on the screening and assessment of young English language learners. For more, go to www.naeyc.org.

- **Encourage home-language and literacy development, knowing that this contributes to children's ability to acquire English language proficiency.** Research confirms that bilingualism is an asset and an educational achievement. When children become proficient and literate in their home language, they transfer those skills to a second language.

- **Help develop essential concepts in the children's first language and within cultural contexts that they understand.** Although some children can seem superficially fluent in their second language, most children find it easier to learn new, complex concepts in a familiar language and cultural framework. Once established, these concepts readily transfer into a second language and contribute to later academic mastery.

By the year 2010, more than 30 percent of all school-age children will come from U.S. homes in which the primary language is not English.

- **Support and preserve home-language usage.** Whether or not staff are proficient in a child's home language, programs should make every effort to use children's home languages and create classroom environments that reflect children's languages and cultures. Within that context, teachers can model appropriate use of English and provide many opportunities for children to learn and practice a new language.

NAEYC Interest Forums

Interest Forums are organized by groups of NAEYC members who share an interest in a particular early childhood issue. Interest Forums focused on the issues in this position statement include Latino Caucus, Black Caucus, Children's Global Issues, and Diversity and Equity. To learn about joining a forum, go to www.naeyc.org/community.

- **Develop and provide alternative, creative strategies to promote all children's participation and learning.** Creativity and collaboration are needed to ensure that all children, whatever their current language proficiency or culture, have the opportunity to participate fully in the program's learning opportunities. Collaborative work groups, including teachers and families, can develop flexible approaches that are developmentally, culturally, and linguistically appropriate.

- **Provide children with many ways of showing what they know and can do.**
  Children have already learned a great deal before they enter an early childhood program, even if this learning has been in a different language and culture. Effective curriculum and assessment systems do not underestimate children's abilities. Instead, they create multiple, often nonverbal ways for children to demonstrate interests, knowledge, and skills.

RECOMMENDATIONS FOR PREPARATION OF EARLY CHILDHOOD PROFESSIONALS

- **Provide professional preparation and development in the areas of culture, language, and diversity.**
  By examining their own cultural background, educators come to see how young children's culture and language influence responses, interactions, and approaches to learning. Competence is further enhanced by professional development in language acquisition, working with diverse families, cross-cultural communication, and other critical content.

- **Recruit and support educators who are trained in languages other than English.**
  Individuals with multilingual and multicultural backgrounds can be advocates and crucial support for diverse young children and families. We must recruit more bilingual educators, give them appropriate professional responsibilities, and link them in collaborative relationships with others in the field.

For More on Diversity

The Early Childhood Research Institute on Culturally and Linguistically Appropriate Services identifies, evaluates, and promotes effective and appropriate early intervention practices and preschool practices that are sensitive to and respectful of culturally and linguistically diverse backgrounds. http://clas.uiuc.edu/links.html

The National Association for Bilingual Education is devoted to representing both English language learners and bilingual education professionals. www.nabe.org

The National Association for Multicultural Education fosters the understanding of unique cultural and ethnic heritage and promotes the development of culturally responsible and responsive curricula. www.name.org

The National Task Force on Early Childhood for Hispanics endeavors to enhance educational achievement and opportunities for children of Hispanic descent and to influence education policy. www.ecehispanic.org/about.html

The National Black Child Development Institute seeks to improve and protect the lives of children, recognizing the pivotal role that all members of the community must play if equity and access are to become a reality. www.nbcdi.org

References

CHAPTER 1

Ballenger, C. (1992, Summer). Because you like us: The language of control. *Harvard Educational Review* 62(2), 199–208.

Bloom, P. J., Eisenberg, P., & Eisenberg, E. (2003, Spring/Summer). Reshaping early childhood programs to be more family responsive. *America's Family Support Magazine*, 36–38.

Bowlby, J. (1969). *Attachment and loss* (Vol. 1, *Attachment*). New York: Basic Books.

Bowlby, J (1973). *Attachment and loss* (Vol. 2, *Separation: Anxiety and anger*). London: Hogarth.

Bronfenbrenner, U. (1979). *The ecology of human development: Experiments by nature and design.* Cambridge, MA: Harvard University Press.

Bronfenbrenner, U. (1994). Ecological models of human development. In T. Husen and N. Postlethwaite (Eds.), *International Encyclopedia of Education, Vol. 3*, 2nd ed. 1643–1647.

Bronfenbrenner, U., & Morris P. A. (1998). The ecology of developmental processes. In *Handbook of child psychology, Vol. 1. of Theoretical models of human development*, New York: Wiley.

Center for the Study of Social Policy (CSSP). (2004). *Protecting children by strengthening families: A guidebook for early childhood programs.* Washington, DC: Author. Online: www.cssp.orghttp://www.cssp.org/doris_duke/index.html, accessed April 15, 2007.

Christian, L. G. (2006). Understanding families: Applying family systems theory to early childhood practice. *Young Children* 61(2), 12–20.

Epstein, J. L. (2001). *School, family and community partnerships: Preparing educators and improving schools.* Boulder, CO: Westview Press.

Fitzgerald, D. (2004). *Parent partnership in the early years.* London: Continuum.

Gonzalez-Mena, J., & Stonehouse, A. (2008). *Making links: A collaborative approach to planning and practice in early childhood programs.* New York: Teachers College Press.

Gordon, I. J. (1968) *Parent Involvement in compensatory education.* University of Illinois Press.

Gordon, I. J. & Breivogel, W. F. (1976). *Building effective home-school relationships.* Boston: Allyn and Bacon.

Hannaford, C. (2005). *Smart moves: When learning is not all in your head.* Salt Lake City: Great River Books.

Hilliard, A. G. (2004). Assessment equity in a multicultural society, copyright March 2004. New Horizons for Learning, www.newhorizons.org

Hilliard, A. G. (2007). What do we need to know now? A speech presented at a conference on Race, Research and Education, held in Chicago at an African-American symposium sponsored by the Chicago Urban League and the Spencer Foundation.

Im, J., Parlakian, R., & Sanchez, S. (2007). Understanding the influence of culture on caregiving practices . . . From the inside out. *Young Children* 62(5), 65–66.

Keyser, J. (2006). *From parents to partners: Building a family centered early childhood program.* Washington DC: National Association for the Education of Young Children, and St. Paul, MN: Redleaf.

Lee, L. (2006). *Stronger together: Family support and early childhood education.* San Rafael, CA: Parent Services Project.

Lee, L., & Seiderman, E. (1998). *Families matter: The parent services project.* Cambridge, MA: Harvard Family Research Project.

Lewis, T., Amini, F., & Lannon, R. (2000). *A general theory of love.* New York: Vintage Books.

Mahoney, Gerald, & Wiggers, Bridgette. (2007). The role of parents in early intervention. *Children and Schools,* 29(1) 7–15.

McGee-Banks, C. A. (2003). Families and teachers working together for school improvement. In J. A. Banks & C. A. McGee-Banks (Eds.), *Multicultural education: Issues and perspectives* (4th ed., pp. 402–410). New York: Wiley.

Maslow, A. (1954). *Motivation and personality.* New York: Harper and Row.

National Association for the Education of Young Children (2005). *Families and community relationships: A guide to the NAEYC early childhood program standards and related accreditation criteria.* Washington, DC: National Association for Education of Young Children.

Olmsted, P. P., Rubin, R. I., True, J. H., & Revicki, D. (1980). *Parent education: The contributions of Ira J. Gordon.* Olney, MD; Association for Childhood Education International.

Olson, M. (2007) Strengthening families: Community strategies that work. *Young Children* 62(2), 26–32.

Pope, J., & Seiderman, E. (2001, Winter). The child-care connection. *Family Support,* 19(4), 24–35.

Powell, D. R. (1986). Research in review. Parent education and support programs. *Young Children,* 41(3), 47–53.

Powell, D. R. (1998). Research in review. Reweaving parents into the fabric of early childhood programs. *Young Children* 53(5), 60–67.

Rogoff, B. (2003). *The cultural nature of human development.* New York: Oxford University Press.

Seiderman, E. (2003). Putting all the players on the same page: Accessing resources for the child and family. In B. Neugebauer & R. Neugebauer (Eds.), *The art of leadership.* Redmond, WA: Exchange Press.

Turnbull, A. P., Turbiville, P. V. & Turnbull, H. R. (2000). Evolution of Family-professional partnerships: Collective empowerment as the model for early twenty-first century. In *Handbook of early childhood intervention,* eds. J. P. Shonkoll & S. J. Meisels, 630–50. New York: Cambridge University Press.

CHAPTER 2

Ainsworth, M. D. S., & Bell, S. (1977). Infant crying and maternal responsiveness. *Child Development,* 48, 1208–1216.

Ainsworth, M. D. S., Blehar, M. C., Waters, E., & Wall, S. (1978). *Patterns of attachment: A psychological study of the Strange Situation.* Hillside, NJ: Erlbaum.

Berk, L. (2001). *Dialogues with children: Creating learning-environments at home and school.* New York: Oxford University Press.

Bower, B. (2000). Attachment disorder draws a closer look. *Science News,* 1157(22), 343.

Bowlby, J. (2000 [1969]). *Attachment and loss: Vol. 1. Attachment.* New York: Basic Books.

Bowman, B., & Moore, E. (2006). *School readiness and social-emotional development: Perspectives on cultural diversity.* Washington DC: National Black Child Development Institute.

Braungart-Rieker, J. M., Garwood, M. M., Power, B. P., & Wang, B. (2001). Parental sensitivity, infant affect, and affect regulation: Predictors of later attachment. *Child Development,* 72(1), 252–270.

Brazelton, T. B., & Cramer, B. G. (1990). *The earliest relationship: Parents, infants, and the drama of early attachment.* New York: Addison-Wesley.

Bronfenbrenner, U. (1979) *The ecology of human development.* Cambridge, MA: Harvard University Press.

Bronfenbrenner, U. (2000). Ecological system theory. In A. Kazdin (Ed.), *Encyclopedia of Psychology.* Washington, DC: American Psychological Association & Oxford Press.

Bronfenbrenner, U. (Ed.) (2005). *Making human beings human: Bioecological perspectives on human development.* Thousand Oaks, CA: Sage.

Butterfield, P. M., Martin, C. A., & Prairie, A. P. (2004). *Emotional connections: How relationships guide early learning.* Washington, DC: Zero to Three.

Caldwell, B. M. (1987, April). The tie that binds. *Working Mother,* 105–107.

Carlebach, D., & B. Tate. (2002). *Creating caring children: The first three years.* Miami: Peace Education Foundation.

Cernoch, J. M., & Porter, R. H. (1985). Recognition of maternal axillary odors by infants. *Child Development,* 56, 1593–1598.

Chang, H. (1993). *Affirming children's roots: Cultural and linguistic diversity in early care and education.* San Francisco: California Tomorrow.

David, M., & Appell, G. (2001 [1973, 1996]). *Loczy: An unusual approach to mothering.* Translated from *Loczy ou le maternage insolite,* by Jean Marie Clark; revised translation by Judit Falk. Budapest: Association Pikler-Loczy for Young Children.

DeCasper, A. J., & Fifer, W. P. (1980). Of human bonding: Newborns prefer their mothers' voices. *Science,* 208, 1174–1175.

Elliot, E. (2003, July). Challenging our assumptions: Helping a baby adjust to center care. *Young Children,* 58(4), 22–28.

Erikson, E. (1963). *Childhood and society.* New York: Norton.

Ferber, R. (1985). *Solve your child's sleep problems.* New York: Simon & Schuster.

Gandini, L., & Edwards, C. P. (Eds.). (2000). *Bambini: The Italian approach to infant-toddler care.* New York: Teachers College Press.

Gerber, M., & Johnson, A. (1998). *Your self-confident baby.* New York: Wiley.

Gonzalez-Mena, J. (1995). *Dragon Mom.* Napa, CA: Rattle Ok.

Gonzalez-Mena, J. (1997, September). Understanding the parent's perspective: Independence or interdependence? *Exchange,* 61–63.

Gonzalez-Mena, J. (2002, September). Working with cultural differences: Individualism and collectivism. *The First Years: Nga TauTuatahi (New Zealand Journal of Infant and Toddler Education),* 4(2), 13–15.

Gonzalez-Mena, J. (2004, September). What can an orphanage teach us? Lessons from Budapest. *Young Children,* 26–30.

Gonzalez-Mena, J. (2008). *Diversity in early care and education: Honoring differences.* New York: McGraw-Hill.

Gray, H. (2004, September). You go away and you come back: Supporting separations and reunions in an infant/toddler classroom. *Young Children,* 100–107.

Greenfield, P. M., Quiroz, B., Rothstein-Fisch, C., & Trumbull, E. (2001). *Bridging cultures between home and school.* Mahwah, NJ: Erlbaum.

Greenough, W., Emde, R. N., Gunnar, M., Massinga, R., & Shonkoff, J. P. (2001, April–May). The impact of the caregiving environment on young children's development: Different ways of knowing. *Zero to Three*, 21(5), 16–24.

Grether, J. K., Shulman, J., & Croen, L. A. (1990). Sudden infant death syndrome among Asians in California. *Journal of Pediatrics*, 116, 525–528.

Hesse, E., & Main, M. (2000). Disorganized infant, child, and adult attachment: Collapse in behavior and attachment strategies. *Journal of the Psychoanalytic Association*, 48(4), 1–5.

Honig, A. S. (2002). *Secure relationships: Nurturing infant/ toddler attachment in early care settings*. Washington, DC: National Association for the Education of Young Children.

Howes, C., & Ritchie, S. (2002). *A matter of trust*. New York: Teachers College Press.

Immordino-Yang, M. H., & Damasio, A. (2007). We feel, therefore we learn: The relevance of affective and social neuroscience to education. *International Mind, Brain, and Education Society* 1(1).

Katz, L. G. (1980). Mothering and teaching: Some significant distinctions. In L. G. Katz (Ed.), *Current topics in early childhood education* (Vol. 3, pp. 47–63). Norwood, NJ: Ablex.

Keyser, J. (2006). *From parents to partners: Building a family-centered early childhood program*. Washington DC: National Association for the Education of Young Children.

Lally, J. R. (1995, November). The impact of child care policies and practices on infant/toddler identity formation. *Young Children*, 58–67.

Lee, L. (2002). *Serving families: A handbook on the principles and strategies of the parent services project approach*. San Rafael, CA: Parent Services Project.

LeVine, R. A. (1977). Child rearing as cultural adaptation. In P. H. Leiderman, S. R. Tulkin, & A. Rosenfeld (Eds.), *Culture and infancy: Variations in the human experience*, (15–27). New York: Academic Press.

Lieberman, A. F., & Zeanah, C. H. (1995, July). Disorders of attachment in infancy. *Infant Psychiatry*, 4(3), 571–585.

Main, M., & Solomon, J. (1990). Procedures for identifying infants as disorganized/disoriented during the Ainsworth Strange Situation. In M. Greenberg, D. Cicchetti, & E. M. Cummings (Eds.), *Attachment in the preschool years: Theory, research and intervention*, (121–160). Chicago: University of Chicago Press.

McKenna, J. J. (1992, Winter). SIDS research. *Mothering* (62), 45–51.

Motz, M., Leslie, M., & DeMarchi, G. (2007, March). Breaking the cycle: Using a relational approach to address the impact of maternal substance use on regulation and attachment in children. *Zero to Three* 27 (4), 19–25.

O'Brien, M. (1997). *Inclusive child care for infants and toddlers: Meeting individual and special needs*. Baltimore: Brookes.

Park, S. (2007, August 27). How not to raise a genius. Is Baby Einstein doing your child more harm than good? *Time* Magazine, 170, 46.

Pawl, J. H. (1995, February–March). The therapeutic relationship as human connectedness: Being held in another's mind. *Zero to Three*, 15(4), 48–49.

Perry, B. D. (2002). Childhood experience and the expression of genetic potential: What childhood neglect tells us about nature and nurture. *Brain and Mind*, 3, 79–100.

Perry, B. (2006). Applying principles of neurodevelopment to clinical work with maltreated and traumatized children. In N. B. Webb (Ed). *Working with traumatized youth in child welfare*. New York: Guilford Press.

Pinto, C. (2001, Spring). Supporting competence in a child with special needs: One child's story. *Educaring*, 22(2), 1–6.

Raikes, H. (1996, July). A secure base for babies: Applying attachment concepts to the infant care setting. *Young Children*, 51(5), 59–67.

Rofrano, F. (2002, January). "I care for you": A reflection on caring as infant curriculum, *Young Children*, 57(1), 49–51.

Schneider, B. H., Atkinson, L., & Tardif, C. (2001). Child-parent attachment and children's peer relations: A quantitative review. *Developmental Psychology*, 37, 86–100.

Sears, W., & Sears, M. (2001). *The attachment parenting book*. NY: Little, Brown and Company.

Shonkoff, J. P., & Phillips, D. (2001, April–May). From neurons to neighborhoods: The science of early childhood development—An introduction. *Zero to Three*, 21(5), 4–7.

Solomon, J., & George, C. (1999). The measurement of attachment security in infancy and childhood. In J. Cassidy & P. Shaver (Eds.), *Handbook of attachment* (287–318). New York: Guilford.

Stack, C. B. (1991). Sex roles and survival strategies in an urban black community. In R. Staples (Ed.), *The black family: Essays and studies* (4th ed.). Belmont, CA: Wadsworth.

Stern, D. N. (1985). *The interpersonal world of the infant*. New York: Basic Books.

Thevenin, T. (1987). *The family bed*. Garden City, NY: Avery.

Thomas, A., Chess, S., & Birch, H. G. (1963). *Behavioral individuality in early childhood*. New York: New York University Press.

Vinson, B. M. (2001, January). Fishing and Vygotsky's concept of effective education. *Young Children*, 56(1), 88–89.

Vygotsky, L. S. (1978). *Mind in society: The development of higher psychological process*. Cambridge, MA: Harvard University Press. (Original works published 1930, 1933, and 1935).

Werner, E. E. (1984, November). Research in review: Resilient children. *Young Children*, 40(1), 68–72.

Werner, E. E. (1995, June). Resilience in development. *Current Directions in Psychological Science*, 4(3), 81–85.

Werner, E. E. (2000, February–March). The power of protective factors in the early years. *Zero to Three*, 20(4), 3–5.

Werner, E. E., & Smith, R. S. (1992). *Overcoming the odds: High risk children from birth to adulthood*. Ithaca, NY: Cornell University Press.

Zimmerman, L., & McDonald, L. (1995). Emotional availability in infants' relationships with multiple caregivers. *American Journal of Orthopsychiatry*, 65(1), 147–152.

CHAPTER 3

Balaban, N. (2006). *Everyday goodbyes: A guide to the separation process*. New York: Teachers College Press.

Balaban, N. (2006 November). Easing the separation process for infants, toddlers, and families. *Young Children* 61(6), 14–19.

Bowlby, J. (1969). *Attachment and loss: Vol. 1. Attachment*. London: Hogarth.

Bowlby, J. (2000a [1972]). *Attachment and loss: Vol. 2. Separation: Anxiety and anger*. New York: Basic Books.

Bowlby, J. (2000b [1980]). *Attachment and loss: Vol. 3. Loss: Sadness and depression*. New York: Basic Books.

Carlebach, D., & Tate, B. (2002). *Creating caring children: The first three years*. Miami: The Peace Education Foundation.

David, M., & Appell, G. (2001 [1973, 1996]). *Loczy: An unusual approach to mothering*. Translated from *Loczy ou le maternage insolite*, by Jean Marie Clark; revised translation by Judit Falk. Budapest: Association Pikler-Loczy for Young Children.

Elkind, D. (2007). *The power of play*. Cambridge, MA: Da Capo.

Erikson, E. (1963). *Childhood and society*. New York: Norton.

Gerber, M. (1979). *The RIE manual*. Los Angeles: Resources for Infant Educarers.

Gonzalez-Mena, J. (2001, September). Making meaning of separation: Contrasting pictures of the first good-bye. *The First Years, Nga TauTuatahi* (New Zealand Journal of Infant and Toddler Education), 3(2), 4–5.

Gonzalez-Mena, J. (2004, September). What can an orphanage teach us? Lessons from Budapest. *Young Children*, 59(5), 26–30.

Gonzalez-Mena, J. (2008). *Diversity in early care and education: Honoring differences*. New York: McGraw-Hill.

Gray, H. (2004, September). "You go away and you come back": Supporting separations and reunions in an infant/toddler classroom. *Young Children*, 59(5), 100–107.

Greenfield, P. M., Quiroz, B., Rothstein-Fisch, C., & Trumbull, E. (2001). *Bridging cultures between home and school*. Mahwah, NJ: Erlbaum.

Greenough, W., Emde, R. N., Gunnar, M., Massinga, R., & Shonkoff, J. P. (2001, April–May). The impact of the caregiving environment on young children's development: Different ways of knowing, *Zero to Three*, 21(5), 16–24.

Jones, E. & Cooper, R. (2006). *Playing to get smart*. New York: Teachers College Press.

Kahwaty, D. H. (2006, March/April). Toilet-training newborns: parents grab hold of trend to potty-train infant twins. *Twins*, 20–23.

Lee, L. (Ed.). (2006). *Stronger together: family support and early childhood education*. San Rafael, CA: Parent Services Project.

McCracken, J. B. (1986). *So many good-byes: Ways to ease the transition between home and groups for young children*. Washington, DC: National Association for the Education of Young Children.

National Association for the Education of Young Children (1996, January). Linguistic and cultural diversity position paper. *Young Children*, 51(2), 4–12.

Parten, M. B. (1932). Social participation among preschool children. *Journal of Abnormal Psychology*, 27, 756–759.

Piaget, J. (1954). *The construction of reality in the child*. New York: Ballantine.

Piaget, J. (1962). *Play, dreams and imitation in childhood*. New York: Norton.

Pikler, E. & Tardos, A. (1968). Some contributions to the study of infants' gross motor activities. In *Proceedings of the 16th International Congress of Applied Psychology*. Amsterdam: ICAP. AMSTERDAM.

Pikler, E. (1971). Learning of motor skills on the basis of self-induced movements. In J. Hellmuth (Ed.). *Exceptional infant* (vol. 2, pp. 54–89). New York: Brunner/Mazel.

Pikler, E. (1973). Some contributions to the study of gross motor development of children. In A. Sandovsky (Ed.), *Child and adolescent development* (pp. 52–64). New York: Free Press.

Szanton, E. S. (2001, January). For America's infants and toddlers, are important values threatened by our zeal to "teach"? *Young Children*, 56(1), 15–21.

Van Hoorn, J., Nourot, P., Scales, B., & Alward, K. (2007). *Play at the center of the curriculum* (4th ed.). Upper Saddle River, NJ: Merrill/Prentice Hall.

Vinson, B. M. (2001, January). Fishing and Vygotsky's concept of effective education. *Young Children*, 56(1), 88–89.

Wittmer, D. S., & Petersen, S. H. (2006). *Infant and toddler development and responsive program planning: A relationship-based approach*. Upper Saddle River, NJ: Merrill/Prentice Hall.

Zepeda, M., Gonzalez-Mena, J., Rothstein-Fisch, C. & Trumbull, E. (2006). *Bridging cultures in early care and education*. Mahwah, NJ: Erlbaum.

CHAPTER 4

Barkley, R. A. (1997). *ADHD and the nature of self-control*. New York: Guilford.

Berk, L. E. (1994, November). Vygotsky's theory: The importance of make-believe play. *Young Children*, 50(1), 30–39.

Chandler, L. (1998). Promoting positive interaction between preschool-age children during free play: The Pals Center. *Young Exceptional Children*, 2(2), 13–19.

Duckworth, E. (2001). *"Tell me more": Listening to learners*. New York: Teachers College Press.

Edmiaston, R., Dolezal, V., Doolittle, S., Erickson, C., & Merritt, S. (2000). Developing individualized education programs for children in inclusive settings: A developmental framework. *Young Children*, 55(4), 36–41.

Eggers-Pierola, C. (2005). *Connections & Commitments .Reflecting Latino values in early childhood programs*. Portsmouth, NH: Heinemann.

Elkind, D. (2007) *The power of play*. Cambridge, MA: Da Capo.

Erikson, E. (1963). *Childhood and society*. New York: Norton.

Ferguson, C. J., & Dettore, E. (2007). *To play or not to play: Is it really a question?* Olney, MD: Association for Childhood Education International.

Fraiberg, S. H. (1959). *The magic years*. New York: Scribner's.

Fromberg, D. P. (2002). *Play and meaning in early childhood education*. Boston: Allyn & Bacon.

Frost, J., Wortham, S., & Reifel, S. (2008). *Play and child development* (3rd ed.). Upper Saddle River, NJ: Merrill/Prentice Hall.

Ferguson, C. J. & Dettore, E. (2007). *To play or not to play: Is it really a question?* Olney, MD: Association for Childhood Education International.

Greenberg, P. (1990, January). Why not academic preschool? *Young Children*, 45(2), 70–80.

Hyson, M. (2004). *The emotional development of young children* (2nd ed.). New York: Teachers College Press.

Jensen, E. (1998). *Teaching with the brain in mind*. Alexandria, VA: Association for Supervision and Curriculum Development.

Jacobs, G., & Crowley, K. (2007). *Play, projects and preschool standards: Nurturing children's sense of wonder and joy in learning*. Thousand Oaks, CA: Corwin Press.

Jones, E. (2003, May). Playing to get smart. *Young Children* 58(3), 32–33.

Jones, E. & Cooper, R. (2006). *Playing to get smart*. New York: Teachers College Press.

Jones, E., & Prescott, E. (1978). *Dimensions of teaching-learning environments: Vol. 2. Focus on day care*. Pasadena, CA: Pacific Oaks.

Jones, E., & Reynolds, G. (1992). *The play's the thing: Teachers' roles in children's play*. New York: Teachers College Press.

Kamii, C. (With L. B. Housman). (2000). *Young children reinvent arithmetic: Implications of Piaget's theory* (2nd ed.). New York: Teachers College Press.

Katch, J. (2001). *Under deadman's skin: Discovering the meaning of children's violent play*. Boston: Beacon.

Katz, L. G., & Chard, S. (2000). *Engaging children's minds: The project approach* (2nd ed.). Stamford, CT: Ablex.

Kelly, J. F., & Booth, C. L. (1999). Child care for children with special needs: Issues and applications. *Infants and Young Children*, 12(1), 26–33.

Kemple, K. M. (2004). *Let's be friends: Peer competence and social inclusion in early childhood programs*. New York: Teachers College Press.

Kern, P., and Wakeford, L. (2007 September). Supporting outdoor play for young children: The zone model of playground supervision. *Young Children* 62(5), 20–25.

Klein, M. D., & Chen, D. (2001). *Working with children from culturally diverse backgrounds*. New York: Delmar.

Kostelnik, M., Onaga, E., Rohde, B., & Whiren, A. (2002). *Children with special needs: Lessons for early childhood professionals*. New York: Teachers College Press.

Levin, D. E. (2002). *Teaching young children in violent times: Building a peaceable classroom* (2nd ed.). Cambridge, MA: Educators for Social Responsibility; Washington, DC: NAEYC.

Martin, B. (1975). Parent-child relations. In F. D. Horowitz (Ed.), *Review of child development research* (Vol. 4). Chicago: University of Chicago Press.

McCathren, R. B. (2000). Teacher-implemented prelinguistic communication intervention. *Focus on Autism and Other Developmental Disabilities*,15(1), 21–29.

Mistry, J. (1995). Culture and learning in infancy: Implications for caregiving. In P. L. Mangione (Ed.), *Infant/toddler caregiving: A guide to culturally sensitive care*. Sacramento: California Department of Education and the Far West Laboratory for Educational Research.

Noonan, M. J. & McCormick, L. (2006). *Young children with disabilities in natural environments*. Baltimore: Brookes.

Odom, S. (Ed.). (2002). *Widening the circle: Including children with disabilities in preschool programs*. New York: Teachers College Press.

Okagaki, L., & Diamond, K. E. (2000). Responding to cultural and linguistic differences in the beliefs and practices of families with young children. *Young Children*, 55(3), 74–78.

Olds, A. R. (1998). Places of beauty. In D. Bergen (Ed.), *Play as a medium for learning and development* (pp. 123–127). Olney, MD: Association for Childhood Education International.

Paley, V. G. (1986). *Bad guys don't have birthdays: Fantasy play at four*. Chicago: University of Chicago Press.

Paley, V. G. (1992). *You can't say you can't play*. Cambridge, MA: Harvard University Press.

Paley, V. G. (1999). *The kindness of children*. Cambridge, MA: Harvard University Press.

Pellegrini, A. D., & Smith, P. K. (Eds.). (2005). *The nature of play*. New York: Guilford.

Perry, J. (2001). *Outdoor play: Teaching strategies with young children*. New York: Teachers College Press.

Rogoff, B. (2003). *The cultural nature of human development*. New York: Oxford University Press.

Sandall, S. R. (2003, May). Play modifications for children with disabilities. *Young Children*, 58(3), 54–55.

Shonkoff, J. P., & Phillips, D. (2001, April–May). From neurons to neighborhoods: The science of early childhood development—An introduction. *Zero to Three*, 21(5), 4–7.

Shore, R. (1997). *Rethinking the brain: New insights in early development*. New York: Families and Work Institute.

Stinger, D. G., Golinkoff, R. M., & Hirsh-Pasek, K. (Eds.). (2006). *Play = Learning: How play motivates and enhances children's cognitive and social-emotional growth*. New York: Oxford University Press.

Thornberg, R. (2006) February). The situated nature of preschool children's conflict strategies. *Educational Psychology*, 26I(1), 109–112.

Trawick-Smith, J. (2001). Play and the curriculum. In J. Frost, S. Wortham, & S. Reifel (Eds.), *Play and child development*. Upper Saddle River, NJ: Merrill/Prentice Hall.

Van Hoorn, J., Nourot, P., Scales, B., & Alward, K. (2007). *Play at the center of the curriculum* (4th ed.). Upper Saddle River, NJ: Merrill/Prentice Hall.

Vygotsky, L. S. (1967). Play and its role in the mental development of the child. *Soviet Psychology*, 12, 62–76.

Wasserman, S. (2000). Serious players in the primary classroom: Empowering children through active learning experiences (2nd ed.). New York: Teachers College Press.

Wellhousen, K., & Kieff, J. (2001). A *constructivist approach to block play in early childhood*. Albany, NY: Delmar.

Wolfberg, P. L. (1999). *Play and imagination in children with autism*. New York: Teachers College Press.

CHAPTER 5

American Academy of Pediatrics, The committee on Communications and Committee on Psychological Aspects of Child and Family Health. (2006, October 9). Clinical report: The importance of play in promoting healthy child development and maintaining strong parent-child bonds. www.aap.org/pressroom/playFINAL.pdf. (Accessed May 3, 2007)

Axtmann, A., & Dettwiler, A. (2005). *The visit: Observation, reflection, synthesis for training and relationship building*. Baltimore: Brookes.

Bredekamp, S., & Copple, C. (Eds.). (1997). *Developmentally appropriate practice in early childhood programs serving children from birth through age 8*. Washington, DC: National Association for the Education of Young Children.

Briggs, D. C. (1975). *Your child's self-esteem*. New York: Dolphin.

Bronson, M. (2000). Research in Review: Recognizing and supporting the development of self-regulation in young children. *Young Children*, 55(2), 32–27.

Butterfield, P. M., Martin, C. A., & Prairie, A. P. (2004). *Emotional connections: How relationships guide early learning*. Washington, DC: Zero to Three.

Carlebach, D., & Tate. B., (2002). *Creating caring children: The first three years*. Maimi: Peace Education Foundation.

Chaille. C. (2008). *Constructivism across the curriculum in early childhood classrooms: Big ideas as inspiration*. Boston, MA: Allyn & Bacon/Pearson Education.

Chaker, A. M. (2006, October 10). Rethinking recess. *Wall Street Journal*.

Clarke, J. I. (1998) *Self-esteem a family affair*. Minneapolis: Winston.

Coopersmith, S. (1967). *The antecedents of self-esteem*. San Francisco: Freeman.

Curry, N. E., & Johnson, C. N. (1990). *Beyond self-esteem: Developing a genuine sense of human value*. Washington, DC: National Association for the Education of Young Children.

David, M., & Appell, G. (2001 [1973, 1996]). *Loczy: An unusual approach to mothering*. Translated from *Loczy ou le maternage insolite*, by Jean Marie Clark; revised translation by Judit Falk, Budapest: Association Pikler-Loczy for Young Children.

Delpit, L., & Dowdy, J. K. (2002). *The skin that we speak: Thoughts on language and culture in the classroom*. New York: New Press.

Derman-Sparks, L. (1989). *Anti-bias curriculum: Tools for empowering young children*. Washington, DC: National Association for the Education of Young Children.

Derman-Sparks, L., & Ramsey, P. G. (2006). *What if all the kids are white? Engaging white children and their famiies in anti-bias/multicultural education*. New York: Teachers College Press.

Diffily, D., & Sassman, C. (2006) *Positive teacher talk for better classroom management: Grades k-2*. New York: Scholastic.

Dorris, M. (1978). Why I'm *not* thankful for Thanksgiving. *Interracial Books for Children Bulletin*, 9(7), 6–9.

Erikson, E. (1963). *Childhood and society*. New York: Norton.

Gartell, D. (2007 May). You worked really hard on your picture! Guiding with encouragement. *Young Children* 62(3), 58–59.

Gerber, M. & Johnson, A. (1998). *Your self-confident baby*. New York: Wiley.

Gilligan, C. (1983). *In a different voice*. Cambridge, MA: Harvard University Press.

Ginsburg, K. R. (2006, Oct. 9) Clinical Report: The importance of play in promoting healthy child development and maintaining strong parent-child bonds. www.aap.org/pressroom/playFinal.pdf. accessed April 6, 2007.

Gonzalez-Mena, J. (2008). *Diversity in early care and education*. New York: McGraw-Hill.

Greenfield, P. M., Quiroz, B., Rothstein-Fisch, C., & Trumbull, E. (2001). *Bridging cultures between home and school*. Mahwah, NJ: Erlbaum.

Grieshaber, S., & Cannella, G. S. (2001). *Embracing identities in early childhood education: Diversity and possibilities*. New York: Teachers College Press.

Gross-Loh, C. (2007, March/April). Give me that old-time recess. *Mothering*, 54–63

Harter, S. (1983). Developmental perspectives on the self-system. In E. M. Heatherton (Ed.) & P. H. Mussen (Series Ed.), *Handbook of child psychology: Vol. 4. Socialization, personality, and social development* (4th ed., pp. 275–386). New York: Wiley.

Hitz, R., & Driscoll, A. (1988). Praise or encouragement? New insights into praise: Implications for early childhood teachers. *Young Children, 43*(5), 6–13.

hooks, b. (2003). *Rock my soul: Black people and self-esteem*. New York: Atria.

Howard, G. (1999). *We can't teach what we don't know: White teachers, multiracial schools*. New York: Teachers College Press.

Kagan, J. (1984). *The nature of the child*. New York: Basic Books.

Kern, P., & Wakeford, L. (2007, September). Supporting outdoor play for young children: The zone model of playground supervision. *Young Children 62*(5), 20–25.

Kohlberg, L. (1976). Moral stages and moralization. The cognitive-development approach. In T. Lickona (Ed.), *Moral development and behavior*. New York: Holt, Rinehart & Winston.

Kranowitz, C. S. (1998). *The out of sync child: Recognizing and coping with sensory integration dysfunction*. New York: Paragee.

Lally, J. R. (1995, November). The impact of child care policies and practices on infant/toddler identity formation. *Young Children, 51*(1), 58–67.

Landy, S. (2002). *Pathways to competence: Encouraging healthy social and emotional development in young children*. Baltimore: Brookes.

Markus, H. R., Mullally, P. R., & Kitayama, S. (1997). Selfways: Diversity in modes of cultural participation. In U. Neisser & D. Jopling (Eds.), *The conceptual self in context* (pp. 12–61). New York: Cambridge University Press.

Marshall, H. H. (2000, November). Cultural influences on the development of self-concept. *Young Children, 56*(6), 19–22.

Martinez, F. (2005) Early care and education for Hispanic children. *Childhood Education 81*(3), 174–176.

Morrison, J. W. (2001, Spring). Supporting biracial children's identity development. *Childhood Education, 77*(3), 134–138.

Noddings, N. (2002). *Educating moral people: A caring alternative to character education*. New York: Teachers College Press.

Noddings, N. (2005). *The challenge to care in schools*. New York: Teachers College Press.

Noonan, M. J., & McCormick, L. (2006). *Young children with disabilities in natural environments*. Baltimore: Brookes.

Paley, V. G. (1992). *You can't say you can't play*. Cambridge, MA: Harvard University Press.

Piaget, J. (1952). *The origins of intelligence in children*. New York, International Universities Press.

Rhodes, M., Enz, B., & LaCount, M. (2006, January). Leaps and bounds: Preparing parents for kindergarten. *Young Children 61*(1), 50–51.

Rogoff, B. (2003). *The cultural nature of human development*. New York: Oxford University Press.

Seligman, M. E. P. (1975). *Helplessness: On depression, development and death*. San Francisco: Freeman.

Teaching Tolerance Project. (1997). *Starting small: Teaching tolerance in preschool and the early grades*. Montgomery, AL: Southern Poverty Law Center.

Vygotsky, L. S. (1978). *Mind and society: The development of higher psychological process*. Cambridge, MA: Harvard University Press.

Wardel, F. (1993, March). How young children build images of themselves. *Exchange*, 90.

Werner, E. E. (1984, November). Research in review: Resilient children. *Young Children, 40*(1), 68–72.

CHAPTER 6

Ballenger, C. (1999). *Teaching other people's children*. New York: Teachers College Press.

Bandtec Network for Diversity Training. (2003). *Reaching for answers: A workbook on diversity in early childhood education*. Oakland, California: Bandtec Network for Diversity Training. Available at the Bandtec Web site (www.bandtec.org).

Barrera, I., & Corso, R. (2003). *Skilled dialog*. Baltimore: Brookes.

Bredekamp, S., & Copple, C. (Eds.). (1997). *Developmentally appropriate practice in early childhood programs serving children from birth through age eight*. Washington, DC: National Association for the Education of Young Children.

Brody, H. (2001). *The other side of Eden: Hunters, farmers, and the shaping of the world*. New York: North Point Press.

Bruno, H. E. (2003, September–October). Hearing parents in every language: An invitation to ECE professionals. *Child Care Information Exchange, 153*, 58–60.

Butterfield, P. M., Martin, C. A., & Prairie, A. P. (2004). *Emotional connections: How relationships guide early learning*. Washington, DC: Zero to Three.

Carlebach, D., & Tate, B. (2002). *Creating caring children: The first three years*. Miami: Peace Education Foundation.

Charney, R. S. (2002). *Teaching children to care: Classroom management for ethical and academic growth*. Greenfield, MA: Northeast Foundation for Children.

Copple, C. (Ed.). (2003). *A world of difference: Readings on teaching young children in a diverse society*. Washington, DC: National Association for the Education of Young Children.

David, M., & Appell, G. (2001[1973, 1996]). *Loczy: An unusual approach to mothering*. Translated from *Loczy ou le maternage insolite*, by Jean Marie Clark; revised translation by Judit Falk. Budapest: Association Pikler-Loczy for Young Children.

Delpit, L., & Dowdy, J. K. (2002). *The skin that we speak: Thoughts on language and culture in the classroom*. New York: New Press.

Derman-Sparks, L. (1989). *Antibias curriculum*. Washington, DC: National Association for the Education of Young Children.

Eggers-Pierola, C. (2002). *Connections and commitments: A Latino-based framework for early childhood educators*. Newton, MA: Educational Development Center.

Epstein, J. L. (2006, January). Families, schools, and community partnerships. *Young Children* 61(1), 40

Friend, M., & Cook, L. (2003). *Interactions: Collaboration skills for school professionals* (4th ed.). Boston: Allyn & Bacon.

Gandini, L., & Edwards, C. P. (Eds.). (2000). *Bambini: The Italian approach to infant-toddler care*. New York: Teachers College Press.

Gerber, M. (1998). *Dear parent: Caring for infants with respect*. Los Angeles: Resources for Infant Educarers.

Gilligan, C. (1982). *In a different voice*. Cambridge, MA: Harvard University Press.

Goldenberg, C., Gallimore, R., & Reese, L. (2003). Cause or effect? A longitudinal study of immigrant Latino parents' aspirations and expectations, and their children's school performance. *American Educational Research Journal, 38*, 547–582.

Goldstein, L. (2002). *Reclaiming caring in teaching and teacher education*. New York: Lang.

Gonzalez-Mena, J. (2002, September). Working with cultural differences: Individualism and collectivism. *The First Years: Nga Tautuatahi, 4*(2), 13–15.

Gonzalez-Mena, J. (2008) *Diversity in early care and education*. New York: McGraw-Hill.

Gonzalez-Mena, J., & Peshotan Bhavangri, N. (2001, March). Cultural differences in sleeping practices. *Exchange, 138*, 91–93.

Goodman, J. F., & Lesnick, H. (2001). *The moral stake in education*. New York: Longman.

Greenfield, P. M. (1994). Independence and interdependence as developmental scripts: Implications for theory, research, and practice. In P. M. Greenfield & R. R. Cocking (Eds.), *Cross-cultural roots of minority child development* (pp. 1–37). Mahwah, NJ: Erlbaum.

Greenfield, P. M., Quiroz, B., & Raeff, C. (2000). Cross-cultural conflict and harmony in the social construction of the child. *New Directions for Child and Adolescent Development, 87*, 93–108.

Greenfield, P. M., Quiroz, B., Rothstein-Fisch, C., & Trumbull, E. (2001). *Bridging cultures between home and school*. Mahwah, NJ: Erlbaum.

Guerra, P., & Garcia, S. (2000). *Understanding the cultural contexts of teaching and learning*. Austin, TX: Southwest Educational Development Laboratory.

Harwood, R. L., Miller, J. G., & Irizarry, N. L. (1995). *Culture and attachment: Perceptions of the child in context*. New York: Guilford.

Hoffman, M. L. (2000). *Empathy and moral development*. Cambridge: Cambridge University Press.

Hofstede, G. (2001). *Culture's consequences: Comparing values, behaviors, institutions, and organizations across nations* (2nd ed.). Thousand Oaks, CA: Sage.

Kaiser, B., & Rasminsky, J. S. (2003, July). Opening the cultural door. *Young Children, 58*(4), 53–56.

Kohlberg, L. (1976). Moral stages and moralization: The cognitive-developmental approach. In T. Lickona (Ed.), *Moral development and behavior*. New York: Holt, Rinehart & Winston.

Lee, L. (2002). *Serving families: A handbook on the principles and strategies of the parent services project approach*. San Rafael, CA: Parent Services Project.

Levin, D. E. (2002). *Teaching young children in violent times: Building a peaceable classroom*. (2nd ed.). Cambridge, MA: Educators for Social Responsibility; Washington, DC: National Association for the Education of Young Children.

Lustig, M. W., & Koester, J. (2003). *Interpersonal competence: Interpersonal communication across cultures* (4th ed.). New York: Addison Wesley Longman.

Martini, M. (2002, February–March). How mothers in four American cultural groups shape infant learning during mealtimes, *Zero to Three, 22*(4), 14–20.

Noddings, N. (2005). *The challenge to care in schools*. New York: Teachers College Press.

Noddings, N. (2002a). *Educating moral people: A caring alternative to character education*. New York: Teachers College Press.

Noddings, N. (2002b). *Starting at home: Care and social policy*. Berkeley: University of California Press.

Patterson, K., Grenny, J., McMillan, R., Switzer, A., & Covey, S. R. (2002). *Crucial conversations: Tools for talking when the stakes are high*. New York: McGraw-Hill.

Poussaint, A. F. (2006, January). Understanding and involving African American parents. *Young Children* 61(1), 48.

Powers, J. (2006 January). Six fundamentals for creating relationships with families. *Young Children* 61(1), 28.

Quintero, E. P. (2004, May). Will I lose a tooth? Will I learn to read? Problem posing with multicultural children's literature. *Young Children, 59*(3), 56–62.

Raeff, C., Greenfield, P. M., & Quiroz, B. (2000, Spring). Conceptualizing interpersonal relationships in the cultural contexts of individualism and collectivism. *New Directions for Child and Adolescent Development, 87*, 59–74.

Reese, L. (2002). Parental strategies in contrasting cultural settings: Families in Mexico and El Norte. *Anthropology & Education Quarterly, 33*, 30–59.

Rogoff, B. (2003). *The cultural nature of human development*. New York: Oxford University Press.

Rothstein-Fisch, C. (2003). *Readings for bridging cultures: Teacher education module*. Mahwah, NJ: Erlbaum.

Shweder, R. A., Goodnow, J., Hatano, G., LeVine, R. A., Markus, H., & Miller, P. (1998). The cultural psychology of development: One mind, many mentalities. In W. Damon & R. M. Lerner (Eds.), *Handbook of Child Psychology: Vol. 1. Theoretical models of human development* (5th ed., pp. 865–937). New York: Wiley.

Siraj-Blatchford, I., & Clarke, P. (2000). *Supporting identity, diversity and language in the early years.* Philadelphia: Open University Press.

Some, S. (2000). *The spirit of intimacy: Ancient African teachings in the ways of relationships.* New York: HarperCollins/Quill.

Sue, S., & Moore, T. (Eds.). (1984). *The pluralistic society.* New York: Human Sciences Press.

Trumbull, E., Greenfield, P. M., Rothstein-Fisch, C., & Quiroz, B. (2001). *Bridging cultures between home and school: A guide for teachers.* Mahwah, NJ: Erlbaum.

Trumbull, E., Rothstein-Fisch, C., & Greenfield, P. M. (2000). *Bridging cultures in our schools: New approaches that work.* Knowledge brief. San Francisco: WestEd.

Trumbull, E., Rothstein-Fisch, C., & Hernandez, E. (2003). Parent involvement—according to whose values? *School Community Journal*, 13(2), 45–72.

U.S. Department of Health and Human Services, Administration on Children, Youth and Families. (2000). *Celebrating cultural and linguistic diversity in Head Start.* Washington, DC: Department of Health and Human Services.

Wong Fillmore, L. (2000). Loss of family languages: Should educators be concerned? *Theory Into Practice*, 39(4), 203–210.

Zepeda, M., Gonzalez-Mena, J., Rothstein-Fisch, C., & Trumbull, E. (2006). *Bridging cultures in early care and education.* Mahwah, NJ: Erlbaum.

CHAPTER 7

Ball, J., & Pence, A. R. (1999). Beyond developmentally appropriate practice: Developing community and culturally appropriate practices. *Young Children* 54(2), 46–50.

Ballenger, C. (1992, Summer). Because you like us: The language of control. *Harvard Educational Review*, 62(2), 199–208.

Ballenger, C. (1999). *Teaching other people's children.* New York: Teachers College Press.

Berk, L. E., & Winsler, A. (1995). *Scaffolding children's learning: Vygotsky and early childhood education.* Washington, DC: National Association for the Education of Young Children.

Brault, L, & Brault, T. (2005). *Children with challenging Behavior: Strategies for reflective thinking.* Phoenix AZ: CPG Publishing.

Brehm, S. S. (1981). Oppositional behavior in children: A reactancy theory approach. In S. S. Brehm, S. M. Kassin, & F. X. Gibbons (Eds.), *Developmental social psychology theory* (pp. 96–121). New York: Oxford University Press.

Bronson, M. (2000). Research in review: Recognizing and supporting the development of self-regulation in young children. *Young Children*, 55(2), 32–36.

Campbell, S. B., Pierce, E. W., March, C. L., Ewing, L. J., & Szumowski, E. K. (1994). Hard to manage preschool boys: Symptomatic behavior across contexts and time. *Child Development* 65, 836–851.

Dahlberg, G., Moss, P., & Pence, A. (1999). *Beyond quality in early childhood education and care: Postmodern perspectives.* London: Falmer.

Diaz, R. M., Neal, C. J., & Amaya-Williams, M. (1996). *The social origins of self-regulation: Vygotsky and Education.* Cambridge: Cambridge University Press.

Dreikurs, R., & Loren, G. (1990). *Logical consequences: A new approach to discipline.* New York: Dutton.

Dreikurs, R., & Soltz, V. (1964). *Children: The challenge.* New York: Duell, Sloan, & Pearce.

Drifte, C. (2004). *Encouraging positive behavior in the early years: A practical guide.* London: Paul Chapman Publishing.

Eggers-Pierola, C. (2005). *Connections and commitments: Reflecting Latino values in early childhood programs.* Portsmouth, NH: Heinemann.

Gil, D. G. (1970). *Violence against children: Physical child abuse in the United States.* Cambridge, MA: Harvard University Press.

Gonzalez-Mena, J. (2008). *Diversity in early care and education: Honoring differences*, 5th ed. New York: McGraw-Hill.

Gonzalez-Mena, J., & Shareef, I. (2005, November). Discussing diverse perspectives on guidance. *Young Children*, 60(6), 34–38.

Goodman, J. F., & Balamore, U. (2003). *Teaching goodness: Engaging the moral and academic promise of young children.* Boston: Allyn & Bacon.

Gordon, T. (2000). PET: *Parent effectiveness training.* New York: Wyden.

Hale, J. E. (1986). *Black children: Their roots, culture, and learning styles.* Baltimore: Johns Hopkins University Press.

Howes, C., & Ritchie, S. (2002). *A matter of trust.* New York: Teachers College Press.

Hyson, M. (2004). *The emotional development of young children* (2nd ed.). New York: Teachers College Press.

Jones, E., & Cooper, R. (2005). *Playing to get smart.* New York: Teachers College Press.

Kagan, J. (1984). *The nature of the child.* New York: Basic Books.

Kaiser, B., & Rasminsky, J. (2003). *Challenging behavior in young children: Understanding, preventing and responding effectively.* Boston: Allyn & Bacon.

Kohn, A. (1999). *Punished by rewards: The trouble with gold stars, incentive plans, A's, praise, and other bribes.* Boston: Houghton Mifflin.

Kohn, A. (2004). *Unconditional parenting: Moving from rewards and punishment to love and reasoning.* New York: Atria.

Kranowitz, C. S. (1998). *The out of sync child: Recognizing and coping with sensory integration dysfunction.* New York: Paragee.

Lee, L. (Ed.). (2006). *Stronger Together. Family support and early childhood education.* San Rafael, CA: Parent Services Project, Inc.

Marion, M. (1999). *Guidance of young children* (5th ed.). Upper Saddle River, NJ: Merrill/Prentice Hall.

Maslow, A. H. (1968). *Toward a psychology of being.* New York: Van Nostrand.

Maslow, A. H. (1970). *Motivation and personality.* New York: Harper & Row.

McLoyd, V. C., Hill, N. E., & Dodge, K. A. (Eds.). (2005). *African American family life.* New York: Guilford.

Nelsen, J., (Ed.). (2001). *Positive discipline: A teacher's a–z guide* (2nd ed.). Rocklin, CA: Prima.

Nelsen, J., & Glenn, H. S. (1996). *Positive discipline.* New York: Ballantine.

Noddings, N. (2002). *Educating moral people: A caring alternative to character education.* New York: Teachers College Press.

Ostrosky, M., & Sandall, S. (2001). *Teaching strategies: What to do to support young children's development.* Denver: Division for Early Childhood of the Council for Exceptional Children.

Pence, A. (2004). Finding a niche in building ECE capacity. *Interaction 18*(1), 31–33.

Phillips, C.B. (1995). Culture: A process that empowers. In J. Cortez & C. L. Young-Holt (Eds.). *Infant/toddler caregiving: A guide to culturally sensitive care.* Sacramento: California Department of Education.

Rand, M. K. (2000). *Giving it some thought: Cases for early childhood practice.* Washington, DC: National Association for the Education of Young Children.

Reynolds, E. (2001) *Guiding young children: A problem-solving approach.* New York: McGraw-Hill.

Sandall, S., McLean, M. E., & Smith, B. (2000). *DEC recommended practices in early intervention/early childhood special education.* Longmonth, CO: Sopris West.

Sandall, S., & Ostrosky, M. (1999). *Young exceptional children: Practical ideas for addressing challenging behaviors.* Denver: Division for Early Childhood of the Council for Exceptional Children.

Sandoval, M., & De La Roza, M. (1986). A cultural perspective for serving the Hispanic client. In H. Lefley & P. Pedersen (Eds.), *Cross-cultural training for mental health professionals.* Springfield, IL: Thomas.

Segal, M., Masi, W., & Leiderman, R. (2001). *In time and with love: Caring for infants and toddlers with special needs.* New York: New Market Press.

Siccone, F., & Lopez, L. (2000). *Educating the heart: Lessons to build respect and responsibility.* Boston: Allyn & Bacon.

Snowden, L. R. (1984). Toward evaluation of black psycho-social competence. In S. Sue & T. Moore (Eds.), *The pluralistic society.* New York: Human Sciences Press.

Trickett, P. K., & Kuczynski, L. (1986). Children's misbehavior and parental discipline strategies in abusive and nonabusive families. *Developmental Psychology, 8,* 240–260.

CHAPTER 8

Ballenger, C. (1992, Summer). Because you like us: The language of control. *Harvard Educational Review, 62*(2), 199–208.

Ballenger, C. (1999). *Teaching other people's children.* New York: Teachers College Press.

Baumrind, D. (1971). Current patterns of parental authority. *Developmental Psychology Monographs, 4,* 99–103.

Baumrind, D. (1986). Socialization and instrumental competence in young children. In W. W. Hartup (Ed.), *The young child: Reviews of research* (Vol. 2, pp. 202–224). Washington, DC: National Association for the Education of Young Children.

Bruno, H. E. (2007, September). Gossip-free zones: Problem solving to prevent power struggles. *Young Children, 62*(5), 26–32.

Butterfield, P. M., Martin, C. A., & Prairie, A. P. (2004). *Emotional connections: How relationships guide early learning.* Washington, DC: Zero to Three.

Chao, R. K. (1994). Beyond parental control and authoritarian parenting style: Understanding Chinese parenting through the cultural notion of training. *Child Development, 65,* 1111–1119.

David, M., & Appell, G. (2001 [1973, 1996]). *Loczy: An unusual approach to mothering.* Translated from *Loczy ou le maternage insolite,* by Jean Marie Clark; revised translation by Judit Falk. Budapest: Association Pikler-Loczy for Young Children.

Dowrick, P. W. (1986). *Social survival for children: A trainer's resource book.* New York: Brunner/Mazel.

Dung, T. N. (1984, March-April). Understanding Asian families: A Vietnamese perspective. *Children Today, 13*(2), 10–12.

Goleman, D. (2000). *Working with emotional intelligence.* New York: Bantam.

Gonzalez-Mena, J. (2007). What to do with a fussy baby: A problem-solving approach. *Young Children, 62*(5), 20–25.

Greenspan, S. I. (1999). *Building healthy minds.* Cambridge, MA: Perseus.

Greenspan, S. I., & Greenspan, N. T. (1985). *First feelings: Milestones in the emotional development of your baby and child.* New York: Viking.

Greenspan, S. I., & Wieder, S. (1998). *The child with special needs: Encouraging intellectual and emotional growth.* Reading, MA: Perseus.

Harter, S. (1998). The development of self-representations. In N. Eisenberg (Ed.), *Handbook of child psychology: Vol. 3. Social, emotional, and personality development* (5th ed., pp. 553–618). New York: Wiley.

Harter, S., & Buddin, B. J. (1987). Children's understanding of the simultaneity of two emotions: A five-stage developmental acquisition sequence. *Developmental Psychology, 22*(3), 388–399.

Hsu, F. L. K. (1970). *Americans and Chinese: Purpose and fulfillment in great civilizations.* Garden City, NY: Natural History Press.

Hyson, M. (2004). *The emotional development of young children* (2nd ed.). New York: Teachers College Press.

Keenan, M. (1996, September). They pushed my buttons: Being put up against myself. *Young Children, 51*(6), 74–75.

Kagan, J. (1985) *The nature of the child.* New York: Basic Books.

Klein, M. D., & Chen, D. (2001). *Working with children from culturally diverse backgrounds.* Albany, NY: Delmar.

Lee, D. (1959). *Freedom and culture.* Upper Saddle River, NJ: Prentice Hall.

Paley, V. G. (1988). *Bad guys don't have birthdays: Fantasy play at four.* Chicago: University of Chicago Press.

Parke, R. D., & O'Neil, R. (2000). The influence of significant others on learning about relationships: From family to friends. In R. S. L. Mills & S. Duck (Eds.), *The developmental psychology of personal relationships* (pp. 15–47). New York: Wiley.

Petersen, S., Bair, K., & Sullivan, A. (2004). Emotional well-being and mental health services: Lessons learned by early Head Start Region VIII programs. *Zero to Three, 24*(6), 47–53.

Rogers, C. R. (1980). *A way of being.* Boston: Houghton Mifflin.

Rogoff, B. (2003) *The cultural nature of human development.* Cambridge, MA: Oxford University Press.

Smith, L. A. H. (1985). *To understand and to help: The life and work of Susan Isaacs.* Cranbury, NJ: Associated University Presses.

Thoman, E. B., & Browder, S. (1987). *Born dancing: How intuitive parents understand the baby's unspoken language and natural rhythms.* New York: Harper & Row.

Van Hoorn, J., Nourot, P., Scales, B., & Alward, K. (2007). *Play at the center of the curriculum* (4th ed.). Upper Saddle River, NJ: Merrill/Prentice Hall.

CHAPTER 9

Bredekamp, S., & Copple, C. (Eds.). (1997). *Developmentally appropriate practice in early childhood programs serving children from birth through age 8.* Washington, DC: National Association for the Education of Young Children.

Briggs, D. C. (1975). *Your child's self-esteem.* New York: Dolphin.

Bronson, M. (2000). Research in Review: Recognizing and supporting the development of self-regulation in young children. *Young Children, 55*(2), 32–27.

Butterfield, P. M., Martin, C. A., & Prairie, A. P. (2004). *Emotional connections: How relationships guide early learning.* Washington, DC: Zero to Three.

Clarke, J. I. (1998). *Self esteem: A family affair.* Minneapolis, MN: Winston.

Coopersmith, S. (1967). *The antecedents of self-esteem.* San Francisco: Freeman.

Copple, C. (2006) *Basics of developmentally appropriate practice: An introduction for teachers of children 3–6.* Washington DC: National Association for the Education of Young Children.

Curry, N. E., & Johnson, C. N. (1990). *Beyond self-esteem: Developing a genuine sense of human value.* Washington, DC: National Association for the Education of Young Children.

Delpit, L., & Dowdy, J. K. (2002). *The skin that we speak: Thoughts on language and culture in the classroom.* New York: New Press.

Derman-Sparks, L. (1989). *Anti-bias curriculum: Tools for empowering young children.* Washington, DC: National Association for the Education of Young Children.

Dorris, M. (1978). Why I'm *not* thankful for Thanksgiving. *Interracial Books for Children Bulletin, 9*(7), 6–9.

Egertson, H. A. (2006, November). Of primary interest. In praise of butterflies: Linking self-esteem and learning. *Young Children 61*(6), 58–60.

Eggers-Pierola, C. (2005). *Connections & Commitments .Reflecting Latino values in early childhood programs.* Portsmouth, NH: Heinemann.

Epstein, J. L. (2006, January). Families, Schools, and Community Partnerships. *Young Children 61*(1), 40

Erikson, E. (1963). *Childhood and society.* New York: Norton.

Goldstein, L. (2002). *Reclaiming caring in teaching and teacher education.* New York: Lang.

Gonzalez-Mena, J. (2008). *Diversity in early care and education.* New York: McGraw-Hill.

Greenfield, P. M., Quiroz, B., Rothstein-Fisch, C., & Trumbull, E. (2001). *Bridging cultures between home and school.* Mahwah, NJ: Erlbaum.

Grieshaber, S., & Cannella, G. S. (2001). *Embracing identities in early childhood education: Diversity and possibilities.* New York: Teachers College Press.

Harter, S. (1983). Developmental perspectives on the self-system. In E. M. Heatherton (Ed.) & P. H. Mussen (Series Ed.), *Handbook of child psychology: Vol. 4. Socialization, personality, and social development* (4th ed., pp. 275–386). New York: Wiley.

Hitz, R., & Driscoll, A. (1988). Praise or encouragement? New insights into praise: Implications for early childhood teachers. *Young Children, 43*(5), 6–13.

hooks, b. (2003). *Rock my soul: Black people and self-esteem.* New York: Atria.

Howard, G. (1999). *We can't teach what we don't know: White teachers, multiracial schools.* New York: Teachers College Press.

Kagan, J. (1984). *The nature of the child.* New York: Basic Books.

Kranowitz, C. S. (1998). *The out of sync child: Recognizing and coping with sensory integration dysfunction.* New York: Paragee.

Lally, J. R. (1995, November). The impact of child care policies and practices on infant/toddler identity formation. *Young Children*, 51(1), 58–67.

Landy, S. (2002). *Pathways to competence: Encouraging healthy social and emotional development in young children*. Baltimore: Brookes.

Markus, H. R., Mullally, P. R., & Kitayama, S. (1997). Selfways: Diversity in modes of cultural participation. In U. Neisser & D. Jopling (Eds.), *The conceptual self in context* (pp. 12–61). New York: Cambridge University Press.

Marshall, H. H. (2000, November). Cultural influences on the development of self-concept. *Young Children*, 56(6), 19–22.

Morrison, J. W. (2001, Spring). Supporting biracial children's identity development. *Childhood Education*, 77(3), 134–138.

Noddings, N. (2002). *Educating moral people: A caring alternative to character education*. New York: Teachers College Press.

Paley, V. G. (1992). *You can't say you can't play*. Cambridge, MA: Harvard University Press.

Rogoff, B. (2003). *The cultural nature of human development*. New York: Oxford University Press.

Rosenthal, R. (1987) Pygmalion effects: Existence, magnitude, and social importance. *Educational Researcher*, 16(9), 37–41.

Seligman, M. E. P. (1975). *Helplessness: On depression, development and death*. San Francisco: Freeman.

Teaching Tolerance Project. (1997). *Starting small: Teaching tolerance in preschool and the early grades*. Montgomery, AL: Southern Poverty Law Center.

Vygotsky, L. S. (1978). *Mind and society: The development of higher psychological process*. Cambridge, MA: Harvard University Press.

Wardel, F. (1993, March). How young children build images of themselves. *Exchange*, 90.

CHAPTER 10

American Psychological Association. (2007). Report of the APA Task Force on the Sexualization of Girls. www.apa.org/pi/wpo/sexualization.html

Bailey, J., Bobrow, D., Wolfe, M., & Mikach, S. (1995). Sexual orientation of adult sons of gay fathers. Special issue: Sexual orientation and human development. *Developmental Psychology*, 31, 124–129.

Bruno, H. E. (2004). Hearing parents in every language. *Exchange*.

Cox, A. J. (2006). *Boys of few words. Raising our sons to communicate and connect*. New York: Guilford.

The Economist, 384(8545), 82–82.

Eiduson, B. T., Kornfein, M., Zimmerman, I. L., & Weisner, T. S. (1988). Comparative socialization practices in traditional and alternative families. In G. Handel (Ed.), *Childhood socialization* (pp. 73–101). Hawthorne, NY: Aldine.

Fagot, B. I. (1978). The influence of sex of child on parental reactions to toddler children. *Child Development*, 49, 459–465.

Gorman, C. (1997, March 24). A boy without a penis. *Time*.

Gurian, M. (1997). *The wonder of boys*. New York: Putnam.

Money, J., & Ehrhardt, A. A. (1973). *Man and woman, boy and girl*. Baltimore: Johns Hopkins University Press.

Paley, V. (1984). *Boys and girls: Superheroes in the doll corner*. Chicago: University of Chicago Press.

Parke, R. D. (2002). Fatherhood. In M. Bornstein (Ed.), *Handbook of parenting* (2nd ed.). Mahwah, NJ: Erlbaum.

Parke, R. D., & Brott, A. (1999). *Throwaway dads*. Boston: Houghton Mifflin.

Patterson, C. J. (2002). Lesbian and gay parenthood. In M. H. Bornstein (Ed.), *Handbook of parenting* (2nd ed.). Mahwah, NJ: Erlbaum.

Pollack, W. (1998). *Real boys*. New York: Random House.

Pomerleau, A., Bolduc, D., Malcuit, G., & Cossette, L. (1990). Pink or blue: Environmental gender stereotypes in the first two years of life. *Sex Roles*, 22, 359–367.

Rheingold, H. L., & Cook, K. V. (1975). The content of boys' and girls' rooms as an index of parent behavior. *Child Development*, 46, 459–463.

Ruble, D. N., & Martin, C. L. (1998). Gender development. In W. Damon (Gen. Ed.) & N. Eisenberg (Vol. Ed.), *Handbook of child psychology* (Vol. 3, pp. 933–1016). New York: Wiley.

Serbin, L. A., O'Leary, F., Kent, R. N., & Tolnick, I. J. (1973, December). A comparison of teacher response to the preacademic and problem behavior of boys and girls. *Child Development*, 44(4), 776–804.

Thorne, B. (1993). *Gender play: Girls and boys in school*. New Brunswick, NJ: Rutgers University Press.

Turner-Bowker, D. M. (1996). Gender stereotyped description in children's picture books: Does "Curious Jane" exist in literature? *Sex Roles*, 35, 461–488.

Weisner, T. S., & Wilson-Mitchell, J. E. (1990). Nonconventional family lifestyles and multischematic sex typing in six-year-olds. *Child Development*, 61, 1915–1933.

Weitzman, L. J. (1979). *Sex role socialization: A focus on women*. Mountain View, CA: Mayfield.

Zeitlin, S. A. (1997, September). Finding fascinating projects that can promote boy/girl partnerships. *Young Children*, 52(6), 29–30.

CHAPTER 11

Akbar, N. (2003). *Akbar papers in African psychology*. Tallahassee, FL: Mind Productions.

Blimes, J. (2004). *Beyond behavior management: The six life skills children need to thrive in today's world*. St. Paul, MN: Redleaf Press.

Bronfenbrenner, U. 1994. Ecological models of human development. In *International Encyclopedia of Education*, *Vol.* 3 (2nd edition.), eds. T. Husen and N. Postleth-waite, 1643–1647.

Carnegie Task Force on Meeting the Needs of Young Children. (1994, July). Starting points: Executive summary of the report of the Carnegie Corporation of New York Task Force on Meeting the Needs of Young Children. *Young Children*, 47(5), 58–60.

Casper, V. (2003, January). Very young children in lesbian- and gay-headed families: Moving beyond acceptance. *Zero to Three*, 23(3), 18–26.

Children's Defense Fund. (2004). *The state of America's children* 2004. Washington, DC: Children's Defense Fund.

Children's Defense Fund. (2005). *The state of America's children* 2005. Washington, DC: Children's Defense Fund.

Christian, L. G. (2006). Understanding families: Applying family systems theory to early childhood practice. *Young Children* 61(2) 12–20.

Crockenberg, S. (1992, April). How children learn to resolve conflicts in families. *Zero to Three*, 12(5), 11–13.

DeJong, L. (2003, March). Using Erikson to work more effectively with teenage parents. *Young Children*, 58(2), 87–95.

Galinsky, E. (1989, May). Problem solving. *Young Children*, 44(4), 2–3.

Hall, E. T. (1981) *Beyond culture*. Garden City, NY: Anchor Press/Doubleday.

Keyser, J. (2006) *From parents to partners: Building a family centered early childhood program*. Washington DC: National Association for the Education of Young Children and St. Paul, MN: Redleaf.

Korfmacher, J., & Marchi, I. (2002, November). The helping relationship in a teen parenting program. *Zero to Three*, 21(2), 21–26.

Lee, L. (Ed.). (2006). *Stronger together. Family support and early childhood education.* San Rafael, CA: Parent Services Project, Inc.

Lee, L., & Seiderman, E. (1998). *Families matter: The Parent Services Project.* Cambridge, MA: Harvard Family Research Project.

Links, G., Beggs, M., & Seiderman, E. (1997). *Serving families.* Fairfax, CA: Parent Services Project.

Luthar, S. S., Cicchetti, D., & Becker, B. (2000). The construct of resilience: A critical evaluation and guidelines for future work. *Child Development*, 71, 543–562.

Morrison, J. W. (2001, Spring). Supporting biracial children's identity development. *Childhood Education*, 77(3), 134–138.

National Association for the Education of Young Children (2005). *Families and community relationships: A guide to the NAEYC early childhood program standards and related accreditation criteria.* Washington, DC: National Association for Education of Young Children.

Odom, S. L., Teferra, T., & Kaul, S. (2004, September). An overview of international approaches to early intervention for young children with special needs and their families. *Young Children*, 59(5), 38–43.

Okagaki, L., & Diamond, K. (2000, May). Responding to cultural and linguistic differences in the beliefs and practices of families with young children. *Young Children*, 55(3), 74–80.

Parke, R. D., & O'Neil, R. (2000). The influence of significant others on learning about relationships: From family to friends. In R. S. L. Mills & S. Duck (Eds.), *The developmental psychology of personal relationships* (pp. 15–47). New York: Wiley.

Payne, R. K. (2003). *A framework for understanding poverty.* Highlands, TX: Aha Process.

Seploch, H. (2004, September). Family ties: Partnerships for learning: Conferencing with families. *Young Children*, 59(5), 96–100.

Stonehouse, A., & Gonzalez-Mena, J. (2004). *Making links: A collaborative approach to planning and practice in early childhood services.* Castle Hills, NSW, Australia: Pademelon Press.

Satir, V. (1972). *Peoplemaking.* Palo Alto: Science and Behavior Books.

Swick, K. (2004). *Empowering parents, families, schools, and communities during the early childhood years.* Champaign, IL: Stipes.

Werner, E. E. (1984, November). Research in review: Resilient children. *Young Children*, 40(1), 68–72.

Werner, E. E. (1995, June). Resilience in development. *Current Directions in Psychological Science*, 4(3), 81–85.

Werner, E. E., & Smith, R. S. (1992). *Overcoming the odds: High risk children from birth to adulthood.* Ithaca, NY: Cornell University Press.

CHAPTER 12

Aronson, S., & Spahr, P. M. (2002). *Healthy young children: A manual for programs.* Washington, DC: National Association for the Education of Young Children.

Axtmann, A. & Dettwiler, A. (2005). *The visit: Observation, reflection, synthesis for training and relationship building.* Baltimore: Brookes.

Balaban, N. (2006, November). Easing the separation process for infants, toddlers, and families. *Young Children* 61(6), 14–19.

Brazelton, T. B., Zigler, E., Sherman, L., Bratton, W., & Sanders, J. (1999). *Quality child care and after school programs: Powerful weapons against crime.* Available on the Fight Crime: Invest in Kids Web site (www.fightcrime.org).

Breaking the link: National forum on child care compensation. (1994, April). National Center for the Early Childhood Workforce.

Bredekamp, S. (Ed.). (1984). *The accreditation criteria and procedures of the National Academy of Early Childhood*

Programs. Washington, DC: National Association for the Education of Young Children.

Bredekamp, S., & Copple, C. (Eds.). (1997). *Developmentally appropriate practice in early childhood programs serving children from birth through age 8.* Washington, DC: National Association for the Education of Young Children.

Butterfield, P. M.(2002, February–March). Child care is rich in routines. *Zero to Three, 22*(4), 29–32.

Campbell, F. A., Pungello, E. P., Miller-Johnson, S., Burchinal, M., & Ramey, C. T. (2000). *Early learning, later success: The Abecedarian study early childhood educational intervention for poor children, executive summary.* Chapel Hill: University of North Carolina, Frank Porter Graham Child Development Center.

Children's Defense Fund. (2000). *The state of America's children yearbook, 2000.* Washington, DC: Children's Defense Fund.

Children's Defense Fund. (2004). *Children with disabilities and other special needs: Opportunities to participate in quality programs must be expanded.* From *Key facts: essential information about child care, early education, and school-age care,* 2003 edition. Retrieved August 19, 2004, from the Children's Defense Fund Web site (www.childrensdefense.org/earlychildhood/childcare/keyfacts2003_childcare.pdf).

Cook, R. E., Tessier, A., & Klein, M. D. (2000). *Adapting early childhood curricula for children in inclusive settings* (5th ed.). Columbus, OH: Merrill.

Copple, C. (2006) *Basics of developmentally appropriate practice: An introduction for teachers of children 3–6.* Washington DC: National Association for the Education of Young Children.

Cost, quality, and outcomes in child care centers: Technical report. (1995). Denver: Center for Research in Economic and Social Policy, University of Colorado.

Curtis, D., & Carter, M. (2000). *The art of awareness.* St. Paul: Redleaf.

Division of Research to Practice, Office of Special Education Programs. (2001). *Synthesis on the use of assistive technology with infants and toddlers.* Washington, DC: U.S. Department of Education.

Dombro, A. L. and Lerner, C. (2006 January). Sharing the care of infants and toddlers. *Young Children 61*(1), 29–33.

Edmiaston, R., Dolezal, V., Doolittle, S., Erickson, C., & Merritt, S. (2000). Developing individualized education programs for children in inclusive settings: A developmental framework. *Young Children, 55*(4), 36–41.

Erikson, E. H. (1963). *Childhood and society.* New York: Norton.

Fromberg, D. P., & Bergen, D. (Eds.). (2006). *Play from birth to twelve: Contexts, perspectives, and meanings* (2nd ed.). New York: Routledge, Taylor & Francis Group.

Gandini, L., & Edwards, C. P. (Eds.). (2000). *Bambini: The Italian approach to infant-toddler care.* New York: Teachers College Press.

Goldstein, L. (2002). *Reclaiming caring in teaching and teacher education.* New York: Lang.

Gonzalez-Mena, J. (2000, July). In the spirit of partnership: High maintenance parent or cultural difference? *Exchange, 134,* 40–42.

Gonzalez-Mena, J. (2002). *Infant/toddler caregiving: A guide to routines* (2nd ed.). Sacramento: California Department of Education, with WestEd.

Gonzalez-Mena, J. & Eyer, D. (2007) *Infants, Toddlers, and Caregivers.* New York: McGraw-Hill.

Gonzalez-Mena, J., & Stonehouse, A. (2000, January). Responding in the spirit of partnership: The high maintenance parent. *Child Care Information Exchange, 131,* 10–12.

Greenman, J. (2003). Places for childhood include parents, too. In B. & R. Neugebauer, (Eds.), *The art of leadership.* Redmond, WA: Child Care Information Exchange.

Greenough, W., Emde, R. N., Gunnar, M., Massinga, R., & Shonkoff, J. P. (2001, April–May). The impact of the caregiving environment on young children's development: Different ways of knowing. *Zero to Three, 21*(5), 16–24.

Greenspan, S. I. (1999). *Building healthy minds.* Cambridge, MA: Perseus.

Greenspan, S. I., & Wieder, S. (1998). *The child with special needs: Encouraging intellectual and emotional growth.* Reading, MA: Perseus.

Illig, D. C. (1998). *Birth to kindergarten: The importance of the early years.* Sacramento: California Research Bureau.

Jacobs, G., & Crowley, K. (2007). *Play, projects and preschool standards: Nurturing children's sense of wonder and joy in learning.* Thousand Oaks, CA: Corwin Press.

Jamblon, J. R., Dombro, A. L., & Dichtelmiller, M. L. (1999). *The power of observation.* Washington, DC: Teaching Strategies.

Karoly, A. (1998). *Investing in our children.* Santa Monica, CA: Rand.

Kids count data book. (2003). Baltimore: Annie E. Casey Foundation.

Kontos, S., & Wilcox-Herzog, A. (1997, January). Teachers' interactions with children: Why are they so important? *Young Children 52*(2), 4–12.

Kostelnik, M., Onaga, E., Rohde, B., & Whiren, A. (2002). *Children with special needs: Lessons for early childhood professionals.* New York: Teachers College Press.

Kranowitz, C. S. (1998). *The out of sync child: Recognizing and coping with sensory integration dysfunction.* New York: Paragee.

Lee, L. (2002). *Serving families: A handbook on the principles and strategies of the parent services project approach.* San Rafael, CA: Parent Services Project.

Lombardi, J. (2003). *Time to care: Redesigning child care to promote education, support families and build communities.* Philadelphia: Temple University Press.

Morgan, G & Nadig, S. (2007) Trends in education and care. Online article accessed August 26, 2009 at http://www.ccie.com/resources/view_article.php?article_id=5017112

Noddings, N. (2002a). *Educating moral people: A caring alternative to character education.* New York: Teachers College Press.

Noddings, N. (2002b). *Starting at home: Care and social policy.* Berkeley: University of California Press.

Noddings, N. (2005). *The Challenge to Care in Schools.* New York: Teachers College Press.

O'Brien, M. (1997). *Inclusive child care for infants and toddlers: Meeting individual and special needs.* Baltimore: Brookes.

Phipps, P. A. (2003). Working with angry parents—Taking a customer service approach. In B. & R. Neugebauer (Eds.), *The art of leadership.* Redmond, WA: Child Care Information Exchange.

Pinto, C. (2001, Spring). Supporting competence in a child with special needs: One child's story. *Educaring,* 22(2), 1–6.

Ramey, C. T., & Campbell, F. (1991). Poverty, early childhood education, and academic competence: The Abecedarian experiment. In A. Huston (Ed.), *Children in poverty: Child development and public policy.* New York: Cambridge University Press.

Raver, S. A. (1999). *Intervention strategies for infants and toddlers with special needs* (2nd ed.). Upper Saddle River, NJ: Merrill/Prentice Hall.

Ruopp, R., Travers, J., Glantz, F., & Coelen, C. (1979). *Children at the center: Final results of the National Day Care Study.* Boston: ABT Associates.

Schweinhart, L., Barnes, H., & Weikart, D. (1993). *Significant benefits: The High/Scope Perry preschool study through age 27.* Ypsilanti, MI: High/Scope Press.

Segal, M., Masi, W., & Leiderman, R. (2001). *In time and with love: Caring for infants and toddlers with special needs.* New York: New Market Press.

Shonkoff, J. P., & Phillips, D. (2001, April–May). From neurons to neighborhoods: The science of early childhood development—An introduction. *Zero to Three,* 21(5), 4–7.

Starting points: Meeting the needs of our youngest children. (1994). Carnegie Corporation of New York.

Stonehouse, A., & Gonzalez-Mena, J. (2004). *Making links: A collaborative approach to planning and practice in early childhood.* Sydney, Australia: Pademelon Press.

Szanton, E. S. (2001, January). For America's infants and toddlers, are important values threatened by our zeal to "teach"? *Young Children,* 56(1), 15–21.

Tobin, J. J., Wu, D. Y. H., & Davidson, D. H. (1989). *Preschool in three cultures: Japan, China, and the United States.* New Haven, CT: Yale University Press.

U.S. Department of Health and Human Services. (2003). *Making a difference in the lives of infants and toddlers and their families: The impacts of early Head Start.* Washington, DC: U.S. Department of Health and Human Services.

U.S. Department of Labor, Bureau of Labor Statistics. (1999, December). Table 48, Marital and Family Characteristics of the Labor Force from March 1999. In *Current population survey, December 1999* (p. 293). Washington, DC: U.S. Government Printing Office.

Vinson, B. M. (2001, January). Fishing and Vygotsky's concept of effective education. *Young Children,* 56(1), 88–89.

Whitebook, M., Howes, C., & Phillips, D. (1993) *The National Child Care Staffing study revisited.* Oakland, CA: Child Care Employee Project.

Whitebook, M., & Sakai, L. (2004). *By a thread: How child care centers hold onto teachers, how teachers build lasting careers.* Kalamazoo, MI: Upjohn Institute for Employment Research.

Whitehead, L. C., & Ginsberg, S. I. (1999). Creating a family-like atmosphere in child care settings: All the more difficult in large child care centers. *Young Children,* 54(2), 4–10.

Zigler, E. F., Finn-Stevenson, M., & Hall, N. W. (2003). *The first three years and beyond: Brain development and social policy.* New Haven, CT: Yale University Press.

Zill, N. (2003, May). *Head Start FACES 2000: A whole-child perspective on program performance, fourth progress report.* Washington, DC: U.S. Department of Health and Human Services.

CHAPTER 13

Alan Guttmacher Institute. (1999). *Facts in brief: Teen sex and pregnancy.* Available on the Web site of the Alan Guttmacher Institute (www.agi-usa.org/pubs/fb_teen_sex.html).

Bennett, R. (2006, January). Future teachers forge family connections. *Young Children* 61(1), 22–28.

Bushman, B. J., & Anderson, C. A. (2001). Media violence and the American public: Scientific facts versus media misinformation. *American Psychologist,* 56, 466–489.

Bushman, D., & Huesmann, L. R. (2001). Effects of televised violence on aggression. In D. Singer & J. Singer (Eds.), *Handbook of children and the media.* Thousand Oaks, CA: Sage.

Children's Defense Fund. (2000). *State of America's children 2000.* Washington, DC: Children's Defense Fund.

Children's Defense Fund. (2004). *The state of America's children 2004.* Washington, DC: Children's Defense Fund.

Clark, K. E., & Ladd, G. W. (2000). Connectedness and autonomy support in parent-child relationships: Links to children's socio-emotional orientation and peer relationships. *Developmental Psychology,* 36, 485–498.

Duncan, G. O., & Brooks-Gunn, J. (2000). Family parenting, welfare reform, and child development. *Child Development,* 71, 188–195.

Golden, O. (2000). The federal response to child abuse and neglect. *American Psychologist,* 55, 1050–1053.

Gonzalez-Mena, J. (2007). *50 early strategies for working and communicating with diverse families.* Upper Saddle River, NJ: Pearson/Merrill/Prentice Hall.

Ispa, J. M., Thornburg, K. R. & Fine, M. A. (2006). *Keepin' on: The everyday struggles of young families in poverty.* Baltimore: Brookes.

Kilgo, J. L. (Ed.). (2006). *Transdisciplinary teaming in early intervention/early childhood special education: Navigating together with families and children.* Association for Childhood Education International.

Lally, J. R. (1998, May). Brain research, infant learning, and child care curriculum. *Child Care Information Exchange, 121,* 46–48.

Lee, L. (Ed.). (2006). *Stronger Together. Family support and early childhood education.* San Rafael, CA: Parent Services Project, Inc.

Maccoby, E. E. (1998). *The two sexes.* Cambridge, MA: Harvard University Press.

McLoyd, V. C., Hill, N. E., & Dodge, K. A. (Eds.). (2005). *African American family life.* New York: Guilford.

National Research Council and Institute of Medicine. (2000). *From neurons to neighborhoods: The science of early childhood development.* Board on Children, Youth, and Families, Commission on Behavioral and Social Sciences and Education. Washington, DC: National Academy Press.

Parke, R. D., & O'Neil, R. (2000). The influence of significant others on learning about relationships: From family to friends. In R. S. L. Mills & S. Duck (Eds.), *The developmental psychology of personal relationships* (pp. 15–47). New York: Wiley.

Payne, R. K. (2003). *A framework for understanding poverty.* Highlands, TX: Aha Process.

Poussaint, A. F. (2006, January). Understanding and involving African American parents. *Young Children 61*(1), 48.

Powers, J. (2006, January). Six fundamentals for creating relationships with families. *Young Children 61*(1), 28.

Ritchie, S., & Willer, B. (2005) *Families and community relationships.* Washington DC: National Association for the Education of Young Children.

Satir, V. (1972). *Peoplemaking.* Palo Alto: Science and Behavior Books.

Schneider, B. H., Atkinson, L., & Tardif, C. (2001). Child-parent attachment and children's peer relations: A quantitative review. *Developmental Psychology, 37,* 86–100.

Shonkoff, J. P., & Phillips, D. (2001, April–May). From neurons to neighborhoods: The science of early childhood development—An introduction. *Zero to Three, 21*(5), 4–7.

Shore, R. (1997). *Rethinking the brain: New insights in early development.* New York: Families and Work Institute.

Signorielli, N., & Morgan, M. (2001). Television and the family: The cultivation perspective. In J. Bryant & J. A. Bryant (Eds.), *Television and the American family* (2nd ed., pp. 333–351). Mahwah, NJ: Erlbaum.

Tan, A. L. (2004). *Chinese American children and families: A guide for educators and service providers.* Onley, MD: Association for Childhood Education International.

Tinsley, B. R. (2002). *How children learn to be healthy.* New York: Cambridge University Press.

White, E. (Qoyawayma, P.). (1992). *No turning back: A Hopi woman's struggle to live in two worlds.* Albuquerque: University of New Mexico Press.

Wright, J. C., Huston, A. C., Murphy, K. C., St. Peters, M., Pinon, M., Scantlin, R., & Kotler, J. (2001). The relations of early television viewing to school readiness and vocabulary of children from low-income families: The early window project. *Child Development, 72,* 1347–1366.

Zigler, E. F., Finn-Stevenson, M., & Hall, N. W. (2003). *The first three years and beyond: Brain development and social policy.* New Haven: Yale University Press.

CHAPTER 14

Anderson, C. A., Berkowitz, L., Donnerstein, E., Huesmann, I., Rowell Johnson, F. D., & Linz., D. (2003). The influence of media violence on youth. *Psychological Science in the Public Interest, 4,* 81–110.

Bandura, A., & Walters, R. H. (1963). *Social learning and personality development.* New York: Holt, Rinehart & Winston.

Boyer, E. L. (1991). *Ready to learn: A mandate for the nation.* Princeton, NJ: Carnegie Foundation for the Advancement of Teaching.

Bushman, B. J., & Anderson, C. A. (2001). Media violence and the American public: Scientific facts versus media misinformation. *American Psychologist, 56,* 466–489.

Bushman, D., & Huesmann, L. R. (2001). Effects of televised violence on aggression. In D. Singer & J. Singer (Eds.), *Handbook of children and the media.* Thousand Oaks, CA: Sage.

Byrnes, D. A., & Kiger, G. (Eds.). (2005). *Common bonds: Anti-bias teaching in a diverse society,* 3rd ed. Association for Childhood Education International. Olney, MD.

Carlsson-Paige, N., & Levin, D. E. (1990). *Who's calling the shots: How to respond effectively to children's fascination with war play and war toys.* Philadelphia: New Society.

Clark, K. E., & Ladd, G. W. (2000). Connectedness and autonomy support in parent-child relationships: Links to children's socio-emotional orientation and peer relationships. *Developmental Psychology, 36,* 485–498.

Derman-Sparks, L., & the ABC Task Force. (1989). *Antibias curriculum: Tools for empowering young children.* Washington, DC: National Association for the Education of Young Children.

Derman-Sparks, L., & Ramsey, P. G. (2006). *What if all the kids are white? Antibias/Multicultural education with young children and families.* New York: Teachers College Press.

Elkind, D. (2007). *The power of play*. Cambridge, MA: Da Capo Press.

Gerbner, G., Gross, L., & Signorielli, N. (1986). Living with television: The dynamics of the cultivation process. In J. Bryant & D. Zillman (Eds.), *Perspectives on media effects*. Hillsdale, NJ: Erlbaum.

Hirsch, K. W. (1997). Media violence and audience behavior. In A. Wells & E. Hakanen (Eds.), *Mass media and society* (5th ed., pp. 479–505). Greenwich, CT: Ablex.

Huesmann, L. R., & Miller, L. S. (1994). Long-term effects of repeated exposure to media violence in childhood. In L. R. Huesman (Ed.), *Aggressive behavior: Current perspectives* (pp. 153–186). New York: Plenum.

Kozol, J. (1991). *Savage inequalities: Children in America's schools*. New York: Crown.

Lally, J. R., (1998, May). Brain research, infant learning, and child care curriculum. *Child Care Information Exchange*, 121, 46–48.

Maccoby, E. E. (1998). *The two sexes*. Cambridge, MA: Harvard University Press.

McKenna, T., & Ortiz, F. I. (Eds.). (1988). *The broken web: The educational experience of Hispanic American women*. Encino, CA: Floricanto.

National Research Council and Institute of Medicine. (2000). *From neurons to neighborhoods: The science of early childhood development*. Board on Children, Youth, and Families, Commission on Behavioral and Social Sciences and Education. Washington, DC: National Academy Press.

Parke, R. D., & O'Neil, R. (2000). The influence of significant others on learning about relationships: From family to friends. In R. S. L. Mills & S. Duck (Eds.), *The developmental psychology of personal relationships* (pp. 15–47). New York: Wiley.

Schneider, B. H., Atkinson, L., & Tardif, C. (2001). Child-parent attachment and children's peer relations: A quantitative review. *Developmental Psychology*, 37, 86–100.

Shonkoff, J. P., & Phillips, D. (2001, April–May). From neurons to neighborhoods: The science of early childhood development—An introduction. *Zero to Three*, 21(5), 4–7.

Shore, R. (1997). *Rethinking the brain: New insights in early development*. New York: Families and Work Institute.

Signorielli, N., & Morgan, M. (2001). Television and the family: The cultivation perspective. In J. Bryant & J. A. Bryant (Eds.), *Television and the American family* (2nd ed., pp. 333–351). Mahwah, NJ: Erlbaum.

Singer, D. G., & Singer, J. L. (2005). *Imagination and play in the electrnoic age*. Cambridge, MA. Harvard University Press.

Tinsley, B. R. (2002). *How children learn to be healthy*. New York: Cambridge University Press.

Wright, J. C., Huston, A. C., Murphy, K. C., St. Peters, M., Pinon, M., Scantlin, R., & Kotler, J. (2001). The relations of early television viewing to school readiness and vocabulary of children from low-income families: The early window project. *Child Development*, 72, 1347–1366.

Zigler, E. F., Finn-Stevenson, M., & Hall, N. W. (2003). *The first three years and beyond: Brain development and social policy*. New Haven: Yale University Press.

CHAPTER 15

Boyer, E. L. (1991). *Ready to learn: A mandate for the nation*. Princeton, NJ: Carnegie Foundation for the Advancement of Teaching.

Carnegie Task Force on Meeting the Needs of Young Children. (1994, July). Starting points: Executive summary of the report of the Carnegie Corporation of New York Task Force on Meeting the Needs of Young Children. *Young Children*, 49(5), 58–60.

Chang, H. N. L., Muckelroy, A., & Pulido-Tobiassen, D. (1996). *Looking in, looking out: Redefining child and early education in a diverse society*. San Francisco: California Tomorrow.

Children's Defense Fund. (2000). *The state of America's children*. Washington, DC: Children's Defense Fund.

Children's Defense Fund. (2004). *The state of America's children*. Washington, DC: Children's Defense Fund.

Compton-Lilly, C. (2004). *Confronting racism, poverty, and power. Classroom strategies to change the world*. Portsmouth, NH: Heinemann.

Connolly, P., Hayden, J., & Levin, D. (2007) *From conflict to peace building: The power of early childhood initiatives*. Redmond, WA: World Forum Foundation.

Cook, R. E., Tessier, A., & Klein, M. D. (2000). *Adapting early childhood curricula for children in inclusive settings* (5th ed.). Columbus, OH: Merrill.

Dahlberg, G., Moss, P., & Pence, A. (1999). *Beyond quality in early childhood education and care*. London: Falmer.

Edmiaston, R., Dolezal, V., Doolittle, S., Erickson, C., & Merritt, S. (2000). Developing individualized education programs for children in inclusive settings: A developmental framework. *Young Children*, 55(4), 36–41.

Feerick, M. M., & Silverman, G. B. (Eds.). (2006). *Children exposed to violence*. Baltimore: Brookes.

Feerick, M. M., Knutson, J. F., Trickett, P. K., & Flanzer, S. M. (Eds.). (2006). *Child Abuse and neglect*. Baltimore: Brookes.

Goffin, S. G., & Lombardi, J. (1989). *Speaking out: Early childhood advocacy*. Washington, DC: National Association for the Education of Young Children.

Goffin, S., & Washington, V. (2007) *Ready or not: Leadership choices in early care and education*. Washington DC: National Association for the Education of Young Children.

Gonzalez-Mena, J. (2001). Cross-cultural infant care and issues of equity and social justice. *Contemporary*

Issues in Early Childhood, 2(3). Available online at the Web site of Symposium Journals, a division of wwwords Ltd. (www.wwwords.co.uk/ciec).

Kelly, J. F., & Booth, C. L. (1999). Child care for children with special needs: Issues and applications. *Infants and young Children*, 12(1), 26–33.

Lee, L. (2002). *Serving families: A handbook on the principles and strategies of the Parent Services Project approach.* San Rafael, CA: Parent Services Project.

Lee, L., & Seiderman, E. (1998). *Families matter: The Parent Services Project.* Cambridge, MA: Harvard Family Research Project.

Links, G., Beggs, M., & Seiderman, E. (1997). *Serving families.* Fairfax, CA: Parent Services Project.

Lombardi, J. (2003). *Time to care: Redesigning child care to promote education, support families, and build communities.* Philadelphia: Temple University Press.

Love, J., Raikes, H., Paulsell, D., & Kisker, E. E. (2000). New directions for studying quality in programs for infants and toddlers. In D. Cryer & T. Harms (Eds.), *Infants and toddlers in out of home care* (pp. 117–162). Baltimore: Brookes.

McLoyd, V. (1998). Socioeconomic disadvantage and child development. *American Psycholgist,* 53(2), 185–204.

National Association for the Education of Young Children. (1996, January). Position statement: Responding to linguistic and cultural diversity: Recommendations for effective early childhood education. *Young Children,* 51(2), 4–12.

Nieto, S. (2000). *Affirming diversity: The sociopolitical context of multicultural education* (3rd ed.). New York: Addison Wesley Longman.

Noddings, N. (2002). *Starting at home: Care and social policy.* Berkeley: University of California Press.

O'Brien, M. (1997). *Inclusive child care for infants and toddlers: Meeting individual and special needs.* Baltimore: Brookes.

Odom, S. (Ed.). (2002). *Widening the circle: Including children with disabilities in preschool programs.* New York: Teachers College Press.

Perry, B (2006). Applying principles of neurodevelopment to clinical work with maltreated and traumatized children. In N. B. Webb (Ed.). *Working with traumatized youth in child welfare.* New York: Guilford Press.

Putname, J. W. (Ed.). (1998). *Cooperative learning and strategies for inclusion* (2nd ed.). Baltimore: Brookes.

Shames, S. (1991). *Outside the dream: Child poverty in America.* (Introduction by J. Kozol; afterword by M. W. Edelman.) New York: Aperture.

Shore, R. (2003). *Rethinking the brain: New insights into early development.* New York: Families and Work Institute.

Thaxton, S. M. (2003). Grandparents as parents—Understanding the issues. In B. & R. Neugebauer (Eds.), *The art of leadership* (pp. 323–325). Redmond, WA: Child Care Information Exchange.

Washington, V. & Andrews, J. D. (1998) *Children of 2010.* Washington DC: National Association for the Education of Young Children.

Whitebook, M., Phillips, D., & Howes, C. (1993). *National Child Care Staffing Study revisited: Four years in the life of center-based child care.* Oakland, CA: Child Care Employee Project.

Zigler, E. F., Finn-Stevenson, M., & Hall, N. W. (2003). *The first three years and beyond: Brain development and social policy.* New Haven: Yale University Press.

Zigler, E., & Styfoco, S. J. (2004). *The Head Start debates.* Baltimore: Brookes.

Index

AFDC. See Aid to Families with Dependent Children (AFDC)
Affirmations/strokes
  defined, 120
  nonverbal, 126
  uses for, 121
Aggression
  causes of, 93–96
  defensiveness and, 95–96
  learned, 93–94
  in preschool children, 93–96
  unreleased frustrations and, 95
Ainsworth, Mary, 27, 39, 40
Alward, K., 84
American Academy of Pediatrics, 112, 338
American Psychological Association (APA), 234, 338
  Report on the Sexualization of Girls, 234
Americans and Chinese (Dung), 185
Americans with Disabilities Act (ADA), 285. *See also* Individuals with Disabilities Education Act
Anderson, C. A., 338
Antibias Curriculum, (Derman-Sparks), 215
Antibias curriculum task force, 145, 215
Anger, 193–194. *See also* Feelings
APA. *See* American Psychological Association
Appell, G., 31, 54, 118
Atkinson, L, 335
Assisted performance, 212–214
Attachment Parenting (Sears and Sears), 37
Attachment
  behaviors, 32
  Bowlby's theory of, 11

child care and, 42–45
child development and, 30–31
children's resiliency and, 30
in cross cultural situations, 42
cultural patterns of, 138
defined, 26
developmental differences and, 35–36
drug abuse effects on, 38–39
embedded families and, 41–42
extended families and, 41–42
factors in developing child-adult relationships, 30–31
full inclusion/special education programs and, 46–47
in infants
  born addicted to drugs, 38–39
  cognitive development and, 27
obstacles to, 33–36
patterns of, 39–41
in preschool children, 27–30
  caregiver sensitivity/responsiveness and, 28
  importance of, 28–29
  professional considerations for educators, 31
single parent families and, 40–41
as a strategy for working with families, 45–46
temperament and, 34–35
types of, 39–40
Attention
  negative, 118–127
  positive, 118–127
  power of adult, 118–120
Attention deficit/hyperactivity disorder (ADHD)
  diagnostic controversy, 81
  example, 81–82
  play, 90–91

Authoritarian parenting approach, 196–197
Authoritative parenting approach, 198
Autonomy
  cultural considerations, 56–57
  developmental milestone in children, 53–61
  independence and, 54–55, 56
  interdependence and, 54–55, 56, 58
  preschool children and, 53–61, 82
  preschool children and, signs of readiness, 58
  self-help skills and, 55–57
  sense of possession and, 59–60
  sharing and, 59–60
  stages of (Erikson's), 52, 82, 109
  toddlers and, 52–53

Balaban, N., 69
Ball, J., 172
Ballenger, Cindy, 10,158, 166,195
Baby Einstein, 26
Bandura, A., 338
Barkley, R. A., 81
Barrera, Isaura, 144
Basics of Developmentally Appropriate Practice: An Introduction for Teachers of Children 3–6, 282
Baumrind, Diana, 196
Becker, B., 262–263
Beggs, M., 264
Behavior
  modification, 126
  positive/negative attention toward, 118–127
  remediating negative, 125
Behavior contagion, 334
Believing game, 172
Bell, S., 39

Berk, L. E., 47, 84
Bias, 216–217
Birch, H. G., 35
Birthright, 314
Biting behavior, 65–66
Blehar, M. C., 39
Bloom, P.J., 8–9
Bolduc, D., 230
Bowlby, John, 11, 28, 39, 69
Boy Without a Penis, A (Gorman), 240
Boyer, E. L., 339
Boys and Girls: Superheroes in the Doll Corner (Paley), 231
Brain research and early education, 349
Bratton, W., 279
Brazelton, T. B., 279
Bredekamp, Sue, 143, 211–212
Briggs, D. C., 209
Bronfenbrenner, Uri, 6
   ecological model, 6–8, 12
Brott, A., 230
Browder, S., 190
Burchinal, M., 279
Bush, George W., 349, 351–352
Bush, Laura, 351–352
Bushman, B. J., 339

Calming techniques, 190
Campbell, F. A., 279
Caregiver role, 44–45
Caring relationships, 118
Carlebach, Diane, 118
Carlsson-Paige, N., 339
Center for the Study of Social Policy, 15
Cernoch, J.M., 32
Chaille, C., 111
Chaker, Anne Marie, 112
Challenge to Care in Schools, The (Noddings), 117, 274
Chandler, L., 91
Chang, H. N. L., 28, 352
Chao, Ruth, 198
Chess, S., 35
Child abuse
   discipline vs., 162–163
   family-centered programs to prevent, 15
Child care
   attachment and, 42–45
   coping with separation, 69–70
Child Care Center Licensing Study (Children's Foundation), 276
Children of 2010, 354

Children: The Challenge (Dreikers and Soltz), 166
Children's Defense Fund, 260, 348, 350, 353, 355
Children's Defense Fund Year Book: State of America's Children 2005, 347–348, 357, 359
Christian, Linda, 17–18
Cicchetti, D., 262–263
Clark, K. E., 335
Clarke, J. I., 221
Clinton, Bill, 280–281, 351
Coelen, C., 281
Cognitive development
   in infants, 27
   internal representations of stages, 64
   Piaget's stages of, 63–64
   theory, 16, 109–110
Comforting styles, 140
Community resources
   availability of, 313–314
   Birthright, 314
   child care, 311
   family connections to, 310–314
   institutions, 303
   isolation due to sexual orientation, 307–308
   Planned Parenthood, 314
   police/fire, 311
   social networks, 300–304
   support, 301–302
   trends influencing need for, 303–304
   Temporary Assistance for Needy Families (TANF), 311–312, 356
   Women, Infants and Children program (WIC), 304, 355
Competence, 207
Conflict management/resolution, 57
   cross-cultural communication and, 145
   cultural differences in, 141
   dialoguing, 142–143
   skills and techniques for, 141–148
Connolly, P., 360
Cook, K. V., 230
Cooper, R., 62, 84, 172
Coopersmith, Stanley, 206
Coping
   dramatic play and, 190
   transition object, 71
Copple, Carol, 143, 211–212
Corso, R., 144

Co-sleeping, 37
Cossette, L., 230
Crockenberg, S., 265
Croen, L. A., 37
Cultural Nature of Human Development, The (Rogoff), 10–11, 198
Cultural patterns
   attachment and, 138
   contrasts between, 137–138
Cultural pluralism
   communicating importance of to children, 148–149
   importance of, 135
Cultural scripts, 184–185
Culture(s)
   child-rearing differences, 158
   effects on education, 134
   goals/values among different, 135–137
   high-context, 253
   influences on individuals, 136
   low-context, 253
Culture and Attachment (Harwood et al), 141
Curry, N. E., 211

Dahlberg, G., 172
Damasio, A, 26
David, M., 31, 54, 118
Davidson, D. H., 288
Decision making and moral development, 116–118
Defensiveness, 95–96
De La Roza, M., 159
DeCasper, A.J., 32
Derman-Sparks, Louise, 145, 215, 216, 332
Developmental psychology, 16
Developmental theory and culture, 16
Developmentally Appropriate Practice (National Association for the Education of Young Children), 282
Developmentally Appropriate Practice in Early Childhood Programs Serving Children from Birth Through Age 8 (Bredekamp and Copple), 211–212
Dialoguing, 142–143
Differential socialization, 234–239
   from parent, 236
   in elementary school, 237–239
   in preschool, 236–237

Discipline
  defined, 157–159
  consequences approach, 159
  cultural considerations, 157–159
  environmental controls, 163
  external locus of control,
    157–158
  guidelines for in young
    children, 160–161
  inner controls/self discipline,
    157
  logical consequences, 166
  natural consequences and, 166
  prevention of unacceptable
    behaviors, 162–170
  punishment approach,
    159–160
  response to unacceptable
    behavior, 165–170
  time out, 168
Diversity
  celebrating, 215–216
  education and, 330–331
  importance of, 134
Doris Duke Foundation, 15
Dorris, Michael, 215–216
Dorwick, P.W., 912
Doubt, 82
Dramatic play, 190
Dreikers, R., 166
Driscoll, A., 211
Drug abuse (adverse effects on
    attachment), 38–39
Dung, T. N., 185

Early care/education programs
  adult-child interactions and,
    282–284
  affordability of, 278–280
  availability of, 278–280
  child care today, 280–281
  as child-rearing
    environments, 276–278
  continuity between home and
    child care, 287–290
  cultural competence and, 288
  descriptions of, 272–276
  inclusion of children with
    special needs, 285–286
  parent-professional
    partnerships, 286–287,
    290–293
  quality of, 281–282
    teachers' salaries and,
      279–280
    teachers' status and,
      279–280
  universal pre-K/preschool for
    all (PFA), 274–275

Early Childhood Education
    (ECE), 8–16
Early education, brain research
    and, 349
ECE. See Early Childhood
    Education
Ecological model/theory
  Bronfenbrenner's, 6–8, 12
  family context and, 5–6
Economist, The, 239
Educating Moral People: A Caring
    Alternative to Character
    Education (Noddings), 117
Education
  accountability linked to
    achievement and,
    329–330
  classroom behavior
    influences, 330–331
  constructivist approach
    to, 111
  communication with families,
    113–115
  diversity in, 330–331
  effects of culture and values
    on, 134
  family-centered approach to,
    8–11
  inequity in schools, 332–333
  problem-solving skills, 96–98
  prosocial skills development,
    114–115, 127–129
  role of recess in, 111–112
  teaching morals, 114–115. See
    also Prosocial skills
  test score accountability, 327
Education of All Handicapped
    Children Act of 1975,
    12–13
Eggers-Pierola, C., 159
Ehrhardt, A. A., 239
Eiduson, B. T., 230
Eisenberg, E., 8–9
Eisenberg, P., 8–9
Elkind, David, 64, 84, 335
Embedded families, 41–42
Empowerment in children,
    61–68
  choices, 65
  self-help skills development,
    64
  environmental
    considerations, 61–62
  preschool children, 98–100
  providing control, 65–66
  role of play in, 62–64
  setting limits, 67–68
Encouragement (vs. praise),
    126–127

Engrossment, 117
Epstein, Joyce, 8–9, 13–14
Epstein Model for School,
    Family and Community
    Partnerships, 13–14
Erikson, Erik, 29, 52, 78,
    101, 108–111, 208,
    209, 283
  psychosocial dilemmas, 29
  psychosocial stages of
    development, 29, 52, 83,
    108–110, 209
  on self-esteem, 209
  stage of autonomy, 52, 82, 109
  stage of initiative, 78, 82, 109
Ethic of caring, 117
ExchangeEveryDay, 274
Extended families, 41–42
External locus of control,
    157–158
Extrinsic rewards, 126–127

FACES, 279
Failure, 214–215
Family(ies)
  characteristics of, 248–250
  characteristics/traits of
    successful, 250–261
  common stressors for
    successful, 260 contexts
    of, 4
  creating partnerships with,
    15–16
  cultural contexts of, 249
  embedded, 41–42
  extended, 41–42
  single-parent, 40–41
  strategies for working with
    accessing community
      services, 313
    advocacy, 359
    attachment, 45–46
    in community, 284
    conflict resolution, 57
    creating partnerships/
      relationships, 72
    expanding social networks,
      301
    feelings, 197
    gender equity, 242
    discipline and guidance,
      171
    parents as advocates, 340
    peacemaking, 361
    problem solving, 197
    RERUN for conflict
      management/
      resolution, 144
    self-esteem, 222

sharing approaches for children in the stage of initiative, 101
using a strength-based perspective, 252
teaching play appreciation, 86
stress as a positive force in, 261–262
Family bed, 37
Family-centered
approach
context of, 16–19
defined, 9
family systems theory, 16–18
to kindergarten, 107
whole child theory and, 18–19
care (history of), 11
movement, 13
programs
benefits of, 9–11
child abuse prevention and, 15
choices for families, 65
collaborative approach to, 21
Family Lifestyles Project, 230
Family systems theory, 16–18
FCC. *See* Federal Communications Commission.
Fear (coping with), 191–193
Federal Child Care Bill, 351
Federal Communications Commission (FCC), 339
Feelings
accepting, 185–186
anger redirection for children, 181
coping with
play and, 190–191
problem solving, 194–195
self-calming, 189–190
cultural considerations, 180–181
cultural scripts, 184–185
importance/value of, 178–181
learning about, 182–189
social referencing, 182
teaching healthy expression of, 187–189
Ferber, R., 37
Fifer, W. P., 32
Fight Crime: Invest in Kids report, 279

First Feelings: Milestones in the Emotional Development of Your Baby and Child (Greenspan and Greenspan), 181
Fitzgerald, D., 8–9
Fraiberg, Selma, 95
From Parents to Partners: Building a Family Centered Early Childhood Program (Keyser), 14
Frost, J., 85
Full-inclusion programs, 46

Galinsky, E., 265
Gartell, D., 126
Gender equity, 240–244
child rearing and, 230–233
guidelines for, 242–244
Gender reassignment, 240
Gender roles
biology and socialization, 239–240
cultural differences and, 235–236
differential socialization and, 234–239
gender reassignment and, 240
language and, 232–233
modeling in teaching teach, 233–234
same-sex families and, 240
sexual orientation and, 240
teaching, 228–229
toys and, 230–232
women's, 229–230
Generative curriculum, 172
George, C., 40
Gerber, Magda, 118
Gilligan, Carol, 116–117
Glantz, F., 281
Goffin, S., 358
Gonzalez-Mena, J., 21, 28, 32, 54, 118, 158
Gordon, Thomas, 165
Gorman, C., 240
Greenfield, P. M., 136, 205
Greenspan, Stanley I., 181
Greenspan, Nancy Thorndike, 181
Grether, J. K., 37
Gross-Loh, C., 112
Guidance (behaviorist view), 157
Gurian, Michael, 239

Hale, Janice, 157, 158
Hannaford, Carla, 19
Harvard Family Research Project, 14
Harwood, R. L., 141

Head Start program, 12, 350
history of, 12
Hierarchy of needs, 19–21
High-context cultures, 253
Hilliard, Asa, 15, 16
Hirsch, K. W., 339
Hitz, R., 211
Howard, G., 216
Huesmann, L. R., 338, 339
Human development theories, 16

"I Am Your Child" (Reiner), 349
IDEA. *See* Individuals with Disabilities Act
IEP. *See* Individualized Educational Plan
IFSP. *See* Individualized Family Service Plan
Illsley Clarke, Jean, 119
Im, J., 11
Imagination/fantasy (in preschool children), 84
Immordino-Yang, M. H., 26
Independence and interdependence
differences in goals, 136–137
importance of, 251
Individualized Educational Plan (IEP), 12–13, 82, 123, 285
Individualized Family Service Plan (IFSP), 12–13
Individuals with Disabilities Act (IDEA), 13, 285, 354
Infants
attachment behaviors in, 32
cognitive development in, 27
drug-addicted, 38–39
Infant mortality, 347
Initiative stage/phase, 78, 82, 109
adult contribution to, 89–90
considerations for children with special needs, 90
environmental factors and, 86–89
guilt and, 82–83
shyness and, 91–93
Inner controls/ self-discipline, 157
International Mind, Brain, and Education Society, 26
Intrinsic rewards, 126–127
Irizarry, N. L., 141
Isaacs, Susan, 187–188, 190

Jenson, E., 90–91
Johnson, C. N., 211
Johnson, Lyndon B., 261
Jones, Elizabeth, 62, 84, 88, 172

Kagan, Jerome, 164–165, 180, 205
Kahwaty, D. H., 58
Katz, L. G., 44, 45, 100
Kent, R. N., 236
Keyser, J., 8–9, 11, 14
King, Dr. Martin Luther, Jr., 362
Kinship networks, 40
Kohlberg, Lawrence, 116–117
Kohn, A., 169
Kontos, Susan, 282–283
Kornfein, M., 230
Kozol, J., 333
Kindergarten, 107
Kohlberg, Lawrence, 116–117
Kohn, Alfie, 169
Kozol, Jonathan, 333

Ladd, G. W., 335
Lally, J. R., 209
Lally, Ron, 30, 35
Lee, D., 185
Lee, L., 8–9, 14, 65, 264
Levin, D. E., 339
Lewis, F. 19
Lieberman, A.F., 33
Life script, 221
Limit-setting, 67–68
Links, G., 264
Long day programs, 274
Loren, G., 166
Loss
    coping with, 36–39, 68–72
    cultural values and, 37
    sudden infant death syndrome (SIDS), 37
Low-context cultures, 253
Luthar, S. S., 262–263

Maccoby, E. E., 334
McCracken, J. B., 69
McDonald, L., 41
McGee-Banks, C. A., 8–9
McKenna, J. J., 37
Magic Years, The (Fraiberg), 95
Mahoney, Gerald, 15
Main, M., 40
Malcuit, G., 230
Martin, Barclay, 94
Maslow, Abraham, 19–21, 165
    hierarchy of needs, 19–21
Miller, J. G., 141
Miller, L. S., 338
Miller-Johnson, S., 279
Mistry, J., 87
Mixed feelings, 191
Money, J., 239
Moral development

decision-making related to, 116–118
theory
    ethic of caring, 117
    and Piaget's cognitive stages, 117
    prosocial skills development, 127–129
Morgan, G., 274
Morgan, M., 339
Moss, P., 172
Mothering (Gross-Loh), 112
Mothers in the workforce, 275
Motivation and Personality (Maslow), 165
Muckelroy, A., 352

Nadig, S., 274
NAEYC. *See* National Association for the Education of Young Children
National Association for the Education of Young Children (NAEYC), 14, 117–118, 281, 282, 352
    Basics of Developmentally Appropriate Practice: An Introduction for Teachers of Children 3–6, 282
    Developmentally Appropriate Practice, 282
National Center for the Early Childhood Workforce, 279
National Day Care Study, 283
Nature of the Child, The (Kagan), 205
NCLB. *See* No Child Left Behind
Negative internal messages, 221–222
Nelson, Jane, 165
Neurotransmitters, 26
New Hope Project, 261
No Child Left Behind (NCLB), 349
    challenges of, 110
    effect on approaches to education, 111
    reduced recess time and, 112
    test score accountability and, 327
Noddings, N., 117, 161, 274
Nourot, P., 84

Ounce of Prevention Fund, 97
O'Leary, F., 236
O'Neil, R., 335,
Ounce of Prevention Fund, 97
Outside the Dream: Child Poverty in America (Shames), 347

Paley, Vivian, 190–191, 231
Parallel play, 62
Parent(s)/parenting
    attachment behaviors in, 32
    authoritarian approach, 196–197
    authoritative, approach, 198
    parenting vs. caregiver role
    permissive approach, 197–198
    styles of, 196–199
Parent Effectiveness Training (PET), 165
Parent Services Project (PSP), 14–15, 65, 264, 354
Parke, R. D., 230, 236, 335,
Parten, M. B., 62
Pawl, J. H., 44
Pence, A., 172
Peoplemaking (Satir), 16–17, 252, 253
Perry, Bruce, 26, 29
PET. *See* Parent Effectiveness Training
Phillips, C. B., 158
Piaget, Jean, 16, 63–64, 109–110, 116–117
    on Kohlberg's moral development theory, 116–117
Pikler, Emmi, 31, 54, 118
Pikler Institute, 31, 43, 118
PL 94–142. *See* Education of All Handicapped Children Act of 1975
Planned Parenthood, 314
Play
    appreciation, 86
    environments, 88–89
    hand regard, 62
    high-mobility activities, 89
    importance/value of, 62–64, 84–86
    low-mobility activities, 89
    parallel, 62
    in preschool children, 62–64
    role of imitation in developing play skills, 63–64
    simple/complex dimensions of environment and, 89
    as strategy for coping with feelings, 190–191
Playing to Get Smart (Jones and Cooper), 62
Pollack, William, 239
Pomerleau, A., 230
Pope, J., 14–15
Porter, R. H., 32

Post-traumatic stress syndrome
(effects on children), 360
Poverty
infant mortality and, 347
Lyndon B. Johnson's War on
Poverty, 261
statistics regarding, 260–261
Powell, Douglas, 13, 21
Power, 207–208
in preschool children, 61–68
Power of Play, The (Elkind), 64, 84
Praise (vs. encouragement),
126–127
Prescott, Elizabeth, 88
Problem solving
coping with feelings, 194–195
cultural considerations and,
195–196
cultural differences in, 195
parenting styles and, 196–198
RERUN process, 195
scaffolding/assisted
performance and,
212–214
Prosocial skills/behavior
development, 114–115, 127–129
in education, 115, 127–29, 169
strategies for development in
children, 127–129
Psychosocial dilemmas, 29
Pulido-Tobiasson, D., 352
Pungello, E. P., 279
Punished By Rewards (Kohn), 169
Punishment, 94
Psychosocial dilemmas, 29

Quiroz, B., 136, 205

Recess
No Child Left Behind and, 112
role in education, 111–112
Raeff, C., 136
Raikes, H., 44
Ramey, C. T., 279
Real Boys (Pollack), 239
Reifel, S., 85
Reiner, Rob, 349
Reinforcement, 126
Report on the Sexualization
of Girls (American
Psychological
Association), 234
RERUN, 143, 144, 195
Resilience
and response to stress in
family life, 262–264
problem solving and, 265
strategies for developing,
264–266

Resources for Infant Educators
(RIE), 31, 54, 118, 286
*Rethinking the Brain: New Insights
Into Early Development*
(Shore), 349
"Rethinking Recess" (Chaker),
112
Rewards
extrinsic, 126–127
intrinsic, 126–127
Reynolds, G., 84
Rheingold, H. L., 230
RIE. *See* Resources for Infant
Educators.
Rogers, C. R., 182
Rogoff, Barbara, 10–11, 16, 87,
134, 182, 198, 205
Rosenthal, R., 220
Rothstein-Fisch, C., 136, 205
Ruopp, R., 281, 286

Safe Start program, 97
Sakai, L., 279
Sanchez, S., 11
Sanders, J., 279
Sandoval, M., 159
Satir, Virginia, 16–17, 252,
253, 300
Savage Inequalities (Kozol), 333
Scaffolding/assisted
performance, 212–214
Scales, B., 84
Schneider, B. H., 335
*School, Family and Community
Partnerships* (Epstein),
13–14
Sears, M., 37
Seiderman, Ethel, 8–9, 14–15,
41, 264, 354
Self-actualization, 20
Self-discipline and inner
controls, 157
Self-esteem
affirmations/strokes and,
220–222
characteristics of, 204–205
cultural considerations and,
205–206
cultural differences and,
217–221
defined, 205–206
dimensions of, 206–208
inception of, 209–210
promotion of, 210–214
experiencing success,
211–212
providing feedback, 211
role of beliefs/expectations in,
208–209

role of bias in, 216–217
self-concept and, 205
self-image and, 205
Self-Esteem: A Family Affair
(Clarke), 221
Self-help skills development, 64
Separation
facilitating adjustment to, 70
and loss
coping with, 36–39, 68–72
cultural values and, 37
sudden infant death
syndrome (SIDS), 37
in preschool children, 69–72
use of transition objects, 71
Serbin, L. A., 236, 237
Sessional programs, 274
Sexual orientation, 240
Shame, 82
Shames, S., 347
Shared care, 293
Shareef, I., 158
Sharing, 59–60
Sherman, L., 279
Shore, R., 349
Shulman, J., 37
SIDS. *See* Sudden infant death
syndrome (SIDS)
Signorelli, N., 339
Simultaneous feelings, 191
Singer, D. G., 338
Singer, J. L., 338
Skilled Dialogue (Barrera), 144
Sleep, 37–38
*Smart Moves: Why Learning is
Not All in Your Head*
(Hannaford), 19
Smith, L. A. H., 188, 190
Smith, R. S., 30, 262
Snowden, L. R., 158
Social-emotional
development, 26
Socialization
differential, 234–239
family and, 320–326
bias and, 321–322
classism and, 322–324
racism and, 324–326
peer groups and, 333–335
school and, 326–333
classroom behavior,
330–331
diversity, 331–332
effect of accountability
through test scores, 327
inequity, 332–333
kindergarten readiness,
327–329
limitations of tracking, 327

Socialization (continued)
  televison/media and, 335–340
    commercial
      advertising, 337
    violent programming,
      338–340
    viewing by children, 335–336
Social policy issues
  access to programs, 346–347
  advocacy, 357–359
  child care, 351
  children's movement, 351
  domestic disputes, 359–360
  economic development,
    354–355
  equality for children, 346–347
  family responsibility for
    children, 346
  full inclusion programs, 354
  health care access, 355–356
  No Child Left Behind (NCLB),
    349
  school readiness for children
    ("ready to learn"),
    348–354
  services for families, 350
  societal responsibility for
    children, 346
  violence, 359–361
  White House Conference on
    Children, 351–352
Social referencing, 182
  feelings and, 181
  neutrality in, 183–184
  overuse of, 184
Social Survival for Children
  (Dowrick), 192
Sociocultural theory, 46–47, 91
Solomon, J., 40
Soltz, V., 166
Solve Your Child's Sleep Problems
  (Ferber), 37
Special Education Law. See
  Education of All
  Handicapped Children
  Act of 1975
Special education programs, 46
Stack, C. B., 40
State Children's Health
  Insurance Program, 348
Stonehouse, A., 21
"Strange Situation, The" 39
  criticism of, 40

Strokes. See Affirmations/
  strokes
Sudden infant death syndrome
  (SIDS), 37

Tardif, C., 335
Tardos, Anna, 31, 54
Tate, Beverly, 118
"Teachers' Interactions with
  Children: Why Are They
  So Important?", 282
Television
  increased aggression in
    children and,
    338–340
  as a teaching tool, 339
Temporary Aid to Needy
  Families (TANF),
  280–281, 304–305
Thevenin, T., 37
Thoman, E. B., 190
Thomas, A., 35
Thorne, B., 237
Time Magazine, 26
Tinsley, B. R., 337
Tobin, J. J., 288
Toilet training, 140
  approaches to, 57–59
  elimination communication
    (EC), 58
  infant potty training
    (IPT), 58
Tolnick, I. J., 236
Toward a General Theory of Love
  (Lewis), 19
Tracking, 327
Transition object, 71
Travers, J., 281
Trumbull, E., 136, 205
Trust, 27–30
Turner-Bowker, D. M., 234
Twins Magazine, 58

Unconditional Parenting: Moving
  From Rewards and
  Punishments to Love and
  Reasoning (Kohn), 169
U.S. Department of Health and
  Human Services, 279

Values (effects on education), 134
Van Hoorn, J., 84
Virtue, 208

Voting Rights Act of 1964, 228
Vygotsky, Lev, 46–47, 91, 212
  assisted performance/
    scaffolding, 212

Wall, S., 39
Walters, R. H., 338
War on Poverty, 261
Washington, V., 358
Waters, E., 39
Way of Being, A (Rogers), 182
Weisner, T. S., 230
Weitzman, L. J., 236
Werner, Emma, 30, 125,
  262, 263
WestEd Program for Infant-
  Toddler Caregivers, 35
Whitebook, M., 279
White House Conference on
  Children, 351–352
Whole child theory, 18–19
"Why I'm Not Thankful For
  Thanksgiving" (Dorris),
  215–216
WIC. See Women, Infants
  and Children (WIC)
  program
Wiggers, Bridgette, 15
Wilcox-Herzog, Amandar,
  282–283
Wilson-Mitchell, J. E., 230
Wolfberg, P. L., 91
Women, Infants and Children
  (WIC) program,
  304–355
Wonder of Boys, The
  (Guran), 239
World Health Organization, 43
Wortham, S., 85
Wright Edelman, Marian, 357
Wright, Frank Lloyd, 231
Wright, J. C., 335
Wu, D. Y. H., 288

Zeanah, C. H., 33
Zeitlin, Stacey, 231
Zepeda, M., 136
Zigler, E., 279
Zimmerman, I. L, 230
Zimmerman, L., 41
Zone of proximal development,
  See sociocultural
  theory.